Though Without Anger

☙

Losses of Transport and Special Duties Aircraft and Assault Gliders 1940 to 1945

☙

Compiled and Edited

by

Colin Cummings

First published in 2008 by

Nimbus Publishing, October House, Yelvertoft,
Northamptonshire, NN6 6LF

ISBN – 13: 978-0-9526619-6-2

Profits from the sale of this book will be donated to
the Royal Air Force Museum and The Assault Glider Trust

By the same author:

RAF Aircraft Losses Series:

Lost To Service (1959 to 1996) – Out of Print } see below
To Fly No More (1954 to 1958) – Out of Print } see below
Last Take-Off (1950 to 1953)
Final Landings (1946 to 1949)
The Price Of Peace (VE-Day to end 1945)

Airborne Forces Series:

Arnhem Sacrifice

In Preparation:

Category Five (A major update and amalgamation of "To Fly No More"
   & "Lost To Service" to cover the period 1954 to 2008)
**Airborne Across The Rhine (6th Airborne Division in Operation
   VARSITY)**
Uncommon Valour (A record of gallantry awards to RAF personnel
   1939-45)
Blades Above The Jungle (RAF helicopters in Borneo 1963-1966)
The Debt of Honour (A novel of Bomber Command)

Contents

ACKNOWLEDGEMENTS

As with the other books I have compiled, the end product is the result of a great deal of help and assistance given by a wide variety of individuals and organisations. Without such willing contributions it would have been immensely difficult to get this book into print and its coverage would certainly have been more cursory in a number of key areas.

The RAF Museum's Department of Research and Information Systems (DORIS) has, as always, provided much help and assistance. The microfilmed Accident Cards and Aircraft Movement Cards are the basis for the individual records in this book and Peter Elliott and his team have always been most helpful in resolving various queries and looking at other sources of information they hold to help resolve thorny problems. The RAF's Air Historical Branch, a somewhat nomadic tribe who have occupied 3 different locations since I first encountered them and who now find themselves recently moved yet again; this time to RAF Northolt, have helped me on many occasions particularly with information difficult to obtain elsewhere and in particular I am grateful to Graham Day, Seb Cox and Flight Lieutenant Mary Hudson for their comprehensive responses and advice and guidance on legal issues, such as the Freedom of Information Act.

Simon Batchelor, a knowledge expert of the Air-Britain (Historians) Ltd, provided information relating to 24 Sqn losses in particular. Air-Britain (Historians) Ltd is an organisation which possesses - corporately - a remarkable and seemingly bottomless, source of information on a very wide range of historical aviation subjects. I have used the individual registers of RAF aircraft serials to track down cases where there is confusion or where the microfilmed records are indistinct or missing and it is from the Air-Britain records that I have compiled the lists of the gliders lost at Normandy, Arnhem and Operation VARSITY. The original research and compilation of these books has been conducted by James J Halley MBE and he has 'saved my bacon' many times in getting problems resolved. In a previous volume of aircraft accidents I suggested that a membership subscription to the organisation would be a remarkably good investment for any aviation history enthusiast or those stuck for a gift to an enthusiast or favourite uncle, and that remains my firm belief.

Although it is customary to record information sources in a bibliography, on this occasion I would have had serious problems in gathering information had it not been for two books, which I consulted frequently. Both helped redress my lack of detailed knowledge of special duties operations and they are:

- Agents by Moonlight
- Flights of the Forgotten

Whilst details appear in the bibliography, I am immensely grateful to the authors; Freddie Clark and Ken Merrick respectively, who have provided me with two fascinating accounts, the former from his personal experience of the sharp end of the business.

On this occasion and mindful of the distances and time taken to get to and from the National Archives at Kew, I have been helped greatly by a professional researcher. I am, therefore, pleased to acknowledge the help given by Pat Wiggins (e-mail: patawig@aol.com). She has taken my often disjointed lists of queries and sought to find the answers, mainly from the Forms 540 and 541 held within the Kew archives.

Finally, my colleague on the RAF Historical Society committee; Wing Commander C G Jefford MBE, has cast his eye over some of my work and made many useful suggestions and some historical corrections, thereby saving my blushes over several 'howlers'. Jeff Jefford is the author of 'Flying Camels' and this is the squadron history by which all others will be judged. He is probably better known, however, for his book 'RAF Squadrons' and I have referred to this publication frequently for background information and particularly the comprehensive and detailed maps showing base locations.

This is the seventh book produced for me by The Short Run Book Co and each seems to be larger or more complex than the last. I am grateful to John Cox for once again making sense of my screed and turning my scripts into a presentable book. Our telephone conversations now comprise 10% business and 90% of mostly enjoyable aviation niff naff, trivia and banter – a most agreeable way to combine business with pleasure!!

Notwithstanding, the help I have received, past experience warns me that regardless of how often I go through the text, there will be errors of both commission and omission. I hope there will not be too many of either but those which occur are my liability and mine alone.

INTRODUCTION

It would probably be true to say that fighter aircraft and those who flew them are generally considered to be the 'glamorous' side of the wartime air force: not for nothing the title; Brylcream Boys! Bombers, coastal and anti-submarine aircraft and their crews also had an obvious combative role and a legion of books and films portray the bomber and anti-submarine offensives. However, transport aircraft and their crews were and to an extent often still are, largely ignored. Of special duties squadrons, little was known of their dangerous and often solitary forays deep into enemy territory and after the war was over, only a relatively few books were produced to record their work.

Of course, the events at Normandy and Arnhem have been recorded in 'blockbuster' films but most other airborne operations are unknown. Ignorance of the hazardous supply dropping tasks to 14th Army in Burma, including the Chindit operations, and the whole of air operations in the Far East theatre in part led the late Air Commodore Henry Probert to write his; "The Forgotten Air Force". The disastrous attempts by British, Commonwealth (particularly South African) and Polish aircrews to bring supplies from Italy to support the Warsaw uprising in the summer of 1944 are also little known and to many students of air force history, the transport task is viewed as a mundane, if essential, undertaking.

From an Army viewpoint, the Parachute Regiment is seen generally as the 'airborne forces' but the glider borne troops, who were an integral part of airborne assault operations, are sometimes overlooked. The contribution of the Glider Pilot Regiment also tends to be underplayed, rather than played down, and the efforts by army and air force staff, working in unison, in the development and training of the parachutists and glider pilots is also neglected.

This book is not an account of transport, special duties and assault glider forces and their aircraft. It is rather a simple attempt to record that over 1000 transport aircraft were lost during the period 1940 to VE-Day. To that total is added the gliders lost in training and on operations and the aircraft, often small or obsolete and often both, used to tow the training gliders.

THE RECORDS

The records in this volume follow the format used in the five volumes of the post-war accident series; that is, listing by date with serial number, aircraft type, operating unit, location of loss and the number of fatal casualties. There are occasional variations to this format, particularly if it is appropriate to record the involvement of several aircraft of different types in a single or related incident.

An important variation from the norm relates to assault gliders and glider pilots, particularly when involved in operations. There are several reasons for this variation:

- First, although small numbers of Horsa, Hamilcar and the occasional Hadrian were held by stations and squadrons for general training purposes, the large numbers required to mount the major operations such as; Normandy, Arnhem and the Rhine Crossings were supplied when needed from storage units. These gliders were flown to the mounting bases and were allotted 'chalk numbers'; literally that, with a large number marked on the glider's side with chalk or paint. Thereafter, loads were allocated to chalk numbers and the loading sheets were related to the chalk number but not always the glider serial number. Although some glider pilots recorded their operational sorties using the aircraft serial number, others used the chalk number. In many cases, the loading sheets have not survived.

- Second, although in Normandy and Arnhem, it is generally possible to link a casualty amongst the glider pilots as having been caused by action in the air, the same has proved more difficult for the attacks in Sicily and the Rhine Crossings; Operation VARSITY.

- Third, almost all gliders flown on operations were never recovered for further use, even when their landing in the operational zone was effected without any significant damage being caused.

The following conventions have, therefore, been adopted when recording gliders lost on operations:

a. The majority of gliders lost on most operations are listed as a schedule of serial numbers in an Appendix, with no attempt to be more precise.

b. Where the fate of a particular Chalk No: can be related to a crash resulting in injury or death of the occupants or where it occurs following enemy action, the Chalk No: is recorded with a summary of circumstances in the usual way.

c. Likewise, glider pilots who deployed to Sicily or the Rhine Crossing are recorded as a nominal roll of casualties, again listed in an Appendix, as it has not been possible to link crews to particular aircraft. In the case of Operation VARSITY, however, it can be accepted that almost all glider pilots listed in the Appendix were killed as a consequence of action in the air or immediately on landing.

This book is not intended to be a definitive Roll of Honour of the Glider Pilot Regiment and hence readers searching for those lost in the ground campaign at Arnhem are directed to: "Roll of Honour – Battle of Arnhem, September 1944" by J A Hey, whilst a Roll of Honour for glider pilots is to be found in Claude Smith's book: 'The History of the Glider Pilot Regiment'.

As an aside, it will be seen that almost half the glider pilots lost on 24 Mar 45 were air force personnel. Following the very serious losses suffered at Arnhem, it was decided to use the emerging surplus of air force pilots to make up the shortfall of Army glider pilots and hence many air force pilots were seconded to the Glider Pilot Regiment, taught to fly the assault gliders and given elementary ground defence and infantry tactics training. Although there was a degree of reluctance from the air force side, probably matched by a similar measure of concern from the army side, the arrangement worked well and the air force personnel acquitted themselves creditably when they found themselves with the smoke of battle in their nostrils!

Unfortunately, it is sometimes very difficult to provide any information with which to enhance the bald statement that; 'aircraft 'X' took off and neither it or the crew was ever seen again'. Some aircraft simply disappeared because they were lost over the sea or crashed into deep jungle, where they remain to this day awaiting discovery. Indeed several Far East transport aircraft have been found in the past 20 or so years and in some cases it has been possible to reclaim the victims and provide them with a proper resting place. In other cases, the political situation in the immediate post-war period made recovery difficult and occasionally the eventual recovery of an aircraft and its crew was never linked back to the original records of the loss. Unlike the Bomber Command Loss Cards, other commands did not record aircraft lost to enemy action but only those subject to an accident or circumstances where there was no direct link between the loss and the presence of the enemy forces.

Dates are also a problem! An aircraft which departs at 2100 hours and is due to return at (say) 0400 hours the following morning could have been lost on either date, unless there is evidence as to the precise time of loss. The record uses the date of departure, therefore, unless there is information to the contrary.

It is said that the RAF fought the Second World War with a volunteer air force, populated by reservists. There is some truth in this statement. The survivors of the peacetime air force; the 'regulars' bore the brunt of the early losses and those who came afterward were mostly enlisted in the RAF Volunteer Reserve and they quickly swamped the regulars and the auxiliaries in numbers. For the purposes of this book, members of the RAF, RAFVR and AuxAF (it became 'Royal' in 1947) and, the Reserve of Air Force Officers (RAFO) are all treated as 'RAF' and a post nominal is not used against their name. Members of the Commonwealth air forces are accorded the appropriate title.

Where rank titles are abbreviated, I have used the current conventions and the title 'Bomb Aimer' is preferred to 'Air Bomber'. I have also used the spelling 'Sergeant' throughout, although many army records use; 'Serjeant'.

The official Operations Record Book (RAF Form 540) and the details of sorties flown (RAF Form 541) are often not as comprehensive as one would wish and occasionally the standard of the documents is such as to make them impossible to read. In some cases the Forms 540 and 541 are missing because they were lost and in other cases, it seems as if some supplementary documents, originally attached to the Forms 540 or 541, have been removed. It must also be remembered that the compilation of the Form 540 was usually done one month in arrears, rather than as a daily diary and hence it is often a summary made from the recollections of the individual compiler and his commanding officer. The latter may or may not have contributed a more strategic review of what ought to be included and whilst some Forms 540 are very informative, others so brief as to provide little help to a researcher.

Where possible, the records in this book include details of the fatal casualties and this information is taken, for the most part, from the Commonwealth War Graves Commission (CWGC) registers. These registers have some variations from the records compiled by the squadrons at the time of the loss. This is usually because the CWGC registers show the official rank to which the casualty was entitled and not the rank in which they were serving at the time of their death. This arises since commissions, promotions or gallantry awards might have been in the 'pipeline' but not yet made known generally by means of a London Gazette entry or similar official promulgation. There are also occasional errors in the CWGC records and these usually relate to incorrect squadron numbers but also sometimes, date of death. One slight anomaly relates to records for South African personnel: very frequently, only an individual's initials are shown not his full christian names. No explanation can be found for this but it does seem incongruous where personnel of other air forces have their names shown in full, SAAF members do not.

In several cases it has not been possible to be absolutely certain about some casualties resulting from an aircraft loss. Where, however, evidence indicates a probability that a given person was in an aircraft, the words; 'believed to be', have been used before the casualty entry.

A complication, for this compiler at least, relates to the interpretation of the various legal requirements imposed by the Freedom of Information Act, the Human Rights Act and the Data Protection Act. This welter of legislation has caused difficulties in obtaining information from public bodies, generally with regards the identities of casualties. Indeed, it has sometimes proved difficult to identify which organisation to consult in the first instance! Nonetheless, I am appreciative of those who helped me understand the laws as they now are and who gave guidance on how to deal with these matters.

THE DEVELOPMENT OF TRANSPORT FORCES

That the RAF was ill prepared for the air transport role at the start of World War II, is probably an understatement. In the years preceding the outbreak of war, most of the available procurement budget went on fighters and bombers to the extent that the main aircraft available for transporting personnel and equipment were three bomber/transport types.

The oldest; the Valentia, was based on the Vickers Victoria and was a twin engined biplane of 1920s design. Many of the type were rebuilt Victorias and notwithstanding its age the Valentia would give good service, within its limitations until May 1944. Indeed, it even participated in its primary bombing role on at least one occasion, worked in various other support roles – such as wireless operator training – and, on at least one occasion, a number were used to carry out an opposed assault landing! At the start of hostilities there were some sixty examples, mostly in the Middle East and a few in India.

The other two aircraft; the Bristol Bombay and the Handley Page Harrow were high wing monoplanes and were not entirely dissimilar in appearance. The Bombay entered service with a Middle East squadron in November 1939 and was used on occasions as a night bomber in that theatre. Only fifty were built and a few remained in UK but the type was withdrawn by 1944. The Harrow had entered service in 1937 as a bomber but at the start of the war it was transferred to the transport role and its gun turrets removed. In its new role it could carry twenty passengers but with the advent of the Dakota, many of the surviving aircraft were converted as casualty air-evacuation aircraft and given the unofficial name 'Sparrow'.

Although on declaration of hostilities, the Government set up National Air Communications (NAC) to coordinate the use of available air transport, it was not until the spring of 1940 that many civilian aircraft were impressed into service and these included the enormous four-engined biplane HP42s, Flamingos, and several small commercial aircraft types. Additionally, a few Hudsons were also used for transport tasks. In the meantime, the deployment of the AASF to France had been accomplished largely by assets managed by NAC.

Although not within the scope of this book, it is worth recording that throughout the war British Overseas Airways Corporation (BOAC) operated many of the strategic and long range passenger and freight services being undertaken. This included a shuttle service to Sweden and priority freight flights to Malta. In addition to civilian crews, BOAC received a significant number of seconded RAF personnel and also employed some crews from the occupied countries. As an example of the risks these crews faced, it might be recalled that the actor Leslie Howard was killed when the Dakota, flying from Lisbon to Whitchurch, was intercepted and shot down by the Luftwaffe; it is said because a large male passenger was taken to be Winston Churchill.

With the fall of France, a new transport requirement; to provide special duties aircraft, arose so that agents and supplies could be flown into France and the other occupied countries. Yet a third role was identified when the decision to form an airborne corps of parachute and glider borne troops, brought forward a requirement for transport aircraft, adapted to carry and drop parachutists and tow gliders.

During the course of the war, the various roles converged and diverged and it is probably best to describe the growth and development of general transport, special duties and airborne forces – including the assault gliders, separately.

General Transport Aircraft:

In the UK the principal transport unit was No 24 Sqn, based at RAF Hendon. In addition to a wide variety of aircraft types, the unit also held a small fleet of aircraft to permit senior officers to retain flying practice. The unit was heavily committed in France and lost or was compelled to abandon, a number of aircraft during the Spring of 1940 and in the autumn of that year it lost a significant number in an air attack on its base.

Additional transport resources were acquired by requisitioning a wide variety of commercial types and a second squadron; No 271 was formed in 1940 by raising No 1680 Flight to squadron status. This unit spent much of its time assisting with moving fighter squadrons between bases, as well as general air transport and overseas flying tasks. It received Dakotas in 1943 and it used Horsa gliders as a way of supplementing its freight carrying capacity whilst providing role training for the glider pilots. The Harrow component of the unit was to develop its casualty evacuation work and continued to use the type to the war's end. The requirement for air transport continued to increase and in October 1942, 510 Squadron was formed from a flight of 24 Squadron, taking on the latter's communications aircraft. At this time, 511 Squadron came to birth with the re-designation of No 1425 (Communications) Flight. This unit was to pioneer and operate long range transport services and in the fullness of time was to provide the nucleus of a second long range squadron; No 246. In its early days, 511 Sqn did have some problems trying to operate the Albemarle as a fast transport but with so poor a single-engined performance, it was completely unsuitable for use on long over sea flights.

In the following Spring, the Dakota element of 24 Squadron was formed into another new unit; 512 Squadron and this left 24 Sqn as the VIP transport squadron.

Two other transport units are worth mentioning here; Nos 231 and 232 Sqns. No 231 Sqn was formed as a trans-Atlantic unit and flew several types, including the exotic Coronado flying boat. There had been a regular trans-Atlantic service already and this was the 'Return Ferry Service'. This service was part of 45 Gp and was instituted as a means of getting those engaged on regular ferrying duties – as opposed to those who did it but once – back to the north American hub more quickly than waiting for a sea convoy. No 232 Sqn, on the other hand, was formed to cover the UK – India routes.

In the Middle East, the general transport squadron was No 216 Sqn, equipped with Valentias at first before receiving the Bristol Bombay. A further squadron was added when the local communications unit was renumbered 267 Sqn and more robust transport types were added to supplement the smaller 'communications' aircraft it was operating initially. Lodestars and Hudsons were added to both squadrons at various times and in 1941 a Flight of 216 Squadron was used to form No: 117 Squadron. All 3 sqns eventually re-equipped with the Dakota.

As the war progressed, 267 Squadron remained in the Mediterranean, where it also became involved in some of the most spectacular special duties operations of the war by flying into airstrips near Warsaw to recover parts of a V2 rocket and other tasks of 'derring do'. Additionally, it carried out clandestine operations over the Balkans. Of the other squadrons, 117 eventually redeployed to South East Asia and whilst 216 Squadron was also detached for operations in Burma, it was to remain in the Middle East for much of the war.

The South African Air Force contributed significantly to the transport force in the Middle East, with two sqns; Nos 28 (SAAF) and 44 (SAAF).

28 (SAAF) Squadron started operations with the Anson in mid-1943 and a trio of Wellingtons was soon added for troop carrying duties. These were followed quickly by the first of the Dakotas, which the unit operated for the rest of the war. The squadron was joined in theatre by 44 (SAAF) Squadron in early 1944, also equipped with the Dakota. Both units flew a wide variety of sorties over the entire Mediterranean and Balkan theatres and occasionally further afield to the Persian Gulf or to France and the UK.

In India, No: 31 Sqn had had a long tenure, indeed the published history of the sqn, written by Norman Franks, has the title; 'First In The Indian Skies' and this is also the unit's motto in Latin. Acquiring Valentias cast off by 216 Squadron in 1939, 31 carried out the dual bomber – transport roles and it soon took delivery of DC2 airliners in the Spring of 1941 and later added some DC3s, as well as Hudsons . The squadron assisted in the Iraqi revolt by flying troops from Basrah to Habbaniya but it subsequently became heavily involved with supporting the withdraw from Burma, losing several DC3s in the process. The arrival of the Dakota in March 1943, signalled the standardisation on the type, which it continued to operate for the rest of the conflict.

Another new squadron; 194, was formed in October 1942 and used the Hudson on internal communications work before being given Dakotas in the Spring 1943, a type it used until after the war's end. 117 Sqn came from the Middle East towards the end of 1943 and 62 Sqn converted to Dakotas during early 1944. These four sqns formed the backbone of transport support for general military operations in eastern India and Burma. Backing up these squadrons was 353 Sqn which, from August 1943, assumed responsibility for general communications and scheduled service flying across India. At a late stage No 238 Sqn, again flying the Dakota, joined the transport force.

In the final quarter of 1944, two RCAF squadrons; Nos; 435 and 436 joined in and these also contributed Dakotas to the transport support task, with 215 Squadron changing from a bomber to a transport unit in April 1945 to add further capacity until the war concluded.

Special Duties Aircraft

The Special Duties part of the air transport equation is probably the most easy to describe in summary but so cold a description denies the reader the intensity of the SD work, the dangers involved and sheer hard work and discomfort of the operations undertaken.

Although some 'casual' – in the sense of being expedient and quickly organised – SD type work was done immediately following the fall of France, it was to be several months before any formal organisation was to be established to undertake the clandestine operations over occupied Europe. In August 1940, therefore, No 419 (Special Duties) Flt was formed at North Weald with a small number of Lysanders, to which several Whitleys were soon added. The first operations were hesitant affairs as experience was gained. Several changes of base occurred, along with 'ownership' of the unit, which was renumbered No 1419 (Special Duties) Flt before being endowed with sqn status in August 1941 as No 138 Sqn within 3 Group, Bomber Command and moving to RAF Tempsford the following March. The Halifax II was brought on strength in August 1941 and this type, to which the Mark V version was added later, was to be the principal aircraft used until the Stirling Mk IV was provided and eventually supplanted the Halifax in the summer of 1944.

In addition to RAF and Commonwealth air and ground crews, Czech and Polish airmen featured heavily in the flying personnel and many sorties were flown from Britain to Poland and Czechoslovakia, although this is not to say that crews only operated to their own homeland. The tempo of special duties work gathered pace and it soon became apparent that further resources were required and a second sqn No 161, was formed at Newmarket on 15 February 1942.

For the rest of the war, these two squadrons worked in unison and 161 Sqn operated, in addition to the aircraft already mentioned, the Hudson.

As Bomber Command units, the position of the Tempsford sqns could be a little difficult at times, since they operated in a completely different way to the main bomber force. However, when required, resources from the main force were deployed to assist in dropping supplies into Europe and some losses of these aircraft appear in this book. 1944 brought an increase in the Stirling and Halifax force in 38 Gp and the initial eight sqns (six of Stirlings and a pair with the Halifax), together with several sqns of Albemarles, joined in with the dropping of supplies to SOE, SIS and SAS forces in France and elsewhere in the low countries. This approach continued for the rest of the war period, the 38 Gp units casting their nets to cover Denmark and Norway. In the latter part of 1944, 138 Sqn swapped its Halifax fleet for the Stirling Mark IV and although the intensity of operations continued, neither squadron long survived the end of the war, with 138 converting to the Lancaster and 161 disappearing from the ORBAT for good.

In the Middle East theatre, some SD work was undertaken with Wellington aircraft taken from the bomber squadrons, but a Special Liberator Flight was formed following the fall of Greece and Crete, so that the additional range and payload offered could be used to reach more distant targets. The Flight was redesignated as 148 Squadron in the early months of 1943 and the Halifax Mk II was added to the Liberator fleet. These two types were used together for about a year before the Liberator was withdrawn and the unit added the Lysander to its inventory; a combination which continued to be used for the remainder of the war, although by this time the unit was based at Brindisi.

The requirement for SD operations in the Mediterranean area and the Balkans, increased and it was decided to expand the force. To do this a number of crews and aircraft from the Tempsford sqns were deployed to North Africa and designated 1575 Flt in May 1943 before being renumbered 624 Sqn in September of that year. Operations by this unit were generally focused to the western end of the Mediterranean from its base at Blida but also extending, when necessary, into Czechoslovakia and Yugoslavia. The sqn made a significant contribution to SD operations into southern France but with that area coming under allied control in September 1944, the unit was disbanded and its tasks undertaken by 148 Sqn.

The second injection of aircraft and resources into the theatre saw the Polish Flight of 138 Squadron moved to North Africa where 1586 (Polish) Special Duties Flight was created. Reinforcements for this unit were also forthcoming from the disbandment of 301 (Polish) Sqn, whose crews were posted to various other heavy units. Whilst by no means exclusively involved with operations to Poland, it was natural for the crews to see support for the Polish resistance organisations as a major and first priority task for their efforts but the official view was not always in tune with that ideal and there were some frictions between the Poles and their RAF 'masters'.

The beginning of August 1944 saw the start of the Warsaw Uprising, in which the Polish Home Army (AK) attempted to wrest the city from the grip of the Nazis and in so doing lay claim to liberating their own capital before the arrival of the Soviet Army. This summary is not the place to discuss this ill conceived venture, other than to record that there was no realistic way that Warsaw could be supplied by air without the cooperation of the Soviets; the deployment of the Polish Parachute Brigade from UK to Poland was totally impractical and the military realities placed on the aircrews, who were given the job of supporting the AK, an impossible task. This was shown up immediately when 1586 Flt and 148 Sqn attempted the first sorties on the night of 4/5th August and the latter promptly lost five of its seven tasked aircraft.

The Warsaw Uprising lasted until early October and cost the two aforementioned SD units heavily. However, the theatre's three Liberator bomber sqns; 178 RAF, 31 (SAAF) & 34 (SAAF) were also committed and again significant losses were sustained by these units, whilst diverted to supply dropping over Poland.

With the failure of the uprising and the surrender of the AK forces, SD work continued with sorties being flown throughout the region. On occasions, bomber sqns flying Wellingtons, Liberators and Halifaxes backed up the special duties units (1586 Flt had been granted squadron status as 301 (Polish) Sqn in early November) and despite the dreadful winter weather there was no slackening of effort as the enemy forces withdrew from the Balkans, were forced northward in Italy or driven inexorably westward by the Soviets.

The end of the war in Europe saw the SD squadrons moved to help establish normal conditions and this included flying supplies into airfields and bringing out allied POWs. Although 148 Sqn remained in theatre for sometime after hostilities were concluded, the Poles were brought to UK, converting first to Warwicks and later Halifax A7s, for general transport duties. The shabby treatment of the Poles at the war's end is not part of this account but reflects poorly on the British government.

In the Far East, special duties work was rather slower to develop because hostilities did not commence until the end of 1941. With the series of defeats in Hong Kong, Malaya, Burma, Borneo and the Dutch East Indies, simple survival was a first priority and there was only modest progress during 1942 and 43. Notwithstanding, the first Chindit operation in 1943 was supported throughout by RAF transport aircraft but attempts to infiltrate agents had little real success. Weather and the great distances involved were particular factors in this enterprise. In addition, the only suitable available aircraft with which to do the SD work was the Hudson and the crews came mainly from the Air Landing School. It was decided to form a special duties transport flight and 1576 (Special Duties) Flt was formed on 1 June 1943 but its operations were handicapped because suitable aircraft, capable of ranging beyond Burma, were not made available. Towards the end of the year, however, some Liberators were redeployed from the Middle East and, being already modified for special duties work, brought into operational use. With the addition of a Catalina flight, located at Redhills Lake, the SD Flt was upgraded to sqn status and allocated the number plate '357'. The wide separation of the Liberators and Hudsons from the Catalinas was quickly exposed as unworkable and a separate squadron for the Catalinas was formed as 628 (Special Duties) Sqn, although its separate existence was remarkably short lived.

The pace of SD work increased during 1944 and a Dakota Flight was added to the unit and in early 1945, a Lysander Flight using aircraft and personnel from 161 Squadron joined the Squadron. Very long range flights were carried out by both Catalinas and Liberators, with the record for the longest flights of 29 ½ and 31 ½ hours being undertaken between Ceylon and the east coast of Malaya by Flight Sergeant C Drummond. In addition, sorties over the Hump to China were made and excursions to Indochina likewise. With long range tanks fitted, the Dakota was also used for operations at great range from base.

Towards the end of 1944 the Liberator training unit; No 1673 Heavy Conversion Unit was disbanded and its twelve aircraft, plus four additional airframes, used to create a new SD unit, to be numbered 358 (Special Duties) Squadron. A significant proportion of the training unit's staff were also transferred and this gave the new squadron a balance of experienced crews. Their operational debut on 22 January 1945, proved a disaster when three aircraft and crews of the force eleven Liberators were lost and only two of the remainder actually managed to deliver their supplies to a DZ, covered in thick cloud and in heavy rain.

As with many other units, the SD sqns did not long survive the end of hostilities and were disbanded after VJ-Day. Although there was a future for the Dakotas, the Liberators were redundant and most were withdrawn to India for scrapping, although a few were taken over by the Royal Indian Air Force. In the fullness of time an example of this fine aircraft was to find its way to the RAF Museum at Cosford where it resides now.

Airborne Forces & Tactical Transports

In summarising the development of airborne forces, the tactical transport fleet and the assault gliders, it is perhaps worth looking in a little more detail as to how this element came about and some of the issues involved.

The birth of airborne forces and with it the development of a transport force to carry paratroops and tow gliders was kick started immediately following the defeat in France. It is common currency that Winston Churchill suggested the formation of airborne forces, when he proposed the formation of an airborne corps of 5000 men. However, during May 1940, the topic was frequently aired in The Times 'letters page' and on 4 June 1940, the MP Frederick Cocks asked the Secretary of State for War whether he intended to organise a corps of parachutists and gliders.

The formation of any such organisation carries with it a need to identify just what is required and it would probably be true to suggest that nobody had a clear idea of what was actually needed and how to go about getting it. It must also be remembered that the tabling of this new idea was but one more cross for the military and air force planners to bear, just a few days after the retreat from Dunkirk had been accomplished. Indeed at this stage there were still substantial numbers of British troops to be withdrawn from other parts of France.

For its part the Army needed to identify, recruit and train the new special troops and starting from a base where they either had no knowledge or often chose to ignore the experience that existed amongst our allies, particularly the Poles. At first, the RAF was lukewarm about the whole idea and reluctant to make over aircraft and personnel for the venture and spent much energy in raising all sorts of problems without pushing for solutions, possibly in the hope that if the whole venture foundered, they could say; 'We told you so'!

Despite having the aforementioned bomber/transport Harrows and Bombays in the inventory, the air force offered early versions of the Whitley bomber as its contribution to setting up the initial training machine, which was to be formed at Ringway. The Whitley was completely unsuitable for the parachute dropping role and all sorts of methods were tried to get the paratroops out of the aircraft in as tight a bunch as possible. At first, the rear turret was removed and replaced with a platform from which the paratrooper dived: later the method was to drop from a hole cut in the floor. It was only when the Mark V Whitleys became available that a stick of ten could be carried, before that it was just eight. The first two airborne attacks by parachutists were flown with Whitleys; that against the Tragino Viaduct in Italy in February 1941 and the more famous sortie against Bruneval a year later. However, these Whitleys came from bomber squadrons and not from the emerging airborne forces establishment.

In their reluctance to become too deeply embroiled in airborne forces, their 'airships' were out flanked to a certain degree by one of the officers they appointed to help with the formation of The Central Landing School, later to become the Air Landing Establishment. In true: 'cometh the hour - cometh the man' fashion, enter - Pilot Officer Louis Arbon Strange. Strange served in World War I and was awarded the DSO, MC and DFC. For flying an unarmed but serviceable Hurricane out of France and escaping from an attack by an Me 109, he received a second DFC, making him one of a small band decorated for gallantry in both wars. When Strange arrived at Ringway and found that nobody had the faintest idea what was going on, he took himself to London and called on various 'mates', extracted some general idea of what was required and returned to Ringway as a Squadron Leader in charge of the RAF's contribution – the man appointed originally to that role having conveniently broken a leg whilst parachuting.

Strange was a maverick but it took somebody with his dynamic approach to make things happen and with his network of contacts he was instrumental in gathering in instructors (men experienced in parachuting and gliding) and obtaining stocks of parachutes and having them adapted for parachuting for its own sake, not in extremis. In fact he thwarted the RAF's 'let's not get too involved' approach and when airborne forces became a certainty and those who had kept their heads below the parapet emerged to take control, poor old Strange and others he had 'tainted' were given the boot. Strange, however, had the last laugh because in the end he returned to airborne forces as deputy chief of plans at the Allied Airborne Army HQ under General Louis H Brereton and finished the war as a Group Captain. The Army side of the new enterprise was led by Major John Rock, a Royal Engineer, and these two men can be credited with much of the early success enjoyed by those setting up the airborne forces business. Regrettably, Rock was killed in a gliding accident and his pivotal role in the development of military gliding was taken on by George Chatterton.

An important element of airborne forces development was the provision of training and assault gliders and this element is a good example of what can be achieved when one sets ones mind and energies to a programme.

No 1 Glider Training School was set up Haddenham and used civilian sailplanes and light aircraft tugs to start training glider pilots but design work on the first assault glider bore fruit within 4 months, when the Hotspur glider was produced. This proved not to be suitable as an assault glider in its initial form, mainly because the original specification called for a sailplane type with a long glide capability. However, during development of the glider, the requirement was altered to specify an aircraft with a steep dive angle, having been cast off the tow almost overhead the landing area. Nonetheless, clipping the Hotspur's wings and adding other modifications produced an aircraft which was to prove a most effective training aircraft but whose limited eight-man capacity made it a non-starter for realistic operational use. In all, about 1000 Hotspurs were built and these formed eventually a vital part of the glider pilot training regime, taking pilots from the basic flying training and producing pilots experienced in the rudiments of gliding and suitable to move to the operational conversion units.

The second glider was also developed with vigour and this was eventually named; Horsa. It was capable of carrying twenty seven soldiers and their kit or a wide range of other loads, such as a 6-pounder anti-tank gun, its limber and a jeep to tow it. The load carrying capacity of this glider actually forced a change in the number of soldiers in a rifle platoon of a glider borne battalion and led in turn to making four platoons to a rifle company and four rifle companies in a battalion, where in an normal infantry unit it was three and three. A Mark II Horsa, introduced later in the war, had a removable nose which made the task of loading and unloading vehicles a good deal easier.

The Americans provided the British with modest quantities of their principal glider; the Waco CG4, which the British christened the Hadrian. This aircraft was of very different construction to the British gliders but it was used in Sicily and most of the remainder were shipped to the Far East. By way of a reciprocal arrangement, numbers of Horsa gliders were passed to the US forces in Europe.

Needless to say, there was always a mismatch between capacity and requirement and this was addressed in part by the third British design; the Hamilcar. Again, the development of this aircraft was accomplished with considerable speed and a team of 100 designers produced a product which was available for test in the Spring of 1942 and which was of such a sound design that its basic flight trials were completed in 4 weeks. The Hamilcar was the only glider which could carry the long barrelled 17-pounder anti-tank gun and its impressive load carrying capacity meant it could carry a bulldozer or a light tank of the size of Tetrarch or Locust. As might be imagined this glider, with its all up weight of 36000 lbs, needed something special to tow it into the air and this was to be the Halifax, mainly in its Mark III or V variants.

Within eight months; on 10 February 1941, a small party of sappers, covered by infantry, were dropped from Whitleys operating from Malta with the task of blowing up the Tragino Aqueduct, which was accomplished. However, one of the Whitleys involved in a diversionary attack, force landed on the very beach assigned to be the exit point from which the troops would be evacuated by submarine. The submarine was cancelled and the raiding party were made POW but the enterprise demonstrated the feasibility of airborne attacks.

During 1941, the development of the airborne forces continued apace with much progress being made in formalising responsibilities and divisions between the RAF and Army and getting the recruitment and training regimes sorted out.

For the RAF's part, they introduced the following:

- Elementary Flying Training Schools (EFTS) for Army pilots destined for gliders.

- A Glider Training Squadron, which eventually expanded into several Glider Training Schools to give basic glider pilot training from those coming from the EFTS.

- The expansion of the Central Landing Establishment to include glider and parachute training squadrons and a development squadron.

Over time these units expanded, changed their names, locations and precise responsibilities several times and these will not be explored in detail here. Suffice to record that in time Nos 296 and 297 Sqns were formed and they in turn spawned 295 and 298 Sqns, with a Wing – No 38 to control them. As the game gathered pace the Wing became a Group in October 1943. The aircraft used by these squadrons were Whitleys, Halifaxes and Albemarles.

Following the attack on the Tragino Aqueduct, there was a break of a year before the next airborne operation was mounted and this involved a company of parachutists, led by Major John Frost, being dropped from a force of Whitleys commanded by Wing Commander P C Pickard, hero of the film 'Target For Tonight'. The target of that night, however, was the Bruneval radar site and the purpose was to seize certain parts of the Wurzburg radar and get these back to UK. This raid, inter alia, brought a Military Medal to Flight Sergeant Charles Cox an RAF radar expert. The first operational deployment of gliders, however, was the attack on the heavy water plant at Rujan in Norway and this ended in disaster when both the Horsa gliders and one of the Halifax tugs crashed in the mountains in awful weather conditions. The surviving glider borne troops, all of whom were volunteers from the Royal Engineers, were murdered by the enemy. Two of the glider pilots were air force men, and all these casualties are recorded later in this book.

From the RAF's viewpoint, one of the most testing enterprises was the ferrying of several dozen Horsa gliders from UK to North Africa in preparation for the subsequent airborne assaults on Sicily and the Italian mainland. There were two broadly similar operations; one conducted with a start date of 3 June 1943 and called Operation BEGGAR, saw 295 Sqn tow Horsas from Portreath to Sale in North Africa in a single 10 hour flight over 1300 miles. Besides the risks of broken tow ropes, the weather and marauding Ju 88s, there was a significant element of fatigue and the gliders each carried 3 pilots. From 15 August, the exercise was repeated with Operation ELABORATE and this time involved both 297 Sqn and 295 Sqn. Inevitably, there were losses to both tugs and gliders but most got through. Once at Sale, there was another long tow to be carried out to move the gliders east along the North African coast to Froha.

The Halifax and Albemarles were involved in the invasion of Sicily and although most of the Horsas brought from the UK were involved, the majority of gliders were the US manufactured Waco CG4. These aircraft had been shipped to North Africa in kit form and it fell to the glider pilots to build these under supervision of US engineers.

As 1943 progressed, the Army continued to expand its part of the airborne forces with the formation of a second division; 6th British (Airborne) Division. As with 1st British (Airborne) Division, which had been operating in North Africa and later Italy since late-1942, the new division comprised two brigades of parachutists and a glider borne brigade of infantry. The supporting arms were also airborne in one form or another.

The growth of the transport force continued apace and additionally it was realised that the Albemarle was of limited use because of its range, payload and single engine performance. However, the Stirling was being withdrawn from the bomber force and it was decided to convert some existing Mark III aircraft to the glider towing and parachute dropping roles. This involved removing the front and dorsal gun turrets, fitting a glider towing bridle and making structural changes to permit parachutists to be dropped. The revamped aircraft was designated as the Mark IV and converted aircraft were subsequently joined by some new build Mark IVs.

With the formation of Transport Command in late 1943, the airborne forces task was the preserve of 38 Gp and a new Gp; No 46, equipped entirely with the Douglas Dakota. One of the convergences between roles happened when the UK special duties squadrons were supplemented in their task of supporting clandestine operations, by use of the Stirlings and Halifaxes of 38 Gp. This increase in tempo was a direct consequence of readying the various resistance movements for the allied landings on mainland Europe.

In summarising the continued development of the RAF units to support airborne forces, by mid-March 1944, the Order of Battle for No: 38 Gp looked something like this:

- Four squadrons, each with 26 Albemarles, paired at Brize Norton or Harwell.

- Four squadrons, each with 26 Stirlings, paired at Keevil or Fairford.

- Two squadrons, each with 20 Halifaxes, at Tarrant Rushton.

- A Heavy Glider Maintenance Unit.

- Two Operational Training Units, one each at Ashbourne/Darley Moor and Tilstock.

- A Heavy Conversion Unit at Tilstock and an Operational & Refresher Training Unit at Hampstead Norris.

- No: 1 Parachute Training Unit at Ringway.

- A variety of other training, experimental, development and support units.

As for No: 46 Gp, this comprised 48, 233, 271, 512 and 575 Sqns each equipped with the Dakota and based in a triangle of airfields in the vicinity of Lechlade; at Down Ampney, Broadwell and Blakehill Farm. Two more Dakota units were to be formed during the summer; 525 Sqn and 437 Sqn, the latter being a Canadian unit. These sqns each had an establishment of 30 aircraft and there was a reserve pool of 20.

By this time all elements of the airborne forces mix were undergoing intensive training in preparation for the Normandy landings and the additional task on the 38 Gp sqns has already been referred to.

The sqns were fully involved with Operation OVERLORD – the Normandy landings and whilst their main task was towing gliders, the pathfinders, troops from 3rd Parachute Brigade and some specialist elements parachuted from Albemarles and Stirlings. Resupply sorties continued apace for the summer, as did specialist tasks, such as supporting the Special Forces in their deep penetration work. The attack at Arnhem needs no rehearsal here but it is worth remembering that a very significant proportion of the casualties suffered in that operation came from the air transport crews and members of the Royal Army Service Corps Air Despatch teams. Furthermore, the losses which befell the Glider Pilot Regiment in the subsequent fighting at Arnhem, resulted in many RAF pilots being transferred to the GPR and trained to fly the Horsa and Hamilcar. These, often reluctant, glider pilots acquitted themselves well and some 50% of the casualties during the attack across the Rhine were RAF personnel.

The 38 Gp squadrons ranged far and wide over Europe during the winter of 1944/45 and on several occasions they were called upon to undertake their supplementary role of tactical bombing, during which they suffered some losses, including an experienced Squadron Commander, whilst another sqn cdr and his crew were lost in a freak accident.

The last major airborne offensive in Europe was Operation VARSITY and the whole of 38 and 46 Groups were involved, mainly towing gliders. Six weeks later the war in Europe ended and with it came the inevitable drawdown and disbandment of the units and the retirement of their aircraft as part of the general retrenchment.

The airborne forces support role in the other theatres of war are more easily described. Outside of north-west Europe, there was little activity which falls into this category. There were no major deployments of parachute or glider borne troops and Operation THURSDAY, the second Chindit expedition, relied heavily on USAAF glider forces to get those infantry brigades which were flown into Burma onto the landing zones deep behind the Japanese lines. As for air resupply of these forces and support for the main army ground offensives, these tasks were undertaken by theatre transport squadrons as summarised elsewhere in this section.

The RAF was never to develop a paratroop transport of any consequence and it was only when the Dakota squadrons of 46 Group came along, that such a capability existed. Even so, most of the major British parachute drops of the war were only accomplished because the C47 squadrons of IXth USAAF Troop Carrier Command provided the bulk of the aircraft for that purpose – the 38 and 46 Group units being used for glider towing and resupply work, with the principal exception being the advanced drops of pathfinders, first in Albemarles and later Stirlings.

Date	Serial	Aircraft	Unit	Place	Casualties

Date Serial Aircraft Unit Place *Casualties*
Brief Circumstances of Accident
        Casualty Details (If Applicable)

13-Jan-40 P1752 Vega Gull 24 Sqn Wentworth Golf Club 0
The aircraft was forced landed on the golf course due to very bad weather. It struck a hedge, swung and its undercarriage collapsed.

12-Feb-40 X9320 DH89A Rapide 24 Sqn Moyenneville, Pas de Calais 0
The aircraft, previously registered as; G-ACYM before being impressed, was being landed on a rough surface. Its tail skid collapsed and it was not repaired.

09-Feb-40 K2797 Valentia 70 Sqn 0
The aircraft was airborne on a weather test and the pilot attempted to land downwind rather than remain airborne until the winds abated. The aircraft was landed downwind and on ground too rough for a normal landing and was damaged beyond repair.

23-Feb-40 W6424 DH89A Rapide 24 Sqn Clisson, France 0
The aircraft, previously registered as G-AEAM, was being used to collect passengers from Nantes. It suffered an engine failure but on landing it overran the airfield and went into a ditch.

21-Mar-40 L4395 Mentor I 24 Sqn Burbage Wood near Hinkley 2
The aircraft was en-route from Hendon to Kirkbride and was being flown in cloud, despite the sortie being described as 'aerial survey and cross country'. It is believed the pilot lost control and the aircraft dived steeply into the ground. The civilian casualty was employed by the Air Ministry as a member of the camouflage department.

Sergeant Raymond Charles EDWARDS 30

Date	Serial	Aircraft	Unit	Place	Casualties
		Brief Circumstances of Accident			
		Casualty Details (If Applicable)			

Mr John F D TANQUERAY 46

| 29-Apr-40 | X9395 | DH89A Rapide | 24 Sqn | Mourmelon France | 0 |

This aircraft, originally built and registered in 1933, was impressed at the beginning of April and sent to the 24 Sqn detachment at Rheims as a VIP transport. The aircraft was damaged in an unspecified take-off accident on this date but before repairs could be completed, the airfield was abandoned because of the enemy's advance and the aircraft was destroyed by the ground crew on 9 May to prevent it being used by the enemy. Before being impressed into military service, it had been registered as; G-ACIU and it was still carrying these serials at the time of its loss.

| 30-Apr-40 | K2798 | Victoria (Valentia) | 70 Sqn | Heliopolis | 0 |

The pilot was engaged in circuit training but during one approach he allowed the aircraft to drift and it undershot and struck the wall of a cemetery. The pilot was criticised for making a low approach and it was commented that he should be supervised more closely. As a squadron leader flight commander of a Stirling transport squadron, he was killed during the attempt to resupply Arnhem in September 1944, by which time he was the holder of the DFC.

| 05-May-40 | P1765 | DH89 Rapide | 24 Sqn | France | 0 |

In common with a significant number of light transports and communications aircraft, this example was unserviceable in France and was lost. In many cases the dates and precise circumstances are unclear but there seem to have been few if any casualties whilst operating 24 Sqn aircraft on the continent.

11-May-40 L5813 Bombay   271 Sqn   Bethenville France   4

The aircraft was being used to transport personnel from 501 Sqn to France from the UK and was one of a number of Bombays and an Imperial Airways Envoy employed on this task. On landing, the aircraft suddenly began to climb and stalled off the top, before its nose and wing dropped and it dived into the ground. It was considered that the cause of the stall was the incorrect distribution of the passengers and freight in the aircraft. In addition to the fatal casualties at the time of the accident, one officer was repatriated but died subsequently and Flying Officer MacGevor, Pilot Officer Duckenfield, Flight Sergeant Avent and Sergeants Adams, Crabtree and Davis were injured.   Sergeant Hugh Adams returned to duty and was killed on 6 Sep 40, during the Battle of Britain, when his Hurricane V6612 was shot down. It was also the day his commission as a Pilot Officer was promulgated.

    Sergeant William Harry WHITFIELD 22 Pilot
    Flying Officer Alistar Charles Jocelyn PERCY 29 501 Sqn Adjutant
    Sergeant Harold James BARNWELL 103 Sqn
    Flying Officer Bernard John Richard BRADY 20 died of injuries 14 Aug 40

15-May-40 P5991 Vega Gull   24 Sqn   RAF Hendon   0

The pilot mishandled an engine failure and the aircraft was damaged.

16-May-40 P1751 Vega Gull   24 Sqn   Coulommiers   0

This aircraft and the two others listed below were destroyed as the result of an enemy air attack on the airfield.

16-May-40 P1764 DH 89A Rapide   24 Sqn   Coulommiers   0

As recorded above.

Date	Serial	Aircraft	Unit	Place	Casualties
		Brief Circumstances of Accident Casualty Details (If Applicable)			
16-May-40	W6423	DH89A Rapide	24 Sqn	Coulommiers	0
		As recorded above.			
21-May-40	X8505	DH89A Rapide	24 Sqn	St Omer France	0
		Destroyed, along with X8506 in an air attack.			
21-May-40	X8506	DH89A Rapide	24 Sqn	St Omer France	0
		As above.			
21-May-40	X8508	DH89A	24 Sqn	Merville, Normandy	0
		Destroyed by an enemy air attack.			
23-May-40	OO-AUI	DC3	24 Sqn	France	0
		This aircraft was being flown by an RAF and civilian crew. It was shot down but is believed to have been forced landed by its crew and was later destroyed by ground troops.			
23-May-40	OO-AGS	SM73	24 Sqn	France	0
		This aircraft was being operated by the RAF with civilian crew in addition. Two other aircraft were reported as missing on this day but were eventually located in Marseilles			
29-May-40	L5853	Bombay	271 Sqn	Hunters Hill Ruislip	0
		The aircraft was on loan from 216 Sqn and was carrying a load of 1680 lbs of ammunition to Deauville. Immediately after take-off, the aircraft entered low cloud and the pilot failed to climb the aircraft to a safe			

height before it struck rising ground and the undercarriage was ripped off by a tree. The pilot was inexperienced in instrument flying and the Board of Enquiry states, in disparaging tones, 'trained out in the Middle East'.

31-May-40 W6457 DH 89 Rapide   Aneuil   0

The aircraft, formerly registered as G-AFSO and owned by Western Airways, was flying an evacuation sortie out of the remaning allied bridgehead in France. It suffered engine failure and the pilot was compelled to land close to enemy lines. All those on board escaped from the crashed aircraft but were fired on by the enemy. Whilst the crew and passengers survived, the aircraft did not and was destroyed by fire.

??-Jun-40 X9329 DH89A Rapide   France   ?

The date on which this aircraft was lost and the precise circumstances have not been traced. It seems probable, however, that it was abandoned in France either because it was unserviceable or had been damaged in an air attack.

17-Jun-40 L5852 Bombay   271 Sqn   East Dean Sussex   5

The aircraft, which was being flown by a 24 Sqn crew, struck the ground whilst descending in cloud.

      Flying Officer Colman O'Shaughnessey MURPHY Pilot
      Pilot Officer Hedley Eric LARGE 23 Co-Pilot
      Leading Aircraftman Wilfred Arnold HARPER 23
      Leading Aircraftman Ernest WRAGG
      Aircraftman 1st Class Leonard BRADBURN 21

18-Jun-40 G-AEBW DH89 Rapide   24 Sqn   France   0

This aircraft was being operated in France by Isle of Man Air Services when it was destroyed.

Date	Serial	Aircraft	Unit	Place	Casualties
Brief Circumstances of Accident					
Casualty Details (If Applicable)					
20-Jun-40	K6996	Harrow II	271 Sqn	France	0

The aircraft is recorded as crashing in France whilst being used to evacuate personnel.

| 21-Jun-40 | L5850 | Bombay | 216 Sqn | El Gubbi | 4 |

The aircraft was undertaking an attack on an enemy target at El Gubbi and was last seen in the target area but how it came to be lost is unclear. In addition to the fatal casualties, one crew member; Leading Aircraftman N P Donelly was taken prisoner.

> Flight Lieutenant John Basil Wentworth SMITH 26 Pilot
> Flight Sergeant Benjamin Thomas Morgan BAKER 27 Pilot
> Corporal William Charles ROYLE 23 Wireless Operator/Ai Gunner (u/t)
> Leading Aircraftman Albert Francis CROHILL

| 12-Jul-40 | P1750 | Vega Gull | 24 Sqn | RAF Hendon | 0 |

The aircraft had an engine failure during take-off and the pilot landed it on the taxyway but a wing tip hit the ground and the aircraft ran into a pile of bricks.

| 14-Jul-40 | L5848 | Bombay | 216 Sqn | Heliopolis | 0 |

The aircraft was making a transit flight to Heliopolis from Fuka Main (also known as LG 17) but on landing after a sortie of about 1½ hours, the aircraft crashed and was damaged beyond repair. The cause of the crash has not been determined.

| 15-Jul-40 | L5815 | Bombay | 216 Sqn | 25 miles south of Mersa Matruh | 3 |

The aircraft was participating in a bombing raid on naval fuel storage tanks at Tobruk and when returning from the raid, the crew was endeavouring to pick out a road by flying low and using the landing light as a search light. The aircraft struck an escarpment and crashed, being destroyed by fire. In addition to the fatal casualties, two other crew; Squadron Leader R G Taylor and Corporal E Hazlitt were injured, both suffering serious burns.

Pilot Officer Ralph Paul Joseph OSBORNE 23 Pilot
Leading Aircraftman Kenneth WEBBER 28
Corporal George NIVEN 24

15-Jul-40   L5849   Bombay   216 Sqn   Lost at sea   5

The aircraft, flown by the pilot involved in the accident to L5848 24 hours earlier, was part of an air raid on Tobruk as outlined above. The aircraft was shot down by an enemy night fighter and crashed into the sea. A few days later the body of one of the crew was washed ashore near Sollum but the others were not found.

Sergeant John George COWLISHAW 23
Pilot Officer Thomas Albert GRUNDY 26
Sergeant Peter Douglas SNOWDEN 21
Leading Aircraftman Thomas MURPHY 23
Leading Aircraftman Matthew Hetherington WINSHIP 22

15-Jul-40   L5819   Bombay   216 Sqn   South west corner of Lake Maruit   0

The aircraft was taking part in a bombing raid against Tobruk and the pilot was unable to locate Fuka Main due to fog and the aircraft suffered an engine failure because the pilot did not investigate the reasons for fuel flow problems, which if properly investigated and remedied would not have led to the engine failure. The aircraft was forced landed on the shores of Lake Maruit and was damaged. Immediately afterwards, the crew was fired upon by Egyptian forces and taken prisoner, only to be released once their identity was discovered.

Date	Serial	Aircraft	Unit	Place	Casualties
		Brief Circumstances of Accident			
		Casualty Details (If Applicable)			

07-Aug-40 AS981 HP42   271 Sqn   1 mile north-east Whitehaven   0
The aircraft suffered an engine failure whilst conveying a 3000 lb cargo of ammunition from Ringway to Prestwick. The pilot could not maintain height and so attempted a forced landing on uneven ground which ripped off the undercarriage.

19-Sep-40 X5000 Ford Model 5 AT 24 Sqn   Location not shown   0
The aircraft was forced landed in poor weather and bad visibility.

01-Oct-40 K3161 Victoria (Valentia) 70 Sqn   Ramleh   0
The pilot took off with one doubtful engine and when its revolutions dropped in flight, he throttled back and attempted a single engine forced landing. The aircraft undershot the approach and struck trees. The pilot was assessed to have a low standard of ability and was sent on a refresher course before being permitted to resume flying the Valentia. In early 1952 the pilot, by now a transport squadron CO, was seriously injured after an engine failed and his aircraft crashed whilst attempting an emergency landing.

04-Oct-40 T5357 Flamingo   24 Sqn   Not Known   ?
There is no Accident Card for this aircraft but the Movements Card records it as being damaged beyond repair but without explaining the circumstances.

08-Oct-40 P1749 Vega Gull   24 Sqn   RAF Hendon   ?
This aircraft and the three listed immediately below were destroyed in an enemy air attack on RAF Hendon. They were amongst 10 aircraft parked in 'A' hangar.

Date	Serial	Type	Unit	Location	?
08-Oct-40	P5635	Petrel Q6	24 Sqn	RAF Hendon	?

As outlined above.

| 08-Oct-40 | L4396 | Mentor I | 24 Sqn | RAF Hendon | ? |

As outlined above.

| 08-Oct-40 | L4400 | Mentor I | 24 Sqn | RAF Hendon | ? |

As outlined above.

| 08-Oct-40 | AS468 | Cleveland I | 24 Sqn | RAF Hendon | ? |

Destroyed as outlined above. The Curtiss Cleveland was the equivalent of the US Navy Helldiver and five of the type were delivered to the RAF from a quantity originally destined for the French. Quite what a two-seater dive bomber was doing in a transport squadron is unclear!

| 08-Oct-40 | L3102 | Roc | 24 Sqn | RAF Hendon | ? |

Destroyed in an enemy air raid on RAF Hendon.

| 08-Oct-40 | L3120 | Roc | 24 Sqn | RAF Hendon | ? |

Destroyed in an enemy air raid on RAF Hendon.

| 08-Oct-40 | K4277 | DH82A | 24 Sqn | RAF Hendon | ? |

Destroyed in an enemy air raid on RAF Hendon.

| 08-Oct-40 | K4284 | DH82A | 24 Sqn | RAF Henson | ? |

Destroyed in an enemy air raid on RAF Hendon.

Date	Serial	Aircraft	Unit	Place	Casualties
				Brief Circumstances of Accident Casualty Details (If Applicable)	
08-Oct-40	X9370	Envoy	24 Sqn	RAF Hendon	?
Destroyed in an enemy air raid on RAF Hendon.					
08-Oct-40	L8212	Magister	24 Sqn	RAF Hendon	?
Destroyed in an enemy air raid on RAF Hendon.					
08-Oct-40	L8345	Magister	24 Sqn	RAF Hendon	?
Destroyed in an enemy air raid on RAF Hendon.					
08-Oct-40	G-AFIE	Vega Gull	24 Sqn	RAF Hendon	?
Destroyed in an enemy air raid on RAF Hendon.					
08-Oct-40	K6814	Hind	24 Sqn	RAF Hendon	?
Destroyed in an enemy air raid on RAF Hendon.					
11-Oct-40	P5025	Whitley	419 Flt	RAF Stradishall	0
The Flight was moving from its base at Stapleford Tawney to RAF Stradishall, a permanent RAF station of the pre-war design. For some reason the pilot of this aircraft, who had no experience of the Whitley and had been posted to fly the Lysander, was entrusted with flying it to the new station. However, on the approach he lost control and the aircraft crashed on the airfield boundary and was written off.					
19-Oct-40	L5816	Bombay	216 Sqn	Missing on sortie to Benghazi	5
The aircraft took off at about 1900 hours for a sortie against Benghazi but it failed to return and its fate is					

38

unknown. The crew, who included one who had survived the crash of L.5848 in mid July, are commemorated on the Alamein Memorial.

Flight Lieutenant Edward Lionel CULLIMORE 21
Pilot Officer Lyon Curtis QUICK 27
Leading Aircraftman William Robert YORK 21
Leading Aircraftman Rolfe Vivian MINTON 26
Leading Aircraftman John Campbell PERRIE

21-Oct-40   R9027   Lysander   419 Flt   Near Oban   0

This aircraft was the first Lysander to be modified for its new role in the special duties business and a ladder was fixed to the fuselage to assist entry and exit, whilst the rear canopy was also removed to help access. The aircraft was pre positioned at RAF Tangmere but its deployment to collect an agent from France was delayed by weather. The aircraft took off in the late evening of 20 Oct and flying through very poor weather, the aircraft's radio was rendered inoperative. The pilot was eventually able to break free from the poor conditions and to make the pick up at an LZ some 4½ miles south of Fontainbleu. On the return flight, the aircraft was shot at from the ground and its compass hit and then it encountered more very bad weather. The pilot climbed the aircraft to 16000 feet and flew above the weather on a rough heading until the fuel was exhausted and he was compelled to make a forced landing, which he did in Scotland. Although both pilot and agent were uninjured, the aircraft was severely damaged. One wonders where the aircraft would have landed had it continued, since it had effectively transitted much of the UK.

23-Oct-40   R2510   Hertfordshire   24 Sqn   Woodlands Way, Mill Hill, London   11

The aircraft took off on a sortie to Belfast and was carrying a crew of five and six passengers. Shortly after taking off the aircraft crashed into some houses and all those on board were killed. The aircraft was the sole Hertfordshire in use with the RAF and it was a military version of the Flamingo aircraft. No Accident card was found for this aircraft nor could any reference to the outcome of the Board of Enquiry be located. AVM Blount was AOC 22 Group at the time of his death and was on a scheduled flight to Belfast to discuss joint training exercises with the GOC Northern Ireland. The website 'RAFWEB' suggests that there was one survivor but this person's identity is not shown in the squadron's Operational Record Book.

Flight Lieutenant Edward Charles Norman JEFFRIES Pilot
Flying Officer William LEDLIE 46 Co-Pilot
Corporal Alexander Hamilton Knighton ROBERTSON 20 Wireless Operator
Leading Aircraftman Leslie Donald RUDLING 24 Flight Rigger
Leading Aircraftman Wlater John WYNNE-HARLEY 29 Flight Mechanic
Air Vice Marshal Charles Hubert Boulby BLOUNT CB OBE MC
Lieutenant Commander Michael Joseph TOOLE 42 RN
Lieutenant (E) Thomas Gwyn James MATHIAS 40 RN
Pilot Officer George GRANT 40
Pilot Officer Frederick Eustace STRONGE 32
Warrant Officer Alfred BERRY 38

Date	Serial	Aircraft	Unit	Place	Casualties
07-Nov-40	W9105	Lockheed 10A	24 Sqn	RAF Hendon	0

This aircraft is recorded as being destroyed on this date an air attack on Hendon.

Date	Serial	Aircraft	Unit	Place	Casualties
07-Nov-40	?????	Dominie	24 Sqn	RAF Hendon	?

A Dominie is recorded as having been destroyed in an air attack on this day but its serial number is not known.

Date	Serial	Aircraft	Unit	Place	Casualties
12-Nov-40	K5605	Valentia	216 Sqn	Maaten Bagush	0

Destroyed on the ground by enemy aircraft following its participation in a bombing raid. The Valentia, which was obsolete, was nonetheless a reliable freighter and was to continue operating in both the transport and training role for sometime, before bowing out of RAF service in 1944. It seems remarkable that, despite being designed originally as a bomber/transport, it should actually be deployed in that role during the war, given that it was obsolete in both roles.

| 06-Dec-40 | AS982 | HP42 | 271 Sqn | Doncaster | 0 |

The HP42 had a normal flying speed of the order of 80 knots but winds being experienced at its base were in excess of this. Despite being properly moored, the aircraft was blown down an embankment and onto a railway line. During the attempt to recover the aircraft it was subjected to further strong gusts of wind and was severely damaged.

| 06-Dec-40 | K6974 | Harrow II | 271 Sqn | Doncaster | 0 |

Although the aircraft was picketed correctly to protect it against the high winds forecast, its port tyre burst and this allowed the starboard wing to lift in the gale and break free of the pickets, causing the undercarriage to collapse.

| 10-Dec-40 | K8848 | Valentia | 216 Sqn | Fuka | 0 |

The aircraft was being landed by the pilot responsible for the accident to K2798. The weather was poor and there was a dust storm blowing which reduced visibility. At the end of the landing run, the aircraft struck a disabled aeroplane and was damaged beyond repair.

| 17-Dec-40 | K7031 | Harrow | 271 Sqn | Nostal Priory near Wakefield | 0 |

The aircraft was being flown from Prestwick to Doncaster and had called at Jurby en-route. Whilst approaching its destination an engine failed from an unspecified cause and the pilot was prevented from turning the aircraft against the dead engine because of poor visibility and obstacles. As height could not be maintained on one engine, the pilot was compelled to make forced landing in a field but did not notice a ridge in the field until about to touchdown. The aircraft's undercarriage struck the ridge and collapsed. Although four

Date	Serial	Aircraft	Unit	Place	Casualties

Brief Circumstances of Accident
Casualty Details (If Applicable)

crew were injured, there were no fatalities.

17-Dec-40   L5821   Bombay   216 Sqn   No 1 Suez Road Bombing Range   10

The aircraft stalled and dived into the ground with insufficient height for the pilot to make a recovery. It is thought that the aircraft's CofG might have been affected by the passengers moving about the aircraft. It was commented that efforts were being made to develop a computing device to help in calculating the safe CofG for a Bombay and other types. It was also observed that the extra passengers were being carried without apparent authority.

Flying Officer Francis Adrian WALTON 22 Pilot
Flying Officer Peter Aveline Slaney BAKER 25 Co-Pilot
Pilot Officer William Edward LACEBY 30 Air Gunner
Pilot Officer John Cottrell Leonard HANMER-STRUDWICK 35 Air Gunner
Pilot Officer Harold Herbert Jordain HOBDAY 31 Air Gunner
Sergeant John Ogilvie PAUL 23 Wireless Operator
Believed to be:
Driver James BLEASDALE RASC
Aircraftman 2nd Class Robert COULSON
Guardsman Arthur GRAHAM 23 2nd Battalion Scots Guards
Piper Robert Shaw KETTLES 19 2nd Battalion Scots Guards

17-Feb-41   T4264   Whitley   419 Flt   Namur Belgium   0

The crew was originally briefed for a sortie to Czechoslovakia but this was changed at short notice and an agent was taken to Belgium, where he was successfully dropped. Shortly after and with the aircraft at only 200 feet, it was hit by enemy AA fire, which disabled one engine, whilst the other engine suffered a coolant leak and seized shortly afterwards. The aircraft crashed on the edge of a wood and the crew of six were all captured.

17-Feb-41   K9754   Hector   CLE   RAF Ringway   0

The aircraft was in the airfield circuit at 300 feet in conditions of poor visibility when its engine cut. The pilot was unable to switch to gravity feed on the fuel system and so landed the aircraft downwind in a ploughed field, resulting in an undercarriage collapse.

14-Mar-41   K6951   Harrow II   271 Sqn   RAF St Eval   0

The aircraft was struck by a bomb during an enemy air attack on RAF St Eval and was damaged substantially.

31-Mar-41   L5854   Bombay I   216 Sqn   Heliopolis   0+1?

The aircraft struck a tree whilst carrying out a mock attack during a demonstration to ground forces. The sortie was also part of an air test and the aircraft was carrying unauthorised passengers. The fatal casualty was described as; 'a native' but there is some doubt as to whether he was struck by the aircraft or whether his death was a consequence of some other factor.

01-Apr-41   L5817   Bombay I   271 Sqn   Little Seabrook Farm Ivinghoe Bucks   0

The aircraft was being operated in poor weather and the crew became lost in the bad visibility. The pilot attempted a forced landing in a field but the aircraft overshot and its undercarriage was ripped off when it crashed through a hedge. The Board of Enquiry was very critical of the navigator, whom it described as 'haphazard' and the pilot; for not checking the navigator and allowing the flight to continue beyond

Date	Serial	Aircraft	Unit	Place	Casualties

Brief Circumstances of Accident
Casualty Details (If Applicable)

Peterborough, when the weather deteriorated.

| 08-Apr-41 | AX682 | Lockheed 14 | 267 Sqn | 10 miles north west of Sollum | 0 |

The aircraft, which was an ex-US registered civilian machine – NC17398, suffered an engine failure immediately after take-off and the pilot forced landed it but the undercarriage collapsed in the process. The aircraft could not be immediately recovered and it was destroyed by artillery fire where it lay.

| 11-Apr-41 | T4165 | Whitley | 419 Flt | RAF Manston | 2 |

The crew was briefed to take a team of six Polish parachutists to blow up a power station near Bordeaux but on the outward leg of the sortie the containers were all released from the aircraft because of a technical fault. Without their equipment and explosives, there was no point in continuing and the party was brought back to UK. The aircraft was directed to RAF Manston but the pilot stalled the aircraft at 100 feet on final approach and it crashed and burst into flames. In addition to the fatal casualties, four crew members were injured but the six Poles were described as being no more than badly shaken. The pilot was to return to operations after recovering from his serious injuries but, unfortunately, he was not to survive his return to operations for very long.

Sergeant Lloyd George MORRIS 28
Sergeant Alfred Julius COWAN 28

| 14-Apr-41 | L5830 | Bombay | 216 Sqn | Lagos | 3 |

The aircraft was being flown from Khartoum to Takoradi and had landed at Lagos to refuel. On take-off, the aircraft's port tyre burst and the undercarriage collapsed. The aircraft swung violently, tipped onto its nose and caught fire when a parachute flare, stowed in the nose compartment, ignited. In addition to the fatal casualties, two others were injured.

    Sergeant Alexander Magowan MCVEA 25 Pilot
    Sergeant Victor Sidney WIMHURST 21 Wireless Operator
    Leading Aircraftman James CROFT 22

20-Apr-41 K7015 Harrow II   271 Sqn   Inwardleigh Near Okehampton   4

The aircraft crashed following an engine fire, which led to the controls being burnt through. Control was lost and the aircraft dived into the ground.

    Pilot Officer E PROCYK PAF
    Aircraftman 2nd Class Kenneth Robert MOORE 25
    Aircraftman 1st Class Kenneth BEEVERS 21
    Aircraftman 1st Class Kenneth ROBBINS

22-Apr-41 L5855 Bombay   216 Sqn   160 miles from Wadi Halfa   0

The aircraft was being flown by a pilot recently arrived from UK and with little experience of flying in the desert. The sortie was to deliver fuel to an aircraft which had been forced landed but was undamaged. The pilot attempted to land in small valley but the aircraft struck a heap of loose rocks and its starboard undercarriage collapsed.

06-May-41 K3609 Valentia   31 Sqn   Missing   0

There is no Accident Card for this loss and the Movements Card simply indicates 'Missing'; the facts, however, are far more exciting and dramatic! A pro-Nazi Iraqi, called Rashid Ali, was attempting to drive the British from Iraq and had besieged the air base at Habbaniya. It was decided to deploy ground troops by air and 31 Sqn was tasked with flying in reinforcements from India. To do this they used a mix of Valentias and DC2s. Three Valentias led by Sqn Ldr Dudley Burnside had taken off from Shaibah on the final stage but encountered a severe dust storm shortly before arriving at Habbaniya. As the crews could not see the ground, the aircraft flew on until clear of the storm. By this stage the aircraft were low on fuel

45

and a decision was made to land at a desert airstrip. Burnside led the three aircraft in to land but as he reached the end of the landing run, his aircraft was struck by bullets, fired from several places on the airstrip. He turned his aircraft around and took off downwind, whilst trying to warn the others of the danger. This Valentia, flown by Sergeants Chalk and Farr, landed after Burnside and gunfire from the rebels holding the airfield struck a fuel tank in the aircraft and it was gutted in the ensuing blaze. Although the crew and passengers escaped, they were taken prisoner by the rebels; being released eventually when the uprising was quelled.

| 06-May-41 | L5823 | Bombay I | 216 Sqn | Kano Nigeria | 0 |

The aircraft was landing in very strong and variable winds and it was forced off the runway following a change of wind direction. The pilot was unable to to correct the swing and the aircraft ran into a ditch where its undercarriage was ripped off.

| 18-May-41 | K9751 | Hector | GTS | Thame | 0 |

The aircraft's engine cut on take-off and it swung before tipping onto its nose. The pilot was alleged to have been careless but there is no evidence as to how he was so implicated.

| 22-May-41 | K9775 | Hector | CLE (GTS) | Thame | 0 |

The aircraft was engaged in a sortie to Hatfield and return. On landing at the conclusion of the sortie, the brakes were uneven and caused a violent swing, leading to the aircraft running into soft ground and tipping onto its nose. The pilot of this aircraft was Malcolm Strathdee, who was destined to pilot a Horsa on the first operation with gliders; Operation FRESHMAN in late 1942.

28-May-41 K9782 Hector   GTS   Haddenham   0

The aircraft was landing but the pilot bounced the aircraft in a heavy touchdown. However, the aircraft's wheels went into a furrow in the surface of a rough landing area and the strain proved too much for the undercarriage, which collapsed.

03-Jul-41 K8119 Hector   GTS   Sydenham   0

The pilot made a bad landing and damaged the undercarriage as a consequence. The aircraft was climbed away and then successfully abandoned by its crew.

06-Jul-41 L5837 Bombay I   OADF   Off RAF North Front   0

The pilot mishandled an engine failure and the aircraft was ditched in the sea off Gibraltar.

06-Jul-41 K9723 Hector   GTS   Sydenham, Oxfordshire   0

During the take-off the aircraft's undercarriage suffered damage and the pilot elected to abandon the aircraft, rather than attempt a forced landing.

25-Jul-41 Z6727 Whitley   419 Flt   Near Newmarket   0

The aircraft was engaged in trials work and had taken off on a test flight with 8 passnegers. On take-off an engine failed and the aircraft crashed into a telegraph pole and thence into the ground.

31-Jul-41 GAFOE Hornet Moth   24 Sqn   16 miles south of Limavady   2

The aircraft, which is shown in the records under its original civilian identity, was being used to try to identify suitable sites for locating heavy anti-aircraft guns in the area. Whilst operating in mist and fog, it struck a mountainside. The duty pilot of the operating unit did not take overdue action on the aircraft for some considerable time, which may have jeopardised the rescue.

Wing Commander Arthur Hammond DALTON 47

Brief Circumstances of Accident
Casualty Details (If Applicable)

+ one other

10-Aug-41 AM261 Liberator I   Ferry Cd   1 mile north of Goat Fell Isle of Arran   22

With the start of ferrying aircraft from Canada to the UK, it became necessary to return those crews engaged on the programme to Canada, so that they could bring another aircraft back to UK. This was initially done by sea but was slow and had inadequate capacity to maintain the ferry programme. The solution was 'The Return Ferry Service', which employed large aircraft to repatriate the crews to Canada. This aircraft took off in very poor weather and it was noted by those watching on the ground that the aircraft was not being climbed at the normal rate despite there being high ground ahead of the aircraft as it flew over the outer islands off the mainland. Nothing further was seen or heard of the aircraft until wreckage was discovered a few days later near the summit of a mountain some 25 miles from the take-off point. It appears that the aircraft drifted off track by 4½ miles in the strong winds and not having reached its safety height because of the pilot's habit of climbing the aircraft slowly, it flew into the ground.

Captain Edward Robert Bristow WHITE Captain
Josiah James ANDERSON Ferry Pilots
Francis Delaforce BRADBROOK
Daniel Joseph DUGGAN
Watt Miller KING
George Thomas HARRIS
Hoyt Ralph JUDY
John Evan PRICE
John James ROULSTONE
Harold Clifford Wesley SMITH
Jack WIXEN

Ralph Bruce BRAMMER Ferry Radio Officers
John Beatty DRAKE
Henry Samuel GREEN
Wilfred Graves KENNEDY
George LAING
Hugh Camerom MCINTOSH
William Kenneth MARKS
Albert Alexander OLIVER
George Herbert POWELL
Herbert David REES
Ernest George REEVES Flight Engineer

| 11-Aug-41 | AX903 | DH91 Albatross | 271 Sqn | Reykjavik | 0 |

The aircraft, formerly registered G-AEVV, swung on landing, left the runway and collided with a Battle, serial number: L5547.

| 14-Aug-41 | AM260 | Liberator I | Ferry Cd | Heathfield, Ayr | 22 |

The aircraft was undertaking a return ferry sortie, similar to that attempted by AM261 a few days earlier. The pilot lined up the aircraft on the wrong runway, which was both out of wind and also 300 yards shorter than that which he should have used. During the take-off run the aircraft drifted off the runway after a swing developed but the crew made no attempt to close the throttles and halt the aircraft, which continued run across the grass. It passed through the boundary fence, struck a telegraph pole and then hit an embankment, breaking up in the process. Although the reason why a pilot, with over 5000 flying hours, would make such an elementary error was not resolved, there is some evidence that he was under considerable stress for a number of reasons and had been working exceptionally long hours.

Captain Richard Charles STAFFORD Pilot
Elbert Beard ANDING - Ferry Pilots

Date	Serial	Aircraft	Unit	Place	Casualties
Brief Circumstances of Accident					
Casualty Details (If Applicable)					

Murray Benjamin DILLEY
Alton Chester EARL
Edward HAMEL
Gerald HULL
John Joseph KERWIN
Philip Francis LEE
James John MOFFAT
Wlater L TRIMBLE
Earl Wellington WATSON
Martin Joseph WETZEL
Richard COATES - Ferry Service Radio Officers
Joseph Patrick CULBERT
Robert Arnold DUNCAN
Wesley Francis James GODDARD
Donald Norman HANNANT
John Joseph MACDONALD
Glenwood MCKAY
Albert TAMBLIN
Roland Fulford DAVIS
Arthur B PURVIS Head, British Purchasing Commission

Date	Serial	Aircraft	Unit	Place	Casualties
21-Aug-41	L5826	Bombay I	117 Sqn	Khartoum	0

This aircraft had acquired a reputation as a rogue, in that on a number of occasions and for no apparent reason, it suddenly dived to starboard. After an incident in Jun 41, the aircraft was carefully examined but no fault could be found and it was returned to service. However, the dive occurred again and the pilot recovered the aircraft to Khartoum, where its engines were removed to provide spares for another Bombay. Whilst languishing at the airfield and despite being securely picketted with heavy ropes, it was badly damaged by an haboob – a tropical storm with severe gusts of wind – after breaking free from its moorings. There seems to have been no expressions of regret that this aircraft had been destroyed!!!

21-Aug-41	K8112	Hector	CLE	Farnborough	0

The aircraft overturned after it was landed on soft ground to the side of the runway.

25-Aug-41	K1312	Victoria	31 Sqn	Haft Khel Iraq	0

The aircraft was one of several landing in formation, so as to give concentrated fire support from the troops they were carrying, as the landing ground was held by the enemy. This aircraft overshot the very restricted airstrip and ran off the end into a nullah. A contributing factor was that in order to obtain surprise, the aircraft landed out of wind and on a sloping strip. Fortunately, there were no injuries to passengers or crew.

25-Aug-41	K3611	Valentia	31 Sqn	Haft Khel Iraq	0

This aircraft was operating with K1312 and crashed in identical circumstances, albeit with injury to one of those aboard.

29-Aug-41	R1987	Lysander II	267 Sqn	15 miles north-west Gaza	0

The aircraft was badly damaged in a forced landing but the circumstances are not known.

01-Sep-41	AM915	Liberator	Ferry Cmd	Achinhoan Head Near Campeltown	10

The aircraft was homed to the overhead at Ayr in poor weather but then continued to Squires Gate Blackpool, which despite a favourable weather report given to the pilot, was unsuitable for landing. The aircraft then

Date	Serial	Aircraft	Unit	Place	Casualties

Brief Circumstances of Accident
Casualty Details (If Applicable)

returned to Ayr and it seems probable that the pilot attempted to get below cloud before ascertaining that it was safe to do so. The aircraft struck high ground at about 700 feet.

Captain Kenneth GARDEN Pilot
Geoffrey Llewellyn PANES Co-Pilot
Samuel Walter SYDENHAM Radio Officer
Charles Alvin SPENCE Flight Engineer
Count Guy de BAILLER-LATOUR 36
Professor Robert Balmain MOWATT 58
Captain PICKERING
Eric TAYLOR
Lieutenant Colonel Lewis Harris WRANGHAM 43 Royal Marines

Date	Serial	Aircraft	Unit	Place	Casualties
22-SEP41	K9762	Hector	GTS	Thame	0

On take-off, the oleo leg tube failed and this caused one of the undercarriage legs to hang loose. A crash landing was made but with an obsolete aircraft type it was not repaired.

Date	Serial	Aircraft	Unit	Place	Casualties
23-Sep-41	L5822	Bombay I	216 Sqn	1 mile south west of Heliopolis	6

The aircraft was approaching to land at the conclusion of a sortie when the pilot lost control and the aircraft dived into the ground. It seems probable that the loss of control was caused by a crew member moving to the rear of the aircraft and creating a change of CofG at a critical moment in the landing.

Pilot Officer Jeffrey TURNER 21 Pilot
Flight Sergeant Pete Charles MCCUE Wireless Operator/Air Gunner
Leading Aircraftman Cyril JENKINS 19

Aircraftman 1st Class Ronald William Joseph WINSLADE 23
Aircraftman 2nd Class Kenneth ADAMSON 24
Aircraftman 2nd Class Thomas Archibald BERRILL 19

05-Oct-41	P5164	Hudson I	267 Sqn	Near Cairo	8

The aircraft suffered an engine failure but the pilot failed to take the appropriate action immediately and the aircraft lost height, stalled and crashed. It seems surprising that a senior Army officer and his staff should be entrusted to a relatively inexperienced pilot and there is no explanation as to why the pilot made no apparent attempt to deal with an engine failure.

Sergeant Lucien Georges LEVY
Sergeant Brain Chadwick GRAY 26 RAAF
Sergeant Frank Derek WARD 23 RAAF
Leading Aircraftman Charles CHAPMAN 26
Lieutenant General Vyvyan Vavasour POPE 50 CBE
Brigadier Hugh Edward RUSSEL 45 DSO
Colonel Eric Sudeley UNWIN 47 MC
Captain George Robert AMERY 21

12-Oct-41	W9104	Lockheed 10A	24 Sqn	Clifton, near York	0

The aircraft, previously registered – G-AFEB, swung on landing after its brakes failed and it ran into a ditch

13-Oct-41	L5834	Bombay I	OADF	RAF North Front	0

The aircraft was being ferried from UK to the Middle east and had flown from Portreath. It was appraoching to land at Gibraltar and the pilot decided to overshoot and so opened the throttles. The engines failed to pick up and so the pilot attempted to brake but the aircraft swung and its undercarriage collapsed. It is interesting to note that the pilot had a total of only 129 flying hours of which 42 were 'on type', yet he was employed on the difficult job of ferrying an aircraft overseas.

Date	Serial	Aircraft	Unit	Place	Casualties
Brief Circumstances of Accident					
Casualty Details (If Applicable)					

24-Oct-41   DG471   Dakota   31 Sqn   Karachi   0

The aircraft crashed on take-off and was destroyed by fire at the end of the runway. The aircraft, which was piloted by Flying Officer Mehar Singh RIAF and Pilot Officer Mike Vlasto, had been loaded with ammunition for transport to Iraq. However, although the load lacked bulk, it certainly had considerable weight but nobody checked this and so another load of ammunition was added!!! The crew boarded the aircraft in the pre-dawn dark and the additional load was not noticed until the aircraft failed to get airborne. Fortunately, there were no casualties. Singh rose to the rank of Air Commodore, whilst Vlasto had a distinguished operational career on transport aircraft in India and Burma. It was he who landed a Dakota on open ground in Burma in order to rescue 17 wounded Chindit soldiers who were returning from the first penetration raid in 1943: a feat for which he was awarded the DFC.

30-Oct-41   Z9223   Whitley   138 Sqn   RAF Stradishall   3

The aircraft was on a flight from Newmarket and was approaching to land. The aircraft's engines were at full power and the flaps were down but the elevator trimming wheel was wound a considerable way back. In this condition, the aircraft's nose would tend to rise quickly and induce a stall if corrective action was not applied rapidly. The Accident Card also states that the passenger was sitting towards the rear of the aircraft which would have exacerbated the taildown trim. The pilot had been in command of Whitley T4165 when it crashed in Apr 41, having stalled on the approach.

   Flight Lieutenant Albert John OETTLE 25 DFC Pilot
   Flight Sergeant Hugh Francis ROCHFORD 24 DFM RNZAF Navigator
   Leading Aircraftman Walter John LEE 21

01-Nov-41 L9612 Halifax   138 Sqn   Tormelilla Sweden   0

The aircraft ran short of fuel on return from a long range sortie to Poland. The cause of the problem was that the hydraulics froze on the outbound leg and the undercarriage came down. Nonetheless, a successful drop was made and the aircraft was set on a course back to UK. Unfortunately, it encountered headwinds and this coupled with the drag of the lowered undercarriage, used the fuel reserves. It crashed in Sweden but without injury to its crew, who were repatriated to the UK in due course.

17-Nov-41 L5847 Bombay I   216 Sqn   Near Gazala   1?

The aircraft made a forced landing after being damaged by enemy fighters.

       Pilot Officer Donald Sunman MARTIN 24 Pilot

26-Nov-41 L5846 Bombay I   OADU   1½ miles south west of Carnaro Point   0

The Air Ministry Form 1180 records this aircraft as L5866, which was an allocation made to a batch of Bombays cancelled before construction. The correct serial number is believed to be as shown above. The aircraft was being ferried from Hampstead Norris to Gibraltar but the engines failed and the aircraft was ditched at sea. The subsequent investigation revealed that the pilot had very little knowledge of the aircraft's fuel system and it was his mishandling of the fuel supply that caused the fuel starvation and subsequent accident.

28-Nov-41 T1771 Lysander III   138 Sqn   Hungry Hill Farnham Surrey   2

Whilst being flown at low level in very bad visibility the aircraft struck trees and crashed. Flight Lieutenant Laurant was a French officer serving with the RAF

       Flight Lieutenant A J DE V LAURANT
       Leading Aircraftman John Arthur Martin HARKNESS 21

Date	Serial	Aircraft	Unit	Place	Casualties
		Brief Circumstances of Accident			
		Casualty Details (If Applicable)			

10-Dec-41 BD145 Whitney Straight 24 Sqn Park Street Herts 2

The aircraft lost its propeller and in taking action to shut down the engine, the pilot allowed the aircraft to stall and it spun to the right and crashed before recovery could be taken.

Flight Lieutenant John Jackson HAMILTON 28 Pilot
Warrant Officer Sidney Charles WILLIAMS 27 Co-Pilot

16-Dec-41 V9115 Hudson III 24 Sqn At sea near Corunna 7

The aircraft was one of a pair en route from UK to Gibraltar and it was seen by the crew of the other aircraft to crash into the sea in the vicinity of several merchant ships which are thought to have fired on it.

Flight Lieutenant John Herbert Morgan DAVIES 21 DFC Pilot
Flying Officer Douglas Veale GILMOUR 26 Pilot (but flying as Navigator)
Flight Sergeant Robert Martin HANNAN 28 Wireless Operator/Air Gunner
Leading Aircraftman William Graham SHEEAN
Lieutenant Commander Edward CROGHAN RNVR
Lieutenant Patrick Lainson FIELD 30 RN
Mr Charles John DAVIDSON 45 HM Dockyard Malta

16-Dec-41 K8103 Hector AFEE Exp Flt Middlewich, Cheshire 0

The pilot was thwarted in his attempts to return to base at Ringway because of gathering darkness and a local storm. Instead of landing at a suitable diversion, the pilot pressed on and became lost. Eventually he landed in an unsuitable field and the aircraft was damaged.

19-Dec-41   BT488   Hotspur II   AFEE   RAF Ringway   8

The aircraft was being used to conduct trials into airsickness amongst passengers flying in troop carrying gliders and the sortie was to be of 3 hours duration. The glider, being towed by a Hawker Hector, and after being airborne for about 90 minutes, the tug pilot decided to return to the area of the airfield because of generally deteriorating weather. After a further 30 minutes, the glider began to fly rather erratically and shortly afterwards, the glider pilot cast off the tow. The glider pulled up steeply, stalled and fell off into a spin, which the pilot corrected. However, the glider entered a vertical dive from 500 feet and control was not recovered before the glider crashed into a field near the base and broke up on impact. The observer had recorded that several passengers had been airsick and it is possible that the glider pilot was similarly affected. However, the steep pull up after casting off was this pilot's 'MO' and it is thought more likely that he lost control because he was not strapped in.

        Sergeant John Victor RUTTER 24 Pilot The Queen's Own Royal West Kent Regt
        Lieutenant David Northmore TIMMS 23 Royal Artillery Observer
        Sergeant Harry HARRISON 31 The Border Regiment
        Private Henry G HORNBY 32
        Private Richard Foster MARSHALL 24
        Private Lewis William FELTON 25
        Private Matthew PILKINGTON 40
        Private George M KEOGH 22

23-Dec-41   AX699   Lockheed 10A   267 Sqn   Near Ismailia   0

The aircraft was damaged beyond repair after during a forced landing. The cause of the emergency is not known and there is no Accident Card.

25-Dec-41   DG475   Dakota   31 Sqn   Near LG138   1

The aircraft, flown by Warrant Officer David Lord and Flight Lieutenant Howell, was attacked by three

Date	Serial	Aircraft	Unit	Place	Casualties

Brief Circumstances of Accident
Casualty Details (If Applicable)

German fighters about 10 miles north east of their objective. Although both pilots were slightly wounded they managed to force land the aircraft in the desert and were then able to walk to the airstrip. However, one of the passengers received fatal injuries in the attack.

One casualty whose name is not known

27-Dec-41   Z9385   Whitley   138 Sqn   UK location not known   4

The aircraft is believed to have been shot down by a Luftwaffe night intruder aircraft whilst returning from a night sortie over France in poor weather. Two other crew members abandoned the aircraft successfully by parachute. Flight Sergeant Reimer had previously served with 51 Sqn and had ditched an aircraft in the North Sea about 8 miles off Scarborough in Jun 41.

Flight Sergeant Alvin Wilbert REIMER 21 RCAF Pilot died of injuries 12 January 1942
Sergeant John Russell PETTS 21 RCAF
Sergeant George Russell Stewart GORDON 19
Corporal Herbert Andrew PICKERING 25 died of injuries 28 December 1941

01-Jan-42 DG474 Dakota 31 Sqn Mingaladon 0
The aircraft was destroyed in an air attack on the airfield by Japanese aircraft.

03-Jan-42 Z9140 Whitley 138 Sqn Malta 0
Whilst parked at Malta, this aircraft and the Whitley below were destroyed during an enemy air raid.

03-Jan-42 Z9295 Whitley 138 Sqn Malta 0
As recorded above

08-Jan-42 T5628 Tiger Moth II 2 GTS Kirklington, Oxon 0
The aircraft was being flown in very hazy weather with poor visibility. The pilot allowed the airspeed to bleed off in a turn and the aircraft side slipped but the pilot corrected this and dived to regain speed. However, in recovering near the ground, the aircraft bounced, nosed in and overturned. It was commented that the pilot, who had been trained in Canada, was unused to flying in the sort of poor weather often encountered in UK.

10-Jan-42 T9375 Hudson II 24 Sqn Sydenham Belfast 0
The aircraft ran along the runway and the tail did not rise nor was flying speed attained. The aircraft stalled when trying to lift off the ground and flames came from the port engine. The aircraft ran off the runway and into the mud where the starboard petrol tank exploded. The Accident Card offers no indication as to the cause of the accident nor why the pilot did not throttle back and attempt to brake when the aircraft was clearly unlikely to get airborne. The thirteen people on board survived.

13-Jan-42 BT484 Hotspur II AFEE Mobberley, Cheshire 0
The pilot lost contact with the tug aircraft, when the combination was compelled to fly through a squall, and he cast off the tow. In the ensuing forced landing, the glider struck a tree and a barbed wire fence.

Date	Serial	Aircraft	Unit	Place	Casualties
				Brief Circumstances of Accident	
				Casualty Details (If Applicable)	

20-Jan-42 K1313 Victoria 267 Sqn Heliopolis 0

The aircraft was being used for a co-pilot conversion check, in order that he would be qualified as captain. On take-off an engine failed and the aircraft began to lose height. Unfortunately, the ground was uneven and hilly and it was impossible to set the aircraft on an even keel before impact and it was damaged on crashing. The aircraft was being flown by Squadron Leader Maurice Booth, who was to distinguish himself as a Dakota squadron commander later in the war. For his war service in the Middle East, he was awarded a DFC a few months after this incident and a bar to the DFC whilst with 271 Sqn.

23-Jan-42 L5811 Bombay I 216 Sqn Near Msus ?

The aircraft was shot down by anti-aircraft fire. However, no record of any casualties could be found and there seems to be no reference to the loss in squadron records.

28-Jan-42 Z6728 Whitley 138 Sqn 20 miles off the English coast 7

The aircraft was returning from Operations MUSJIDE and MAJOR DOMO but was ditched after an engine failed and height could not be maintained. Although the remains of 2 of the crew were eventually washed ashore, the others were not found and are commemorated on the Runnymede Memorial.

Sergeant Emrys Evan JONES 20 Pilot
Sergeant David GOLD 21
Flight Sergeant George Edward Albert BAXTER
Sergeant Albutt BRITTAIN 20
Pilot Officer Dennis Owen WEEKS Air Gunner
Sergeant Francis William SMITH 21Despatcher
Wing Commander Jack Elkan David BENHAM 41 Observer

29-Jan-42   T1508   Lysander III   138 Sqn   Issoudun Indre   0

The aircraft was returning from a pick-up of two agents in France but the pilot was compelled to return to the original landing site, after his aircraft was affected badly by heavy icing and he was unable to either fly round or through the bad weather. He managed to make a forced landing in bad weather and although his aircraft was not badly damaged, it was completely destroyed by a train during an attempt to salvage it.

01-Feb-42   DG478   Dakota   31 Sqn   Chittagong   0

The aircraft was damaged at Chittagong and temporary repairs were made, sufficient to fly it to Lahore. However, it was then grounded for more extensive repairs to be made but these were later suspended, when the full scale of the damage was revealed, and the aircraft was scrapped.

22-Feb-42   AL574   Liberator I   108 Sqn   RAF Fayid   0

This aircraft was one of a small batch of Liberators made available for special duties work in the Middle East and it had undertaken a number of sorties, including a long range flight to Palembang Sumatra, carrying spares for 84 Sqn aircraft. On take-off, the undercarriage was raised before flying speed was attained and the aircraft sank back on the ground and was damaged badly. Although repairs were started, it became apparent that these were not economic and the aircraft was written off.

23-Feb-42   BT718   Hotspur II   2 GTS   RAF Weston on the Green   0

The hood blew open and the pilot lost control of the glider whilst trying to close it and the tow broke. In trying to land, the pilot put the glider down in a ploughed field and it was damaged badly.

02-Mar-42   W5555   Wellington II   148 Sqn   4 miles off Daba Point   0

This aircraft's crew, captained by Pilot Officer D M Crossley, had made several attempts to deliver supplies to partisan forces in Crete but had been thwarted several times for various reasons. Whilst making a further attempt, an engine failed and the aircraft began to lose height quickly in the general area of the DZ. The

Date   Serial   Aircraft   Unit   Place   Casualties
Brief Circumstances of Accident
Casualty Details (If Applicable)

load was jettisoned immediately and much other equipment was thrown out in an attempt to arrest the descent and the aircraft turned for base. Eventually, the other engine failed and the aircraft was ditched and the crew was able to board the dinghy. Unfortunately, although a convoy was passing nearby, they were unable to attract attention but after about 4 hours afloat, they were seen by an aircraft which directed a boat to their position and they were rescued. Pilot Officer Crossley was awarded a DFC in June 1942 and then undertook a second tour of operations with 70 Sqn and received a bar to the award as a Squadron Leader a year later.

08-Mar-42   BT639   Hotspur II   1 GTS   RAF Thame   0

The tug's quick release mechanism failed shortly after take-off and the glider was cast off. The glider pilot attempted a turn back to the airfield, for a downwind landing but the Hotspur was damaged.

10-Mar-42   Z9125   Whitley   138 Sqn   RAF Stradishall   5

The pilot, who had been posted from 24 Sqn to be a flight commander, was taking off for the first time as captain of a Whitley. The sortie, code named FRENSHAM, had been attempted the previous night but the aircraft used then had returned to base. Immediately after take-off the aircraft lost height and crashed beyond the airfield. All on board, except the rear gunner, who was rescued by the crash crew, were killed. The crew were all Czechs serving with the RAF.

Squadron Leader Boris ROMANOFF 27
Sergeant Jan JANEC 23
Sergeant Maxmillian POLITZER 22
Sergeant Ladislav FORNUSEK 21
Flying Officer Vaclav JELINEK 26

12-Mar-42   BT563   Hotspur II   102 GOTU   Bodicote, Oxfordshire   0

The tug pilot accidentally released the glider with the tow rope still attached and the pupil flying the glider did not jettison the tow rope by pulling his own cable release. On approach for a forced landing, the tow rope fouled a hedge and the glider dived into the ground from 50 feet. As a result of this accident, it was forbidden for retain the tow rope on the glider – a practice developed to reduce speed in the event of forced landing – and cockpit drills were revised to ensure the tow rope release is always operated in a glider after a release by the tug.

16-MAR-42   AL577   Liberator   108 Sqn   Jenkinstown, Dundalk, Eire   15

With the fall of Greece and Crete and with the long distances involved, it was impossible to infiltrate supplies etc into Yugoslavia and other locations in the Balkans. The solution was to use some Liberator aircraft, as these became available and they were attached to 108 Sqn, which was to convert to the type anyway. Many problems were encountered with the early aircraft, which did not have powered gun turrets and these were solved with typical ingenuity. For example, a Wellington turret was adapted and fitted to a Liberator and the turrets' slow rotation increased by fitting a more powerful motor. SD sorties started to be flown and the sqn cdr was closely involved in this work with this particular aircraft was one of the early airframes to be used. It was decided to send sqn crews to UK to collect other Liberators and two had already been flown out from England a week earlier. This aircraft, with a crew of seven and eleven passengers was routed via Gibraltar to Hurn, from where the passengers would return to Egypt with other aircraft. The aircraft left Gibraltar for UK but its crew encountered very poor weather and a diversion was made to Aldergrove. However, whilst approaching Aldergrove the aircraft crashed into hills and the operating crew and eight passengers were killed or died of injuries. The three survivors were; Flying Officer J R Anderson DFC, Sergeant C R Amos and Sergeant S F Hayden. Pilot Officer Tolson's father and Flight Lieutenant Barrett's brother both died on active service.

Flight Sergeant Lindsay Ross WILLIAMS 26 RAAF Pilot
Wing Commander Richard John WELLS 28 DFC & Bar Pilot Squadron Commander

Date	Serial	Aircraft	Unit	Place	Casualties

Brief Circumstances of Accident
Casualty Details (If Applicable)

Pilot Officer John Peile TOLSON 21
Flight Sergeant Paul Herrick MOREY 22 Observer
Sergeant Charles Joseph INGRAM Wireless Operator
Sergeant Henry James GIBBONS 20 Wireless Operator
Flight Lieutenant Francis Charles BARRETT 32 DFC Air Gunner
Passengers:
Sergeant Walter Paul Brooks 20 Wireless Operator
Sergeant Andrew McMillan Smith BROWNLIE 29
Flight Sergeant George BUCHANAN 22 Pilot
Flight Sergeant Carlton Stokes GOODENOUGH 28 RCAF Observer
Flight Sergeant Leslie George JORDAN 20 Observer
Pilot Officer George Frederick KING 25 RCAF Observer
Flight Sergeant Herbert William Thornley SLOMAN 22 RAAF
Pilot Officer Wilfred Bertrand STEPHENS Pilot

Date	Serial	Aircraft	Unit	Place	Casualties
18-Mar-42		Hotspur III	101 GOTU	Kidlington	1

The glider was landing at night on an airfield lit with a mixture of 'lead in' lights, open goose neck flares and glim lamps. The aircraft was too high and on landing it overshot the area and crashed into a parked Hurricane BD768.

Pilot Officer William Richard CLARK 31

Date	Serial	Aircraft	Unit	Place	Casualties
19-Mar-42	BT562	Hotspur III	1 GTS	Kingston Bagpuize	0

The glider's undercarriage had been incorrectly fitted at manufacture and the pilot accidentally knocked the release mechanism when he entered the cockpit. After take-off, the aircraft's nose dropped and it crashed

64

without the protection of the undercarriage.

19-Mar-42   BT481   Hotspur II   296 Sqn   RAF Netheravon   0
The pilot was flying a fully laden glider but made the turn into land at too low a speed and the aircraft stalled off the turn and crashed from about 100 feet. It was commented that some pilots were becoming over confident and had little experience of flying more heavily loaded aircraft and the training syllabus needed changing to address this.

25-Mar-42   HM498   Hornet Moth   24 Sqn   RAF Bicester   0
The aircraft failed to get airborne and struck an Avro Tutor K4811. The pilot, a senior officer from the Dutch forces in exile, was criticised for his poor airmanship in failing to take-off into wind and displaying poor discipline. This particular aircraft was formerly the Danish registered OY-DOK and was typical of the hotch-potch of aircraft which were pressed into service during the war.

27-Mar-42   K2807   Victoria   31 Sqn   Akyab   0
The aircraft was destroyed on the ground during an air attack by a force of Japanese Ki 43s.

28-Mar-42   T4166   Whitley   138 Sqn   At sea off Den Helder south of Texel   6
This aircraft took off on Operations WATERCRESS/CATARRH with the intention of dropping a Dutch agent; Lt A A Baatsen, near Steenwijk in northern Holland. This part of the mission was accomplished but the aircraft crashed shortly afterwards and the crew was killed. What was not known at that time, was that the Dutch Resistance had been penetrated by the enemy and a radio operator captured and compelled to work for the Germans, who had then used him to signal the landing site to be used for Lt Baatsen's infiltration. Baatsen was captured immediately after landing and was subsequently murdered.

Flight Sergeant John THOMPSON 21 Pilot
Pilot Officer Stanley WIDDUP

Date	Serial	Aircraft	Unit	Place	Casualties
				Brief Circumstances of Accident Casualty Details (If Applicable)	

Pilot Officer Robert William FRANKLIN 26
Sergeant Kenneth HAILSTONE 20
Sergeant George Robert WOOD
Sergeant William Charles EVANS 26

Date	Serial	Aircraft	Unit	Place	Casualties
07-Apr-42	AX904	DH91 Albatross	271 Sqn	Reykyavik	0

The aircraft was operating a mail service and was landing at about 1830 hours. On touchdown the aircraft started to swing and this was corrected by the pilot but then a further swing developed suddenly and the undercarriage collapsed. Subsequent investigation suggested that the second swing resulted from partial brake failure.

Date	Serial	Aircraft	Unit	Place	Casualties
11-Apr-42	W6456	DH89A Rapide	24 Sqn	RAF Hendon	0

Whilst taxying, the aircraft's port tyre burst and the aircraft swung off the perimeter track and was damaged badly.

Date	Serial	Aircraft	Unit	Place	Casualties
11-Apr-42	K8126	Hector	2 GTS	½ mile south of Weston on the Green	1

The aircraft was towing a glider and the combination entered cloud. The glider pilot released the tow and made a forced landing safely but the tug carried on in cloud before reappearing at about 300 feet above the ground in a gentle descent but on an even keel. The aircraft continued in this attitude until it struck the ground. The cause of the accident is obscure but it it seems possible that the tug pilot did not revert to visual flying when he cleared the cloud, although one might have thought he would be aware of his surroundings, even if flying on instruments. The patch of cloud had formed in the area because of a sudden deterioration in the weather.

12-Apr-42 BT730 Hotspur II 101 GOTU Yarnton, near Oxford 0
This glider was on a twin tow but it became too high behind the tug aircraft and the pilot released the tow. Unfortunately, the pilot made a poor forced landing, resulting in serious damage to the aircraft.

13-Apr-42 AX755 DC2 31 Sqn Akyab 0
The aircraft was abandoned by the RAF after it ran into a bomb crater. This was an ex-US civilian registered aircraft: NC-14268.

13-Apr-42 K9738 Hector 101 GOTU Kelmscott, Oxfordshire 0
The aircraft was engaged on a cross country sortie and was towing a pair of Hotspurs. During a turn, one of the gliders got above the tug aircraft and caused the tug's nose to be pulled down, at which point both glider pilots pulled off the tow and landed but the tug pilot was unable to recover from the induced dive before his aircraft struck the ground. Although it was judged that the tug pilot was too low, a decision was made to cease double towing of gliders.

14-Apr-42 BT619 Hotspur II 102 GOTU Kidlington 0
The pilot was practising a dive approach onto the airfield but pulled out of the dive too sharply and this caused the glider to sink and strike trees at the airfield's boundary.

16-Apr-42 BT745 Hotspur II 296 Sqn Near Everleigh, Wilts 4?
The glider was taking part in a demonstration of an airborne assault but the pilot undershot the landing zone and in attempting a turn at low level, a wing tip struck the boundary fence and the glider crashed.

Date	Serial	Aircraft	Unit	Place	Casualties
		Brief Circumstances of Accident			
		Casualty Details (If Applicable)			

20-Apr-42   V9776   Halifax   138 Sqn   Kreuth, south of Munich   10

The aircraft was being used to ferry Soviet NKVD agents into Austria but it struck a hill whilst flying in dense fog and all aboard were killed.

Wing Commander Walter Robert FARLEY 38 DFC
Flying Officer Ryszard ZGMUNTOWICZ 26 PAF Pilot
Flight Lieutenant Antoni Henryk VEOLLNAGEL 31 PAF
Flying Officer James Ansford PULTON Air Gunner
Flight Sergeant Bronislaw KARBOWSKI PAF
Sergeant Czeslaw MADRACKI 34 PAF
Sergeant Leon WILMANSKI 28 PAF
Sergeant Mieczslaw WOJCIECHOWSKI PAF
Vsevolod TROUSSEVITCH Soviet Agents
Peter STARISKY

20-Apr-42   Z9158   Whitley   138 Sqn   Porton Wiltshire   4

The aircraft had been engaged on a leaflet dropping sortie over France with two others from the same sqn. On return to Tangmere, the airfield was found to be covered by mist and so a diversion to Boscombe Down was initiated. However, the aircraft struck high ground near Porton and all on board were killed with the exception of the rear gunner.

Pilot Officer Ivan Anderson MILLER 29 RCAF Pilot
Sergeant Raymond Fred SHADDICK 19
Flight Sergeant Walter John Edward LINES RCAF
Sergeant Sydney William Francis LEIGH 21

68

20-Apr-42 BD143 DH Dominie   24 Sqn   Dalmillingto, Ayr   0

The aircraft lost an engine and the pilot elected to make a forced landing, having judged he could not safely continue. In the final stages of an approach into a field, the aircraft's tail struck a hedge and was torn off.

21-Apr-42 X7374 DH89A Rapide   24 Sqn   RAF Hendon   0

Destroyed by a fire on the ground.

22-Apr-42 AM725 Hudson   24 Sqn   RAF Hendon   0

The aircraft was destroyed after it caught fire in a hangar. The cause of the blaze is not recorded but the Accident Card comments that if the First Aid Fire Appliances had worked, the fire could have been contained before it took a hold.

24-Apr-42 BT787 Hotspur II   101 GOTU   Kidlington   0

The glider was being landed in a strong wind and its downwind leg was being flown close into the airfield's side, which necessitated a sharp turn crosswind. As the pilot made the turn, the glider's ground speed decayed rapidly and it was unable to reach the touchdown point before striking a stone wall. The Board of Enquiry had some strong comments to make about the landing techniques being taught at the Glider Training Schools and how many students were ignoring proper circuit procedures.

24-Apr-42 BT791 Hotspur II   102 GOTU   Kidlington   0

The aircraft had been on a cross country training sortie with a full load, in a formation practice. On return and having cast off the tow, the glider pilots misjudged their approach because the wind was stronger than expected. When it became clear that the glider would undershoot, the pilots raised the flaps in an attempt to stretch the glide but this did nothing more than increase the stalling speed of the glider, which duly obliged and it crashed short of the runway. The Board of Enquiry comments that pilots are continually told that raising the flaps of a fully loaded glider will gain nothing but it has to be queried – from a comfortable

Date	Serial	Aircraft	Unit	Place	Casualties
				Brief Circumstances of Accident	
				Casualty Details (If Applicable)	

distance of 65 years – what sort of aerodynamics instruction was being given to pilots in training if they did not appreciate the different stalling characteristics with flaps raised and lowered.

| 26-Apr-42 | K9765 | Hector | 1 GTS | Thame, Oxfordshire | 0 |

The aircraft made a normal landing but it then struck a ridge in the grass surface, causing the port wing to drop and the undercarriage to fracture under the strain.

| 28-Apr-42 | W7878 | Stinson 10C | 24 Sqn | Mill Hill | 0 |

Whilst being flown on an airtest, following a 30 hours' inspection, the aircraft had an engine failure and the pilot was compelled to force land it in a ploughed field, causing the aircraft to turn over.

| 30-Apr-42 | R2764 | Flamingo | 24 Sqn | Great Ouseburn Yorkshire | 10 |

The aircraft was being used to take a group of Soviet military personnel on a tour of inspection. In flight an engine failed after a piston broke away and the Accident Card suggests that the accident might have been avoided if the engines had been fitted with automatic propellers rather than constant speed units but does not elaborate on this point. The card also says that the fuel tanks disintegrated in the air but again there is no further information about this.

Pilot Officer Iain RAMSAY 35 Pilot
Flight Sergeant James Bennett SMITH 24 DFM Navigator
Flight Sergeant Alan James STRIPP 22 DFM Wireless Operator
Leading Aircraftman James LEWIS 25 Fitter
Squadron Leader Kenneth Wykeham EDWARDS 33 believed to be escorting officer
Flight Lieutenant Francis William WILTON

Colonel ROUSACHEW (correct spelling of name uncertain) Soviet Military Delegation
Major Petre BARANOV 36
Major Sergei ASIMOR 34
Major Boris SHVETZOU 31

05-May-42	N6246 DH86B	24 Sqn	RAF Hendon	0

The aircraft, from which the engines had been removed, was destroyed by a fire. The cause of the fire is not recorded.

06-May-42	LR230 Dakota	31 Sqn	Myitkyina	0

This aircraft and the one below were the first pair of four aircraft sent to Myitkyina to evacuate personnel and civilians in the face of the advancing Japanese forces. This aircraft was flown by Sqn Ldrs Withers and Mackie and its take-off from base had been delayed by poor weather for over 3½ hours. On landing at Myitkyina enemy air activity was noted but was thought to be simply a recce aircraft and both Dakotas were loaded and prepared for the return sortie. As it was taking off, the enemy attacked and a bomb exploded in front of the port wing of the aircraft, destroying it and causing the aircraft to veer round sharply. At the same time, a bomb exploded alongside LR231 as it was taxying out and its starboard mainwheel was damaged. Both aircraft were evacuated and the passengers and crews took shelter as best they could. Shortly after the other pair arrived and landed and during the course of the next few hours, several sorties were flown to continue the evacuation.

06-May-42	LR231 Dakota	31 Sqn	Myitkyina	0+3

This aircraft was flown by Sqn Ldr W H Burbury and Flt Lt Howell and was damaged in the incident summarised above. Two women and a child were killed during the attack but their names are not recorded and it is probable that they were civilian evacuees and their presence on the aircraft not documented or if they were, the records did not survive. This aircraft was attacked again in the afternoon as it lay abandoned and it was set on fire. As a consequence of their work during this period of operations Sqn Ldrs Withers

71

and Burbury were awarded the DFC. An account of this and other 31 Sqn activities are recorded in the book; "First In The Indian Skies" by Norman Franks.

06-May-42 BT637 Hotspur II   1 GTS   East of Thame   1

The glider approached the airfield correctly in a right hand circuit but was both too high and too slow. The crew then turned the aircraft away from the airfield and it stalled at a height of 150 feet and crashed off the resulting spin. At this stage, the Hotspur was not fitted with primary instruments in the rear cockpit and so an instructor in the rear depended on the student in the front seat for readings from the vital instruments, unless he is sufficiently experienced to judge speed, height etc accurately for himself.

Pilot Officer Frederick WALL

06-May-42 BT561 Hotspur II   2 GTS   RAF Weston on the Green   1

The glider took off behind the tug but immediately got into a very high position relative to it. At about 50 feet , the glider's right wing dropped, the tow rope detached and the glider stall turned to the right and dived vertically into the ground. The cause of this accident was the incorrect setting of the elevator trim to the 'fully tail down' position, which of itself means that the pilot's ability to push the nose forward would have been seriously limited. In addition, the tow rope release toggle was located by the pilot's right knee and hence he would have had to change hands quickly in order to cast off the tow. Having got into the predicament outlined, there would have been insufficient height to effect a safe recovery.

Major Francis Anthony Goss ROBINSON 28 MC Royal Artillery

14-May-42 K9770 Hector   296 Sqn   Shrewton L G, Wiltshire   0

The pilot was undertaking his first night solo on type and at the conclusion of the sortie, was given permission to land. However, another aircraft had been delayed at the take-off point and the airfield controller ordered a red aldis signal to be flashed at the pilot of this aircraft, to indicate he should not land. The aldis lamp failed at this point and unaware of the potential obstruction, the pilot continued his approach but then saw the other aircraft in the darkness and swung to avoid a collision and crashed, sustaining serious injuries and writing off the aircraft.

18-May-42 BT674 Hotspur II   2 GTS   RAF Weston on the Green   0

At the conclusion of a towing exercise, the pilot misjudged his approach and turned in to land too late and too far back from the touch down point. Thie wings fouled an obstruction and the glider overturned.

19-May-42 K9747 Hector   102 GOTU   Kidlington   0

The pilot came in low and misjudged his approach, striking a 2 foot high pile of gravel on the airfield boundary with the left wing and causing the aircraft to overturn. The gravel was for use in filling bomb craters but dumping it in line with the runway seems unwise. The pilot, who is said to have a bad habit of 'creeper' approaches, was injured. It has to be queried why, if the pilot's bad habits were known, they were not corrected by his supervisors.

29-May-42 V9595 Lysander III   161 Sqn   le Fay near Issoudin France   0

The aircraft became bogged down after landing at a small airstrip. It could not be freed and the pilot abandoned it and made his escape.

31-May-42 BD371 Whitley V   297 Sqn   Porton Down   1

The crew was engaged in night flying practice and after touchdown, the pilot opened the throttles to overshoot for another circuit. Immediately after take-off, he retracted the flaps instead of the undercarriage and the aircraft lost height and crashed. The Enquiry revealed that this was a fairly frequent happening amongst the less experienced pilots and the CO suggested that the Flap lever be graduated in such a way as

73

to prevent it being moved from 'fully-up' to 'fully-down' in a single movement and thereby avoid large, sudden, changes to the aircraft's trim, which are uncontrollable on heavy aircraft.

Sergeant Donald George GREEN 21 Wireless Operator

02-Jun-42   K9746   Hector   296 Sqn   Shrewton LG, Wiltshire   0

The pilot took off but immediately put the aircraft into a steep climbing turn to starboard. At about 150 feet, on a reciprocal heading, the aircraft stalled and crashed into the ground.

03-Jun-42   P1386   Albemarle I   AFDU   Near Ringway   0

The aircraft was being used by the Airborne Forces Development Unit on parachute dropping trials. The parachute with its dummy were dropped at 500 feet and the parachute snagged the tailplane causing the pilot – Fg Off A S Lucas - to lose partial control of the aircraft as the control surfaces were fouled. Nonetheless, a forced landing was made in an orchard and the pilot was commended for his airmanship.

03-Jun-42   BT500   Hotspur II   AFEE   Densford, near Chelveston   0

The aircraft was being flown on a training flight to assess the aircraft's performance. At 7500 feet, the pilot cast off the tow and dived the glider at 150 mph. On commencing the pull out, the tailplane detached and the wings folded, with the two crew being thrown out of the aircraft but subsequently able to pull their parachutes. The original findings blamed the pilot for mishandling the glider and causing a serious overstress, leading to the breakup. However, this incident was but one of series which led to structural modifications being made to strengthen the spars and alter the tailplane incidence.

74

04-Jun-42   Z9431   Whitley V   Irthlingborough   3

The Accident Card records a cryptic 'EF' for engine failure but gives no other information and the location of the crash is unreadable. In addition to the fatalities, two crew were injured.

     Sergeant Quinton Shirley MOORE 27 Pilot
     Sergeant Tom Lawson JACOBS 29
     Sergeant Herbert JOHNS 29

04-Jun-42   BT568   Hotspur II   101 GOTU   Kidlington   0

On take-off as leader of a formation of 3 gliders, the pilot of this aircraft held it down but in doing so, found himself below the tug aircraft's slipstream and was unable to lift the glider. The tow was released and the glider went through a hedge.

10-Jun-42   BT839   Hotspur II   296 Sqn   RAF Netheravon   0

The aircraft was taking off on an airsickness trial but the tug's engine cut and the tow was released. The pilot of this glider could not land ahead as the ground was unsuitable with air raid shelters and other obstructions. A turn back for a downwind landing was attempted but in the final stage of the turn, the port wing struck the ground and the glider swung onto the ground broadside.

11-Jun-42   BT728   Hotspur II   102 GOTU   Kidlington   0

The glider was undershooting the landing and the pilot raised the flaps and dived in an attempt to hit the field and then bounce the glider over the boundary wall! Unfortunately, the pilot misjudged this and the aircraft hit the wall.

14-Jun-42   BT682   Hotspur II   1 GTS   Kingston Bagpuize RLG 0

During the downwind leg to land with a full load, the wind changed and the aircraft overshot into a bank.

Date	Serial	Aircraft	Unit	Place	Casualties

Brief Circumstances of Accident
Casualty Details (If Applicable)

Date	Serial	Aircraft	Unit	Place	Casualties
14-Jun-42	DG473	Dakota	31 Sqn	60 miles east of Bangalore	0

The crew became lost in poor weather, caused by the tropical monsoon and the crew was unable to get any assistance from the wireless. The aircraft struck a ridge whilst making a forced landing in the gathering darkness, and its undercarriage collapsed.

| 14-Jun-42 | K9743 | Hector | 102 GOTU | Kidlington | 0 |

The aircraft was being landed downwind but it swung at the end of the landing run and the pilot checked this with rudder and brake but a swing developed in the opposite direction and the aircraft tipped onto its nose.

| 17-Jun-42 | BT485 | Hotspur II | AFEE | Near Snaith | 0 |

The aircraft was one of a pair of Hotspurs being used to trial the dual tow technique. After getting airborne, the glider encountered the tug's slipstream and the pilot lost control. In view of the proximity of the other glider, the tow was cast off and a forced landing attempted but in trying to stretch the glide to reach a suitable field, the pilot allowed the aircraft to stall and crash.

| 18-Jun-42 | BT789 | Hotspur II | 102 GOTU | ½ mile east of Kidlington | 1 |

The aircraft was making a dive approach and the pilot failed to pull out in time. The glider struck the ground and although the second pilot was injured, the handling pilot was killed.
Corporal John Harold KEENAN 21 The Glider Pilot Regiment

| 20-Jun-42 | BT771 | Hotspur II | AFEE | Tatton Mere, Cheshire | 0 |

This sortie was a deliberate ditching in Tatton Mere, as part of experiments to see the survivability aspects of landing the glider in water when fully loaded. The front of the glider disintegrated and Flight Lieutenant Kronfeld, the test pilot, was injured. The report records criptically, that water landings were impractical unless extensive modifications were made to the glider.

22-Jun-42   Z9224   Whitley   161 Sqn   RAF Tempsford   0
The airspeed indicator failed to operate properly during the take-off and the aircraft crashed.

22-Jun-42   K8093   Hector   101 GOTU   Kidlington   0
The pilot made a heavy touchdown and the aircraft bounced. He attempted to correct this with use of throttle but the aircraft bounced again several times and its undercarriage collapsed, before tipping onto its nose. After coming to rest, the aircraft was damaged further when it fell back onto its tail.

26-Jun-42   BT771   Hotspur II   296 Sqn   Chilbolton   0
The tug pilot was waved off by the ground handling party and took off with with its glider. Unfortunately, there was no pilot in the glider!

29-Jun-42   AE533   Hudson   24 Sqn   RAF Luqa   0
The aircraft was destroyed in an air raid after being hit by a bomb.

29-Jun-42   K9755   Hector   1 GTS   Thame   0
During the take-off run with a Hotspur glider in tow, the pilot felt a bump on the undercarriage but he continued the detail and climbed to 2000 feet before releasing the glider. On looking over the side, the pilot noticed the port wheel was hanging loose and so made a circuit and crash landed as best he could but the aircraft cartwheeled on to its nose. The pilot Sergeant C M Ward, was praised for his handling of the situation.

30-Jun-42   BT618   Hotspur II   102 GOTU   Bletchington near Oxford   2
The aircraft was struck by the discarded tow rope of another glider and tug combination and crashed.
        Sergeant George KENWORTHY 28
        + 1 other believed to be RAF

30-Jun-42   BT844   Hotspur II   102 GOTU   Kidlington   0
The tug pilot was given incorrect signals and then attempted a take-off with an unoccupied glider! One must query how the tow rope can be connected to an empty glider, if a set of operating procedures have been drawn up and are understood by those operating the aircraft.

01-Jul-42   BT622   Hotspur II   101 GOTU   Blockley, near Morton in the Marsh   0
The glider was engaged in a cross country towing exercise when the combination flew into cloud. The tow was released but the glider did not emerge from the cloud until it was 100 feet above the surrounding countryside. A suitable field could not be reached in the short time available and the aircraft flew into trees and crashed, causing serious injuries to Corporal H G Protheroe, the pilot.

01-Jul-42   BT565   Hotspur II   296 Sqn   1 mile south-east of Withycombe Church   0
The tug and glider combination were participating in a tactical troop carrying exercise and had been airborne for about 90 minutes. The pilot of the tug aircraft felt unwell and wanted to land immediately and so ordered the glider pilot to cast off the tow. This was done at low level and the glider overshot a barley field, crashing into a bank beyond.

01-Jul-42   K8108   Hector   296 Sqn   Croydon Hall, near Washford, Somerset   0

This aircraft was towing glider BT565 and the pilot cast off the tow because he was suffering from a severe headache. An emergency landing was made in a field but the pilot did not make full use of the space available and the aircraft ran into a wood. The pilot's station commander was unkind enough to suggest that the pilot was losing his nerve.

01-Jul-42   DL307   Master II   2 GTS   Slade Farm, near Bicester, Oxfordshire   1

The pilot was undertaking his first solo on type, which was to have been confined to circuits and landings. However, his aircraft flew into the ground at high speed during a gentle descending turn to starboard. An AIB investigation failed to determine the cause of the crash or to offer any plausible reasons for the crash.

Sergeant John Eric GOODRICH 26

13-Jul-42   BD534   Whitley   296 Sqn   Weston Zoyland   1

During take-off, the pilot was unable to pull the control column back properly and the aircraft failed to gain height and struck a gun post on the airfield. It transpired that the aircraft had probably been trimmed excessively nose heavy and this might have been caused by the removal of the stop on the elevator trim tab and the failure to remark the trim wheel.

Sergeant Laurence Edmond FAIRCHILD 38

14-Jul-42   K8140   Hector   1 GTS   Thame, Oxforshire   0

The aircraft's oleo leg collapsed on take-off due to failure of the rivets following continued landings on poor airfield surfaces. The pilot continued the take-off, flew a circuit and made a safe landing. With an aircraft of this vintage, no repair of substance would be made and the aircraft was scrapped.

15-Jul-42   BT569   Hotspur II   4 GTS   Kidlington   0

The tug and glider combination was engaged in a night towing exercise and had been airborne for 75

79

Date	Serial	Aircraft	Unit	Place	Casualties

Brief Circumstances of Accident
Casualty Details (If Applicable)

minutes. The glider pilot released the the tow prematurely and undershot the landing point by about 30 yards. The glider then struck a semi sunken pillbox which could have been avoided, had the pilot used his landing lamp during the approach.

| 19-Jul-42 | HH232 | Hotspur II | 5 GTS | Mixbury Hill Farm, near Bicester | 1 |

The aircraft was heavily loaded for a dual training sortie but for reasons not established, the pilot pulled off the tow prematurely at a low height. The glider was then turned, its nose dropped in a stall and it dived into the ground.

Sergeant John George FRUCHTL 26 RCAF Pilot

| 23-Jul-42 | HH141 | Hotspur II | 5 GTS | Kidlington | 0 |

The glider pilot cast off the tow at the start of a dive approach to landing. However, the starboard half of the tailplane and elevators broke away and the glider landed very fast and overturned. The structural failures of various parts of the Hotspurs' back end were by this time well known and a modification had been introduced to strengthen the attachment points and adjust the tailplane settings.

| 23-Jul-42 | K9740 | Hector | 296 Sqn | RAF Netheravon | 0 |

The pilot was approaching to land after completing a glider tow. On making a turn to avoid a tractor, the aircraft struck a moving tank, which wrenched off the port wheel. The pilot put the aircraft down on its starboard wheel but when the port oleo dug into the ground, the aircraft turned onto its back.

| 24-Jul-42 | AX768 | DC2 | 31 Sqn | Nandi State Forest | 11 |

The pilot was following a road but was not sure of his position, having failed to pinpoint his location. The

80

aircraft then entered a valley and having flown into cloud, the aircraft struck a hillside and burst into flames. This aircraft had started life as a civil airliner with American Airlines and coded; NC14966. It was sold to the US Treasury and eventually passed to the RAF in Khartoum in October 1941, serving with 117 Sqn before being transferred to 31 Sqn in India. Its early use is similar to several other DC2 and DC3 airliners acquired by the RAF before a steady flow of C47s became available.

Flight Lieutenant Paul GEAREY 25 Pilot
Flying Officer Terence Frederick James CRUDDEN 21 Co-Pilot
Flight Sergeant Stewart John MILES 22 Observer (Navigator)
Brigadier Edward Miles Gisborne BRITTAN 46
Brigadier Cecil Thomas BROWN OBE 47 Royal Marines
Group Captain Charles Anthony Hugh EVANS
Lieutenant Ronald Scott MCALPINE 29 The Loyal Regiment (North Lancashire)
Flight Sergeant Harry BRIGGS 25
Sergeant William Brailsford SPENCER 35
Aircraftman 1st Class Cyril Percival BIRD
Aircraftman 2nd Class Dennis Edgar Barton ATTWOOL 22

24-Jul-42 L5824 Bombay I 216 Sqn Western Desert location not specified ?
The aircraft was attacked by enemy fighters and the pilot was compelled to make a forced landing in the desert. It is unclear as to why the aircraft could not be recovered and there is scant evidence as to the circumstances surrounding the loss.

25-Jul-42 BT684 Hotspur II 4 GTS Kidlington 0
The glider was landing at night, in strong wind conditions and the pilot misjudged his approach. The aircraft crashed into the undershoot area short of the flarepath.

Date	Serial	Aircraft	Unit	Place	Casualties
		Brief Circumstances of Accident			
		Casualty Details (If Applicable)			

26-Jul-42   Z9282   Whitley   138 Sqn   Vire near Caen   4

The aircraft was one of nine Whitleys from 138 and 161 Sqns detailed to attack a power station at Cholet. On return from the raid, this aircraft crashed in Normandy. One of the crew; Sergeant P H Avery survived and was made a POW, spending some time in Stalag Luft 8B.

   Flight Sergeant John OWEN 21 Pilot
   Sergeant Douglas THORNTON 23
   Sergeant James WHALLEY 28
   Flight Sergeant William George ROCK 23 Wireless Operator

26-Jul-42   BT685   Hotspur II   2 GTS   ½ mile south-east of Weston on the Green   2

The glider was released from the tug at about 1000 feet but it broke up following an identical failure to that suffered by HH141 (see above). It dived into the ground, with the complete tail unit falling away separately.

   Pilot Officer Albert Farish JACKSON 22
   Sergeant Peter Hay CAMPBELL

27-Jul-42   L5835   Bombay I   216 Sqn   Western Desert location not specified   ?

The aircraft was parked when it was attacked and destroyed by enemy fighters.

29-Jul-42   BT852   Hotspur II   296 Sqn   Shrewton, Wiltshire   0

The aircraft was damaged when its crew undershot a night approach.

30-Jul-42   Z9230   Whitley   138 Sqn   5 miles west north west of Rijssen   7

The aircraft was shot down by a night fighter as it was approaching the dropping zone. The aircraft was the first aircraft to be lost as a result of being lured into a trap by the Germans who were controlling a captured Dutch radio operator.

Squadron Leader William Twiston DAVIES 23 DFC Pilot
Flight Sergeant LeonardSidney FRANKLIN 28
Flight Sergeant Trevor Morgan GRAY Wireless Operator
Sergeant Eric Henry KERRY 21 Wireless Operator
Sergeant Derek Frank STANTON 24
Sergeant Philip Thomas WRIGHT 22
Sergeant Geoffrey Barrington WOOD 20 Air Gunner

30-Jul-42   K8151   Hector   4 GTS   Hill House Farm, Somerton, Oxfordshire   0

The pilot allowed the main tank to run dry, before attempting to switch over to the gravity tanks and the engine stopped. The pilot landed in a field of standing wheat which caused the aircraft to flip onto its back. Higher authority was unimpressed by the pilot's performance and he was described as 'careless' and 'lacking commonsense' and his Log Book was endorsed accordingly.

03-Aug-42   BD639   Whitley V   HGCU   Black Bourton Oxfordshire   0

The aircraft was towing a glider and failed to climb away after take-off and struck some trees. It seems possible that the cause was the engines overheating because of the use of boost settings during a take-off with a glider.

05-Aug-42   DP714   Horsa I   HGCU   Bampton, Oxfordshire   2

The aircraft's tail detached in flight, due to structural failure, and it crashed. The reason for the failure is not disclosed but it is worth noting that the first glider lost during the Arnhem attack on 17 Sep 44, lost its

Date	Serial	Aircraft	Unit	Place	Casualties

Brief Circumstances of Accident
Casualty Details (If Applicable)

tail from presumed structural failure.

Flying Officer Colin Joseph Edward BOUSTEAD 22
+ one

06-Aug-42 BT546 Hotspur II AFEE Allerton Park, Yorkshire 1
The glider was being towed behind a Halifax in a triple tow configuration. The glider's cockpit hood came off and may have struck the pilot. The tow was immediately cast off and and a forced landing attempted but the glider struck a tree. The pilot was not wearing goggles and this might have affected his vision.

Flight Sergeant Eric Gordon TRAVIS

06-Aug-42 BT799 Hotspur II 296 Sqn RAF Netheravon 1
The glider became caught in the tug aircraft's slipstream and was uncontrollable. The glider pilot was unable to fly the glider into a position above the slipstream and it slipped to starboard and into the ground. An RAF 2nd pilot and four non RAF personnel were injured but the 1st pilot was killed.

Sergeant John Edward SMITH The Glider Pilot Regiment

07-Aug-42 L5814 Bombay I 216 Sqn Near LG90 18
This aircraft was engaged on a routine passenger carrying sortie but on this occasion was carrying wounded troops to the rear area, as well as Lieutenant General W H E Gott, the commander designate of 8th Army. The aircraft was attacked by fighters of the Luftwaffe JG27 and its starboard engine was set on fire, followed by more general damage and the loss of the port engine. The fuel tanks were ruptured and the aircraft crashed in flames. Although a few men escaped from the wreck through the cockpit and forward emergency hatches, most were trapped in the rear and were unable to clear the already burning aircraft because the

main door was jammed. For his bravery both during and following this action, the pilot Sergeant H G James was awarded a DFM. Subsequently commissioned, he received an AFC in 1946.

Lieutenant General William Henry Ewart GOTT 44 CB CBE DSO MC
Leading Aircraftman Peter Noel HOWARTH
Leading Aircraftman John Charles MANNING 21
Private Robert Thomas CHARLESWORTH 24 2nd Bn West Yorkshire Regt
Gunner John CLEARY 52 LAA Regt Royal Artillery
Signalman Joseph Taverner COX 29 Royal Corps of Signals
Lance Corporal George David DODD 34 1st/4th Bn Essex Regt
Driver Nochum UNDI RASC
Trooper John Joseph LAMB 35 50th Regt Reconnaissance Corps
Gunner Thomas MCDONALD 32 1 LAA Regt Royal Artillery
Sapper Frank PRICE 32 588 Field Coy Royal Engineers
Private Arthur Robert SAGGERS 22 RAOC
Corporal J E SMART Regiment President Steyn South African Forces
Private William WILSON 42 2nd Bn West Yorkshire Regt
+ four others whose names were not found

11-Aug-42   DP717   Horsa I   HGCU   RAF Brize Norton   0

At the conclusion of a 15 minute sortie, the aircraft was landing in a strong wind with full flaps set. The pilot misjudged the approach in this configuration and the glider hit the boundary fence.

13-Aug-42   BT536   Hotspur II   GPEU   4 miles west of Lisburn, Ulster   0

The glider was being ferried when the tug pilot towed the combination into cloud and conditions of rain and poor visibility, contrary to instructions. The intercom between the tug and glider, which was generally unsatisfactory in any event, had failed in this case. The glider pilot elected to pull off the tow and then attempted a forced landing in a small field but the glider was damaged.

Date	Serial	Aircraft	Unit	Place	Casualties

Brief Circumstances of Accident
Casualty Details (If Applicable)

16-Aug-42 N7357 Hudson 267 Sqn ???????? ?

The aircraft is recorded as being lost on this date but there is no explanation of the cause nor any reference to casualties amongst the crew.

16-Aug-42 K8145 Hector 4 GTS Kidlington 0

The pilot, who had little night flying experience, was attempting a landing in the dark but held off too high and the aircraft stalled onto the ground, landed heavily and its undercarriage collapsed.

17-Aug-42 BT793 Hotspur II 1 GTS Chapel Lane, Charlbury, Oxon 1

The combination was engaged in a cross country training sortie when the engine of the Hector tug aircraft failed because of the pilot's faulty cockpit drill. The glider and its tow rope were released but although the glider appeared to fly normally at first, its nose rose, it stalled at low level and crashed before a recovery could be made. The glider pilot's failure to reset the elevator trimming lever and not to jettison the tow rope, were contributing factors in the loss of control.

Corporal Edgar Sanderson BEEVERS 26 Glider Pilot Regiment

17-Aug-42 HH519 Hotspur II 3 GTS Near Stoke Orchard 1

The glider pilot did not climb his aircraft above the tug's slipstream and then decided to pull off the tow as a precaution. This was done but he then attempted a turn back to land but in doing so the glider crashed.

Corporal Nigel Guthrie MCQUEEN 27 Glider Pilot Regiment

20-Aug-42 BD536 Whitley V 296 Sqn RAF Leuchars 7

The aircraft stalled on the approach to land in gusty wind conditions and dived into the ground. It was

86

judged that the pilot had probably aproached at too low a speed and the passengers might not have been properly distributed in the aircraft causing a rearward shift in its centre of gravity when the flaps were lowered.

Pilot Officer John WOODS 31 Pilot
Flight Sergeant Joseph Harold KELLY 26 RCAF
Flight Sergeant James Joseph MAJOR 28 RCAF
Aircraftman 2nd Class Denham Frederick ARMSTRONG 20
Aircraftman 2nd Class Reginald Ford FISHER 21
Aircraftman 2nd Class Raymond Frederick George PADFIELD 21
Aircraftman 2nd Class William INGLIS 19

20-Aug-42	BT551	Hotspur II	2 GTS	Slade Farm, Oxfordshire	0

This was another red faced occasion when the tug towed off an empty glider!

22-Aug-42	AX681	Lockheed 14	117 Sqn	Bilbeis	0

The aircraft ground looped on landing, its undercarriage collapsed and it caught fire. The Accident Card – rather quaintly – states; 'the undercarriage collapsed because the aircraft was old and had a "bad reputation"'. The aircraft was left derelict for sometime in Kenya and was then offered to AOC Iraq but he (probably wisely) discarded it.

23-Aug-42	BD417	Whitley V	296 Sqn	Andreas Isle of Man	5

The loss of this aircraft is a rather bizarre episode! The crew had been tasked to tow a glider from Netheravon to Nutts Corner but over the Irish Sea, the glider had broken loose and had been ditched successfully and stayed afloat long enough for the five people on board to take to their dinghy. The Whitley crew called for assistance and remained in the area until a warship arrived to rescue the glider's occupants. The Whitley was then diverted to Ronaldsway because its fuel was running low. At Ronaldsway the pilot contacted his base and was advised to return to Netheravon but he needed first to refuel and there was no 100 octane aviation fuel at Ronaldsway and so a short flight was made to Andreas. On arrival, the crew was met by the station commander who coerced the pilot into letting him fly the Whitley, a type with which he had plenty of experience. The station commander took with him on the sortie an Army officer, the station's duty pilot, a civilian female friend and four airmen, the last group being positioned in the rear of the aircraft. Immediately after take-off the aircraft stalled and dived into the ground at West Kimmeragh Farm and broke up on impact with the forward section catching fire. Those in the nose section were killed immediately and whilst three of the four airmen in the rear section were able to escape relatively unscathed, but the fourth suffered serious head injuries from which he died. Major Wait's son, Richard, was killed serving in Burma in early 1945 and is buried at Taukkyan War Cemetery. The cause of the accident is thought to have been due to the aircraft taking off with full flaps set, no flaps at all or being badly out of trim. The Board of Enquiry, however, is certain of one thing – the pilot had been drinking! Wing Commander Knowles had served with considerable distinction and commanded 138 Sqn, participating in many of the early special duties sorties and been responsible for the development of some of the techniques and tactics used. That he should die in these circumstances is particularly unfortunate.

Wing Commander Edward Vincent KNOWLES DFC
Flying Officer Andrew Bryce PATON
Major Geoffrey Killigrew WAIT MC The Wiltshire Regiment
Miss Thelma KERSLEY daughter of Sir Robert Kersley
Corporal Alfred HENDERSON

23-Aug-42   BT666   Hotspur II   GPEU   Irish Sea off Isle of Man   0
This was the glider referred to in the previous accident. The glider suffered the structural failure of the tailplane which caused a number of other accidents and as it became uncontrollable, the glider pilots cast off the tow and ditched the aircraft in the sea.

25-Aug-42 Z9232 Whitley 138 Sqn 6 miles south east Romorantin-Lamthenay 0
The aircraft was being used to drop supplies when it crashed and was destroyed by fire. The crew all escaped and were successful in evading capture and returned safely to the UK in due course.

25-Aug-42 BT597 Hotspur II 2 GTS RAF Weston on the Green 0
The glider landed short because the pilot misjudged his approach.

26-Aug-42 BT790 Hotspur II 1 GTS RAF Croughton 0
The pilot made a poor approach and turned in steeply and late, striking a building with the port wing in the process.

27-Aug-42 K8155 Hotspur 4 GTS Kidlington 0
The aircraft was damaged when it swung on landing in light wind conditions.

27-Aug-42 Z9275 Whitley 138 Sqn Merville Nord France 3
The aircraft crashed in the vicinity of a German airfield and although two of the crew survived to become POWs, the others were killed. The cause of the loss is not known.

Flight Sergeant David Harrison FREELAND
Flight Sergeant Edmund George HAYHOE 19
Flight Sergeant Frederick George GREEN 21 Wireless Operator

29-Aug-42 BT594 Hotspur II 2 GTS RAF Weston on the Green 0
The aircraft was cast off by the tug, as the pilot of the latter was having trouble controlling his aircraft. A landing was made heavily within the airfield.

Date	Serial	Aircraft	Unit	Place	Casualties
		Brief Circumstances of Accident			
		Casualty Details (If Applicable)			
31-Aug-42	BD667	Whitley V	HGCU	RAF Brize Norton	0

On take-off with a glider in tow, the aircraft struck a hangar and crashed. The cause of the accident was due to one of several possible reasons: first the pilot throttled back the starboard engine to correct a swing, the airfield surface was soft following a heavy shower and this impeded acceleration or third, the glider pilot pulled the glider off early, thereby increasing the drag. This accident took place at 0135 hours and the accident reported below happened 2120 hours the same day: the pilot in each case was the same!

Date	Serial	Aircraft	Unit	Place	Casualties
31-Aug-42	BD438	Whitley V	HGCU	Black Bourton Oxfordshire	2

The aircraft was towing a glider off on a calm night and the pilot was unable to clear trees which were in line with the take-off path selected. It was commented that the Whitley had a poor rate of climb when towing a glider in still conditions. The glider was cast off but it too struck trees. Flying Officer Thornley's two brothers also died on military service during the war.

Flying Officer Walter THORNEY 28 Pilot
+ one other

Date	Serial	Aircraft	Unit	Place	Casualties
31-Aug-42	DP755	Horsa I	HGCU	Black Bourton, Oxfordshire	0

As outlined above, this glider struck trees after its tug had hit some other trees during the take-off. The 3 crew of the glider were injured.

Date	Serial	Aircraft	Unit	Place	Casualties
31-Aug-42	K8154	Hector	GPEU	Shrewton LG, Wiltshire	0

The pilot failed to overshoot for another attempt, after a poor approach. The aircraft overshot and ran into a ridge of earth and turned over. The pilot was disciplined for bad airmanship.

01-Sep-42 V9597 Lysander III   161 Sqn   Arbigny 12 miles north north east Macon   0
The aircraft, flown by Sqn Ldr Guy Lockhart – who was to become a renowned Pathfinder pilot – taxyed into a ditch after landing and was then deliberately set on fire. Lockhart escaped back to the UK

02-Sep-42 V9230 Hudson III   24 Sqn   RAF Luqa   0
Whilst the aircraft was taking off, its port tyre burst. It swung to port and the pilot was unable to correct this; the undercarriage collapsed and the aircraft caught fire.

02-Sep-42 K8139 Hector   4 GTS   Hook Horton, Oxfordshire   0
The engine failed because the pilot did not change over the fuel feed quickly enough to gravity feed. The aircraft was at 600 feet and the pilot attempted a forced landing but the aircraft turned over in the process.

02-Sep-42 DL425 Master II   2 GTS   Witney, Oxfordshire   2
The aircraft was towing a glider (Hotspur HH518) on a low level cross country flight not below 200 feet and to avoid built up areas. It flew into a church steeple, which was 165 feet high, and crashed.
       Sergeant G F H COUGH (or GOUGH)

04-Sep-42 BD543 Whitley V   296 Sqn   Hampshire (location obscured)   7
The aircraft had been flown on an automatic pilot test and at the conclusion of the sortie was returning to land. The port engine failed and the aircraft stalled before entering a spiral turn, striking some trees, crashing and catching fire.

       Flying Officer John CALLAHAN 23 RAAF Pilot
       Pilot Officer William Richard STEPHENS
       Sergeant Alfred DOUGHERTY
       Pilot Officer Kenneth Graham AVERY
       Flight Sergeant Richard John MAYES 31

91

Date	Serial	Aircraft	Unit	Place	Casualties
Brief Circumstances of Accident					
Casualty Details (If Applicable)					

Believed to be:
Captain Hubert Ray TAYLOR Royal Warwickshire Regt
2nd Lieutenant Arthur Edward Godstone TWELVETREES 24 The Hampshire Regt

Date	Serial	Aircraft	Unit	Place	Casualties
04-Sep-42	HH263	Hotspur II	3 GTS	Stoke Orchard	0

The glider struck the ground with its port wing after the pilot turned in to land at too low an altitude.

| 04-Sep-42 | HH332 | Hotspur II | 3 GTS | Beddington House Farm, Cheltenham | 1 |

The aircraft stalled and in the subsequent dive its tailplane failed and it crashed out of control.

Corporal Wallace Charles PALMER 21 The Glider Pilot Regiment

| 05-Sep-42 | EW944 | Hudson VI | 267 Sqn | Kabrit | 0 |

The undercarriage collapsed after the aircraft ground looped following a swing that the pilot was unable to halt, despite closing the throttles.

| 07-Sep-42 | EW964 | Hudson VI | 117 Sqn | Asmara, Eritrea | 0 |

The aircraft was being landed in a strong crosswind. The technique for doing so is to keep the tail up for as long as possible, thereby retaining some rudder control to assist maintaining direction. The pilot did not do this and was faced with the option of correcting the swing with throttles and differential braking or braking to try to avoid aircraft towards which the aircraft was heading. He chose the latter option but the undercarriage collapsed.

07-Sep-42   DL519 Master II   1 GTS   Fritwell, Upper heyford, Oxfordshire   1

This aircraft was towing the Hotspur listed below on a glider pilot training exercise. The tug dived into the ground in a side slipping attitude and was destroyed in the subsequent fire. The glider was pulled down in a steep dive and crashed with the tug. Whilst it seems possible that the start of the accident sequence was the glider getting too high behind the tug and pulling its tail up, the investigation looked at but was unable to discover, why neither pilot pulled off the tow.

Pilot Officer James Ilott EVANS 21

07-Sep-42   HH402 Hotspur II   1 GTS   Fritwell, Upper Heyford, Oxfordshire   1

Destroyed in the accident summarised above. It is considered possible that the pilot might have had difficulty operating the tow rope release.

Corporal Thomas Edward ELLIDGE 20 The Glider Pilot Regiment

11-Sep-42   DL532 Master II   3 GTS   Stoke Orchard   0

The aircraft was taking off with a crew of 2 RAF pilots for a training sortie but the cockpit checks had not been done prior to starting the roll and the rudder trim was set to full starboard deflection. In consequence as speed built and the flying controls started to 'bite', the aircraft swung and in doing so it struck a stationary glider.

11-Sep-42   HH296 Hotspur II   3 GTS   Stoke Orchard   0

This aircraft, which was parked and unmanned, was struck by Master DL532 as summarised above.

12-Sep-42   K9780 Hector   4 GTS   Kidlington   0

The pilot held off too long and the aircraft stalled from 10 feet and struck the ground heavily with its wing before turning over.

93

Date	Serial	Aircraft	Unit	Place	Casualties

Brief Circumstances of Accident
Casualty Details (If Applicable)

| 14-Sep-42 | HH376 | Hotspur II | 1 GTS | RAF Croughton | 0 |

The tug pilot could not maintain his aircraft's airspeed after take-off because the glider, which was fully laden, had got into the low position and its drag was affecting the tug's angle of attack and hence its ability to accelerate. The glider was cast off and damaged in the subsequent forced landing.

| 14-Sep-42 | BT489 | Hotspur II | GPEU | Maiden Bradley, Wiltshire | 0 |

The combination encountered bad weather and pressed on despite entering thick cloud, instead of turning back. The glider lost the tug in the cloud and the glider pilot pulled off the tow. In attempting a forced landing, the pilot encountered trees and in overshooting these he struck a fence.

| 14-Sep-42 | BT490 | Hotspur II | GPEU | Hampshire | 0 |

During a tactical troop carrying training exercise, the combination encountered poor weather and at a height of 150 feet the glider was released. Unfortunately, the glider was not fully under control at the time of release and it hit the ground heavily, injuring 6 of those on board.

| 14-Sep-42 | K8112 | Hector | GPEU | Eversleigh, Wiltshire | 0 |

The pilot was taking this aircraft to retrieve gliders, which had earlier been released as part of an exercise to demonstrate a landing of glider bourne troops. The landing at the retrieval site was made down a slope and the when the pilot realised the aircraft was in danger of overshooting he applied the brakes harder and the aircraft skidded before tipping onto its nose. As visibility was indifferent, the pilot was unable to gain a clear impression of the lie of the land and the ground party set up the landing 'T' in the wrong direction, as iven the field's slope, it would have been more appropriate to lay the 'T' in the other direction.

15-Sep-42   K9706   Hector   4 GTS   Wytham, Oxfordshire   1
The aircraft was towing the glider listed below at night and low level. The combination ran into cloud at about 600 feet, when the forecast weather deterioration took place earlier than expected. Whilst still on tow both aircraft flew into the ground south of Kidlington.

    Sergeant Alistair William ALLEN 20 RNZAF

15-Sep-42   BT505   Hotspur II   4 GTS   Wytham, Oxforshire   2
Flew into the ground whilst being towed by the Hector shown above.

    Pilot Officer Hugh Thomas WELLER-POLEY 20
    Corporal Hugh Walter Charles CORKE 18 The Glider Pilot Regiment

16-Sep-42   EM260   Master II   5 GTS   Shobdon, Herefordshire   2
The aircraft was being used for a glider towing sortie and after releasing the glider, the aircraft went into a steep turn to starboard but then spun off the turn. Although the spin was stopped at 100 feet, there was insufficient height to recover from the dive. Although the investigation suggested a poorly executed turn before dropping the tow rope, there was also a theory that the pilot's ability was impaired by carbon monoxide poisoning but the true cause of the accident was not found.

    Pilot Officer Peter John Ernest MASON
    + one other

17-Sep-42   FH464   Hudson IIIA   24 Sqn   RAF North Front   0
Whilst being refuelled, the aircraft caught fire and was damaged beyond repair. The fire was caused because the fuselage fuel tank had not been bonded properly to the aircraft.

17-Sep-42   BT776   Hotspur II   5 GTS   Shobdon, Herefordshire   0
The glider pilot failed to acknowledge a signal from the air control party and the tug pilot believed the

Brief Circumstances of Accident
Casualty Details (If Applicable)

glider had pulled off and so he dropped the tow rope! The glider was left to make a downwind landing and whilst doing so it ran into a drainage ditch on the edge of the airfield.

18-Sep-42   AX687   Lockheed 18   117 Sqn   1 mile north of Bilbeis   0

The aircraft was being used for single engined flying practice and had a crew of an instructor and two students. The instructor inadvertently feathered both propellers and then made a belly landing but the aircraft was damaged when it went over a 4 feet high drop. The investigation revealed that the feathering buttons were very close together and it was very easy to press both at the same time.

19-Sep-42   Z6940   Whitley V   161 Sqn   Near Boulogne   6

The crew was detailed for a sortie coded TERRIER, to be flown into Belgium. However, the aircraft crashed near Boulogne with the loss of its complete crew.

    Flight Sergeant James David WALLS 20 Pilot
    Flight Sergeant Frank McLeod MACDONALD 26 RCAF Pilot
    Pilot Officer Michael Robert SYMONDS 19 Wireless Operator
    Sergeant Walter Ernest Ruskin WRIGHT 31
    Sergeant Alan Richard ASHFORD Wireless Operator
    Sergeant Harry PATEMAN 29 Wireless Operator

23-Sep-42   HH242   Hotspur II   4 GTS   Leckhampstead, Bucks   0

Despite instructions to the contrary, the tug pilot towed the glider into cloud in the vicinity of rain and thunderstorms. The glider pilot lost sight of the tug and so cast off the tow as a precaution. A forced landing was then made but the glider was damaged by the rough ground.

24-Sep-42 BT624 Hotspur II 2 GTS Chesterton, Oxfordshire 1

The aircraft was on tow behind Master DL516 and both aircraft crashed and were destroyed, with fatal injuries to their pilots. From evidence available it seems the glider was very high above the tug and that the glider suffered structural failure during the descent. It is also known that the tow rope was not released, either because the mechanism failed or the glider pilot did not try to release the cable.

   Corporal Reginald Frederick ATKINSON 21 Glider Pilot Regiment

24-Sep-42 DL516 Master II 2 GTS Chesterton, Oxfordshire 1

This aircraft was destroyed in the circumstances summarised above. There is a suggestion that the reason for the glider pilot being unable to maintain station was that the tug pilot was flying too fast.

   Sergeant Albert Victor WATSON 32

25-Sep-42 L5833 Bombay I 216 Sqn Kufra ?

This aircraft and the two others listed below were destroyed during an enemy air attack on the Kufra Oasis.

25-Sep-42 L5843 Bombay I 216 Sqn Kufra ?

Destroyed as outlined above.

25-Sep-42 L5857 Bombay I 216 Sqn Kufra ?

Destroyed as outlined above.

25-Sep-42 Z9131 Whitley 161 Sqn Sevigny-Waleppe Ardennes 1

The crew was engaged on a double sortie coded; MONGOOSE and PRIMO. Two agents and half a dozen containers were dropped but the aircraft was subsequently abandoned by its crew, all of whom evaded capture and returned to UK, with the exception of one member who was fatally injured.

   Sergeant Ronald Eden FRANKLIN 28 (died of wounds)

Date	Serial	Aircraft	Unit	Place	Casualties

Brief Circumstances of Accident
Casualty Details (If Applicable)

27-Sep-42	AX769	DC3	31 Sqn	Lahore	0

The aircraft undershot the runway whilst landing and its undercarriage struck a pile of cement and collapsed. The aircraft was dismantled and taken to Bangalore with the intention of rebuilding it but this was abandoned and the aircraft was struck off charge on 1 Apr 43.

27-Sep-42	BT676	Hotspur II	GPEU	Shrewton	1

At 400 feet on the climb after take-off, the tow rope broke. The pilot attempted a forced landing off the airfield but the glider struck a telegraph pole and the 2 crew were injured, when they were crushed by the load of ballast being carried, with one dying of his injuries several weeks later. A recommendation that the gliders should be fitted with landing lamps was made – and had been as the result of other accidents – and that a reliable intercom be provided. Colonel Rock was one of the 'founding fathers' of British airborne forces and his death was felt keenly within both the Army and RAF. At the time of his death he was the Army's senior glider pilot.

Lieutenant Colonel John Frank ROCK 37 RE died of injuries

29-Sep-42	EB308	Whitley V	HGCU	Brize Norton village	0

The aircraft was towing a glider and it swung on take-off before climbing steeply and then stalling. It dived into the ground about 250 yards beyond the airfield boundary and caught fire: the glider pilot released his aircraft from the tow and made a forced landing. The accident was caused by the pilot's relative inexperience and difficulty wil handling the swing as it developed.

29-Sep-42	DP763	Horsa I	HGCU	Brize Norton Village	0

At about 100 feet on the climb after take-off, the glider pilot realised that the tug pilot was having difficulty and so cast off the tow. With little room and time to spare, the glider pilot force landed the aircraft in an orchard. Although the instructor was uninjured the student pilot sustained injuries.

| 01-Oct-42 | FK491 | Hudson VI | 267 Sqn | Bilbeis | 0 |

The aircraft swung to port during its take-off run and then pivoted completely around, breaking off the undercarriage legs, damaging the wing tip and fracturing the main spar. The pilot was not quick enough in correcting the initial swing, which he ought to have anticipated, as the was a strong crosswind.

| 01-Oct-42 | W7776 | Halifax | 138 Sqn | Goldsborough Yorkshire | 0 |

The all Polish crew was tasked to fly to a DZ near Minsk and drop 4 men on that location or at 2 alternatives. They were successful in accomplishing the primary task but having been airborne for 13½ hours, the aircraft ran out of fuel and it crashed landed at Goldsborough, a village north-west of Whitby and close to the coast; a close run thing with a ditching in prospect.

| 02-Oct-42 | BT688 | Hotspur II | 3 GTS | Stoke Orchard | 2 |

The aircraft had been airborne for only 10 minutes and the pilot was to practice a dive approach. The glider was seen to be diving at a steeper than normal angle but the pilot did not initiate a pull out until very late and although the glider was seen to flatten out its angle of dive, it mushed into the ground with considerable vertical velocity.

Corporal George Geoffrey ASHWORTH 25 Glider Pilot Regiment

| 02-Oct-42 | HH227 | Hotspur II | 4 GTS | Kidlington | 2 |

The pilot started a dive approach to the airfield from too low a height and then delayed the pull out and the aircraft crashed heavily into the ground.

Corporal John Edward DENWOOD 22 The Glider Pilot Regiment
Corporal John Nicol GULLAN 20

99

Date	Serial	Aircraft	Unit	Place	Casualties

Brief Circumstances of Accident
Casualty Details (If Applicable)

02-Oct-42   HH146   Hotspur II   4 GTS   Kidlington   2

Twenty minutes after the accident recorded above, there was an essentially repeat performance from the crew of this aircraft, with the glider pilot failing to pull his aircraft out of the dive in time.

Sergeant Arthur Henry Rufus BASKETT 23 The Glider Pilot Regiment
Corporal Frank Ainge QUARRELL 22

03-Oct-42   Z6653   Whitley   161 Sqn   Off the Netherlands Coast   4

This aircraft was one of a pair sent to drop supplies into the Netherlands. It developed engine trouble and was ditched off the coast. Two of the crew; Pilot Officer E Edge, the pilot, and Sergeant D L Taafe, were rescued by the enemy and became POW.

Sergeant John Reginald Simpson SCOTT 21 Pilot
Pilot Officer Joseph Alec Charles KITE 23
Sergeant Kenneth Thorpe HARBRIDGE 22
Sergeant Alfred GANDER 20

03-Oct-42   T9429   Hudson   24 Sqn   Off Gibraltar   0

The starboard engine had failed in flight and the pilot was making an asymmetric approach to RAF North Front. As the undercarriage was lowered the port engine also cut and the aircraft was ditched short of the runway. The cause of the sequential engine failure is not recorded.

03-Oct-42   X9734   Wellington 1C   SD Flt   70 miles south of Crete   1

The aircraft was flown by 2 experienced SD captains; Pilot Officers E R Ridgeway and F A Wood, with a navigator who was well into his tour with 23 sorties completed on 104 Sqn; Pilot Officer L Manfield. After a successful drop of supplies to a DZ controlled by partisan forces on Crete, the crew set course for base but the aircraft's port engine failed and it steadily lost height before being ditched in the sea. The rear gunner is thought to have been killed or seriously incapacitated on impact and despite attempts to extricate him from the wreck, he could not be recovered and was lost when the aircraft sank. Having taken to their dinghy, the surviving crew discovered that the rations had been stolen and the water container was so perished that the water was contaminated and undrinkable. The weather was very poor and the crew was adrift for nearly 2 days before being rescued by a Royal Navy motor torpedo boat. Subsequently, Leslie Manfield, a Welsh international rugby player, received the DFC for his work with special duties units. Flight Sergeant Goldsmith had been awarded the DFM for outstanding bravery in August 1941, when serving on 90 Sqn. The citation for his award suggests that he might so easily have received higher recognition for his actions.

Flight Sergeant Norman Frederick Temple GOLDSMITH DFM Rear Gunner

---

06-Oct-42   HH142 Hotspur II   4 GTS   Wootton, Oxfordshire   0

The tug entered a dive and the glider pilot found himself in the tug's slipstream and so cast off the tow. The pilot then attempted a forced landing in a field but struck a tree in the process.

08-Oct-42   FK509 Hudson VI   31 Sqn   5 miles south-west Karachi   0

The aircraft suffered an engine failure on take-off and the pilot forced landed it when it became impossible to maintain height or fly a successful single engined circuit.

13-Oct-42   K8097 Hector   GIS   Thame   0

The pilot landed at too high a speed and then used his brakes harshly to attempt to stop, rather than overshooting and flying another approach. The aircraft's wing struck the ground when a swing was induced and the aircraft tipped onto its nose.

Date	Serial	Aircraft	Unit	Place	Casualties
		Brief Circumstances of Accident			
		Casualty Details (If Applicable)			
14-Oct-42	EW961	Hudson VI	267 Sqn	Kufra Oasis	0

The aircraft was struck by a bomb during an enemy air attack on the oasis.

| 14-Oct-42 | EW968 | Hudson VI | 216 Sqn | Khartoum | 0 |

The aircraft was taking off in a crosswind and it started to swing. The pilot was unable to correct the swing and the undercarriage collapsed, followed by a fire which destroyed the aircraft.

| 15-Oct-42 | DP373 | Horsa I | GPEU | RAF Wroughton | 2 |

The combination was taking off in a strong crosswind and as the glider became airborne, its port wing dropped and touched the ground. The glider climbed steeply at which point the tug pilot cast off the tow and the glider stalled off the top and crashed to the ground. The pilot of the tug aircraft had made the decision to use a longer runway, which was 'out of wind' rather than that into wind but at this stage in development it was unlikely that the full handling characteristics of the Horsa had been examined. In consequence a crosswind component of 8 mph was specified as the maximum for a Horsa.

Sergeant Douglas Harrison STEWART RCAF
Sergeant Leslie Albert George BUCKTON 22

| 22-Oct-42 | BD228 | Whitley | 161 Sqn | Tempsford | 1 |

The crew had attempted a sortie to Belgium but having received no reception at the DZ, they returned. The aircraft crashed on landing and caught fire. Besides the captain being fatally injured, two crew members were seriously injured and three others sustained minor injuries. Smith's DFC, which was not gazetted until 2 months after his death, was awarded for his work with the squadron.

Pilot Officer Wreford William George SMITH 22 DFC Pilot

102

22-Oct-42   EW984 Lodestar II   267 Sqn   Bilbeis East   13

The aircraft was taking off on a passenger sortie to Lydda. Immediately after take-off the pilot made a steep climbing turn through 90 degrees and commenced a beat up of the Officers' Mess. The aircraft then turned through 270 degrees close to the ground, its port wing struck the top of a tent and it crashed partly inverted into the ground. The blame for the accident was laid firmly on the pilot and he was held to have been guilty of culpable negligence. The contemporary RAF magazine 'Tee Emm' published a critical report of this accident and accusing the pilot of killing twelve RAF personnel by his actions: a fairly hard hitting summary by any account.

    Wing Commander John Patrick Stracey SMYTH 31 DFC Pilot
    Flight Lieutenant Ernest Francis Victor COPSEY 23
    Flying Officer Roy Anderson HARPER 25 RAAF
    Corporal Reginald BENSON 21
    Corporal Gerald Alexander GRANT 25
    Pilot Officer Corliss St Leger HAWKES 21
    Warrant Officer II Vern Selby IRWIN RCAF Observer
    Sergeant George Rollinson MACBRYDE Wireless Operator/Air Gunner
    Sergeant Arthur William MILLS 25 Wireless Operator/Air Gunner
    Flight Sergeant Brian Joseph O'CONNOR 26 Observer
    Warrant Officer I Walter H PLANT 23 RCAF Observer
    Pilot Officer John Cecil Oliver TRENCH 19
    Pilot Officer David Maxwell WALKER 29

22-Oct-42   P5029   Whitley   138 Sqn   At sea off Eastbourne   0

This aircraft, flown by a very experienced SD captain – Pilot Officer Gervase Newport-Tinley – and the crew had completed successfully a drop of eight containers into a DZ in France. On return, an engine failed and the aircraft was ditched close in-shore and near the pier at Eastbourne. The crew was quickly rescued by the Royal Navy.

Date	Serial	Aircraft	Unit	Place	Casualties

Brief Circumstances of Accident
Casualty Details (If Applicable)

23-Oct-42   BT723   Hotspur II   GPEU   Queens Drive, Liverpool   3

The glider was towed into cloud and the glider pilot lost contact and his glider got out of position, leading to the tow rope parting. The glider pilot then had very little time to find a suitable landing place as the aircraft only emerged from the cloud at very low level. It crashed and there were three fatal casualties and four men injured.

Lieutenant Richard James BURKE Duke of Cornwall's Light Infantry
+ two other Army personnel, one of whom is believed to be:
Signalman Wilson HALL 22 Royal Corps of Signals

25-Oct-42   EM338   Master II   GIS   Thame, Oxfordshire   1

The aircraft was taking off with a glider in tow but having become airborne it began to swing. The glider pilot immediately cast off the tow and the tug then struck trees, turned onto its back, before crashing and catching fire. It was not clear why the tug pilot took off on the heading selected as there was a longer run available and without the hazard of trees close to the take-off line.

Flight Lieutenant Charles Frederick RIDOUT 35

28-Oct-42   AM717   Hudson   24 Sqn   Near Redruth Cornwall   0

The aircraft had suffered an engine failure in flight and it crashed in a forced landing whilst attempting to reach Portreath. The pilot of this aircraft was Pilot Officer Prchal, a Czech officer, who was destined to be the captain of the aircraft involved in probably the most hotly debated aircraft accident of the War; that involving General Sikorski at Gibraltar in July 1943.

30-Oct-42   V8983   Hudson III   24 Sqn   Bordon Woods Wendover Bucks   12

The aircraft crashed into woods on a hillside after the pilot descended below safety height in cloud, in an attempt to establish his position.

Flying Officer Raymond COOK 29 Pilot
Sergeant Walter John MORBIN Navigator
Sergeant Arthur George HUDD 21 Wireless Operator
Brigadier Donald Stewart MIDDLETON 42 Late RAMC, Commands & Staff
Lieutenant Commander Frank Alan Winson RAMSAY 45 DSO DSC
Lieutenant Commander David John TEES
Flight Lieutenant Philip Meyer DAVIS 37
Squadron Leader John Forbes Andre DAY 52 AFC
Mr Gilbert F QUARTERMAIN 31
Mr Eric Roff STYLES 36
Mr Charles LUMBY 50
Mr Harold William DODDS 30

30-Oct-42   W7774   Halifax   138 Sqn   Off the coast at Sheringham   0

On return from an SOE sortie to Poland – Codename: WRENCH, the aircraft was ditched in the sea short of Sheringham and the crew rescued by the lifeboat. The sortie was to be a bombing mission against the Gestapo HQ in Warsaw but on arrival it was decided that pinpoint accuracy could not be guaranteed and so an alternative target that did not hazard Polish civilians was chosen. On the return flight, the aircraft was attacked by a pair of Me 110s and serious damage caused. The crew was able to get their aircraft towithin sight of the English coast and as their ditching was observed the alarm was raised quickly and they were rescued propmptly.

105

30-Oct-42 W7773 Halifax   138 Sqn   Between Helleran and Refsland, Norway   10

The Polish system of captaincy usually rested with either the pilot or the navigator, if the latter was of senior rank to the pilot. This crew was captained by Flying Officer Wodzicki, who himself held an RAF DFC, and the Polish Order of Virtuti Militari and the Cross of Valour, and was an experienced bunch. They were tasked with taking three Polish agents to their home country on a sortie code named; PLIERS. The aircraft was shot down over Norway and all on board died.

> Flight Sergeant Franciszek SOBKOWIAK Pilot
> Warrant Officer Franciszek ZAREMBA 28 Co-Pilot
> Flying Officer Mariusz A WODZICKI 27 DFC Navigator & Captain
> Pilot Officer Franciszek PANTOWSKI 24 Wireless Operator
> Sergeant Czeslaw KOZLOWSKI 33 Flight Engineer
> Flight Sergeant Tadeusz MADEJSKI 23 Air Gunner
> Flight Sergeant Waclaw ZUK 21 Air Gunner
> Lieutenant Stanislaw H HENCEL Polish agents
> Lieutenant Wieslaw SZPAKOWICZ
> Second Lieutenant Jerzy BICHNIEWICZ

31-Oct-42 AL516 Liberator II   511 Sqn   Gibraltar   14

The aircraft was returning to UK and crashed at Gibraltar. There were a number of survivors, amongst whom was 'Screwball' Beurling, the Canadian fighter pilot.

> Flight Lieutenant E L HETHERINGTON DFC RAFVR
> Flying Officer J W WILLIAMS DFC RCAF
> Flight Sergeant C E MUTCH RCAF

Flight Lieutenant E H GLAZEBROOK RCAF
Sergeant R H DAVEY RCAF
Sergeant D W SPENCER RAF
+ eight civilians who are believed to be:
Isabella Josephine ASTON (wife of Major W G S Aston RM)
Simon ASTON 2
Thomas CHASE (infant)
Edna Patricia CHASE 27 (wife of K M Chase)
Mabel HUCKLEBRIDGE 30 (wife of Marine Hucklebridge)
Edward James ROWE 40 BEM
Hannah Eunice ROWE 44
Elizabeth Priscilla SHELDON 42 (widow of Herbert Sheldon)

| 31-Oct-42 | BT821 | Hotspur II | RAE | Hartford Bridge Flats | 1 |

The glider was being used to conduct parachute retarded dive landings and a descent rate of 8000 feet/minute was achieved. The recovery was commenced too late and the glider struck the ground heavily, climbed steeply to about 50 feet and then cartwheeled to starboard, before crashing near the runway's edge. The pilot; Lieutenant C J H Cranmer was seriously injured but the Flight Test Observer was killed.

Mr David H M HORNER 23 Flight Test Observer

| 01-Nov-41 | Z9159 | Whitley | 138 Sqn | Near Abbeville France | 6 |

The aircraft came down near Abbeville in France but the cause of its loss, on mission; PRODUCER 2, is not known.

Pilot Officer John Edward TURNHAM Pilot
Flight Sergeant Jack Robert O'LEARY RCAF
Pilot Officer Laurence WHEATLEY 33
Sergeant Falconer MORRISON Wireless Operator

Date	Serial	Aircraft	Unit	Place	Casualties

Brief Circumstances of Accident
Casualty Details (If Applicable)

Sergeant Arnold HALLEWELL 21
Sergeant Sydney WHITE Air Gunner

02-Nov-42 DP752 Horsa I   296 Sqn   RAF Netheravon   0
The aircraft was undershooting its approach and the pilot attempted to stretch the glide but succeeded only in stalling the glider, which then crashed heavily.

04-Nov-42 EW900 Hudson VI   216 Sqn   El Khanka   7
The aircraft, which was heavily laden, stalled and crashed after an engine failed immediately after take-off.

Flight Lieutenant Ronald Thomas BRADSHAW 34 Pilot
Sergeant Max Otto BROWN 27 Wireless Operator
Flying Officer Francis Valentine BROWN 30 RAAF
Flight Sergeant David Aird MACDONALD 22 Navigator
Leading Aircraftman Frederick HOLLAND
Leading Aircraftman Clive William Frederick IRONMONGER 30
+ one other

04-Nov-42 LR232 DC3   31 Sqn   1 mile east of Allahabad   0
The aircraft was landed at Allahabad after engine failure and No: 308 MU was tasked with resolving the fault. The following day the aircraft was taken on an airtest during which the port engine failed and the propeller would not feather. The pilot; Pilot Officer Graham Smeaton, turned back to the airfield but the second engine failed!! The pilot forced landed the aircraft wheels up about one mile from the airfield. The precise cause of a double engine failure is not recorded.

06-Nov-42   AL595   Liberator II   1445 Flt   1/2 mile south-east RAF Lyneham   5

The aircraft struck the ground on approach to land and caught fire. The Accident Card implies that the pilot was neither watching the flarepath nor using his instruments but was relying on his knowledge of the local area to fly his approach.

    Flight Lieutenant George John LE MAR 27 Pilot
    Flying Officer Samuel Alexander Bruce GORDON 21 Co-Pilot
    Flying Officer John Henry FULLER 22 Navigator
    Flying Officer Deiniol DAVIES 27 Wireless Operator
    Sergeant Gilbert Henry GREGG 23 Wireless Operator

06-Oct-42   BT658   Hotspur II   5 GTS   1/4 mile east of Shobdon   1

The pilot released the glider at 200 feet and dived to convert height to speed, with the intention of pulling up to reach the airfield. However, the glider struck trees and although the pilot survived, his passenger received fatal injuries.

    Sergeant Gerard MCALEER The Glider Pilot Regiment

09-Nov-42   K9781   Hector   GPEU   Near Shrewton LG, Wiltshire   1

Whilst engaged in a night glider towing exercise, the aircraft stalled. The pilot failed to recover from the subsequent dive before the aircraft struck the roof of a house with its undercarriage and then crashed into a field beyond. The Accident Card is obscured but there is some reference to the glider being towed in a way which helped bring about the stall by pulling the tug to one side and there are other comments, relating to the precise cause of the accident, which cannot be seen because of the poor copy.

    Sergeant William Herbert Cyril COLE 25 RCAF

12-Nov-42   FK501   Hudson VI   267 Sqn   LG 125   0

The pilot decided to overshoot his approach to land and opened the throttles to go round again. Both engines cut and the aircraft crashed, injuring the three occupants. An inspection of the carburettors revealed that they were clogged with dust.

15-Nov-42	K8099	Hector	GPEU	Dorset (precise location not given)	0

The pilot became lost whilst on a night training sortie and ground fog impeded his vision. Despite searching for a gap, a forced landing was made in a ploughed field when the aircraft's fuel ran out. Although the squadron commander states that the pilot made a good effort, the station commander was concerned that the aircraft was being flown without wing tip flares to illuminate the ground but it transpired that this particular aircraft had been configured in anticipation of night circuit work, not a sortie away from the airfield.

17-Nov-42	EB291	Whitley V	295 Sqn	RAF Netheravon	8

The aircraft was taking off in the middle of the afternoon for a paratroop dropping exercise. In a light crosswind, the aircraft began to swing and the pilot overcorrected, inducing a violent swing in the opposite direction. Control of the aircraft was lost and it struck the side of a hangar and burst into flames. The soldiers were members of one of the early parachute battalions, formed by taking an ordinary infantry unit, retaining a cadre of good soldiers, clearing out the deadwood and then building the unit with fresh troops. In this case, the unit was 10th Bn The Royal Welch Fusiliers. Looking at the home towns for both Corporal Lewis and Private Williams, it seems possible that they were members of the original unit and were retained as the Bn was re-roled.

    Flying Officer John Keith MATTHEWS 29 Pilot
    Sergeant Frederick Edward HEWITT Navigator
    Sergeant James Maden SUTCLIFFE 25 Wireless Operator

110

Private Robert Edmund BROWNRIGG 6th Battalion The Parachute Regiment Army Air Corps
Private Raymond Stanley TOWLER 22
Corporal James John LEWIS 22
Private Stanley Samuel READER 17
Private Albert Edward WILLIAMS 22

18-Nov-42 Z9160 Whitley	161 Sqn	Armacao de Pera Portugal	0

The aircraft forced landed in the Algarve region of Portugal and the crew of four was interned. A similar long stay in this area would probably cost them an arm and a leg nowadays!!! The background to this loss is that the aircraft had been left in Gibraltar for an engine change and the crew, captained by Flying Officer O A Cussen had been sent to collect the aircraft. Whilst off Cape St Vincent, the replacement engine began to give trouble but the crew continued with the flight until forced to return to Gibraltar. However, the problems intensified and the captain elected to land in Portugal, where the crew and their aircraft were detained, although the former returned to UK in mid-Jan 43.

18-Nov-42 K9752 Hector	4 GTS	Shilton, Oxfordshire	0

The pilot became lost on a night training sortie and made a forced landing in a field.

19-Nov-42 W7801 Halifax II	38 Wg	Helleland Norway	7

One of the first attacks made by British airborne forces was the attempt to disrupt the heavy water research and production facility at Rjukan near Vermork Norway. This attack, named Operation FRESHMAN, involved two parties of Royal Engineers being flown by Horsa glider to Norway in order to sabotage the plant. Two Halifax/Horsa combinations were used and these flew from RAF Skitten. The weather was poor, the intercommunication between aircraft and gliders failed and the radio navigation aids also failed. Both gliders were lost as was one of the Halifaxes. The glider crews and troops carried in the gliders were all killed when they crashed or were subsequently murdered by the Nazi forces. There are numerous accounts available on the WWW describing this operation in detail and it forms the basis for the film; "The

Heroes of Telemark". This aircraft crashed shortly after its glider cast off.

Flight Lieutenant Arthur Roland PARKINSON 26 RCAF Pilot
Pilot Officer Gerard Walter Sewell DE GENCY 20 Co-Pilot
Flight Lieutenant Arthur Edwin THOMAS 32 Navigator
Flight Sergeant Albert BUCKTON 23 Wireless Operator
Sergeant James FALCONER 20 Flight Engineer
Flight Sergeant George Mercier EDWARDS 24 Air Gunner
Flying Officer Arnold Thomas Hayward HAWARD 28 Observer

19-Nov-42   HS114   Horsa I   38 Wg   North of Hellelandl   17
This glider crashed about 3 miles away from the tug aircraft and the two pilots and Driver Pendlebury were
killed on impact. The remaining soldiers, several of whom were injured, were taken to an army barracks
at Slettebo near Egersund where they were murdered and their bodies buried on the sea shore at Brusand.

Pilot Officer Norman Arthur DAVIES 28 RAAF
Pilot Officer Herbert John FRASER 28 RAAF
Lieutenant Alex Charles ALLEN 24 RE
Lance Sergeant George KNOWLES 28
Corporal John George Llewellyn THOMAS 23
Lance Corporal Frederick William BRAY 29
Lance Corporal Alexander CAMPBELL 24
Sapper Ernest William BAILEY 31
Sapper Howell BEVAN 22
Sapper Thomas William FALKNER 22

Sapper Charles Henry GRUNDY 22
Sapper Herbert J LEGATE 24
Sapper Leslie SMALLMAN 22
Sapper James May STEPHEN 25
Sapper Gerald Stanley WILLIAMS 18
Driver John Thomas Vernon BELFIELD 26
Driver Ernest PENDLEBURY 25

19-Nov-42 DP349 Horsa I   38 Wg   Fylgjdal   17

This glider crashed into the mountains killing the crew and several soldiers. The enemy forces rounded up the others and four seriously wounded men were immediately killed by their captors, whilst the others were subsequently murdered about 2 months later. Staff Sergeant Strathdee was one of the original glider pilots, having served previously in the pre-war RAF but resigning his commission – it is said – because he was not permitted to fly in the Spanish Civil War. Lieutenant Methven had been awarded the George Medal as a 19 year old for his gallantry in rescuing people from a minefield at Mapplethorpe on Christmas Day 1941.

Staff Sergeant Malcolm Frederick STRATHDEE Pilot The Glider Pilot Regt
Sergeant Peter DOIG Co-Pilot
Lieutenant David Alexander METHVEN 20 GM RE
Lance Sergeant Frederick HEALEY 29
Corporal James Dobson CAIRNCROSS 22 (murdered 20 Nov 42)
Lance Corporal Trevor Lewis MASTERS 25 (murdered 20 Nov 42)
Lance Corporal Wallace Mahlon JACKSON 21 (murdered 18 Jan 43)
Sapper James Frank BLACKBURN 28 (murdered 18 Jan 43)
Sapper Frank BONNER 25 (murdered 18 Jan 43)
Sapper William Jacques 30
Sapper Robert NORMAN 22
Sapper Eric John SMITH 24 (murdered 20 Nov 42)

Date	Serial	Aircraft	Unit	Place	Casualties
				Brief Circumstances of Accident	
				Casualty Details (If Applicable)	

Sapper John Wilfred WALSH 21 (murdered 18 Jan 43)
Sapper Thomas William WHITE 23 (murdered 18 Jan 43)
Driver Peter Paul FARRELL 26 (murdered 20 Nov 42)
Driver John Glen Vernon HUNTER 22
Driver George SIMKINS 30

Date	Serial	Aircraft	Unit	Place	Casualties
19-Nov-42	Z9134	Whitley	42 OTU	Honsham, near Grantham	?

The Movements Card refers to a collision with another aircraft but it has proved difficult to obtain any details of this loss.

Date	Serial	Aircraft	Unit	Place	Casualties
20-Nov-42	EW945	Hudson VI	117 Sqn	Near Qaret Somara	1

The aircraft was returning from El Adem to Bilbeis and was being flown solo. Towards the end of the sortie, a severe dust storm was encountered and after the aircraft failed to arrive, a search found it crashed and burnt out.

Flying Officer Alastair Easson DINNIE 24 RNZAF Pilot

Date	Serial	Aircraft	Unit	Place	Casualties
21-Nov-42	P1452	Albemarle V	511 Sqn	Off Gibraltar	4

The aircraft took off shortly after midnight but crashed into the sea almost immediately. The cause of the loss was not determined.

Flight Lieutenant Gordon Webster THOROGOOD Pilot
Flight Sergeant Leo Clifford WEBSTER 26 RNZAF 2nd Pilot
Flight Sergeant Denison Charles HENDERSON 25 RNZAF Navigator
Sergeant Grant Lawrence HENNING 23 RCAF Wireless Operator

22-Nov-42 Z6629 Whitley   161 Sqn   In the North Sea   7

This aircraft and its crew were carrying out a double sortie to Belgium, one part of which included the dropping of an agent. The aircraft was lost without trace and is assumed to have crashed in the North Sea on the outbound leg of the task.

    Flight Sergeant John Alistair HEY 30 Pilot
    Sergeant Gordon Llewelyn HARRISON 23 RCAF Navigator
    Sergeant Cyril Raphael KENZIE 20 Air Gunner
    Sergeant Harry MOXON 24
    Sergeant Richard William ANDREWS 32
    Sergeant Herbert METCALF 24
    Lieutenant FERNAND DE BISSCHOP

23-Nov-42 K9696 Hector   GPEU   Shrewton LG   0

The pilot was engaged in a night training sortie to gain experience with towing a glider in the dark. At the conclusion of the detail, he attempted to land the aircraft but found himself blinded by the port wing tip flare and could not see the flarepath properly. The aircraft overshot the landing strip and the pilot swung it to avoid a hedge but it tipped onto its nose. The cause of the blinding was fairly elementary in that the pilot used the port wing tip flare and was landing on the right hand side of the landing strip and hence was looking into the direct light of the flare. He should have used the starboard flare which would have then have had the light source out of the pilot's direct line of vision.

24-Nov-42 BD506 Whitley V   HGCU   Near Wanborough, Wiltshire   0

The aircraft was towing a Horsa glider (DP743) and was operating in relatively poor weather conditions. The tug pilot lost the flare path on his approach and circled a cluster of lights he located from 500 feet. Whilst making the orbit, the pilot allowed the aircraft to descend and it struck the ground. The glider pilot released the tow and landed in a nearby Army camp.

Date Serial Aircraft Unit Place Casualties
Brief Circumstances of Accident
    Casualty Details (If Applicable)

24-Nov-42 DP743 Horsa I HGCU Near Wanborough, Wiltshire 0
As outlined above, the tug pilot made some mistakes in trying to orientate himself, having lost the flarepath. However, in circling the tug aircraft lost height and struck the ground but the glider was forced landed in an Army camp with injuries being sustained by the RAF glider pilot.

26-Nov-42 HH284 Hotspur II GPEU RAF Netheravon 8
The glider was being used to give air experience flying to glider troops and it was released from the tow over the airfield at 500 feet. As the glider was apparently going to overshoot the airfield, the pilot made a steep 360 degree turn to port but the turn became ever steeper, until at about 70 degrees of bank, the glider's nose dropped and it dived into the ground.

    Sergeant George Steven MALCOLM 22 Glider Pilot Regiment
    Sergeant Joseph Lowden SALOMONS 2nd (Airborne) Bn Ox & Bucks LI
    Believed to be:
    Corporal Arthur BRADSHAW 25 died of injuries 27 Nov 42
    Private George Henry CAREY 27
    Private Ronald Joseph CORDAS 20
    Private Leonard E MANN
    Private Leonard Frederick MARKS
    Private H G THOMPSON

27-Nov-42 EB294 Whitley V 297 Sqn 3 miles south west Yeovilton 0
The pilot encountered poor weather and thick cloud when in the vicinity of Boscombe Down and was diverted to Yeovilton but the aircraft then suffered a starboard engine failure due to an air lock and resulting

in fuel only being supplied to the port engine. A forced landing was made in a field.

29-Nov-42 FK388 Hudson VI 117 Sqn Solluch 0
The aircraft had an engine fire whilst in flight and shortly before arriving at the destination airfield. This was followed in the final stages of the approach to land, by a fire in the starboard wing and the port engine then cutting. The pilot was able to land the aircraft with its wheels down and on good ground but the aircraft hit an obstruction and the undercarriage collapsed.

30-Nov-42 K9764 Hector 4 GTS Kidlington 0
The pilot, who appears to have been on his first night solo on type, made a low approach to land, struck telephone wires and undershot the landing strip. The aircraft hit the ground, turned onto its back and was destroyed by fire but fortunately, the pilot escaped uninjured.

03-Dec-42 DP821 Horsa I Horsa Flt Not stated 0
The aircraft crew could not maintain the tow during deteriorating weather and it was cast off. A forced landing was made but the aircraft was damaged beyond repair but the two pilots were uninjured.

04-Dec-42 FK387 Hudson VI 216 Sqn LG 224 0
The aircraft swung on take-off and its undercarriage collapsed. The cause of the swing is not known and there is no Accident Card.

08-Dec-42 BD541 Whitley V 296 Sqn Burghclere 4
The crew was engaged on a low level cross country sortie and had been airborne for just over 2 hours. They encountered low cloud and although the aircraft had considerable fuel reserves, the pilot elected to stay low, rather than climb to a safe height. In attempting to avoid the cloud the pilot made a turn away from rising ground but struck trees on top of a hill and the aircraft crashed.

Date	Serial	Aircraft	Unit	Place	Casualties
			Brief Circumstances of Accident		
			Casualty Details (If Applicable)		

Flying Officer Robert Leslie EWART 26 RNZAF Pilot
Sergeant Egbert Julian WESTFIELD 23
Flying Officer Geoffrey O'CONNELL 22
Flight Sergeant John Eli WESTFIELD 23

Date	Serial	Aircraft	Unit	Place	Casualties
08-Dec-42	BD556	Whitley V	296 Sqn	Near Andover	0

The aircraft was returning to base at the conclusion of a 6½ hour operational sortie dropping leaflets over enemy held territory. The pilot attempted an overshoot from his landing approach but the flaps remained set to the landing configuration and the aircraft failed to accelerate. It crashed beyond the airfield, injuring four of the crew.

Date	Serial	Aircraft	Unit	Place	Casualties
09-Dec-42	K8142	Hector	GIS	Thame	0

The pilot was engaged in night glider towing detail and had been on task for about 50 minutes towing off gliders as required. Have been airborne for about 4 minutes on this particular tow and having released the glider, the aircraft's engine stopped and the pilot made a forced landing in soft ground during which the aircraft turned over. The pilot mishandled the fuel system in that he failed to change from gravity feed to the main tanks.

Date	Serial	Aircraft	Unit	Place	Casualties
10-Dec-42	AE578	Hudson III	24 Sqn	Cantra, near Lisbon Portugal	0

The aircraft suffered fuel starvation because of problems with bomb bay fuel tank. A forced landing was made in a neutral country and the aircraft was interned.

118

10-Dec-42   L9618   Halifax I   138 Sqn   At sea between Egypt & Malta   15

The crew had been engaged on some special sorties, which involved seven crews from 138 Sqn and a further pair from 161 Sqn, being deployed to the Middle East for the purpose of moving a large amount of urgent supplies to North Africa. At the conclusion of the detachment, this aircraft was returning to UK and had left Cairo West but never arrived at Malta. Amongst the additional passengers were five pilots who had completed their tours of duty in the Middle East and were posted back to UK. Although thought possible that the aircraft fell victim to an enemy night fighter, this is conjecture.

Flying Officer Leo M ANDERLE DFC
Warrant Officer Vaclav PANEK
Pilot Officer Viktor KRCHA
Sergeant Frantisek VANICEK
Pilot Officer Josef TESAR
Flight Sergeant Bohuml HAJEK
Pilot Officer Miroslaw ROZPRYM
Pilot Officer William Thomas Charles CHAMBERS
Warrant Officer II John Rosebery MILLIGAN 21 RCAF ex-70 Sqn
Flight Sergeant Calman BENTLEY 29 ex-37 Sqn
Flight Sergeant Emlyn Barclay DAVIES ex-40 Sqn
Flight Sergeant George Geoffrey ORGAN 30 RNZAF Pilot
Sergeant John Alexander TOVEY 28 RNZAF Pilot
Corporal Roy Edward CHANDLER 22
Aircraftman 1st Class Harold Henry HUTCHINSON 20

12-Dec-42   BD437   Whitley V   295 Sqn   Near Abbeville France   5

The aircraft was lost on a leaflet dropping raid over the town of Roubaix. However, it was shot down about 60 miles south west of the target area and its crew killed.

Date	Serial	Aircraft	Unit	Place	Casualties

Brief Circumstances of Accident
Casualty Details (If Applicable)

Flying Officer Clifford WOOD 31 Pilot
Flying Officer D'Arcy Clive Melville DRUCKER 23 RNZAF Wireless Operator
Flight Sergeant Douglas Lambert GRANT 24
Flying Officer William Archibald HINSELWOOD 32
Sergeant Cecil Graham George HOBSON 20

13-Dec-42	FK407	Hudson VI	267 Sqn	10 miles south of El Agheila	?

The aircraft disappeared whilst on an operational sortie and was found subsequently crashed and burnt out. The Accident Card records the crew as 'missing' but details have not been traced in any Commonwealth War Graves register or the squadron Form 540 and it may be that the crew were not accounted for when the card was raised but that they were subsequently found safe or had been made POW.

15-Dec-42	AL513	Liberator II	1445 Flt	Rota Spain	0

The Accident Card is sparsely written with the basic information about type and serial number and the pilot's name. There is no indication as to what happened to the aircraft but there are shown as 11 fatal casualties. However, it appears that the aircraft was being ferried overseas but for some reason it made a forced landing near Rota in Spain and was destroyed by its own crew.

16-Dec-42	FK474	Hudson VI	194 Sqn	Near Sitakund	0

The aircraft was attacked and damaged by Japanese aircraft, which put the port engine out of action and damaged the undercarriage. The crew, captained by Flying Officer Salvesen, forced landed it on a beach at low tide, apparently without casualties. They were then faced with a march to the nearest habitation at Sitakund and after a visit to hospital in Chittagong, returned to their unit.

17-Dec-42   FH431   Hudson IIIA   194 Sqn   Fort Hertz Near Nhkang Ga   5

The aircraft, which was being flown by a mixed crew from 194 and 353 Sqns, took off from Tezpur for a supply dropping sortie in the area of Sumprabum in Northern Burma. About 15 miles from the DZ, the aircraft was attacked by 3 Japanese aircraft and it crashed and exploded in the tree tops in position 26 degrees 48 North/97 degrees 46 East. The crew's remains were not recovered and their names are commemorated on the Singapore Memorial. Foot had been attached from 353 Sqn and was helping convert crews of 194 Sqn to the Hudson.

    Pilot Officer William Easton FOOT Pilot
    Sergeant Leonard Keith TEMPEST 22 RNZAF 2nd Pilot
    Flight Sergeant William Caverhill CAMERON
    Flight Sergeant Ralph MACLEAN
    Warrant Officer II Giles James Daniell KERSWILL RCAF

17-Dec-42   DT542   Halifax   138 Sqn   Near RAF Luqa Malta   17

This aircraft was another of the 138/161 Sqns detachment to the Middle East. The aircraft took off in the early hours of the morning but had barely become airborne when it crashed beyond the runway's end and was destroyed.

    Flying Officer Krzysztof Leon DOBROMIRSKI Pilot
    Flying Officer Stanislaw PANKIEWICZ 27
    Flying Officer Zbigniew August IDZIKOWSKI 31
    Sergeant Roman WYSOCKI 27
    Flight Sergeant Alfred Edmund KLENIEWSKI 25
    Flight Sergeant Oskar Franciszek ZIELINSKI 33
    Sergeant Alexander Chubb WATT 21 Flight Engineer
    Squadron Leader Jefferson Heywood WEDGEWOOD DFC
    Flight Lieutenant Peter EARLE 28

Flight Lieutenant Leonard Arthur VAUGHAN 42 DSO DFC
Major The Lord Allen Algernon Bathurst APSLEY 47 DSO MC TD
Major Arthur David Curtis MILLAR 38
Sergeant Dennis SPIBEY
Corporal Douglas Sidney HOUNSLOW
Leading Aircraftman Cyril Dennis BROWNE 21
Leading Aircraftman Richard CLEGG 21
Aircraftman 1st Class Stanley Edward KELLY 40

17-Dec-42   W1002   Halifax   138 Sqn   200 miles south of Oran Algeria   0

This aircraft was also part of the detachment to the Middle East and was returning to UK after a refuelling stop at Malta. The pilot decided to take an overland route and so headed for Algeria but then experienced engine problems due to overheating. The problem spread from one engine to the others and eventually the pilot; Flight Lieutenant J C K Sutton made a forced landing near some buildings but the aircraft caught fire from fuel spilled from the overload tanks. Subsequently, the crew examined the aircraft's oil filters and found them to be clogged because the wrong type of oil had been used to replenish the systems.

19-Dec-42   K7011   Harrow II   271 Sqn   Missing Bay of Biscay   11

The aircraft was en route to Gibraltar from Portreath and disappeared into the Bay of Biscay. There was no evidence as to what happened after the aircraft took off from UK at about 0215 hours. The location of the loss is assumed because the remains of four of those aboard were washed ashore between Cherbourg and Finisterre. Squadron Leader Brown had been the pilot of Albatross AX904 which crashed in Iceland on 7 April 1942.

Squadron Leader Godfrey Allison BROWN 33 Pilot

Flight Lieutenant Edward Thomson HALLEY Co-Pilot
Flying Officer Edward Buckley BOWEN 27
Flight Sergeant Richard George BRETT
Flight Sergeant John BRISTER 21
Pilot Officer Peter Marsh BURTON 20
Flying Officer William Milton HENDERSON 24
Flying Officer John Glen MCCAULEY 30 RNZAF
Leading Aircraftman Philip CASHMORE 22
Major Harold John PALMER 48 Royal Artillery
Lieutenant Andrew Jervis HAWKINS 21 Royal Navy HMS Formidable

| 23-Dec-42 | W7775 | Halifax | 138 Sqn | Near Meppel | 6 |

The aircraft crashed after being attacked shortly after midnight and only two members of the crew survived as POWs. One of the other crews reported an attack and it seems it was probably this aircraft's destruction that they witnessed. The pilot was a very experienced SD operator despite his relative youth.

Flying Officer Gervase Francis Benton NEWPORT-TINLEY 20 DFC Pilot
Sergeant Ben Michael PICK 21
Sergeant Bernard Stearman NIXON 30
Warrant Officer Charles Anthony HOWARD DFC
Flight Sergeant Henry Charles TAYLOR Wireless Operator
Sergeant Cyril Clifford HAYES

| 24-Dec-42 | EB289 | Whitley V | HGCU | Stormy Down Gloucestershire | 0 |

The aircraft was landing on a slippery grass airfield and the pilot raised the undercarriage to prevent a collision with parked aircraft.

Date	Serial	Aircraft	Unit	Place	Casualties
		Brief Circumstances of Accident			
		Casualty Details (If Applicable)			

25-Dec-42   FK605   Hudson VI   194 Sqn   6 miles north-east of Talabok   4

The aircraft crashed into the jungle in the position shown but the cause is not known. There is some confusion as to who was aboard this aircraft and the pilot's date of death is recorded as being a week after the accident.

    Sergeant James Bernard WALENN 25 Pilot
        + three others

27-Dec-42   FK389   Hudson VI   117 Sqn   Thelepte   4

The aircraft was attacked and shot down by USAAF fighter aircraft. Whilst some excuse for mis-identification might be tolerated when an obscure aircraft type is involved, when the aircraft is a widely used and an easily recognisable type of US manufacture, the question has to be asked as to the standards of training in aircraft recognition provided for USAAF pilots and also the mechanisms used to ensure they correctly identify an aircraft before attacking it.

    Flying Officer Cyril Lloyd Winston POPPLESTONE 30 Pilot
    Sergeant Thomas HOLLIDAY 21
    Flight Sergeant Arthur Alfred James MILLS 20 Navigator
    Sergeant Wilfred John PYE 20 Air Gunner

28-Dec-42   EM295   Master II   5 GTS   Shobdon, Herefordshire   0

The aircraft was forced landed in a field shortly after take-off when its engine failed. The cause of the failure is not recorded.

04-Jan-43   EW986 Lodestar   173 Sqn   2 miles south of Heliopolis   11

The aircraft was returning from a trip by Air Marshal McClaughry, Lady Tedder and their staff to a number of units. During the approach to land, the aircraft crashed but the Accident Card is unclear as to the cause. Lady Tedder was the wife of Air Chief Marshal Sir Arthur Tedder, AOCinC Middle East. Their son had died on 3 Aug 1940 whilst a pilot with 139 Sqn and he is buried in Bayeau Cemetery France.

    Flying Officer Graham Grant COWLING 22 Pilot
    Flying Officer Eric Ralph Dalton JAMES 25 Pilot
    Sergeant Norman Louis CLARKE
    Squadron Leader Richard George CHESTER 37
    Air Vice Marshal Wilfred Ashton MCCLAUGHRY 48 CB DSO MC DFC
    Lady Rosalinde TEDDER
    Squadron Leader Hugh Wynston CLELAND 34
    Pilot Officer William Alfred HAWKINS 32
    Wing Commander Gerard Basil NICHOLAS 42 DFC
    Flight Lieutenant James Ronal RITCHIE
    Leading Aircraftman Albert John William HURDLE 20

09-Jan-43   EB300 Whitley   295 Sqn   RAF Upavon   3

The aircraft was engaged in a night flying sortie and was approaching to land. The pilot overshot the line of the flarepath during the turn in to land and in attempting to recover and turn back to the flarepath, he stalled the aircraft and it entered a spin. Recovery from the spin was made at low level and the pilot then attempted to fly straight ahead but the aircraft flew into rising ground, which was 150 feet higher than the airfield. The weather was recorded as poor with 8/10th cloud at 1500 feet.

    Pilot Officer John Guy CURTIS 23 Pilot
    Sergeant James O'DONNELL 22
    Sergeant Ronald Roy PHILLIPS 19

Date	Serial	Aircraft	Unit	Place	Casualties
				Brief Circumstances of Accident	
				Casualty Details (If Applicable)	

12-Jan-43 LR235 Dakota 31 Sqn 2 miles from Tezpur 0

The aircraft, flown by a crew captained by Pilot Officer David Lord, lost an engine almost immediately after take-off, which then caught fire. An immediate return to base was made and the aircraft descended through mist and drizzle before being forced landed, then skidding into a clump of bamboo, which swung the aircraft around and caused severe damage.

13-Jan-43 DP518 Horsa I 9 MU Oakengates, Shropshire 0

The aircraft was being flown on an airtest and delivery sortie. The aircraft adopted a port wing low attitude and the pilot found he was unable to correct this, even with the flaps lowered. The aircraft was eventually crash landed but despite many ideas as to the cause of the problem, including the affect of hot gasses from the steel works over which the aircraft was flying, no satisfactory explanation was found.

16-Jan-43 DG285 Halifax 161 Sqn Near Rennes Northern France 7

Pilot Officer Harry Sanford READHEAD 31 Pilot
Pilot Officer Ronald GRAY 21
Sergeant Stewart McKenzie ANDERSON 21
Pilot Officer William Wallace ROY 23 RCAF
Sergeant William WILSON 25
Sergeant Leslie Percy MANNING 19 Air Gunner
Sergeant Hedley Geoffrey MARTINS Air Gunner

19-Jan-43 L5841 Bombay I 216 Sqn Sedada 0

The aircraft was taking off on rough ground when a main wheel tyre burst and the aircraft's undercarriage collapsed.

20-Jan-43   HH752 Hotspur II   GPEU   Chilbolton, Hampshire   0

The pilot released the tow too early and the glider undershot the landing strip and struck a tree.

22-Jan-43   K8167   Hector   4 GTS   Kidlington   0

The aircraft was taking off with a glider on tow when it struck a taxying aircraft. This aircraft's undercarriage was damaged and it collapsed on landing. The state of the airfield, the fact that the other aircraft was camouflaged and against a dark background, together with the two pilots not keeping a good enough lookout were all contributing factors but it does seem surprising that a taxying aircraft was within the normal take-off lane of this grass airfield.

24-Jan-43   HH603 Hotspur II   2 GTS   RAF Weston on the Green   0

The aircraft was approaching to land in conditions of hazy calm during the late morning. The pilot realised he was too high on the approach and so initiated some 'S' turns to bleed off excess height. However, he over did this and the aircraft struck a bus parked just inside the boundary fence.

24-Jan-43   HH145 Hotspur II   2 GTS   RAF Weston on the Green   0

During night flying at the same base as HH603, the aircraft was being landed in conditions of increasing and gusty wind and with an altimeter which was known to have an excessive lag in readings. The pilot undershot the landing and struck a hut on the boundary of the airfield.

27-Jan-43   MA929 DC3   31 Sqn   Between Tezpur and Dinjan   ?

In some accounts, this aircraft was missing but it has not been possible to confirm the circumstances of the loss nor to identify the crew and sortie details.

Date	Serial	Aircraft	Unit	Place	Casualties
		Brief Circumstances of Accident			
		Casualty Details (If Applicable)			

29-Jan-43   AM913   Liberator I   511 Sqn   Talbenny   4

The aircraft was approaching the airfield at the end of a ferry flight from Africa (departure airfield not known) when its No: 4 engine caught fire and there was a major failure of the electrics. The engine subsequently fell off and the fire went out. The pilot lowered the undercarriage in preparation for a landing but the No: 3 engine then failed and the aircraft undershot the airfield, collided with various obstructions, broke into several pieces and was destroyed. The severity of the engine fire made it impossible to determine the cause of the initial blaze.

Flying Officer Kenneth Charles Robert MASKELL 29 Co-Pilot
Brigadier Vivian DYKES 44 CBE
Brigadier Guy Milton STEWART 42
+ one other

29-Jan-43   BD668   Whitley V   297 Sqn   Yeldham Essex   0

The crew was engaged in a 'Nickel' sortie and the starboard engine temperature started to rise and flames and sparks started to come from the engine. The aircraft's radio was unserviceable and the compass was affected by a thunderstorm. In addition the weather conditions were poor. The pilot decided to abandon the aircraft and this was done successfully by the crew.

29-Jan-43   BT939   Hotspur II   4 GTS   Kingston Bagpuize   0

The aircraft was behaving abnormally on the tow, which lasted for 1½ hours, but not to such an extent as to make it unmanageable. After release from the tow over the base, the aircraft dived and no amount of pulling back on the control column or use of the flaps had any effect. At this point the two pilots baled out but subsequently it seems that higher authority did not believe the pilots' accounts and suggested the 1st pilot had mishandled the controls and nearly caused a stall in the tug aircraft. Furthermore, it was also considered that the two crew had jumped out unnecessarily but the evidence for this is not recorded. It is also worth noting that there are several cases of structural failure recorded in this volume and it is entirely possible that the glider was displaying the symptoms of control restrictions.

30-Jan-43   DP798 Horsa I   HGCU   RAF Brize Norton   0

The pilot was landing the glider at the conclusion of his first night solo on type. At the point of touchdown, the glider was struck by a very strong gust of wind which moved the aircraft bodily sideways and backwards, causing the starboard wheel to collapse.

30-JAN43   HG985 Horsa I   Horsa Flt   Somerford Churchyard   0

31-Jan-43   HG747 Horsa I   Horsa Flt   RAF Netheravon   0

Damaged beyond repair during a severe gale.

03-Feb-43   HH649 Hotspur II   1 GTS   Membury, Northants   0

The glider pilot was flying dual with an instructor and on approach to land, the glider started to undershoot but the instructor did not intervene and the aircraft crashed through the boundary hedge and was written off when it hit a tree stump.

04-Feb-43   DG271 Halifax   138 Sqn   RAF Tangmere   0

The aircraft swung on take-off for a return to base at Tempsford and the undercarriage collapsed.

05-Feb-43   EW877 Hudson VI   117 Sqn   El Adem   12?

The aircraft crashed on take-off after a loss of power. The full details of the accident are not recorded and the reason for General Willans being on this flight are unknown.

Date	Serial	Aircraft	Unit	Place	Casualties
		Brief Circumstances of Accident			
		Casualty Details (If Applicable)			

Flight Sergeant Leslie John CORFIELD 22 Navigator
Flight Sergeant George Wallace DIXON 22 Wireless Operator
Sergeant William Henry GLADWELL 22 Pilot
Flight Sergeant Brian Godfrey HANCORN 24 Wireless Operator
Flight Lieutenant Howard Otis KNOWLES 22 Pilot
Sergeant Jack Herbert MANNING 28
Flight Lieutenant Denis Joseph PASSADORO
Squadron Leader Reginald John PEACOCK 25 DFC
Sergeant Thomas Charlton TOY 21 Navigator
Major General Harry WILLANS 50 CB CBE DSO MC TD
Colonel Cyprian Francis Thurlow BAKER 46 OBE
Warrant Officer Albert George EDDY 29 RAAF

Date	Serial	Aircraft	Unit	Place	Casualties
05-Feb-43	K9744	Hector	4 GTS	Kingston Bagpuize	0

The undercarriage collapsed on landing after the rivets in the oleo legs sheared off.

| 10-Feb-43 | BD494 | Whitley V | 295 Sqn | Off French Coast | 4 |

The aircraft was being flown on a 'Nickel' leaflet dropping raid at Chateaux Roux but failed to return. No trace of the aircraft was found nor were the circumstances of its loss determined but the navigator's body was washed ashore and it is assumed the aircraft crashed into the sea whilst returning from the sortie.

Sergeant William Ronald ERASMUS 21 Pilot
Sergeant Sidney Albert George WRAIGHT 22 Observer
Sergeant Jack Heaton BEEBE 21 RNZAF Wireless Operator

Flight Sergeant Edward FROGGATT 22 Air Gunner

14-Feb-43   V9675   Lysander IIIA   5 GTS   1 mile west of Shobdon   0

Shortly after take-off on a glider towing sortie, the pilot changed the propeller pitch from 'fine' to 'coarse' and the engine promptly stopped! The glider was cast off and the tug pilot landed the aircraft in a field but it ran into a deep rut and cartwheeled.

17-Feb-43   X9441   DH86B   24 Sqn   RAF Hendon   0+1

The aircraft caught fire whilst starting and an airman rushed forward with the fire extinguisher but was struck by a propeller and was killed. The aircraft was destroyed. The aircraft was, unusually for the time, given a name: 'The Cathedral'.

Leading Aircraftman Alexander NIXON 21

19-Feb-43   W1012   Halifax   138 Sqn   12 miles south of Tours   0

The crew was returning after completing two out of three elements of their sortie. Whilst flying at low level in foggy conditions and attempting to gain a position fix, the aircraft passed over an enemy airfield and was subjected to intense AA fire which caused both starboard engines to fail. Unable to climb, the pilot was left with no alternative but to force land in a field and this was done without injury to the crew, who were all made POW.

19-Feb-43   BD538   Whitley V   295 Sqn

A force of twelve Whitleys and two Halifaxs from this unit were detailed for an attack as summarised below but two were destroyed in the attack. The precise circumstances in which the aircraft were brought down are not known.

Wing Commander Philip Michael Vaughan LYSAGHT 29 Pilot
Flying Officer James Hamish Cameron MCILWRICK 28 Co-Pilot

131

Date	Serial	Aircraft	Unit	Place		Casualties
		Brief Circumstances of Accident				
		Casualty Details (If Applicable)				

Warrant Officer Joseph Elzear Sahl SASSEVILLE 28 RCAF Wireless Operator
Sergeant Ivor William ARNOLD 30 Navigator
+ 1 Casualty not identified

20-Feb-43	DK123	Halifax V	295 Sqn	Near Distre France	7

The aircraft was flown by one of 14 crews detailed to attack a transformer station at Distre but it was shot down near the target and its crew killed. This aircraft included amongst its crew a staff officer from the Group HQ who was flying on this sortie as part of a familiarisation sortie.

Squadron Leader Campbell CRICHTON-MILLER 28 HQ 38 Gp Staff Officer
Flight Lieutenant Michael Edward Jackson CROKER 34 Air Gunner
Flight Sergeant Thomas William HOLLAND 31 Air Gunner
Sergeant Walter MATHER 32 Navigator
Flying Officer Malcolm Cedric HAYES 24 Pilot
Flight Sergeant Keith Reynolds MARSHALL 34 RNZAF Wireless Operator
Flying Officer David Herbert UPSHER 25 Co-Pilot

21-Feb-43	FK485	Hudson VI	194 Sqn	Bangalore	0

On landing, the aircraft bounced and the co-pilot retracted the undercarriage without telling the pilot or being requested to do so. A belly landing followed and the aircraft skidded into a DC2 and a B17 Fortress.

26-Feb-43	HH545	Hotspur II	GPEU	Chilbolton, Hampshire	0

The aircraft was landing in ideal weather conditions but the pilot misjudged his approach, undershot the airfield compeletely and crashed through the boundary hedge.

01-Mar-43 HH719 Hotspur II   2 GTS   Near Slade Farm LG, Oxfordshire   0

This aircraft was baulked by another glider having lined up to land. The pilot attempted to dive and get some speed for a longer low approach but failed to check the dive and the aircraft struck the ground.

04-Mar-43 P1393 Albemarle V   296 Sqn   Hartford Bridge Flats   0

The brakes failed due to faulty installation and the aircraft overshot.

04-Mar-43 Z6747 Whitley V   42 OTU   Thruxton   0

The crew was undertaking a long cross country flight and the aircraft had been airborne for just over 3 hours, when an engine failed due to a glycol leak. The pilot attempted a single engine landing but undershot the runway and the aircraft stalled and crashed. Although the crew of four all suffered injuries, it was noted that engine failures on the Whitleys at the OTU were prevalent with thirteen in 283 flying hours and it had been decided to increase the amount of instructional time devoted to asymmetric flying.

05-Mar-43 BT619 Hotspur II   5 GTS   Shobdon, Herefordshire   0

The aircraft crashed during an approach at the conclusion of a short flight of about 10 minutes and the pilot said that the controls were ineffective, although an inspection of these didn't reveal any faults.

06-Mar-43 FK527 Hudson VI   117 Sqn   Marble Arch   0

The aircraft was taking off on an operational sortie when the pilot realised that he had not removed the pitot cover. An attempt to stop the aircraft was made but it overshot the runway and its undercarriage was damaged.

07-Mar-43 HH250 Hotspur II   3 GTS   Northleach, Gloucesterhire   0

The aircraft was picketed against a storm but the gusts of wind were such that the pickets pulled out and the glider overturned.

133

Date	Serial	Aircraft	Unit	Place	Casualties
Brief Circumstances of Accident					
Casualty Details (If Applicable)					

13-Mar-43   FK615   Hudson VI   117 Sqn   Castel Benito   0

The aircraft was landing but it ran over some shrapnel left on the airfield and a tyre burst. The aircraft swung and its undercarriage was damaged.

14-Mar-43   BB281   Halifax   138 Sqn   Near Munich   8

The aircraft crashed whilst en-route to Czechoslovakia, as part of an SIS operation code named: BRONZE. The circumstances surrounding the loss are not recorded. The award of the DFC to Squadron Leader Gibson was not promulgated until 12 days after his death, whilst that to Sergeant Stokes had been awarded for his service on 90 Sqn in 1941.

Squadron Leader Christopher Francis GIBSON 31 DFC Pilot
Flight Sergeant Douglas Clark LISSON 24 RCAF
Sergeant Malcolm John HUDSON 19 Flight Engineer
Flight Sergeant John Stanley RIGDEN
Flight Sergeant Arthur STOKES DFM Wireless Operator
Sergeant Leo Peter WARD
Sergeant Harold John SHAROOD 21
Flight Sergeant Maurice Tallier Peter MYERS RCAF Wireless Operator

15-Mar-43   DG245   Halifax   161 Sqn   Southern Germany   7

This aircraft was another engaged on a sortie to Czechoslovakia. The award of the DFC to Flight Lieutenant Taylor was promulgated on the same day as that to Squadron Leader Gibson (see previous record) but surprisingly a Bar was awarded as late as 1945. Flight Lieutenant Prior was a very experienced operator and his DFM was awarded in April 1941 for services on 51 Sqn.

Flight Lieutenant Alfred Ellis PRIOR DFM Pilot
Pilot Officer Alfred John KINGHAM
Sergeant Felix James MOWLES
Flying Officer Richard Winter TAYLOR DFC & Bar RCAF
Flight Sergeant George MCWILLIAM 23
Sergeant John Henry KEMPTON 29
Sergeant Francis Douglas BELL 22

15-Mar-43   DG283 Halifax   161 Sqn   Fawley Buckinghamshire   2
About 30 minutes after take-off the aircraft lost an engine and the crew jettisoned the load and attempted a return to base. Height could not be maintained and the aircraft crashed near Henley on Thames. The pilot; Flying Officer Geoffrey Alan Osborn was awarded the George Medal on 13 Jul 43 for his efforts to evacuate his crew from the wrecked aircraft on this occasion but also for saving life after an aircraft accident at RAF St Mawgan on 29 Nov 42.

     Sergeant Hugh SHEARER 20
     Sergeant Barrie Lincoln CRANE

15-Mar-43   DT620 Halifax   138 Sqn   South east of Koge, Denmark   7
This crew was the fourth from Tempsford lost on this night and they were engaged on a long range sortie to Poland. In almost full moon conditions, the aircraft crashed in Denmark.

     Flight Sergeant Leslie Rowland SMITH 26
     Sergeant Horace Robert HARRAP 25 RNZAF
     Sergeant Thomas MAIRS 23
     Sergeant Colin Frederick CHAMBERS
     Flight Sergeant Eugene Shadrack MASSON RCAF Air Gunner
     Sergeant Donald Robb ROSS 23 RCAF Wireless Operator
     Sergeant Arthur Cyril SIXSMITH

135

Date	Serial	Aircraft	Unit	Place	Casualties
		Brief Circumstances of Accident Casualty Details (If Applicable)			
16-Mar-43	LH971	Horsa I	296 Sqn	West Parley, Hampshire	0

After take-off, the glider pilot was unable to keep position above the slipstream of the tug aircraft because he found the aircraft nose heavy, possibly because the 'self loading freight' (passengers) might have moved after take-off. Flying in the tug's slipstream compounded the problem in that it prevented the tug from accelerating to a sufficient speed to give the glider the extra lift needed. The glider pilot pulled off the tow but but then crashed the glider during a turn at low level.

Date	Serial	Aircraft	Unit	Place	Casualties
20-Mar-43	DG244	Halifax	161 Sqn	Lost without trace	7

The crew was engaged in an SIS sortie coded; VIGA 3, to a DZ in Norway. However, the aircraft was lost without trace.

Flying Officer Herbert Lloyd WYNNE DFM
Flight Sergeant Raymond Robert Seppings ROLFE 23
Sergeant Thomas Bell COLWELL
Flying Officer William Harry FRANKLIN 20 DFC
Sergeant James Cornelius INSOLE 21
Sergeant Eric William FOSTER
Pilot Officer Thomas William CHALLONER 22 DFC

Date	Serial	Aircraft	Unit	Place	Casualties
20-Mar-43	EB297	Whitley	297 Sqn	Chaigny	?
22-Mar-43	FH406	Hudson IIIA	24 Sqn	Tougourt Algeria	0

The aircraft was being used for a shuttle service and about 5 minutes after take-off its port engine failed. This was followed almost immediately by a complete loss of oil pressure in the starboard engine. The pilot carried out a wheels up landing in soft sand.

| 23-Mar-43 | AL587 | Liberator II | 511 Sqn | Missing Gibraltar to Lyneham | 19 |

The aircraft departed from Gibraltar at 1036 hours local time on a transit flight to RAF Lyneham. However, the aircraft did not arrive and was lost without trace. Errol Martyn records in his book 'For Your Tomorrow' Vol 2, that the aircraft was attacked and shot down by fighters over the Bay of Biscay at 1420 hours and that one of the attacking aircraft crashed into the sea during the engagement.

Flight Lieutenant Geoffrey Thomas Raleigh FRANCIS 35 RAFVR Pilot
Flight Sergeant Carlo Ernesto FERRO 20 RCAF Co-Pilot
Flying Officer John Stanley RENOUF 27 RCAF Navigator
Sergeant Richard Price MARVIN 32 RAFVR Flight Engineer
Sergeant Lloyd George BURRY RAFVR Wireless Operator/Air Gunner
Pilot Officer Richard Sidney TEDDER 26 Wireless Operator/Air Gunner
Air Vice Marshal Robert Parker Musgrave WHITHAM 47 CB OBE MC RAF
Flying Officer John Gordon GREEN 23 RAFVR
Sergeant Frederick William BOUSTEAD 29 RAFVR
Flight Sergeant William John HOUGH 29 RNZAF
Pilot Officer Albert Henry BOWLER RAFVR
Pilot Officer Frank STUART 31 RAAF
Flying Officer Owen Albert SMITH 23 RCAF
Flying Officer Terence James MARRIOTT RCAF
Sergeant Wilfred Archibald UPSTON 26 RAFVR
Lieutenant Paul Seymour SKELTON 28 RN HMS Medway
Lieutenant Colonel Lucius William ARMSTRONG-MACDONNELL Irish Guards
Colonel J E MORIN Free French Forces

Date	Serial	Aircraft	Unit	Place	Casualties
		Brief Circumstances of Accident Casualty Details (If Applicable)			
23-Mar-43	BD422	Whitley V	296 Sqn	Fothergay Northamptonshire	5

This aircraft was flying in formation with other Whitleys on a 'Spartan' sortie but because of the bumpy conditions it collided with Whitley LA827 and crashed out of control. LA827 was able to return to base where it made a forced landing.

Flight Lieutenant Derek Woodhead JACKSON 23 Pilot
Sergeant Henry Thomas BROWN 23
Sergeant Leslie Lawrence BULL 32
Flight Sergeant Frank NICHOLSON 25
+ one other

Date	Serial	Aircraft	Unit	Place	Casualties
25-Mar-43	HR665	Halifax	138 Sqn	Ijsselmeer Netherlands	1

The aircraft was being used to fly in two Dutch agents but before its crew could deliver them, the aircraft was shot down by AA fire. The pilot; Flying Officer E Clow RNZAF, was able to make a controlled ditching in the Ijsselmeer on its western side at Enkhuizen. Although the crew escaped from the wreckage, they were made POW and one of the agents was able to escape from the scene, however, the other was drowned.

A BERGMAN SOE Agent

Date	Serial	Aircraft	Unit	Place	Casualties
26-Mar-43	FK567	Hudson VI	194 Sqn	Nirmatud	0

The Accident Card merely records 'fuel shortage' but does not explain any further.

Date	Serial	Aircraft	Unit	Place	Casualties
26-Mar-43	DL472	Master II	2 GTS	RAF Weston on the Green	2

The aircraft spun into the ground south west of the airfield.

Flying Officer Warren Wainwright Duncan PEARL 22
Corporal Roland RENFREY Glider Pilot Regiment

27-Mar-43 DL517 Master II   5 GTS   Delwyn, Herefordshire   ?
The aircraft spun into the ground after the pilot lost control during a slow roll.

03-Apr-43 BD533 Whitley V   296 Sqn   Trowbridge   0
The crew was engaged on a low level cross country and when flying at 500 feet, about an hour after take-off, the port engine failed because the flame traps burst, after the securing studs in the rear camshaft bearing failed. At the height involved the pilot had no option but to make a forced landing straight ahead and this was done successfully.

03-Apr-43 HG975 Horsa I   6 MU   Near Kidlington   0
The pilot made a forced landing after difficulties with the tow rope. However, the problem is not detailed further but possibly involved the rope wrapping around some control surfaces when the glider got out of position relative to the tug.

05-Apr-43 BD554 Whitley V   297 Sqn   Weighill Railway Station Hampshire   2
The aircraft was returning from an operational sortie after 6¼ hours airborne and the pilot was attempting to land off a beam approach, having refused a diversion despite the poor weather. Possibly due to his inexperience of beam approaches, the pilot undershot and the aircraft crashed short of the airfield. In addition to the fatal casualties, the other three crew members were injured.

    Flying Officer Louis Andrew SPROULE 27 Pilot
    Warrant Officer John Benjamin BURROWS 21 RAAF

06-Apr-43 FK384 Hudson VI   117 Sqn   RAF Luqa   1?
The aircraft was struck by a Baltimore whilst parked at RAF Luqa. However, the squadron suffered a fatal

139

casualty on this date and the two incidents might be related, although no such link was found.

Sergeant Paul STRINGFELLOW 22

| 07-Apr-43 | DP419 | Horsa I | ABN | RAF Foulsham | 0 |

The aircraft was damaged during a very severe gale, despite being picketed correctly.

| 08-Apr-43 | BT989 | Hotspur II | 3 GTS | Northleach, Gloucestershire | 1 |

On landing, the glider ballooned into the air and stalled into the ground. The Accident Card records that the instructor did not take control soon enough but then comments that a contributory cause was the instructor's seat breaking away from its cradle. Clearly, if this happened before the initial touchdown, there would have been little the instructor could have done to have brought the glider under control.

Sergeant Reginald HULME 24

| 13-Apr-43 | BB340 | Halifax | 138 Sqn | Douvres la Delivrande Calvados | 1 |

The crew, which was a mixed RAF and Polish team, was engaged on dropping two agents in France. Whilst crossing the coast at 500 feet, the aircraft was struck by a burst of AA fire and a fire was started in one engine. The pilot; Flying Officer P Korpowski, made a forced landing about 7 miles north north west of Caen but the aircraft was completely gutted and one of the crew killed. Of the remainder, Korpowski and two RAF men evaded capture, with Korpowski – who had been quite badly injured - and one of the others reaching UK via Spain and Gibralar some six weeks later but four others became POW. The two agents also evaded capture at first but were arrested and imprisoned later

Sergeant Jan LESNIEWICZ PAF

13-Apr-43   DG409   Halifax   161 Sqn   RAF Tempsford   0

The aircraft was being flown on an airtest but its port inner engine failed on take-off and the pilot was unable to retain control. The aircraft was destroyed in the subsequent crash but there were no injuries amongst the crew.

14-Apr-43   HG857   Horsa I   5 MU   RAF Kemble   0

The pilot deliberately stalled the glider to avoid an aircraft which had landed on the runway. The Accident Card contains some confusing comments about whether or not the glider should have been landing so close to the runway. The outcome was that the glider pilot was found to be in error and he was subject of disciplinary action.

14-Apr-43   BB363   Halifax   138 Sqn   English Channel off Bournemouth   9

The aircraft was being flown by an experienced pilot who was nearing the end of his tour. For reasons not determined, the aircraft crashed into the sea off the south coast. Although the records show the crash site as near Bournemouth, the pilot was recovered from the sea at Newhaven. The extra crew members were on board to gain operational experience. Warrant Officer Ward's DFC was not gazetted until 10 days after his loss but Sergeant Davidson had received his DFM whilst serving with 102 Sqn in 1940. The circumstances of Davidson's award are worth repeating. He was the wireless operator to Pilot Officer Leonard Cheshire and their Whitley was damaged and set on fire, during which time Davidson was badly burnt. Although the aircraft was burning for sometime and was subjected to enemy AA fire, Davidson remained at his post despite being in very considerable pain and and temporarily blinded. He continued to operate the wireless with the assistance of Richard Rivaz, the rear gunner, who helped guide Davidson's hands to the knobs and dials. Davidson refused to leave his post and insisted the aircraft get back to its home base. His gallantry was probably worthy of a higher award than the DFM and it is sad to record that, having returned to operational duties, he lost his life in this accident.

Sergeant William Arthur COOK 27 RNZAF Pilot
Sergeant Jack DOY Co-Pilot
Sergeant Edwin George HAMMETT 20
Warrant Officer Robert Weavers WARD 21 DFC
Sergeant William SKELTON 32
Flight Sergeant Henry Eugene DAVIDSON 25 DFM
Flight Sergeant Archie Ernest KING 31
Sergeant James Richard CALLAN 23
Sergeant Edward Joseph KIMBERLEY 22

16-Apr-43 FK411 Hudson VI   194 Sqn   Palam   2

The aircraft started to swing on take-off and the pilot failed to correct this. The aircraft became airborne but immediately stalled and crashed. In addition to the fatal casualties, four others were injured.

Sergeant Ansell Edward BRITTEN-JONES 21 RAAF Pilot
Believed to be:
Flight Sergeant Arthur BROWN Navigator

17-Apr-43 DT725 Halifax   138 Sqn   Ussy Calvados France   6

This crew was in one of five squadron aircraft on sorties on this date. Having completed the task, coded; LIME 9, the aircraft crashed about 5 miles north-west of Falaise in circumstances which are not known.

Flying Officer Tadeusz GINTER 24 PAF Pilot
Sergeant James Henry ASPEN 29 Flight Engineer
Flight Lieutenant Bogdan Seweryn LAWRENCZUK 31 PAF

Sergeant Stefan GADOMSKI 25 PAF
Flight Sergeant Jan Kazimierz MIRONOW 29 PAF
Sergeant Franciszek ULASIUK 24 PAF

17-Apr-43	BT675	Hotspur II	GPEU	By Chilbolton airfield, Hampshire	1

The pilot was attempting to stretch the aircraft's glide but whilst in a gentle turn, the glider stalled and spun off the turn into the ground.

Sergeant Geoffrey Ernest REYNOLDS The Glider Pilot Regiment

| 17-Apr-43 | DP825 | Horsa I | ?????? | Location unclear | 0 |

The aircraft caught fire on the airfield for no apparent reason and the circumstances were treated as suspicious.

| 21-Apr-43 | P1565 | Albemarle I | 511 Sqn | Blida North Africa | 0 |

The aircraft had landed and was taxiing to its parking slot when the pilot inadvertently selected the undercarriage lever 'UP' and the main wheels collapsed.

| 21-Apr-43 | BT979 | Hotspur II | GPEU | Chilbolton, Hampshire | 0 |

The pilot misjudged the approach and struck some buildings when the glider undershot the landing.

| 27-Apr-43 | R9553 | Dominie I | 24 Sqn | Rednal Shropshire | 0 |

The aircraft had an engine failure immediately after take-off and the pilot attempted to regain the airfield but was unable to do so and the aircraft crashed and overturned, injuring all four occupants.

| 28-Apr-43 | FK390 | Hudson VI | 117 Sqn | Monastir | 10 |

The aircraft stalled in a turn at low altitude and spun into the ground.

Sergeant James Frank COWBURN 21 Pilot

Date	Serial	Aircraft	Unit	Place	Casualties
Brief Circumstances of Accident					
Casualty Details (If Applicable)					

Sergeant Peter George LEACH 20 Wireless Operator/Air Gunner
Sergeant Ronald Alfred MARTIN 23 Wireless Operator/Air Gunner
Believed to be:
Major Frank Edward Norman CROUCHER 27 Kings Royal Rifle Corps
Sergeant John WALLS
Corporal Arthur PLATT
Leading Aircraftman James LEMMON
Leading Aircraftman William PARKER
+ two others whose details are not known

Date	Serial	Aircraft	Unit	Place	Casualties
28-Apr-43	FK507	Hudson VI	267 Sqn	RAF El Adem (Staging Post 12)	0

The aircraft was taking off when its port engine failed because of a fatigue failure of the air intake shutter.
The pilot made a wheels up landing and there were only minor injuries amongst the four people on board.

Date	Serial	Aircraft	Unit	Place	Casualties
29-Apr-43	FH307	Hudson IIIA	24 Sqn	1 mile north north west of Chivenor	9

The aircraft had left RAF Hendon and was scheduled to land at RAF Portreath, to be refuelled before making the flight to Gibraltar and onwards. However, weather conditions at Portreath were poor and it was decided that the aircraft should stage through RAF Chivenor instead. On the approach to land, the aircraft stalled, entered a spin and crashed. It appears that the undercarriage was lowered while the flaps were still retracted and this induced the stall. The pilot had survived an earlier accident whilst flying another Hudson in North Africa. The two senior officers killed in this accident were both very distinguished officers. Admiral Mack had commanded a destroyer flotilla with great daring and courage and had returned to UK earlier as he was unwell. General Salmon was amongst the most senior Canadian officers serving in UK and had commanded an infantry division. Both officers were travelling to the Middle East to participate in a planning conference in preparation for operation HUSKY – the attack on Sicily - and both were destined for higher command had they survived.

Flight Lieutenant Gordon Leslie MACINTYRE 27 DFC Pilot
Flying Officer Frederick Ronald FORD Navigator
Warrant Officer Percy Frederick LAVER 21 Wireless Operator
Aircraftman 1st Class Harold John Anthony NEWTON 21
Rear Admiral Philip John MACK 50 DSO & Bar
Major General Harry Leonard Nowell SALMON 48 MC RCIC
Captain Sir Thomas Lubbock BEEVOR 6th Baronet
Lieutenant Colonel Charles Francis Geoffrey FINLAY 29 RCASC
Lieutenant Colonel Guy Gervers Holmes WILSON 38 RA

30-Apr-43   P1556   Albemarle I   511 Sqn   6 miles east of Gibraltar   0
The aircraft ditched after the pilot was unable to maintain height on one engine. Although not confirmed it is thought the engine may have lost its oil supply through a leak in the constant speed unit and this led to the initial engine failure.

02-May-43   HR661   Halifax   148 Sqn   Derna   0
The aircraft swung on take-off and its undercarriage collapsed, followed shortly afterwards by the starboard inner engine catching fire and the aircraft being destroyed in the ensuing blaze. This aircraft had been compelled to return early from an operational sortie 10 days before after its port inner engine had failed in flight.

06-May-43   EB313   Whitley V   HGCU   RAF Brize Norton   0
The aircraft had been airborne for about 15 minutes on a night training sortie when its port engine failed. The pilot was unable to maintain height on one engine and so made a wheels up forced landing.

Date	Serial	Aircraft	Unit	Place	Casualties
		Brief Circumstances of Accident			
		Casualty Details (If Applicable)			

07-May-43 BD548 Whitley V HGCU 300 yards south of Stanton Harcourt 0

The aircraft had just taken off on a glider towing sortie when its starboard engine failed because of a broken valve in the No: 1 cylinder. The pilot attempted to reach base on one engine but delayed releasing the glider until his aircraft had descended to 300 feet above the ground. The pilot made a forced landing short of the airfield and was criticised for not casting off the glider (Horsa LF887) immediately.

11-May-43 DG350 Halifax V 295 Sqn Holmsley South 0

The pilot was practising asymmetric flying and was landing in a slight crosswind. The aircraft swung after a poor landing and the brakes failed to slow the aircraft on soft ground and it struck a pile of earth and fractured its undercarriage.

12-May-43 BB328 Halifax 138 Sqn Pont Audemer Eure France 6

Flying Officer Thomas NOBLE 27 Pilot
Sergeant James WOODS 23
Sergeant Dudley Frank WEST
Sergeant Kenneth HUBBARD 23 Wireless Operator
Sergeant Douglas Albert BALL 21
Sergeant John Patrick KEATING 20 RCAF Air Gunner

12-May-43 DT627 Halifax 138 Sqn Crashed at sea, position not known 7

The aircraft crashed in the sea off the Dutch coast and all on board were killed

Flying Officer Jan POLNIK 24 PAF
Flight Sergeant Bronislaw WOJNO 29 PAF

Sergeant Edward PIATKOWSKI 24PAF
Flying Officer Jerzy Henryk POLKOWSKI 30 PAF
Sergeant Jerzy KURZAK 35 PAF
Sergeant Karol GERMANSINSKI 29 PAF
Sergeant Piotr BEDNARSKI 28 PAF

12-May-43   FK471   Hudson VI   267 Sqn   Gardabia Main   0

On landing the starboard tyre burst, followed by the starboard undercarriage collapsing. Although there was no fire, the report states that the damage is such as to prevent a further examination of the wreck but tyre bursts in the hostile climate were fairly common and resulted in the loss of several aircraft, as recorded in these records.

13-May-43   BB313   Halifax   138 Sqn   West of Troyes Aube France   0

This aircraft was shot down on its way back from a successful drop coded; LIME 16. Several of the crew were able to bale out and evade capture, whilst another who was still on board also evaded. However, the pilot; Squadron Leader C G S R Robinson, and four others were made POW.

13-May-43   HH253   Hotspur II   5 GTS   ????????????????   0

The tug and glider combination had been airborne for about 50 minutes and the glider pilot was having difficulty keeping station properly. Eventually the tow rope broke and the glider was forced landed but hit a tree. In what must count as a rare burst of humour in an official document, the glider pilot's station commander commented: 'glider pilot needs more dual – when he gets out of hospital'!

15-May-43   EB306   Whitley V   HGCU   Carterton Village   0

The aircraft suffered an engine failure on take-off, when a valve stem fractured and there was also evidence of a coolant leak. The pilot made a forced landing just off the airfield and the was commended for his handling of the situation. The aircraft caught fire after landing and the blaze spread to the airframe.

147

Date	Serial	Aircraft	Unit	Place	Casualties
		Brief Circumstances of Accident			
		Casualty Details (If Applicable)			

16-May-43　DG390　Halifax　295 Sqn　2 miles north east of Sopley　5

The aircraft was being used to retrieve gliders but its starboard inner engine failed because of a serious glycol leak. The pilots lost control at low altitude and the aircraft spun into the ground.

Flying Officer Peter Sutherland THOMAS 21
Flying Officer Melvin Wilson COLLINS 21 RCAF
Flying Officer Donald James SMITH 21 RCAF
Sergeant Francis Joseph DAVIES 28 The Glider Pilot Regiment
Sergeant Roland Davies SUNTER 32

16-May-43　R9106　Lysander III　161 Sqn　RAF Tempsford　1

Shortly after mid-day, the aircraft stalled and crashed onto the airfield, where it burst into flames. The pilot received multiple injuries and subsequently died.

Flight Lieutenant Jack Edward BARTRUM 29

18-May-43　JB802　Halifax　138 Sqn　Maison Blanche　0

The aircraft overshot the runway on landing at the end of a flight from UK, ran into a building and was badly damaged.

19-May-43　DK122　Halifax　295 Sqn　Damerham Wiltshire　5

The aircraft was engaged in a 10 hour towing sortie but had only been airborne for a short time when the pilot instructed the glider pilot to cast off the tow. Shortly afterwards, the tug crashed. The cause of the accident was not determined but the aircraft was fully laden with its overload fuel tanks full, as well as a glider. It follows that any loss of engine power shortly after take off might have been critical.

Flying Officer Frank HILTON 29
Sergeant Patrick John PHIPPS 25
Sergeant Frank William WILSON 21
Flying Officer Russell Melvin REISNER 21
Flying Officer Edward Bradley BLACKBURN 21 died 2 Jun 43

19-May-43 FH168 Hudson IIIA   38 Wg   7 miles south of RAF St Eval   2

The port engine failed immediately after take-off and the aircraft crashed during an attempted forced landing. Air Commodore Norman was a 'major player' in the development of airborne warfare and is believed to have been travelling to the Middle East as part of the planning team for the invasion of Scilly.

    Air Commodore Sir Nigel St Valery NORMAN 45 CBE Bt
    Flying Officer Arthur ROTENBURG 22 RCAF Navigator

22-May-43 BB329 Halifax   138 Sqn   Polder Noordbemster Netherlands   2

The crew of this aircraft were detailed for a double drop coded; MARROW 35 and 36 and it was intended to deliver a total of fourteen containers and four packages. Having been hit by enemy AA fire, the aircraft crashed in the early hours of the moring 9 miles east-south-east of Alkmaar. Although the pilot and four of his crew were taken POW, two others were killed.

    Sergeant Stanley BOOTHROYD 31 Flight Engineer
    Sergeant William Henry WILDE 21

23-May-43 AM911 Liberator I   511 Sqn   Gibraltar   0

The aircraft, captained by the same pilot involved in the Talbenny crash in January, suffered a No: 3 engine failure on take-off. The engine fire was extinguished and the propeller feathered. The pilot then landed the aircraft which was close to its maximum weight but the port tyres burst and the undercarriage collapsed.

Date	Serial	Aircraft	Unit	Place	Casualties
					Casualty Details (If Applicable)

Brief Circumstances of Accident

23-May-43 BD419 Whitley V   HGCU   Carterton Village   0

The aircraft was forced landed immediately after take-off after the pilot suspected a loss of power during take off. It will be seen from the this and previous reports that Carterton Village could be a dangerous place to live!

25-May-43 MA928 DC3   31 Sqn   Argatala   0

This appears to be the result of the typical cockpit 'foul up'. The co-pilot misunderstood the pilot's orders and raised the aircraft's undercarriage during the take-off.

25-May-43 HH295 Hotspur II   5 GTS   Grove Farm, 4 miles north-wset of Shobdon   0

Within a few minutes of taking off, the tug pilot instructed the glider pilot to release the tow immediately and this was done. However, not being at a time and place of his own choosing, the glider pilot was then compelled to make the best he could of the situation but the aircraft was damaged when forced landed in a field. The glider pilot instructor; Flight Sergeant R P Bartrum and his student; Sergeant R C Creed were both injured.

26-May-43 Z6797 Whitley V   PTS   Tatton Park   0

The aircraft was forced landed immediately after take-off following an engine failure caused by a coolant leak.

29-May-43 P1503 Albemarle I   305 FTU   Perthshire   1

The pilot, a Russian officer being trained to fly the aircraft as part of an arrangement to supply them to the Soviets, made a shallow dive but failed to appreciate the rising ground ahead and was unable to pull out and clear the hill.

Major Alexander Gruisdin IVANOVITCH Soviet Air Force

29-May-43   LJ170   Horsa I   297 Sqn   RAF St Mawgan   0
The pilot misjudged his landing and crashed on the cliff adjacent to the the airfield when the glider undershot. The eight people aboard the aircraft were injured: the pilot; Lieutenant D M Shuttleworth, was to be killed in action at Arnhem the following year.

31-May-43   HH369 Hotspur II   GPEU   RAF Netheravon   0
Whilst landing at the conclusion of a 25 minute sortie, the glider stalled off a steep turn and crashed into a car and a building.

03-Jun-43   LG733   Horsa I   1 OADU   200 miles north-west of Cape Finisterre   0
This glider was one of a batch of four Horsas being towed to North Africa on this date, as part of Operations BEGGAR/TURKEY BUZZARD, an attempt to get a number of troop carrying gliders into the theatre for use during the pending attack in Scilly. Two of this batch made the non-stop 10 hour leg from Portreath in Cornwall to Sale but one aircraft turned back and this glider's tow rope snapped. The tug pilot; Flying Officer J A G Sizmur, transmitted a ditching position report before turning back to base. The glider crew; Major Alastair Cooper and Staff Sergeants Dennis Hall and Sotirios Antonoupoulis went into the sea at about 1000 hours, having escaped from the glider with their dinghy. Although the glider had filled with water rapidly after landing in the sea, it did not sink but remained awash with its tailplane and upper fuselage visible. At 2200 hours that evening, they were picked up by a Royal Navy frigate and taken back to Northern Ireland. None of the men was any the worse for their ordeal and all returned to the ferrying task within a few days. For Hall and Antonoupoulis, this ditching was merely a taster of what was to come less than two weeks later!

Date	Serial	Aircraft	Unit	Place	Casualties
		Brief Circumstances of Accident			
		Casualty Details (If Applicable)			
05-Jun-43	DP837	Horsa I	295 Sqn	Denbighshire location not specified	0

The poor visibility made it necessary for the tug to fly through cloud for a short period. The glider pilot pulled off the tow and made a forced landing.

| 05-Jun-43 | DP764 | Horsa I | HGCU | RAF Brize Norton | 0 |

The crew was practising flapless landings and the pilot undershot the approach.

| 07-Jun-43 | Z9419 | Whitley V | AFEE | Sherburn – in – Elmet | 0 |

The aircraft suffered a starboard engine failure because of a sheared magneto drive shaft. The pilot attempted a wheels down forced landing near the airfield but the undercarriage collapsed.

| 07-Jun-43 | HH125 | Hotspur II | 3 GTS | Stoke Orchard, Gloucestershire | 1 |

Whilst being towed at low level, the glider side slipped into the ground, fatally injuring the pilot. There was no obvious cause of the accident although it thought possible that the pilot, who was fairly inexperienced, might have lost control.

Believed to be:
Sergeant John Cyril PRATT 27 The Glider Pilot Regiment died of injuries 11 Jun 43

| 07-Jun-43 | BT603 | Hotspur II | 3 GTS | Stoke Orchard, Gloucestershire | 0 |

Whilst approaching to land, the glider was subjected to an increase in wind velocity and it undershot the landing.

09-Jun-43 LG932 Horsa I 38 Wg Det Frotha 0

At the conclusion of a ferry sortie, the glider pilot landed his aircraft off the runway and in doing so struck an oil drum, damaging the glider's undercarriage.

11-Jun-43 EB132 Halifax 295 Sqn Ashley Combe, Porlock Weir, Somerset 4

The aircraft was en-route from Holmsley South to Portreath but it flew into a hill near Porlock whilst flying in fog. Although the pilot and flight engineer survived, the other crew members were killed. This pilot had already completed a round trip to North Africa, towing a Horsa glider on the outward leg. The survivors were rescued due to the efforts of three local men; Messers H Pollard, T Cook and J Ridler, the last of whom was seriously injured when petrol vapour exploded

      Flight Sergeant Frederick Carl SCHULTZ 25 RAAF Co-Pilot
      Flying Officer William Angus Bartlett STOKES 24 RCAF Wireless Operator
      Warrant Officer John Nelson HANSEN Air Gunner
      Flying Officer Alan Douglas GARDNER 23 Navigator

11-Jun-43 P1527 Albemarle I 296 Sqn Algeria 0

On landing on a rough ground airfield at the end of a cross country flight, the port tyre burst and the aircraft swung, before its undercarriage collapsed.

12-Jun-43 DG406 Halifax 161 Sqn In English Channel 7

The crew was flying on a double sortie and was taking Squadron Leader Walker along as an observer, as he had just taken over the squadron's Halifax flight, having previously flown a tour with 49 Sqn, from whence he was awarded a DFC. It appears that the sortie had been completed successfully but the aircraft never returned to base and its fate and that of its is unknown but it probably crashed into the sea. Foster, O'Brien and Roberts, all received their awards on the squadron, although O'Brien's was not gazetted until after his death.

Date	Serial	Aircraft	Unit	Place	Casualties
		Brief Circumstances of Accident			
		Casualty Details (If Applicable)			

Flight Lieutenant Alfred Francis FOSTER 28 DFC
Squadron Leader Anthony De' Quincey WALKER 21 DFC
Sergeant John Smith RIDDELL
Pilot Officer James Thomas O'BRIEN 31 DFM
Pilot Officer LLewellyn ROBERTS 23 DFM
Sergeant Arthur MOON 22
Pilot Officer Frederick Lionel WILLIAMS 20

Date	Serial	Aircraft	Unit	Place	Casualties
12-Jun-43	HH784	Hotspur II	GPEU	RAF Netheravon	0

This is another instance of an aircraft being subjected to an unexpected increase in wind speed in the final stages of the approach, resulting in an undershoot.

Date	Serial	Aircraft	Unit	Place	Casualties
14-Jun-43	DK190	Halifax	295 Sqn	100 miles north west of Cape Finisterre	6

The aircraft was engaged on an Operation BEGGAR sortie but it and the glider it was towing were lost. The Luftwaffe reported that an aircraft and glider combination had been shot down and it is assumed to relate to this aircraft.

Warrant Officer William Armando MCCRODDEN 21 Pilot
Sergeant George Richard HALE 21
Sergeant Arthur SELVES 26 Flight Engineer
Sergeant Herbert Francis UPPERTON 22 Air Gunner
Flight Sergeant Frederick Charles PAYNE 29 Navigator
Flight Sergeant Victor James NORMAN 22 Wireless Operator

14-Jun-43　LG945　Horsa I　　　　1 OADU　　　　100 miles north west of Cape Finisterre　　　0

The Accident Card records the crew of this aircraft as 'missing', since they were in the glider being towed by DK190 when it was attacked and shot down, apparently by a pair of Focke Wulf Kondors and after a spirited defence. The glider had been cast off and the crew had ditched it in the sea. They escaped from the wreckage and boarded their dinghy but were adrift for 11 days before being rescued by the crew of a Spanish trawler and having drifted to within 20 miles of Oporto. The glider pilots were; Staff Sergeants Antonopoulos, Hall and Conway and it will be noted that Antonopoulos and Hall had previously ditched on 3 Jun 43, both were subsequently awarded the Air Force Medal.

16-Jun-43　DK130　Halifax　　　　295 Sqn　　　??????????????　　　?

17-Jun-43　P1443　Albemarle　　　296 Sqn　　　Froha Algeria　　　?

The aircraft crashed on landing at this base after a transit flight from UK

18-Jun-43　HH264　Hotspur II　　　3 GTS　　　Stoke Orchard　　　0

The glider was baulked on its final approach by another aircraft and the glider lost height whilst its pilot was making a turn in an attempt to land in a small field on the airfield boundary. However, in doing so, the glider's wing struck a tree and it crashed into a hedge.

19-Jun-43　W1229　Halifax　　　　138 Sqn　　　RAF Tempsford　　　0

The aircraft was landing in a cross wind when control was lost and it crashed.

21-Jun-43　FK592　Hudson VI　　　117 Sqn　　　Castel Benito　　　0

This is another occasion when a tyre burst, caused by sharp fragments or shrapnel, led to the collapse of the undercarriage. In this case the aircraft caught fire after coming to a stop and was damaged extensively.

Date	Serial	Aircraft	Unit	Place	Casualties
		Brief Circumstances of Accident			
		Casualty Details (If Applicable)			

22-Jun-43	DT727	Halifax	138 Sqn	RAF Tempsford	0

The aircraft was being used to carry out asymmetric landings but control was lost and the aircraft swerved into a hangar and was damaged badly. The pilot on both this occasion and that on 19 Jun, involving W1229, was Warrant Officer Stanislaw Klosowski. This pilot was a very experienced bomber pilot who had been awarded an honorary DFM on completion of a tour with 301 Sqn and had recently received the DFC for his work at Tempsford on special duties operations. The following year he was heavily involved with the Polish Special Duties Flight in Italy, especially during the Warsaw uprising.

22-Jun-43	V9316	Lysander IIIA	5 GTS	Shobdon	0

The pilot failed to take proper care whilst landing and the aircraft crashed into Hotspur HH615.

23-Jun-43	DG405	Halifax	161 Sqn	Ijsselmer Netherlands	8

This crew, flying their seventh sortie of the month, was shot down over Ijsselmeer. The Dutch underground had been comprehensively penetrated by the German Abwehr and almost every agent flown into the country was immediately captured because the enemy knew precisely what was going on. On many occasions, the Germans used this information to trap the SD crews and it appears that a significant number of losses amongst both 138 and 161 Sqns over the Netherlands came about because of this infiltration. It is worth noting also that when the first radio operator was compelled to transmit signals to London, he did his best to alert the 'handlers' that his cover was blown by making various errors in procedure. It seems, however, that nobody bothered to question why this was so and hence the lives of many Dutch agents and special duties aircrew were lost as a result.

Pilot Officer Robert Geoffrey HIGGINS 20 Pilot
Sergeant Norman BLANCHARD 27
Sergeant Maynard Hazelet MOORE 29 RCAF Navigator

Sergeant Charles William HARTIN 32
Sergeant Gordon GEORGE 27
Sergeant Frank GROOM 19
Sergeant Robin Douglas PRYDE-WATSON 27
Sergeant George Noel COCHRANE 27

23-Jun-43   DJ989   Halifax V   295 Sqn   Furndown Hants   0

Both port engines lost power immediately after take-off and the pilot made a forced landing. The aircraft was damaged extensively in the post crash fire but the crew survived without injury. The pilot; Flying Officer J A G Sizmur had recently made two successful round trips to North Africa to deliver Horsa gliders and on another occasion had returned early, after the glider's tow rope snapped and it was ditched in the sea.

23-Jun-43   FK452   Hudson VI   267 Sqn   Marble Arch   0

The aircraft was taking off in a crosswind and it started to swing to port. The pilot applied compensating brake but the aircraft swung to starboard and control was lost. The aircraft crashed off the runway and was destroyed in the subsequent fire.

24-Jun-43   BB379   Halifax   138 Sqn   Oostzaan Netherlands 4

This aircraft was shot down by flak. In addition to the fatal casualties, the other three crew were made POW.

Flight Sergeant Tadeusz Piotr ZABICKI 23 PAF Pilot
Flight Sergeant Walenty SICINSKI 30 PAF
Flying Officer Waclaw Stanislaw KALKUS 21 PAF
Flight Sergeant Kazimierz KIDZIAK 28 PAF

Date	Serial	Aircraft	Unit	Place	Casualties

Brief Circumstances of Accident
Casualty Details (If Applicable)

26-Jun-43 LJ175 Horsa I   Skinner's Bottom, near Redruth, Cornwall   0
The aircraft was leaving Portreath en route to North Africa. The procedure after take-off required the undercarriage to be jettisoned, so as to reduce drag and the aircraft would then land at the other end on its skids. Spare undercarriages were made available and in some cases carried by the gliders, for fitment once arrival was made at Sale. On this occasion, the handling pilot pulled the tow rope release instead of the undercarriage jettison handle and the glider was cast off. A landing was made in a field but the glider struck a stone wall and was damaged badly.

27-Jun-43 EB135 Halifax   295 Sqn   Missing   6
The aircraft was missing from an Operation BEGGAR/TURKEY BUZZARD sortie. The glider was also lost together with its crew. The German forces claimed that the combination had been intercepted by their aircraft over the Bay of Biscay and both had crashed into the sea after the tug aircraft was shot down.

> Flying Officer William Robert Lynden HORNE 22 RCAF Pilot
> Flying Officer James Andrew SMITH 20 RCAF
> Warrant Officer Michael TRAVALE 25 RCAF
> Sergeant Ronald Buckland MINCHIN 22
> Flight Sergeant Cyril Harry WEST 24
> Sergeant Jack STRETTON 22

27-Jun-43 LG833 Horsa I   295 Sqn   Missing   3
Lost in the circumstances summarised above.

> Staff Sergeant Daniel Stephen CASSELDEN 23 The Glider Pilot Regiment
> Sergeant Mark Albert Charles CHANDLER 27 The Glider Pilot Regiment

Sergeant Harold NORRIS 25 The Glider Pilot Regiment

| 27-Jun-43 | ????? | Waco CG4 | GPR | North Africa | 15 |

In preparation for the invasion of Scilly, a number of gliders had been flown out from UK and the losses suffered during this long range ferry flight have been summarised above. To provide sufficient gliders for the invasion, the US Army made over a substantial number of Waco CG4 gliders to the British. These aircraft were for the most part assembled by the British with assistance from the US personnel and training to operate the gliders commenced as soon as a stock of gliders had been constructed. Subsequently, it was necessary to move the airborne forces from their main assembly area, eastwards along the North Africa coast to some desert airstrips which would be used as the mounting bases for the airborne attack. Unfortunately, during this ferry operation, one of the Waco gliders suffered a structural failure and its tail unit came off. The aircraft crashed and all on board were killed.

Sergeant Arthur HIGGINS 26 Glider Pilot Regt
Sergeant James Edmund HARRISON 24 Glider Pilot Regt
Warrant Officer II (CSM) Reginald GLYNN 27 The South Staffordshire Regt
Lance Sergeant George Frederick MANNING 31
Corporal Alan HOLMES 24
Lance Corporal Frederick Albert BAILEY 30
Private Cyril Gordon ALLIN 22
Private George Henry ANDREWS 31
Private Raymond CRESSWELL 19
Private Albert William HAWKINS 23
Private William Isaac MASON 25
Private Arthur John REEDER 23
Private Douglas Gowe WILLIAMS 26
Lance Corporal William CLARKE 24 RAMC
Private John Arthur MARSHALL 29 RAMC

Date   Serial   Aircraft   Unit   Place   Casualties
Brief Circumstances of Accident
Casualty Details (If Applicable)

30-Jun-43   BD351   Whitley V   42 OTU   30 miles from St David's Head   0

The crew was engaged on a night training sortie and the aircraft had been airborne for 3 ¼ hours. The aircraft started to lose height following engine failure and was eventually ditched in the sea. The crew had some initial difficulties launching their dinghy and subsequently in using their distress flares. However, they were eventually picked up by a passing ship but none suffered serious injuries.

03-Jul-43   V9376   Lysander IIIA   5 GTS   Shobdon   0

The pilot failed to correct a swing which developed on landing and the aircraft struck another and was damaged beyond repair. The pilot did not carry out the normal corrective action and the station commander commented that his training was at fault.

04-Jul-43   AL523   Liberator II   511 Sqn   Gibraltar   16

The loss of this aircraft has probably generated more column inches of print over the years and aroused much controversy as to the precise circumstances of the crash etc than almost any other aircraft accident. In addition, it has proved a cause celebre for conspiracy theorists the world over. The aircraft was being used by the head of the Polish Government in Exile and was on the final stage of a tour of the Middle East. It had landed in Gibraltar and the passengers and crew were accommodated and entertained during their short stay by the Governor and his staff. Amongst the additional passengers who joined the aircraft was a member of the Polish Home Army who was carrying documents and despatches for the Polish Government and who had made the long and hazardous journey from Warsaw to Gibraltar. The aircraft was prepared for a night time transit to UK and it took off but did not seem to climb before it descended and struck the sea. The sole survivor was the Czech pilot; Flight Lieutenant Prchal. A great many theories were advanced as to the reason for the crash and these included sabotage by members of a Russian delegation, who were also in Gibraltar, a deliberate assassination plot sanctioned by Winston Churchill, pilot error and a mail bag blowing out of an open hatch and jamming the controls. The 'mystery' also extends to the two men listed at the end of the casualty roll but there is an innocent explanation for their presence. Madame Lesniowska was Sikorski's daughter but also his ADC. It is believed that Colonel Marecki was the author of a major paper dealing with the formation of airborne forces, which was written and presented to the British but the value of which has rarely been acknowledged by the latter, even though much of the information was accepted and formed the basis of British airborne doctrine in the early years. General Sikorski's remains were recovered from the sea and were repatriated to UK. He was buried in a focal position within the Polish forces plot at Newark Cemetery but, following the end of the 'Cold War', he was taken to Warsaw and is now buried in his homeland.

Squadron Leader Wilfred Stanley HERRING 29 DSO DFM
Warrant Officer Lewis ZALSBERG
Sergeant Francis Simpson KELLY 26
Flight Sergeant George Brotchie Robertson GERRIE 21 DFM
Flight Sergeant Dobson HUNTER 30
General Wladyslav SIKORSKI Head of Polish Government in Exile
Major General Tadeusz KLIMECKI
Colonel Andrzej MARECKI
Madame LESNIOWSKA
Mr Adam KULAKOWSKI
Colonel GRALEWSKI
Brigadier John Percival WHITELEY 45 OBE TD MP for Buckingham
Colonel Victor Alexander CAZALET MC MP for Chippenham, Liaison Officer to Polish Government
Lieutenant Jozef PONIKEWSKI
Mr Walter Heathcote LOCK 42 MA
Warrant Telegraphist Harry PINDER 42 RN HMS Nile

Date	Serial	Aircraft	Unit	Place	Casualties
Brief Circumstances of Accident					
Casualty Details (If Applicable)					

08-Jul-43   FD888   Dakota I   216 Sqn   RAF North Front   0

The aircraft swung on landing and the pilot was unable to correct it. The aircraft's wing struck a road roller and the aircraft overshot into the sea.

08-Jul-43   P1522   Albemarle   296 Sqn   Goubrine Tunisia   4

This aircraft crashed during an attempted overshoot whilst being air tested prior to the start of Operation LADBROOKE. It collided with the one below and both were wrecked.

    Flying Officer Geoffrey Frederick Laing HOPKINSON 21 Pilot
    Sergeant John CHARLEY 21
    Flying Officer Oscar Edward COATES 33
    Sergeant George Richard HUTCHINS 32

08-Jul-43   P1552   Albemarle   296 Sqn   Goubrine Tunisia   0

Destroyed as shown above.

09-Jul-43   FD774   Dakota   267 Sqn   At sea, west of Malta   2

The aircraft was en route from Tunis to Malta, to take on cargo destined for Gardabia West in Libya. After being airborne for only just over an hour, the aircraft was ditched apparently after its fuel supply ran out. The aircraft floated for sometime in the rough seas and the crew launched several dinghies but these drifted away as they were not secured by a lanyard to the aircraft. The navigator experienced trouble after entering the water and the wireless operator attempted to save him but neither man could then return to the aircraft nor reach a dinghy and they were drowned. The pilot; Flight Sergeant W L Cargill DFM, did manage to get into a dinghy and was eventually washed up on a beach many hours after the ditching. He had previously flown with the Special Liberator Flight from whence he was awarded a DFM

Flight Sergeant Daniel James Arthur HANNAN 23 RNZAF Wireless Operator

Warrant Officer John James SMITH 22 RAAF Navigator

| 09-Jul-43 | FD876 | Dakota | 267 Sqn | At sea | 0 |

It is unclear as to precisely what happened to this aircraft, although there is reference to an enquiry being convened to look into the circumstances of the loss of both this aircraft and that listed above.

| 11-Jul-43 | FD815 | Dakota III | 267 Sqn | 5 miles west of El Aouina | 6 |

This aircraft was one of a group of four from the squadron whose crews were detailed to drop flares and dummy parachutists over parts of Sicily. The aircraft was seen to be on fire in the air and then to dive into the ground. The cause of the accident was not determined.

Flying Officer Gowan Vernon GIBSON RCAF Pilot

Flying Officer Harry Grant SPENCER 21 RCAF Pilot

Lieutenant S A YALDWYN 26 SAAF Navigator

Warrant Officer Kennedy PATERSON Wireless Operator/Air Gunner

Wing Commander Reginald Frederick Stewart LESLIE 52 DSC DFC AFC

Major Frank Godrey BAXTER 39 RE

| 12-Jul-43 | JD155 | Halifax | 138 Sqn | St Paul sur Risle Eure France | 7 |

The aircraft crashed whilst one of a group of a dozen aircraft from the squadron operating in the same general area. The cause of the loss is not known.

Flight Lieutenant Julian MORAWSKI 30 PAF Pilot

Flight Sergeant Edward JONSKI 27 PAF

Sergeant Konrad Jozef TOMASZEWSKI 23 PAF

Flight Lieutenant Napoleon Stanislaw LEWICKI 30 PAF

163

Date	Serial	Aircraft	Unit	Place	Casualties
				Brief Circumstances of Accident Casualty Details (If Applicable)	

Flight Sergeant Leon Stanislaw BONK 24 PAF
Flight Sergeant Edmund RUSINSKI 26 PAF
Flight Sergeant Jan NAWROT PAF

Date	Serial	Aircraft	Unit	Place	Casualties
12-Jul-43	P1446	Albemarle	296 Sqn	Lost without trace	5

During air operations over and around Sicily, this aircraft failed to return. It was one of a pair of aircraft (the other was Albemarle P1526 flown by Flight Lieutenant P H Smulian AFC) detailed to drop two parties, each comprising 10 SAS troops, at Randazzo or Enna with the intention of disrupting enemy communications. The sorties were code named Operation CHESTNUT. Wing Commander May was the CO of 296 Sqn and had been awarded his AFC on 1 Apr 41. In preparing for the Sicily operations, May had asked Colonel Chatterton of the Glider Pilot Regiment, if he could have the latter's desert boots if the Chatterton did not return from the attack on Sicily. Chatterton agreed but Wing Commander May 'jumped the gun' and was wearing the desert boots when he was lost; Chatterton survived!

Wing Commander Peter Rodriguez MAY 35 AFC DFC (US) OC 296 Sqn
Warrant Officer Frank Holman Hintington ELLIOT 27
Flight Lieutenant John CLARKE 25 DFM
Flight Lieutenant George HOOD 28
Flight Lieutenant Terence Dlancey NEILL 39

Date	Serial	Aircraft	Unit	Place	Casualties
13-Jul-43	P1437	Albemarle	296 Sqn	At sea off Sicily	0

The aircraft was engaged in Operation FUSTIAN and was dropping parachute troops from 1 Para Bde on the Catania Plain. The aircraft was damaged by AA fire and the fuel tanks were holed, causing the engines to cut, and further damaged was inflicted on the control surfaces. The pilot, Flying Officer Buzeta, ditched the aircraft successfully and the crew escaped, being picked up from the water and taken to Malta.

13-Jul-43   P1466   Albemarle   296 Sqn   Froha   0

The aircraft crashed on take-off but apart from injuries to the pilot, the crew was unharmed.

13-Jul-43   P1521   Albemarle   296 Sqn   Location not known   0

The aircraft was towing a Horsa glider as part of Operation FUSTION/MARSTON. It failed to return to base but the precise circumstances in which it was lost are not known. The crew; captained by Fg Off Houchin, was reported as safe and rejoined their unit shortly afterwards.

13-Jul-43   Z9463   Whitley V   30 miles north west of Hartland Point   0

The aircraft was undertaking a training sortie and was carrying a crew of 6. The port engine failed following a loss of oil pressure probably due to a fractured feed pipe and the pilot was unable to maintain height on one engine and so made a successful ditching. Although a MAYDAY message was transmitted none was received and the crew experienced some problems with their safety equipment and emergency rations.

14-Jul-43   P1444   Albemarle   296 Sqn   Sicily   5

The aircraft was engaged in towing a Waco glider as part of Operation FUSTIAN and it and the glider were shot down. Major Lander was a remarkable Army officer who was the commanding officer of 21st Parachute Pathfinder Company. Despite his age and his service in the 1st World War, Lander had raised and trained the airborne pathfinders and although not deploying himself, he had gone in this aircraft to observe the work of his Company. The loss of this officer was keenly felt but he was succeeded by an equally larger than life character called 'Boy' Wilson, who was to lead the Company in action at Arnhem.

Flying Officer Robert Tope HAMER 30 Pilot
Warrant Officer James Jonathan KUNZ 23 RCAF
Sergeant Hugh SLOAN 28
Flight Sergeant James Berry 23

Date	Serial	Aircraft	Unit	Place	Casualties
Brief Circumstances of Accident					
Casualty Details (If Applicable)					

Major John LANDER 47 OC 21st Parachute Pathfinder Coy

Date	Serial	Aircraft	Unit	Place	Casualties
14-Jul-43	EB145	Halifax V	295 Sqn	Missing	6

This aircraft was missing from a sortie related to the invasion of Sicily but the cause of its loss is not known. Squadron Leader Wilkinson was the captain of one of the aircraft used to tow gliders on Operation FRESHMAN the previous November.

Squadron Leader Arthur Bernard WILKINSON 26 DFC (USA) Pilot

Flying Officer Roy Ingle HARGREAVES 23

Sergeant Eric Spencer BARBER 21

Sergeant George BEANS 23

Sergeant Alan CLARKE 22

Sergeant George MILLAR 25

Date	Serial	Aircraft	Unit	Place	Casualties
16-Jul-43	BD550	Whitley V	HGCU	Inkberrow Worcestershire	0

The aircraft was engaged in a glider towing sortie but it suffered a starboard engine failure due to a failure of the camshaft drive and other related components. The pilot attempted a single engined landing at Pershore but overshot the airfield and struck some trees.

Date	Serial	Aircraft	Unit	Place	Casualties
18-Jul-43	DP304	Horsa I	HGCU	RAF Brize Norton	0

The tug aircraft encountered performance problems immediately after take-off and the glider pilot pulled off the tow and made a forced landing straight ahead.

18-Jul-43   T9465   Hudson III   161 Sqn   Blida   0

This aircraft was flown by Group Captain E H Fielden DFC, the station commander at Tempsford. The sortie involved a landing in a field some 20 miles east of Lyon but on arrival there was no reception party and so continued to Algerai with the intention of refuelling before returning to UK. The aircraft was parked and the crew went off to rest, only for their aircraft to be struck and written off by a Blenheim, whose pilot was making an emergency landing having lost a propeller.

19-Jul-43   DK131   Halifax V   295 Sqn   Missing   6

The aircraft was returning to UK after delivering a glider to North Africa. It failed to arrive in UK and there is no indication of its fate. It is known, however, that the aircraft was refuelled at Ras El Ma but that was the last heard or seen of it. The crew had already made three successful round trips to North Africa, towing gliders and hence would have been experienced and alert to the hazards posed by this particular journey.

    Flying Officer John Winston BEWICK 29 Pilot
    Sergeant Edward Alfred ANCELLE 20
    Sergeant William Herbert SHAW 21
    Sergeant Russell Edward TOMLIN 22
    Flight Sergeant Joseph TRAVIS 26
    Flight Sergeant Robert Henry COWLEY 28 RCAF

19-Jul-43   DL373   Master II   3 GTS   Northleach   0

The aircraft was returning from a training sortie lasting about 1¾ hours when the pilot elected to make a low approach to land. He flew the aircraft beneath some telephone cables but then collided with a stone wall.

19-Jul-43   DL491   Master II   3 GTS   Stoke Orchard   1

The aircraft had completed a glider towing exercise at night and having dropped the tow rope, the pilot decided to carry out unauthorised low flying, during which the aircraft hit a telegraph pole.

167

Date	Serial	Aircraft	Unit	Place	Casualties

Brief Circumstances of Accident
Casualty Details (If Applicable)

Sergeant Arden Roy THOROUGOOD 21

21-Jul-43 DG391 Halifax V   295 Sqn   Missing North Africa to UK   7

Within two days of another Halifax going missing, this aircraft was lost in similar circumstances. It took off at about 0900 hours but never arrived in UK. The pilot had made several transits to and from North Africa and had generally been successful apart from one early return because of trouble with the glider.

Flying Officer Peter Thomson MUIRHEAD 26 DFC Pilot
Flying Officer Edwin Herbert OTTWAY 26
Wing Commander Wallace Stanley BARTON 25 DFC
Sergeant Robert John BROAD 21
Flight Sergeant Sidney MCCORMICK 34
Sergeant Norman Richard WAITE 20
Flight Sergeant Eddie WILLIAMS 23

22-Jul-43 BD532 Whitley V   295 Sqn   Dorset   0

The aircraft was being used for a dummy parachute dropping sortie and had been airborne for just over 1½ hours when its starboard engine failed following a coolant leak. The pilot forced landed the aircraft in a field with undercarriage and flaps retracted and the aircraft subsequently caught fire, making post crash investigation difficult. The pilot; Flying Officer H T Gwynne and his crew were highly commended for their crash discipline.

22-Jul-43 P1440 Albemarle   296 Sqn   Goubrine II   0

The aircraft was towing off a glider but the latter got too high because it was enveloped in dust and the glider pilot lost his visual cues. The nett result was that the tug's tail was pulled up, it crashed and caught fire but the crew was unhurt.

23-Jul-43	DK119 Halifax	161 Sqn	St Sauvier Allier France	1

On completion of their sortie, the crew were compelled to force land their aircraft after serious engine problems. Unfortunately, the rear gunner was killed in the landing and the navigator injured and made POW.

Flight Sergeant Louis Max LAVALLE 23 RCAF Air Gunner

23-Jul-43	V9373 Lysander	5 GTS	Shobdon	0

This aircraft and the Moth Minor listed below were both recorded as damaged at Shobdon on this date. However, no further information was discovered and it is possible their loss might have involved a collision.

23-Jul-43	W6458 DH94 Moth Minor 5 GTS		Shobdon	0

Damaged in a taxying accident but see note above.

Date	Serial	Aircraft	Unit	Place	Casualties
Brief Circumstances of Accident					
Casualty Details (If Applicable)					

24-Jul-43 LA856 Whitley 295 Sqn Hurn 3

The aircraft was being used for a type conversion sortie and its port engine failed on take-off. The crew lost control of the aircraft, it crashed and was destroyed by fire.

Flight Lieutenant John Noel Wilmot KERR 27 Pilot
Flight Sergeant Thomas Harold PAYNE 27 RAAF Pilot under instruction
Flight Sergeant Geoffrey Maurice CONNELL 20 RAAF

27-Jul-43 L5838 Bombay I 1 AAU Phillipeville, Tunisia 0

The aircraft was landing on a casualty evacuation flight and it overshot into a depression after a total run of 1100 yards. Unfortunately for the pilot, the wind was very gusty and at a crucial moment some children ran across the landing strip and he was forced to take avoiding action.

27-Jul-43 Z9189 Whitley V 42 OTU Edlaston Hall, Derbyshire 5

Almost immediately after take-off the port engine failed because the flame traps collapsed. The trainee pilot lost control and the aircraft struck the tops of some trees and crashed adjacent to Edlaston Hall.

Flight Sergeant John Alfred WATKINS Pilot (Staff Pilot)
Flying Officer Ian Bert MANN Pilot
Warrant Officer Ian WALLACE-COX Navigator
Sergeant Albert John SHORTER Wireless Operator
Sergeant Kenneth Alfred GOODING Air Gunner

28-Jul-43 FK573 Hudson VI 117 Sqn Lentini West 0

The aircraft was landing at the end of a freight carrying sortie and it started to swing in a strong crosswind.

The pilot checked the swing but then a tyre burst and the aircraft swung once more before its undercarriage collapsed.

31-Jul-43   L5844   Bombay I   216 Sqn   Francesco   0?
The aircraft was written off after its undercarriage collapsed following a tyre burst on take-off.

31-Jul-43   P1474   Albemarle   296 Sqn   Goubrine II   0
On landing the aircraft suffered a tyre burst and the undercarriage collapsed. The investigation revealed that the aircraft had stood for a long time at the maintenance unit without its tyres being rotated and this had weakened the tyre wall. In addition the prevailing conditions at airfields in North Africa were particularly harsh on tyres.

05-Aug-43   P1468   Albemarle   296 Sqn   Telergma Algeria   0
The aircraft took off on a parachute dropping sortie but suffered a tyre burst. A wheels down landing was made but the aircraft was damaged. Once again the climatic conditions prevailing were judged to be a major factor.

05-Aug-43   EM288   Master II   5 GTS   Shobdon, Herefordshire   0
The aircraft was being landed back after a towing sortie. Whilst approaching in a strong crosswind, the aircraft stalled and crashed.

06-Aug-43   EB141   Halifax V   1575 Flt   Blida, Tunisia   0
The aircraft was landing at the end of 4½ hour cross country sortie but the pilot made a heavy landing, causing a tyre to burst, which in turn induced a swing from which the undercarriage collapsed.

Date	Serial	Aircraft	Unit	Place	Casualties
				Brief Circumstances of Accident Casualty Details (If Applicable)	
07-Aug-43	DP777	Horsa I	HGCU	RAF Brize Norton	0

The glider undershot the approach and struck a crane with the port wing. The release height would have allowed the glider to fly an approach, overshoot and then fly a second approach to land. However, the pilot delayed raising the flaps and lost so much height that he left insufficient margin to complete a second circuit.

| 09-Aug-43 | L5827 | Bombay I | 216 Sqn | Francesco Sicily | 0 |

During the take-off on a casualty evacuation flight, a tyre burst and the undercarriage collapsed.

| 10-Aug-43 | P1433 | Albemarle | 511 Sqn | Missing off Gibraltar (105 miles west Tarifa) | 13 |

The aircraft was on a passenger carrying sortie and a MAYDAY message was transmitted giving a position over the sea 105 miles west of Tarifa, after which nothing more was heard. The stark comment is made in the Accident Card that it is not sensible to have an aircraft which cannot carry a reasonable load whilst flying on one engine, used for passenger carrying sorties over the sea.

Flight Lieutenant Harold Anthony KIDD-MAY 21Pilot
Flying Officer Albert William LITTLE 26 RCAF Navigator
Flying Officer Jack Collingridge VALDER 34 RAAF
Flying Officer Douglas Charles Walter CLARKE RCAF Air Gunner
Flight Sergeant William Robert MCLELLAN 23 RCAF Air Gunner
Flying Officer James Hannen CHARNOCK 20
Sergeant William Brownlie CLARKSON 20
Sergeant Jack OXLEY 21
Sergeant Desmond Arthur WOODS

Flying Officer Philip Oscar DAVIS 22
Corporal Keith Treffa ALEXANDER
+ two others

10-Aug-43 DP772 Horsa I   HGCU   RAF Brize Norton   0

The glider's crew was engaged in a night training sortie and they were landing at the end of a 30 minute detail. The landing was made short and the aircraft drifted into another Horsa waiting to take off. To try to prevent a repeat performance. Some changes to the flare path were instituted.

11-Aug-43 V9228 Hudson III   AFEE   Sherburn in Elmet   0

The aircraft was taking off on a sortie to RAF Hendon and was being flown by a Group Captain with three others on board. Immediately after take-off, the pilot moved the elevator trim control wheel in the wrong direction and consequently ran out of elevator control authority. The aircraft lost height, crashed through a hedge and caught fire. This embarrassing 'gaff' did not deter the officer and he was promoted to Air Vice Marshal in 1954 and retired 4 years later.

13-Aug-43 BB334 Halifax   138 Sqn   Ecorceai Orne   2

This aircraft was one of fifteen despatched by the squadron and the crew was attempting to complete a sortie coded SPRUCE 20 and 21 which they had been unable to finish the previous evening. There are some conflicting accounts about what actually happened but whether shot down by night fighter or hit by flak, the aircraft crashed into a field and two of the crew were killed. Warrant Officer II Scott RCAF and Sergeant Trusty, the pilot and despatcher respectively, evaded capture and returned to UK but three others were made POW.

Flight Sergeant Donald Alexander Joseph CAMERON RCAF Wireless Operator
Flight Sergeant Allan Gerald FOSTER RCAF Air Gunner

173

Date	Serial	Aircraft	Unit	Place	Casualties
			Brief Circumstances of Accident		
			Casualty Details (If Applicable)		

13-Aug-43 HH412 Hotspur II 3 GTS Stoke Orchard, Gloucestershire 0

The aircraft landed well but the surface at the point of touchdown was poor. The aircraft tipped violently forward onto its skid and was damaged.

15-Aug-43 FD838 Dakota 31 Sqn Area of Alangdunaku 6

The aircraft had taken off from Dinjan at about noon for a supply dropping sortie to position 27 degrees 17 North/97 degrees 43 East. The aircraft was seen in the area of the drop zone but it failed to return to base and the cause of its loss is uncertain.

Flying Officer Arthur Valentine BARY 22 RNZAF Pilot
Sergeant Raymond George HINTON
Sergeant Kenneth Edward LAMOND
Leading Aircraftman Albert George JOHN
+ one other RAF
Lance Corporal George Robert HENDERSON 24 62 Field Coy Royal Engineers

15-Aug-43 JD180 Halifax 138 Sqn Meythet Haute-Savoy 6+5

This aircraft was one of twelve sent to France and it was shot down after being hit in the engines. It was, at the time, dropping leaflets over a town and one must wonder why high value assets like an SD squadron aircraft were risked on that sort of caper. When the aircraft crashed, the pilot; Squadron Leader F C Griffiths AFC and Sergeant J Maden were the only survivors, although Griffiths was badly injured. Griffiths was immediately captured but the aircraft blew up at this stage and the Italian captors fled, giving the pilot a chance to escape, which he took and eventually returned to UK via Spain and Gibraltar. Sergeant Maden is thought to have been shot whilst trying to evade capture. Unfortunately, the crashing aircraft claimed

174

the lives of five French civilians.

Sergeant Frederick Ronald DAVIES 25 Flight Engineer
Flying Officer Sydney John CONGDON 26 DFM Navigator
Pilot Officer Roderick Alexander MACKENZIE 22 Bomb Aimer
Flight Sergeant Robert William PETERS 22 DFM Wireless Operator
Flight Sergeant Francis POLLARD 22
Sergeant John MADEN 20 (shot by the Italian forces)

15-Aug-43 DP388 Horsa I   1 OADU   At sea   0

The glider was one of five being towed to the Middle East as the first part of Operation ELABORATE, another attempt to move Horsa gliders into an operational area. The glider was cast off and crashed but it seems the crew of Staff Sergeant E Johnson and Sergeants P A Attwood and N E Brown, were rescued.

16-Aug-43 JD312 Halifax   138 Sqn   Arx Landes   0

The aircraft suffered engine problems shortly after completing its drop and was forced landed safely. The crew were about to destroy the aircraft when some French arrived and drained some of the fuel away before the aircraft was set on fire. The entire seven man Polish crew evaded capture and eventually returned to UK.

16-Aug-43 DP329 Horsa I   1 OADU   At sea   0

Lost at sea during an Operation ELABORATE sortie. The three glider pilots; Sergeants Saunders, Jackson and Wedge survived.

16-Aug-43 DJ994 Halifax V   295 Sqn   Missing en route to Sale   1

The aircraft was towing a glider to Sale but it and the glider failed to arrive.

Sergeant Manassah COX 21

Date	Serial	Aircraft	Unit	Place	Casualties
		Brief Circumstances of Accident			
		Casualty Details (If Applicable)			

16-Aug-43 DP284 Horsa I   HGCU   Harcourt Estate, Oxfordshire   0

The glider was being used for a routine pilot training sortie and after 1 hour airborne its tow rope broke. A forced landing was made but the aircraft was damaged.

18-Aug-43 DG253 Halifax   138 Sqn   RAF Tempsford   0

The aircraft was damaged after it overran the runway on return from operations. The record indicates that this was an 'early return' and in this case there was a pre-existing problem with the aircraft, caused by a possible serious fuel leak from the overload tanks, before its landing.

18-Aug-43 JD179 Halifax   138 Sqn   l'Aigle Orne   7

This crew failed to return from a sortie to France and their aircraft crashed killing all on board.

Flight Sergeant Norman Wood HAYTER 24 RAAF Pilot
Sergeant William Stuart DAVIES 24
Sergeant Francis BOLES 20 Navigator
Sergeant Horace George ANSELL 21 Bomb Aimer
Sergeant John Albert HUTCHINSON 22 Wireless Operator
Flight Sergeant Allan Blakiston ROBINSON 25 Air Gunner
Sergeant George William Francis DUCKETT 22 Air Gunner

18-Aug-43 DP293 Horsa I   HGCU   Stenlake, Oxfordshire   0

The glider pilot got his aircraft into an awkward position, relative to the tug aircraft and so pulled off the tow. This was followed by a bad forced landing and damage to the glider.

22-Aug-43   DG393   Halifax   295 Sqn   Sale French Morocco   4

The aircraft was towing a glider to a forward base and had just taken off when its starboard inner engine caught fire. The glider cast off and the aircraft's pilot brought the aircraft back for a landing. Unfortunately, the aircraft undershot the approach, crashed short of the runway and was burnt out.

    Flight Sergeant Irwin James CLARK 27 RCAF Co-Pilot
    Flying Officer Gordon Cecil ROLLS 25 Navigator
    Sergeant Edward Frank JARRET 21 Wireless Operator
    Flying Officer Richard Alfred CHARTER 26 Pilot died of injuries 29 Aug 43

22-Aug-43   EB299   Whitley   296 Sqn   Middle Wallop   0

The aircraft's starboard engine failed because of a glycol coolant leak and the pilot was unable to maintain height. The pilot attempted to land at Middle Wallop when he was unable to control the aircraft but it crashed and four of the crew were injured.

23-Aug-43   T4339   Whitley V   42 OTU   Gold Cliffe, Newport Monmouthshire   4

The aircraft was on a night training sortie and was seen to dive into the River Severn. The cause for the loss of control and accident was not determined.

    Pilot Officer Robert Warren CONWAY 26 RCAF Pilot
    Flight Sergeant Roy Hamilton SMITH 26 RCAF Air Gunner
    Flight Sergeant Harold Claude WARD21 RCAF Wireless Operator
    Flight Sergeant Clement John JAMISON 29 RAAF Navigator

23-Aug-43   P1478   Albemarle   297 Sqn   Missing   4

The aircraft is recorded as missing and the Accident Card states 'suspected EA' and it may be assumed therefore that there is some evidence that the aircraft was shot down. In consulting the Accident Cards, there is some confusion as records show peoples' names incorrectly and also show several officers with

Date	Serial	Aircraft	Unit	Place	Casualties
Brief Circumstances of Accident					
Casualty Details (If Applicable)					

the same personal serial number. However, it is believed this crew list is accurate.

Warrant Officer Herbert Edward CURTIS 34 Pilot
Flying Officer John Bruce BOWDEN 23 RCAF
Flight Sergeant Albert Edward George NUNN 21
Flight Sergeant Robert Angus MOORE 23

Date	Serial	Aircraft	Unit	Place	Casualties
23-Aug-43	LH122	Horsa I	1 OADU	Portugal	0

The glider was was one of four being flown to Sale as part of Operation ELABORATE and was being towed by Halifax DK198, captained by Flying Officer Clapperton. For some reason not explained, the glider was forced landed on a beach in Portugal and is assumed that whatever the problem, it was possible for the tug aircraft to take the glider fairly close in shore to permit a landing to be made on dry ground. The glider crew of Sergeants C Robinson, L Wright and L Ridings eventually made their way back to UK.

Date	Serial	Aircraft	Unit	Place	Casualties
23-Aug-43	LH232	Horsa I	9 MU	RAF Cosford	0

The aircraft was being flown on a airtest and had been airborne for about 15 minutes. As he was preparing to land, the pilot executed a turn downwind too close to the ground and the glider side slipped in, striking the ground and colliding with a parked Spitfire VIII serial number JF664.

Date	Serial	Aircraft	Unit	Place	Casualties
24-Aug-43	LG929	Horsa I	297 Sqn	Hurn, Bournemouth	0

The pilot landed the glider on the runway at the end of his night flying detail but then allowed it to run off the side and over rough ground and into a ditch. The cause was attributed to the pilot's inexperience and the comment was made that glider pilots needed more night flying training before carrying out similar exercises with large gliders.

24-Aug-43 DP396 Horsa I   297 Sqn   Hurn, Bournemouth   0

The aircraft, flown by Squadron Leader T C Musgrave and with Lieutenant Colonel I A Murray as his co-pilot, landed short at the conclusion of an exercise and collided with Horsa LG929, which had crashed just a short while before, and it then ran into an anti-tank ditch. The exercise in which this crew were involved, required a number of aircraft to land in quick succession and it had not proved possible to mark the wreck of LG929 with lights. Both Musgrave and Murray were to have distinguished careers in transport forces. Musgrave lost a leg in an accident but returned to flying duties and commanded a squadron later in the war, being awarded an OBE in the 1944 New Years' Honours List and DFC in 1945. Murray on the other hand became the principal glider pilot flying operationally and was involved in the assaults in Europe during 1944 and 1945 being awarded both the DSO and a first bar to the award.

27-Aug-43 FK584 Hudson VI   194 Sqn   Bamrauli   10

The aircraft was landing in a dust storm and the pilot made a flat turn at about 80 feet on final approach, causing the aircraft to stall with no height for recovery.

Pilot Officer Kenneth BROOKMAN 26 Pilot
Pilot Officer William Clayton WALSH 24 RCAF Navigator
Flight Sergeant Leonard YEALLAND 30 Wireless Operator
Squadron Leader Lewis Richard Conway CARTWRIGHT 33
Squadron Leader Colin METCALFE 31
Major General Thomas George Gordon HEYWOOD 56 CB OBE
Brigadier Hugh Poynton RADLEY 49 CIE MC
+ three others

31-Aug-43 DM404 Master II   3 GTS   Bishops Cleeve, Glocestershire   1

The aircraft was being flown on an air test and had been airborne for about 15 minutes. The pilot was undertaking unauthorised low level aerobatics and the aircraft stalled, crashing into a field.

Date	Serial	Aircraft	Unit	Place	Casualties
				Brief Circumstances of Accident	
				Casualty Details (If Applicable)	

Sergeant Charles Eric PETRE 22

03-Sep-43 LG671 Horsa I OADU At sea 0
This glider was one of three being sent overseas and towed by Halifaxes; in this case DK199 flown by Flight Sergeant Crossley and his crew. It was ditched in the sea and the three glider pilots were picked up by a naval vessel.

04-Sep-43 P1526 Albemarle 296 Sqn Gouribine II Tunisia 0
The aircraft ran into a hole whilst taxying and sustained serious damage.

05-Sep-43 FD786 Dakota 31 Sqn Imphal 0
The aircraft was landing at the conclusion of mail delivery sortie. It drifted on final approach because of a light crosswind and struck a tar barrel situated close to the runway edge. On touchdown, the aircraft ran off the side of the runway and into a ditch where its starboard engine caught fire.

06-Sep-43 V9672 Lysander IIIA 5 GTS Dilwyn Herefordshire 0
The aircraft was engaged in a glider towing sortie and the combination had been airborne for about 5 minutes. The tug's engine failed because some components in the throttle linkage came adrift and the engine could not be controlled. The glider was cast off and made a safe landing, whilst the tug pilot; Sergeant N E Burlow, was compelled to force land the aircraft in a field.

07-Sep-43 AE881 Ventura II 624 Sqn Missing 4
The aircraft was flown by a very experienced special duties pilot but it failed to return from a sortie to Italy

and no trace of it or the crew was found. It seems probable that the aircraft crashed in the sea but it is unclear whether the crew had completed their task or if they were on the outbound leg and as there were no known claims for its destruction, its loss as a direct consequence of enemy action seems unlikely.

Flight Lieutenant Cyril Dennis BOOTHBY DFC DFM
Flying Officer Donald Burnard POPE 34
Flight Sergeant William Herbert LOWE 33
Warrant Officer Lancelot WILLIAMS 23

07-Sep-43   BB435   Halifax II   148 Sqn   Missing on sortie to Greece   8

The aircraft was missing from an SOE sortie.

Pilot Officer William Leslie TOPP 20 RAAF Pilot
Flying Officer George KAY Navigator
Flying Officer Wilfred KING Bomb Aimer
Sergeant Dennis Vivian HUMBERSTON 22 Wireless Operator
Sergeant Alfred Charles GOSS Flight Engineer
Sergeant Charles DOVE Air Gunner
Sergeant George Ernest SMITH 21 Air Gunner
Flight Sergeant James Edward WINTIE 28 Air Gunner

07-Sep-43   EB178   Halifax   295 Sqn   South of Lisbon Portugal   0

This tug aircraft and the glider listed below, crashed in Portugal and were destroyed by fire. The cause of this accident is not known but it may have been related to an attempt to ensure that a damaged glider was not released over the sea or it may be that the tug was in distress and hence turned towards land.

07-Sep-43   DP824   Horsa I   OADU   South of Lisbon Portugal   0

Destroyed by fire.

181

Date	Serial	Aircraft	Unit	Place	Casualties
					Brief Circumstances of Accident
					Casualty Details (If Applicable)

09-Sep-43   FH275   Hudson IIIA   353 Sqn   Palam   0
The aircraft undershot the airfield after an engine failed during the approach to land.

09-Sep-43   HR670   Halifax II   148 Sqn   RAF Fayid   0
The aircraft was returning from a night operational sortie but its starboard undercarriage would not lower completely. A crash landing was made but the aircraft caught fire and was destroyed. The undercarriage problems were judged to have been caused by a mechanical failure due to a previous heavy landing, damage on take-off or a problem with the hydraulics system.

09-Sep-43   EB197   Halifax V   624 Sqn   Blida   0
The aircraft was returning from a successful sortie and at the moment of touchdown, all the airfield lighting failed. The aircraft was slightly off line and it went off the side in the pitch darkness as the pilot lost all his visual cues. Despite the pilot trying to recover, the aircraft collided with several Wellington aircraft (BB468 and HZ274) and these were written off in addition the this aircraft. Fortunately, the crew survived and as the pilot had cut the ignition switches there was no fire. The pilot; Flight Sergeant G F Regan RAAF was into his second tour of duty and subsequently received the DFC on its conclusion.

10-Sep-43   EB130   Halifax V   295 Sqn   RAF Portreath   0
The aircraft was positioning for a flight to the Middle East and was landing in a crosswind. The pilot failed to correct a swing that developed and the aircraft swung and ran into the control tower.

10-Sep-43   HS102   Horsa I   OADU   At sea   0
The aircraft was being towed to Sale by Halifax DG396. About 3½ hours after take-off and when well out to

sea, the combination was attacked by 12 Ju 88 twin engined enemy fighters. The glider pilot ordered the tow to be dropped and the flying pilot did this immediately and the glider was ditched successfully in rough seas. The glider crew of Lieutenant Prout, Sergeant P B Hill and Sergeant H Flynn drifted in their dinghy but were found first by a Sunderland flying boat and then rescued by HMS Crane. The Halifax crew fought off the concerted attack and one Ju 88 was shot down resulting in the air gunner, Sergeant John Patterson Grant, being awarded the DFM in Nov 43. The damaged Halifax eventually returned to Portreath.

Date	Serial	Aircraft	Base	Casualties
13-Sep-43	EM262	Master II	5 GTS	RAF Shobdon, Herefordshire	0

The aircraft ran into Oxford HM783 after a swing developed on landing.

| 14-Sep-43 | JD269 | Halifax | 138 Sqn | Esberg Denmark | 10 |

During the outward leg of its sortie to Poland, where its crew was to have dropped 3 agents onto DZ Pierzyna 206 near Minsk, the aircraft was struck by enemy AA fire from a number of batteries. It crashed close to a railway track about 4 miles north of Esberg and there were no survivors. A Danish researcher; Soren C Flensted, records that the Germans found $US 180000 in the wreckage, together with significant quantities of arms and ammunition.

Flight Lieutenant Augus John Mathewson MILNE 21 DFC
Flight Sergeant Frank SHUTTLEWORTH 24 Flight Engineer
Pilot Officer Thomas Richardson WILSON 22 Bomb Aimer
Flying Officer Ian MACLEAN 35 DFC Navigator
Pilot Officer Philip Eaton ROLLINS 21 Wireless Operator
Pilot Officer Jack Robert SCARLES 22 Air Gunner
Sergeant Edward Joseph SMYTH 22
Lieutenant Wladyslaw SIAKIEWICZ Polish Army (Code Name – MRUK)
Lieutenant Kazimierz LEWKO (Code Name – PALEC)
Lieutenant Ryszard Kazimierz SKOWRONSK (Code Name – LECHITA)

Date	Serial	Aircraft	Unit	Place	Casualties

Brief Circumstances of Accident
Casualty Details (If Applicable)

15-Sep-43 HR666 Halifax   138 Sqn   At sea off Korsor Denmark   5

The aircraft crashed into the Store Baelt after being hit by enemy AA fire, in a position between the island of Sprogo and Halskov Rev Lightship. Although Pilot Officer James was picked up alive, he died before reaching hospital. The remains of the others, excepting Sergeant Irwin, were recovered in various places over the following weeks and laid to rest in cemeteries nearby.

Pilot Officer William Henry JAMES 23 Pilot
Flying Officer Dennis Barton IRELAND 33 Navigator
Sergeant Jack Edward IRWIN 21
Sergeant Bernard Alan Cavendish HUNT 20
Sergeant Roy Hedley David BOUTTELL 22

15-Sep-43 JD154 Halifax   138 Sqn   Skalmierzyce Nowe Poland   7

This aircraft and its crew were engaged on sortie FLAT 22 to a target in western Poland. With some considerable irony, the aircraft struck a block of flats about 6 miles south-west of Kalisz Pomorski and all on board were killed. It is unclear whether the aircraft had descended to very low level for operational reasons or whether it had already been seriously damaged by flak or a night fighter.

Flight Lieutenant Franciszek Jozef JAKUSZ-GOSTOMSKI 26 DFC PAF Pilot
Flight Sergeant Ludwig Henryk MISIAK 30 PAF
Sergeant Zdzislaw KUCZKOWSKI 29 PAF
Flight Lieutenant Karol Piotr GEBIK 30 DFC PAF
Flight Sergeant Wiktor JABLONSKI 29 PAF
Sergeant Henryk FOJER 21 PAF
Warrant Officer Kazimierz PACUT 28 PAF

15-Sep-43   JN910   Halifax   138 Sqn   In the Baltic near Rugenwalde   7
The crew had completed their task; FLAT 12 to Poland and the aircraft crashed into the sea on its return flight.

    Flying Officer Edward Chichester HART Pilot
    Sergeant Kenneth Charles WINDSOR 23 RCAF Flight Engineer
    Flying Officer Joseph Darie Louis CLOUTIER 23 RCAF Navigator
    Sergeant Leonard Charles GAY
    Sergeant Sidney John SMITH
    Sergeant William Henry MUDGE
    Sergeant Kenneth Ross NORRIE 26

17-Sep-43   BB309   Halifax   138 Sqn   Slaglille Denmark   5+5
The crew was engaged on NEON 3 to dropping zone Obraz 108 in Poland. Having left Tempsford at about 1830 hours the previous evening, the aircraft had been flown to its target and its cargo and two Polish officers; Lieutenants M Kryszezukajtis and B Augustyn, had been dropped successfully. Whilst returning over Denmark, the aircraft was attacked by a JU88C-6 night fighter of 11/NJG 3, flown by Leutnant Richard Burdyna and Obergefreiters Leo Klotz and Fritz Merten. The Halifax struck a house in its crash landing and three adults and two children from the eleven occupants of the house were killed. Soren C Flensted, in his research states that the night fighter crew only had a couple of minutes to savor their victory, as their aircraft struck trees and crashed whilst circling the wreckage.

    Sergeant Eugeniusz Piotr KASPRZAK 21 PAF Flight Engineer
    Flight Lieutenant Wincenty WASILEWSKI 27 PAF
    Flight Sergeant Julien MICHALSKI 35 PAF Wireless Operator
    Sergeant Wladyslaw Stanislaw PATLEWICZ 33 PAF Air Gunner
    Flight Sergeant Wladyslaw BARZDO 27 PAF

Date	Serial	Aircraft	Unit	Place	Casualties

Brief Circumstances of Accident
Casualty Details (If Applicable)

17-Sep-43   JD156   Halifax   138 Sqn   Off the Jutland Peninsula   3

The aircraft was outbound on sortie FLAT 5 to a DZ at Obraz Poland. The weather forecast proved to be badly in error and the aircraft was attacked by a night fighter, which set fire to the aircraft's overload fuel tanks and disabled two engines. The pilot ditched the aircraft and the crew who survived spent a couple of hours in the water until rescued by a fishing boat crewed by Danes but with SS troops on board.

Flying Officer James Reid BRADLEY RCAF Navigator
Sergeant Henry JOHNSON
Flight Sergeant Graham Ernest SNOOK RAAF

17-Sep-43   DP745   Horsa I   HGCU   1 mile south-west of Brize Norton railway stn   0

The aircraft had been airborne for just over an hour on a training sortie. The pilot instructor decided to execute a 360 degree turn to bleed off excess height but in doing so he allowed the glider to carry him away from the airfield. On completion of the turn, his glider was then out of position and a landing in a field made.

18-Sep-43   FD832   Dakota III   216 Sqn   Antimachia Kos   0

This aircraft and the three Dakotas listed below were destroyed during an air attack by German forces against the airbase at Kos.

Sergeant Gerard Eric NEWALL Wireless Operator

18-Sep-43   FD892   Dakota III   216 Sqn   Antimachia Kos   0

As outlined above

186

| 18-Sep-43 | FD893 | Dakota III | 216 Sqn | Antimachia Kos | 0 |

As outlined above

| 18-Sep-43 | FD921 | Dakota | 216 Sqn | Antimachia Kos | 0 |

As outlined above

| 18-Sep-43 | P1389 | Albemarle | 296 Sqn | Grottaglie | 0 |

Whilst parked on the airfield, this aircraft was struck by a Kittyhawk and burnt out in the subsequent blaze.

| 18-Sep-43 | P1528 | Albemarle | 296 Sqn | 3 miles north of Tafaroui, Oran | 1 |

Following take-off, the aircraft failed to climb and the pilot elected to make a wheels down forced landing off the airfield. Unfortunately, the aircraft struck a ditch and was destroyed. The Accident Card records that there were six fatal casualties but further research suggests there was just one as shown below.

Warrant Officer II Edward Handley ROBINSON RCAF Navigator

| 19-Sep-43 | BB317 | Halifax | 138 Sqn | North Sea | 3 |

The crew had dropped successfully their load of containers and packages onto 2 DZs but their aircraft was then shot down by AA fire and crashed into the North Sea. Although the pilot and two crew were killed, the other four survived to be made POW.

Flight Sergeant Norman Louis SHERWOOD 20 Pilot
Sergeant Bertram Sidney BURCH 22
Sergeant Richard Thomas CHINN 20

| 19-Sep-43 | FD806 | Dakota I | 216 Sqn | At sea off Kos | 0 |

The aircraft was taking part in the delivery of troops and supplies to Kos and the pilot had been instructed to fly at low level but the aircraft had not been fitted with extra dinghies because of the urgency of the sortie.

Date	Serial	Aircraft	Unit	Place	Casualties

Brief Circumstances of Accident
Casualty Details (If Applicable)

The pilot misjudged the height over the water and the aircraft struck the sea and was ditched, fortunately without injury to those on board.

| 20-Sep-43 | DG252 | Halifax | 138 Sqn | North Sea | 5 |

This aircraft was flown by a five man crew, three of whom had been decorated for service on the squadron and the pilot had been with the unit for 2 years overall. The crew was assigned two targets in Holland but in common with the crew of BB317 above, they were trapped by the enemy who were operating the DZ and the aircraft was hit by AA fire and crashed into the sea with loss of all on board. Both Squadron Leader Wilkin and Flight Sergeant Hughes were holders of the Czech Military Cross.

    Squadron Leader Richard Pennington WILKIN DFC Pilot
    Pilot Officer George Alfred BERWICK 26 DFM Flight Engineer
    Flying Officer James Wilfred Henry BROWN 35 DFM
    Flying Officer Hugh BURKE 27 DFM
    Flight Sergeant Albert HUGHES 23

| 20-Sep-43 | EB188 | Halifax V | 624 Sqn | Blida | 0 |

The aircraft crashed on take-off.

| 21-Sep-43 | DG354 | Halifax V | 624 Sqn | Blida, Algeria | 0 |

During the take-off for an operational sortie, the aircraft developed a swing because of a temporary trouble with the port outer engine. The pilot over corrected the swing and the aircraft ran off the side of runway, where the undercarriage collapsed.

188

22-Sep-43 BD531 Whitley 295 Sqn Thruxton 0

The inlet valve on a cylinder in the port engine was jammed open by a foreign body and this in turn caused the flame traps to burn through. On take-off the port engine failed and the pilot; Squadron Leader J R Grice, closed the throttles, raised the undercarriage and forced landed the aircraft, which passed through a boundary fence and was badly damaged.

23-Sep-43 FD909 Dakota 31 Sqn Chittagong 0

On landing, the aircraft struck a concrete block, the undercarriage was torn off and the aircraft skidded into a lorry. The Flying Control Officer was cited for negligence for not having the obstruction removed.

23-Sep-43 HS109 Horsa I OADU Atlantic Ocean, position not stated 3

Flying Officer Sizmur, who was an experienced aircraft captain with a number of sorties between Portreath and Sale, was flying Halifax DG384 and the aircraft was towing this glider. The circumstances of the loss appear to be that somewhere off the coast of Portugal, the glider was ditched in the sea with its tow rope still attached. The three crew were lost. The tow rope is said to have parted due to the excessive strain and the weather was very poor with low cloud, heavy rain and strong winds. The glider crew were unable to follow instructions being given by the Halifax rear gunner or to respond to aldis lamp signals, eventually the glider drifted over to starboard and the tow rope broke.

Sergeant Laurence James BAKER 22 The Glider Pilot Regiment
Sergeant John Kenneth BARON The Glider Pilot Regiment
Sergeant Hugh Wilfred SARGENT 23 The Glider Pilot Regiment

24-Sep-43 P1382 Albemarle I 296 Sqn Off Pantelleria 1

The aircraft was ferrying mail and had been airborne for nearly 2 hours when its starboard engine failed. As it became impossible to maintain height, the pilot carried out a successful ditching but one member of the crew was killed.

Date	Serial	Aircraft	Unit	Place	Casualties
Brief Circumstances of Accident					
Casualty Details (If Applicable)					

Flight Sergeant Herbert LIDGETT 26

25-Sep-43   EB139   Halifax V   295 Sqn   Missing   0

The aircraft was ditched but the reasons are not recorded

25-Sep-43   AL506   Liberator II   148 Sqn   Brindisi, Italy   1

The aircraft had been sent to a DZ near Sugric in Yugoslavia and the crew picked up the correct signals etc and prepared to drop the first set of containers. However, an electrical fault prevented the containers from dropping but just after the bomb doors were closed, most of them released inside the aircraft's bomb bay and crashed through the closed doors. The captain turned for base but during the transit the two starboard engines failed and diversion was initiated for Brindisi. After 9 ¾ hours airborne, the aircraft arrived at the airfield and commenced its landing approach but without the flarepath being available. At this stage, the starboard inner engine caught fire and wheels up landing was made, following which the fire spread and the aircraft was completely gutted. Unfortunately, one of the crew jumped from the aircraft whilst whilst it was still moving and received fatal injuries. The pilot Flying Officer R A Callander was commended for his handling of the situation.

Warrant Officer I Charles Melville HOWES 31 RCAF Air Gunner

27-Sep-43   EM377   Master II   GPEU   RAF Netheravon   0

On landing, the pilot was distracted by people walking near a glider and he taxied the aircraft into the side of truck.

01-Oct-43 P1516 Albemarle 296 Sqn Missing 5

The aircraft was undertaking a mail run and was crewed by four airman and carried a passenger from 1st Airlanding Sqn RAC. It took off from Gioia delle Colle en route for Tunisia but it never arrived and the circumstances of its loss remain unknown.

    Flying Officer Ian Robertson HYDE 24 Pilot
    Flying Officer Norman Lee BURTON 29 RNZAF Navigator
    Flying Officer Ivan William HALL 31 RNZAF Wireless Operator
    Warrant Officer Brendan Hilary MCISAAC 36 RCAF Air Gunner
    Captain Arthur John WATERMAN 1st Airlanding Recce Sqn

02-Oct-43 HH549 Hotspur II 3 GTS Northleach, Gloucestershire 0

The aircraft was landing in conditions of gusty winds with down draughts. The pilot undershot the landing and the glider struck a wall on the edge of the airfield.

02-Oct-43 FR568 Hadrian 295 Sqn Hurn 0

The crew was undertaking a type conversion to the Waco CG4 glider, which was being supplied to the British in small numbers. Whilst landing, the glider was caught in a down draught and it undershot the landing area and was damaged.

06-Oct-43 FD899 Dakota III 512 Sqn Regents Park London 9

The aircraft was being flown on an air test and had been airborne for about 25 minutes. It struck Barrage Balloon cables whilst flying above Regents Park, crashed and caught fire.

    Flying Officer James Alan ROBERTSON 27 Pilot
    Flying Officer Theodore Myroslaw HAWRYLUK 25 RCAF
    Flight Sergeant Henry Edgar DENNIS 31 RAAF
    Aircraftman 2nd Class Ronald Douglas BROWN 20

191

Date	Serial	Aircraft	Unit	Place	Casualties
Brief Circumstances of Accident					
Casualty Details (If Applicable)					

Aircraftman 1st Class Ronal Eric PENN 22
Aircraftman 2nd Class Kenneth Thomas DING 20
Aircraftman 1st Class Hugh Richard PHILLIPS 22
Aircraftman 2nd Class Dudley Austin WESTCOTT 37
Leading Aircraftman Jack Leonard HOUGHTON 21

| 07-Oct-43 | P1553 | Albemarle | 296 Sqn | Between Tunisia and Goia delle Colle | 4? |

The aircraft is recorded as missing but there is no information as to how it was lost. Although the Accident Card records the pilot's name, rank and number, there is no matching record in the CWGC database nor in the 38 Group Roll of Honour.

| 09-Oct-43 | BZ858 | Liberator | 138 Sqn | 20 miles north of Varberg Sweden | 0 |

This aircraft was one of three examples delivered to the squadron for use by the Polish Flight. The crew, captained by Flight Lieutenant M Malinowski the navigator with Warrant Officer B Hulas DFC as pilot, was attempting a single sortie to Poland, coded COTTAGE 7. The flight engineer warned the captain that the fuel consumption was such that the aircraft would not have sufficient to return to its base and when finding themselves in daylight and still not over Denmark, a decision was made to turn north for Sweden and then abandon the aircraft. This was done safely and the crew was eventually interned by the Swedes.

| 10-Oct-43 | P1405 | Albemarle | 297 Sqn | 2 miles north of Stoney Cross | 4 |

Whilst on a training flight and just a few minutes after take-off, the aircraft's port engine failed. The pilot allowed the aircraft to stall and it spun into the ground from a low level, making recovery impossible.

Flight Sergeant George Mendel GROSSMAN 22 Pilot

Flying Officer Alfred Hugh JACKSON 35
Sergeant Leonard BARKER 28
Flight Sergeant John JACKSON 21

14-Oct-43 P1401 Albemarle 296 Sqn Near Goubrine Tunisia 4

During an air test one of the engines was either shut down deliberately or failed – the latter being the most likely because a piston ring was found in the oil scavenge filter. The pilot was unable to maintain height and the aircraft crashed and was destroyed.

Flight Sergeant Henry Charles MARSHALL 20 Pilot
Flight Sergeant Thomas Alexander HOUSTON 23
Flight Sergeant Ronald Frederick NEILL 20
Flying Officer Reginald WESTERLAND 33

15-Oct-43 K7012 Harrow II 271 Sqn Doncaster 0

The pilot undershot the approach and the aircraft ran into a ditch.

17-Oct-43 FH422 Hudson IIIA 1576 Flt Dum Dum ?

The aircraft crashed into a swamp after an engine failure on take-off.

18-Oct-43 LW281 Halifax 138 Sqn 20 miles east of Antwerp Belgium 0

The crew was searching for their allotted DZ and the aircraft was flying at low level when both its starboard engines were hit and the aircraft set on fire. The pilot; Squadron Leader C W Passey, crashed landed the aircraft and all those on board survived, two of whom were agents. The crew of eight evaded, with the exception of one man who was captured. The Belgian and Dutch agents also made good their escapes but in the case of the Dutch agent, he was used, unbeknownst to himself, as a pawn in an enemy plot to expose and destroy one of the escape networks, which they achieved by passing him down the route along with one of their own. Considerable causalties were inflicted on the resistence movements by this action.

193

Date	Serial	Aircraft	Unit	Place	Casualties
		Brief Circumstances of Accident			
		Casualty Details (If Applicable)			

19-Oct-43   HR674 Halifax II   148 Sqn   Southern Albania   9

The crew was detailed for Operation SAPLING 7, a supply drop over the Biza Plain in the Chermenika Mountains of Albania. The aircraft did not return and a subsequent report from the reception party stated that the aircraft had appeared to catch fire in the air and then to strike a hillside at position 40 degrees 16 north/ 19 degrees 34 East (which is near Dukati about 16 miles south south east of Vlore). A comment made about this loss was that the pilot had previously briefed his commanding officer about the dangers of operating over this DZ. He provided the CO with a sketch map of the area with the caution; 'Climb quickly, left handed or else'.

Flight Lieutenant William Ross FORESTER 22 Pilot
Flying Officer Francis Jack HUNTER 25 RNZAF Bomb Aimer
Flight Sergeant Harold WILLIAMS 18 Air Gunner
Flight Sergeant James Clement COLE 28
Flying Officer Peter Raymond FLYTE 23
Flying Officer Edmond Frank MYERS 30
Sergeant Peter TWIDDY
Captain Alfred CARELESS 31 Royal Armoured Corps attached SOE
Believed to be:
Signalman David William ROCKINGHAM 21

19-Oct-43   HH665 Hotspur II   3 GTS   Gloucestershire, location not specified   0

The glider was towed into cloud during the climb after take-off, due to a rapid build up of cloud and the glider pilot lost sight of the airfield. When he believed he had pinpointed a landmark, the pilot released the tow and then descended in cloud but on breaking out at 700 feet he was unable to orientate himself or to select a suitable field and so ended up crashing through a high hedge.

20-Oct-43   FR569   Hardrian   1 HGMU   RAF Netheravon   0

The station received a severe gale warning only about 2 hours before it struck the area. There were fifty six light aircraft and gliders to be picketed and placed in parking positions to ride out the storm. Unfortunately, in a gust of 55 mph, this glider was damaged.

21-Oct-43   EB239   Halifax   161 Sqn   Valenciennes Nord France   7

This aircraft crashed with the loss of all its crew whilst engaged on a triple sortie to Belgium. The circumstances of the loss are not known.

    Flight Sergeant Trevor Washington LEWIS Pilot
    Sergeant Charles Edward YOUNG 27 Wireless Operator
    Sergeant Henry James CRAWFORD 22
    Sergeant John RAMSDEN 33
    Sergeant Thomas Bertram YOUNG 22 Flight Engineer
    Sergeant Walter CROUCH 21
    Sergeant Desmond Robert FEELY

21-Oct-43   Z9490   Whitley V   42 OTU   Near Isle of Anglesea   0

The aircraft was being flown by a student crew and had been airborne for nearly 5 hours on a night cross country training sortie. The starboard engine failed because of a serious coolant leak and height could not be maintained on one engine. The pilot ditched the aircraft successfully and without injury to his crew, all of whom were then picked up safely. The pilot; Pilot Officer J Le Bouvier, was commended for his handling of the incident.

21-Oct-43   HH149   Hotspur II   5 GTS   Shobdon, Herefordshire   1

The glider was landing but the pilot failed to check the descent and it made a heavy landing and then rose almost vertically, stall turned off the top and crashed into the ground. It appears that the pilot's seat back

Date	Serial	Aircraft	Unit	Place	Casualties

Brief Circumstances of Accident
Casualty Details (If Applicable)

collapsed and he was thrown backwards, pulling the control column in the process and being unable to take any action. There had been a number of other instances where the seat back failed or collapsed and a modification was proposed to address this.

Corporal Norman Michael WESTON

| 27-Oct-43 | LJ285 | Horsa I | 2 HGMU | RAF Feltwell | 0 |

The aircraft was picketed and parked but it caught fire and was destroyed after an unknown person introduced a naked light into the fuselage. Although the destruction of the aircraft was deliberate, there is no indication that the culprit was found.

| 30-Oct-43 | DP817 | Horsa I | 297 Sqn | Elton Farm, Cirencester | 0 |

The glider was being operated in very poor weather and the pilot misjudged his approach and overshot the landing.

| 01-Nov-43 | FD829 | Dakota I | 216 Sqn | Location not shown | 0 |

The aircraft was engaged on a supply dropping sortie and had been airborne for nearly 10 hours. The crew became lost because important navigational information had not been passed to them at their briefing and the aircraft's fuel consumption was high because it was carrying two banks, each of three containers, underneath its wings. After searching for and being unable to locate a suitable landing site the crew abandoned the aircraft.

| 04-Nov-43 | DT726 | Halifax | 138 Sqn | Marcols les Eaux Ardeche France | 7 |

This aircraft was operating deep into south eastern France and it crashed in mountainous country about 10 miles north west of Privas. There was a single survivor; the air gunner Sergeant J F Brough, whose turret broke off during the crash and remarkably escaped with minor injuries. The US pilot had been attached to the squadron for some operational experience before joining the USAAF's own SD force.

Pilot Officer Henry Fitzgerald HODGES 21 Pilot
Captain James E ESTES USAAF
Sergeant Harold Thomas PENFOLD RCAF
Flight Sergeant Harry SMITH 27
Pilot Officer Ronald Edward PULLING 26
Sergeant Jacques BARTHELEMY 19 Wireless Operator
Flight Sergeant Reginald Lance NOTT RAAF

| 04-Nov-43 | AL509 | Liberator II | 148 Sqn | Kosinjski Zamost Yugoslavia | 7 |

The crew was undertaking sortie FUNGUS 33, a supply drop to partisan groups. The weather was extremely poor and several aircraft turned back or were recalled, including one with serious structural damage resulting from the conditions. A report indicated that AL509 was seen to be apparently on fire and to pass over a village, circle the area before striking the ground and being destroyed.

Flight Lieutenant Maurice PASSMORE 23 Pilot
Flight Lieutenant Hugh Irvine CRAWFORD 25 RNZAF Wireless Operator
Warrant Officer I James Herbert Stevenson CLARKE 23 RCAF Bomb Aimer
Flight Sergeant William Joseph DOWLE Air Gunner
Flight Lieutenant Eldon Burke ELLIOTT 33 RCAF Navigator
Warrant Officer I Ralph Edward HAWKEN 30 RCAF Air Gunner
Flight Sergeant Edwin Archibald TOOLE 24 RCAF Flight Engineer

| 05-Nov-43 | DK232 | Halifax | 161 Sqn | RAF Tempsford | 0 |

The aircraft swung off the runway during its take-off, went over a sodium flare and its undercarriage collapsed.

Date	Serial	Aircraft	Unit	Place	Casualties
Brief Circumstances of Accident Casualty Details (If Applicable)					
06-Nov-43	EM284	Master II	5 GTS	Shobdon	0

The aircraft was being landed in a crosswind at the conclusion of a glider towing detail. On touchdown, the aircraft bounced, the port wing rose and the aircraft tipped onto its nose.

Date	Serial	Aircraft	Unit	Place	Casualties
07-Nov-43	JN921	Halifax	138 Sqn	Near Liesse Aisne France	8

The crew was operating in the vicinity of several enemy airfields located near Laon and it appears that it was shot down with the loss of all on board, either by a night fighter from one of these bases or the AA defences of a base.

Flight Sergeant Kenneth Richard COPAS 21 Pilot
Sergeant Reginald Thomas BROWN 33 Flight Engineer
Flying Officer Ronald MORRISH 24
Sergeant Charles William CHARRO
Sergeant William AITKENHEAD 26 Bomb Aimer
Sergeant FFrederick LAWRENSON 21 Wireless Operator
Sergeant Joseph Robert George DAY 19
Sergeant Albert Reginald FLATTERS 23

Date	Serial	Aircraft	Unit	Place	Casualties
09-Nov-43	BD502	Whitley V	HGCU	2 miles north east of RAF Brize Norton	2

These two aircraft collided whilst flying in the circuit.

Flying Officer Peter Charles BELL 25
Flying Officer Morris Robert James CRUTCHER 21

09-Nov-43   BD512   Whitley V   HGCU   2 miles north east of RAF Brize Norton   2

This aircraft and the Whitley listed above collided at night in the circuit, mainly because the other aircraft was flying against the circuit pattern.

09-Nov-43   V9723   Lysander III   161 Sqn   RAF Tangmere   0

The aircraft was landing at Tangmere, on conclusion of an operational sortie, when its undercarriage collapsed and the aircraft was damaged badly.

11-Nov-43   EB129   Halifax   161 Sqn   Brunelles, 27 miles west of Chartres   7

The aircraft crashed with the loss of all aboard, except one crew members who was made a POW. The USAAF officer was another member of that force attached for operational experience. In this case Lieutenant Gross was a Bombardier.

    Pilot Officer Murray Alfred LINE 26 RAAF Pilot
    Lieutenant B W GROSS USAAF
    Sergeant Ronald COTTERILL 23
    Sergeant Ernest Reginald WATTS 23 Navigator
    Sergeant Harold Royston BATTEN Wireless Operator
    Flight Sergeant Ernest HARRISON 32RAAF
    Flight Sergeant Wilfred Raymond Rus SHORE 22 RCAF Air Gunner

11-Nov-43   EM344   Master II   5 GTS   Shobdon   ?

The aircraft is recorded as being ' damaged beyond repair in an accident'.

16-Nov-43   FD790   Dakota   216 Sqn   Missing   0

The crew was reported missing on a sortie, which the Form 540 states was a round trip between Cairo West and Kasfareet but then, confusingly states that the misson was supply dropping on Leros! The aircraft

Brief Circumstances of Accident
Casualty Details (If Applicable)

ditched in the sea off Turkey and the crew, comprising four RAF and two South African Army despatchers, was picked up by the Turks and returned to their squadron in due course.

| 16-Nov-43 | V9548 | Lysander III | 161 Sqn | Niort France | 0 |

The pilot, who had correctly declined to land at 2 air strips a few days before because they were too soft, landed on a strip and his aircraft promptly became bogged down! As it proved impossible to extricate the Lysander, it was destroyed and the pilot made good his escape.

| 18-Nov-43 | AL540 | Liberator II | 1675 HCU | RAF Lydda | 4 |

The aircraft was being flown on a crew training sortie to convert transport and bomber crews to the type. An instructor had chosen to terminate his training detail and he handed the aircraft over to another instructor, who then took off with a trainee captain. On their first circuit and whilst approaching to land the aircraft was struck by a Hurricane (BV168) which was being flown on a delivery sortie. The Liberator's starboard fin, rudder and tailplane were severed and the aircraft crashed about 1000 yards short of the runway threshold. Whilst the Hurricane's pilot was seriously injured, he survived but the operating crew of this aircraft was killed. It was recommended that rear turrets should be occupied in future, to give warning of hazards from the rear of the aircraft. The training captain was a very experienced transport and special duties pilot, who had been awarded the DFC in March and also one of Yugoslavia's highest awards; The White Eagle.

Squadron Leader Desmond Malcolm ROLPH-SMITH 24 DFC Instructor Pilot
Flight Sergeant Michael Joseph COYNE 28 Pilot
Sergeant George HALL 30 Wireless Operator
Flying Officer Herbert HARTNETT 22 Wireless Operator/Air Gunner

23-Nov-43 BB301 Halifax II 148 Sqn Italy 0

The aircraft was being used for a special operation and was fitted with two overload tanks for extra fuel because of the sortie's anticipated duration. It arrived over the drop zone but the crew could not detect any sign of a flare path and so the aircraft returned to base with its cargo. Throughout the sortie the fuel consumption was higher than anticipated at 360 gallons per hour and eventually the aircraft ran out of fuel and was abandoned safely by its crew. No explanation was offered for the reason the fuel consumption was so high but the weather is recorded as poor and with the load still being carried on return, this would have contributed to the continued high consumption.

23-Nov-43 K6947 Harrow II 271 Sqn Auchinblae Kincardineshire 1

The pilot displayed poor airmanship in not obtaining a weather forecast, failed to make use of his radio and then flew in cloud below safety height. The aircraft struck high ground.

24-Nov-43 FD960 Dakota 216 Sqn Catania 0

The aircraft was being taxyed in a strong wind and it was blown off the side of the runway, where it became bogged down in soft ground. It is unclear as to what happened subsequently but the aircraft became a write-off and it is assumed that it was damaged during the recovery process. The pilot, an RCAF Warrant Officer, had been responsible for the loss of another Dakota due to an error of judgement and it was decided to take him off transport flying.

25-Nov-43 LT192 Anson 28 SAAF Near Bari, Italy 0

The aircraft's starboard engine failed on take-off and crashed through high tension cables, injuring all on board. Although water in the fuel was identified as the cause and an investigation and remedial action put in hand, it could not have been effective, given the accident recorded immediately below.

Date	Serial	Aircraft	Unit	Place	Casualties
		Brief Circumstances of Accident Casualty Details (If Applicable)			
27-Nov-43	LT279	Anson	28 SAAF	1 mile south-west of Bari, Italy	0

The aircraft was being used for a freight sortie and immediately after take-off its port engine failed, it then lost height, struck trees and crashed, injuring the pilot. The engine failure was caused by water in the fuel, dirty sparking plugs and oil on the magneto points. A thorough investigation into the fuel systems was instigated and the systems of all the aircraft at the unit were drained and flushed through.

| 28-Nov-43 | FD793 | Dakota | 31 Sqn | Near Tiddum | 5 |

The aircraft crew was conducting a morning supply dropping sortie at Tiddum and had already off loaded 5000 lbs of supplies when their aircraft was attacked and shot down by a Japanese fighter.

Warrant Officer Robert Ian Mckay RICHARDS 23 Pilot
Flying Officer Arthur HOPKINS 27 Co-Pilot
Sergeant Andrew Patrick MCKEE 32 Navigator
Warrant Officer Aloysius LOW 23 Wireless Operator
Sergeant Richard Stanley YATES 29 Wireless Operator

| 30-Nov-43 | FL515 | Dakota | 511 Sqn | In the sea north of Portreath airfield | 12 |

The aircraft took off shortly after midnight on a transport sortie but shortly afterwards it spun into the sea. The initial findings suggested that the aircraft had been incorrectly loaded giving it a tail down trim, which the pilot would not have realised probably until after the aircraft was airborne. Additionally, there were strong vertical air currents which would have affected the aircraft as it was climbing away after take-off. The AOC in C disagreed with the findings of the Board of Enquiry, stating that the aircraft was correctly loaded but accepting that better supervision of the loading process was required.

Warrant Officer John Herbert GILLIES 26 RAFVR Pilot

Flight Sergeant James BENNETT 25 Co-Pilot
Flight Lieutenant S PATALON Navigator PAF
Flight Sergeant Thomas William PEARMAN 32 Wireless Operator
Sergeant William BROWN 30 RAFVR
Leading Aircraftman Philip Gilbert HODGKINS RAFVR
Aircraftman 2nd Class Alfred Edward WORT 19 RAFVR
Aircraftman 2nd Class Douglas SHAW 19 RAFVR
Aircraftman 2nd Class Harry Robert AVES RAFVR
Aircraftman 2nd Class Roy HURLEY 19 RAFVR
Aircraftman 2nd Class Willie KENNEDY 19 RAFVR
Aircraftman 2nd Class John Dudley HAMES RAFVR

01-Dec-43   EB140   Halifax   624 Sqn   Koplesiagraphn, near Neokhorcan, Greece   12
The aircraft failed to return from a special duties sortie which was to include infiltrating a five man Army liaison team into Koritza, Albania. However, the aircraft crashed on the outbound leg of the sortie and was destroyed.

Flight Sergeant Dennis John HOWLETT Pilot
Flight Sergeant Arthur Edward HICKERTON Navigator
Flight Sergeant John Kenneth HUGHES Wireless Operator/Air Gunner
Flight Sergeant Raymond Percival ATKINSON Flight Engineer
Flight Sergeant Arthur Ernest EDWARDS
Flight Sergeant Vernon Leslie MILLER 19 RCAF Air Gunner
Flight Sergeant James Kenneth SHEWRING Air Gunner
Major Ian Albert SMART 26 2nd Battalion Cameronians (Scottish Rifles)
Captain John Corry STEPHENSON 26 Royal Armoured Corps
Lieutenant Alan Willoughby TOLEY 26 Royal Armoured Corps
Corporal Ian Douglas KESTERTON 22 Royal Corps of Signals

Date	Serial	Aircraft	Unit	Place	Casualties
			Brief Circumstances of Accident		
			Casualty Details (If Applicable)		

Gunner George Hughes MCKENNA 23 Royal Artillery

Date	Serial	Aircraft	Unit	Place	Casualties
01-Dec-43	DP813	Horsa I	1 HGMU	Shrewton LG, Wiltshire	0

The inexperienced pilot undershot the landing and the glider struck a bank of earth.

| 01-Dec-43 | LG928 | Horsa I | 1 HGMU | Shrewton LG, Wiltshire | 0 |

This is the second similar accident and it took place at almost the same time as that recorded above.

| 01-Dec-43 | DP816 | Horsa I | | 295 Sqn | Shrewton LG, Wiltshire | 0 |

On landing the pilot applied the brakes and the aircraft ran over rough ground lurching heavily. On inspection, it was found that the top of the fuselage behind the cockpit area was cracked.

| 01-Dec-43 | LG984 | Horsa I | | HGMU | 4 miles south of Shaftsbury, Dorset | 0 |

The tow rope broke and during the subsequent forced landing, the undercarriage was damaged.

| 05-Dec-44 | FL545 | Dakota III | | 512 Sqn | Portreath | ? |

The aircraft crashed whilst taking off but all those on board survived.

| 06-Dec-43 | P1434 | Albemarle | | 296 Sqn | Near Hurn Christchurch Hants | 3 |

The aircraft was being flown on a formation training sortie by a crew of four. The starboard engine lost oil pressure and the pilot broke away from the formation to attempt a precautionary landing at Hurn. The pilot decided to overshoot his first approach but in going round again, the starboard engine cut and the with the port engine at a high power setting, the aircraft rolled inverted and crashed. The cause of the starboard engine's loss of oil pressure and subsequent failure was the break up of the piston rings and then the collapse of the piston in the No: 4 cylinder. The investigation commented on problems with engines which had been used on Albemarle aircraft previously deployed to North Africa and it seems that the conditions experienced in the Middle East had affected many engines adversely.

Flying Officer James WYLLIE 21 Pilot
Sergeant Tom Ellis ROBINSON 33
Flying Officer Richard Mercer 23

07-Dec-43   BT822   Hotspur II   GPEU   Near Collingbourne Ducis, Wiltshire   8

The tug pilot disobeyed orders and towed the glider into cloud during a flight in very poor weather. The glider pilot cast off the tow but stalled the aircraft and lost control before the aircraft crashed into high ground, killing all those aboard. The subsequent enquiry revealed very poor standards of briefing and a haphazard approach to flying supervision etc.

Staff Sergeant Eric Andrew JEFFS 21 The Glider Pilot Regiment
Sergeant Phillip Douglas TAYLOR 20 The Glider Pilot Regiment
Lance Sergeant Maurice KING 6th Airborne Divisonal Signals
Signalman Colin CAMPBELL
Signalman Charles DAWSON
Signalman Stanley JACKSON
Signalman Arthur PALLETT
Signalman Harry SIMPSON

10-Dec-43   V9673   Lysander III   161 Sqn   la Ville aux bois Pontavert Aisne France   2

The aircraft crashed about 12½ miles north-west of Reims in the area of Juvincourt

Flying Officer James Robertson Grant BATHGATE 23 DFC RNZAF Pilot
Captain Claudius FOUR French Agent

Date	Serial	Aircraft	Unit	Place	Casualties
Brief Circumstances of Accident					
Casualty Details (If Applicable)					

10-Dec-43   ED825   Lancaster   617 Sqn   Meharicourt, Somme   7

This aircraft was one of three from the 'Dambusters' to be detached to Tempsford for SD operations. The aircraft and their crews had arrived on 8 Dec but bad weather had prevented their operational use for a couple of days. Unfortunately, this aircraft and that listed below were both shot down. The third aircraft, flown by the very experienced Flight Lieutenant Clayton – who was to end the war with a DSO, CGM and DFC but was to lose his life in a Hastings crash in the early 1950s – was the only one to return safely after successfully completing its sortie.

Flying Officer Gordon Herbert WEEDEN 23 RCAF Pilot
Sergeant Arthur William RICHARDSON 19 Air Gunner
Pilot Officer Ralph Neville JONES 22
Flight Sergeant Edward Joseph WALTERS 26 RCAF
Flight Sergeant Robert Geoffrey HOWELL 22 Wireless Operator
Sergeant Brook ROBINSON 31 Air Gunner
Warrant Officer II Robert CUMMINGS RCAF Air Gunner

10-Dec-43   ED886   Lancaster   617 Sqn   Terramesnil, Somme   2

This was the second aircraft lost from the squadron, as outlined above. The pilot; Warrant Officer G F Bull, and three others were taken POW and one man evaded capture but the other two were killed.

Sergeant John McLean STEWART 22 Wireless Operator
Flight Sergeant Donald Menzies THORPE 24 Air Gunner

11-Dec-43   R9289   Stirling I   214 Sqn   RAF Tempsford   0

Occasionally the main force bomber squadrons were drawn in to SD work to assist the two permanent squadrons, who were always tasked heavily. This aircraft was taking off when a swing developed and it ran off the runway and struck a sodium light, which caused the undercarriage to collapse.

11-Dec-43   BB344   Halifax II   148 Sqn   Tocra, Cyrenniaca   0

On landing at the conclusion of its sortie, the aircraft swung off the runway and collided with Spitfire EN264 of 680 Sqn, before overturning. Both aircraft were destroyed in the subsequent fire but the CO of the Spitfire detachment was held to be responsible for allowing the aircraft to be parked so close to the runway.

11-Dec-43   BB378   Halifax   138 Sqn   Tostrop Denmark   0

The crew was engaged in sortie TABLEJAM 18/19, which included dropping the senior Danish agent; Dr Fleming Muus, by parachute on his return from a period in UK. The aircraft had been only partially defrosted before the crew was ordered off and whilst the crew was preparing to drop the agent, the aircraft was attacked by a Ju 88 several times. A crash landing was made and everybody escaped from the wreckage before the aircraft blew up. The crew split into 2 groups and one was successful in evading capture but the others were made POW.

11-Dec-43   AE733   Ventura   299 Sqn   Kingston Warren, Watchfield, Wilts   5

The aircraft crashed during a snow storm. The precise circumstances were not recorded but it is assumed the aircraft was being operated in restricted visibility because of the weather.

Flying Officer Albert Henry SALT 31 RAAF
Flying Officer John Burnett SELTH 31 RAAF
Warrant Officer II William Roy CHESTER 23 RCAF Wireless Operator
Flight Sergeant James McNae THOMSOM 20 RCAF Air Gunner
Flight Sergeant Raymond Louis SANDERS 24

Date	Serial	Aircraft	Unit	Place	Casualties
		Brief Circumstances of Accident			
		Casualty Details (If Applicable)			

14-Dec-43   K7005   Harrow II   271 Sqn   Inishowen Head Co. Donegal Eire   4

The aircraft took off in poor weather which did not improve. Whilst flying on instruments and in cloud at 1000 feet, the pilot made a change of course and the aircraft flew into the top of a hill killing all aboard, except the pilot. The enquiry considered that the pilot should not have taken off in the prevailing weather conditions and was at fault for flying below safety safety height in the prevailing weather.

    Pilot Officer Carol Herbert BROWN 24 Co-Pilot
    Leading Aircraftman Albert Edward JAMES 25
    Flight Sergeant Arthur Bain SHAW 22 Navigator
    Leading Aircraftman John Thurston TABERNER 27

16-Dec-43   FK537   Hudson VI   AFEE   Sherburn in Elmet   1

The aircraft was being flown on an air test and was returning to land in conditions of fog. The port engine failed and the aircraft crashed about 200 yards short of the runway before striking an embankment. The fatal casualty was apparently a passenger and it was recommended that station standing orders should prohibit the carrying of passengers on test flights.

    Corporal Wilfred MAWSON 46

17-Dec-43   DK206   Halifax   161 Sqn   Capel St Andrews   3

On this occasion the special duties squadrons were flying on the same night as a major operation by the main bomber force to Berlin. The weather on return was thick fog and a very large number of aircraft were lost in crashes whilst attempting to land at bases in the UK. This aircraft crashed whilst rtrying to get into RAF Woodbridge and the pilot and two others of the crew were killed.

Flight Lieutenant Stanley Nicholson GRAY 24 Pilot
Flight Sergeant Peter Austin FRY 24 Flight Engineer
Flying Officer Leslie Howard THOMAS 23 Navigator

17-Dec-43 LK899 Halifax   161 Sqn   Near RAF Debden   0

This aircraft was first diverted first to Little Staughton and thence to Woodbridge, where the crew were given to believe the cloudbase was 200 feet. The pilot flew out to sea and then descended on the reverse leg. However, the aircraft struck part of the radio tower at RAF Bawdsey Manor, which ripped off a section of the port wing. The pilot managed to retain some control and the aircraft was crashed onto the banks of the River Deben. Unfortunately, the navigator had remained in the nose of the aircraft in order to relay GEE fixes to the pilot, and when the aircraft crashed he was unable to save himself and by time he was found and despite intensive attempts to revive him, he died from drowning.

Flying Officer Wilfred Frederick MCMASTER DFM Navigator

17-Dec-43 LL115 Halifax   138 Sqn   Capel Green Near RAF Woodbridge   5

The aircraft crashed at Capel Green near Woodbridge.

Flight Sergeant John George Addison WATSON 22 Pilot
Sergeant Norman Montague GILLIS RCAF Flight Engineer
Sergeant John Robert HODDINOTT
Sergeant Hubert Donald KING 26
Sergeant George OSBORNE 20

17-Dec-43 LL119 Halifax   138 Sqn   At sea off Felixstowe   0

The aircraft was abandoned by its crew, who all survived.

17-Dec-43 LL120 Halifax   161 Sqn   At sea off Skegness   0

The aircraft was returning from a sortie to Angouleme, north-east of Bordeaux but its crew encountered the

209

same poor weather as all other aircraft that night on return.   The captain; Warrant Officer W A Caldwell, was unable to get into the 2 diversions at Swinderby and Woodbridge and ordered the crew to abandon the aircraft.   This was done successfully and crew, including a pet dog, all survived and landed in the vicinity of Spilsby, whilst their aircraft ended up in the North Sea off Skegness.

17-Dec-43   LW280   Halifax   138 Sqn   Off Harwich   4
On return, the pilot was unable to land and so elected to abandon the aircraft.   Although all left the aircraft, only three survived and the aircraft crashed into the sea off Harwich.

    Sergeant Tom Bailey HAWKES 21 Flight Engineer
    Sergeant John LYNCH 20
    Sergeant Robert MARSHALL 31
    Sergeant James Johnson HANNAH 20 Wireless Operator

17-Dec-43   V9367   Lysander III   161 Sqn   Near RAF Tangmere   1
The aircraft was one of the many caught out by thick fog on this evening.   The aircraft crashed whilst attempting a landing.   The two agents being carried were uninjured.

    Flying Officer James McAllister MCBRIDE 25

17-Dec-43   V9674   Lysander III   161 Sqn   Near Ford (Yapton) Sussex   3
The aircraft was part of the same operation as V9367 and was returning to UK.   Having been diverted to Ford naval air station, the aircraft crashed at Yapton and all those on boardwere killed.

    Flight Lieutenant Stephen Alers HANKEY 28 Pilot
    Albert KOHAN

Jacques TAYAR

19-Dec-43   BB364   Halifax   Near RAF Henlow   9

This aircraft, captained by Sergeant H D Williams and including some additional crew members acting as 'screens' for the new crew, was being used for container dropping practice at RAF Henlow. However, whilst flying about 1 mile south east of RAF Henlow, the aircraft struck the chimney of one of the numerous brickwork kilns in the area and it crashed.

Sergeant Hugh Gwyn WILLIAMS 21 Pilot
Sergeant Stanley HIGHAM 23 Flight Engineer
Sergeant Harold Maitland HOUGHTON 22
Sergeant Joseph Norman POLLAND 31 Bomb Aimer
Sergeant Frank Henry ADAMS 22 Wireless Operator
Sergeant Cyril Addison KIDD 37
Sergeant John Edward MOONEY 28
Pilot Officer Cyril Arthur WOOLLDRIDGE 32 Navigator
Sergeant Alexander John MCINTYRE 36

19-Dec-43   HH556   Hotspur II   3 GTS   Northleach   0

The glider's cockpit hood was not properly secured and it caused the glider to sink more rapidly than usual. This was unfortunate because the exercise was the pilot's first solo low level release and after dropping the tow, he then found his aircraft descending more rapidly than it should have done in normal circumstances. The aircraft undershot the airfield and was damaged.

21-Dec-43   P1462   Albemarle   297 Sqn   Near Alton Hampshire   13

The aircraft was engaged in a paratroop dropping exercise in the early hours of the morning. The pilot commenced the descent to the dropping height earlier than had been briefed and because of a small error in the dead reckoning plot, the aircraft was slightly off track but sufficient for it to strike high ground at a height of 750 feet. In addition to the fatal casualties, 3 others were injured. This was the second major parachute training loss suffered by this battalion. Several months earlier a stick of parachutists had been dropped in the sea because of a navigational error. Weighed down with their equipment, most were drowned but a few survived.

Flight Sergeant George William JUBB 22 Pilot
Sergeant Joseph Frederick HUGHES 21
Flight Sergeant Charles RUSSELL 28
Sergeant Caleb Hugh DRAKEFORD 25
Flying Officer Lionel Victor JONES 24
Corporal William George FIRKINS 8th Battalion The Parachute Regiment
Private Reginald Clarence CAPON 21
Private William John HILL 19
Private Albert Harry JONES 19
Private Vernon Donald JUKES 18
Private Norman Joseph Peter ROGERS 20
Sergeant Sidney William WILKES 31
Private Ernest Edward WOOTTON 19

22-Dec-43   V1697   Albemarle   570 Sqn   Staverton Gloucestershire   0
The aircraft was being landed, having just been collected from the makers but in attempting to land on a short runway, the pilot landed the aircraft heavily on its nosewheel and the aircraft was damaged.

24-Dec-43   FD903   Dakota   512 Sqn   Missing   3

The Accident Card records the aircraft as missing but gives no indication of the sortie being undertaken. However, the book "They Shall Grow Not Old" records that the aircraft was en route from Lyneham to Gibraltar and that a radio call was made giving a position off the coast of Spain.

   Flying Officer Roy Lloyd Acton HAMMILL 29 Pilot
   Flying Officer James BATTERSBY 26 BEM
   Warrant Officer II Cyril Frederick Dean STEEL 24 RCAF

24-Dec-43   FH274   Hudson IIIA   353 Sqn   Dum Dum   0

The aircraft was damaged beyond repair after an engine failure during take-off. The detailed circumstances are not known.

28-Dec-43   HH539   Hotspur II   3 GTS   Wanborough, Gloucestershire   1

Following a low level release, the pilot continued to fly crosswind for too long and this necessitated him to execute a steep turn near the ground to avoid obstructions. However, whilst doing this, the aircarft's wing tip struck a hedge and the aircraft crashed. Although the pilot survived, another member of the crew did not.

   Believed to be:
   Corporal Cyril John TYLER 23 The Glider Pilot Regiment

29-Dec-43   HH522   Hotspur II   3 GTS   Northleach, Gloucestershire   0

The pilot failed to monitor the airspeed and the glider stalled on final approach and landed heavily. The Accident Card states ominously; 'pilot to have a suspension test'.

30-Dec-43   EB287   Whitley V   42 OTU   Home Farm Yeldersley   1

The aircraft's undercarriage would not lock down and after attempts to resolve the problem had failed, the pilot was instructed to make a wheels up landing beside the runway. During the final stages of the

213

Date	Serial	Aircraft	Unit	Place		Casualties

Brief Circumstances of Accident
Casualty Details (If Applicable)

approach, the air traffic controller realised the aircraft was positioned to land on the left side of the runway in use and not the right as had been directed. Since there was a line of houses obstructing the approach path to the left, the pilot was ordered to overshoot the approach. The throttles were opened normally but the sudden increase in power caused the aircraft's nose to rise sharply and before the pilot could correct this attitude change, exacerbated by the crew being at crash stations and hence moving the aircraft's CofG rearwards, it stalled, crashed and burst into flames. Although the other crew members survived, the pilot received fatal injuries.

Sergeant Edmund Anthony FARTHING Pilot

214

03-Jan-44 LG745 Horsa 9 MU Churchill, Worcestershire 0

The aircraft was being flown on a delivery sortie and had been airborne for about 15 minutes. The glider pilot lost control and so pulled off the tow, however, in attempting a forced landing the aircraft's wing tip struck the ground.

06-Jan-44 FD802 Dakota I 31 Sqn Tibual (93 degrees 22E/23 degrees 07N 3

The aircraft took off at 0710 hours for a supply dropping sortie and arrived at the drop zone, which was subject to thick cloud and heavy rainstorms. The first pass of the drop zone was accomplished successfully but on the second pass the aircraft lost height and crashed before catching fire. Although Warrant Officer Evans the co-pilot and Flight Sergeant Fox an air gunner survived, three others did not.

Pilot Officer Jack GARRETT 22 RNZAF Pilot
Flight Sergeant Errington George McEvoy DAVIS 23
Pilot Officer William HOWITT 26

06-Jan-44 BZ949 Liberator III 1586 Flt Near Villa Castelli 8

The crew was returning from a sortie to Poland, having failed to locate the DZ and after their aircraft was subjected to severe gale force winds and heavy icing during the flight. Whilst attempting to land at Grottaglie, not far from Taranto, the aircraft crashed into high ground and all on board were killed.

Flight Sergeant Zygmunt DUNSKI
Flight Sergeant Franciszek OLKIEWICZ
Flight Lieutenant Witold PASZKIEWICZ
Flight Lieutenant Tadeusz DOMARADZKI
Sergeant Jozef MARCHWICKI
Sergeant Piotr HALIK
Flight Sergeant Stefan MAGDZIAREK
Sergeant Julian BUCKO

06-Jan-44   BZ859   Liberator   1586 Flt   Off Brindisi   7

The crew of this aircraft had been undertaking the same sortie as the one above, together with another Liberator and a Halifax from the same unit. The Halifax had lost an engine and returned early whilst the third Liberator had been subjected to severe winds and despite being flown by Warrant Officer Klowoski and his experienced crew, the drop had been abandoned and the aircraft returned to base. This aircraft's crew, however, had completed their mission successfully but the aircraft had lost an engine and been damaged by AA fire. Whilst attempting a landing at Brindisi, the aircraft crashed into the sea and although the second pilot; Flight Lieutenant Kazimierz Dobrowolski, survived the ditching, the rest of the crew drowned.

Flight Lieutenant Witold BOHUSZEWICZ
Flight Lieutenant Anton PULCZYNSKI
Flight Lieutenant Mieczyslaw KUZMICKI
Sergeant Jerzy DRONG
Flight Sergeant Zdzislaw TACZALSKI
Flight Sergeant Romuald BLAZENSKI
Flying Officer Roman FINDER

06-Jan-44   LG672   Horsa   HGMU   Hurn   0

The glider undershot the approach during a night landing and crashed into a wood. The pilot misjudged the distance between the 'funnel' lights and the start of the flarepath.

08-Jan-44   LK743   Halifax   138 Sqn   Tetworth Hill, Bedford   10

The aircraft was returning to base after about 5 hours airborne. Its crew had part completed a dual sortie coded; TYBALT 3 and THERSITES 4, during which time they had parachuted two agents into Belgium. Unfortunately, it did not prove possible to drop three more agents and the aircraft was flown back to UK. During the return flight, the port outer engine failed and the propeller could not be feathered, causing considerable additional drag and creating control problems. Whilst making its approach to land, the aircraft crashed about 1½ miles east of the airfield and all those aboard were killed.

Pilot Officer Harry Murray KENNEDY 23 Pilot
Sergeant Victor Albert Edward THEEDOM
Sergeant Stanley WHITELEY
Sergeant Edwin THRIPP 23 Wireless Operator
Flight Sergeant David Fisher DAVIES DFM
Sergeant Peter Sidney BARLOW 22
Sergeant Thomas Samuel HOWLETT 22 Flight Engineer
Captain Henri P VERHAEGEN 25 Belgian Forces Agent
Sergeant Hector GOFFIN 23
Sergeant Rene MICHAUX 21

10-Jan-44	BB445 Halifax	148 Sqn	Albania	0

The aircraft lost its port outer engine during the outbound transit but the captain; Squadron Leader John Brotherton-Ratcliffe, elected to continue the sortie. Having completed the first drop successfully, the aircraft's port inner engine failed and the aircraft could not maintain height and this in a mountainous area. The crew then attempted to fly down various valleys in order to reach the coast but this proved impossible when they became trapped in a blind valley. All except the captain baled out at low level and the pilot made a forced landing in a maize field. The entire crew survived without injury and were evacuated subsequently. Brotherton-Ratcliffe, who completed two tours of duty on this squadron, was awarded a DSO subsequently.

Date	Serial	Aircraft	Unit	Place	Casualties

Brief Circumstances of Accident
Casualty Details (If Applicable)

12-Jan-44	FD913	Dakota III	62 Sqn	Nowgong	0+2

The aircraft was returning after a supply dropping exercise and the pilot was not advised of the wind speed or direction and the only windsocks were not visible from the direction of the aircraft's approach. The airstrip, in addition, had a number of natural hazards about its western boundary and was fairly small. The pilot landed downwind with a tail wind speed of about 20 knots. The aircraft overshot the strip, crashed into trees beyond and killed two native children.

17-Jan-44	FZ632	Dakota III	45 Gp	15 miles off Lagens, Azores	1

The aircraft ditched at sea off the Azores en route to UK. Although most of the crew were rescued uninjured, the navigator drowned.

Pilot Officer Thomas Davidson THOMSON RCAF Navigator

18-Jan-44	HH604	Hotspur II	5 GTS	Near Shobdon	0

The pilot lost control of the glider after the hood came open. Although he had less than an hour's solo on type he was criticised for faulty cockpit drill and his injuries were exacerbated because he was not wearing his helmet properly.

20-Jan-44	HH961	Hamilcar	1 HGMU	RAF Tarrant Rushton	0

The aircraft crashed into a building after it overran the landing area.

23-Jan-44	DG272	Halifax	161 Sqn	Missing	7

This aircraft and the one below were being flown on an air sea rescue sortie to search for downed aircrew over the North Sea. The aircraft departed RAF Tempsford within a few minutes and neither they nor their crews were ever seen again. There is an assumption that the aircraft collided but there is no evidence for this.

Flying Officer Kenneth Ferris SMITH 23 Pilot
Flight Sergeant Kenneth James ROBERTS 21
Flying Officer Wilfred PRESTON 22 DFC
Sergeant Keith CUSHING
Sergeant John Richard BRADSHAW
Flight Sergeant John Anderson WHYTE 23
Flight Sergeant Matthew LIVINGSTON 28 DFM

23-Jan-44	LL182	Halifax	161 Sqn	Missing	7

Lost without trace in the circumstances summarised above.

Flight Sergeant James William ROBERTSON Pilot
Flying Officer John Morrice KEAY
Sergeant Edward HEATON 21
Sergeant Edward Robert RICHARDSON 19
Sergeant Henry Charles WALTON 22
Sergeant William MEIKLE 20
Sergeant Lyal HARVEY 29

23-Jan-44	LG722	Horsa	1 HGMU	Downward Farm, Hants	2

The aircraft was being delivered and was approaching to land in the darkness having, it is thought, lost sight of the tug. The aircraft crashed and both pilots received fatal injuries.

Sergeant Robert Sidney BAIRD 24 The Glider Pilot Regiment
Sergeant William HOBBS 25 The Glider Pilot Regiment

23-Jan-44	DP292	Horsa	HGCU	RAF Brize Norton	0

The undercarriage collapsed following a heavy landing and the glider was subsequently converted into a

Date Serial Aircraft Unit Place Casualties
Brief Circumstances of Accident
Casualty Details (If Applicable)

ground instructional airframe.

25-Jan-44   DP346 Horsa   HGCU   'B' Site, Black Burton, Oxon   0
Whilst flying a height of 75 feet, the glider's port towing bridle detached, followed shortly afterwards by the starboard bridle. The glider was forced landed straight ahead but the 2 crew; Staff Sergeant H Leary and Sergeant H Josephs were both injured.

28-Jan-44   LG746 Horsa   1 HGMU   Shrewton, Wilts   0
Whilst approaching to land, the pilot judged that the glider was too high and so dropped the flaps to the half setting and then selected full flaps. However, in doing so the glider sank more rapidly than intended and was damaged when it undershot the landing area.

28-Jan-44   LH245 Horsa   1 HGMU   ?????   0
The glider pilot pulled off the tow because the tug pilot was flying too fast and control was difficult. The glider was forced landed but damaged. The tug pilot was disciplined for his poor performance.

28-Jan-44   FD811 Dakota I   31 Sqn   2 miles west north west of Kharpur   11
The aircraft took off at about 0600 hours in the dark with a crew briefed to carry out a mail run for 221 Group to Calcutta. The aircraft was making a circuit of the airfield but the pilot allowed it to descend and it struck the ground 8 minutes after take-off. The Accident Card records that the pilot was inexperienced at night flying and his skills should have been checked before being allowed to operate at night. The book "First In The Indian Skies" suggests, however, that the pilot had been dancing on the roof of a basha the night before and hence might not have been at his most alert!

Flying Officer Thomas William TOWNLEY 28 Pilot
Warrant Officer Donald Ashley THOMPSON 21 RCAF Co-Pilot
Flying Officer George Edward BESWICK 22 Navigator
Flight Sergeant Albert James WALLIS 22 Wireless Operator
Flight Sergeant Lionel Beaumont KNIGHT 25 Wireless Operator
Aircraftman 2nd Class Arthur James MILES
Corporal Ronald PARRY 22 (described as a Wireless Operator/Air Gunner)
+ four US personnel whose names were not found

31-Jan-44   LA765   Whitley V   81 OTU   Dilhorne Cheadle   4

The aircraft was engaged on a night cross country sortie but about 20 minutes after take-off and whilst flying below its safety height, it struck rising ground, bounced into the air, turned over and crashed inverted into a gulley and was destroyed. The aircraft had been flown throughout the sortie at low level, despite warnings from the navigator and it was heading in the wrong direction. The sole survivor was the rear gunner who was seriously injured.

Sergeant Ian Leslie WILKINSON Pilot
Flying Officer John Frederick CUSWORTH Navigator
Sergeant George Victor BOURNE Bomb Aimer
Flight Sergeant Andrew Harkes ROBERTSON 30 Wireless Operator

31-Jan-44   LJ325   Horsa   1 HGMU   1 mile south-south-west of Downton, Wilts   0

The pilot allowed the glider to get caught in the tug's slipstream and an uncontrollable swing developed. The tow was cast off but the glider pilot then selected a field, which was crossed by HT cables, as his landing point. An attempt was made to fly beneath the cables but the glider's tail was ripped off and it was damaged further when it went through a hedge.

221

02-Feb-44   BB444   Halifax II   624 Sqn   Lost over Albania   6
The crew was engaged, with two others, on supply dropping in Albania, whilst another crew from the squadron flew a sortie into Greece. The other two crews sent to Albania both failed to pick up the ground signals and aborted their mission but this aircraft reached the DZ (SCULPTURE 16) but crashed on it. Although the rear gunner survived, the others were killed

  Flight Sergeant Edward Drake Steele TENNANT 31 RAAF Pilot
  Sergeant Francis Cecil Rudolph BURLFINGER 26 Wireless Operator/Air Gunner
  Sergeant George GARDNER 19 Air Gunner
  Flight Sergeant Dennis Hilton POTTER 21 RAAF Bomb Aimer
  Flying Officer Ronald Edwin STANLEY 21
  Sergeant James Leo DEVINE 22

03-Feb-44   DK199   Halifax V   298 Sqn   RAF Tarrant Rushton   0
Destroyed as a result of being struck by the aircraft listed below.

03-Feb-44   BK771   Stirling III   196 Sqn   RAF Tarrant Rushton   0
The aircraft was taking off on a short runway and it started to swing, in part because of the strong crosswind. The pilot failed to correct the swing or to follow the standard procedures and attempting a further take-off after stopping the aircraft. In consequence, the aircraft left the runway and crashed into Halifax DK199.

03-Feb-44   LH181   Horsa   1 HGMU   Hurn   0
The glider pilot cast off the tow too early and the aircraft undershot the landing.

04-Feb-44 LH297 Horsa   1 HGMU   Tarrant Rushton   0

The glider pilot misjudged his approach at night and the glider undershot.

04-Feb-44 LH136 Horsa   1 HGMU   Oatlands Hill   0

The glider was damaged after it overshot its landing field.

05-Feb-44 EJ110 Stirling IV   196 Sqn   FTR   7

This aircraft was one of a mixed force from five of the transport sqns sent to support SD operations. It failed to return from its task but the details of its loss are not clear.

Pilot Officer Henry Ivan PRYKE 21 Pilot
Sergeant Denis Tunnard VINCE 23 Navigator
Warrant Officer James DONALDSON 22 RCAF Bomb Aimer
Sergeant Kenneth Albert GLEW 20 Wireless Operator
Sergeant Robert DOWZER 21 Flight Engineer
Sergeant Kenneth Thomas STAPLE 20 Air Gunner
Sergeant Alfred SPRAY 20 Air Gunner

05-Feb-44 LK395 Stirling IV   620 Sqn   Near Bourges   7

The crew was one of four operating with aircraft from other squadrons and based temporarily at Hurn. The mixed force was tasked with drops mainly in south-east France and although initially the weather was good it deteriorated en route. The aircraft was hit by enemy light AA fire and crashed shortly afterwards with the lss of its crew. The following night, other aircraft operating in the same area were subjected to very heavy concentrations of AA fire but what was worth protecting in this area is not known.

Squadron Leader Edward Creighton FYSON 27 Pilot
Flying Officer George SALTER 27 Navigator
Sergeant Eric BENNETT 31 Bomb Aimer

Sergeant Albert Victor Robert EDWARDS 23 Flight Engineer
Sergeant Leslie Frederick DARLINGTON 22 Wireless Operator
Sergeant Frederick William Christian DEAN 23 Air Gunner
Sergeant George Harold KENT 20 Air Gunner

06-Feb-44   EF469   Stirling IV   196 Sqn   Cornimont   3

A force of six Stirlings, drawn equally from 196 and 620 Sqns, (the latter unit providing the crews which had survived the previous night's operations and a further pair of crews detached that morning) and a pair of Albemarles from 295 Sqn were sent on SOE sorties mainly to northern and central France but only one aircraft made a successful drop. This aircraft failed to return. The crews reported intense enemy activity in the general area where LK395 was lost the previous night. A 620 Sqn aircraft, flown by Flight Sergeant McNamara, was very badly damaged but was flown back to Hurn where a successful belly landing was made on the grass. Photographs of the aircraft show it to look quite badly damaged in the landing but it was repaired and returned to service.

Flying Officer Thomas MOORE 22 Pilot
Flying Officer John Rothwell LINDLEY 32 Navigator
Warrant Officer Lionel Howard WOODRUFF 21 RCAF Bomb Aimer

07-Feb-44   K6984   Harrow II   271 Sqn   RAF Sumbrugh   0

The aircraft was pushed by the force of a gale into a fuel bowser and damaged badly, despite it being properly picketted. By some ironic twist, the bowser was fully laden and was being used to assist with the picketing of aircraft.

07-Feb-44   V1067   Magister   3 GTS   Eynsham   ?

The aircraft dived into the ground following a stall whilst making a steep turn.

08-Feb-44   FD775   Dakota   31 Sqn   Arakan   3?

This aircraft was one of a large formation of Dakotas from 62 and 31 Sqns detailed to drop supplies to the forces defending the 'Admin Box' during the Arakan offensive by the Japanese. The formation was escorted by Hurricanes but, nonetheless, one of the Dakotas was chased northwards and shot down by an enemy fighter. Apparently, two of the crew; Flying Officer Nat Gould DFM and Warrant Officer A Young, survived and returned to allied lines but the others did not. Squadron Leader Walker and his brother were both awarded DFCs and there is some evidence that Squadron Leader Walker deliberately put his aircraft in harms way to draw off the enemy fighters and permit other crews to scatter and make their escape. It has proved difficult to confirm the precise number killed in this aircraft or to confirm that Flying Officer Baptie lost his life in this aircraft.

    Squadron Leader James Arthur WALKER 25 DFC and Bar RCAF Pilot
    Flying Officer Thomas Wilfred BAPTIE 34 Navigator
    Flight Sergeant Neville Walker SMETHURST 22

08-Feb-44   LL114   Halifax   138 Sqn   Autrans Isere France   7

The aircraft crashed about 9 miles west of Grenoble whilst on task JOHN 35. The circumstances of the loss are not known.

    Flying Officer Gerald Dennis CARROLL 21 Pilot
    Pilot Officer Arthur Edward REID 22 RCAF Navigator
    Sergeant Ronald Denis CLEMENT 22
    Sergeant Peter Theodore THOMPSON 21
    Flight Sergeant James Alvin TAYLOR 19 RCAF Bomb Aimer
    Sergeant Gordon Stanley WOODROW 20

225

Date	Serial	Aircraft	Unit	Place	Casualties
		Brief Circumstances of Accident			
		Casualty Details (If Applicable)			

Sergeant Kenneth William RADFORD 20

08-Feb-44 LW275 Halifax   138 Sqn   Hauterives Drome France   0

The crew, captained by Squadron Leader T C Cooke, was engaged in on task JOCKEY 5 to France. On the outbound leg, the aircraft's starboard inner engine caught fire but this was extinguished and the aircraft continued but could not maintain height on three engines with its load. The aircraft descended gradually but it subsequently entered cloud which caused serious icing problems. Eventually, the crew abandoned the aircraft and all landed safely and were able to evade capture and return to the UK about 4 months later.

10-Feb-44 V9822 Lysander III   161 Sqn   3 miles north of Dun sur Auron Cher   1

The aircraft was being used to deliver 2 agents to an LZ south east of Bourges and the pilot made two unsuccessful approaches to land. On the third attempt the aircraft touched down too fast, overran the flarepath and tipped onto its nose and caught fire. Although the pilot was killed, the two agents survived, although one of them was badly injured.

Flying Officer John Walter MCDONALD 26 RAAF

11-Feb-44 LH377 Horsa   1 HGMU

The tug had control problems and the pilot ordered the glider to be cast off. Unfortunately, there was no suitable landing site and the glider was damaged in the forced landing.

12-Feb-44 EF350 Stirling I   1665 CU   Hawarden   0

The aircraft was being landed at Hawarden in poor visibility and it overshot the runway and ran into an air raid shelter, causing damage to the undercarriage.

13-Feb-44 FL505 Dakota III   62 Sqn   Comilla   3+2

The aircraft swung on take-off and the pilot failed to correct this before the aircraft left the runway and collided with several USAAF C47's, which were parked close to the runway. Although the hazard of having aircraft parked so close was appreciated, the intensity of the flying operations and the crowded nature of the airfield meant the risk had to be accepted. The US aircraft were serial numbers: 42/210699, 2100706 and 2100701. It is unclear whether the two casualties on the ground were RAF or US personnel, although there is an unconfirmed report that the two men were sleeping in or working on one of the aircraft and hence were probably USAAF.

　　　Warrant Officer Frederick Henry William KINGSWOOD 22 RAAF Pilot
　　　Sergeant Ralph Joseph CUNNINGHAM 23 Wireless Operator
　　　Flight Sergeant Charles Frederick WRIGHT 23 Wireless Operator
　　　Two others outside the aircraft

13-Feb-44 LH413 Horsa   1 HGMU   Hurn   0

This glider was part of a mass glider exercise and it could so easily have become a serious accident. In order to allow the glider to be towed off downwind, the heavy ballast load was replaced by a number of troops who had neither seats nor safety harnesses. The glider pilot took evasive action to avoid another glider, bounced on touchdown, struck a heap of rubble and then crashed into a building. There were 17 people in the glider and 8 of these were injured to varying degrees.

13-Feb-44 LH342 Horsa   1 HGMU   Hurn   0

The aircraft overshot and was damaged when it crashed through a fence.

14-Feb-44 HH605 Hotspur II   3 GTS   Stoke Orchard   0

The pilot was bringing the glider into land but he continued to fly crosswind so that when he turned the glider onto the finals leg, the aircraft was too low and a wing struck the ground and was ripped off.

Date	Serial	Aircraft	Unit	Place	Casualties
				Brief Circumstances of Accident	
				Casualty Details (If Applicable)	

15-Feb-44 BD420 Whitley V 81 OTU Snailbach, 1½ miles south of Minsterley 5

The aircraft was towing a Horsa glider, serial number HA443, in turbulent conditions at low level and near high ground. The aircraft broke up and all its crew died but the glider was released and its crew made a successful forced landing. Sergeant Hodges brother – Warrant Officer R B Hodges was killed in action on 7 Jun 43 when the airfield on which he was based was attacked by enemy aircraft.

    Flight Sergeant Ronald Richmond BROUN 21 RNZAF Pilot
    Sergeant Jack Thomas BROWNHILL 21
    Warrant Officer Edward Alan CREBERE 24
    Sergeant Ronald Frederick HODGES 19 RCAF Bomb Aimer
    Sergeant Henry LITTLE 20

15-Feb-44 JN959 Halifax 148 Sqn ????????????????? ?

The aircraft is known to have been lost by the squadron on the night of 15/16 February but the circumstances of its demise were not found.

20-Feb-44 EF468 Stirling III 196 Sqn Near RAF Keevil 6

The aircraft had just completed a night cross country sortie and had returned to base. It then crashed in the circuit whilst attempting to land and although the cause was not established it is thought the pilot lacked proficiency in instrument flying and was also out of general flying practice.

    Warrant Officer Calvert Hamilton HUNTER 31 RCAF Pilot (died 21 Feb 44)
    Flight Sergeant Ronald Cecil LYSONS 23
    Warrant Officer Charles Arthur SIMPSON 23 RCAF
    Flight Sergeant Patrick William SULLIVAN 24 RCAF

Sergeant John Edward SAWFORD 20
Sergeant Duncan Malcolm MCCANNELL 24 (died 21 Feb 44)

20-Feb-44   LA619 Lockheed 12A   NAS Maydown, Northern Ireland   0
Deicing paste had been applied to the wings, which might have affected the stalling speed.   On take-off the port wing stalled but the pilot picked this up but the wheels touched the ground.   The throttles were closed and the aircraft crashed into a fence.

20-Feb-44   LA927   Whitley V   42 OTU   Gate Inn, Upper Longdon Staffs   4
The aircraft crashed, collided with a tree and was destroyed in a forced landing, possibly because of engine icing problems.

   Sergeant William Ivor ROBERTS 21 Pilot
   Sergeant William John CONSTABLE 21 Navigator
   Sergeant Vincent Joseph ASHMORE 21 Wireless Operator
   Sergeant Frederick HILL 24 Air Gunner

20-Feb-44   DP350 Horsa   1HGMU   Hurn   0
The glider had landed and completed its landing run but had then stopped to await retrieval by a tractor. The pilot of another glider did not see this aircraft's tail lights and a collision took place.

20-Feb-44   LH391 Horsa   1 HGMU   East Ragley, Hants   0
During a night towing exercise, the intercom between tug and glider failed and instead of waiting for the tug crew to flash a white light to indicate the release point, the glider pilot pulled off the tow but his aircraft was out of reach of the airfield and it was forced landed short of its base.

229

Date	Serial	Aircraft	Unit	Place	Casualties
Brief Circumstances of Accident					
Casualty Details (If Applicable)					

20-Feb-44   PF701   Horsa   1 HGMU   Hurn   0

The aircraft was undershooting its landing and it touched down nose first, causing the floor to be pushed up.

22-Feb-44   EW906   Hudson VI   48 Sqn   Estrela Mountains, Portugal   6

The aircraft is shown in the Accident Card to belong to 46 Group of Transport Command, as the role of this maritime patrol squadron was about to change to that of a Dakota transport unit. It is probable, therefore, that this crew and their passengers were en route to UK to dispose of their aircraft and commence training in their new role. The aircraft was making a night transit and it struck mountains at a height of 5300 feet. The reason for it being off course and flying over neutral territory is unknown.

    Captain Robert Taverner HILDICK 21 SAAF Pilot
    Lieutenant Daniel De Waal WALTERS SAAF Navigator
    Lieutenant J BARBOUR 29 SAAF Wireless Operator
    Lieutenant J P THOM 25 SAAF Wireless Operator
    Corporal Henry Ernest HEDGES 30
    Corporal Jack Learoyd WALKER 26

23-Feb-44   LA948   Whitley V   PTS   Ringway   0

The aircraft was taking off for a night parachute dropping sortie when it collided with another Whitley (LA895) taxiing down the runway from the opposite direction! This aircraft swung violently to starboard after the collision and its undercarriage collapsed before it caught fire and was destroyed. It does not say much for the standard of flying control that this happened.

24-Feb-44   V1707   Albemarle   42 OTU   RAF Ashbourne   0

The aircraft was being landed at its base after a night cross country of 3½ hours duration. The presence of patches of low cloud on the approach made it difficult for the pilot to line up with the runway accurately and the aircraft touched down heavily and too fast, causing the undercarriage to collapse. The pilot, who had only 48 hours on type, was not blamed and the accident was recorded as being due to inexperience. The crew was uninjured.

24-Feb-44   LH401 Horsa   1 HGMU   Preston Court, near Tarrant Rushton   0

The glider was released early and undershot the airfield.

25-Feb-44   BB330   Halifax   138 Sqn   RAF Tempsford   0

This aircraft had been damaged in an unspecified accident and was struck off charge on this date.

26-Feb-44   EM291 Master II   5 GTS   Shobdon   ?

Damaged in an accident, no details and no Accident Card found.

29-Feb-44   EF297   Stirling IV   196 Sqn   RAF Netheravon   0

The aircraft was engaged on a glider retrieval sortie and a swing developed on landing, resulting in the port main tyre bursting followed by the undercarriage collapsing. The comment was made that despite the poor standard of the airfield it was necessary for Stirlings to use it for operational reasons.

29-Feb-44   LG723 Horsa   575 Sqn   Woodside Farm, Oxford   0

At a height of 100 feet and immediately after take-off, the tow rope broke. The aircraft was forced landed straight ahead in a field but in trying to avoid high tension cables, the glider pilot allowed the glider to hit a stone wall.

Date	Serial	Aircraft	Unit	Place	Casualties
				Brief Circumstances of Accident Casualty Details (If Applicable)	

01-Mar-44 BB387 Halifax 148 Sqn ????? ?
The aircraft is recorded as being struck off charge on this date but no details were found.

01-Mar-44 LA647 Hamilcar 1 HGMU France Farm, Blandford Forum 0
The aircraft cast off from the tug after the latter suffered an engine failure whilst flying at 250 feet. The crew was left with no option but to put down where possible and the glider was crash landed in a sunken lane.

03-Mar-44 V1641 Albemarle 570 Sqn FTR 5
The aircraft was one of a mixed tasking of Albemarles and Stirlings engaged in SOE work but it failed to return.

Flying Officer Christopher James ELMER 22 Pilot
Flying Officer John Herbert HOOD 30 Navigator
Flying Officer Thomas Johnston ADAMSON 34 Bomb Aimer
Sergeant Edward James ATKINSON 33 Wireless Operator
Sergeant James DAVIES 21 Air Gunner

03-Mar-44 HR660 Halifax 148 Sqn Near Ancona 5
The aircraft was hit by flak in the general area of its DZ at Ancona. However, the crew continued with the sortie and the supplies were dropped on target before the aircraft crashed in the DZ vicinity. In addition to the fatal casualties, there were apparently 5 survivors who baled out. Flight Lieutenant Lancaster had just joined the unit and was flying as supernumery for operational experience. Flight Lieutenant Botham, on the other hand, was almost at the end of his second operational tour and had amassed nearly 600 hours of operational flying.

Flight Lieutenant James Harold BOTHAM 23 Pilot

Flying Officer Henry George LANCASTER 28 Pilot
Flight Sergeant John Walter SOLE Wireless Operator
Warrant Officer II John Caldwell CALHOUN 24 RCAF Flight Engineer
Sergeant William THURNALL 20 Air Gunner

| 03-Mar-44 | FP161 | Catalina | 628 Sqn | Bay of Bengal | 14 |

The aircraft was undertaking a ferry flight from Willingdon Reach to China Bay, on the east coast of Ceylon, so as to position for a long range special duties sortie. There was some confusion about the responsibilities for briefing the crew and it appears that adverse weather conditions were not brought to the attention of the crew. The aircraft was lost without trace over the Bay of Bengal and it is thought probable that it was lost in the severe cyclone storm experienced on route. Those lost comprised an operating crew of ten and four agents. Flight Lieutenant Lawrence's wife; Flight Officer Pamela Lawrence nee Thorpe aged 22, died in service some 15 months prior to her husband's death in this accident.

Flying Officer Frederick AISTON 23 Pilot
Flight Sergeant Abraham GARCIA 34 Co-Pilot
Sergeant James William HOLLAND 27
Sergeant Henry WHITBY 21
Flight Lieutenant George Henry LAWRENCE RCAF
Sergeant Robert Higginson OWEN 31
plus four other crew who may have been:
Sergeant Robert William Cowan YEAMAN 23
Sergeant Robert Cuthbert WILD
Flying Officer Thomas Reginald HOLLAND
Sergeant Charles Neville TASKER
plus four ISLD agents, whose names were not found

Date	Serial	Aircraft	Unit	Place	Casualties
Brief Circumstances of Accident					
Casualty Details (If Applicable)					
03-Mar-44	LH354	Horsa	1 HGMU	Knighton Farm, Hants	0

The pilot allowed the glider to get into the tug's slipstream and this caused control problems. The pilot cast off the tow but then struck trees, stalled the glider and made a heavy landing whilst trying to avoid overhead power lines in the field selected for the landing.

Date	Serial	Aircraft	Unit	Place	Casualties
03-Mar-44	LH174	Horsa	1 HGMU	RAF Welford	0

The aircraft was struck by Stirling EF456, after the latter had swung on landing.

Date	Serial	Aircraft	Unit	Place	Casualties
03-Mar-44	LH404	Horsa	1 HGMU	Kinson Manor Farm, Hants	0

The pilot, who was not very experienced on the type, found it difficult to retain control having entered the tug's slipstream. He cast off the tow and the aircraft descended rapidly into a field and was damaged in the landing.

Date	Serial	Aircraft	Unit	Place	Casualties
03-Mar-44	BT836	Hotspur II	5 GTS	½ mile south-west of Hockley Heath	0

The pilot first thought he could reach his base but then realised that the glider would be unable to do so. He then set up a forced landing before concluding that he would crash into a cottage and so he put the aircraft down in a ploughed field.

Date	Serial	Aircraft	Unit	Place	Casualties
04-Mar-44	LL279	Halifax	138 Sqn	Bernay area Eure (location not stated)	5

The crew was engaged on sortie JOHN 23 but the aircraft crashed in the vicinity of a German airfield and it is possible it was shot down. Two members of the crew survived and were captured. Sergeant Dutton had served in the 1st World War and had enlisted in 1940 before training as a flight engineer. He was probably amongst the oldest men to have flown on operations.

Flying Officer William Charles KINGSLEY RCAF Pilot
Flying Officer George Albert ROBERTS RCAF Navigator
Flying Officer John Edgar WRIGHT RCAF Bomb Aimer
Flight Sergeant Kenneth Fredrick Hill HART 29 Wireless Operator
Sergeant James Roy DUTTON 47 RCAF Flight Engineer

04-Mar-44 V9405 Lysander III 161 Sqn Plumetot Calvados 0

The aircraft, flown by Flying Officer D S Bell DFC, had engine trouble and the pilot elected to return to UK. However, when over the sea, he decided to return to France and crashed landed 5 miles north of Caen, Normandy. Bell and the two agents he was flying escaped from the area and Bell was eventually repatriated to UK.

04-Mar-44 BB386 Halifax II 624 Sqn 5 miles north-west of Blida 7

The crew was detailed for a sortie involving a force of seventeen aircraft from the squadron. The weather was marginal and this aircraft took off first but crashed shortly afterwards with the loss of all on board. It was judged unsafe to continue and the sortie was cancelled.

Warrant Officer II George Thomas JACKSON 23 RCAF Pilot
Sergeant Donald Garforth BROWNE
Flying Officer Francis Era ELLIOTT 28 RCAF Air Gunner
Sergeant Willian Dennis HAZELDINE
Flight Sergeant Roy Wesley MOLLER 21 RCAF Air Gunner
Flying Officer Gordon MUNDELL 31 RCAF Bomb Aimer
Pilot Officer Harry Alexander Edward SMITH 33 RCAF Navigator

05-Mar-44 EH906 Stirling III 90 Sqn St Hilaire de Gondilly 1

This aircraft was from a main bomber group squadron, whose crews had been coopted to help with SD work. Whilst flying near Bourges at low level, the aircraft was illuminated by a searchlight and hit by light flak which destroyed both starboard engines and started a fire in the port wing. The pilot attempted to climb to a safe height for his crew to abandon the aircraft by parachute but was unable to escape himself and he died in the subsequent crash. Following a report made by one of the crew, French was awarded a posthumous Mention in Despatches.

Flight Lieutenant Cyril Vincent FRENCH Pilot

05-Mar-44	EF215	Stirling III	75 Sqn	Rochfort Montagne, Clarmont-Ferrand	6

A force of seventy six aircraft were sent on SD sorties of which fourteen came from 75 Sqn, a predominantly New Zealand unit. This particular crew was tasked with TRAINER 124, which required supplies to be dropped to a DZ in the Pay de Dome west of Clarmont-Ferrand. The aircraft struck a mountainside and only one member of the crew survived to be taken POW. The weather was low cloud down to 500 feet with hazy conditions otherwise and very few crews from this unit were successful.

Squadron Leader Raymond Johnson WATSON 27 DFC RNZAF Pilot
Sergeant Cyril BEECH 20 Flight Engineer
Flying Officer Hugh William HENDERSON 24 RNZAF Navigator
Pilot Officer Arthur Stanley JONES 28 RNZAF Wireless Operator
Flight Sergeant Robert James Ian MELVILLE 26 RNZAF Air Gunner
Flight Sergeant Ralph Morley WOODS 29 Bomb Aimer

05-Mar-44	LA793	Whitley V	ORTU	Hampstead Norris	0

The aircraft was engaged in a night training sortie and was approaching to land at about 0300 hours in the morning. The pilot initiated an overshoot but the aircraft was drifting to port and it struck a Dakota parked too close to the runway without lights. Although the pilot is cited for an error of judgement the poor old Flying Control Officer is subjected to disciplinary action for not ensuring the Dakota could be seen. It must be commented that it is not clear how the Whitley pilot was to have avoided the Dakota since he had already allowed his aircraft to drift into harms way.

05-Mar-44 KG375 Dakota III   271 Sqn   Hampstead Norris   0
Damaged beyond repair as indicated above.

05-Mar-44 KG396 Dakota   45 Gp   Meeks Field Iceland   3
The aircraft crashed en route to UK but the circumstances are not recorded.

    Pilot Officer Lester James TINGLE RCAF Pilot
    Pilot Officer Donald Keith NELSON RCAF Navigator
    Pilot Officer Philip Joseph ASSEFF RCAF Wireless Operator

05-Mar-44 EE944 Stirling III   218 Sqn   RAF Tempsford   5
This aircraft was from a main force bomber squadron and had been loaned for SD sorties, as often happened particularly if there was a backlog of tasks to be completed. The aircraft had returned from its sortie following a failure of the port outer engine but was still carrying its load of supplies. An overshoot on three engines was attempted but a wingtip struck the ground and the aircraft crashed with the loss of five of its seven man crew.

    Pilot Officer Elwyn Hinto EDWARDS 22
    Flying Officer Bernard DENNESS 23
    Sergeant Douglas Graham DAVIES
    Sergeant Ernest VAMPLOUGH 19 Flight Engineer
    Flight Sergeant Peter Henry KILSBY 22 Bomb Aimer

06-Mar-44 KG446 Dakota   45 Gp   Atlantic Ocean   3
The aircraft went missing after departing Reykjavik en route to UK. There is no evidence as to how it was lost.

Date	Serial	Aircraft	Unit	Place	Casualties
			Brief Circumstances of Accident		
			Casualty Details (If Applicable)		

Sergeant James Gerard BRUEN Pilot
Pilot Officer Kenneth William RAPER RCAF Navigator
Sergeant Andrew THORPE Wireless Operator

| 06-Mar-44 | LH290 | Horsa | 2 Wg GPR | Leicester Forest East | 0 |

The glider was part of a mass landing formation and the pilot found himself baulked by 2 other gliders. Instead of landing on the grass, as briefed in an emergency, he attempted to overshoot and then land back on. However, he misjudged this and the glider landed in a field.

| 07-Mar-44 | V1747 | Albemarle | 295 Sqn | Hurn | 0 |

The aircraft ran into an electricity transformer after its brakes failed during taxying.

| 09-Mar-44 | FZ677 | Dakota | 45 Gp | 15 miles from Reykjavik | 3 |

The aircraft struck a mountain in the position shown.

Sergeant Bernard Vincent ARNEY Pilot
Pilot Officer John Nisbet THOMSON RCAF Navigator
Sergeant Noel Arnold THOMAS Wireless Operator

| 09-Mar-44 | LH434 | Horsa | 1 HGMU | RAF Stoney Cross | 1 |

The intercom between tug and glider was u/s and the pilot was dazzled by the glare of lights on a misted windscreen. Having dropped the tow, he misjudged the approach and alignment of the landing area and the aircraft crashed into a Nissan Hut.

09-Mar-44 HH711 Hotspur II   126 A/F HQ   1 mile north-west of RAF Biggin Hill   0

The two pilots, who were RCAF officers, had almost no gliding experience between them!! The glider broke loose from the tug but the tow rope was not jettisoned and hence acted as a dead weight on the aircraft's nose. A forced landing was attempted but the glider dived into the ground from about 15 feet. The reason why the tow rope was not jettisoned is not explained, other than to say the briefing would need to be improved. It must be commented that one of the vital actions briefed and taught to glider pilots is that after a cable break (for a winched launch) or any disconnection not initiated by the glider pilot during an aero tow, the cable release mechanism should be activated vigorously to make sure any cable or tow rope has been discarded.

10-Mar-44 FD848 Dakota III   267 Sqn   Bari Italy   0

The aircraft swung on take-off, and although the pilot throttled back, it left the runway and collided with a Fairchild aircraft before running into trees.

10-Mar-44 FD880 Dakota III   194 Sqn   Chandina Bengal   0

An engine suffered a severe internal detonation whilst this aircraft was taking-off and at 100 feet the engine failed completely. The pilot then encountered very considerable loss of visibility as he attempted an asymmetric landing because of all the dust blown up by other aircraft. The aircraft touched down late, overshot the runway and was damaged badly.

11-Mar-44 FL539 Dakota III   194 Sqn   94 degrees 48 East/24 degrees 18 North   0

The crew was tasked to fly to Tamu landing ground to pick up 15 passengers but the pilot mistook his destination for this airstrip, which was short and very obviously unsuitable for larger aircraft. The aircraft overshot the landing area, struck a bund about 30 yards beyond the end and tipped onto its nose.

Date	Serial	Aircraft	Unit	Place	Casualties
		Brief Circumstances of Accident Casualty Details (If Applicable)			
11-Mar-44	LH270	Horsa	1 HGMU	Leicester Forest East	0

There was some considerable confusion during a mass landing practice and many gliders were landing downwind. The tug pilot brought this glider into the wrong runway and it overshot the landing.

| 11-Mar-44 | LH524 | Horsa | 1 HGMU | Hurn, Hants | 0 |

The aircraft was stopped after its landing run and was struck by Horsas LH573 and DP801 in turn.

| 12-Mar-44 | V1604 | Albemarle | 42 OTU | Bradley Pastures Farm, Ashbourne | 5 |

The aircraft was returning to base after a 3½ hour night cross country exercise. The pilot called for assistance but did not acknowledge the response and subsequently asked for floodlights. However, almost immediately the aircraft crashed at high speed and with the flaps and undercarriage raised. Although the weather was poor and deteriorating, it was considered that the pilot was unsuitable for the role for which he was being trained and that it was most probable that his instrument flying was inadequate and led to loss of control.

Flying Officer James Duncan MacTavish BAILLIE Pilot
Flying Officer Willebrodus Maria Antoine VAN LEEMPUTTEN Navigator
Sergeant Norman WHITE Wireless Operator
Flight Sergeant Basil Herbert SYMES Air Gunner
Sergeant James Robertson GRAHAM Air Gunner

| 13-Mar-44 | FH229 | Hudson IIIA | 353 Sqn | Yelahanka | 0 |

The aircraft swung on landing at the end of a sortie and its undercarriage collapsed.

240

13-Mar-44 V1711 Albemarle 295 Sqn 2 miles north-west of St Catherines 0

The aircraft was flying through cloud when it struck a hill at an altitude of 800 feet, whilst the altimeter was registering 1050 feet. The pilot had failed to reset the altimeter after leaving the target area and made too small an allowance for the change in barometric pressure. There can be little doubt that the crew was extremely fortunate to survive flying into high ground.

14-Mar-44 EB399 Whitley V ORTU East Ilsley 4

The crew was engaged in a glider towing sortie on a dark night in poor weather. Almost immediately after take-off and as the aircraft passed 500 feet, it dived into the ground, killing four of the five crew. It is thought that the pilot might have been too slow in changing from visual to instrument flying or that he lost control looking back at the airfield lights. There was criticism of the decision to send so inexperienced a crew on a sortie in such poor weather. The crew of the glider was able to cast off the tow and make a safe landing in a field.

    Flight Sergeant Colin Arthur BRADFORD 21 RAAF Pilot
    Sergeant Alan Clarence EDWARDS 19
    Sergeant David Hugh KERR 22
    Flight Sergeant Harold KILDUFF 23

15-Mar-44 AM949 Hudson 357 Sqn 85 miles north-east of Lashua Burma 5

The aircraft was engaged in a 'Buffin' sortie dropping supplies to clandestine forces operating in the Burma-Siam border area in position 23 degrees 44 North/98 degrees 48 East. An engine had been giving trouble during the dropping and after 4 containers had been released on the DZ, it burst into flames and the aircraft subsequently, struck a tree, cartwheeled and crashed into a hillside, at about 0300 hours and in extremely poor weather conditions. Four crew were killed instantly and two were injured critically but Flight Lieutenant Ponsford was able to pull the navigator; Flying Officer W Prosser, from the wreckage and guard him until help arrived. The initial Force 136 team who reached the scene radioed for immediate help

Date	Serial	Aircraft	Unit	Place	Casualties

Brief Circumstances of Accident
Casualty Details (If Applicable)

but Ponsford died of his injuries a few hours later, leaving Prosser as the sole survivor. At base, no parachute trained doctor could be found but the newly appointed squadron MO; Flight Lieutenant George Graham MBE, volunteered to parachute into the jungle, despite never having jumped before. Flight Sergeant Thomas White, a parachute jumping instructor attached to the squadron, then offered to help Graham and the pair set out for the crash site. Their aircraft left Chittagong at 0315 hours the following morning and the load included two containers of medical supplies. On arrival at the crash site, which was 5500 feet up a mountain, the DZ was covered in fog and White helped Graham by showing him how to steer the parachute. Having reached the surviving casualty, it was then necessary to treat him and evacuate him overland and through enemy controlled territory, a journey that took a total of 33 days to complete. Flying Officer Prosser spent many months in hospital before recovering and Graham received a DSO, whilst White was awarded the CGM (Flying) for their exceptional efforts. Flight Lieutenant Graham was a leading light in the establishment of mountain rescue teams, for which he received the MBE.

Flight Lieutenant Richard Blake PALMER RCAF Pilot
Flight Lieutenant James Cecil Spencer PONSFORD 44 Co-Pilot
Flight Lieutenant Lorne PATTERSON 32 RCAF Wireless Operator
Pilot Officer Bruce Adam OGILVIE RCAF 2nd Wireless Operator
Flight Sergeant Joseph WILKINSON 25 Despatcher

Date	Serial	Aircraft	Unit	Place	Casualties
15-Mar-44	BB337	Halifax	148 Sqn	Brindisi	0

The aircraft swung on take-off and crashed.

Date	Serial	Aircraft	Unit	Place	Casualties
15-Mar-44	LH383	Horsa	1 HGMU	RAF Tarrant Rushton	0

The tow rope came away from the tug aircraft and the glider pilot then released it from the glider. A forced landing was carried out in difficult circumstances, in order to avoid various obstructions.

242

15-Mar-44   HH591 Hotspur II   3 GTS   Stoke Orchard   0
The glider was struck by Master DL433, which was taking off. The glider had previously landed and was waiting to be towed back to the towline by a tractor.

15-Mar-44   DL433   Master II   3 GTS   Stoke Orchard   0
This aircraft struck a glider whilst taking off and was then forced landed in a field beyond the airstrip.

16-Mar-44   DK198 Halifax V   644 Sqn   RAF Tarrant Rushton   0
At the end of a 5 hour cross country sortie, the aircraft was flown back to its base. All attempts to lower the undercarriage failed and eventually the aircraft was belly landed on the airfield without injury to its crew.

16-Mar-44   LJ834   Stirling IV   196 Sqn   RAF Tarrant Rushton   0
The aircraft's undercarriage collapsed on landing after the pilot initiated a swing to avoid the boundary fence. The accident was judged to be the pilot's fault and he was deemed unsuitable for the type and was posted off the squadron.

18-Mar-44   LA832   Whitley V   81 OTU   Staverton, Gloucester   0
Whilst about 55 minutes into a day cross country sortie, the aircraft's starboard engine failed because the 'B' block camshaft sheared. The pilot was unable to maintain the aircraft's height and elected to make a wheels up landing on the airfield.

20-Mar-44   HH925 Hamilcar   1 HGMU   RAF Tarrant Rushton   0
The crew was carrying out local night flying practice but the glider was cast off too far from the airfield and the pilot undershot the approach and crashed into a hedge.

243

Date	Serial	Aircraft	Unit	Place	Casualties
Brief Circumstances of Accident					
Casualty Details (If Applicable)					

20-Mar-44 HG851 Horsa   1 HGMU   Marnhull, Dorset   0

A forced landing was made after the tow rope broke.

20-Mar-44 LH171 Horsa   1 HGMU   In the sea off Bournemouth   2

The tug took avoiding action to stay clear of another aircraft but the glider pilot could not keep his glider clear of the slipstream and the tow rope broke. A ditching was made in the sea off Bournemouth and two of the five men on board did not survive.

21-Mar-44 FD910 Dakota III   62 Sqn   Chandina Bengal   0

Prior to starting the take-off, the pilot did not lock the tailwheel and it caused a swing port, then starboard and finally to port, with the pilot attempting to correct each swing in turn. Eventually, the aircraft ground looped and its starboard undercarriage collapsed. In mitigation, it was observed that the pilot was taking off in a dust storm raised by aircraft in front and he did not realise the extent of the swings.

21-Mar-44 KG366 Dakota   512 Sqn   Model Farm North End Watlington   5

The crew was taking part in a general flying exercise, involving a sortie to Doncaster and return to base after a night stop. The aircraft was being flown in poor visibility and below its safety height because the pilot was uncertain of his correct position. The aircraft struck high ground at 750 feet in an area with a cloud base of 600 feet. It crashed and was destroyed by fire.

　　　　Flight Lieutenant Robert Henry James MOUNTFORD 32 Pilot
　　　　Flying Officer John Creighton BECK 23 Wireless Operator (died 22 Mar 44)
　　　　Flying Officer Clarence Edward ROBERTSON 30 Air Gunner
　　　　Flying Officer Colin LEVINGS 32 RAAF

244

Flying Officer James Garnet FALLOON 26 RCAF

23-Mar-44 LT191 Anson 28 SAAF Rio de Oro, Spanish Sahara 0

The crew were engaged on a transport sortie and there were seven people on board. En route, bad weather was encountered with a sandstorm and bad visibility. However, the pilot elected to continue the sortie rather than return or land. With only weak radio reception and no other cues, the crew became lost and when fuel ran low a forced landing was made in Spanish territory.

24-Mar-44 LA774 Whitley V HGCU Near Empingham Rutlandshire 0

Whilst engaged in a night flying test, the aircraft's starboard engine was feathered at a height of 3500 feet. Subsequently, it could not be unfeathered and the aircraft started to lose height. An approach was made to land but the runway was obstructed and the pilot could not reposition for another runway nor did he land on the grass to the side of the runway which was obstructed. With the drag from the undercarriage that had been pumped down and could not be raised, the pilot elected to force land and this he did without injury to himself or the other occupant.

25-Mar-44 FD850 Dakota III 267 Sqn Map Ref Napoli 913299 8

The aircraft took off from Bari and were en-route to Trigno near Vasto but on arrival a flare was fired to indicate the airfield was unserviceable. On heading away from the airfield, the aircraft encountered very severe winds and snow storms and about 24 miles west of Foggia, the aircraft struck the summit of a 3000 feet high mountain at the map reference indicated.

Flying Officer David William McEwan WOOD 20 Pilot
Pilot Officer Lester Cameron GRAHAM 22 RCAF Co-Pilot
Flight Lieutenant James Gabriel KNIGHT 26 RNZAF Navigator
Flight Sergeant Harry William Owem PIGRAM 23 Wireless Operator
+ four non-RAF

245

Date	Serial	Aircraft	Unit	Place	Casualties
				Brief Circumstances of Accident Casualty Details (If Applicable)	

25-Mar-44 FL511 Dakota III   194 Sqn   Imphal Assam   0

The aircraft had swung on landing and had then bogged down in soft sand but was undamaged, although it was in such a position as to cause a hazard to aircraft using the runway. Inevitably, before it could be towed clear, a USAAF C47 ran into it, causing serious damage.

25-Mar-44 FL641 Dakota III   271 Sqn   1½ miles west south west of Blunsdon   6

During a formation flying sortie and after being airborne for 1 ¼ hours, this aircraft which was flying in the No: 2 position at about 700 feet, collided with the leader, flying Dakota FZ592. This aircraft crashed out of control with the loss of all on board. The other aircraft was landed safely

    Flight Sergeant John Hargreaves SANDERSON 21 Pilot
    Flight Sergeant Frank Attenborough SHAKESPEARE 34
    Aircraftman 2nd Class James Edward MARKEY 18
    Flight Sergeant George Thomas FENNELL 26 Navigator
    Aircraftman 2nd Class John WINDER 19
    Leading Aircraftman Harry Alfred STONE 33

25-Mar-44 LH202 Horsa   1 HGMU   Poole Harbour   0

The tow rope broke after the glider got into the tug's slipstream. The aircraft ditched in the sea but the twelve men on board survived. It was commented that glider pilots should be supplied with waterproof torches and that passengers be issued with Mae Wests when flying over water.

26-Mar-44 LJ814 Stirling IV   299 Sqn   RAF Brize Norton   1

The aircraft had the starboard outer engine fail on take-off and the pilot feathered it but the airscrew

246

subsequently unfeathered itself and caused the aircraft to sink and strike the ground. The pilot was not strapped in and sustained fatal injuries.

Flight Lieutenant Duncan James CAMERON 21 RCAF Pilot

26-Mar-44   LH330   Horsa   1 HGMU   RAF Brize Norton   0

The aircraft was parked and a very cartridge, fired by the airfield controller, landed on the glider which promptly caught fire!

27-Mar-44   FZ590   Dakota   117 Sqn   6

The aircraft was lost whilst its crew was undertaking a supply dropping sortie in the vicinity of the 'White City' airstrip, in direct support of the Chindit operation. The aircraft apparently failed to clear the high ground beyond and to the north of the DZ and it crashed and burnt.

    Pilot Officer Albert Jack LUSTED 28
    Flying Officer Francis Arthur PFEFFER RCAF Pilot
    Flight Sergeant Albert CLARKE
    Flight Sergeant Eric MCLOUGHLIN
    Pilot Officer Charles Lennox O'NEIL RCAF
    + one non-RAF

28-Mar-44   FK767   Hudson   161 Sqn   Arsley Bedfordshire   4

The crew was engaged on a local night training sortie to include low level parachute dropping. Having been airborne for about 90 minutes, the aircraft was approaching RAF Henlow but the pilot missed his first approach because he was unable to pick out the flarepath lights. An overshoot was initiated and the aircraft climbed away to about 400 feet and the pilot made a steep turn to port to commence a crosswind leg. Unfortunately, the aircraft stalled off the turn and dived into the ground, with the loss of the entire crew.

Flying Officer Robert Leonard BAUGHAN 21 Pilot

Date	Serial	Aircraft	Unit	Place	Casualties

Brief Circumstances of Accident
Casualty Details (If Applicable)

Flying Officer Norman BROCKLEHURST 22 Navigator
Flight Sergeant Eric Clive BREWER 23 RNZAF
Warrant Officer II David Stuart GILLANDER 35 RCAF Wireless Operator

28-Mar-44	LJ839	Stirling IV	196 Sqn	RAF Marham	0

The aircraft had been flown to RAF Marham to collect a glider. However, on landing the pilot found himself dazzled by the sun and he allowed the aircraft to overshoot and strike the end of a hangar.

28-Mar-44	LJ312	Horsa	1 HGMU	Near RAF Harwell	0

The crew had been flying a short night cross country sortie and were returning to base. The pilot, who had misunderstood the pre-flight briefing regarding distances between the perimeter track and the drem lighting, pulled off the tow too soon and undershot the airfield, landing in a field outside.

30-Mar-44	P1385	Albemarle I	295 Sqn	RAF Harwell	0

The aircraft was landing without brakes and was advised by Flying Control to swing to starboard to avoid any risk of colliding with other aircraft. In doing so, the aircraft ran into a ditch and its undercarriage collapsed.

30-Mar-44	P1463	Albemarle	42 OTU	Wigber Low, Bradbourne, Near Ashbourne	4

The aircraft was operating on a dual night sortie of circuits and landings and was being operated by an instructor pilot, two trainee pilots and a wireless operator. Almost immediately after take-off the aircraft failed to gain sufficient height to clear some high tension cables which were only 200 feet above the airfield altitude and flew through these before crashing and exploding in flames. From the flight path of the aircraft, it is apparent that the crew had initiated a turn back to the airfield during which the cables were hit. The Board of Enquiry considered the possibility that the flaps had been raised at too low a speed, leaving the aircraft semi-stalled condition or that the aircraft or engines had been affected by icing. The possibility of a loss of engine power was not considered and given the Albemarle's known poor performance on a single engine, this is surprising.

Pilot Officer Douglas Reginald REVITT Pilot
Flying Officer Eric Matthew Montagu O'CONNOR RAAF Pilot
Flight Sergeant Samuel MORRISON Pilot
Sergeant George Bruce SCAMMELL Wireless Operator

31-Mar-44	LL287 Halifax	138 Sqn Near Hansweert Netherlands	5

The crew, captained by Flight Lieutenant B B Mill and including a 2nd pilot who was gaining operational experience, was engaged on OSRIC 27 but was shot down by enemy AA fire. The aircraft crashed into a river. Although Mill evaded capture, four others were made POW and three crew and a pair of Belgian agents were killed.

Flying Officer Eric FRANCIS DFC
Flight Sergeant Edwin BATES 30
Warrant Officer II Frederick ANDERSON RCAF
Lieutenant R DEPREZ Belgian Agent
Lieutenant A GIROULLE

31-Mar-44	BT841 Hotspur II	5 GTS Shobdon	0

The aircraft was struck by a Master DL482 because the latter's brakes failed and it ran into the glider.

31-Mar-44	FR576 Hadrian I	1 HGSU ?????????	0

The crew was undertaking a ferry flight but they encountered bad visibility caused by hail and snow storm. The tow was released and the glider was forced landed.

01-Apr-44   FL543   Dakota III   31 Sqn   'Aberdeen'   0

The aircraft was landing on a forward airstrip during a sortie in direct support of the Chindits. It was at night and there had been a heavy rainstorm which made the runway surface greasy. The brakes locked and the aircraft overshot the airstrip and crashed.

01-Apr-44   LL252   Halifax   138 Sqn   Vallee de Cousse ndre et Loire   2

This aircraft's crew was captained by Flying Officer F B Clarke, the author of the books 'Agents By Moonlight' and 'Peter 5'. Having failed to get any response from the two DZs, the pilot set course for home but was lured to investigate a torch light which was flashed at the aircraft. In doing so, the aircraft flew across an enemy airfield, was illuminated by a searchlight and shot down.

        Sergeant Eric MacDonald KEEP 21 Bomb Aimer
        Sergeant Ronald Granville THOMPSON 22 Wireless Operator

04-Apr-44   LJ842   Stirling IV   196 Sqn   1 miles south west of Romsey   6

The aircraft was engaged in a large glider exercise, code named Exercise DREME, which involved some 140 gliders being towed off from Keevil and carrying a large component of the 1st Air Landing Brigade. This combination descended through cloud and whilst low flying the tug aircraft struck a tree and about 15 minutes later stalled, possibly because the port outer engine had failed, and crashed. Although the weather was judged suitable for the exercise, there were some local areas of very low cloud which had not been forecast.

        Warrant Officer John Hugh LEES 28 RAAF Pilot
        Sergeant Sidney CLAYPOLE 23
        Sergeant Shayrene MEERA 19

Flight Sergeant Kenrick PAYNE 21 RAAF
Flying Officer John Robert TEECE 32
Flight Sergeant John Thomas WILKINSON 29

04-Apr-44 LG999 Horsa I   Warneford   28

This was the glider being towed by Stirling LJ842. Its occupants were two glider pilots and the members of No: 3 Platoon 'A' Company, 7th (Airborne) Battalion The King's Own Scottish Borderers. All were killed when the glider crashed following the collision with a tree mentioned above. During this exercise a total of eighteen gliders crashed but this was the only accident involving fatal injuries.

Staff Sergeant Henry JOEL The Glider Pilot Regiment Pilot
Sergeant William Geoffrey WALKER 24 Co-Pilot
Lieutenant L A EASTMAN 26 Officer Commanding 3 Platoon
Private B P BAMFORTH 20
Private William Henry BATTYE 25
Lance Corporal John Murdock DIROM 22
Corporal Robert Fowler FOLEY 24
Private George Frederick JONES 34
Private William LOVE 23
Private Joseph LUCAS 27
Corporal T MCGREGOR 28
Private William MCMILLAN 37
Private Thomas MCNAMARA
Private J MCPHERSON 21
Private William MCWHIRTER 22
Private Charles MYLES 28
Private George MOLE 18
Private John PARK 21

Lance Corporal David PROVAN
Lance Sergeant Henry James READ 27
Private Thomas Harper REID 26
Private Kenneth William SCOTT-BROWNE 23
Private Frank STAPLETON 24
Private John William STEEL 29
Lance Corporal Roy Murray STEWART 37
Private Robert Donald WELLS
Lance Corporal Horace Alex Bertram POPE 25 RAMC attached Kings Own Scottish Borderers

04-Apr-44   LH289   Horsa   1 HGMU   RAF Brize Norton   0

The tug and glider combination took off immediately after the previous combination and shortly after take-off ran through their slipstream. The glider pilot lost control and cast off the tow but then failed to use the flaps in the subsequent forced landing. The aircraft was damaged badly and both crew were injured.

04-Apr-44   DP418   Horsa   1 HGMU   East Meon, Hants   0

After nearly 2½ hours airborne on a towing exercise the combination entered thick cloud whilst flying over high ground. The glider pilot lost sight of the tug and so pulled off the tow and then attempted a forced landing. The glider first struck a hedge and then landed heavily in a field. None of the twenty two persons on board was injured and the glider; Staff Sergeant A E Coates, was commended for his handling of the situation.

06-Apr-44   BZ952   Liberator III   357 Sqn   30 miles west of Weining China   13

The crew of this aircraft and that of another from the same unit, were briefed to fly supplies of petrol to Kunming in order to sustain operations from that base during the monsoon period. The two aircraft collected their cargoes and then positioned at Chabua, where they received their briefing. As the weather was forecast to be very bad, both captains were offered the option to delay their departure until the following day but they elected to continue as planned originally. This crew took off first and was last seen by the second crew just before encountering the severe weather. The second crew later reported the extreme conditions they encountered, which included violent turbulence and wind shear and they were eventually forced to make a landing at a forward airstrip. However, this crew was not heard from again and their aircraft was eventually located by a missionary on a mountainside about 1500 feet above the surrounding countryside. The precise circumstances surrounding their loss could not be determined but it seems probable that they were overwhelmed by the weather. The other aircraft was eventually flown out of the forward airstrip, having been stripped of most of its equipment but it was found to have suffered significant structural damage.

Flight Sergeant Frederick SULLIVAN 23 Pilot
Flight Sergeant Victor Albert GRAHAM Pilot
Flight Sergeant Eric Leo Burrows VANES 22 Navigator
Sergeant James Walton RIDLEY 22 Wireless Operator
Sergeant Thomas George RUTTER Wireless Operator
Sergeant Frederick Joseph UNSWORTH 25 Flight Engineer
Flight Sergeant Richard Applegarth DUNN 24 Air Gunner
Flight Sergeant Howard Ross HUGHES 24 Air Gunner
Corporal Charles Fred DUGDALE 23
Leading Aircraftman John Alexander STEWART 24
Aircraftman 1st Class Charles Henry HUTT 21
Aircraftman 1st Class Selwyn George JONES 22
Aircraftman 2nd Class Douglas Maurice LEONARD

Date	Serial	Aircraft	Unit	Place	Casualties

Brief Circumstances of Accident
Casualty Details (If Applicable)

| 06-Apr-44 | LL228 | Halifax | 644 Sqn | FTR Southern France | 1 |

This sortie was the first flown by Flight Lieutenant R F W Cleaver and his crew. The aircraft was attacked and the crew, except Cleaver, abandoned the aircraft which the pilot crash landed without injury to himself. Unfortunately, the air gunner baled out too late and was killed, whilst several of the others evaded capture and returned to UK. Cleaver had been awarded a DSO whilst serving with 295 Sqn and subsequently the award of the DFC whilst on 644 Sqn, in part because of his actions on this occasion.

Flight Sergeant Donald John HODDINOTT 31 Air Gunner

| 07-Apr-44 | BL537 | Whitley V | HGCU | Peterborough | 0 |

The aircraft was towing a glider at a height of 400 feet when the port engine failed because of the failure of the reduction gear. The tow was released and the aircraft returned to base for a single engined landing. However, the airfield controller failed to notice the Whitley approaching and gave permission for a Martinet to land and it baulked this aircraft. The pilot attempted to land on the grass but this was wet and the brakes proved ineffective and so he was compelled to swing the aircraft to avoid going through the boundary fence but the undercarriage failed as a result.

| 07-Apr-44 | DP334 | Horsa | HGCU | Helpston, near Peterborough | 0 |

The tug's port engine failed shortly after take-off and at a height of 400 feet the glider was released. Whilst attempting a forced landing, the glider stalled in a 45 degree bank with full flaps set at an airspeed of 65 mph. It was damaged on landing in a ploughed field.

| 08-Apr-44 | K7009 | Harrow | 271 Sqn | RNAS Eglinton | 0 |

The pilot, a Polish warrant officer with nearly 2000 flying hours experience, made a landing approach which was both too high and too fast. After touchdown, the aircraft ran off the end of the runway, over the perimeter track and fell into a deep drainage ditch.

09-Apr-44   FD911 Dakota III   194 Sqn   'Aberdeen'   7

This aircraft was one of several carrying out troop transport and supplies delivery into the Chindit airstrip at Aberdeen. The pilot began his approach and switched on his wing tip lights as a signal to the ground controller that his aircraft was landing. As he did so, he noticed other navigation lights nearby and took these at first to be a 'friendly' aircraft. However, his aircraft was attacked and one engine was destroyed and the other damaged, whilst many cannon shells struck the fuselage. The approach was continued and after landing the pilot, with his aircraft still under attack, turned off the strip so as not to block it and in doing so narrowly avoided a bomb dropped by the enemy aircraft but the aircraft crashed into a tree. Although nobody was hurt in the crash, seven Ghurkha soldiers had been killed by gunfire during the attack.

09-Apr-44   JN911 Halifax   1586 Flt   Near Bari   0

The aircraft, flown by Flight Sergeant Zygmunt Wieczorek and his crew, had been sent to drop supplies to the 27th Volhynian Infantry Division of the Polish Home Army but the DZ could not be located, as it had been moved from the briefed position. The aircraft then developed engine trouble and the sortie was abandoned. Whilst attempting to make a landing at Bari, the pilot decided that the aircraft should be abandoned and all the crew baled out safely, although four were injured in doing so.

10-Apr-44   KG369 Dakota IV   512 Sqn   Chedworth Gloucestershire   4

The aircraft was being flown on a night navigation exercise and was returning to its base at Broadwell in poor weather having been airborne for about 2½ hours. The crew mistook this airfield for their base and with an altimeter set incorrectly they attempted to land off a non-standard night circuit at an airfield with a 500 foot height differential from their own. Whilst overshooting, the aircraft struck trees and crashed.

Flying Officer Thomas William BRUMWELL 29 Pilot

Pilot Officer Ronald TEED 22 Navigator (shown as 2nd pilot on Accident Card)
Sergeant John George SMITH 23 Wireless Operator
Flight Sergeant Douglas EASTELL 26 Navigator

10-Apr-44   P1398   Albemarle I   297 Sqn   RAF Broadwell   0

The aircraft was returning from a night training sortie of 3 hours duration and it broke cloud at 450 feet above ground level but with its windscreen iced up and, as was to become obvious shortly, poor brakes. The pilot joined the wrong airfield circuit – Broadwell instead of Brize Norton - and touched down too fast on an airfield with which he was not familiar and with restricted visibility from the iced up windscreen. The aircraft overshot the runway because of the faulty brakes, and fell into a 15 foot deep gully.

11-Apr-44   FL540   Dakota III   194 Sqn   Near 'Aberdeen' Strip   19

The aircraft was tasked with bringing troops into the Chindit airstrip at 'Aberdeen'. The pilot overshot the first approach to land but the aircraft failed to clear high ground beyond the strip and it crashed and was destroyed. The tally of casualties varies between several information sources but it seems that in addition to the RAF crew of three, sixteen soldiers were killed and a further seven were injured. Although the fatal casualties were buried on the crash site, it appears that after the war the location could not be found and the RAF casualties are commemorated on the Singapore Memorial.

Flying Officer Raymond Gilmour MELLSOP 33 RNZAF Pilot
Flying Officer Neal BRIDGES RCAF Wireless Operator
Flight Lieutenant James Roland SCOTT 34 Navigator

It has proved difficult to identify positively the names of the army personnel aboard the above named aircraft and the entry in the main table suggests there were 16 army soldiers. An examination of a 'Chindit'

Roll of Honour suggests that those army personnel listed below may have been amongst the casualties but no corroborating evidence was found to confirm this

Fusilier Harry ANDREWS 23 1st Bn Lancashire Fusiliers
Fusilier George ARNOTT 29
Fusilier Leo CONWAY 21
Fusilier Gilbert DANTON 25
Fusilier Lawrence FISHER 25
Fusilier Thomas GRAHAM 34
Fusilier James OATES 20
Fusilier Frederick PRESS 32
Gunner Clifford ASHWORTH 267 Bty 69 Light Anti-Aircraft Regt Royal Artillery
Gunner William John CHAPMAN 40
Sergeant Neil DOOGAN 22
Gunner George Henry EASTELL 32
Bombardier Charles HAYES 35
Gunner James McPherson KERR 22
Gunner Frank Edwin OULD 22
Gunner Victor SCHOFIELD 22
Gunner James SCOBIE 22
Gunner Jesse SMITH 22
Gunner Alfred Harry Sidney TOMKINS 25

| 11-Apr-44 | LJ822 | Stirling | 190 Sqn | Hampreston south east of Tarrant Rushton | 6 |

On a night take off, the aircraft swung badly twice but the pilot continued the take off run and the aircraft became airborne for an SOE sortie, dropping supplies into France. Shortly afterwards the aircraft dived into the ground and exploded on impact. Although not positively determined, it seems possible that the pilot, who was inexperienced on type, might have initiated a turn at too low an airspeed and the heavily laden aircraft stalled, with flaps retracted, and spun in. This crew and the one below were the only pair lost from a total of fifty five aircraft operating from Tarrant Rushton that night.

Flight Sergeant Peter CROUDIS 24 RNZAF Pilot
Flight Sergeant Douglas John SAMPSON 24 RNZAF Navigator
Flight Sergeant Leslie Ernest ZIERSCH 20 RAAF Air Bomber
Flight Sergeant Kenneth Stanley NUNN 20 RAAF Wireless Operator
Sergeant John Willie MITCHELL 31 Flight Engineer
Flying Officer Robert Stewart HADLEY 19 RCAF Air Gunner

11-Apr-44   LJ867   Stirling   620 Sqn   50 miles south-east of Bordeaux   0

The aircraft failed to return from an SOE sortie but the squadron ORB subsequently records the aircraft as 'not missing'. The correct situation is that the crew; led by Flight Sergeant L J S Brown, flew the aircraft to make a drop of supplies near Bordeaux. Unfortunately, having been hit by enemy AA fire, the aircraft crashed and the navigator was injured fatally. The others escaped from the aircraft but three were captured and the pilot and air gunner evaded. Eventually, the air gunner was captured but Brown remained at large and was eventually repatriated, having crossed into Spain and reached Gibraltar. Brown was sent to 81 OUT, where he formed a new crew before returning to operations with the sqn. In June 1945, Brown – by now a Warrant Officer – was awarded the Military Medal in recognition of his evasion and escape to safety.

Flight Sergeant Alec David BARNETT Navigator

11-Apr-44   LK738   Halifax   161 Sqn   St Hilaire sur Risle Orne   8

The crew was engaged on a dual sortie; JOHN 98 and BREUGEL but their aircraft crashed and all, including a 2nd pilot being carried for operational experience, lost their lives.

Flight Sergeant James Edmund MCGIBBON 25 RCAF Pilot
Sergeant Ernest James FIRTH 22 RCAF Navigator
Sergeant Ernest MERSER 22 Wireless Operator
Sergeant Duncan Alfred JOHNSON Flight Engineer
Flying Officer John Rivers Herbert WILSON 23 Flight Engineer
Sergeant George Oliver PARKER 19 Air Gunner
Sergeant George Temple DOYLE 32 RCAF Air Gunner
Flying Officer Peter William BOOTH-SMITH Co-Pilot

12-Apr-44 HH965 Hamilcar 1 HGMU 2½ miles west-north-west of Fordingbridge 0
The aircraft overshot its landing area whilst flying in very bumpy conditions.

12-Apr-44 LH277 Horsa 1 HGMU Oxfordshire 2
The combination was engaged in a night training exercise and cross country. Having been airborne for about 15 minutes and whilst flying at 1300 feet, the combination entered cloud and the glider was cast off. Precisely what happened in unclear but the glider, apparently travelling at high speed, first struck a haystack and then crashed.

Staff Sergeant Bob Julius LEVY 21 Pilot The Glider Pilot Regiment
Sergeant Noble FRENCH Co-Pilot

13-Apr-44 LJ475 Stirling IV 620 Sqn Blackford Farm, Kempsford 5
The aircraft was engaged on a glider towing sortie and the tow was released rather late. The pilot then dived the aircraft towards the rope dropping area more steeply than would normally be the case. However, the pull out was delayed and the aircraft struck the ground. Only the air gunner survived and he was seriously burned.

Flight Sergeant Huia Nelson BURNS 22 RAAF
Flight Sergeant Edmund Christopher WILLARD 22

Flying Officer John Alfred AMY 26
Sergeant George Whitton LEWIS 29
Sergeant Ernest William TOOTILL 24

13-Apr-44	LG696	Horsa	512 Sqn	RAF Broadwell	0

The glider pilot pulled off the tow too soon and the glider undershot the landing. The glider's starboard wing struck the ground and the aircraft tipped onto its nose and partially overturned.

14-Apr-44	DL368	Master II	5 GTS	1 miles south-east of ??disland, Herefordshire	0

The combination was engaged in a towing exercise and the glider pilot advised the tug pilot that smoke was coming from the tug. The glider pilot cast off the tow and the tug was then climbed until the engine stopped, at which point the tug pilot baled out as the country was unsuitable for a forced landing. The engine was recovered and sent for a strip examination but the findings are not recorded.

15-Apr-44	FL569	Dakota III	62 Sqn	Mowdock	6

The aircraft crashed on a hillside after the pilot lost control at low level whilst attempting to drop supplies in very turbulent conditions

Flight Sergeant William Frederick HOUSTON Pilot
Pilot Officer Reginald FIFOOT 32
Sergeant Gordon SCULLY 22
Flight Sergeant Colin Graham SMITH
+ two non RAF, probably air despatchers

15-Apr-44   V1609   Albemarle   42 OTU   Hartford, Northwich Cheshire   4

The crew was undertaking a general training sortie but the aircraft was over 50 miles away from its intended track. The pilot was seen to be carrying out steep turns at low level over the village of Hartford and it collided with a chimney stack and crashed, killing all but one of those on board.

> Flight Sergeant Robert Philip Henry BROWN 31 RAAF Pilot
> Warrant Officer Faulkner Adrian Andrew ORMISTON 22 RAAF
> Flight Sergeant John CRICHTON 22
> Sergeant Aubrey Gerald CROWE 32

15-Apr-44   KG508   Dakota   113 Wg   8 miles east of Assei Brazil   3

The aircraft crashed in a flat spin with its wing tips missing after flying into a heavy thunderstorm. The pilot and navigator abandoned the aircraft before it crashed but their parachutes were not used.

> Sergeant Ronald Jack UDEN 21 Pilot
> Pilot Officer Gwilym Deiniel MORRIS 23 Navigator
> Sergeant William John POLING 22 RAAF Wireless Operator

17-Apr-44   FZ552   Dakota III   271 Sqn   Bitterne Farm Collingbourne Wilts   4

The crew was engaged in a night glider towing sortie but flying in cloud and poor weather, which caused the pilots some difficulty. The aircraft entered a steep diving turn from 1000 feet and it crashed and caught fire. The glider – a Horsa LG850 – was cast off by its crew and landed safely.

> Flight Sergeant Frederick Ernest MOODY 22 Pilot
> Flight Sergeant Herbert John RALPH 27 Pilot
> Warrant Officer II James Angus BROWN RCAF Navigator
> Sergeant Dennis John FAZAKARLEY 23 Wireless Operator

Date	Serial	Aircraft	Unit	Place	Casualties
Brief Circumstances of Accident					
Casualty Details (If Applicable)					

17-Apr-44 LG263 Horsa   1 HGSU   RAF Fairford   1

The combination was engaged on a night training sortie and the glider had a crew of five undertaking the flight, of whom three were RAF and two Army. The intercom between tug and glider failed not long after take-off and the tug pilot believed the glider was in distress and released the glider at the wrong place in the circuit. The glider pilot was left with a difficult situation approaching from the wrong end to a flarepath and when the glider started to drift, this was corrected by rudder instead of ailerons. In addition, the night was dark and hazy and the airfield obstruction lights were incomplete. On landing, the glider struck the control tower and the 1st pilot received fatal injuries, whilst three of the others were hurt.

Staff Sergeant William CLARKE 1st Pilot

17-Apr-44 BV247 Warwick   525 Sqn   Off RAF St Mawgan   14

The aircraft was on a routine flight to Maison Blanche Algeria, via Gibraltar and had a crew of three and eleven passengers. Shortly after take-off the aircraft collided with an enemy aircraft and crashed into Newquay Bay and all on board were killed. The passengers were; two French officers, two Polish couriers, a staff officer travelling to Cairo, an expert in Greek affairs travelling to that country, a Canadian/Hungarian en route to an SOE assignment, three SOE officers and an MI6 officer. Unfortunately, their names were not confirmed.

Flying Officer Arthur Douglas GAVEL 23 RCAF Pilot
Sergeant Michael Kingston ROWE 22 Pilot
Flying Officer Harold Calven AUSTEN 26 RCAF Wireless Operator
+ eleven others
It is believed that three of the casualties were:
Lieutenant Colonel Ivor Watkins BIRTS 34 Royal Artillery
Lieutenant Colonel Stanley CASSON 54 Intelligence Corps

Lieutenant Stephen MATE (thought to be the Canadian/Hungarian referred to above)

18-Apr-44   FZ683   Dakota III   Rock Manor Farm, Carterton   1
The aircraft was towing Horsa glider HG871 on a night training sortie but immediately after take-off the aircraft entered a steep turn and crashed. Five of the six people aboard the aircraft were injured but the pilot was killed.

   Pilot Officer Hubert Francis DELHAYE 25 RCAF Pilot

18-Apr-44   BT872   Hotspur II   5 GTS   Shobdon   0
The glider was parked when it was struck by a Master DL483, whose brakes had failed.

19-Apr-44   T9439   Hudson   161 Sqn   Gothenberg Sweden   0
The aircraft, carrying a crew of four and an aircrew cadet as a passenger, took off in the early afternoon for a training sortie over Wales, after first flying to Cornwall. The radio became unserviceable and there appears to have been some serious navigational errors because the aircraft was eventually forced to land at a Swedish airbase!

20-Apr-44   FD846   Dakota III   62 Sqn   Chandina   0
The aircraft swung on take-off and the pilot failed to correct this in time. The aircraft left the runway and its undercarriage was ripped off when it ran into a ditch.

21-Apr-44   V1739   Albemarle   296 Sqn   Southwick, near Trowbridge   1
The pilot selected the wrong fuel tanks and the both engines failed shortly after take-off. The pilot raised the undercarriage and the aircraft crashed landed, injuring four crew members but causing fatal injuries to the fifth.

   Sergeant Clifford Victor LAKE 22

263

23-Apr-44   V1610   Albemarle   42 OTU   Kirton Fen near Boston Lincolnshire   3

This aircraft was the second to take-off on a night flying detail and it departed Ashbourne at 0230 hours. The route was to be flown at 2500 feet, to give the crew experience of flying at night at relatively low level. The aircraft flew north into Yorkshire and then tracked south over Lincolnshire. The sortie was uneventful until about 0400 hours when the aircraft was struck by fire, thought to be from an Me410 night intruder of the Luftwaffe's KG51. The aircraft quickly became uncontrollable and the wireless operator and air gunner; Sergeants Davis and Thorogood were the only two who were able to escape.

    Sergeant John Edward HUTCHINSON 21 Pilot
    Sergeant Kenneth RUSBY 33 Navigator
    Sergeant Anthony Arthur WHITTOME 29 Bomb Aimer

23-Apr-44   LA648   Hamilcar   1 HGMU   200 yards short of Tarrant Rushton   0

The glider was being towed on a night exercise and had been airborne for just over 1½ hours. The pilot cast off the tow in the circuit without warning as he was concerned about the proximity of another aircraft. The unplanned landing resulted in the glider being in a far from ideal position and it struck a tree

24-Apr-44   JP224   Halifax   148 Sqn   Near Rudnik   0

This aircraft was one of nineteen (eight Polish and eleven from 148 Sqn), making various drops to partisans and Polish AK Home Army units. Although a few aircraft made reasonable drops the majority were thwarted by the weather. This aircraft, captained by Warrant Officer T Storey, suffered mechanical problems and was abandoned by its crew. Although two crew were captured and made POW, Storey and the rest of his crew evaded captaure and joined an AK unit.

24-Apr-44   DP530   Horsa   1 HGSU   Fordown, Kincardine   0

The aircraft was damaged in a storm.

24-Apr-44   LJ275   Horsa   1 HGSU   RAF Fairford   0

The pilot lost sight of the flarepath and forced landed the glider in the undershoot.

24-Apr-44   PW812   Horsa   1 HGSU   Bulkington Drove, Wiltshire   0

At 1500 feet during a night training sortie, the aircraft's co-pilot pulled off the tow. The 1st pilot took control and forced landed ina field but the glider struck a tree. The 1st pilot was critised for not preventing the 2nd pilot from pulling off but it is difficult to see how he might have prevented this, unless he had sufficient time to react.

25-Apr-44   EF269   Stirling IV   299 Sqn   Rowde Wiltshire   0

The crew was engaged in a fighter affiliation exercise and was being flown with two pilots and seven other crew. Whilst flying at 3000 feet the aircraft's wing mounted dinghy hatch came open and the dinghy came out and wrapped itself around the rudder jamming it hard to port. Despite the best efforts of the pilots the dinghy could not be dislodged and the crew abandoned the aircraft which crashed and burnt. Apparently there was a modification to prevent this happening, which comprised a doped fabric strip being glued to the edges of the hatch. In the case of this aircraft, the modification had not been embodied.

25-Apr-44   EW148   Liberator   45 Gp   Montreal   5+10

The aircraft was being ferried from Canada to Bermuda but it suffered a structural failure to the tailplan and fins, probably due to severe weather. The ten casualties outside the aircraft were civilians in a building struck by the Liberator.

    Flight Lieutenant Kazimierz BURZYNSKI Pilot
    Pilot Officer Andrzej KUZNIACKI Co-Pilot

Date	Serial	Aircraft	Unit	Place	Casualties

Brief Circumstances of Accident
Casualty Details (If Applicable)

Flight Lieutenant Adolf Jan NOWICKI Navigator
Pilot Officer James Smith WILSON RCAF Wireless Operator
Flight Sergeant Islwyn JONES Flight Engineer

25-Apr-44 FD952 Dakota III   62 Sqn   60 miles south-west Imphal   4

This aircraft and the one below were detailed to fly supplies to Sapam and both unloaded their stores and took off to return to base. However, they were intercepted and shot down by enemy fighters and were lost with their crews. Unfortunately, the records do not clearly show who was in which aircraft and apart from the pilots, all the crews are listed in this entry.

Flying Officer Charles Rae PORTER 23 RCAF Pilot
Flight Sergeant Percy James ADSHEAD 27
Pilot Officer Ian Albert EDWARDS 33
Flight Sergeant Edward Arthur James HEALEY 24
Flight Sergeant William Howard HIGGINS 24
Flight Sergeant John Charles Herbert Layle HUNTER 24
Flight Sergeant Tom RAMAGE 29

25-Apr-44 FL602 Dakota III   62 Sqn   60 miles south-west Imphal   4

Lost as summarised above.

Flight Sergeant Ernest Joseph WINTERS Pilot

25-Apr-44 KG462 Dakota III   194Sqn   Location not known   4?

This aircraft had left Agartala at 0720 hours to deliver supplies into the same general area as the pair of 62 Sqn Dakotas mentioned above. However, it did not arrive and is assumed to have been shot down by enemy fighters. The pilot was a Pole serving with the RAF, rather than the Polish forces. These three Dakotas were amongst five lost to enemy action on this day, the others being a pair of USAAF C47s. The day was rounded off by the loss of the aircraft below.

Warrant Officer Teofil GRYNKIEWICZ Pilot
Flight Sergeant John Hayden MANTLE
Warrant Officer Ronald George PILE
Warrant Officer Stephen James SHEPHERD

25-Apr-44 FL601 Dakota III   117 Sqn   'Aberdeen' Airstrip Burma   0

The crew was engaged on an operational sortie, flying in support of the 2nd Chindit operation Operation THURSDAY. The pilot approached the strip, which was strewn with obstructions and very short, too fast. To prevent an overshoot the pilot attempted to ground loop the aircraft but in doing so its undercarriage struck a ridge in the ground and was fractured. None of the crew of four or the eight passengers was injured.

25-Apr-44 LA649 Hamilcar   1 HGSU   RAF Tarrant Rushton   0

The glider struck a tree whilst landing at night.

26-Apr-44 P1592 Albemarle I   42 OTU   RAF Ashbourne   0

The crew was engaged in a night training sortie and had only been airborne a short time when the pilot noticed that the air pressure in the braking system was dropping. As he was inexperienced on type, with only 9 hours solo, he sought advice from flying control by radio but received no reply. He returned to the circuit and landed the aircraft without brakes but as it overran the runway he retracted the undercarriage to stop. Subsequent investigation revealed that the air pressure had escaped through a blown union coupling.

26-Apr-44   LA648   Hamilcar   1 HGSU   RAF Tarrant Rushton   0

The aircraft was landed fast because the flaps would not lower. In order to prevent the aircraft going over the end of the runway and down a cliff, a heavy landing and ground loop resulted in serious damage. It was subsequently stated that the flaps would not lower because of the speed of the initial approach and the glider pilot was found to have been careless and he was reduced in rank.

27-Apr-44   JN960   Halifax   624 Sqn   At sea off French coast   6

The crew was engaged on a PRETTYTOES operation over southern France but failed to return. A search operation involving a Liberator, three Halifaxes and a trio of USAAF B17s was called off after over 5 hours on task but by then the weather had deteriorated at Brindisi, from which the searchers had set out and they were diverted to Maison Blanche. Six aircraft landed safely at the diversion airfield but a B17 from the 122nd Bomb Sqn attempted to reach Blida and struck a hill near Algiers, killing all on board.

      Flight Sergeant William HOUGHTON
      Flying Officer George Joffre HUDDART
      Sergeant Eric Furlow HUDSON
      Pilot Officer Sidney Richard STEAD
      Sergeant Kenneth Norman WARD
      Sergeant David GEMMELL

27-Apr-44   PW818   Horsa   1 HGSU   Kingsteighton, Devon   0

The glider and its tug flew through the slipstream of another combination and the glider got out of position in relation to its own tug aircraft and so the glider pilot therefore cast off the tow. The aircraft was then damaged when it forced landed in a field.

28-Apr-44   LL356   Halifax   138 Sqn   Missing off the Netherlands coast   7

This crew was lost when the aircraft crashed into the sea off the Dutch coast whilst inbound for a drop in Belgium. From other reports, it seems possible that the aircraft was shot down by an enemy flak ship.

Flight Sergeant George Herbert WILLIAMSON 29 RAAF Pilot
Sergeant Herbert DOOTSON 33
Sergeant Hubert Francis BENBOW 23
Sergeant George Partridge CROAD 19
Flight Sergeant Arthur John George BARNES 22 RCAF
Sergeant Eric Raymond CLAYWORTH 25 RAAF
Sergeant James Ethelred SMYTH 21 RCAF

28-Apr-44   V1613   Albemarle   295 Sqn   Near Welford Berks   6

This aircraft and V1770 were both being flown on a container dropping and moonlight map reading exercise and they had been airborne for about 10 minutes. They were flying on a parallel courses but probably because of poor lookout, they collided and crashed.

Flying Officer Horace John MORRIS 30 Pilot
Flight Lieutenant William Glyn EVANS 25 Navigator
Sergeant Norman Henry POWELL 26 Bomb Aimer
Sergeant Edward George Arthur MARNHAM 23 Wireless Operator
Sergeant Robert Malcolm LANE 23 Air Gunner
Air Mechanic 2nd Class Stanley Richard WARNER 18 Royal Navy Passenger

28-Apr-44   V1770   Albemarle   295 Sqn   Near Welford Berks   5

Destroyed as summarised above.

Flying Officer Philip James CRANK 22 Pilot
Flight Sergeant Walter James Thomas CROSSMAN 35 Navigator

Date	Serial	Aircraft	Unit	Place	Casualties
		Brief Circumstances of Accident			
		Casualty Details (If Applicable)			

Flying Officer Richard Bertram IDIENS 34 RCAF Bomb Aimer
Warrant Officer Edward Terence DONOVAN 23 Wireless Operator
Flight Sergeant Albert George ROWLAND 27 Air Gunner

Date	Serial	Aircraft	Unit	Place	Casualties
28-Apr-44	BB431	Halifax	148 Sqn	FTR Albania	0?

The aircraft, captained by Warrant Officer M S Bruce, failed to return from a sortie to Albania. It is believed the entire crew survived the loss and Bruce was still serving on the squadron during the Spring of 1945, as will be found later in this book.

Date	Serial	Aircraft	Unit	Place	Casualties
28-Apr-44	Z9164	Whitley V	42 OTU	3 miles north-east of Hucknall Notts	0

The aircraft had been airborne for about 2½ hours on a night training cross country sortie when because of a glycol leak the port engine failed at 1700 feet. The pilot could not maintain height on a single engine and so made a forced landing in a field, without any injury to his crew.

Date	Serial	Aircraft	Unit	Place	Casualties
28-Apr-44	LH438	Horsa	1 HGSU	7 miles south of Hungerford	2

The glider's tail unit detached, possibly because of looseness in the front part of the tail fin. The tow rope to the glider pulled out and the glider went into a spiral dive and crashed. Both occupants were killed. Subsequently, the squadron commander; Major R S Croot and Lieutenant M J Dauncey, his adjutant, conducted some test flying to determine the affect of flying a Horsa in the tug's slipstream and in an effort to restore confidence in the structural integrity of the aircraft.

Staff Sergeant Jack NEDDLEMAN 24 The Glider Pilot Regiment
Sergeant Frederick Charles BROWN The Glider Pilot Regiment

30-Apr-44 HH472 Hotspur II   3 GTS   Wanborough, Gloucestershire   0

On landing, the glider struck a ridge in the ground and bounced. The pilot, who was on his first solo, forgot the method of recovering from a bounce and the aircraft was damaged when it landed again on the ground.

30-Apr-44 BB437 Halifax   148 Sqn   Brindisi   0

The aircraft was formally 'struck off' charge following an assessment of its condition. No details were found but it could have been that the aircraft suffered severe structural damage as a consequence of enemy action, a heavy landing or even having its fuselage distorted by flying through some of the appalling weather conditions in the area.

01-May-44 FL549 Dakota III   216 Sqn   'Aberdeen' Airstrip Burma   16

The aircraft was evacuating mules and troops from a jungle airstrip, which was located deep in enemy territory. At about 200 feet immediately after take-off, the nose of the aircraft dropped and it crashed and caught fire. Although not confirmed, it is believed that the co-pilot may have mishandled the flaps and undercarriage levers and this caused the flaps to extend again after they had been raised.

    Warrant Officer Kenneth Edwin ROBINSON
    Flight Sergeant William Frank MITCHELL 27
    Sergeant, SYDNEY CROOK 22
    Warrant Officer Arthur JONES
    + twelve Army personnel whose identities have not been found

01-May-44 HG751 Horsa   HGSU   RAF Brize Norton   0

The crew was engaged in a night navigation exercise and their glider was returning to land. The wind speed had increased since the crew was briefed and they dropped the tow earlier than they should have done for conditions actually prevailing. The glider undershot the landing and was damaged when it hit an air raid shelter.

01-May-44   LG698   Horsa   HGSU   RAF Keevil   0

The combination had been airborne for about 2 hours, when it encountered adverse weather, including low cloud. The tow rope became entangled round the glider's nose wheel and the glider was then subjected to the tug's slipstream. The glider pilot released the tow and then attempted to position his aircraft in line with the flare path. Unfortunately, the glider undershot the approach and crashed into trees.

02-May-44   FL534   Dakota III   194 Sqn   Lalagaat   0

The aircraft was landing at its base at the end of a 5 hour supply dropping sortie when it struck a Buffalo just as it was about to touch down. The port undercarriage was damaged and the aircraft was belly landed at another location.

03-May-44   V9664   Lysander   161 Sqn   Modesir Airfield   1

The aircraft had landed at a field near Ouarville, about 12 miles south-east of Chartres and the pilot was waiting for his return load. However, an RAF air attack was developing nearby and the pilot elected to make an immediate departure. Unfortunately, after take off he flew his aircraft over an enemy airfield and was promptly shot down.

    Flight Lieutenant Leslie Lawrence WHITTAKER DFC

04-May-44   BB318   Halifax   148 Sqn   Brindisi   0

The aircraft, captained by Group Captain Rankin, crashed on take-off for an operational sortie. Apart from the flight engineer, who suffered leg injuries, the crew escaped unscathed.

04-May-44 FH461 Hudson IIIA   353 Sqn   Dum Dum   0

During the take-off the engines failed to deliver full power and the take-off was abandoned. The undercarriage was raised to stop the aircraft running off the end of the runway.

04-May-44 PW873 Horsa   1 HGSU   ¼ mile north of RAF Keevil   2

The glider stalled and the pilots, who were not strapped in, were thrown forward against the control column and the aircraft dived into the ground.

    Staff Sergeant Eric Herbert LOWE 23 The Glider Pilot Regiment
    Sergeant David John HUNT 23 The Glider Pilot Regiment

05-May-44 BB438 Halifax   148 Sqn   Poland   5

This aircraft was lost on a sortie to Poland and the circumstances of its loss are not known.

    Warrant Officer Eric Alfred ALDRED Pilot
    Flight Sergeant Ralph DAWES 33 Wireless Operator
    Flight Sergeant Michale Edwin AGAR Flight Engineer
    Flight Sergeant Norman Wilson JOHNSTONE Air Gunner
    Flight Sergeant Ronald Albert MENDAY Air Gunner

05-May-44 FZ599 Dakota III   194 Sqn   Broadway   9

The aircraft crashed into hills on approach to 'Broadway'. From the limited evidence it seems possible that the pilot commenced his let down before he had cleared the last ridge of hills near his destination. At the time there was a storm and is probable that the aircraft was in cloud. It is interesting to note that despite the summary above, taken from the Accident Card, another report suggests the aircraft was actually taking off, struck a wing and then struck a hillside. What is not in dispute, is that the wreckage was not discovered for a month.

    Flight Lieutenant Peter William Henry WOOD 21 Pilot

Flying Officer Clare Kenneth THAIN 23 RCAF
Sergeant Robert ROBERTS 21
+ one RAF and five Army

05-May-44 EF117 Stirling III   1665 CU   RAF Tilstock   0

The aircraft was engaged in a training sortie comprising night circuits and landings and was captained by Flight Sergeant W J Jennings RNZAF. The starboard inner engine caught fire and the pilot feathered it and raised the undercarriage before carrying out an emergency landing. After landing the other three engines caught fire and the blaze spread to the rest of the aircraft. All the crew escaped successfully and although some had minor injuries, none was hurt seriously. Jennings was commended for his coolness and initiative in getting his crew out of the aircraft and his handling of the situation.

06-May-44 LH152 Horsa   1 HGSU   1 mile south of Ecklington, Worcestershire   0

Having been airborne for 1¾ hours on a night training exercise, the combination got itself out of position viz a viz glider to tug because they passed through the turbulent slipstream of another combination. The tow was dropped and the glider made a forced landing in a field.

06-May-44 LH207 Horsa   1 HGSU   1 mile south of Spitlesbury   0

The crew was engaged in a high release training exercise which was quite difficult for a crew with their experience. Whilst in free flight, the pilots lost their position and could not land in the field they had selected and so were compelled to force land in another field, causing damage to the glider.

07-May-44 AL545 Liberator II 511 Sqn RAF Lyneham 0

The aircraft caught fire whilst being serviced inside an aircraft hangar and it was damaged beyond repair.

07-May-44 FL506 Dakota III 194 Sqn Jorhat 0

The pilot suspected that the aircraft had fuel flow problems as the fuel pressure in the port wing fuel system dropped. An emergency landing was decided upon but then the pilot was faced with low cloud at the diversion airfield. A poor approach was made but after landing the aircraft started to swing and ran off the runway and collided with a train.

07-May-44 LH558 Horsa 1 HGSU RAF Tarrant Rushton 0

The crew was taking part in a mass take-off and landing exercise, as part of the D-Day preparations. Having landed safely and come to a stop, another Horsa (DP699) ran into this aircraft.

07-May-44 RF788 Horsa 1 HGSU 2 miles from RAF Tarrant Rushton 0

The crew was engaged in a high release training exercise. This required the crew to release the tow at high level and then steer various courses for pre determined periods before setting up a landing at the selected base. This is quite a difficult exercise to fly in a glider. Unfortunately, the crew could not pinpoint the landing spot in the dark, despite there being a moon. In accordance with the procedures, the crew turned on their landing lights and this was supposed to result in the airfield control party, flashing a signal to the glider crew. Unfortunately, this aircraft's signal was not seen and so no response was made. The crew then carried out a forced landing in a field.

07-May-44 LJ331 Horsa GETR RAF Netheravon 0

This aircraft, operated by the Glider Echelon Tarrant Rushton, was part of a mass landing at Netheravon. Its crew had completed their landing successfully and the aircraft had stopped and was awaiting retrieval by the ground handling party. Unfortunately, before it could be towed away by a tractor, it was struck by

Date	Serial	Aircraft	Unit	Place	Casualties
				Brief Circumstances of Accident	
				Casualty Details (If Applicable)	

Horsa LH208.

Date	Serial	Aircraft	Unit	Place	Casualties
07-May-44	LH208	Horsa	GETR	RAF Netheravon	0

Damaged in the circumstances outlined above.

Date	Serial	Aircraft	Unit	Place	Casualties
07-May-44	PF794	Horsa	GETR	RAF Netheravon	0

Just to compound matters, as the 2 gliders listed above lay locked together, this glider ran into them. This sort of accident was accepted as a natural hazard when carrying out mass landings, particularly at night.

Date	Serial	Aircraft	Unit	Place	Casualties
08-May-44	BZ923	Liberator III	357 Sqn	1 mile west of Buwmwan railway station	3

The aircraft was returning from a long range SD sortie and it ran short of fuel and was forced landed by its pilot. Unfortunately, two crew were killed and a 3rd died of his injuries later.

Pilot Officer James Duffield SPENCER RCAF Wireless Operator
Flying Officer George Duncan VAN PATTER 23 RCAF Air Gunner (died of injuries 8 May 1944)
Flight Lieutenant William James CORBETT RAAF

Date	Serial	Aircraft	Unit	Place	Casualties
08-May-44	LJ886	Stirling IV	620 Sqn	50 miles north-west Lyon	6

This aircraft was one of ten, split equally amongst 190 and 620 Sqns, operating from Tarrant Rushton in support of SOE operations. Six of the crews were successful, three failed for various reasons and this crew was shot down at Poisson.

Flying Officer Archie Campbell SWAN 30 RAAF Pilot
Sergeant James Henry LISTER 27 Navigator

Flying Officer William Joseph TAY 29 Bomb Aimer
Sergeant Aubrey Louis Arthur ASH-SMITH 26 Flight Engineer
Sergeant Donald JONES 24 Wireless Operator
Sergeant Eric George SWALLOW 19 Air Gunner

08-May-44 LK652 Halifax V 298 Sqn RAF Tarrant Rushton 0

The aircraft had been on a glider towing exercise and after 1¼ hours it returned for a landing. The undercarriage was lowered on approach, green 'undercarriage locked' lights were obtained and confirmed by the crew. As the aircraft slowed for its landing, the undercarriage warning horn sounded and after touchdown the undercarriage collapsed.

08-May-44 LL192 Halifax 138 Sqn North Sea off north-west Danish coast 7

This crew was engaged on TABLEJAM 46, their aircraft one of a pair operating over Denmark that night. The crew completed the delivery of the twelve containers and two packages to a DZ at Sonderholm Heath, a few miles from the town of Nibe, itself just west of Albourg, and set course for UK. However, the aircraft crashed into the sea at about 0215 hours some 38 miles north of Thisted having been attacked by an enemy aircraft.

Flight Lieutenant Harcourt Hunter MCMULLAN 24 RAAF Pilot
Flying Officer Leslie Frank STANNARD 33
Sergeant Bernard STYNES 20 Wireless Operator
Sergeant Ronald BOFFEY 23
Flying Officer Kevin James MURPHY RCAF Bomb Aimer
Sergeant Angus Alexander MCPHERSON 22
Sergeant Leslie Leonard John SMITH 20

08-May-44 LL280 Halifax 138 Sqn St Denis de Orques Sarthe 7

These airmen, captained by the squadron commander, were second tourists and it would have been difficult to find a more experienced SD crew. Their aircraft was one of six from the squadron sent to France but they were shot down by a night fighter about 25 miles west of Le Mans.

Wing Commander William McFarlane RUSSELL 35 DFC & Bar Pilot
Flying Officer Donald BROWN 23 DFC Navigator
Flying Officer James Alexander ARMOUR 22 DFC DFM Wireless Operator
Flight Sergeant George CABLE 23 DFM Flight Engineer
Flying Officer Bernard Pierce MCGONAGLE 21 DFC bomb Aimer
Flying Officer Alexander Frederick BRYCE 22 Air Gunner
Flying Officer Norman SIMISTER 32 DFM Air Gunner

08-May-44   P1404   Albemarle   295 Sqn   RAF Netheravon   0

The aircraft was landing at the end of a short sortie to retrieve gliders and had touched down normally. After running for about 300 yards along the airfield the nosewheel ran over a bump in the ground, causing the undercarriage to collapse. There were injuries sustained by two crew members but the other three plus a non-RAF passenger were unhurt.

08-May-44   LJ496   Horsa   1665 HCU   500 yards north of RAF Tilstock airfield   4

The pilot was recorded as being in the habit of making dive approaches, despite this being contrary to safe practice. On this occasion he made a dive approach with the glider's left wing very low and it struck some cables and the ground, throwing the aircraft onto its back, after which it crashed about 100 yards further on. It is believed that the two RAF officers were undertaking a familiarisation flight, having been recently posted to the unit.

Staff Sergeant John Charles DYER 22 The Glider Pilot Regiment

Sergeant Gordon Dennis COE 23 The Glider Pilot Regiment
Flight Lieutenant Sidney Godfrey FALCONER 23 DFC DFM
Flight Lieutenant Alan AUSTIN 22 DFC

08-May-44 BT783 Hotspur II   3 GTS   Stoke Orchard   0

The pilot who was very inexperienced, held off too long and was distracted by other gliders at the landing point. He also did not appreciate fully the effectiveness of controls at low speed and the glider landed heavily and its back was broken.

09-May-44 KG548 Dakota III   3 ADU   Castel Benito   0

The undercarriage retracted during the take-off run and the starboard wing dropped and the aircraft then caught fire.

09-May-44 LA714 Hamilcar   23 MU   RAF Lyneham   4

The aircraft crashed after the pilot made a dive approach, in order to lose height, when attempting to land after a test flight.

  Sergeant Frederick Henry MOORE 21
  Believed to be;
  Wing Commander George Guy MEAGER 54
  Squadron Leader Frederic John POPE 44
  Flying Officer John Lindsay BENNETT 30

09-May-44 RX776 Horsa II   644 Sqn   Sudanese desert   0

The glider and tug combination, which was being used on an airborne support exercise, had been airborne for about 4 hours and was flying at 8000 feet. The engines of the Halifax tug were overheating and one eventually failed. The glider was released and a safe forced landing, without damage to the glider was made in position; 19 degrees 59 North/31 degrees 30 East. Unfortunately, having been left exposed to fierce

Date   Serial   Aircraft   Unit   Place   Casualties
Brief Circumstances of Accident
Casualty Details (If Applicable)

sun for 2 days, shrinkage took place and the glider was deemed irrecoverable.

10-May-44 LL183 Halifax 161 Sqn Rochechouart Haute-Vienne 0
This aircraft was on loan from 161 Sqn and was being operated by a 138 Sqn crew, captained by Flying Officer A S Coldridge RCAF. Their task, together with four other crews, was to drop supplies onto an area south of Limoges. For reasons not disclosed, the aircraft was abandoned on the outbound journey and although one of the crew was made POW, the others evaded. It is clear from the reports of these men that they 'enjoyed' an eventful period, some helping with the Maquis in both active and training roles before eventually returning to UK.

12-May-44 FZ582 Dakota III 194 Sqn 'Clydeside' 0
The aircraft was landing at the hastily prepared strip of 'Clydeside' which had trees on the approach, very rough ground and shell holes only partially filled. The cargo was several sacks of mail and 600 lbs of petrol. After touchdown, the aircraft's port wheel ran into a shell hole and snapped off. The aircraft crashed and immediately caught fire but the crew escaped without injury. Realising the mail sacks were still in the aircraft, the pilot; Flying Officer Joe Simpson, returned and retrieved them.

12-May-44 V1612 Albemarle 297 Sqn Windrush, Oxfordshire 0
On landing after a sortie of 1¼ hours, the pilot, navigator and bomb aimer all failed to identify the correct airfield for various reasons and the aircraft landed at small airstrip, which it overran. The undercarriage was retracted to stop. Fortunately, none of the crew was injured, except possibly their professional pride!

280

12-May-45 LH389 Horsa   N/R   RAF Keevil   0

The aircraft was landing at the conclusion of a cross country flying exercise but it crashed into trees on the approach. The pilot reported heavy bias to the starboard side but this is thought to have been due to passing through another aircraft's slipstream.

13-May-44 FD859 Dakota III   216 Sqn   Near Kohima   4

During a pass over the drop zone near Kohima, the aircraft suffered an engine failure. The aircraft crashed and although two crew members survived, the pilot and others, including an air despatcher were killed.

   Flight Lieutenant Claude Hose Hubert BIGNELL 26
      Sergeant Hugh MCHARDIE 20 Wireless Operator
      + two Army

13-May-44 HG753 Horsa   GETR   RAF Netheravon   0

This aircraft crew was engaged in what the Accident Card describes as; 'a very difficult exercise' at the end of a cross country flight. The crew was required to land in a small field with no lights to guide them in the early hours of the morning. The aircraft overshot and was damaged. The crew were in fact; Staff Sergeants Jim Wallwork and John Ainsworth who, 4 weeks later, would carry Major John Howard and his party of troops from 1st Bn Oxfordshire & Buckinghamshire Light Infantry to Pegasus Bridge at the start of the D-Day landings.

13-May-44 LH520 Horsa   1 HGSU   RAF Tarrant Rushton   1

The aircraft overshot its landing point and collided with Halifax LL334, which was properly parked and marked with hazard lights. Although the 1st pilot survived, the co-pilot received fatal injuries.

   Sergeant Ernest BLACKBURN 24 The Glider Pilot Regiment

Date	Serial	Aircraft	Unit	Place	Casualties

Brief Circumstances of Accident
Casualty Details (If Applicable)

| 14-May-44 | FD937 | Dakota III | 117 Sqn | 'Clydeside' LG Burma | 0 |

This airstrip was of very poor quality and several aircraft came to grief because of the ground surface. However, the detail of this aircraft's loss is not known.

| 15-May-44 | V1709 | Albemarle | 297 Sqn | Near RAF Brize Norton | 0 |

The aircraft had been airborne for nearly 3 hours and rejoined the circuit to land at the conclusion of an exercise. The port engine failed and could not be feathered, so the pilot attempted an overshoot but could not then safely maintain height and so he then decided on a forced landing but in doing so the aircraft struck trees and crashed into a field. The original engine failure was though to be a fuel flow restriction but the failure of the propeller feathering mechanism was made the subject of defect report and examination by the manufacturers.

| 16-May-44 | FP191 | Catalina IB | 628 Sqn | Redhills Lake | 5 |

The pilot, who was experienced on operational duties, had been undertaking an air test and compass swing and the aircraft had been airborne for nearly an hour. Although alighting in daylight and on smooth water, the pilot failed to level out sufficiently and the airplane landed heavily on the water with a high rate of descent. Its bows dug into the water and it turned over and sank. In addition to the fatal casualties, three of the crew were injured. It was commented that a failure to wear mae wests and to strap in, probably increased the number of fatal casualties.

Flight Lieutenant Robert Brander LEVACK 22 Pilot
Flying Officer Keith Bertram LEAVER 21 Co-Pilot
Flying Officer Frederick WALSH 28 Navigator
Flight Sergeant Thomas MURRAY 22

282

Flight Sergeant Claude Frederick GARDINER 23 Air Gunner

17-May-44   LK736   Halifax   138 Sqn   Great Barford Bedfordshire   1

The pilot, who had barely 5 hours solo on type and had not completed a formal conversion course to type, was engaged with his crew on circuit training and three-engined flying. Having taken off normally, the pilot feathered the starboard inner engine but closed the fuel cocks for the starboard outer engine. Shortly afterwards, the starboard outer engine failed through fuel starvation and the pilot managed to restart the starboard inner and regain some control before making a crashed landing in a field, whereupon the aircraft caught fire and was destroyed. Besides commenting about the pilot's training – or lack thereof – it was noted that he had not observed the rule that practice asymmetric flying should not be undertaken below 3000 feet and it transpired that this order did not appear in the Conversion Unit Order Book. The pilot, who was serving in the RNZAF at the time, was subsequently decorated with both the DFC and a first Bar. He was killed in April 1950 when a Vampire he was collecting from Istres, broke up in mid air.

Flying Officer Victor Charles CARTER 24 Bomb Aimer

18-May-44   DM322   Master II   5 GTS   1 mile west of Staunton on Arrow   0

The aircraft had been engaged in glider towing in the local area of its base at Shobdon for about 15 minutes when the engine failed. The pilot crash landed the aircraft but was injured in doing so. The engine was sent for a strip examination but the fault is not recorded.

19-May-44   EF244   Stirling IV   620 Sqn   1 mile west-south-west of Kempsford   6

At the conclusion of a glider towing exercise, involving a large formation converging on Netheravon, the crew of this aircraft based at RAF Fairford flew back to an area near their station on which the crews were to drop the tow ropes. This aircraft had broken away from the formation but then attempted to rejoin by flying into the dropping area on a different track to that briefed. The crew failed to keep a good lookout and the aircraft flew into another from the same squadron. Both aircraft crashed from about 400 feet after breaking up.

Date	Serial	Aircraft	Unit	Place	Casualties

Brief Circumstances of Accident
Casualty Details (If Applicable)

Flight Sergeant Arthur Bruce HAYNES 20 RAAF Pilot
Sergeant Robert Max COTTERELL 23
Sergeant Albert Thomas FRANKS 24
Sergeant Garmon Peter JONES 22
Flight Sergeant Gwilym POWELL 21
Sergeant James Walter TAYLOR 19

| 19-May-44 | LJ880 | Stirling IV | 620 Sqn | 1 mile west-south-west of Kempsford | 6 |

Aircraft destroyed as outlined above.

Flight Lieutenant Richard Owen FRANCIS 20 RCAF Pilot
Flying Officer Keith Alexander HILLS 25 RCAF
Flying Officer Llewellyn Quinlan JENKINS 23
Sergeant Norman Harry FLACK 19
Flight Sergeant Richard KENNEDY 21
Flight Sergeant Anthony Edmund HILL 22

| 20-May-44 | BD503 | Whitley V | HGCU | RAF Down Ampney | 0 |

The aircraft was engaged in ferrying a Horsa glider to another base and after barely 30 minutes airborne, its starboard engine failed and caught fire. The glider was released and made a safe landing and the pilot of this aircraft then landed wheels up on the airfield and close to the fire tender. A subsequent examination of the engine showed that the big end bolts in the pistons of three cylinders had failed. The pilot was commended for his handling of the emergency and then criticised for not turning off the fuel supply to the failed engine!

20-May-44   FD948   Dakota III   194 Sqn   Agartala   0

The crew was detailed to undertake an air test on this aircraft but during the take off it veered to starboard, ran off the runway and its starboard undercarriage collapsed as it ran into a ditch. The pilot was at fault because of poor cockpit drills and his failure to check the rudder and aileron trim, both of which were set fully to starboard. The pilot, who had over 1000 flying hours, was killed shortly afterwards with his crew during a supply dropping sortie.

23-May-44   DG286   Halifax   138 Sqn   RAF Tempsford   0

The aircraft was being used for crew training but whilst taking off, the port main tyre burst and the aircraft swung off the runway, at which point the undercarriage collapsed and the aircraft was damaged severely. There were no injuries amongst the crew, although they were lost 7 weeks later on operations.

24-May-44   FL576   Dakota III   31 Sqn   38 miles east north east of Imphal   5

The aircraft was one of three Dakotas undertaking the third sortie of the day, carrying supplies between Agatala and Sylhet, where they dropped them near the Irrawaddy river. The crew is known to have delivered its supplies but failed to return. The wreckage of the aircraft was found many months later by an Army patrol and the remains of three crew were buried at the site but were not recovered after the war and all are commemorated on the Singapore Memorial.

Sergeant David Frank Boyce BELL 31
Flight Sergeant Alan Michael CAREW-GIBBS
Sergeant Edwin Maurice JOHN
Sergeant Gerald Patrick O'CONNOR
Warrant Officer George Heptinstall SHEARER 25 RNZAF Wireless Operator

24-May-44   HH972   Hamilcar   1 HGSU   RAF Tarrant Rushton   0

The glider undershot its landing and struck an obstruction, which damaged the undercarriage badly.

Date	Serial	Aircraft	Unit	Place	Casualties
Brief Circumstances of Accident					
Casualty Details (If Applicable)					

24-May-44   LG770   Horsa   271 Sqn   RAF Down Ampney   0

The crew was engaged in a mass landing exercise and theirs was the last glider to land. In consequence, the airfield was full of other gliders, scattered at random. The pilot was compelled to land as near to the boundary as possible but in doing so, he undershot and his glider was damaged.

26-May-44   FL574   Dakota III   31 Sqn   North of Kumbhirgram   9

This aircraft was one of five detailed for a supply dropping sortie and it took off at about 1500 hours. It crashed into a hill in the area indicated (2½ miles north west of Silchar) but the cause is not known, although other crews had reported ground fire including the use of mortars, on previous occasions. The Accident Card suggests that the aircraft's load had not been secured and this might have shifted in the severe monsoon turbulence and caused a loss of control. After the crash a hurricane lamp ignited some petrol fumes and the aircraft caught fire.

    Flight Sergeant Roy Newton HILL 22 Pilot
    Warrant Officer Reginald JAMIESON 23 Navigator
    Flight Sergeant Gomer Glyndwr REES 23 Wireless Operator
    Warrant Officer George COWDREY 24 Wireless Operator
    Flight Sergeant Gordon Frederick REMNANT 21 Navigator
    Sergeant Wilfred WALKER 20 Air Gunner
    + three non-RAF

27-May-44   LL346   Halifax III   644 Sqn   1 mile west of RAF Tarrant Rushton   3

The aircraft was taking off at night with a Hamilcar glider on tow but it did not climb away as expected and when the pilot realised the situation and began to climb the aircraft, it then stalled and crashed into trees which were below the level of the runway. The accident was deemed to have been surviveable but none of the crew of five was strapped in.

Warrant Officer Arthur Lawrence WOOD 22 RCAF Pilot
Pilot Officer Waldemar Frederik WOLF 19 RCAF
Pilot Officer Thomas Murray STEWART 23 RCAF

27-May-44   V1702   Albemarle   570 Sqn   USAAF Grove, Berkshire   0
The aircraft was taking part in a glider towing exercise and immediately after take-off the engines lost power and the aircraft would not climb. The pilot released the glider and then attempted to land at a USAAF base but could not reach it and so forced landed short. The loss of power was traced to several defective spark plugs.

28-May-45   EF121   Stirling III   1665 CU   RAF Tilstock   0
The aircraft's undercarriage collapsed after a swing developed on landing.

29-May-44   LL300   Halifax   161 Sqn   RAF Tempsford   0
This aircraft was written off as a consequence of damage caused when it caught fire during maintenance.

29-May-44   V1817   Albemarle   297 Sqn   France (location not stated)   1
This aircraft was one of a mixed force of eight Albemarles, five Stirlings and a brace of Halifaxes sent to drop supplies in France. Although most sorties were successful, this aircraft did not return and its pilot was killed although the other crew survived.

Flight Lieutenant Ian George Gore HART 23 Pilot

30-May-44   FH417   Hudson IIIA   353 Sqn   Palam   0
The aircraft's starboard engine failed on take-off because the engine driven fuel pump drive shaft sheared. The aircraft's height and speed made it impossible for the pilot to retain control at so critical a stage and the

Date   Serial   Aircraft   Unit   Place   Casualties
Brief Circumstances of Accident
Casualty Details (If Applicable)

aircraft crashed on the airfield and burst into flames.   Although there were no fatalities, four of the eight occupants were injured.

31-May-44 KG517 Dakota III   62 Sqn   Imphal   0
The aircraft swung to starboard on landing at the end of a supply dropping sortie and headed towards a row of parked Spitfires.   The pilot applied port rudder and starboard throttle but this induced a severe swing to port and the undercarriage collapsed.   The Accident Card contains the ominous comment 'pilot being watched'!

31-May-44 V9155 Hudson   161 Sqn   Near Gilze-Rijen Netherlands   6
The aircraft was flying a mission to Holland to drop two agents but it strayed too close to the enemy airfield at Gilze-Rijen and was shot down.   The four crew and the pair agents were killed.

Flight Lieutenant Warren Macauley HALE 24 RCAF Pilot
Flying Officer John GALL 20 DFC RNZAF
Flying Officer Arthur George MASKALL 33 DFM Wireless Operator
Flying Officer Michael Henry HUGHES Air Gunner
2nd Lieutenant C M DEKKERS – Dutch Agent
2nd Lieutenant J KUENEN

31-May-44 JD172 Halifax   148 Sqn   Poland   7
This aircraft was flown by one of four crews detailed for a sortie to Poland, whilst ten other aircraft from the unit mounted operations to Yugoslavia.   This crew failed to return but another crew reported seeing air to air firing in the vicinity of the DZ and it is assumed the aircraft was shot down by a night fighter.

Flight Sergeant Thomas Johnson MAKEPEACE 21 RCAF Pilot
Warrant Officer II John Stewart MCWILLIAMS 31 RCAF Navigator
Flight Sergeant James Henry ROBSON 26 Bomb Aimer
Sergeant William Wycliffe BRIGHT 21 Wireless Operator
Sergeant Ronald Charles James CHESSMAN Flight Engineer
Sergeant George Francis HANCOX 28 Air Gunner
Sergeant George Henry HALL 19 Air Gunner

31-May-44	PF804	Horsa	1 HGSU	5 miles north of Wimborne????	0

The aircraft was forced landed after the tug crew released the glider in the wrong place.

01-Jun-44	LL276	Halifax	138 Sqn	Halsteren The Netherlands	5

The crew was engaged on sortie OSRIC 74 but the aircraft was attacked by enemy night fighter. There were three survivors who were captured but the others were killed, including Flying Officer Solomon a supernumerary navigator.

Warrant Officer Henry Francis Graham MURRAY 23 Pilot
Sergeant Thomas MCCLUSKY 29 Flight Engineer
Sergeant Alexander Peter CLIFF-MCCULLOCK 28 Air Gunner
Sergeant Roy ROBINSON 20
Flying Officer Leonard John SOLOMON Navigator

01-Jun-44	LL419	Halifax	138 Sqn	Tholen-Lepelstraat, Netherlands	8

This crew was engaged in sortie OSRIC 78 to Holland but their aircraft was intercepted and shot down by a German night fighter: there were no survivors.

Flying Officer Joseph Patrick GALLAGHER 29 RCAF Pilot
Flying Officer Thomas CARNEGIE 21 RCAF Navigator
Sergeant Wilbur Joseph JEFFREY 28 RCAF Wireless Operator/Air Gunner

Sergeant Cyril JONES 24
Flying Officer John ZYWINA 24 RCAF Bomb Aimer
Flying Officer Herbert John Patrick BRENNAN 20 RCAF Navigator
Pilot Officer Herbert BARKER 32 RCAF Wireless Operator/Air Gunner
Flying Officer Gordon William HEMSLEY 23

Date	Serial	Aircraft	Unit	Place	Casualties
01-Jun-44	FZ563	Dakota III	117 Sqn	FTR	4

The aircraft was being used for a supply dropping sortie and it appears that it was crewed by a mix of personnel from the owning unit and also 215 Sqn, who had provided a number of crews to reinforce 117 Sqn. The cause of the loss is not known.

Pilot Officer Clare Pymer MCWILLIAMS 23 RCAF Wireless Operator/Air Gunner
Flying Officer Harold Gordon TACKABERRY RCAF
Flight Sergeant Dennis Robert JONES
Flight Sergeant Ernest SQUIRE

Date	Serial	Aircraft	Unit	Place	Casualties
02-Jun-44	LL284	Halifax	138 Sqn	Sandy Bedfordshire	0

The aircraft took off on sortie TYBALT 29 to a DZ in Belgium. Immediately after take-off and at a height of 100 feet, the port inner engine failed, whilst the port outer suffered a drop in power. At this stage of flight and whilst the aircraft was fully laden, the pilot; Flight Lieutenant Hugh Stiles, was left with no options but to crash land the aircraft and this he did on a hillside covered in young trees not far from the airfield. The aircraft broke into several pieces and caught fire, seriously injuring four of the crew. This was Stiles final sortie of his second operational tour and in Aug 44 he was awarded a bar to the DFC.

02-Jun-44   LL289   Halifax   138 Sqn   Longue-Jumelles Maine et Loire   5

This crew was one of three sent to PERCY 7 but it crashed in flames about 8 miles north-north-west of Saumur. There were two survivors; Pilot Officer G G Houston and Sergeant A Lyall but the others were killed.

Pilot Officer Douglas Anthony HAYMAN 24 RAAF Pilot
Flying Officer Dennis Dennis HARGREAVES 22 Navigator
Flight Sergeant Alfred Henry DICKEL 22 Wireless Operator
Sergeant Dennis Arthur PAGE
Pilot Officer John Charles FARNDON 25 RAAF

03-Jun-44   FD866   Dakota III   216 Sqn   34 degrees 44North/01 degrees 07 West   16

The aircraft was being flown on a routine courier sortie but after being airborne for 2½ hours it was some distance off track. It was climbing through cloud when it struck the side of a mountain at a height of 5200 feet. The Board of Enquiry commented that the radio aids were not used to assist navigation but that the pilot, who had flown over 100 hours in the previous month, was probably fatigued.

Flying Officer Harold Kent THOMPSON Pilot
Lieutenant Denis Oswald BILSE 21 SAAF Co-Pilot
Captain Philip COHEN 30 SA Medical Corps
Captain John Arthur FORKNALL 23
Lieutenant Colonel Cullis William GAV RE
Pilot Officer Clifford James HIGGINS
Warrant Officer Thomas Atherton HINDMARSH 33 Navigator
Flight Sergeant Ralph John HODGSON 22
Flight Sergeant Francis Vincent MCFARLANE 21
Flight Sergeant Thomas William SPARK 31
Flying Officer Wesley John WHITE 28

291

Date	Serial	Aircraft	Unit	Place	Casualties

Brief Circumstances of Accident
Casualty Details (If Applicable)

Warrant Officer I Frederick Henry Theodore WHITTARD 21 RCAF
Flying Officer John St Clair WOOTTON RCAF
+ three others

03-Jun-44   LA770   Whitley V   81 OTU   Belton Farm Myddle Shropshire   1

The aircraft was being used for the crew to practice asymmetric approaches and overshoots. The Accident Card is not particularly well written and it implies that the aircraft had made a single engined approach with the starboard engine feathered but on the climb out and at 200 feet, the port engine failed and the aircraft gradually lost height until its tail plane struck a tree. However, the summary then goes on to record a criticism of the pilot for not being able to maintain height on one engine, although it accepts that he was relatively inexperienced on type. This, therefore, suggests that the starboard engine had actually been restarted before the overshoot was commenced or otherwise the aircraft would have had no power at all.

   One RAF crew

03-Jun-44   LL307   Halifax   138 Sqn   Stavenisse, Isle of Tholen The Netherlands   9

The crew was engaged in twin sorties; RODERIGO 1 and OSRIC 77 and their load included three Belgian agents. The aircraft crashed about 1 mile from Stavenisse on the north shore of Oosterschelde and the only survivor was a Belgian agent, who was badly wounded and taken prisoner.

   Flight Lieutenant Thomas Morgan THOMAS
   Flying Officer Derek Albert John SMITH Navigator
   Flight Sergeant Eric NELSON Wireless Operator
   Sergeant Eric PARRY 20 Flight Engineer
   Flying Officer Leslie Victor WARBOYS Bomb Aimer
   Flight Sergeant John Keith Robert VINCENT 22 Air Gunner

Sergeant James Albert VICK
Sergeant H FILOT – Belgian Agent
Sergeant L STROOBANTS

06-Jun-44   P1442   Albemarle   42 OTU   Missing   7

This aircraft was one of four Albemarles from 42 OTU, detached with their crews to Hampstead Norris, to contribute to the air plan for D-Day. It was lost without trace and there is no indication as to what caused its loss.

Flight Lieutenant James Andrew FINN 29 Pilot
Flying Officer Douglas Frank SMART 24 Navigator
Pilot Officer Geoffrey Rogers WELLSMAN 20 Navigator
Flight Lieutenant Percy Cyril MORGAN 30 DFM Navigator
Flying Officer Albert Louis ANDREWS 23
Flight Sergeant Roy DUNK 23 Wireless Operator
Sergeant Wilfred Thomas FRANCIS 22 Air Gunner

06-Jun-44   V1745   Albemarle   ORTU   Near St Sylvain, Normandy   7

This aircraft and that above, were part of a contribution of nine aircraft provided by the ORTU and 42 OTU to the airborne element of the D-Day invasion. It failed to return but the circumstances of its loss are not known.

Flying Officer Graydon Raymond HOWE 24 RAAF Pilot
Sergeant Ernest Leonard BELCHER 22 Bomb Aimer
Sergeant Bernard Percy CANE 21 Navigator
Flight Sergeant Alan Albert CLARK 29 Navigator
Sergeant Stanley NEALE 21 Wireless Operator
Sergeant Henry Edward PEARSON 19 Air Gunner
Sergeant Clifford SCARGILL 22 Wireless Operator

Date	Serial	Aircraft	Unit	Place	Casualties

Brief Circumstances of Accident
Casualty Details (If Applicable)

| 06-Jun-44 | BB441 | Halifax | 148 Sqn | Near Brindisi | 0 |

The aircraft, piloted by Pilot Officer C W Crabtree, was destroyed after an engine fire resulted in a crash landing being made away from the airfield.

| 06-Jun-44 | JP285 | Halifax | 148 Sqn | Brindisi | 0 |

Whilst taking off, this aircraft crashed and was written off as a consequence of the damage caused. The crew, captained by Warrant Officer Browne, survived. The cause of the accident is not recorded.

| 06-Jun-44 | EF268 | Stirling | 620 Sqn | Normandy | 0 |

The aircraft was forced landed in a field but all the crew, captained by Flying Officer G H Thring, survived and returned to their unit a short time later.

| 06-Jun-44 | EF295 | Stirling IV | 620 Sqn | Chateau de Granguesn near Dives sur Mare | 16 |

The aircraft was carrying the officer commanding 591 Parachute Sqn RE (Major A Wood) and his HQ party. Shortly after crossing the coast it was hit by enemy AA fire, caught fire and began to lose height rapidly. Major Wood, Lieutenant Bartlett and two sappers were able to jump from the aircraft but another soldier was killed when his parachute caught fire. The remainder of the stick were still aboard the aircraft, as were the crew, when it crashed. Lieutenant Shinner and three soldiers escaped from the downed aircraft, as did the aircraft's wireless operator and rear gunner, and despite their own injuries attempted to rescue the others. Unfortunately, enemy troops arrived and fired into the aircraft and it became impossible to continue the rescue attempt. Squadron Leader Pettit's OBE, an unusual award for a sqn ldr, was made in recognition of his brave conduct, rather than for conspicuous service. He was responsible for rescuing the crew of an aircraft which had crashed into marshy ground near the home base and caught fire, whilst night flying.

His DFC was awarded for pressing home an attack on Berlin despite his aircraft being badly damaged before reaching the target.

Squadron Leader Wilmot Reginald PETTIT 32 OBE DFC RCAF Pilot
Flying Officer Richard George WATKINS 23 Navigator
Flight Sergeant Edward Harry Frederick ATKINSON 22 Bomb Aimer RNZAF
Sergeant Geoffrey Albert MAUND 19 Flight Engineer
Sapper John Joseph EVANS 24 591 Parachute Sqn RE
Sapper John YOUELL 20
Sapper Albert Edwin AUSTIN
Lance Corporal Kenneth William BRANSTON
Lance Corporal Thomas Andrew FRASER
Driver Arthur HANDLEY
Corporal William Alexander KELLY
Driver George THOMSON
Sapper David Henry WHEELER
Sapper Frank WOLFE
Sapper Peter GUARD
Lance Corporal John Readon PARKER died of injuries 7 June

06-Jun-44	EJ116 Stirling	620 Sqn Normandy	27

This aircraft and the Stirling above, both crashed in the grounds of the Chateau de Grangues. The crew and a large contingent of parachutists from the Reconnaisance Regt and 7th Bn The Parachute Regt were all killed.

Flying Officer Albert Hamilton BARTON Pilot
Flight Sergeant Henry Mark BITTINER 22 Navigator
Sergeant Donald REID 28 Bomb Aimer
Sergeant Geoffrey CROSSE 19 Flight Engineer
Sergeant William Eric WALLIS Wireless Operator

Date	Serial	Aircraft	Unit	Place	Casualties

Brief Circumstances of Accident
Casualty Details (If Applicable)

Sergeant John Gillies SMITH 23 Air Gunner
Lieutenant Raymond Charles BELCHER 6th Airborne Div Recce Regt RAC
Trooper Michael Percy DONE 19
Trooper George Wilson LAMONT 31
Corporal Peter Thomas EARWICKER 25
Trooper Arthur Harry WILSON 21
Private Geoffrey COPSON 19 7th Bn Parachute Regt
Private Vincent Patrick Cole FROST 21
Lance Corporal John GASCOIGNE 27
Craftsman George William HUNT 21 (attached from REME)
Warrant Officer II (CSM) John Edward Philip HUTCHINGS 26
Corporal Alfred Ronald KEMP 26
Lance Corporal George Henry LEAMER 26
Lance Corporal Robert Laurence MITCHELL 20
Private Walter SCOTT 29
Private Robert William STOBBART 32
Lance Corporal Robert TWIST 29
Corporal Albert VAN RYNEN 28
Private Reginald Albert Edward FRANCIS
Private Dennis SHUTT

| 06-Jun-44 | LJ288 | Stirling IV | 620 Sqn | East of Dives sur Mare | 26 |

This aircraft, carrying a large 'stick' of parachutists, crashed in the vicinity of an enemy artillery battery and all aboard were killed. In two aircraft, 7th Bn The Parachute Regt had lost a significant number of men before even getting into action. Before the day was out, the unit would lose a total of 68 men.

Pilot Officer Ian Nathaniel CASKEY 24 RCAF Pilot
Flying Officer Thomas Frederick BARKER 27 RCAF Navigator
Sergeant James HEWITT 23 Wireless Operator
Flight Sergeant Robert Alfred SPARKES 23 Air Gunner
Flight Sergeant Arthur Welch JACKSON 25 Bomb Aimer
Sergeant Arthur Lacy SMITH 22 Flight Engineer
Lance Corporal Alfred Henry James BEARD 7th Bn The Parachute Regiment
Sergeant Joseph Albert BEECH
Private John CAVEY
Corporal Henry DENHAM
Private Peter Sidney FINCH
Private Frederick GARNETT
Private William HECK
Private Patrick HUGHES
Sergeant Ernest William JARVIS
Private Dennis KERR
Private Robert KINGSLEY
Lance Corporal Leslie Henry PHILLIPS
Private John William SMITH
Private Charles Kenneth STRINGER
Private Cyril John SURMAN
Private Montague James TRUEMAN
Private John WALKER
Private Leslie Charles WEY
Sergeant Ernest Sidney HOUNSLOW
Private Cyril Cooper STUBBINS

06-Jun-44   FZ690   Dakota   512 Sqn   12 miles off French coast   0

This aircraft was flown by the leader of a sortie which was part of Operation MALLARD and had taken off at 1840 hours on D-Day. The objective was to tow Horsa gliders from 'F' Squadron GPR with cargoes of reinforcements and supplies for 6th Airborne Division. Unfortunately, the aircraft and gliders had been pitched to use a particular runway but by time departure came, the wind was at 20 knots from port and at 80 degrees to the runway heading. The weather was generally poor but the formation made its landfall and the leading glider, flown by Captain Thomas, was cast off successfully. The pilot of this aircraft; Squadron Leader Rae, then flew to the south of the LZ, where the rope dropping zone was established. On turning away to starboard, the aircraft was coned by light flak and badly damaged, with the navigator and wireless operator; Flying Officer Cullingford and Flight Sergeant Standen respectively, being wounded. The starboard engine failed and the port engine was not delivering full power, with the consequence that the aircraft was losing height. A ditching was made off the French coast and the crew was picked up within about 15 minutes. Other crews of aircraft in the formation saw what had happened to this aircraft and so turned to port on dropping their ropes.

06-Jun-44   KG347   Dakota   512 Sqn   Location not shown   8?

The aircraft was engaged on Operation ROB ROY, which involved supplies being dropped to LZ 'N' during the night of 'D' Day. Five aircraft from this squadron were detailed to take part in this operation but two did not return. It is believed that this aircraft was fired at by allied shipping as it ran up to the coast of France. The 'colours of the day' were fired but it was only after a second firing that the anti aircraft fire ceased. This aircraft is believed to be the Dakota seen to be on fire on a beach.

Flying Officer William Stanley BRENNAN 32 RAAF Pilot
Flying Officer Keith Anzac COOMBE 24 RAAF
Sergeant Ivan Charles SEAGER 21 Navigator

Pilot Officer William Henry Stacey TOYNE
+ four RASC air despatchers

06-Jun-44   KG480   Dakota   512 Sqn   Missing   8?

This aircraft was shot down and lost without trace in similar circumstances to KG347. It has proved to be difficult to identify the air despatchers from the RASC who were flying in the 46 Gp Dakotas but they are believed to have come from 398th, 63rd and 716th (Airborne) Companies of the RASC

Flight Lieutenant Maurice Henry CARTER 30 Pilot
Warrant Officer Walter Bernard NORTHALL
Warrant Officer William Henry Kenneth TREWIN 36
Warrant Officer Norman John WOODCOCK 22
+ four RASC air despatchers

Compiler's Note:

It has proved difficult to accurately record which aircraft particular RASC soldiers flew in. Listed below are those members of the RASC Air Despatch Coys who were killed on 6 or 7 Jun 44 and most of these personnel will have been aboard the Dakotas or Stirlings taking part in the D-Day invasion.

Corporal A STANNARD 63 (Airborne) Composite Company RASC
Corporal S WOOLLARD
Lance Corporal A BUTCHER
Lance Corporal A G O WILLIAMS
Driver F A CORDELL
Driver J A DALBY
Driver P MCNALLY
Driver B T O'LOUGHNANE
Driver D E ROE
Driver D J SMITH
Driver R TURNER

Driver F W PARKER 398 (Airborne) Composite Company RASC
Driver W T I SMURTHWAITE
Driver B H EDDINGTON
Lieutenant P SILVERT 716 (Airborne) Light Composite Company RASC
Corporal F J CRAWFORD
Driver W CANNING
Private R E FIELDER
Driver I R HARPER
Driver B S HOSEGOOD
Driver J W LUNN
Driver J E MCKEE
Driver F RIPO

06-Jun-44   KG356   Dakota   233 Sqn   Bassenville, east of Caen   1

The aircraft was flying No: 2 in a 'Vic' of three aircraft when it was attacked and set on fire during the run up to the DZ. The paratroops being carried were all dropped successfully and then two of the crew baled out. The wireless operator; Warrant Officer Corby Engleberg RCAF, was unable to escape in time but was rescued from the wreckage and repatriated to UK. Unfortunately, the aircraft's captain was killed, having refused his parachute and remained at the controls in order to ensure the troops and crew were able to leave the aircraft.

Flying Officer Harvey Edgar JONES 26 RCAF

06-Jun-44   KG429   Dakota   233 Sqn   Normandy (location not known)   22

Shot down but the detailed circumstances are not known. It appears that Company Sergeant Major Jones

300

of 8th Bn Parachute Regt was the sole survivor of this crash and he joined up with a Dakota crew and having been captured and then escaped from the enemy, served with the Maquis for several months.

Warrant Officer Munro Murdoch MCCANNELL 22 Pilot
Flight Sergeant Alexander Robert PORTER Navigator
Warrant Officer Albert Theodore DOWNING 23 Navigator
Warrant Officer Nathan Louis BERGER 22 RCAF Wireless Operator
Lance Corporal John Patrick BOYLE 25 8th Bn The Parachute Regt
Private Roger Frank CANTIN 21
Private Sidney George COX 19
Sergeant Alfred DOCKERILL 32
Corporal Samuel Reuben FEWINGS 34
Private Charles Frederick HOLLIS 21
Private Arthur HUMPHRIES
Private Dennis JOHNSON
Private Edward JONES 23
Private Ronald Peter KENT 24
Corporal Robert Thomas Henry LONGMAN 23
Private James Arthur MILLS 21
Sergeant James Albert MOIR 22
Private William PIGGOTT 21
Private John ROBINSON 21
Corporal Leonard Frank SMITH 31
Private William Harold Robert THORPE 22
Private John Halse WATKINS 19

| 06-Jun-44 | KG426 | Dakota | 48 Sqn | Normandy, positon not known | 1 |

The aircraft had taken off with a Horsa glider on tow at 1850 hours and the glider was released successfully at 2107 hours. Two minutes later the aircraft was hit by AA fire in the starboard engine and it began to lose height. Two of the crew baled out but one fell into a canal and drowned before he could be rescued. The pilot; Flying Officer J Le Huray, crash landed the aircraft and together with Flying Officer J M Woodcock and Flying Officer H A Farrell, eventually returned to UK

Sergeant Raymond CARR 21 Wireless Operator

06-Jun-44   KG434   Dakota III   575 Sqn   RAF Broadwell   0

The aircraft was taking off on Operation ROB ROY and was towing a heavily laden glider. The wind was at 25 mph at 40 degrees to the runway and shortly after take-off and after the undercarriage locks had released, the aircraft sank back, its starboard wing dropped and the propeller hit the runway. The pilot closed the throttles and belly landed the aircraft. The Accident Card comments that the take-off would not have been authorised for a non operational sortie in the prevailing winds.

06-Jun-44   LJ819   Stirling   299 Sqn   8 miles north west of Caen   6

This aircraft crashed after being damaged by enemy AA fire but after delivering its glider successfully.

Flying Officer James Harrison CLARK 24 RCAF Pilot
Flying Officer Francis Allan BOYCE RCAF
Pilot Officer Albert Lance COATES
Warrant Officer James Henry MUNROE 23 RCAF
Warrant Officer Theodore Henry SCHRUMP 26 RCAF
Sergeant Ernest Henry MILLS 20

06-Jun-44   LJ881   Stirling IV   196 Sqn   South-east of Caen, Normandy   6
The aircraft was seen by a number of crews to be on fire east of its DZ

    Flight Lieutenant Fred GRIBBLE 32 Pilot
    Flying Officer Alexander Edward BOTHWELL 27 Navigator
    Flight Sergeant Philip Charles GODDARD 21 Bomb Aimer
    Flight Sergeant Harry Edgar WOOTTON Wireless Operator
    Sergeant Edward WHITEHEAD Flight Engineer
    Flying Officer Sydney Frank YARDLEY 23 Air Gunner

06-Jun-44   LJ885   Stirling   299 Sqn   France, location not known   6
The aircraft failed to return from its sortie and its crew was lost

    Flight Sergeant Leslie John GILBERT 30 DFM RAAF Pilot
    Flying Officer Arthur George FRANKLIN 27
    Sergeant Leslie George KNIGHT 21
    Flight Sergeant Barry Alan CROFT 20 RAAF
    Sergeant Ronald Herbert PIZER 22
    Sergeant Francis Louis MCMAHON 19

06-Jun-44   LL407   Halifax V   298 Sqn   Ditched 8 miles of French coast   0
The aircraft, captained by Flying Officer R I Carpenter, ran up to the DZ and successfully released its glider (Hamilcar Chalk No: 235) before being struck by flak and catching fire. The pilot turned away and attempted a return to UK but was blinded and choked by smoke in the cockpit and so made a successful ditching about 8 miles off the French coast. Another Halifax, flown by Squadron Leader G H Briggs from the same squadron, flew around the aircraft until the crew could be rescued by a naval vessel. On the previous evening, it was Carpenter's crew, captained on that occasion by Wing Commander Derek Duder, that had towed one of the six 'coup de main' Horsas which had been landed right against the Orne River and canal

Date | Serial | Aircraft | Unit | Place | Casualties
Brief Circumstances of Accident
Casualty Details (If Applicable)

bridges. The troops from the Ox & Bucks Light Infantry, commanded by Major John Howard, then captured and held the bridges until relieved later on D-Day.

06-Jun-44 LL348 Halifax V 298 Sqn France, location not known 0

The aircraft was struck in the port wing by flak and set on fire after releasing its glider (Chalk No: 124, serial LF912). The crew, captained by Flying Officer C E Anderson, abandoned the aircraft and all fell into an area controlled by British troops and were repatriated to UK safely.

06-Jun-44 P1374 Albemarle 295 Sqn 1½ miles west of RAF Harwell 0

The aircraft was taking off on the evening of D-Day to tow a glider to Normandy but on take-off the aircraft could not maintain height and so the glider was cast off and the pilot carried out a wheels up landing on a hilltop. The AOC comments that the aircraft was probably overloaded but that this was not investigated by the Board of Enquiry. It is worth remembering that the Albemarle was underpowered and was barely adequate for towing a laden Horsa glider, let alone being at a high all up weight itself.

06-Jun-44 LH583 Horsa 1 HGSU Grange Farm, near Harwell 0

This is the glider towed off by P1374 above. After releasing the tow, the glider pilot attempted to clear some trees across his track but stalled the glider which then crashed. The two pilots and their six passengers were unhurt.

06-Jun-44 V1605 Albemarle 296 Sqn Normandy 1

The crew of this aircraft was engaged on an Operation MALLARD sortie and after releasing its glider, the aircraft was struck by enemy AA fire when flying at 250 feet. The pilot; Flying Officer G L Wilson, climbed to 1000 feet and ordered his crew to abandon the aircraft and this they did with the exception of one man. The reason for his failure to leave the aircraft is not known.

Pilot Officer Joseph SMITH 22

06-Jun-44   Albemarle   297 Sqn   Bienville   5

The crew failed to return from an Operation MALLARD sortie but the cause of their loss is unknown.

V1773

Flying Officer Richard Hughes LONG 21 Pilot
Flying Officer Stephen Percy COOPER Navigator
Sergeant Henry John CHATTERTON 21 Air Gunner
Sergeant Robert Telford MUIR Wireless Operator
Sergeant Henry William APARIGIO 20 Bomb Aimer

06-Jun-44   LH388 Horsa   1 HGSU   RAF Brize Norton   0

The Accident Card describes this sortie as 'training' but then goes on to record that the undercarriage locking plate has been removed as is the custom on overseas flights. Furthermore, as the timing of the accident fits in with the fly in of gliders on D-Day, it is more likely to have been an operational sortie, possibly that being towed behind Albemarle V1743 (Flying Officer J Coxell). The combination was taking off in a crosswind of 15 mph from 15 degrees across the runway when the undercarriage detached, smashed into the tail unit and rendered the glider uncontrollable. The aircraft crashed onto the airfield and none of those on board was badly injured.

06-Jun-44   LH550 Horsa   1 HGSU   Sussex, Map Reference: 133 588217   0

The glider suddenly yawed to port and caused the tug to partially stall. The tug pilot cast off the tow and the glider was ditched but there is some confusion based on the map reference quoted. This aircraft is thought to have been carrying the Chalk Number: 77 and is identified by its serial number because the ditching was treated as an accident rather than an operational loss.

Date	Serial	Aircraft	Unit	Place	Casualties
Brief Circumstances of Accident					
Casualty Details (If Applicable)					

06-Jun-44   C/N 35 Horsa   B Sqn GPR   LZ 'N'   2+

The glider crashed on landing and the two pilots were killed. The aircraft was carrying a load destined for 5 Parachute Bde but the other fatal casualties are not known.

Staff Sergeant Colin Harold HOPGOOD 26 The Glider Pilot Regiment
Sergeant Daniel Francis PHILLIPS 27 The Glider Pilot Regiment

06-Jun-44   C/N 39 Horsa   B Sqn GPR   LZ 'N'   1

The glider struck an obstruction whilst landing and the 2nd pilot received fatal injuries.

Staff Sergeant Henry BEVERIDGE 25 The Glider Pilot Regiment

06-Jun-44   C/N 42 Horsa   B Sqn GPR   At sea   2+

The glider was conveying a load for the Royal Engineers but short of the Normandy coast the tow rope broke and the aircraft was ditched in the sea. Although one of the glider pilots was found drowned, the other was not recovered and the fate of the passengers is unknown, although some are thought to have been killed.

Staff Sergeant John Pascal BRABHAM 23 The Glider Pilot Regt
Sergeant Eric LIGHTOWER 24 The Glider Pilot Regiment

06-Jun-44   C/N 74 Horsa   A Sqn GPR   LZ 'N'   2

The 2nd pilot received fatal injuries when the glider crashed on landing and his 1st pilot was killed by the enemy after being taken prisoner.

Staff Sergeant Duncan Frank WRIGHT 25 The Glider Pilot Regiment
Sergeant Barry POWELL 22 The Glider Pilot Regiment

06-Jun-44   C/N71   Horsa   A Sqn GPR   Normandy   0

Shortly before reaching the scheduled release point, the glider's tow rope broke and a forced landing was made about 4 miles east of the LZ 'N'. Unfortunately, this was in the middle of an enemy minefield but the pilots; Major J P Royle and Lieutenant S R Smith and their passengers from HQ 6th Airborne Divison HQ survived!!

06-Jun-44   C/N 68   Horsa   A Sqn GPR   7½ miles suth west of LZ 'V'   0

The 2nd pilot was seriously injured when the glider crashed into a tree during the landing.

06-Jun-44   C/N 69   Horsa   A Sqn GPR   Villers sur Mer   0

The glider's tow rope broke before the combination reached the release point and the pilots were compelled to make a forced landing, which they did in a wooded area.

06-Jun-44   C/N 90 Horsa   A Sqn GPR   Chateau de Grangues   6?

This glider was carrying the Forward Observation Officer's (FOO) team attached to 5 Parachute Bde and all the occupants were killed when it crashed into trees on landing.

Staff Sergeant Roy Samuel LUFF 23 The Glider Pilot Regiment
Lieutenant John Lee BROMLEY 25 MA The Glider Pilot Regiment
Captain Robert Arbuthnot HUNTER 34 Royal Artillery
Telegraphist Spencer Charles PORTER 18 Royal Navy
Believed to be:
Captain John Hornsby MAX 25
Telegraphist Arthur Frederick MARTIN Royal Navy

06-Jun-44   C/NU/K   Horsa   A Sqn GPR   Normandy   1

The glider collided within another Horsa on the LZ and the aircraft's 2nd pilot received fatal injuries, when

Date	Serial	Aircraft	Unit	Place	Casualties

Brief Circumstances of Accident
Casualty Details (If Applicable)

his aircraft turned over.

Sergeant Alex Rigg 27 The Glider Pilot Regt

| 06-Jun-44 | C/NU/K | Horsa | A Sqn GPR | Normandy | 6 |

The aircraft crashed into a farm building on landing and the 1st pilot was killed as were all the passengers.

Staff Sergeant Alan Trevor STEAR 23 The Glider Pilot Regiment

| 06-Jun-44 | C/N267 | Horsa | E Sqn GPR | Normandy | 3 |

The glider, carrying a load for 4 Air Landing Anti-Tank Battery RA, crashed about 7 miles from its allotted LZ and the pilots were killed as was the gun commander. The other pair of soldiers escaped.

Staff Sergeant Victor Charles SAUNDERS 28 The Glider Pilot Regiment
Sergeant John Henry FUELL 24 The Glider Pilot Regiment
Lance Sergeant Frederick Lewis WOODCOCK 32 4th Air Landing Anti-Tank Battery

| 06-Jun-44 | HS129 | Horsa | A Sqn GPR | Normandy | 1 |

This glider was Chalk No: 69. The aircraft crashed on landing and its pilot was killed.

Staff Sergeant Herbert Victor OCKWELL 27 The Glider Pilot Regiment

| 06-Jun-44 | C/N 67 | Horsa | A Sqn GPR | Normandy | 2+ |

The glider, which was carrying some of the equipment for 9th Parachute Bn, crashed into the sea off the coast and the pilots were killed. It is unclear how many others lost their lives.

Staff Sergeant William Kenneth MARFLEET 24 The Glider Pilot Regiment
Sergeant Victor HAINES 25 The Glider Pilot Regiment

06-Jun-44   C/N 99 Horsa   D Sqn GPR   Normandy   7

The glider's tow rope was severed by anti-aircraft fire and it crashed. In addition to the two pilots, it is believed that some of the passengers, who were five soldiers from 4 Air Landing Anti-Tank Battery, were also killed.

Staff Sergeant Roland George NEW 30 The Glider Pilot Regiment
Sergeant John Robert Maurice GIBBONS 27 The Glider Pilot Regiment

06-Jun-44   C/N 102 Horsa   D Sqn GPR   Near Bures   0

This glider, flown by Captain J M Walker and Sergeant F Carpenter, was carrying a jeep and an anti-tank gun of 4th Air Landing Anti-Tank Battery. The glider was released by its tug in the wrong position after the tug crew mistook the ground features. The glider crashed into the River Dives and Sergeant Carpenter was seriously injured and two of the passengers were also casualties. The 1st pilot and the other passenger were later taken prisoner by the enemy.

06-Jun-44   C/N 110 Horsa   D Sqn GPR   Near Briqueville   6

On landing, the glider crashed into a tree.

Sergeant William Henry STONEBANKS 29 The Glider Pilot Regt
Captain Frank Alan KILBEY 25 4th Air Landing Anti Tank Battery
Bombardier Alfred John LANE 30 RA
Gunner Paul LAZAROPOULO 30 RA
Private John Edgar LEACH 33 224 Parachute Field Ambulance RAMC
Private Jack LEWIS 24 RAMC

06-Jun-44   C/N 119 Horsa   D Sqn GPR   Normandy   1

The glider undershot the LZ by nearly ½ mile and crashed. Although the glider broke in half on landing, all those on board survived but the 2nd pilot was subsequently killed by small arms fire.

Date	Serial	Aircraft	Unit	Place	Casualties
		Brief Circumstances of Accident			
		Casualty Details (If Applicable)			

Sergeant Stanley Wood PERRY 22 The Glider Pilot Regt

06-Jun-44	PF715	Horsa	D Sqn GPR	Normandy	2

The tug pilot commenced evasive action when the combination came under enemy anti-aircraft fire. Unfortunately, in trying to maintain position relative to the tug, the glider got out of formation and the tow rope broke. The glider crashed into the sea but the 1st pilot was killed, probably by enemy fire from the shore, whilst the soldier drowned. This glider was Chalk No: 123

Staff Sergeant William Richard HOWE 28 The Glider Pilot Regt
+ one soldier Royal Corps of Signals

06-Jun-44	C/N 125	Horsa	D Sqn GPR	At sea off Normandy	9

The glider exploded after receiving a direct hit from enemy anti-aircraft fire. In addition to the pair of glider pilots, seven troops of 3 Parachute Bde FOO were also killed.

Staff Sergeant George Edward PHILLPOTT 28 The Glider Pilot Regt
Sergeant Eric Manley TAYLOR 25 The Glider Pilot Regt
+ seven soldiers believed to be from 3 Parachute Brigade

06-Jun-44	C/N 501	Hamilcar	C Sqn GPR	St Vaast en Auge	4

After its tow rope broke, the glider's crew attempted a forced landing but the aircraft crashed into an orchard, fatally injuring the 1st pilot.

Staff Sergeant Leslie RIDINGS 23 The Glider Pilot Regt
Bombardier William Cornealous WHITNEY25 3rd Air Landing Anti Tank Battery
Gunner Douglas Stanley 35

Gunner Frederick Ernest NEWHAM 21

06-Jun-44 KG424 Dakota   233 Sqn   Orne River estuary area   0

This aircraft was one of four bringing in supplies but as the formation approached the Normandy coast, they were fired on by anti-aircraft guns on allied ships. Although two aircraft were damaged, they were able to deliver their supplies but this aircraft was shot down. The pilot and navigator; Squadron Leader C Wright AFC and Flying Officer B Cowie RNZAF, along with Driver Alexander RASC, were taken prisoner but Flying Officer E G Sample RCAF(Co-Pilot) and Flying Officer C J Williams Wireless Operator, escaped, with Drivers Ackley and Allen and returned to their unit about 4 weeks later.

07-Jun-44 FZ667 Dakota III   271 Sqn   Off Normandy Coast   5

The aircraft failed to return from a glider towing sortie in support of D-Day and some wreckage was subsequently discovered in the sea

     Flying Officer Lorne Cheatham FLATHER 26 RCAF Pilot
     Warrant Officer I William Henry OAKLEY 21 RCAF Co-Pilot
     Flight Sergeant Stanley HOPE 21 Navigator
     Flight Lieutenant Leslie MILLER 26 Wireless Operator
     + one other

07-Jun-44 KG329 Dakota   233 Sqn   Orne River estuary area   1

This aircraft was engaged in the same detail as KG424. Although the pilot was killed, the other three crew; Flight Sergeant A S Illingworth, Pilot Officer D W B Carr and Sergeant L Thomas survived but were made POW. The same fate befell Drivers Cullen and Duffy, two of the despatchers.

     Flying Officer Edwin Ernest WOOD 23 Pilot

07-Jun-44 LL390 Halifax   138 Sqn   RAF Tempsford   0

This aircraft; flown by Squadron Leader Michael Brogan and his crew, was one of a pair tasked to a DZ in

Date	Serial	Aircraft	Unit	Place	Casualties
Brief Circumstances of Accident					
Casualty Details (If Applicable)					

the Orleans area, coded HISTORIAN 10. The brakes proved ineffective on wet grass and the aircraft swung on take-off and was written off in the subsequent crash.

08-Jun-44	LL416	Halifax	138 Sqn	la Fert St Cyr Loire et Cher	6

This was the second aircraft of the pair flying HISTORIAN 10. It was struck by enemy flak and crashed before reaching its target. One member of the crew survived and was hidden by local people until the area was liberated by US forces 3 months later.

Pilot Officer Francis Harold LYNE 20 RCAF Pilot
Sergeant John HAMILTON 31 RCAF Navigator
Flight Sergeant Ralph William WESTERGARD 22 RCAF Wireless Operator
Sergeant Willie Beaumont BISHOP 19 Flight Engineer
Flight Sergeant Arthur Roy SMITH RCAF Bomb Aimer
Sergeant William Howard MOFFAT 19 RCAF Air Gunner

07-Jun-44	LL466	Halifax	138 Sqn	Doudeville Seine Maritime	7

This aircraft crashed on its outbound flight about 25 miles east of Le Harve and there were no survivors.

Flight Sergeant Angus Donald MCKAY 24 RCAF Pilot
Sergeant William John CHESHIRE 22 Navigator
Flying Officer Kenneth BATEMAN 26 Wireless Operator
Sergeant John Roland IRELAND 19 Flight Engineer
Flying Officer Clifford John ENNIS 20 DFC Bomb Aimer
Sergeant David Watt DRUMMOND 20 Air Gunner
Sergeant Ernest William Bernard CARLSON 21 RCAF Air Gunner

07-Jun-44 BT861 Hotspur II 5 GTS Shobdon, Herefordshire 0

The glider was being towed by a tractor to the flying point but it struck some large stones concealed in the grass and its skin was damaged.

08-Jun-44 LL306 Halifax 138 Sqn Veauville les Baons Seine Maritime 7

The crew was lost when their aircraft crashed taking part in the dual SIS sorties; PERWINKLE and WALT 3. The cause of the loss is unclear.

Flight Lieutenant Herbert Clifford JONES 28 RAAF Pilot
Flight Sergeant Harold Annalls MONSEN-ELVIK Navigator
Flight Sergeant John Grant CHADWICK 22 Wireless Operator
Sergeant Douglas James Ashley KEMP 20 Air Gunner
Flying Officer Douglas Scott JOHNSTONE 22 RNZAF Bomb Aimer
Sergeant Graham Bernard Charles MOORE 20 Air Gunner
Sergeant Frederick William HERBERT 23

09-Jun-44 LH562 Horsa 1 HGSU RAF Fairford 2

This glider had landed and was being retrieved, when it was towed across the runway in use and without displaying any lights. A Stirling (LJ869) of 620 Sqn, flown by Flight Sergeant Peter Jordan and his crew, was cleared for take-off and commenced its run, towing a glider. At about the point of lift off, the Stirling pilot saw the obstruction but could do nothing to avoid it and the two aircraft collided. Whilst the glider on the ground was destroyed, the Stirling remained under control and the pilot climbed to 1000 feet and reported to flying control and asked permission to release the glider under tow. This was given and the glider landed safely. Whilst the runway was cleared, the Stirling flew in the local area and eventually belly landed safely and was repaired, being struck off charge only in late 1947. The cause of the accident was the failure to display lights on the glider being retrieved and the failure of flying control in allowing a glider being towed by a tractor to enter the active runway.

313

Date	Serial	Aircraft	Unit	Place	Casualties
		Brief Circumstances of Accident			
		Casualty Details (If Applicable)			

Staff Sergeant Sidney FLETCHER The Glider Pilot Regiment
Sergeant Leonard Roy HEBBERD 20 The Glider Pilot Regiment

10-Jun-44	BZ959	Liberator III	357 Sqn	Digri	0+5

The aircraft was on a taxying test but the pilot exceeded the limitations and the aircraft's brakes burnt out.
The aircraft overran the runway and crashed into a lorry carrying local civilians, of whom five were killed.

11-Jun-44	FZ548	Dakota III	62 Sqn	Near Karimganj	27

The aircraft was being flown by a 215 Sqn crew and was ferrying Army reinforcements. The book 'Air War For Burma' records that the aircraft crashed in flames but the Accident Card offers no clues to what happened. The passengers and crew are buried together in a Collective Grave at Kohima, which suggests that the aircraft was probably destroyed by fire after the crash, even if not on fire at the time of its loss.

Flying Officer Neville William Barton BRADY 21 RAAF Pilot
Warrant Officer Henry James DEESTER 28 RAAF
Pilot Officer Douglas Edward JONES 24 RCAF
Flying Officer Arthur James READ 21 Wireless Operator
2nd Lieutenant Roy Henry HARRIS 24 3rd Carabiniers Royal Armoured Corps
2nd Lieutenant John Denys CROASDALE 19 The Black Watch attached 2nd Bn KOSBs
Sergeant David ANDERSON 36 2nd Bn Kings Own Scottish Borderers
Private John AIRLIE 19
Private Charles Robert BRADWELL 30
Private George BROTHERSTON 30
Private John George GAMMAGE 32
Private William John HARRIS 20

Private John KERR 30
Private George Septimus MAITLAND 29
Private James Tuite SLANE 21
Private Thomas STEIN 27
Rifleman James COUTTS 20 1st Bn Cameronians (Scottish Rifles)
Private Joseph DICKSON 30 Gordon Highlanders
Fusilier Patrick MATTHEWS 21 Royal Inniskilling Fusiliers
Fusilier Leo QUINN 19
Fusilier Arthur Thomas ROBERTS 19
Fusilier Albert Arthur ROLLINS 33
Fusilier George William ROWBOTHAM 32
Fusilier Percival John SAUNDERSON 23
Fusilier Jack SCOTT 19
Fusilier Albert SHANKS 23
Fusilier Stanley WHAPSHOTT 22

| 11-Jun-44 | K7014 | Harrow II | 271 Sqn | Hatston | 0 |

The aircraft was badly damaged whilst taxiing in a strong wind in the Orkney islands.

| 11-Jun-44 | P1472 | Albemarle | 42 OTU | RAF Ashbourne | 0 |

At the end of a 1½ hour circuit training detail, the pilot landed the aircraft heavily, bursting the starboard tyre in the process. The starboard propeller then struck the ground and the engine was torn from its mounting. The pilot, who had only 6 hours solo on the type was excused because of his inexperience, although it was accepted that he had made an error of judgement.

| 14-Jun-44 | V1618 | Albemarle | 42 OTU | Hollington, Derbyshire | 0 |

The aircraft had been airborne for just 8 minutes on a daylight training sortie and was at about 1000 feet above ground level when the starboard engine oil pressure dropped to zero. The pilot, who had only 6 hours solo on type, throttled back the engine but did not attempt to feather the propeller because he had been given no instruction on how to do this in the air! The windmilling propeller contributed to the loss of height and the pilot tried a forced landing in a field but struck a tree and a hedge whilst doing so. Whilst two of the crew were injured, the aircraft was badly damaged. Subsequent investigation found large deposits of metal in the sump filters and other indications of serious internal damage to the engine.

| 15-Jun-44 | P1563 | Albemarle | 9 FP | RAF Ashbourne | 1 |

The aircraft was being ferried to the unit and had made an apparently normal touchdown and landing run. About 300 yards from the runway's end, the pilot opened the throttles to go round again but the aircraft struck the boundary fence, then a barn before crashing and bursting into flames. The reason for the pilot's decision is not clear, although possible brake fade could not be discounted. Unfortunately, the co-pilot had raised the flaps and opened the engine gills during the landing run, without the pilot's order and it follows that the aircraft was not configured for a take-off.

1st Officer Henry John Norman ROWE 47 ATA Pilot

| 16-Jun-44 | JP238 | Halifax | 624 Sqn | Blida | 1 |

The aircraft crashed on take-off.

Flight Sergeant Donald Loren SMALL 20 RCAF Air Gunner

| 17-Jun-44 | FD935 | Dakota | 44 SAAF | Takoradi | 0 |

The aircraft crashed on take-off from this base

17-Jun-44   KG343   Dakota   575 Sqn   B5 Camilly, Normandy   0

The aircraft was landing during an artillery exchange, which was producing a good deal of dust and obscuring visibility. The aircraft ran into another Dakota and was destroyed by fire.

18-Jun-44   LJ850   Stirling IV   620 Sqn   At sea off France   21

The crew was engaged in supply dropping to special forces units and this aircraft was the only one of a mixed force of Stirlings and Halifaxs which failed to return. In this case, the squadron had contributed three aircraft to an operation called HOUNDSTOOTH 5, which called for forty five troops and forty two containers to be dropped. There was reported to be very heavy cloud cover and it is thought possible the aircraft flew into high ground shrouded in cloud but as no trace has ever been found, it is more likely the aircraft crashed into the sea.

Warrant Officer Robert William CRANE 24 RAAF Pilot
Flight Sergeant Frank Norman JOHNSON 29 Navigator
Warrant Officer John Percy CLASPER 28 RCAF Bomb Aimer
Sergeant David Wynne EVANS 23 Flight Engineer
Flight Sergeant Granville William STOPFORD 25 Wireless Operator
Sergeant Benjamin James PROFIT 31 RCAF Air Gunner
Private John Seymour BOWEN
Lance Corporal Harold BROOK
Corporal William BRYSON
Lieutenant Leslie George CAIRNS
Private William John CREANEY
Private Donald Maurice GALE
Private Geore Malgwyn HAYES
Private George Dalton LAW
Corporal William LEADBETTER

Date	Serial	Aircraft	Unit	Place	Casualties
			Brief Circumstances of Accident		
			Casualty Details (If Applicable)		

Private Charles MACFARLANE
Private Dominic MCBRIDE
Sergeant Ronald MILLER
Private James O'REILLY
Private John Kenneth ROGERS
Sergeant Reginald Josiah WORTLEY

Date	Serial	Aircraft	Unit	Place	Casualties
18-Jun-44	HG849	Horsa	1 HGSU	RAF Tarrant Rushton	0

This glider was written off after it was struck by another Horsa (LH549) which had undershot its landing spot.

| 19-Jun-44 | FZ600 | Dakota III | 194 Sqn | North east of Kohima | 4 |

The crew attempted to fly beneath the cloud base in conditions of poor visibility, which compelled other aircraft to turn back. It was seen at very low altitude and its wreckage was subsequently found burnt out on a hillside.

Pilot Officer Burton Roxborough CHRISTIE 22 RCAF Pilot
Warrant Officer I George Wellington HANSFORD 26 RCAF Wireless Operator
Pilot Officer Charles Esley TATTRIE RCAF Wireless Operator
Warrant Officer Walter Douglas PEARCE 24 RAAF Navigator

| 21-Jun-44 | LH115 | Horsa | 1 HGSU | Bulkington, Wiltshire | 0 |

The glider was being flown on an airtest but in turbulent conditions which created a good deal of bumpiness. The tow rope snapped and the glider pilot attempted to return to the aerodrome but had to force land in a field.

22-Jun-44 BT847 Hotspur II 5 GTS Shobdon 0

On approach to land, the instructor corrected the pupil's flying but the glider undershot, passed through two hedges and then landed heavily on the airfield and broke up, with the cockpit detaching and then being run over by the glider.

23-Jun-44 FL504 Dakota III 194 Sqn Imphal 0

The pilot, who was inexperienced on type, found the crosswind and general weather conditions at a difficult airstrip beyond his skill and he landed the aircraft heavily. The aircraft swung off the runway and was completely wrecked when ran into a ditch beside the runway.

23-Jun-44 FZ598 Dakota III 62 Sqn Comilla 4

The aircraft had been loaded with a cargo of full 40 gallon petrol drums by an Army party and these had probably not been secured correctly. On take-off, the aircraft made a very short run, the nose rose sharply, followed by the port wing dropping and the aircraft crashed out of control and was completely destroyed by fire. It is thought probable that one or more drums came adrift and shifted to the rear of the aircraft and caused a change in the aircraft's trim outside the CofG limits. The pilot should have checked the security of the load prior to take-off but the O i/c the Army loading team was held partly to blame.

    Flying Officer Godfrey John Clifford WILLIAMS Pilot died of injuries 24 Jun 44
    David Gordon Stewart MCCARTNEY 21
    Pilot Officer John Allan FRASER 26 RCAF Wireless Operator
    Warrant Officer Dennis Aubrey ORR 21 RNZAF Wireless Operator

23-Jun-44 KG413 Dakota 194 Sqn Sylhet 0

Overran the runway. There is some confusion as to whether this aircraft and the one below are the same aircraft and that there has been a transposition of serial numbers but although only one Accident Card was

Date	Serial	Aircraft	Unit	Place	Casualties
		Brief Circumstances of Accident Casualty Details (If Applicable)			

found, other information suggests there were two incidents on this date.

23-Jun-44   KG493   Dakota III   194 Sqn   Sylhet   0

The aircraft was returning from the first sortie of the day and was approaching to land in monsoon conditions with poor visibility. The pilot's first approach was off the runway line and so an overshoot was initiated but from a low airspeed. The pilot, who was inexperienced in terms of general flying experience and time on type, was unable to get the aircraft to accelerate in the climb and at low altitude it struck a tree with its starboard wing and crashed. Although the five crew were injured, all survived.

24-Jun-44   JP237   Halifax   148 Sqn   23 miles north-east of Genoa   7

This aircraft failed to return from a sortie to drop supplies near Genoa.

> Flight Lieutenant Donald Ernest HILLMAN 26 RCAF Pilot
> Flight Sergeant James Ross ROBERTSON 21 RCAF Bomb Aimer
> Sergeant Edward Geoffrey CHAPMAN 21 Wireless Operator
> Sergeant Arthur PINDER Flight Engineer
> Sergeant Dixon FINLAYSON 35 Air Gunner
> Sergeant John Michael SUMNER Air Gunner
> Flying Officer Nicholas HOLYK 35 RCAF Bomb Aimer

24-Jun-44   P1568   Albemarle I   ATA   Shottesbrooke Park   0

The crew was conducting an air test and practicing single engined approaches and overshoots and had been airborne for 1 hour 20 minutes. During an approach and as the aircraft passed 700 feet on the descent, the pilot attempted to unfeather the starboard propeller but without success and so an overshoot was

320

initiated immediately. The port engine failed to deliver sufficient power and so the overshoot was converted into a forced landing in a field with the undercarriage retracted. The pilot was found to blame in that it was judged he should have proved the unfeathering system whilst at height and not whilst in the final stages of an approach. Although the Accident Card records the aircraft as being Category 'E', the Aircraft Movements Card suggest that the aircraft was not struck off charge until autumn of the following year. This may, however, be an administrative issue rather than an indication that the aircraft was recovered for use.

Date	Serial	Type	Unit	Location	Fatalities
24-Jun-44	LH450	Horsa	81 OTU	RAF Tilstock	0

The glider pilot got his aircraft in to the slipstream of the tug aircraft and had difficulty controlling his glider. The tow was released but then the pilot undershot the approach and landed in a field, striking the port wing on a wooden hut.

| 25-Jun-44 | JP240 | Halifax | 624 Sqn | France | 8 |

The aircraft failed to return from a sortie to Cabriolet, France. Whilst other crews reported seeing a crashed aircraft in the area of the DZ, a subsequent report confirmed that this aircraft had crashed and all on board had been killed.

Warrant Officer II Earl Duncan MCDERMID 26 RCAF Pilot
Warrant Officer II Lloyd Weldon BURNSIDE 22 RCAF Navigator
Flight Sergeant Francis Anthony COADY 19 RCAF Wireless Operator/Air Gunner
Flight Sergeant Dalton Morgan CORBETT 29 RCAF Wireless Operator/Air Gunner
Sergeant William Charles ELLIS 20 RCAF Flight Engineer
Flying Officer Robert Howard SNEATH 23 RCAF Bomb Aimer
Sergeant Robert William WHITELAM 21 Flight Engineer
Captain Brian George DALZIEL 25 The Gordon Highlanders

| 25-Jun-44 | FR596 | Hadrian I | TSTU | Chaklala, India | 0 |

The aircraft was damaged when it broke free from its moorings during a strong gale.

Date	Serial	Aircraft	Unit	Place	Casualties
				Brief Circumstances of Accident	
				Casualty Details (If Applicable)	

26-Jun-44 KG519 Dakota III 194 Sqn Imphal 0+1

The pilot, who was another inexperienced captain on the squadron, attempted to land a fully loaded aircraft in a strong crosswind. It swung off the runway, ran into a ditch and swung round on its belly, before colliding with a lorry, killing the Indian Army soldier driver.

27-Jun-44 JP206 Halifax 624 Sqn Lamastre near Valence 7

This aircraft was one of a group of nine from the squadron operating in the area to the west of the Rhone Valley in the Monts du Vivarais. It failed to return and its crew did not survive.

Warrant Officer Peter Edward GODSELL Pilot
Warrant Officer Leslie John ANSTEE 22 Navigator
Sergeant Ernest Henry William COLES Flight Engineer
Sergeant James MERCER 20 Air Gunner
Sergeant Douglas Hugh ROBINSON 23 Wireless Operator
Flying Officer Walter St. Xavier JAMIESON 26 RCAF Bomb Aimer
Flying Officer Frederick Nelson HACK 20 RCAF Air Gunner

28-Jun-44 BD505 Whitley V AFEE Tackbrook, Leamington Spa 0

The undercarriage failed after the pilot made a fairly fast landing and the aircraft's brakes did not hold on the wet grass, following which the aircraft ran into a ditch.

30-Jun-44 JP253 Halifax 624 Sqn Blida, Algeria 0

This aircraft, flown by Flight Lieutenant Atkins and his crew, was engaged on a operational task when it developed engine trouble, requiring a return to base. On landing the aircraft crashed and was destroyed

322

but the crew survived.

02-Jul-44   FH383   Hudson IIIA   353 Sqn   Jalso, near Jodhpur   4

The pilot had not obtained a Met report before departure and did not turn back or attempt to fly round the extremely violent storm encountered en route. The aircraft caught fire and broke up in the air.

    Flight Lieutenant Owen Archibald BUDGELL 22 Pilot
    Flight Lieutenant Robert Ernest GABBITAS Pilot
    Flight Lieutenant John Leonard Gostwyche WATES RCAF Wireless Operator
    + one non-RAF

04-Jul-44   LA869   Whitley V   HGTU   Poole Harbour   ?

The aircraft suffered an engine failure whilst on a glider towing sortie. The glider was cast off but the tug was then ditched in Poole Harbour when height could not be maintained on a single engine.

04-Jul-44   JP179   Halifax   148 Sqn   Yugoslavia   4

The squadron was scheduled to send out a tasking of fourteen Halifaxes; seven to Poland, three to Yugoslavia and four to Italian targets. In addition a single Lysander was to undertake a pick up in Greece. This aircraft was one of the Yugoslavian serials and was flown by Warrant Officer L J Blattman. It failed to return and the precise circumstances of its loss are not known. It is believed, however, that the crew survived.

04-Jul-44   JP247   Halifax   148 Sqn   Poland   2

Of the seven aircraft scheduled to drop supplies over Poland, three failed to return, of which this was one. The precise fate is not known but it is believed that four crew survived and were made POW.

    Flight Lieutenant George Raymond WOOD 22 Pilot
    Flight Sergeant James William HERN 22 Air Gunner

323

Date	Serial	Aircraft	Unit	Place	Casualties

Brief Circumstances of Accident
Casualty Details (If Applicable)

04-Jul-44   JP286   Halifax   148 Sqn   Hungary (location not known)   8

Squadron Leader Bird had completed a tour with another squadron before flying a full tour with this unit. He elected to remain with his crew and fly additional sorties so that they might finish as a team. The aircraft failed to return and the entire crew and some extras were all lost. There is an indication that there were four passengers aboard but there is no trace of these men in the records found and it follows that they may have already been delivered before the aircraft was lost. Warrant Officer Tilmont was a Frenchman serving with the RAF.

    Squadron Leader Surry Philip Victor BIRD 24 Pilot
    Flight Sergeant Peter LAKE Navigator
    Warrant Officer I Donal David Charles STEWART 21 RCAF Navigator
    Pilot Officer Harold PEARSON Flight Engineer
    Flying Officer Kenneth Peter McLeod CRAN 35 Air Gunner
    Flight Sergeant Arthur Archer LEE Wireless Operator
    Flight Sergeant Ronald RADFORD 20 Air Gunner
    Warrant Officer Marcel TILMONT 24 Air Gunner
    + possibly four passengers

04-Jul-44   JP292   Halifax   148 Sqn   Poland   7

The pilot of this aircraft was within a few hours of completing his second operational tour with the squadron and his was the fourth aircraft lost, again with its entire crew. The night's tally was an awful return for the sacrifice made since only four sorties were successful.

    Warrant Officer Charles Thomas FAIRWEATHER 24 Pilot
    Flight Sergeant John EASTON 20 Air Gunner
    Pilot Officer Allen HAIGH Navigator

324

Flying Officer John Stanley BROWN RCAF Bomb Aimer
Flight Sergeant Ronals Frederick HOUGHTON 23 Wireless Operator
Sergeant Richard JACQUES Flight Engineer
Flight Sergeant Leonard James SMITH 22 Air Gunner

04-Jul-44   LJ897   Stirling IV   299 Sqn   RAF Tarrant Rushton   0

The aircraft was being delivered to the unit and the pilot landed on a runway which had a brow on it, preventing the pilot seeing the runway's end. Realising he was going to overshoot the runway, the pilot ground looped the aircraft but its undercarriage collapsed as the aircraft ran over a steep bank near the boundary.

04-Jul-44   RJ190   Horsa   1 HGSU   Southborne, Christchurch   0

The glider was being towed by an Albemarle but the tug's starboard engine failed and the glider was cast off, whilst the tug made an emergency landing. The glider forced landed but was damaged. The glider pilot; Sergeant L Hotchkin, was considered to have done well under the circumstances.

04-Jul-44   219704   Hadrian I   1 HGSU   RAF Netheravon   2

This Hadrian, which was still assigned its US markings, was being used for 'snatch pick up' trials with a Dakota as the 'snatching' aircraft. The glider was snatched and climbed steeply to a height of 200 feet when the tow was cast off and the glider carried on to about 250 feet, where it stall turned and dived into the ground. The causes of the crash were that the pilots were unfamiliar with the technique but importantly that the pilot could not reach the elevator trimmer controls when seated. This last factor suggests some sloppy preparation since one expect the crews to have been briefed on the techniques involved in the this unusual evolution and certainly to have done some 'dry runs' to familiarise themselves with the controls.

Staff Sergeant Fredrick Whyte SIMPSON 26 The Glider Pilot Regiment
Staff Sergeant Dennis SHAW The Glider Pilot Regiment

Date	Serial	Aircraft	Unit	Place	Casualties
05-Jul-44	FH254	Hudson IIIA	353 Sqn	10 miles west of Surat	0?

The aircraft was forced landed on mud flats after its engines cut.

Date	Serial	Aircraft	Unit	Place	Casualties
05-Jul-44	FK790	Hudson	161 Sqn	Waddenzee Netherlands	7

The crew was engaged on a sortie; FIVES 1 and were carrying three agents to be dropped in Holland. Whilst inbound towards the DZ, the aircraft was shot down by an enemy night fighter before reaching the Dutch coast and all on board were killed.

Flight Lieutenant John Watherston MENZIES 28 DFC

Flying Officer Kenneth Ralph BUNNEY 30 Navigator

Sergeant Dennis James WITHERS 22 Wireless Operator

Sergeant Eric Marshall ELIOT

Peter J QUINT (alternative spelling of KWINT also seen) – Dutch Agents

Johannes A WALTERS

Jan BOCKMA

Pleun VERHOEF

Note: The names of Bockma and Verhoef appear as alternatives in various records and it is uncertain as to whether one name was an alias for the other or if Bockma was not on board the aircraft.

Date	Serial	Aircraft	Unit	Place	Casualties
05-Jul-44	FZ585	Dakota	31 Sqn	Imphal Plain	4

The squadron was in the process of moving bases but operational sorties continued. This aircraft is described as being on a 'special duties sortie' and was routed over the Imphal Plain. Its loss is described as possibly being weather related, rather than as the result of enemy action but the aircraft wreckage was not found and its crew are all commemorated on the Singapore Memorial.

Flight Sergeant Eric Forrester STORRIE 22 Pilot
Sergeant Thomas Herbert Boothman CARDEN 22 Co-Pilot
Warrant Officer II Jack MANNING 21 RCAF Wireless Operator
Warrant Officer I James BICKNALL 21 RCAF Wireless Operator

07-Jul-44   LJ564   Stirling IV   196 Sqn   Keevil   0

The aircraft was returning from a night bombing sortie in the early hours of the morning and the pilot, who was inexperienced on type and tired after the sortie, misjudged the approach and the aircraft landed heavily, damaging the undercarriage, which then collapsed after the aircraft ran into a ditch.

07-Jul-44   V9490   Lysander   161 Sqn   English Channel   2

The aircraft, flown by Captain Per Hysing-Dahl – a Norwegian officer, was engaged on operation PALAISE but was prevented from delivering the three agents and so the pilot set course for home. By this time, safety corridors had been established over the various beachheads, through which allied aircraft could pass but the pilot misjudged this and his aircraft was struck by American AA fire and the aircraft's engine seized, forcing a ditching, during which the aircraft turned over. Although wounded in the hand, the pilot escaped from the aircraft, as did one of the agents but two others were fatally injured.

J M L BESNARD
M LESEUR

10-Jul-44   P1593   Albemarle I   ORTU   Near Peterhead, Aberdeenshire   9

The aircraft was en route to retrieve a glider and had been airborne for 2½ hours. It was seen to be flying at low level in very poor visibility and rain and to enter a spin from which it did not recover before striking the ground. Although, the Board of Enquiry was of the view that the pilot should have returned to the nearest suitable airfield, the possibility of defective instruments was also suggested as a possible factor.

Flying Officer Harvey Oswald FAIRBAIRN 27 Pilot
Flight Sergeant Godfrey Vernon John BELL 23

Date	Serial	Aircraft	Unit	Place	Casualties

Brief Circumstances of Accident
Casualty Details (If Applicable)

Flight Sergeant John Corrie CHEN 23 RAAF
Sergeant Frederick Henry William FINCH 23
Sergeant Alfred James MILTON 20
Sergeant Hugh O'REILLY 23
Sergeant Leonard George STARNES 23
Staff Sergeant Henry McLean DOWDS 27 The Glider Pilot Regiment
Sergeant Herbert James ANSELL 25 The Glider Pilot Regiment

| 10-Jul-44 | LA634 | Hamilcar | 1 HGSU | RAF Tarrant Rushton | 0 |

On landing at the conclusion of a short daytime training sortie, the glider was caught in a strong down draught. It struck the ground heavily and the undercarriage was damaged badly.

| 11-Jul-44 | V1774 | Albemarle V | 296 Sqn | Missing | 6 |

The aircraft took off shortly after midnight on an SOE sortie to deliver supplies near Valencay at position 47 degrees 12North/01 degrees 31East. The aircraft was lost without trace and although two members of the crew were recovered from the sea, two others and a Parachute Regiment air despatcher are commemorated on the Runnymede and Brookwood Memorials respectively.

Flight Sergeant John Bernard JOHNSON 20 Pilot
Warrant Officer Richard Alan SIMPSON 21
Flight Sergeant Wesley Benjamin HUNNIFORD 24 RNZAF Bomb Aimer
Sergeant William Richar BUSH 19
Flying Officer Stanley Morrison MASTERS 27
+ one Parachute Regt believed to be:
Sergeant Samuel DACE 26 6th Battalion The Parachute Regiment

328

11-Jul-44   MA925 Dakota   31 Sqn   New Delhi   0

The aircraft was parked at the dispersal when it was struck by Anson LT895 and damaged beyond repair.

11-Jul-44   LH323 Horsa   1 HGSU   Huntingdon Farm near Ludlow   0

The combination of tug and glider entered cloud, whilst flying over hilly country and after the intercom between the two aircraft had become unserviceable. The glider pilot cast off the tow and whilst attempting to land, the aircraft struck a tree and crashed whilst being pivoted around by the force of the collision. The glider pilot was criticised for not using the cable angle indicator, which would have helped him in maintaining his glider's position relative to the tug.

11-Jul-44   BT538 Hotspur II   3 GTS   Near Stoke Orchard   1

The pilot released the glider from its tow in the wrong place and was downwind instead of upwind of the airfield. He then started a circuit but flew across the airfield instead of losing height by flying figures of '8'. He did not use flaps and was flying at high speed and then attempted to avoid a railway line by landing short. Unfortunately, the aircraft struck the ground heavily and it broke up. The pilot was thought to have found it difficult to cope with the situation as he was inexperienced and his reactions were slow. The Accident Card records that he was 49 but was in fact several years older. He is also listed as being the CO of No: 2 Wing GPR but it does seem somewhat incongruous to appoint an officer of this age and experience to an active flying appointment.

Lieutenant Colonel Charles Ronald FRYER 54 MC & Bar Kings Royal Rifle Corps

12-Jul-44   LL251 Halifax   138 Sqn   Mediterranean Sea   1

The crew of this aircraft, captained by Flight Lieutenant Harold Walker DFC, had been one of several to undertake a mission from RAF Tempsford and then carry on to Blida in Algeria, rather than return direct to UK. On the return sortie, the aircraft was climbed to 8000 feet but the port outer engine began to cause problems with the revolutions fluctuating and black puffs of smoke emitting from the exhausts. Eventually,

329

the engine failed but by this time the aircraft was already returning to Blida and the cargo was jettisoned. Despite lightening the load, height could not be maintained and a ditching was made. The dinghy did not release automatically and some members of the crew were badly affected by petrol fumes from the bomb bay overload tanks, which had ruptured during the ditching. However, apart from the navigator, the crew was picked up quickly. This sortie proved to be Walker's last and in Aug 44 he was awarded a DSO to go with the DFC he had received as a Warrant Officer on the same squadron. The sequel to this accident is that Flight Lieutenant Walker and his surviving crew were flown home to Lyneham in a BOAC Liberator and a Hudson was sent from their home base to bring them back to Tempsford. On landing at the conclusion of this short flight, the Hudson was destroyed in a landing accident but everybody survived with a good shaking up!

Flying Officer Micahel Anthony FARR 24 Navigator

12-Jul-44   ?????   Lysander   148 Sqn   St Vulbas, southern France   0

The aircraft was being operated from an airfield at Borgo, south of Bastia on Corsica, on one of a series of missions into southern France. This sortie was coded THICKET 2 and the contact was made and the landing carried out successfully. Unfortunately, when Lieutenant Georges Libert a French pilot attached to the squadron, attempted to restart the engine it resisted all efforts to do so and so the aircraft was destroyed on the ground.

14-Jul-44   JN888   Halifax   624 Sqn   Nistos, Hautes Pyrennes   7

This crew was one of ten sent to various locations in southern France but it failed to return to Blida and wreckage was eventually located 62 miles south-west of Toulouse.

Pilot Officer Leslie Arthur PEERS RCAF

Flying Officer Albert John BAYTHORP
Sergeant Jack BROOKE
Sergeant Harry CLARKE
Flying Officer Charles Spencer GOBLE
Sergeant James Arthur WALSH
Sergeant William Ronald WHARMBY

16-Jul-44	JP284	Halifax	148 Sqn	FTR SOE operations	?

No details were found of this loss.

16-Jul-44	KG472	Dakota	267 Sqn	Yugoslavia	11

This aircraft was being flown by a very experienced captain with a squadron training officer as the co-pilot. The sortie involved a total of seven Dakotas being flown into two airstrips in Yugoslavia to bring in supplies and evacuate wounded and others. The aircraft stalled and crashed at the end of the runway during the take-off, killing the five crew and six passengers. It appears that the flaps had been raised at too low a speed and before the undercarriage had been retracted. It is unclear why an experienced crew would have made this mistake. Amongst the nine injured were; Major Randolph Churchill - the Prime Minster's son, Captain Evelyn Waugh - the author, and Air Commodore G L Carter. Unfortunately, the last named died of his injuries having been evacuated to Italy. Air Cdre Carter had commanded the fighter force in the desert and despite his senior rank had flown many operational sorties himself. In early 1943, his leadership in that role was recognised by the award of the DSO.

Flight Lieutenant Desmond Edward James GARDINER 41
Captain H W SOLMS SAAF Pilot
Flying Officer Francis Alexander Barclay CAMERON 29 Navigator
Flight Sergeant Henry Alfred BURRILL 23 Wireless Operator
Corporal George HOLROYD 32
Corporal Harry PELL-ILDERTON

Date	Serial	Aircraft	Unit	Place	Casualties

Brief Circumstances of Accident
Casualty Details (If Applicable)

Leading Aircraftman Leslie John HOLT 23
Private Douglas John SOWMAN 24 The Suffolk Regiment
Air Commodore Guy Lloyd CARTER 44 DSO AFC
+ two others

16-Jul-44	LL129	Halifax	298 Sqn	Larre near Alencon	6

The pair of squadrons based at Tarrant Rushton (298 and 644) were tasked to provide fifteen aircraft for a variety of SOE operations over occupied France. This crew was allotted STATIONER 5, a drop of supplies near Chatellerault le Blanc. The aircraft crashed in the area shown and its crew was lost. The other aircraft were all successful and returned to base safely.

Warrant Officer James Foxall CROSSLEY 24
Flying Officer Derwood William SMITH 28 RCAF Navigator
Sergeant Enzo Biagge GRASSO 23 Bomb Aimer
Flying Officer William Edward LINNING 24 RCAF Wireless Operator
Warrant Officer Joseph Wilfred Romeo FOURNIER 27 RCAF Air Gunner
Sergeant Edward Maurice Cyril WILKINSON 20 Flight Engineer

17-Jul-44	DT543	Halifax	138 Sqn	RAF Tempsford	0

The aircraft was struck off charge as being uneconomic to repair but the nature of the damage or structural deterioration is not recorded.

18-Jul-44	LL364	Halifax	138 Sqn	Marigny l'Eglise, Nievre	7

Whilst over the DZ, the aircraft which was taking part in a drop coded; DICK89, collided with a USAAF Liberator from the 'Carpetbaggers' 801st Bomb Group at Harrington in Northamptonshire. The crews of both aircraft were killed and it is unclear how the pair were tasked to the same DZ.

Flight Lieutenant John Alan KIDD 20 Pilot
Flying Officer Kenneth Robinson URQUART 23 RCAF Navigator
Sergeant Charlie TAYLOR Wireless Operator
Sergeant Cyril Frederick Thomas MILES 24
Flight Sergeant Bernard STROUD
Sergeant Graham Bancroft BYRNE 21
Sergeant James Revill MOODY

18-Jul-44   11987   Liberator   850 BS   Marigny l'Eglise, Nievre   8

This aircraft, a B24H of the 850 Bomb Sqn of the 801 Bomb Group and carrying the full code; 42-511987, was based at the airfield of Harrington, between Northampton and Market Harborough. It was tasked to drop supplies to the same DZ as Halifax LL364 of 138 Sqn but records suggest that neither crew was aware of the other's tasking. Details of the USAAF crew have only recently been found and are now included.

1st Lieutenant David A MICHELSON Pilot
2nd Lieutenant John P SHAW Jr Co-Pilot
2nd Lieutenant Donald Clarke BOYDE Navigator
1st Lieutenant Melvin WEISS Bomb Aimer
Technical Sergeant Duncan Locklin PATTERSON Flight Engineer
Staff Sergeant William J HOVANEC Wireless Operator
Staff Sergeant Arnold MARINOFF Air Gunner
Staff Sergeant Enoch K WOOTEN Jr Air Gunner

Note: The crew designations are the British equivalents as used elsewhere in this record

---

18-Jul-44   LL387   Halifax   138 Sqn   At sea off St Pair sur Mer Manche   7

The crew of this aircraft was undertaking SHIPWRIGHT 9 when they were shot down. One member of the

333

Date	Serial	Aircraft	Unit	Place	Casualties

Brief Circumstances of Accident
Casualty Details (If Applicable)

crew survived but was subsequently murdered by an enemy soldier.

Flying Officer Nigel Leslie St George PLEASANCE 25 Pilot
Sergeant Thomas FERGUS 29
Sergeant Raymond Leslie LEE 22 Wireless Operator
Sergeant Eric Richard HEARN 21
Flight Lieutenant Herbert Denis BINNS
Sergeant William Logan DALGLISH RCAF Air Gunner
Sergeant John ALLISON 21 Air Gunner

| 18-Jul-44 | V9106 | Hudson III | 353 Sqn | Near RAF Maurpur | 10 |

Immediately after take-off and as the aircraft climbed through 1000 feet, both engines failed. The aircraft stalled, crashed out of control and burst into flames on impact. The engine failure was probably due to either water ingress into the fuel system or incorrect selection of the fuel cocks on the rear tank. The post crash examination also found some 35 lbs of lead weights had been left in the tail of the aircraft and the fuel filters had not been drained. In addition, the hazy conditions prevailing at the time of the accident may have contributed to the loss of control

Pilot Officer Lawrence Garner GREENWOOD 23 Pilot
Flying Officer Donald William KING 24 Navigator
Sergeant George Thomas Watson Hugh COCKSEDGE 18
Group Captain John Wood HOMER 37
Wing Commander Ernest Archie WOLLASTON 33
Flight Lieutenant William George WAINWRIGHT-FAHEY
Flying Officer Arthur Henry SQUIRES
Lieutenant Colonel Edward John COLE 28 RA

Major Robert Bain ROACH Indian Army Corps of Engineers + one non-RAF

18-Jul-44   HH710 Hotspur II   3 GTS   Northleach, Gloucestershire   0
The pilot failed to check the descent and the glider landed nose first and was damaged.

20-Jul-44 FD836 Dakota   117 Sqn   Near Ukhrul   5
The aircraft failed to return from a supply dropping sortie. It transpired that the pilot attempted to reach the DZ by descending into a valley in poor visibility and rain and in doing so crashed into a hill.

    Flight Sergeant Dennis Hodge NOISE 31 Pilot
    Flight Sergeant William Joseph EDWARDS Navigator
    Flight Sergeant Denis GUEST 22 Navigator
    Flight Sergeant Fred CROWTHER 22 Wireless Operator
    Flight Sergeant Joseph Morrison MAXWELL 27 Wireless Operator

23-Jul-44 LJ864 Stirling IV   620 Sqn   North west of Limoges   6
The aircraft was shot down by flak near Le Harve whilst supporting SOE operations as part of a mixed force of forty four Stirlings, Halifaxs and Albemarles. This crew's particular task was a drop to a DZ coded: STATIONER 117.

    Flying Officer Ernest Cameron OKE 22 RCAF Pilot
    Flight Sergeant Thomas Michael GALVON 21 RCAF Navigator
    Sergeant Luke Anthony HIGGINS 27 RCAF Bomb Aimer
    Sergeant Reginald Alfred WILKINS 20 Flight Engineer
    Pilot Officer Angus Sutherland MIDDLETON 25 Wireless Operator
    Sergeant Robert George CARROTHERS 21 RCAF Air Gunner

Date	Serial	Aircraft	Unit	Place	Casualties
		Brief Circumstances of Accident Casualty Details (If Applicable)			
23-Jul-44	LJ882	Stirling	190 Sqn	1½ miles west of Graffigny-Chemin	13

The aircraft left RAF Fairford to deliver an SAS party to France but flew into a hillside near Bourmont, killing 5 crew and 8 parachutists. Two crew members and one parachutist survived and whilst one of the crew evaded capture the other two became POWs.

Flying Officer Leonard Alfred Arthur KILGOUR 24 Pilot RNZAF
Flying Officer Blake Gordon FOY Wireless Operator/Air Gunner RCAF
Pilot Officer Frank COPLAND 29
Flight Sergeant Henry Lester GUY 22 Flight Engineer
Sergeant Albert William SWINDELL 24 Flight Engineer
Captain Felix John Stewart SYMES 27 Special Air Service Regiment
Private Leonard William CURTIS 22 Special Air Service Regiment
Lieutenant Ian Maxwell GRANT 24 Special Air Service Regiment
Signalman Lachlan TAYLOR 21 Royal Corps of Signals
Signalman Wilfred LEACH Royal Corps of Signals
Sergeant Douglas Hays MCKAY 26 Special Air Service Regiment
Private James William Beattie REILLY 25 Special Air Service Regiment
Private James SIMPSON 30 Special Air Service Regiment

Date	Serial	Aircraft	Unit	Place	Casualties
24-Jul-44	BD230	Whitley V	42 OTU	Near Weston Underwood	5

The aircraft dived into the ground

Sergeant John William Edward COOPER Pilot
Sergeant Henry COWAN Navigator
Sergeant William Brooksbank SMITH Bomb Aimer
Sergeant William Clifford NORCROSS Wireless Operator

Sergeant Maurice Mitchell LYON Air Gunner

24-Jul-44   V1621   Albemarle   42 OTU   RAF Ashbourne   3+3

Shortly after take-off the port engine failed and the aircraft returned to land. An overshoot was made on one engine and the aircraft then turned in to land from 800 feet and the pilot initiated an 'S' turn to bleed off some height. The undercarriage was lowered too soon and the aircraft undershot the runway, struck a telegraph pole, crashed on some buildings in the dispersal area and caught fire. The Board of Enquiry considered the pilot made some errors of judgement in lowering the undercarriage too soon and in using 'S' turns to attempt to line up with the runway, however, the CO and the AOC both considered that the poor visibility made it very difficult for the pilot to see the runway and to line up for landing. It is also worth noting that the pilot, despite having over 1500 flying hours, only had 16 hours on type. In total there were five RAF and one other person injured on the ground and two crew, including the pilot, injured in the aircraft, in addition to the fatal casualties.

Flying Officer John Frederick ROSE 33
Sergeant Selwyn THOMPSON 21
Sergeant Stephen Boag TUFF 20
Leading Aircraftman William MCGREGOR 27
Leading Aircraftman Royston Hubert HARWOOD 23
Leading Aircraftwoman Ivy LITCHFIELD 21 WAAF died of injuries 25 July

26-Jul-44   FZ610   Dakota III   512 Sqn   County Angus   2

The aircraft was being flown on a daylight training exercise and the crew had been briefed to discontinue the exercise if they encountered poor weather. The co-pilot failed to caution the pilot about rising ground and whilst flying in cloud at about 700 feet, the aircraft struck the ground. Although the two pilots survived, the navigator and wireless operator did not. The Accident Card records that the pilots did not set a maximum boost climb when they should have done.

Flight Lieutenant Walter James MATTOCKS RCAF Navigator

Date	Serial	Aircraft	Unit	Place	Casualties
			Brief Circumstances of Accident		
			Casualty Details (If Applicable)		

Warrant Officer John Robert WEST 27 Wireless Operator

26-Jul-44   MW119   York I   511 Sqn   RAF North Front   0

The aircraft, which was configured in a VIP fit and which had only been on the squadron for a couple of weeks, was landing at Gibraltar at the conclusion of a 6½ hour flight from UK. The port outer engine had failed because of an oil leak through a cracked pressure pipe and the pilot approached the runway too high and hence decided to overshoot for another attempt. On opening the throttles the aircraft would not stay straight and the pilot then decided to stall the aircraft onto the runway so as not to overshoot into the sea. This he did but all 25 people on board were injured. The air speed indicators were giving different readings and the pilot's was fluctuating between 70 and 130 mph.

26-Jul-44   RJ262   Horsa   1 HGSU   RAF Tarrant Rushton   0

The glider was landing at night after some circuit training and the pilot turned off the runway too quickly, contrary to his brief and in doing so the glider collided with a parked Halifax.

28-Jul-44   P1400   Albemarle   297 Sqn   France   3

The aircraft was one of a large force from 38 Gp sqns operating over France. It was seen in flames on the ground, having crashed shortly before crossing the coast on the return leg.

Squadron Leader Lawrence Denis EMBLEM 25 Pilot

Flying Officer David PICKARD 29

Flight Sergeant Fulke Henry Arthur BRAYBROOKE 25 Passenger

338

28-Jul-44   P1605   Albemarle I   ORTU   RAF Cottesmore   0

The aircraft was being employed on a glider towing exercise and was flown by a crew of five, whose captain had over 100 hours on type. The pilot mishandled the fuel system and attempted to run the fuselage tanks down to the last 10 gallons, which equates to some 3 minutes flying, instead of changing to the wing tanks in good time. Both engines failed and an attempt was made to land wheels down in a corn field short of the runway. However, after a successful touchdown at about 80 mph, the undercarriage collapsed. Whilst the pilot was judged to have been negligent, a general warning about increased fuel consumption whilst glider towing was issued and the correct use of the fuel system was re emphasised to all crews. It has to be observed that increased fuel consumption at high all up weight or when towing a glider is self evident and the correct manipulation of the fuel system might be regarded as a fairly elementary skill, not to say important one.

29-Jul-44   LK133   Stirling IV   570 Sqn   Near Dijon   7

The aircraft was one of a force of 37 Halifaxes, Stirlings and Albemarles tasked to SOE work and its particular task was HERMIT 15 in the Dijon area. It failed to return.

Pilot Officer Douglas ROBSON 26 Pilot
Flying Officer Arthur Walter William NIPPER 22 Navigator
Flying Officer Dallas Eugene BELT 25 RCAF Bomb Aimer
Warrant Officer Lionel Wilfred Lawrence HAMBROOKE 34 RCAF Wireless Operator
Flight Sergeant Miles Alphonsus MURPHY 22 Air Gunner
Sergeant Stanley William THOMPSON 32 Flight Engineer
Sergeant Leslie HODGSON 20 Air Despatcher

30-Jul-44   JP239   Halifax   148 Sqn   North of Corsica   5

The crew was tasked for a sortie to a DZ in Northern Italy and the drop had been completed successfully. During the return flight at medium level, one of the starboard engines malfunctioned and the aircraft filled

Date	Serial	Aircraft	Unit	Place	Casualties

Brief Circumstances of Accident
Casualty Details (If Applicable)

with smoke. The captain ordered the aircraft abandoned but only one member of the crew survived to be rescued by a US launch after a short period in the water. The cause of the engine problems were never discovered but were sufficient to result in the aircraft's loss within a very few minutes.

Flying Officer Peter William CLIFFORD 21
Sergeant John Brown HUMPHREY 28
Flying Officer John Reginald MACKNEY 23
Sergeant Robert William MCCORMICK
Sergeant Ronald James POCOCK

30-Jul-44	KG461	Dakota	117 Sqn	East of the Chindwin	3

A pair of Dakotas were tasked with a sortie to Mogaung from their base at Sylhet. Whilst en route, the aircraft encountered Japanese aircraft which were attacking targets in the area of Myitkyina and both Dakotas were shot down with the loss of all on board.

Flight Lieutenant Reginald Shirley SMITH DFC RCAF Pilot
Flying Officer John Clifford BYRNE 23
Warrant Officer Harry MCIVER 27
Warrant Officer Edward James PARKER

30-Jul-44	KG537	Dakota	117 Sqn	East of the Chindwin	3

Lost as outlined above.

Flight Lieutenant Bernard Gerrard Levens O'REILLY DFC
Flight Lieutenant Thomas Stephens MCCARTNEY 30 RAAF
Pilot Officer Hugh Crawford YOUNG 23

Flying Officer Francis Henry BAGGS 25 RAAF

31-Jul-44   KG690   Dakota III   44 SAAF   30 miles from Salalah Persian Gulf   32

The aircraft was approaching Salalah at the end of a ferry flight from Riyan, which had taken about 3 hours. Besides an operating crew of five there were twenty seven passengers on board, most from 244 Sqn, a Wellington equipped unit flying anti-submarine patrols in the Gulf region. The pilot had been correctly briefed and warned that approaches to Salalah in bad weather were unsafe below 5000 feet on a heading of 051 degrees magnetic. Wireless reception was good and the HF/DF station was working and had transmitted five QDMs to the aircraft, all of which gave readings of between 054 and 051 degrees magnetic. Whilst flying in cloud with 10/10ths cover at 800 feet, the aircraft struck cliffs at a height of 630 feet and was destroyed. From the position of the wreckage, it is thought possible that the pilot believed he would miss the promontory of rock into which the aircraft flew.

Lieutenant C J SHUTTE 29 SAAF Pilot
Lieutenant John Henry Stevenson GLENNY 20 SAAF Co-Pilot
Lieutenant G C PENNINGTON 19 SAAF Navigator
Air Corporal R HOSNER 28 SAAF
Air Corporal R B BORAINE 19 SAAF
Flying Officer Noel O'Brien BUTLER Passengers
Pilot Officer Lewis William CHAPMAN DFM
Aircraftman 2nd Class Alan Grant CLARK
Aircraftman 1st Class Vincent James COLLETT
Leading Aircraftman William George COLTON 42
Aircraftman 1st Class George Gibb EDMONSTON 35
Leading Aircraftman Richard Edward GILES
Leading Aircraftman Thomas GOWLAND 23
Leading Aircraftman Peter Leonard HEATH 21
Aircraftman 2nd Class William Edward HOLDER 21

341

Date	Serial	Aircraft	Unit	Place	Casualties

Brief Circumstances of Accident
Casualty Details (If Applicable)

Corporal Alexander JOHNSON 27
Sergeant Albert John LINEGAR
Warrant Officer II Roy James LOVE 23 RCAF
Corporal James Adam Bridges MCINTOSH 23
Aircraftman 1st Class Leslie MAWER
Flying Officer John Kendell NEWTH 22 RAAF
Corporal Arthur Stanley Gilbert PERRING
Pilot Officer Derek Vivian RANDALL 24
Leading Aircraftman Jack RATHBONE
Flying Officer Conrad Clifford SWIRE 35 RAAF
Aircraftman 1st Class Cyril Wilfred TURNER 19
Corporal James WHELAN 36
+ five civilian personnel whose names are not known

Date	Serial	Aircraft	Unit	Place	Casualties
31-Jul-44	DL961	Master II	5 GTS	Smethwick Park, Birmingham	2

The pilot was beating up his home area in direct contravention of his brief. The aircraft stalled, dived into the ground and caught fire on crashing.

Flight Sergeant Allan Charley COX 22
Flight Sergeant Gordon PRESTON 22

Date	Serial	Aircraft	Unit	Place	Casualties
01-Aug-44	N7263	Hudson	161 Sqn	RAF Tempsford	0

This aircraft was returning from RAF Lyneham, where it had collected the crew of another aircraft (see account of the loss of Halifax LL251 on 12 Jul 44). The aircraft swung on landing and struck a building, being written off in the process.

01-Aug-44 P9129 Lysander 161 Sqn

02-Aug-44 KG457 Dakota III 62 Sqn Uisi, Falam, Burma 5

The crew was detailed for a supply dropping sortie in the Lushai Hills, which is in the Falam area of Burma, and the aircraft took off at about 1400 hours. The aircraft did not return and an aerial search did not locate it. A couple of weeks later, a patrol found the burnt out wreck of the aircraft on a hillside but there was no evidence to suggest why the aircraft crashed.

    Flight Sergeant John Edward Ray COURTHOPE 24 Pilot
    Flight Sergeant Russell Gordon BROWN Co-Pilot
    Warrant Officer Albert Ronald RIX 24 RAAF Navigator
    Warrant Officer Hildebrand Alfred JOHANSSON 22 RNZAF Wireless Operator
    Sepoy Augustine PINTO 21 1007 Air Supply Section RIASC Air Despatcher

02-Aug-44 LJ969 Stirling 624 Sqn Blida 0

On return from a sortie over southern France, the aircraft was approaching to land at its base but the starboard undercarriage would not release from its bay, as the up lock was jammed. After trying for some time to clear the problem, the pilot; Flight Sergeant K V Pole, made a wheels up landing and although the aircraft was little damaged, it was not repaired and struck off charge at the end of the month.

02-Aug-44 HH721 Hotspur II 3 GTS Northleach 0

Collided with another aircraft on landing.

03-Aug-44 JP294 Halifax 148 Sqn Near Venice 7

The aircraft was shot down whilst on a supply dropping sortie on to a DZ in Northern Italy.

    Warrant Officer Kevin Joseph BEETLES 22 Pilot
    Flight Sergeant Wilfred EDMONDSON 24 Navigator

Date	Serial	Aircraft	Unit	Place	Casualties

Brief Circumstances of Accident
Casualty Details (If Applicable)

Flight Sergeant Reginald Jack WARD BARRETT Bomb Aimer
Flight Sergeant Frank WHARAM Wireless Operator
Sergeant Norman Jack HOBBS Flight Engineer
Sergeant James John BIRTLES 20 Air Gunner
Flight Sergeant William Clark MCINTOSH 20 Air Gunner

04-Aug-44   FH460   Hudson IIIA   24 Sqn   Coombe Hill, Wendover near Aylesbury   6

The aircraft was being ferried back to its base at RAF Hendon after an overseas operation and it had been airborne for nearly 8 hours. Whilst approaching the end of the sortie, the aircraft crashed into high ground, having descended below its safety height whilst still in cloud. The pilot failed to follow the correct procedures for a descent through cloud and it appears that the navigator did not maintain his dead reckoning plot.

Flight Lieutenant Robert William HARDCASTLE 31 Pilot
Flying Officer Edward John SMITH 24 Co-Pilot
Flying Officer Arthur Milford TINDALE 33 RAAF Navigator
Leading Aircraftman Ronald Joseph WALTER 23
Flight Lieutenant George Frederick ROBERTS 33 Pilot
Flight Sergeant Leonard James REASON 37

04-Aug-44   FZ597   Dakota   353 Sqn   11 miles north east of Mohavia India   17

The aircraft was undertaking a routine mail run sortie between Calcutta and Delhi and had been airborne for about 2½ hours. The aircraft was flown into a developed cu-nim cloud and encountered heavy rain and severe turbulence. The pilot lost control and the aircraft broke up with an initial fracture of the port mainplane root fillet, leading to a more general disintegration. In addition to the pilot being fatigued after flying over 130 hours in the previous month, the aircraft's artificial horizon was unserviceable and this could have contributed to the pilot's inability to maintain control.

Flying Officer David Crawford FORMAN 23 AFC RAAF Pilot
Sergeant Charles Edward CHURCH 24 Flight Engineer
Aircraftman 1st Class William John LEWIS 22
Flight Sergeant Kenneth Martyn Anthony SEXTON 21
Aircraftman 1st Class Oliver TAYLOR
Flight Sergeant Stanley WILSON 25
Pilot Officer John BEEBAR 22 RAAF
Flying Officer Frederick William CAWTHORNE Wireless Operator
Lieutenant Colonel Paul Evan Rodgers DAWSON OC 21 Mountain Regiment RA
Warrant Officer Frederick Walter HANDLEY 30 RAAF
Major Ernest HICKS IEME
Flight Lieutenant Frederick Grant JACKSON RCAF
Major Gerald Francis KEEN 24
Lieutenant Colonel Edward Ronald PETTIT MC 9th Queen's Royal Lancers
Major Thomas Atkinson WALTON 31 Sherwood Foresters
Lieutenant Colonel Robert Frank Courtney WEALLENS 39 RE
+ one other

04-Aug-44	KG827 Liberator	1586 Flt	Brindisi	0

The aircraft, flown by Flight Lieutenant Jan Mioduchowski, was one of a mixed force of three Liberators and four Halifaxes from the Polish forces, tasked with a supply drop into Poland. Unknown to the RAF authorities, four of the Polish crews were sent to Warsaw on the orders of their own staff, including this crew. Attacked and damaged by a Ju 88 whilst en-route, the aircraft was hit by AA fire as it flew over Krasinki Square in the Polish capital and one engine was put out of action. The aircraft was attacked again on its return journey and a second engine disabled. With great skill Mioduchowski flew his aircraft back to Italy On landing the aircraft crashed and was written off but without injury to the crew. For his

345

gallantry and perseverance on this unit, Mioduchowski was awarded the DFC by the British.

05-Aug-44   FZ674   Dakota   575 Sqn   Northern France   5

The aircraft was being flown on a freight transport and casualty evacuation sortie and had been airborne for 1½ hours, having taken off from Broadwell on the outbound (freighting) part of the sortie. The aircraft struck ground in what is described as 'zero visibility' but the cause is not known and there are no comments on the state of the radio aids etc. The Accident Card makes the unusual note that 'Command has tried to assemble a Court of Enquiry but no individuals available; all deceased or deployed from UK'.

    Flying Officer Peter Carl HAKANSSON Pilot
    Flying Officer Norman LOMAS Navigator
    Flight Sergeant Ernest Francis GUY Wireless Operator
    Flying Officer John Alexander MORRISON Navigator/Bomb Aimer
    Corporal William Edward BRENNEN

05-Aug-44   JP181   Halifax   148 Sqn   Poland   7

This aircraft and the three listed below were all destroyed whilst attempting to supply the Polish Home Army (AK) during the uprising in Warsaw. There is some suggestion that at least some of the aircraft were attacked by Soviet fighters and it is certainly true that the Soviet authorities did all their power to prevent the British and US forces from providing help to the Poles fighting in Warsaw. Whilst beyond the scope of this book, it is worth noting that the Soviets encouraged the Poles in the belief that their capital was about to be relieved and this led the Home Army (AK) to begin an uprising against the Nazi forces. The Soviets were aware of the violent reaction this would provoke from the enemy and were content, for their own long term ends, to see any form of Polish resistance and nationalistic feeling destroyed anf thence to fill the vacuum with communist 'placemen'. It is also worth noting that the pleas by the AK leadership for help, ignored advice they had been given that it was impossible to support effectively the uprising with the air forces available. The subsequent attempts by British, Commonwealth and Polish aircrews to provide some supplies to the AK forces in and around Warsaw, would result in very heavy losses to all those involved in the airlift and for no gain.

Pilot Officer Charles William CRABTREE 23 Pilot
Sergeant Dennis AIRD 19 Flight Engineer
Warrant Officer John Aloysius CARROLL Wireless Operator
Warrant Officer Alexander SANDILANDS 23 Air Gunner
Flight Sergeant Dennis John MASON 23 Navigator
Flight Sergeant Alexander BENNETT 29 RAAF
Flight Sergeant Charles Alec BEANLAND 20 RCAF Air Gunner

05-Aug-44 JP276 Halifax   148 Sqn   Poland   7
Lost as indicated above.

Flight Lieutenant Arnold Raymond BLYNN RCAF Pilot
Flight Sergeant Charles Burton WYLIE RCAF
Pilot Officer George Alfred CHAPMAN 24 RCAF Navigator
Flying Officer Harold Leonard BROWN 20 RCAF Flight Engineer
Flight Sergeant Arthur George William LIDDELL RCAF Air Gunner
Sergeant Kenneth James ASHMORE
Warrant Officer Frederick George WENHAM 21 Flight Engineer

05-Aug-44 JP162 Halifax   148 Sqn   Poland   3
Lost as indicated above. Four members of the crew survived and were sheltered by the AK.

Flight Lieutenant James Girvan MCCALL 23 Pilot
Sergeant Clifford ASPINALL Air Gunner
Warrant Officer John Frederick Cairney RAE 33 Air Gunner

Date	Serial	Aircraft	Unit	Place	Casualties
Brief Circumstances of Accident Casualty Details (If Applicable)					
05-Aug-44	EB147	Halifax	148 Sqn	Poland	0

This aircraft, captained by Flying Officer L G King was shot down whilst engaged on supply dropping to the Polish Home Army. All the crew survived, although six were made POW and and the other evavded capture and was hidden by the AK forces'

Date	Serial	Aircraft	Unit	Place	Casualties
05-Aug-44	KG779	Dakota III	45 Gp	Lagens	0

See summary below.

Date	Serial	Aircraft	Unit	Place	Casualties
05-Aug-44	KG801	Dakota III	45 Gp	Lagens	0

During the take of run, the aircraft's port engine failed and it swung off the runway, striking both Dakota KG779 and a B17 Fortress serial 230252.

Date	Serial	Aircraft	Unit	Place	Casualties
05-Aug-44	LJ920	Stirling	620 Sqn	Notre Dame de Livaye, near Lisieux	9

The aircraft was part of a ten aircraft package taking part in a supply drop over France and this crew was tasked to HOUNDSWORTH 44, with a drop for SAS forces. However, when outbound and about 1½ hours after take-off it was shot down by flak.

Pilot Officer Edward Grigg ROBINSON 21 RNZAF Pilot
Warrant Officer Ihaia William TRAINOR 32 RNZAF Bomb Aimer
Sergeant Richard George GLANVILLE 21 Flight Engineer
Warrant Officer Peter STURGES 21 RAAF Air Gunner
Flight Sergeant Kenneth Jefferies JOHNSON 20 Wireless Operator
Flight Sergeant James Frederick LEWIS 24 Navigator
Flying Officer Ramsey McKenzie HABKIRK 25 RCAF

Corporal J E SMITH 31 RASC
Driver Ralph WRIGHT 30 RASC

05-Aug-44 LL248 Halifax   Near Huiron Marne   8
The aircraft was shot down during sortie BOB 166, in the area of an enemy airfield. One of the crew survived and was able to evade capture. There are also two unnamed French agents who are buried in the same grave.

Flight Lieutenant Albert Edward LOOS DFC Pilot
Flying Officer Ian Armstrong BLAIKIE 26 RNZAF Navigator
Pilot Officer Kenneth Frederick MORGAN 21 RNZAF Wireless Operator
Sergeant Basil Featherstone HOLLAND 28 Flight Engineer
Flight Sergeant David Gordon PATTERSON 22 Bomb Aimer
Flying Officer Robert Buchan HALL 36 Air Gunner
+ two French agents

05-Aug-44 V9748 Lysander III   Messac Ille et Vilaine   2
This aircraft was shot down by an RAF Mosquito.

Flying Officer John Perry ALCOCK 30
Lucien GERMERAU Agent

06-Aug-44 LJ878 Stirling   4 miles east-south-east Auray   6
The aircraft was being flown on mission IAN 7 to Baden but failed to return. When in the area of Plougoumelen and whilst flying at about 1500 feet, it was shot down by enemy anti-aircraft fire.

Flying Officer Henare Whakatau URU 23 RNZAF Pilot
Warrant Officer Robert Jack BRADDOCK 26 RNZAF Navigator
Sergeant Alfred Anthony HULL 20
Warrant Officer Gordon Fletcher HARRISON 24 RCAF

Date	Serial	Aircraft	Unit	Place	Casualties
Brief Circumstances of Accident					
Casualty Details (If Applicable)					

Flight Sergeant Leonard Allan EUNSON 24 RAAF
Pilot Officer Walter Nelson IRVING 26 RCAF

| 06-Aug-44 | LL334 | Halifax | 298 Sqn | 60 miles south-east Rheims | 1 |

The aircraft was engaged in a sortie; DIPLOMAT 9, in support of SAS operations and was part of a mixed package totalling 28 Stirlings and Halifaxs. The aircraft was intercepted by an enemy night fighter and shot down. The pilot was able to make a crash landing and all the crew except himself survived.

Flying Officer Charles Edward ANDERSON 23 RCAF Pilot

| 07-Aug-44 | EF305 | Stirling | 299 Sqn | RAF Keevil | 0 |

The aircraft overshot its landing, a swing developed and the undercarriage failed.

| 07-Aug-44 | P1519 | Albemarle I | 42 OTU | RAF Ashbourne | 0 |

The aircraft was landing at base and the pilot selected flaps down but despite the lever being moved to the fully down setting, the flaps only travelled to the 25 degree position. The aircraft landed too fast and in attempting to avoid overshooting the runway, the pilot turned the aircraft but its undercarriage collapsed. The pilot was blamed for not checking the flaps in the air but it is unclear how he was supposed to do so.

| 07-Aug-44 | LJ974 | Stirling IV | 624 Sqn | Blida | 0 |

The aircraft is shown in the records as having been categorised; 'CAT 'B' FB', meaning it had sustained damage during a 'flying battle' and was not repairable. Details of the incident are not recorded.

07-Aug-44 LK182 Stirling IV   624 Sqn   Blida   ?

The aircraft was taking off for a sortie to Langoustine, France but crashed after a violent swing developed. There were no injuries amongst the crew, captained by Pilot Officer D H Solin.

09-Aug-44 LL308 Halifax   138 Sqn   Near Geraudot Aube   6

This aircraft was shot down on sortie OSRIC 45 and there was only one survivor; Flight Sergeant F E O Evans RNZAF. Evans evaded successfully and was repatriated 3 weeks later.

    Pilot Officer Graham Warren PATERSON 22 RNZAF Pilot
    Pilot Officer Arthur William ATTERTON 32
    Sergeant Horace BEDFORD 35
    Sergeant Stanley Raymond CURTIS 20
    Sergeant Condor Charles DOWSE 22 Air Gunner
    Flight Sergeant Lewis Paul SEARELL 20 RNZAF Bomb Aimer

09-Aug-44 LL358 Halifax   161 Sqn   Cugny Aisne   7

The crew of this aircraft were flying sortie TOM 53, with another aircraft from the squadron but it did not return. The other crew reported that whilst they were running up to the DZ, they saw this aircraft crash in flames.

    Flight Sergeant Joseph William NICHOLLS Pilot
    Warrant Officer I John Bruce GRADY 26 RCAF Navigator
    Sergeant Anthony Albert RIVERS
    Sergeant Bryan Charles Frederick DEAN 27
    Pilot Officer George Edwards RHEAD 28
    Sergeant Clifford George BRAGG 20
    Sergeant Ellis MARKSON 38

Date	Serial	Aircraft	Unit	Place	Casualties
		Brief Circumstances of Accident Casualty Details (If Applicable)			
09-Aug-44	P1501	Albemarle I	296 Sqn	Missing	6

The aircraft was one of four from the squadron operating on SOE sorties with thirty two Stirlings, nine Halifax aircraft from 298 Sqn, and three Albemarles from the sister squadron No: 297. It failed to return but the circumstances of its loss are not known.

Flight Sergeant Edwin Raymond ABELL 32
Flight Sergeant Francis Charles ELWOOD 24
Sergeant Ralph COWHAM 23
Warrant Officer Bruce STENNING 27 RAAF
Flight Sergeant Frederick Norman MANTON 30
Flight Sergeant Charles Alfred HAMMOND27

Date	Serial	Aircraft	Unit	Place	Casualties
09-Aug-44	P1600	Albemarle I	N/K	RAF Llandow	0

The aircraft's undercarriage collapsed whilst it was taxying but its unit is not shown.

Date	Serial	Aircraft	Unit	Place	Casualties
09-Aug-44	LK177	Stirling IV	624 Sqn	Blida	0

Whilst taking off for sortie TWEEDSMUIR to France, the undercarriage was retracted prematurely and the aircraft bounced. Subsequently it was belly landed but written off.

Date	Serial	Aircraft	Unit	Place	Casualties
09-Aug-44	DP312	Horsa	1 HGSU	RAF Netheravon	0

This glider was landing after a flight of 1¾ hours as part of Exercise MOLE. During final approach, the pilot was compelled to take avoiding action because another aircraft was in the way. Unfortunately, the outcome was that this aircraft crashed on touchdown.

09-Aug-44 LH490 Horsa   1 HGSU   RAF Netheravon   0

This aircraft was taking part in the same exercise as the glider listed above. Whilst landing in poor and misty visibility on an airfield with poor lighting and in close proximity to other gliders, accidents were bound to happen. In this case the pilot lost visual contact with the ground because of the mist and the glider was damaged in a heavy landing.

09-Aug-44 PW638 Horsa   1 HGSU   200 yards south-west of Netheravon   0

This accident was another caused during Exercise MOLE. There was poor marking of the LZ and the pilot, who was relatively inexperienced, had difficulty seeing the landing area. The glider undershot the airfield and was damaged. This pilot was Squadron Sergeant Major E J Blackwood, who was to be awarded a Military Medal for his gallant actions during Operation VARSITY.

10-Aug-44 EF256 Stirling IV   620 Sqn   Off French coast   2

This aircraft, flown by Flying Officer William Bell RAAF and his crew were carrying five French members of 3rd SAS Bn and were part of a four aircraft tasking to a DZ north west of Lyon. However, there was no reception committee at the site and the aircraft returned to base but this one was shot down by AA fire off the French coast in the vicinity of the Jersey. Although the operating crew and three of the parachutists survived, two others did not.

        Trooper Daniel SELLES 3rd Special Air Service Battalion
        Trooper Roger DASTIS

12-Aug-44 KG625 Dakota III   512 Sqn   France   0

The aircraft was landing in a crosswind, estimated at 20 mph and 90 degrees to the runway in use. The aircraft started to swing to starboard and the pilot used the engines to correct the swing. The port tyre burst, the aircraft swung to port and the starboard undercarriage collapsed.

Date	Serial	Aircraft	Unit	Place	Casualties

Brief Circumstances of Accident
Casualty Details (If Applicable)

12-Aug-44 EF210 Stirling III 1665 HCU Alne Yorkshire 4

The aircraft was attempting an emergency landing but then an overshoot was initiated. The aircraft would not gain height and it struck a railway bridge and was destroyed.

    Flight Lieutenant Vernon Terence Joseph HAND 22
    Flight Lieutenant Robert Edwards HARVEY 31
    Flying Officer Godfrey William ARNOLD 27
    Sergeant Leslie SANDERSON 23

12-Aug-44 EM344 Master II 3 GTS Northleach, Gloucestershire 0

The pilot, who was an experienced instructor, flew the aircraft for about 30 minutes longer than the normal safe endurance of the aircraft. On approach to land, the engine cut and the aircraft crashed into a bank and a wall when the pilot attempted a forced landing. There was no fuel remaining in the port fuel tank and only 3 gallons in the starboard tank.

13-Aug-44 DP348 Horsa HGCU RAF North Luffenham 0

At 300 feet on the approach to land, the instructor took control because the student was overshooting. A 360 degree turn was then initiated in order to lose height but the aircraft was still about 60 degrees off the direction of landing when it stalled off a very tight turn and struck the ground. It was commented that the minimum height to start a 360 degree turn in a Horsa was 800 feet and the instructor did not help himself by raising the flaps, which induced a loss of height.

14-Aug-44 JN896 Halifax 624 Sqn 6 miles north-east Palamos 9

The aircraft took off from Blida, Algeria at about 2300 hours on a sortie over occupied territory in France. At

0420 hours, the crew signalled that the sortie had been completed and they were returning. Subsequently, an unidentified aircraft was seen to explode in the air in the position shown, which is at sea about halfway between Barcelona and Perpignan. An extensive search by the Spanish air-sea rescue organisation plus a number of sorties by other squadron aircraft did not find any survivors or their remains and the crew is commemorated on the Malta Memorial. The 14 Aug was Fg Off Neale's birthday.

Flying Officer Walter George DRISCOLL
Sergeant Edmund HURST
Sergeant Norman SOULSBY
Flight Sergeant Edwin Garnet LAMBERT
Pilot Officer Frederick Davidson LAING 21 RCAF Wireless Operatot/Air Gunner
Flying Officer Leopold William NEALE 35 RNZAF Navigator
Flight Sergeant James Maxwell HULMES RAAF
Warrant Officer William Norman PROCTOR 21 RCAF Wireless Operator/Air Gunner
Flying Officer Cecil Henry LUXON 22

14-Aug-44   EV961   Liberator   178 Sqn   Poland   6

The aircraft failed to return from a supply dropping sortie to Polish Home Army (AK) units in the Warsaw area. The crew are buried together in a Collective Grave at Krakow. At this time, aircraft from the three Liberator bomber squadrons based in the area were being used to supplement the efforts of the special duties and transport crews. It consequence, losses below will be recorded against 31 and 34 SAAF Sqns and 178 Sqn.

Flying Officer George Dougal MACRAE RCAF Pilot
Lieutenant Percy Gordon COUTTS SAAF Navigator
Sergeant John Edward PORTER Wireless Operator
Sergeant Richard Herbert Charles SCOTT 21 Flight Engineer
Sergeant Arthur SHARP 22 Air Gunner
Flight Sergeant Hugh Valance MCLANAGHAN Air Gunner

355

Date	Serial	Aircraft	Unit	Place	Casualties

Brief Circumstances of Accident
Casualty Details (If Applicable)

14-Aug-44 EW105 Liberator   31 SAAF   Near Kiev   1

This aircraft was the second from the squadron to be lost whilst dropping supplies to the Poles. It was being flown by a crew of RAF and SAAF personnel, captained by Lieutenant R R Klette SAAF. Whilst over the target area, the aircraft had been badly damaged and the crew baled out, all but one of whom survived to be made POW.

Warrant Officer II H J BROWN SAAF

14-Aug-44 EW138 Liberator   31 SAAF   Poland   0

The circumstances surrounding the loss of this aircraft are unusual. The crew was detailed for a supply dropping sortie to the Warsaw area and approaching the target, their aircraft was attacked by a night fighter and subjected to heavy AA fire. The pilot ordered the supply containers to be jettisoned short of the target and commenced a climbing turn to starboard to evade enemy fire and searchlights. An AA shell struck the port outer engine and it was put out of action, with the co-pilot feathering the propeller. The aircraft was then 'coned' by about a dozen searchlights and subjected to further AA fire, which the pilot attempted to avoid. Quite suddenly, the pilot left his seat, grabbed his parachute and without a word to the others he abandoned the aircraft! The co-pilot; Second Lieutenant Robert Burgess, whose flying experience in the Liberator was negligible, took control of the aircraft and managed to prevent it from diving into the ground. The aircraft was flown away from the immediate target area but was difficult to control and a further assessment revealed problems with the hydraulics and other systems, which made it unlikely that the aircraft could return to its base at Foggia Italy. The navigator; Lieutenant Noel Sleed and the bomb aimer; Sergeant Allan Bates, assisted Burgess with Bates taking over the role of co-pilot. A 'crew conference' was held and it was decided to attempt to get to allied territory, rather than bale out and this they commenced. During the next hours the crew encountered many problems but eventually a wheels down forced landing was made in Russian held territory, where there were further adventures at the hands of the Russian authorities before the survivors were taken to Moscow on 19 August. After a few weeks in the Soviet capital, the crew flew to Cairo on 4 September and then were repatriated to South Africa a month later. For their efforts, Burgess was awarded the DSO, the only such award to a second lieutenant in the SAAF, whilst Sleed received the DFC and Bates the DFM. The citation for their joint awards is remarkably brief but is worth reproducing:

Distinguished Service Order

Second Lieutenant Robert Christopher Wickham BURGESS (542738V) SAAF 31 (SAAF) Squadron

Distinguished Flying Cross

Lieutenant Noel SLEED (542348V) SAAF 31 (SAAF) Squadron

Distinguished Flying Medal

1673535 Sergeant Alan Herbert BATES RAFVR 31 (SAAF) Squadron

One night in August 1944, these officers and airman were second pilot, navigator and air bomber of an aircraft detailed for a vital supply dropping mission. In the operation great difficulties and considerable danger were faced and the skill bravery and fortitude displayed by these members of aircraft crew set an example of the highest order.

It is fitting to record that the other members of the crew, who were all RAFVR personnel were: Sergeant I G Payne, Sergeant D E D Lewis, Sergeant J S Appleyard and Sergeant W Cross. It is known that the pilot was made POW immediately following his departure from the aircraft but what happened to him subsequently is not recorded.

357

14-Aug-44 KG784 Dakota III   98 Staging Post At sea off the coast of Brazil   0

The aircraft was flying at 9000 feet on a delivery flight and had been airborne for about 2¾ hours. Both engines failed and the crew had no option to ditching the aircraft and this was carried out successfully without injury to them. The cause of the double engine failure was not established.

Date	Serial	Aircraft	Unit	Place	Casualties
		Brief Circumstances of Accident			
		Casualty Details (If Applicable)			

15-Aug-44 EW275 Liberator   1586 (SD) Flt   Olszyny near Tarnow   7

This aircraft was shot down during the return flight from the Warsaw area.

Flight Lieutenant Zygmunt PLUTA 31
Sergeant Brunon MALEJKA 27
Flying Officer Tadeusz JENCKA 26
Sergeant Jan MARECKI 23
Flight Sergeant Jozef DUDZIAK 20
Flight Sergeant Bernard WICHROWSKI 21
Flight Sergeant Jan FLORKOWSKI 24

15-Aug-44 JP220 Halifax   1586 Flt   Poland   1

The aircraft was destroyed during the return from Warsaw and besides one member of the crew being killed, the pilot; Warrant Officer Leszek Owsiany, was wounded and made POW, whilst the other six were given shelter by the AK.

Warrant Officer Stafan BOHANES 30

15-Aug-44 KG890 Liberator   1586 Flt   Warsaw   7

At the start of the Warsaw uprising, one of the Polish pilots made an impassioned plea to the crews of other squadrons to do their best to bring relief and aid to the Polish Home Army in Warsaw; that pilot was Szostak. The precise circumstances of the loss of this crew are unclear but the aircraft crashed in the centre of the city whilst dropping supplies from a low level and all on board were killed.

Flight Lieutenant Zbignew Michael SZOSTAK 28 DFC
Warrant Officer Jozef BIELICKI 22

Flight Lieutenant Stanislaw DANIEL 34
Flight Sergeant Wincenty Tudeusz RUTKOWSKI 23
Flight Sergeant Jozef WITEK 29
Warrant Officer Tudeusz DUBOWSKI 21
Sergeant Stanislaw MALCZYK 28

15-Aug-44	EW264 Liberator	178 Sqn	Poland	7

Lost on a sortie to Warsaw.

Warrant Officer Murray Alexander BAXTER 23 RAAF Pilot
Flight Sergeant Richard William ROBINSON 21 Navigator
Sergeant Gordon Waalace JOSLYN 20 Bomb Aimer
Flight Sergeant Bernard Joseph BARRETT 23 Wireless Operator
Sergeant Richard Herbert Charles SCOTT 21 Flight Engineer
Flight Sergeant Jasper Victor LEE Air Gunner
Sergeant Arthur SHARPE 22 Air Gunner

15-Aug-44	KG873 Halifax	178 Sqn	Poland	6

Lost on a sortie to Warsaw.

Flight Lieutenant Edwin Charles THYER 22 Pilot
Lieutenant Keith FAIRWEATHER SAAF Navigator
Sergeant Cecil Edward FOREMAN 28 Wireless Operator
Sergeant Sidney Frank HORNE 21 Flight Engineer
Sergeant Matthew Thomas MOUNTAIN Air Gunner
Sergeant Sydney John DAVIS 34 Air Gunner

15-Aug-44	JN926 Halifax	148 Sqn	Poland	4

There is some confusion regarding the identity of this aircraft but it is believed to be that captained by Pilot

Date	Serial	Aircraft	Unit	Place	Casualties

Brief Circumstances of Accident
Casualty Details (If Applicable)

Officer M L Casey. A total of twenty six aircraft from four squadrons were sent to drop supplies to the AK in Warsaw. As will be seen from the losses listed, the task proved costly in terms of aircraft and crews. This one was shot down and although the pilot and two others survived, four men did not. These men are believed to be those listed below. Sergeant Hartog was of Belgian origin and he served under the assumed name of HARWOOD

Sergeant Robert Samuel DARLING Wireless Operator
Sergeant Thomas LAW Air Gunner
Sergeant Peter Henry ROOTS Flight Engineer
Sergeant Ronald HARTOG Air Gunner

15-Aug-44	KG828	Liberator	178 Sqn	Poland	7

In the confused situation around Warsaw, several aircraft were seen to be on fire or to crash and whilst this crew was lost in these circumstances, it is impossible to identify which of those incidents, reported by crews at debriefing, relate to this aircraft.

Lieutenant R L LAWSON 21 SAAF Pilot
Lieutenant A D E STOTT 24 SAAF Navigator
Sergeant Rupert Vincent STONIER 23 Bomb Aimer
Sergeant Ronald Charles PAIN 24 Wireless Operator
Sergeant William George Clement GARNER 36 Flight Engineer
Warrant Officer Ernest Henry John PAGE 26 Air Gunner
Sergeant William HUDDERT 22 Air Gunner

15-Aug-44	KG836	Liberator	31 SAAF	Warsaw	7

The aircraft was flying in the central city area of Warsaw in an attempt to deliver supplies to the Polish

Home Army. It was so low that a wing struck a rooftop and the aircraft crashed into the Central Square.

Lieutenant Grattan Chesney HOOEY 25 SAAF Pilot
Lieutenant P H ANDREWS 20 SAAF Co-Pilot
Lieutenant Cedric Arthur COOKE 30 SAAF Navigator
Lieutenant H A R MALE 26 SAAF Wireless operator
Lieutenant G B PITT 20 SAAF Wireless Operator/Air Gunner
Warrant Officer I T D O'KEEFE 20 SAAF Wireless Operator/Air Gunner
Sergeant Peter Henry George LEES 20 Bomb Aimer

15-Aug-44 KG871 Liberator   31 SAAF   Poland   7
The aircraft failed to return from a supply dropping sortie to Warsaw

Captain N VAN RENSBURG SAAF Pilot
Lieutenant R A LAVERY 25 SAAF Co-Pilt
Lieutenant J C BRANCH-CLARK 18 SAAF Navigator
Warrant Officer I Richard Walter STAFFORD 26 SAAF Air Gunner
Warrant Officer II Ben Nevis WOODS 36 SAAF Air Gunner
Warrant Officer II J A MEYER 21 SAAF Air Gunner
Sergeant Edward Hall TURNER Wireless Operator

15-Aug-44 KG939 Liberator   31 SAAF   Near Warsaw   3
The aircraft was badly damaged by anti-aircraft fire and crashed near Warsaw whilst attempting to return to base. Although five of the crew survived, three others did not.

Second Lieutenant R G HAMILTON SAAF
Sergeant Leslie MAYES 24 Wireless Operator
Sergeant Herbert HUDSON 20 Bomb Aimer

361

Date	Serial	Aircraft	Unit	Place	Casualties
		Brief Circumstances of Accident			
		Casualty Details (If Applicable)			

15-Aug-44 LJ940 Stirling IV 299 Sqn Mereau France 6
The aircraft failed to return from an SOE sortie 'DICK 108' but no further details are known.

Pilot Officer William HOUGH 23 RAAF Pilot
Flight Sergeant Charles Richard DUTTON 30
Sergeant Anthony Gilbert SHIPTON 19
Sergeant Frederick FIELDER 21
Flight Sergeant Peter WALKER 23
Sergeant James Terence HENRY 23

15-Aug-44 EM293 Master II 3 GTS Stoke Orchard 0
The pilot attempted to land short in order to avoid rough ground. In doing so, he turned the aircraft onto finals at low level, struck some trees 300 yards short of the runway and then hit a hedge before the aircraft caught fire.

16-Aug-44 EV941 Liberator 31 SAAF Near Krakow 8
The crew had made their second sortie to Moscow but their aircraft was shot down as it returned to base.

Captain L V ALLEN 27 SAAF Pilot
Lieutenant A J MUNRO 24 SAAF Co-Pilot
Lieutenant W KLOKOW 27 SAAF Observer
Lieutenant E B H IMPEY 25 SAAF Navigator
Warrant Officer I D B BRANDSMA 24 SAAF Wireless Operator
Warrant Officer I D J PALMER 23 SAAF Wireless Operator
Warrant Officer Edward BRADSHAW Air Gunner

362

Sergeant John Ricahrd William NICKERSON 22 Air Gunner

16-Aug-44 EW161 Liberator 31 SAAF Lysagora, Southern Poland 7
The aircraft was shot down whilst en route to drop supplies over Warsaw. The entire crew was killed

    Captain G LAWRIE 27 SAAF Pilot
    Lieutenant A J MCINNES 22 SAAF Co-Pilot
    Lieutenant G COLEMAN 20 SAAF Navigator
    Lieutenant H H LEWIS SAAF
    Flying Officer Albert Milvron BONNEY 22 Air Gunner
    Flight Sergeant Ronald ZAMBRA 22 Air Gunner
    Sergeant George SWIFT 20 Bomb Aimer

17-Aug-44 EW248 Liberator 31 SAAF Warsaw 7
The aircraft was seen to explode in the air whilst attempting to deliver supplies to Warsaw. Although most
of the crew died in the subsequent crash, Lieutenant J J C Groenwald survived.

    Major I J M ODENDAAL SAAF
    Lieutenant B T LOXTON SAAF
    Lieutenant A J HASTINGS SAAF
    Lieutenant T T WATSON SAAF
    Warrant Officer I J B ERASMUS SAAF
    Warrant Officer II J A C STEEL SAAF
    Sergeant A B ROBINSON

17-Aug-44 KG933 Liberator 178 Sqn Krakow 3?
The aircraft was shot down by enemy flak whilst flying over Krakow during a sortie to Warsaw.

    Flight Lieutenant William Douglas WRIGHT Pilot
    Flight Sergeant John Douglas CLARKE Air Gunner

Date	Serial	Aircraft	Unit	Place	Casualties
Brief Circumstances of Accident					
Casualty Details (If Applicable)					

Squadron Leader John Philip LIVERSIDGE 31 RAAF

17-Aug-44 EB154 Halifax V 148 Sqn Avezzano 9

The crew of this aircraft was detailed for a solo sortie to drop supplies in northern Italy but it failed to return and was eventually found crashed near Avezzano, in mountains to the east of Rome. Unfortunately, for a squadron whose aircrew resources were already at a premium, two newcomers to the squadron were undertaking their operational familiarisation on this occasion and were lost.

Flying Officer David TABOR 22 Pilot
Warrant Officer Douglas Malcolm QUARENDON 26 2nd Pilot
Flight Sergeant Bruce George Harold Robert BEAN 23 RCAF Navigator
Sergeant Patrick Joseph GALLIVAN Bomb Aimer
Warrant Officer II James Howard INCH 21 Bomb Aimer
Sergeant Charles Edward BAINES 23 Wireless Operator
Sergeant Patrick KING Flight Engineer
Sergeant Frank Stephen KNIGHT 22 Air Gunner
Sergeant Stanley Keith MORRISON 20 Air Gunner

18-Aug-44 JP221 Halifax V 624 Sqn ? 8
??????????????

18-Aug-44 LJ984 Stirling IV 624 Sqn 5 miles west of Rehaia North Africa 7

The aircraft, which was one of four operating from Blida that night, was returning from a sortie to Quincaille in Vichy France on a task for SOE. Visibility at Blida was greatly reduced and all the aircraft were diverted to Biskra, where two were able to land safely. This aircraft crashed and all except the air gunner were killed.

Flight Sergeant Kenneth Vincent POLE
Flight Sergeant George William BROWN
Flight Sergeant William James ROBERTS
Sergeant John Alexander FRASER
Sergeant Raymond William MEADOWS
Sergeant Ronald Charles WILSON
Sergeant Dennis Alfred Edgar TAYLOR

18-Aug-44   LK178   Stirling IV   1 mile east of Beni Mared   1

This aircraft was diverted as per LJ984 above but as it was short on fuel, the pilot decided to make a forced landing in a field. In the poor visibility, he misjudged the approach and the aircraft crashed having flown into some trees. Although most of those on board escaped with just minor injuries, a crewman acting as the despatcher was injured fatally.

Sergeant George Whitehead EMERSON

18-Aug-44   FL605   Dakota   216 Sqn   Cairo West   0

The aircraft was engaged on a passenger flight between Cairo West and Bari. On take-off, the pilot held the aircraft down to build up speed but in doing so, struck a 50 feet high sand hill about 500 yards beyond the end of the runway. Although all twenty two people on board escaped without injury, the aircraft was write-off.

19-Aug-44   KG789   Dakota III   113 SA Wg   Nigeria   0

The aircraft was forced landed in position 12 degrees 34 North/06 degrees 03 East having run out of fuel. The crew had encountered an unexpected line squall and instead of landing at an emergency airstrip or diverting to the north of the poor weather, the pilot elected to press on and after nearly 8½ hours airborne, belly landed the aircraft.

Brief Circumstances of Accident
Casualty Details (If Applicable)

21-Aug-44 KG421 Dakota III   48 Sqn   Jurques   0

The aircraft, flown by Wing Commander John Sproule the squadron commander, took off from its base at Down Ampney at 0530 hours to drop supplies to the advancing forces in France. En route bad weather with very low cloud, having a base of about 300 feet, was encountered and the aircraft was kept beneath this. Approaching the DZ, which was lit by fires, the aircraft was fired on by enemy guns and damaged in the wings and engines and the co-pilot and navigator were wounded. A course was set for the airstrip at Amblis (B14) but the aircraft became progressively more difficult to control and the rudder ceased to function. The aircraft then struck the tops of some trees and the pilot made a skilful forced landing. Being close to the front lines, the crew and air despatchers needed to find a safe haven and eventually they located friendly forces and were evacuated to UK.

21-Aug-44 KG752 Dakota III   267 Sqn   Near Trieste   5

The aircraft's crew was engaged in dropping supplies and ammunition to partisans in the general area around Trieste. Six other aircraft from the squadron were tasked similarly, including the squadron commander. During the course of the night, the CO's aircraft passed over the drop zone assigned to this aircraft and was subjected to anti-aircraft fire and searchlights, suggesting the drop zone had been compromised. This aircraft and its crew were lost without trace and it seems possible that they were 'ambushed' when setting up to drop from low level.

Flying Officer Leslie Thomas WHITAKER 27 RNZAF Pilot
Flight Sergeant Henry Francis BOLT 32
Flying Officer Daniel Joseph CHRISTENSEN 35
Flying Officer Maurice SIMS
Flying Officer John James WALSH

21-Aug-44 KG938 Liberator 178 Sqn FTR Warsaw ?

Details of this loss were not found.

21-Aug-44 LJ813 Stirling IV 299 Sqn Morenchie 6

The aircraft was engaged on sortie to an SOE DZ. There is some suggestion that the aircraft encountered poor weather and may have been struck by lightning. The crew is buried at Excideuil and each year there is a ceremony organised by local residents to honour the crew and some French personnel.

    Flight Lieutenant Ernest Albert TAYLOR 30 Pilot
    Flight Sergeant Ronald Victor COOLING 23
    Flight Lieutenant Carl Victor MASON 30
    Sergeant Arthur Arnold BEALE 24
    Pilot Officer Reginald DUTTON 33
    Flying Officer George James ELLIOTT 24

21-Aug-44 RJ162 Horsa RAF Tarrant Rushton 0

The pilot made a slow speed approach with the flaps raised but the glider, which was fully laden as part of a training exrcise, stalled and was damaged in the subsequent heavy landing.

21-Aug-44 HH584 Hotspur II 5 GTS 1 mile east-north-east of Presteigne 0

The tug pilot was compelled to increase speed to the maximum towing to counter an oiling of the plugs and to 'clear' the engine. The instructor cast off the tow and forced landed the glider in a small field.

22-Aug-44 EV839 Liberator 178 Sqn FTR Warsaw 7

The aircraft failed to return from a supply dropping sortie, apparently to Warsaw. The circumstances of its loss are not known but the aircraft crashed in Yugoslavia.

    Flying Officer John William MCDONALD 21 Pilot

367

Date	Serial	Aircraft	Unit	Place	Casualties
		Brief Circumstances of Accident			
		Casualty Details (If Applicable)			

Lieutenant Alan Edward FARROW 23 SAAF Navigator
Sergeant John Mather EVANS 27 Bomb Aimer
Sergeant Francis William HUNWICK 21 Wireless Operator
Sergeant Thomas Newton HOWE Flight Engineer
Sergeant John GILFILLAN Air Gunner
Sergeant Hugh THOMSON Air Gunner

| 24-Aug-44 | FZ550 | Dakota III | 194 Sqn | Agartala | 0 |

The aircraft was taking off on the first sortie of the day, an operational supply dropping flight. The pilot tried to 'yank' the aircraft off the ground in a stalled condition and when it would not lift, he held the control column back. The aircraft failed to become airborne, ran off the runway and the pilot then retracted the undercarriage before the aircraft ran into a gully and was wrecked.

| 24-Aug-44 | FZ644 | Dakota III | 194 Sqn | Burma | 6 |

The crew was engaged in an operational supply drop in conditions of low cloud and poor visibility. The aircraft flew into a mountainside in position 25 degrees 09 North/94 degrees 29 East and was destroyed by fire.

Sergeant Alan DOWNIE 20 Pilot
Pilot Officer Leonard Francis FLETCHER 20 RCAF Wireless Operator
Warrant Officer Michael Graham Gregory HUNTER-MUSKETT 24 Wireless Operator
Flying Officer Thomas Grant LEISHMAN 22 Navigator
Warrant Officer Neil Black Jarvie MELROSE 25 Wireless Operator
Flying Officer Paul Walter Wallace RICHARDSON 26 RAAF

24-Aug-44 JP226 Halifax   148 Sqn   Brindisi   0

This aircraft was one of a pair from the unit sent to drop supplies on a DZ in Northern Italy. However, after take-off the undercarriage malfunctioned and the pilot was compelled to make a wheels up landing. The aircraft was not repaired but the cause of the defect is not recorded.

25-Aug-44 Lj631 Stirling IV   570 Sqn   Belleme   1

This aircraft was shot down by allied AA fire whilst returning from a successful sortie to drop supplies to the SOE on sortie BOB 209. The crew abandoned the aircraft with the exception of the captain, who was killed in the crash.

Flight Lieutenant Stanley Frederick MAUNDER 28 Pilot

25-Aug-44 LL401 Halifax   298 Sqn   Le Mans area   3

The aircraft had been one of nine aircraft from the squadron engaged on SOE operations, in this case PIMENTO 98 to the Lyons area. A successful drop had been made but on return and whilst flying over territory occupied by the allies, the aircraft was fired on by anti-aircraft guns. Despite firing the correct colours of the day, the AA fire continued and both starboard engines were set on fire with the aircraft flying at 4000 feet. The fires were extinguished but then the port inner engine failed and the pilot; Warrant Officer G P Bain, had no option to make a crash landing with the undercarriage retracted and this he did most skilfully. Unfortunately, three crew were killed and the other trio injured. It will come as no surprise to learn that the AA fire came from US forces!

Flight Lieutenant Leslie Jack ROWELL 26 Navigator
Flight Sergeant Robert BENSLEY 22 Flight Engineer
Flight Sergeant Ivan Alexander WEEKS 24 Air Gunner

26-Aug-44 Lj827 Stirling IV   190 Sqn   Villebougis, France   6

The aircraft failed to return from an SD sortie. It was one of eighty one aircraft flying supplies into enemy occupied French territory that night and was the only loss to befall the force. The second flight engineer listed below was attached from 1665 HCU for operational experience and it is unclear whether he was to join an existing crew as a replacement. The sole survivor of this loss was the Bomb Aimer; Flight Sergeant Fulcher.

Flying Officer Norman Harry PORT 27 RAAF Pilot
Pilot Officer Cyril Martin ROSAY 22 Navigator
Flight Sergeant Kenneth Charles GARNER 22 Wireless Operator
Pilot Officer Frank Cecil NEWMAN 24 Flight Engineer
Sergeant William Thomas BUSSELL 28 Flight Engineer
Flight Sergeant Ernest Thomas CORNELIUS 20 Air Gunner

27-Aug-44 LK641 Halifax   644 Sqn   RAF Tarrant Rushton   0

The crew was engaged in three engined practice landings and they had been airborne for 30 minutes. The aircraft landed very heavily from the approach and bounced twice before swinging. The pilot attempted an overshoot whilst also unfeathering the fourth engine but in doing so the aircraft stalled and crashed. It transpired that the pilot had not been briefed on the difficulties and dangers associated with overshooting a landing which required changes to throttle and pitch settings, moving flaps from landing to take-off position and also unfeathering a propeller and building up power on the idling engine. An investigation revealed that the teaching methods at 1665 HCU were at fault and changes were made to prevent a repeat of this accident.

27-Aug-44 V1782 Albemarle VI   297 Sqn   1 mile south of RAF Brize Norton   6

The aircraft returned to base at the conclusion of an operational sortie (HAROLD 4) and the pilot was attempting to land in rapidly deteriorating weather, with reducing visibility below 1500 yards and stratus at

200 feet. The aircraft overshot the approach and the pilot turned it very steeply on to the downwind leg with the undercarriage lowered. The aircraft rapidly lost height, struck a tree with its wing tip, crashed and was destroyed by fire.

Flight Sergeant Alan Henry BUSBRIDGE 20 Pilot
Flight Sergeant William Frederick INSLEY 23 Bomb Aimer
Flight Sergeant Bernard Vincent MOWAN 23 Navigator
Sergeant Edgar Frederick BONSER 19 Air Gunner
Sergeant Kenneth James SHAY 22 Wireless Operator

27-Aug-44   Halifax   JD171   Draz, Yuogslavia   6

The aircraft was shot down by enemy anti-aircraft fire whilst flying over Yugoslavia. Only one member of the crew; Sergeant Aleksander Danilkiewicz, survived as a POW

Flight Sergeant Boleslaw GRAFF
Flying Officer Boleslaw JASINSKI
Sergeant Antoni SZYLLER
Pilot Officer Wladyslaw KOZIOL
Sergeant Jan PASZKIEWICZ
Pilot Officer Adam MUHLM

27-Aug-44   JN895   Halifax   1586 Flt   Over Hungary (location not known)   7

This crew and the one below were new arrivals to 1586 Flt and this was their first sortie to Warsaw. Concerns that the position in Warsaw was now hopeless and the crews were being sent to reinforce a lost cause were probably ignored in the desparate struggle to provide support for the Polish Home Army. Both were lost over Hungary.

Flight Sergeant Jozef Henryk WOROCH 27 Pilot
Sergeant Wlodzimierz AUGUSTYN 23
Sergeant Alfred Jan SZMIGIELSKI 31

Date	Serial	Aircraft	Unit	Place	Casualties

Brief Circumstances of Accident
Casualty Details (If Applicable)

Sergeant Ludmik WANTULOK 22
Sergeant Jan KANTOWSKI 23
Sergeant Bronislaw KLOSOWSKI 31
Sergeant Rudolf MAJEWSKI 27

| 27-Aug-44 | JD362 | Halifax | 1586 Flt | Baksbokod, Hungary | 7 |

This aircraft, crewed by a novice crew newly arrived from UK, was shot down by flak over Hungary.

Flight Sergeant Jan RADWAN-KUZELEWSKI 25 Pilot
Pilot Officer Stafan Gabrjel KLENIEWSKI 31
Sergeant Leon Zygmunt WITKOWSKI 29
Sergeant Karol WALASZEK 20
Flying Officer Kazimierz SOROWKA 25
Sergeant Tadeusz OGRODNIK 26
Sergeant Edward JODIE 23

| 28-Aug-44 | EW160 | Liberator | 178 Sqn | Poland | 1 |

It has proved difficult to trace details of this aircraft but it is believed to have been lost on a sortie to Poland and the bomb aimer was killed.

Flight Sergeant Robert Edgar NORTH 25 Bomb Aimer

| 28-Aug-44 | EF311 | Stirling IV | 196 Sqn | Off Selsey Bill | 0 |

The aircraft was returning from and SOE sortie and had been airborne for about 3½ hours. The port inner engine failed and because of a loss of oil pressure the pitch and feathering control would not work. The propeller eventually came off and struck the port outer propeller, causing that engine to fail. The pilot was unable to maintain height or directional control with asymmetric power and so ditched the aircraft in the sea, from whence the crew was rescued with only minor injuries. The pilot; Flying Officer D R Campbell RCAF and his crew were commended for their performance and handling of the emergency and it was commented that their drills were a credit to the training received at 1665 HCU. Campbell was subsequently awarded the DFC, in part for his skill and courage on this occasion, and was later to receive a bar to the award the following Spring, having flown several times to Arnhem and participated in Operation VARSITY.

28-Aug-44   JP295   Halifax II   1586 Flt   Branica near Tarnow   7

This aircraft disappeared without trace and was first assumed to have crashed into the Adriatic. However, sometime after the end of the war an unidentified aircraft wreck was found in the area quoted above. It seems that this aircraft was JP295.

            Pilot Officer Kazimierz WIDACKI Pilot
            Flight Lieutenant Franciszek OMYLAK
                Sergeant Andrzej BALCAREK
                Sergeant Jan OZGA
            Pilot Officer Konstanty DUNIN-HORKOWICZ
                Sergeant Jozef SKORCZYK
            Pilot Officer Tadeusz MROCZKO

28-Aug-44   KG927   Liberator   1586 Flt   Brindisi   0

This aircraft was engaged on flying supplies to Warsaw and was being flown by Flight Lieutenant Mioduchowski and his crew. It was badly damaged over Mokotow near Warsaw with the despatcher; Flying Officer Jozef Bednarski being seriously wounded and the rear turret being put out of use. The aircraft's hydraulics were damaged and the bomb bay doors would not close but two engines failed at some stage during the return flight and the aircraft was completely wrecked on landing.

Date	Serial	Aircraft	Unit	Place	Casualties

Brief Circumstances of Accident
Casualty Details (If Applicable)

29-Aug-44 LL388 Halifax 161 Sqn Hedel The Netherlands 3

This aircraft was being flown by an experienced crew, captained by Flight Lieutenant P Green, and was engaged on a dual sortie to Holland. It crashed having been struck by enemy cannon fire and although three agents survived a fourth did not. Of the crew, the pilot and four others were made POW.

Flying Officer Arnold Keith Michael DEAN Bomb Aimer
Warrant Officer Norman Francis SLADE Navigator died of wounds 30 Aug 44
G KROON – Dutch Agent

30-Aug-44 LL343 Halifax V 298 Sqn 51 degrees 46 North/05 degrees 34 East 6

The crew was tasked to drop supplies to partisans near Diest at position 51 degrees 03 North/05 degrees 34 East. However, the mission was not accomplished and it seems probable that this was the aircraft seen by another crew to be shot-down in the position reported above.

Flying Officer William Wallace BROWN 30 RCAF Pilot
Flying Officer Robert Denver MACDUFF 26 RNZAF Navigator
Flying Officer Francis SAYLES 22 DFM Bomb Aimer
Flight Sergeant Frederick PEARSON 21 Wireless Operator
Sergeant William BRADLEY 33 Flight Engineer
Flight Sergeant John Bonsall SMITH 33 Air Gunner

31-Aug-44 LL400 Halifax III 644 Sqn Believed at sea off French coast 6

The paired squadrons at Tarrant Rushton (298 and 644) had sent a total of sixteen aircraft out this night and both units lost an aircraft, one being that recorded above and the second being this one. An aircraft was seen to be on fire and to crash at sea off Dover, having been shot down by a flak ship off Calais.

Flying Officer Walter John CALVERLEY 26 RCAF Pilot
Flying Officer William Alexander MACLENNAN 34 RAAF Navigator
Sergeant Stanley George KENCH 21 Bomb Aimer
Flight Sergeant Samuel Albert FOLBIGG 34 RAAF Wireless Operator
Sergeant George Bernard FITZGERALD 30 Flight Engineer
Sergeant Brian Joseph TUHEY 21 Air Gunner

31-Aug-44 LJ503 Stirling Lombard Doubs 8

This mostly Australian crew was flying one of the first squadron missions using Stirling aircraft instead of Halifaxes. Their aircraft is thought to have hit trees in the area of the DZ before crashing. As one of the other crews reported heavy cloud in the area, extending to near ground level, it may be that the pilot descended below safety height whilst in cloud with fatal results.

Flying Officer Robert Blackburn HARDIE 34 RAAF Pilot
Flight Sergeant Morris STANLEY 22 RAAF
Sergeant John Campbell ALEXANDER 30 Navigator
Flight Sergeant Gordon Wesley MCLEOD 26 RAAF
Flight Sergeant Norman Edward BARNES 20 RAAF
Flight Sergeant Stuart James HAYES 19 RAAF
Flight Sergeant Robert Alexander ASHTON 22 RAAF
Flight Sergeant George McPherson JACK 19

01-Sep-44 LK131 Stirling Near Gilze-Rijen The Netherlands 7

This crew, on their maiden sortie, were shot down by flak near the enemy airbase at Gilze-Rijen.

Flight Lieutenant Alfred Jerry WALLACE 23 RCAF Pilot
Flying Officer Paul Edwin MCNAMARA 24 RCAF
Sergeant Royston William BULLEN 21
Sergeant Roger Francis Geoffrey BAILEY 21

375

Sergeant George Charles HANSON 21
Sergeant William Alan BAXTER 19
Flying Officer Charles Bruce THOMPSON 23 RCAF Bomb Aimer

01-Sep-44   BB389   Halifax   1586 Flt   Baki Brestovac   6

This crew was one of only a pair to make a successful drop to the assigned location. Unfortunately, both aircraft were shot down during the return journey; this one at Baki Brestovac, and whilst Flight Sergeant Tadeusz Jawor, the navigator, was able to bale out from this aircraft and was made POW, his crew mates all perished. Sergeant Pialucha, the Flight Engineer, was the only Polish airman to receive the Conspicuous Gallantry Medal (Flying) during the war, whilst he was serving with 300 Sqn. During operations over France the aircraft was struck by enemy fire and severely damaged, with the rear turret traversing round beyond its normal limits and the sliding doors opening and partially sucking out the rear gunner, who was only prevented from falling because his shoe was trapped. When attempts to help the gunner proved fruitless, Pialucha squeezed himself through the gapand tied a rope round the air gunner and secured him to the aircraft. It will be realised that that with just a small gap, Pialucha could not wear a parachute and so was himself in great danger of being sucked out. The aircraft was flown back to UK and in the subsequent emergency landing, made with a full bomb load which could not be jettisoned, the air gunner had to ensure his head did not contact the ground during the landing run.

Warrant Officer Jozef NALEPA Pilot
Sergeant Jozef PIALUCHA CGM Flight Engineer
Sergeant Konrad STANIEWICZ
Flight Sergeant Jozef JAS
Sergeant Adam BIALOSZEWSKI
Flight Sergeant Jozef DEREWIENKO

01-Sep-44 JP180 Halifax   1586 Flt   Jaszfennszaru, east of Budapest   7

The aircraft was shot down by anti-aircraft fire at Jaszfennszaru, to the east of Budapest and crashed in flames with the loss of its entire crew. The aircraft itself was something of a veteran having completed twenty sorties to Poland. .

Flight Sergeant Mieczyslam WALCZYK 23
Flying Officer Michal Rudolf BAWOROWSKI 27
Flight Sergeant Tadeusz BANASIK 25
Sergeant Micczslaw LOJAS 20
Flight Sergeant Wawrzniec BLAZEJEWSKI 28
Flight Sergeant Ernest POLACZEK 24
Flight Sergeant Stanislaw PAETZ 28

01-Sep-44 DK124 Halifax   1586 Flt   Mohacz, Hungary   1

This aircraft was shot down by a night fighter over Hungary and although most of the crew escaped, the pilot did not survive.

Flight Lieutenant Wladyslaw ROSINIUK Pilot

01-Sep-44 JN889 Halifax   1586 Flt   Yugoslavia (position not known)   3

This aircraft, which the Poles had borrowed from 624 Sqn, was shot down by a night fighter. Sergeant Tadeusz Michalkiewicz was badly injured and became a POW but three others; Flying Officer Abcynski, Warrant Officer Sibilski and Sergeant Francowiak, were found by the Yugoslav resistance forces and were evacuated to Italy within a few weeks.

Sergeant Reynhold TYROL Pilot
Flight Sergeant Zbigniew BAR Air Despatcher
Sergeant Mieczylaw MARYNOWSKI Air Gunner

Date	Serial	Aircraft	Unit	Place	Casualties
				Brief Circumstances of Accident	
				Casualty Details (If Applicable)	

04-Sep-44 KG471 Dakota 28 SAAF ½ mile north-east Delabole Slate Quarry 0

The aircraft was en route from Algiers to RAF St Mawgan and had made a refuelling stop in France. In formation with another Dakota, the journey continued but the formation leader was unfamiliar with the weather conditions often faced in UK and the formation flew in and out of cloud, with the crew of this aircraft attempting to maintain station. Eventually, with fuel running low, the crew of this aircraft attempted a diversion to a nearby airfield but the aircraft ran out of fuel and was forced landed in a field. The formation leader had received reports of deteriorating weather whilst en route and ought to have returned to the refuelling stop or landed at an interim airfield before the conditions got below the crew's ability to deal with.

05-Sep-44 V1781 Albemarle V 297 Sqn RAF Brize Norton 0

The crew was tasked with towing a glider to an operating base and the aircraft was taking off with Horsa RN829 on tow. Unfortunately, due to some delay in taking off, the sparking plugs oiled up and the engines failed to deliver sufficient power for the tug and glider to get airborne. The pilot cast off the tow and selected undercarriage up before belly landing to avoid overshooting the airfield. No blame attached to the pilot for this accident as the Hercules XI engines had a tendency to overheat rapidly when towing a glider and the cylinder head temperatures would rocket. The pilot of this aircraft went on to become a heavy bomber captain in later years and was heavily involved with live dropping of nuclear weapons in the late 1950s.

06-Sep-44 EF296 Stirling IV 620 Sqn RAF Fairford 0

The aircraft was being landed at the conclusion of an airtest when its port main tyre burst on the landing run. The aircraft swung to port and the pilot attempted to use engine power to correct the swing, despite this not being the correct techniques in a Stirling. The aircraft's port wing was seriously damaged and although though to be repairable the aircraft was scrapped.

06-Sep-44   P1643   Albemarle I   ORTU   RAF Harwell   0
The pilot failed to level off prior to touchdown and the aircraft's starboard leg struck the ground heavily and fractured. The aircraft then swung around and significant further damage was caused.

06-Sep-44   RN606   Horsa   HGSU   RAF Brize Norton   0
During a training exercise, the tow rope broke and wrapped around the glider's nosewheel. On touchdown for a forced landing the glider tipped onto its nose

09-Sep-44   LK200   Stirling   138 Sqn   Cocksdorp Texel   3
This aircraft was flown by Squadron Leader Gerald Rothwell DFC & Bar and his crew and they were tasked with a dual sortie to Holland to drop two agents. Outbound, very bad weather was encountered and the aircraft was flown at low level, using its landing lights to illuminate the sea. They crossed in bound at Vlieland and were successful in dropping the agents, after which they turned for home. Subsequently, the aircraft struck something which was thought to have been the cable of a balloon, the starboard inner engine caught fire and its propeller came off. The aircraft became uncontrollable and was crashed landed on a beach but three of the crew were killed and the others taken POW. Rothwell had already completed two tours of operations before coming to 138 Sqn and had been awarded a DFC at the conclusion of each.

Flying Officer John HULME Wireless Operator
Flying Officer Thomas Roger COURT DFC Bomb Aimer
Flying Officer George William Evans WALTON 32 DFC BEM

09-Sep-44   LH376   Horsa   1 HGSU   29 miles south-south-west of Needles   0
Whilst being ferried by a Dakota, the cable locking device on the tug failed and the glider was released. A successful ditching was carried out and the crew was rescued by a US Navy cutter.

379

Date	Serial	Aircraft	Unit	Place	Casualties

Brief Circumstances of Accident
Casualty Details (If Applicable)

11-Sep-44 BB422 Halifax II 148 Sqn 25 miles north east of Turin 13

The aircraft was tasked to drop supplies to resistance groups in north-west Italy and it had taken off from Brindisi at about 1930 hours. The aircraft struck a mountain just below its summit and all on board comprising eight crew, a British Army officer, two Czech Army and two Italian air despatchers were killed. The remains of those on board could not be identified separately and they are buried together in a collective grave in Milan War Cemetery. The formal ranks of the Czech and Italian Army personnel are not known.

Pilot Officer John Ervin O'BRIEN 21 RCAF Pilot
Warrant Officer II Richard Alvinzie CROWELL 21 RCAF Wireless Operator
Flight Sergeant Bruce Woodward ELLISON 26 RNZAF Navigator
Flight Sergeant James Howard IRELAND 20 RCAF Air Gunner
Flight Sergeant Douglas Julius IVES 21 Flight Engineer
Sergeant Ronald MCKEEN 19 Air Gunner
Flying Officer Joseph Miller PARKINSON 20 RCAF Bomb Aimer
Flight Sergeant Albert Major VANDERHART RCAF Air Gunner
Captain Charles F WHITAKER 3rd Battalion The Parachute Regiment
Kudolf HRUBEC 29 Czechoslavakian Army
Bohuslav NOCAR 23
Rudolfo MARCHIORI Italian Army
Guido VOGLINO

11-Sep-44 BB412 Halifax 148 Sqn Location not known 0

A mixed force of Liberators and Halifaxes from 148, 178, 34 SAAF Sqns and 1586 Flt carried supplies to Warsaw and the surrounding area. However, new tactics to avoid the numerous light AA fire, which was lethal at low level, was attempted by dropping from much higher level using modified equipment.

Nonetheless, 148 and 34 Sqns each lost an aircraft, whilst the Poles had three of theirs destroyed. This loss has been difficult to substantiate. First, the aircraft serial number is in doubt and, second, it is recorded as being operated by the Polish SD Flight, whilst elsewhere it is shown as being flown by an RAF crew. It seems probable that the aircraft serial is as shown and it was being flown by a crew captained by Pilot Officer D D Bryden. It was shot down whilst operating to Warsaw and its crew was made prisoner.

11-Sep-44   EW198 Liberator   34 SAAF   Yugoslavia   5

The aircraft crashed in Yugoslavia following a sortie to delivery supplies to Polish Home Army forces within Poland. It is believed the aircraft ran out of fuel and whilst five of the crew were killed, two others were made POW.

Captain Eric Arnold ENDLER SAAF Pilot
Lieutenant T A STEWART 24 SAAF Navigator
Sergeant Clifford MANLEY Bomb Aimer
Lieutenant A G MCCABE 22 SAAF Air Gunner
Flying Officer Ronald George DEVINE 22 Air Gunner

11-Sep-44   JP288   Halifax   1586 Flt   Hungary   7

This crew is thought to have made a drop but was lost on its return to base. Although supposed to have crashed in Hungary, in 1946 a wreck was found in Yugoslavia which appears to have been this aircraft.

Flight Sergeant Wlodzimierz FEDZINSKI 20
Pilot Officer Tadeusz LACH 28
Sergeant Stanislaw Jozef MUCHA 31
Pilot Officer Zbignew Jerzy KOZLOWSKI 28
Sergeant Witold PAZDZIOR 35
Sergeant Boleslaw PODSIADLY 21
Sergeant Franciszek DZIADULA 32

Date	Serial	Aircraft	Unit	Place	Casualties
		Brief Circumstances of Accident			
		Casualty Details (If Applicable)			

11-Sep-44   JP161   Halifax   1586 Flt   Yugoslavia   0

The aircraft ran out of fuel and the entire crew baled out safely.

11-Sep-44   EW278   Liberator   1586 Flt   Yuogslavia   3

This aircraft was destroyed on the outbound leg of a sottie to Warsaw. Whilst four of the crew baled out and were made POW, the others were killed.

    Flying Officer Stanislaw Zbigniew FRANCZEK 24 Pilot
    Flying Officer Mieczyslaw FOCZPANIAK 22 Co-Pilot
    Warrant Officer Jerzy Jozef TRUSZKOWSKI 23 Wireless Operator

11-Sep-44   LL273   Halifax V   298 Sqn   10 miles south-west of Dijon   4

The pilot had been briefed not to descend into the valley within which the DZ (BOB 264) was located but to drop the supplies from the height of the surrounding hills. However, the pilot failed to heed this instruction and the aircraft struck high ground and was destroyed by fire.

    Flight Sergeant Willaim Morton CHRISTIE 22 RAAF
    Flight Sergeant Alan LAVERICK 20
    Flying Officer Sonny SOLOMON 25
    Flying Officer Owen Keith SMITH 23 RAAF

12-Sep-44   FD835   Dakota III   194 Sqn   Near Nakingant   0

The crew, comprising an instructor pilot, two 2nd pilots as well as five others, was practicing formation flying and had been airborne for about 1½ hours. The port engine failed and its propeller flew off, whilst the aircraft was at a height of 50 feet. The aircraft could not be climbed and was forced landed in a paddy field, without injury to those on board. The cause of the engine failure and the reason for the propeller detaching were not determined.

12-Sep-44   KG553 Dakota III   1 mile north-west Imphal   0

Immediately after take off on an operational supply dropping sortie and at a height of 300 feet, the aircraft's port engine failed and this was followed almost immediately by a failure of the starboard engine. The pilot had no option but to force land the aircraft straight ahead but in doing so, the port wingstruck a tree and was ripped off. The cause of a double engine failure was not recorded.

12-Sep-44   P1659 Albemarle I   42 OTU   RAF Ashbourne   0

The crew had been engaged on a circuit training sortie, during which time the aircraft's brakes had been heavily used. At the conclusion of the final landing and whilst taxiing to dispersal with hot brakes, which became ineffective, the aircraft overran the dispersal area and ran down a slope towards a very long drop (the Accident Card says 200 feet!). The pilot raised the undercarriage as the only means of preventing this potentially fatal accident.

13-Sep-44   K6937 Harrow II   271 Sqn   Temporary airstrip Normandy   0

The aircraft, being flown by a crew of five was returning to France following a minor maintenance inspection in UK. At a height of 700 feet whilst over Normandy, its starboard engine failed and the pilot found he was unable to maintain height. As he was adjacent to an emergency airstrip: A220, operated by the USAAF, he elected to make an emergency downwind landing but then found his forward visibility obscured by an aircraft blowing up a dust cloud as it tried to manoeuvre clear of the runway. The two aircraft collided and this one sustained damage which was judged not worth repairing.

13-Sep-44   KG934 Liberator VI   178 Sqn   Tortorelli   0

The aircraft lost height soon after take-off and the pilot jettisoned the bombs, which were set to 'safe'.

However, three bombs exploded and caused damage to the aircraft's hydraulics. The aircraft was then landed with a partially retracted undercarriage. It was commented that it was probable that the crew failed to raise the flaps properly or that the engine gills were opened, causing substantial drag. No faults were found with the engines.

13-Sep-44   KG838   Liberator VI   31 SAAF   Foggia   0

The aircraft had returned from a 3½ hour 'nickelling' sortie (leaflet dropping) and taxyed to its dispersal, after which the auxiliary power unit was started. However, during the sortie some leaflets had been blown into the nose compartment and had become lodged near the power unit. The hot exhaust from the unit ignited the leaflets and these in turn caused a serious fire which destroyed the aircraft. Apparently, there was no shielding around the power unit exhaust and the fire fighting arrangements were fairly basic. It also has to be wondered at the allocation of priorities when aircraft as valuable as a Liberator are deployed for dropping propaganda over enemy territory, with the attendant risks of doing so.

13-Sep-44   KH101   Liberator   1586 Flt   Madaras, Hungary   7

This aircraft was one of a pair sent to drop supplies to Warsaw. Although the other Liberator, flown by Warrant Officer Henryk Jastrzebski and his crew, delivered its load, this aircraft was shot down over Hungary with the loss of its entire crew.

    Pilot Officer Edmund RYGIEL 34 Pilot
    Flying Officer Lucjan P WOYTANOWICZ 24
    Warrant Officer Edward WEINZ 37
    Warrant Officer Roman Jakub SIKORSKI 34
    Warrant Officer Boleslaw WAWRZAK 35

Flight Sergeant Bernard WEBER 24
Sergeant Edmund ZIELINSKI 24

13-Sep-44   LK187   Stirling IV   624 Sqn   At sea 5 miles east of Castiglione   3

The aircraft was being flown from its base to 144 Maintenance Unit at Maison Blanche and on take off the pilot had performed a beat up of the dispersal area before departing the circuit. About half an hour later and whilst flying low level (estimated 80 feet) contrary to orders, the starboard outer engine failed, the starboard wing dropped and the aircraft dived into the sea. Whilst four of the crew escaped, three did not. The Accident Card contains the comment that the Flight Engineer had not told the pilot that the starboard outer engine had only just been installed and it is not obvious how that might be relevant to a deliberate case of low flying. The pilot was court martialled.

Flight Sergeant Thomas Percival OWEN
Flight Sergeant James Henry Russell PLATT
Flight Sergeant Russell Hall TERRY

15-Sep-44   HH140   Hotspur II   5 GTS   Hockley Heath   0

The glider was released into a crosswind but the glider pilot was unable to make the airfield and the aircraft crashed into the boundary hedge.

16-Sep-44   LA691   Hamilcar   1 HGSU   At sea   0

The glider was ditched in the sea after the tug aircraft suffered an engine failure and could not maintain height with the glider still on tow.

17-Sep-44   HG804   Horsa   48 Sqn   At sea   0

The glider was being towed by a Dakota as part of Operation MARKET but the tug developed engine trouble and the glider was cast off and ditched successfully, with the crew being picked up by an ASR launch.

Date	Serial	Aircraft	Unit	Place	Casualties

Brief Circumstances of Accident
Casualty Details (If Applicable)

Date	Serial	Aircraft	Unit	Place	Casualties
17-Sep-44	HG766	Horsa	48 Sqn	At sea	0

This glider, flown by Staff Sergeant P A Hobbs who had been awarded a DFM as one of the pilots who flew to Pegasus Bridge on the eve of D-Day, was ditched at sea after the tug's engines gave trouble.

Date	Serial	Aircraft	Unit	Place	Casualties
17-Sep-44	HG930	Horsa	1 HGSU	At sea	0

The glider lost its tow rope after the tug lurched when it passed through the slipstream of another combination. A successful ditching was made.

Date	Serial	Aircraft	Unit	Place	Casualties
17-Sep-44	RN619	Horsa	1 HGSU	At sea off the Dutch coast	0

The tow rope broke after the glider got out of position when being towed in cloud. The aircraft, which was part of operation MARKET, was ditched at sea.

Date	Serial	Aircraft	Unit	Place	Casualties
17-Sep-44	HS101	Horsa	271 Sqn	Bessels Leigh, near Abingdon, Oxon	1

The pilot cast off the tow in cloud and during the subsequent forced landing, the glider struck HT cables and crashed. This pilot's rank is recorded as 'Sergeant', when most 1st pilots were ranked Staff Sergeant but no explanation for this can be found.

Sergeant Thomas JOYCE

Date	Serial	Aircraft	Unit	Place	Casualties
17-Sep-44	HG873	Horsa	HGSU	Water Eaton, Oxon	0

The tow was cast off when the combination entered cloud. The forced landing was made without injury to the 28 men on board but the glider was a write-off.

The loss of this glider was the first major setback during Operation MARKET. The glider and its tug had taken off from RAF Keevil and was carrying soldiers from 9th Airborne Field Company. The tail unit was seen to fail and the glider started to fall back and commenced to drag the tug with it. However, the tow rope broke and the glider crashed at a place called Double Hills, which has given its name to the accident, with the glider now often called 'The Double Hills Glider' or similar description.

Staff Sergeant Leonard Jack GARDNER 27 1st Pilot The Glider Pilot Regt

Sergeant Robert Augustine FRASER 25 2nd Pilot

Lance Sergeant Roy H ALLEN 31 9th Airborne Field Company Royal Engineers

Sapper Joseph Charles BEALES 18

Lance Corporal William Henry BURROWS 29

Sapper Cyril Walton CALVERT 25

Sapper Robert CARNEY 23

Lance Corporal Arthur Lewis CLAMPITT 24

Sapper Arthur CUTHBERTSON 24

Sapper Frederick Arthur Samuel DAVIS 26

Sapper John EVANS 25

Sapper John FERNYHOUGH 24

Sapper Edward J GODFREY 25

Sapper Arthur HALL

Sapper Douglas Edward HOLTHAM 25

Sergeant Arthur Francis OAKEY 30

Lance Corporal Edward Valentine PICKBURN 27

Sapper Edward Eric SHEPPARD 21

Sapper Arthur Raymond STREET 22

Sapper Cyril TURNER 27

Sapper Arthur George WATT 26

Date	Serial	Aircraft	Unit	Place	Casualties
					Brief Circumstances of Accident *Casualty Details (If Applicable)*

Sapper Jack WESTFIELD 32
Sapper John Sanders WILLIAMSON 25

| 18-Sep-44 | FL640 | Dakota | 52 Sqn | Between Dinjan and Kunming | 4 |

The aircraft was flying 'The Hump' in conditions of bad weather but it never reached its destination. Although the USAAF flew 10 sorties in an attempt to locate the wreckage they were unsuccessful and the cause of the loss was not resolved.

Warrant Officer Edward Douglas Haig COLLARD 27 Pilot
Warrant Officer Maurice Leonard CLAYDON 27 Navigator
Flight Sergeant Alfred William SMELT 22 Wireless Operator
Aircraftman 1st Class James Cowan CALLENDER

| 18-Sep-44 | KG570 | Dakota III | 512 Sqn | Near Tiel | 0 |

The aircraft, flown by Sqn Ldr Southgate a flight commander, made a crash landing following damage sustained.

| 18-Sep-44 | LJ594 | Stirling IV | 570 Sqn | Zegge near Bosschenhoofd | 1 |

This aircraft, flown by Pilot Officer D H Balmer, was hit by enemy AA fire and a forced landing was made. One of the air despatchers received injuries from which he died in hospital but the other crew and two supernumeries who were flying for operational experience, survived.

Corporal Alfred Ernest BARKER 31 Air Despatcher 253 Air Despatch Coy RASC (died of wounds)

18-Sep-44   LJ913   Stirling IV   570 Sqn   Schaarsbergen   0

The aircraft was belly landed following damage sustained from enemy AA fire. The crew, captained by by Flight Lieutenant Liddle, survived.

18-Sep-44   LK121   Stirling IV   570 Sqn   Opheusden   7

The aircraft was towing a glider when it was hit by enemy flak at Tiel and caught fire before crashing.

Pilot Officer George Samuel Crawford BELL 23 RAAF Pilot
Pilot Officer Charles William CULLING 29 Pilot
Pilot Officer John Douglas BAKER 21 RCAF Navigator
Sergeant Vincent WILLIAMS 19 Flight Engineer
Flight Sergeant Henry Ernest BROWNE Bomb Aimer
Flight Sergeant Edward Philip POPE 21 Air Gunner
Corporal John Redmond COLEMAN 26 RCAF

18-Sep-44   LK560   Stirling IV   570 Sqn   RAF Harwell   0

During the take off the pilot found he was unable to reach a safe take off speed, in part due to a badly loaded glider which was being towed off to Arnhem. Importantly, however, the pilot had failed to run-up his engines before take-off and the sparking plugs of the starboard inner engine were oiled or fouled and hence the engines were not delivering full power. The glider cast off safely and the pilot corrected a swing which developed but the undercarriage collapsed.

18-Sep-44   PF???   Horsa   1 HGSU   At sea off East Anglia   1

The glider overshot the tug and was then cast off and ditched in the sea. Apart from the 1st pilot who drowned, all others on board were rescued.

Lieutenant Norman Vere Maxwell ADAMS 27 1st Pilot

Date	Serial	Aircraft	Unit	Place	Casualties

Brief Circumstances of Accident
Casualty Details (If Applicable)

18-Sep-44   C/N 5000 Horsa   A Sqn GPR   Hemnen   8

The glider was being towed from RAF Harwell by a Stirling of 570 Sqn. The glider was struck by anti-aircraft fire and crashed with the loss of all on board. The glider was carrying members of an RAF radar party whose role was to establish an air control radar to assist in the direction of allied fighters.

Staff Sergeant John W R HARRIS 28 The Glider Pilot Regt
Sergeant Jesse BOSLEY 24
Flight Lieutenant Alexander John TISSHAW 28
Leading Aircraftman John McKenzie ANDERSON 20
Leading Aircraftman James Chaffels BROOKS
Leading Aircraftman Edwin Herbert LASCELLES 34
Aircraftman 1st Class John Richard SWANN 37
Aircraftman 2nd Class Harold HIGHTON

18-Sep-44   C/N 901 Hamilcar   D Sqn GPR   Off Felixstowe   2

The glider was being towed by a Halifax, flown by Wing Commander V A Pope the CO of 644 Sqn. The tug's port inner engine failed, after the combination had coasted out and height could not be maintained, so Wing Commander Pope turned back and positioned the combination close to one of the chain of air sea rescue launches. At this point the glider pilots pulled off the tow and set up a ditching close to the vessel. The glider ditched but the load, comprising a 17 pdr anti-tank gun and its tractor, broke loose and trapped two men in the cargo hold and they were killed. The two pilots and the other six soldiers were quickly rescued. The tug aircraft returned to Tarrant Rushton on three engines and landed safely.

Lieutenant Robert L MCLAREN 30 2nd Air Landing Anti-Tank Battery RA
Sergeant Robert J CRAWFORD 33

19-Sep-44   EF248   Stirling IV   196 Sqn   North west of Arnhem   7

The aircraft was shot down whilst dropping supplies and crashed. The pilot, wireless operator and the air gunner escaped but the only naval casualty of the battle, who was flying as a passenger, was killed as were four crew and the two air despatchers. This aircraft was also carrying a second navigator.

Flying Officer Frank Douglas CHALKLEY 23 Navigator
Flying Officer George Henry POWDERHILL 33 Navigator
Flying Officer Reginald Cuthbert GIBBS 32 RCAF Bomb Aimer died of injuries 21 Sep 44
Sergeant Dennis Alec MATTHEWS 25 Flight Engineer
Air Mechanic 2nd Class Leonard Augustus HOOKER 23 Royal Navy
Driver William John CHAPLIN 35 63 (Airborne) Composite Coy RASC died of injuries 11 Nov 44
Driver Frederick George SMITH 33

19-Sep-44   EF263   Stirling IV   190 Sqn   St Michielsgestel   8

The aircraft was destroyed by a direct hit from enemy anti-aircraft fire whilst dropping supplies to the Arnhem force. It crashed in the late afternoon and all on board were killed. Coeshott had flown on the D-Day sorties and had lost his bomb aimer – Sergeant C W Bavan – killed by a single bullet which entered the aircraft.

Warrant Officer Stanley Herbert COESHOTT 23 Pilot
Flight Sergeant Stanley Vincent DAVIS 21 Navigator
Flight Sergeant John Garfield JEFFERY 22 Bomb Aimer
Flight Sergeant William Charles MOSS 21 Wireless Operator
Sergeant George Lancelot WOOD 19 Flight Engineer
Flight Sergeant George Stanley BRECKELS 19 Air Gunner
Private George Cyril CADLE 22 253 (Airborne) Coy RASC
Private James COURTNEY 33

Date	Serial	Aircraft	Unit	Place	Casualties

Brief Circumstances of Accident
Casualty Details (If Applicable)

19-Sep-44   EF267   Stirling IV   299 Sqn   Wijchen   0

The aircraft was crashed landed following serious damage received whilst dropping supplies. All those aboard survived but Pilot Officer C A R Bayne and his crew were taken prisoner..

19-Sep-44   EF319   Stirling IV   299 Sqn   Kempenbergerweg, Arnhem   4

Shot down whilst on its dropping run. Wg Cdr Davis was the squadron commander and had had a long and distinguished career with airborne forces, being involved in the early stages of development and holding positions of responsibility as well as taking part in several major operations.

Wing Commander Peter Brian Newsom DAVIS 28 DSO Pilot
Flight Lieutenant Fred MASON 25 Navigator
Squadron Leader Cecil Aubrey Gerald WINGFIELD 31 staff officer flying as observer
Driver Richard Entwhistle ASHTON 29 63 (Airborne) Coy RASC

19-Sep-44   EH897   Stirling   570 Sqn   Schaarsbergen   0

The aircraft crashed in the vicinity of the DZ and all the crew made POW, except Flying Officer Mortimore (the pilot) and Flight Sergeant Marcham (wireless operator).

19-Sep-44   FD865   Dakota III   267 Sqn   Missing   21

The aircraft was flying on a transport sortie, supporting operations in the Balkans and it had taken off from Capodichino, climbing into deteriorating weather conditions. Although radio transmissions suggested nothing was wrong, the aircraft did not reach its destination and it was reported missing. A subsequent comment on the Accident Card suggests the wreckage had eventually been located and the impact had been severe.

Flying Officer Clinton Richard RYERSE 24 RCAF Pilot
Flight Sergeant Joseph PURDHAM 23 Co-Pilot
Flight Sergeant Thomas Charles PASSEY 32 RCAF
Flying Officer James Gordon STABLES RCAF
Air Mechanic E H CRANMER SAAF
Air Corporal J F MYBURGH SAAF
Air Mechanic N SCOTT SAAF
Air Mechanic J SLOAN SAAF
+ thirteen others comprising
  Three Italian civilians
  Three US Navy personnel
  Five AAF personnel
  One member of 16 AACS
  One Army Nursing Corps

19-Sep-44	FZ574	Dakota III	28 SAAF	3 miles west of Maison Blanche	0

At the conclusion of a transport flight of some 3 hours duration, the aircraft was on the downwind leg to land and at a height of 800 feet with the undercarriage down. The port engine failed because of water in the fuel and height could not be maintained on one engine. The pilot raised the undercarriage and forced landed the aircraft in a field.

19-Sep-44	FZ626	Dakota	271 Sqn	Bakenbergseweg, Arnhem	5

The aircraft was dropping supplies and was shot down by enemy flak, crashing into a house; Bakenbergseweg 262, which it demolished. The navigator; Flight Sergeant Leslie Gaydon and two of the air despatchers; Drivers Vincent Dillworth and Wilfred Jenkinson survived.

Pilot Officer John Leonard WILSON 32 Pilot
Flight Sergeant Herbert OSBOURNE 23 Co-Pilot

Flight Sergeant Reginald Francis FRENCH 24 Wireless Operator
Lance Corporal James GRACE 28 223 (Airborne) Coy RASC
Driver Richard Charles NEWTH 35

19-Sep-44 KG374 Dakota   271 Sqn   North of Wolfheze   7

This aircraft was seen by very many soldiers within the perimeter of the Arnhem defences, to fly around the DZ several times before its wing collapsed and the aircraft crashed. The sole survivor was Flight Lieutenant H A King, the navigator, who was thrown from the aircraft and subsequently made a POW. Post war he received a Dutch gallantry award. The circumstances of this loss can best be summarised in the citation for the pilot's Victoria Cross which is below. David Lord had served with distinction in both the Middle and Far East theatres with 31 Sqn. He had been shot down previously whilst flying in the desert and had endured more than his fair share of adventure and drama. He was a popular and respected officer and had been awarded an Air Officers' commendation before receiving the DFC in Jul 43. His crew had flown two sorties to Arnhem already and their aircraft had been damaged the previous day when towing a glider. Flying Officer Medhurst's father was an air marshal and Medhurst junior was straight from training.

    Flight Lieutenant David Samuel Anthony LORD 30 VC DFC Pilot
    Flying Officer Richard Edward Hastings Medhurst 19 Co-Pilot
    Flying Officer Alexander Forbes BALLANTYNE 25 Wireless Operator
    Corporal Philip EdwardNIXON 29 Air Despatcher 63 (Airborne) Composite Coy RASC
    Driver Leonard Sidney HARPER 29
    Driver James RICKETTS 27
    Driver Arthur ROWBOTHAM 28

The London Gazette 13 November 1945:

On 19th September 1944, Flight Lieutenant Lord was pilot and captain of an aircraft detailed to drop supplies to our troops who were closely surrounded at Arnhem. For accuracy this drop had to be done from 900 feet. While approaching the target at 1500 feet the aircraft was severely damaged and set on fire.

Flight Lieutenant Lord would have been justified in withdrawing or even abandoning his aircraft but, knowing the supplies were desperately needed, he continued on his course. Twice going down to 900 feet under intense fire, he successfully dropped his containers.

His task completed, he ordered his crew to abandon the aircraft, making no attempt himself to leave. A few seconds later the aircraft fell in flames only one of the crew surviving.

By continuing his mission in a damaged and burning aircraft, twice descending to 900 feet to ensure accuracy, and finally by remaining at the controls to give his crew a chance to escape, Flight Lieutenant Lord displayed supreme valour and self sacrifice.

19-Sep-44 KG388 Dakota	575 Sqn	Zijpendaal Cemetery Arnhem 8

The aircraft was struck by enemy anti-aircraft fire and crashed in the area of the DZ. Two of the despatchers abandoned the aircraft at low level and landed behind a farmhouse occupied by the enemy and they were promptly killed, as a fire fight was underway between opposing troops around the farm.

Flight Lieutenant Charles Raymond SLACK 23 Pilot
Pilot Officer Ivor Llewellyn William HOLLOWAY Navigator
Flying Officer William Stewart MONGER 22 Navigator
Pilot Officer Joseph Earl Walter CAOUETTE 21 RCAF Navigator
Driver James BOWERS 41 Air Despatcher 63 (Airborne) Composite Coy RASC
Driver William Desmond CROSS 33
Driver Robert HODGKINSON 33
Driver George Leslie WESTON 23

Date	Serial	Aircraft	Unit	Place	Casualties
		Brief Circumstances of Accident			
		Casualty Details (If Applicable)			

19-Sep-44 KG428 Dakota 48 Sqn 3 miles north-north-east of Wolfheze 1

Both engines were damaged during a pass over the supply dropping zone and the aircraft was crashed landed. Three of the four air despatchers became POWs but the aircrew evaded capture and returned safely. Unfortunately, one of the air despatchers received fatal injuries.

Driver Henry William THOMPSON 22 223 Air Despatch Coy RASC

19-Sep-44 LJ647 Stirling IV 570 Sqn Grave 0

The pilot forced landed the aircraft after it had suffered significant damage over the Arnhem drop zones. The crew survived and quickly returned to UK.

19-Sep-44 LJ868 Stirling Iv 299 Sqn Driel 0

The aircraft was forced landed at Driel south of the river and all the crew were able to escape to allied lines and return to the unit. It was this crew, captained by Flying Officer Geoff Liggins, that had been towing a glider on the first day of the Arnhem attack when the Horsas tail detached and it crashed and exploded, killing all 21 on board. Fortunately for Liggins and his crew, the tow rope broke and he was able to recover his aircraft to base on that occasion.

19-Sep-44 LJ939 Stirling IV 190 Sqn Bilderberg 4

The aircraft was shot down whilst dropping supplies and it crashed southwest of the Bilderberg sports stadium, which is in the northwest suburbs of Arnhem. Squadron Leader Gilliard was a very experienced transport and bomber pilot having flown at home and overseas throughout the war. Amongst the survivors was Squadron Leader F N Royle-Bantoft, who was a staff officer flying as an observer.

Squadron Leader John Philip GILLIARD 24 DFC Pilot

Flying Officer Norman Sutherland MCEWEN 37 Bomb Aimer
Driver Denis BREADING 21 253 (Airborne) Coy RASC
Driver Frederick TAYLOR 21

| 19-Sep-44 | LJ944 | Stirling IV | 570 Sqn | Ghent | 0 |

The aircraft was badly damaged by flak and both port engines were affected. The pilot decided that he would fly to allied territory, rather than attempt to return to base and he made a successful belly landing near Ghent, without injury to the crew.

| 19-Sep-44 | LK170 | Stirling IV | 295 Sqn | Aardenburg | 8 |

The aircraft crashed having been hit by flak whilst dropping supplies

Flight Sergeant Ray Ashley HALL 22 Pilot
Flight Sergeant Arthur MARSTON 22 Navigator
Flight Sergeant Eugene Peter MCDONALD 28 Bomb Aimer
Sergeant Bernard FANTHORPE 20 Wireless Operator
Sergeant John S EWART 28 Flight Engineer
Sergeant Alfred Stanley WHEELER 23 Air Gunner
Driver Norman ENDERBY 21 253 (Airborne) Composite Coy RASC
Driver Francis Cliffe HOLDSWORTH 33

| 19-Sep-44 | PF714 | Horsa | 1 HGSU | Winthorpe Farm, Bourn End, Bucks | 0 |

The combination was en route to Arnhem as part of the 3rd day's lift of supplies to the forces fighting there. The tug aircraft had a double engine failure and there was no option but to cast off the tow. The glider pilot had little time to select a landing area and the glider struck a telegraph pole and a truck before crashing across a road.

Date	Serial	Aircraft	Unit	Place	Casualties
Brief Circumstances of Accident					
Casualty Details (If Applicable)					

19-Sep-44 RN857 Horsa   1 HGSU   20 miles off Dutch coast   0
The glider was ditched after its tow rope broke.

19-Sep-44 C/N 994 Horsa   1 HGSU   5 miles off Ostend   1
The combination ran into cloud and the glider was released. In doing so, one of the end attachments of the tow rope broke through the plywood side of the glider and struck the 1st pilot on the head and rendered him unconscious. The aircraft was ditched in the sea but although the others on board abandoned the glider, the 1st pilot did not leave the aircraft and drowned.

Staff Sergeant James B C ELLIN 21 The Glider Pilot Regt

19-Sep-44 C/N 126 Horsa   1 HGSU   St Michielsgestel   4
The glider was carrying a gun, trailer and tractor belonging to the Polish Parachute Bde's Anti-Tank Company (Dyon Artylerii Przeciwpancernej). The combination passed directly overhead an enemy anti-aircraft concentration and the glider had its tail destroyed and it crashed.

Staff Sergeant Ronald E OSBORN 26 The Glider Pilot Regt
Sergeant Norman K WHITEHOUSE 26
Ogniomistrz (Artillery Sergeant) Piotr MASLORZ 37 1st Polish Independent Parachute Bde Gp
Kanonier (Gunner) Kazmierz NOWAK 21

19-Sep-44 256320 Hadrian I   ATTDU   2 miles north-east of Holworthy Devon   0
The crew was engaged of a trials flight to assess the fuel consumption characteristics for the tug aircraft type when towing a Hadrian. The tug flew into cloud and the glider got badly out of position in the poor

visibility and the pilot cast off the tow. A forced landing was made in a field but the aircraft struck a bank.

| 20-Sep-44 | LJ829 | Stirling IV | 190 Sqn | Doorwerth | 9 |

The aircraft crashed at about 1440 hours whilst on a resupply sortie.

Flying Officer Roderick James MATHESON 26 RCAF Pilot
Pilot Officer Reginald Austin DAVIS 27 RAAF Pilot
Pilot Officer Keith WILLETT 29 RAAF Navigator
Warrant Officer Thomas William ALLEN 21 RCAF Wireless Operator
Warrant Officer David Lourne BROUSE 23 RCAF Air Gunner
Sergeant Stanley James COOKE 27 Flight Engineer
Sergeant Edward Francis KEEN 21 Flight Engineer
Lance Corporal Frederick REXSTRAW 30 Air Despatcher 253 (Airborne) Composite Coy RASC
Driver Joseph Francis LEECH 22

| 20-Sep-44 | EF260 | Stirling IV | 190 Sqn | Eldense Zeeg, Valburg | 0 |

This aircraft; piloted by Flying Officer John Le Bouvier, was carrying the usual crew of six and two despatchers but also a war correspondent from the Daily Telegraph; Mr Edmund Townshend. As the aircraft ran up to the DZ, it was hit by flak and set on fire. The drop was completed and then the pilot climbed the aircraft to about 2000 feet and all on board abandoned it safely. That experience must have afforded Mr Townshend the opportunity of an unusual 'by line'!

| 20-Sep-44 | KG324 | Dakota | 512 Sqn | Schaijk | 2 |

The aircraft was struck by anti-aircraft fire and the crew were ordered to bale out, which most did. The pilot and navigator were killed when the aircraft crashed.

Pilot Officer William Henry PERRY 24 DFM Pilot

Warrant Officer Ivan Olaf Morrow GILBERT 29 Navigator

20-Sep-44   KG418 Dakota   512 Sqn   Buunderkamp   0

The aircraft was badly damaged by flak and was forced landed by its pilots. Two of the despatchers are reported to have baled out with one being killed but this cannot be confirmed.

20-Sep-44   LJ618 Stirling IV   295 Sqn   South bank of River Waal at Druten   1

Having been struck by anti-aircraft fire in the area of the DZ, the aircraft caught fire and the order was given to abandon the aircraft after the pilot had managed to climb the aircraft to a safe height. The wireless operator subsequently reported that he helped both despatchers with their parachutes, as well as assisting the air gunner who was trapped in his turrent. He then returned to clip on the pilot's parachute and having done so made to abandon the aircraft. As he exited the aircraft through the hatch, the aircraft exploded and it is certain the pilot did not leave the aircraft.

        Pilot Officer Neil Banks COUPER 21 RNZAF Pilot

20-Sep-44   LJ831 Stirling IV   190 Sqn   Ghent airfield   0

This aircraft was badly damaged by anti-aircraft fire and the pilot; Flight Lieutenant D R Robertson RCAF, made a successful forced landing at Ghent and the entire crew returned safely to UK. Robertson and his crew continued with the squadron and during Operation VARSITY(24 Mar 45) the crew took part in the glider towing sorties with their AOC; Air Vice Marshal James Scarlett-Streatfield, flying as second pilot. Unfortunately, during the repossession of Norway some 7 weeks later the crew, again with their AOC on board, a Norwegian liaison officer and a stick of parachutists from 1st Airborne Division, were all lost when the aircraft crashed in appalling weather north of Oslo – the wreck not being located for several months. (See "The Price Of Peace" pages 35 & 36 for a summary this later accident).

20-Sep-44 LJ840 Stirling IV Betuwe 0

This crew, captained by Flight Sergeant Averill, had already flown glider towing sorties on both 18 and 19 Sep. Their aircraft was heavily damaged by anti-aircraft fire but all six crew and two RASC despatchers escaped by parachute when the aircraft was shot down.

20-Sep-44 LJ851 Stirling IV South-west of Eindhoven 0

The aircraft; flown by Warrant Officer George Oliver RAAF and his crew, was hit by enemy anti-aircraft fire whilst within the airspace above the corridor along which the land forces were advancing. The aircraft was set on fire in the port wing area and this quickly spread to the tail unit. As the aircraft was too low to permit the crew to abandon by parachute, the pilot made a forced landing in a piece of open ground. After some difficulty, the crew of six and a pair of air despatchers, managed to get out of the aircraft and were quickly rescued by some ground troops nearby. Within a couple of days they returned to RAF Keevil.

20-Sep-44 LJ947 Stirling IV Aalst, west of Brussels, Belgium 0

The crew had dropped their load of twenty four containers and four panniers on the DZ before the aircraft was hit in both port engines. Control became increasingly difficult and eventually the pilot; Pilot Officer Marshall, was compelled to make a forced landing, which was accomplished successfully, although he and his bomb aimer; Pilot Officer Tole, were injured.

20-Sep-44 LJ988 Stirling IV Natuurbad Doorweth 7

The cause of this loss is not known but the crew was engaged on a resupply sortie.

Warrant Officer I William Robert TAIT 23 RCAF Pilot
Flight Sergeant Cyril MABBOT 22 Navigator
Warrant Officer I Ernest Walter BANCROFT 21 RCAF Bomb Aimer
Flight Sergeant Andrew Joseph MURPHY 29 Navigator
Flight Sergeant Terence Bowers CRAGG 21 Wireless Operator

Date	Serial Aircraft	Unit	Place	Casualties

Brief Circumstances of Accident
Casualty Details (If Applicable)

Pilot Officer Donovan Geoffrey BENNING 22 Air Gunner
Driver Gordon NEALE 18 Air Despatcher 63 (Airborne) Composite Coy RASC

20-Sep-44 LK127 Stirling IV   620 Sqn   Polderstraat, Heteren   6

The aircraft was dropping supplies at about 1800 hours when it was shot down and dived into marshy ground. Although two members of the crew survived with injuries and were taken POW, the others and the pair of air despatchers were killed.

Flying Officer Athol Richard SCANLON 29 RAAF Pilot
Warrant Officer Edward Joseph MCGILVRAY 31 RAAF
Flight Sergeant Raymond Joseph LAMONT 21 RCAF Bomb Aimer
Sergeant John William MARSHALL 22 Air Gunner
Corporal George Andrew FOWLER 29 Air Despatcher 253 (Airborne) Composite Coy RASC
Driver John Thomas HADLEY 25

20-Sep-44 LK548 Stirling IV   620 Sqn   Vorstenbosch   5

The aircraft was shot down at about 1730 hours. The aircraft had already been hit before reaching the DZ but the crew continued and released their load over the DZ before turning away. The aircraft was then hit by heavy flak, which killed the pilot, air gunner and wireless operator and one of the despatchers. The bomb aimer, navigator and flight engineer survived but the second despatcher did not.

Pilot Officer Maurice MCHUGH 21 RAAF Pilot
Flight Sergeant Eric Arthur BRADSHAW 21 Wireless Operator
Flight Sergeant Thomas VICKERS 19 Air Gunner
Lance Corporal John WARING 35 Air Despatcher 398 (Airborne) Divisional Composite Coy RASC

Driver Ernest Victor HECKFORD 19

20-Sep-44 LK556 Stirling IV   196 Sqn   Between Elst and Valburg   3
The aircraft crashed during a resupply sortie but the cause of its loss is unclear.

    Sergeant David Nicholson CLOUGH 22 Flight Engineer
    Corporal Alfred William James PESCODD 38 Air Despatcher 63 (Airborne) Coy RASC
    Driver Robert Frank PRAGNELL

20-Sep-44 LL256 Halifax V   298 Sqn   Middle Wallop   2

The loss of this aircraft was the consequence of a series of operational problems, poor airmanship and circumstances beyond the crew's control. The crew was tasked for an SAS support sortie; LOYTON 27 and the load comprised an embedded 'jeep' and three soldiers who were to be dropped behind the enemy's lines in occupied France. The crew spent some time in the area of the DZ awaiting the correct signal to drop the load and when this was not forthcoming, the aircraft returned to UK with the load intact and, of course, consuming more fuel than calculated had the load been despatched. When approaching base at Tarrant Rushton, the crew found the airfield closed by fog and were diverted to Harwell, south of Oxford. Instead of proceeding to the diversion straight away, the crew circled base for sometime calling 'DARKY' for assistance. During the transit, the flight engineer – who had not been keeping a fuel consumption log - advised that the fuel supply was very low and hence a further diversion was made Middle Wallop but the pilot did not jettison the jeep nor order the parachutists to jump. A wheels up forced landing was then attempted but the aircraft undershot the airfield and crashed. In addition to the fatal casualties, the six operating crew, an extra wireless operator, an air despatcher and two soldiers survived. Subsequently, it was found that there was at least 115 gallons of fuel in the aircraft's tanks.

    Sergeant Geoffrey O'KEFFE 29 Wireless Operator
    Private Richard Frederick IRELAND 30 Special Air Service Regiment

Date	Serial	Aircraft	Unit	Place	Casualties
				Brief Circumstances of Accident	
				Casualty Details (If Applicable)	

21-Sep-44   EW141 Liberator VI   178 Sqn   Amendola   0

The aircraft was being taxyed over rough ground when its undercarriage collapsed and it sustained significant damage.

21-Sep-44   FZ620 Dakota   48 Sqn   In River Rhine near Doorwerth   0

This aircraft made its first pass over the DZ, during which time it was hit by AA fire but the crew continued to drop the load, on completion of which the pilot opened the throttles and made a climbing turn to port onto a south westerly heading. Shortly afterwards the aircraft was hit in the port wing, suffering major damage and it entered an uncontrollable role to starboard, with the cabin filling with smoke and flames appearing towards the rear. The pilot; Flight Sergeant Stanley Webster, ordered the aircraft abandoned and all escaped with several landing in the river and swimming to the south bank of the Rhine. The only member of the crew who did not cross the river was found by the enemy and made POW the following day.

21-Sep-44   FZ656 Dakota   437 Sqn   Turnhout Melven, Belgium   0

The aircraft was hit by flak and despite getting to the Belgian border, it was eventually crash landed on heathland. The crew, captained by Flying Officer Kenny, was captured with the exception of two of the despatchers who evaded.

21-Sep-44   KG340 Dakota   271 Sqn   Achterstraat, Heteren   3

This crew were on their third sortie to Arnhem and they had already released most of their load over the DZ. However, with three panniers left, it was decided to make another run across the DZ and at that time the aircraft was struck by AA fire, the controls severed and the aircraft set on fire. The pilot immediately ordered everybody to bale out but Driver High is thought to have been killed already and Warrant Officer Anderson's parachute caught fire and he was killed. The pilot did not abandon the aircraft and was found dead in the wreckage.

Pilot Officer Frank CUER 23 Pilot
Warrant Officer Charles Allen ANDERSON 23 Wireless Operator
Driver George HIGH 34 223 Air Despatch Coy RASC

21-Sep-44   KG346 Dakota   48 Sqn   Dengey Flats, near Bradwell, Essex   7

The aircraft had been badly damaged by anti-aircraft fire in the area of the DZ but the crew had flown it back to UK. An unsuccessful forced landing was attempted and the RAF crew and two of the air despatchers were killed whilst one died from his injuries later.

Captain Colin Herbert CAMPBELL SAAF Pilot
Flying Officer John Christoper Colston GARVEY 21 Co-Pilot
Flying Officer John Percival MUDGE 32 Navigator
Flight Sergeant John Leslie ANDERSON 28 Wireless Operator
Driver George Patrick SLEET 23 Air Despatcher 223 Air Despatch Coy RASC
Driver Owen MORGAN 20
Corporal Herbert Arthur AUSTIN 26

21-Sep-44   KG376 Dakota   437 Sqn   South-west of Keldonk   2

This aircraft was set upon by up to nine enemy aircraft and badly damaged. Most of the crew escaped but those listed below died in the crash.

Flying Officer Michael Stanley Reece MAHON 28 RCAF Navigator
Flight Sergeant John Charles Henry HACKETT 36
Lance Corporal James ADAMSON 800 Air Despatch Coy RASC

Date	Serial	Aircraft	Unit	Place	Casualties

Brief Circumstances of Accident
Casualty Details (If Applicable)

21-Sep-44   KG387   Dakota   437 Sqn   Sonniushoeve Farm, Son near Eindhoven   5

The aircraft had not been damaged whilst dropping its supplies and the pilot climbed it to 7000 feet and set course for UK in the hazy conditions existing at that time. The aircraft was well clear of Arnhem when it was attacked by an enemy fighter, which caused serious damage and either fatally wounded or killed the aircraft's captain with its first burst of fire. Three of the despatchers were also killed at this point and the co-pilot ordered the aircraft abandoned and the navigator, wireless operator and the surviving despatcher baled out just as the aircraft went out of control. Squadron Leader Alexander had initially qualified as a navigator and had flown a tour of operations with 148 Sqn in the Middle East and was awarded the DFC in Apr 1942 at the conclusion of his tour. He returned to Canada and trained as a pilot, qualifying in mid-1943.

Squadron Leader Robert Wilfred ALEXANDER 24 RCAF Pilot
Flying Officer William Stewart MCLINTOCK 22 RCAF Co-Pilot
Corporal Albert E HALL 32 799 Air Despatch Coy RASC
Driver Harold WOODWARD 30
Driver Frederick George William YEO 19

21-Sep-44   KG399   Dakota   233 Sqn   Arendonk (Belgian/Dutch border)   2

The aircraft was hit over the DZ but the crew flew it southward at about 4000 feet. The aircraft was subsequently hit again and the navigator, wireless operator and four despatchers baled out. The two pilots remained with the aircraft but were killed when it crash landed alongside the Dessel to Schoten Canal at the position shown.

Flying Officer Michael Tony ADES 20 Pilot
Flight Sergeant George Kenneth DORVILLE 20 Co-Pilot

21-Sep-44   KG404 Dakota   48 Sqn   Achel Belgium   0

Having delivered its supplies to the DZ, the aircraft was climbed to 4000 feet and set course for home. Near Eindhoven, it was attacked by two fighters and set on fire. Some of the air despatchers abandoned the aircraft and the flying crew crash landed it, during which time it hit a tree head on. All those aboard this aircraft survived.

21-Sep-44   KG417 Dakota   48 Sqn   Near Driel   8

The aircraft was running in to the target when it was struck by the load from another Dakota. A wing failed and the aircraft dived into the ground on the southern bank of the river, just north of Driel. It appears that a formation of aircraft from 233 and 437 Sqns were dropping from between 2000 and 3000 feet and as they were ahead of the aircraft from 48 and 271 Sqns, their loads presented a hazard to aircraft flying behind and at a lower altitude.

    Pilot Officer Jack Gordon WILLS 21 RCAF Pilot
    Flying Officer James William ERICKSON 23 RCAF Co-Pilot
    Pilot Officer Desmond George HARDY 24 Navigator
    Flight Sergeant David Stenhouse BLACK 22 Wireless Operator
    Lieutenant Herbert Arthur EDWARDS 27 223 Air Despatch Coy RASC
    Lance Corporal Eric ROSCOE 36
    Driver Jack TAYLOR 27
    Driver Ben WELHAM 38

21-Sep-44   KG444 Dakota   271 Sqn   Between Oploo and Gemert   3

The pilot of this aircraft was to achieve post-war fame as 'Professor' Jimmy Edwards but his 'Sunday title' was Flight Lieutenant James Keith O'Neill Edwards. This crew had delivered their load of supplies and the pilot climbed to 6000 feet and carried out a circuit of the dropping areas before setting course to the south and climbing to 8000 feet. South of Nijmegen, the aircraft was attacked by a fighter and after a running battle amongst the broken cloud, the aircraft was severely damaged and set on fire. After deciding to bale out initially, the pilot elected to crash land the aircraft, when he realised that several of the despatchers had been wounded and this he did. Unfortunately, the wounded soldiers could not be saved and they were killed when the aircraft crashed or died of their injuries immediately afterwards. Flight Lieutenant Edwards, his wireless operator and a soldier were able to reach allied lines but the other two crew were made POW.

Lance Corporal George CHISHOLME 26 RASC
Driver Lionel Henry Samuel ABBOTT 22
Driver Roy ABBOTT 19

21-Sep-44	KG489	Dakota	437 Sqn	Eerschot near St Oedenrode	8

The aircraft was attacked whilst flying at low level by two enemy fighters and was shot down immediately, with no chance for the crew to bale out.

Flying Officer John Spencer BLAIR 21 RCAF Pilot
Flying Officer Charles Herbert CRESSMAN 21 RCAF Co-Pilot
Flying Officer Paul STEFFIN 21 RCAF Navigator
Flying Officer Thomas John BRENNAN 21 RCAF Wireless Operator
Corporal George Henry RHODES 33 799 Air Despatch Coy RASC
Lance Corporal Reginald Arthur ADAMS 29
Driver Rowland John CLAXTON 31
Driver Donald Frederick TITE 19

21-Sep-44	KG516	Dakota	271 Sqn	Near Leygraafbridge, Uden	0

The aircraft was attacked shortly after its cargo was dropped and despite being hit by fire from the enemy

408

aircraft, it was not badly damaged. Later, whilst flying back to UK and having passed Nijmegen, it was attacked again by two FW 190 fighters, whose fire disabled the flying controls and stopped both engines. The crew, captained by Flight Lieutenant Charles Mott, abandoned the aircraft safely and all returned to UK in due course.

21-Sep-44	KG566 Dakota	233 Sqn	Oirschotse Dijk, near Eindhoven	8

The aircraft was returning to base having completed its supply drop when it was attacked by enemy fighters. The aircraft was seen to dive vertically into the ground in a position north west of Einhoven and there were no survivors and no evidence that anybody attempted to abandon the aircraft.

Flying Officer Charles Douglas HAMILTON 28 RAAF Pilot
Flight Sergeant William Burnaby WHEELER 19 Co-Pilot
Pilot Officer Frederick Benbow KNIGHT 26 RAAF Navigator
Warrant Officer Louis James FIRTH 21 RAAF Wireless operator
Corporal Joseph DELLANZO 30 800 Air Despatch Coy RASC
Lance Corporal Robert SHARPE
Driver Robert Winter CROOKS 32
Driver George VAN INGEN 20

21-Sep-44	KG579 Dakota	48 Sqn	Volkel Airfield	4

The aircraft was shot down by a large formation of enemy fighters at about 1730 hours and crashed on the airfield. The wireless operator and the air despatcher were killed during their parachute descent, when the enemy aircraft continued to fire on them, but the navigator survived as a POW and the three other air despatchers made good their escape.

Flight Sergeant Dennis Harry Ralph PLEAR 26 Pilot
Pilot Officer Davis Arthur WEBB 22 RCAF Co-Pilot
Warrant Officer Gordon BIRLISON 24 Wireless Operator
Lance Corporal James PILSON 223 Air Despatch Coy RASC

Date	Serial	Aircraft	Unit	Place	Casualties
				Brief Circumstances of Accident	
				Casualty Details (If Applicable)	
21-Sep-44	LJ982	Stirling IV	190 Sqn	Near Zetten	9

The aircraft was shot down by flak and crashed about 500 yards south of the river at Zetten, having dropped its load of supplies near the Hartenstein Hotel. Wing Commander Harrison was an experienced Stirling pilot and squadron commander, having been awarded his DFC whilst with 149 Sqn. There are a number of photographs of this officer, one talking to his station commander after the first sortie to Arnhem, when he towed a glider containing Major General Roy Urquhart, and also another posing with his crew.

Wing Commander Graeme Elliott HARRISON 29 DFC Silver Star (US) Pilot
Warrant Officer Thomas Barry BRIERLEY 21 RNZAF Co-Pilot
Warrant Officer Donald Meldrum MATHEWSON 36 RNZAF Navigator
Flying Officer Neil MACKAY 35 Bomb Aimer
Flight Lieutenant Norman Edward SKINNER 32 DFC Wireless Operator
Flight Sergeant Robert PERCY 25 Flight Engineer
Pilot Officer Le Comte Jacques Fernand Gabriel DE CORDOUE 29 RCAF Air Gunner
Lance Corporal Leslie CALDECOTT 22 253 (Airborne) Composite Coy RASC
Driver Harold GREGORY 28

Date	Serial	Aircraft	Unit	Place	Casualties
21-Sep-44	KG586	Dakota	233 Sqn	Buunderkamp	0

This aircraft crashed after dropping its supplies and its crew of eight was taken prisoner.

Date	Serial	Aircraft	Unit	Place	Casualties
21-Sep-44	LJ810	Stirling IV	196 Sqn	Between Niftrik and Heren	2

This aircraft was attacked by three fighters and although one was shot down by the air gunner, the others pressed home their attack successfully. This crew had completed their tour on 19 Sep but agreed to fly another sortie due to the shortage of crews. Azouz and his bomb aimer were Jewish and this day was the Day of Atonement. Having baled out, Azouz was machine gunned by the enemy fighters which had been attacking his aircraft and he was killed.

Warrant Officer Mark AZOUZ 22 DFC Pilot
Flight Sergeant Peter Harold BODE 21 Air Gunner

21-Sep-44 LJ823 Stirling IV   Haren south west Demen   3

Initially, this aircraft was damaged by flak and was then attacked by enemy fighter aircraft. A running battle ensued, during which the despatchers baled out and then other members of the crew followed at intervals. The pilot crashed landed the aircraft and was thrown out before the aircraft was destroyed by fire.

Warrant Officer Leslie John BILLEN 22 Bomb Aimer (supernumerary for operational experience)
Flight Sergeant William Louis Pretsell CAIRNS 22 Bomb Aimer
Flight Sergeant William Henry SKEWES 23 Wireless Operator

21-Sep-44 LJ830 Stirling IV   Renkum   1

This aircraft was hit by flak and also attacked by fighters and its rear gun turret was shot away. A forced landing was made and after evacuating the aircraft, the crew split into two groups; one group being made POW quite quickly whilst the others evaded before returning to allied lines in Oct 44.

Flying Officer John Russell THOMAS RCAF Air Gunner

21-Sep-44 LJ833 Stirling IV   River Mass at Ravenstein   6

The aircraft was shot down by enemy fighters and crashed into the River Mass. Whilst some of the casualties were trapped in the wreck several others were drowned in the river but two aircrew and one of the air despatchers survived.

Flight Lieutenant Alexander ANDERSON Pilot
Flight Sergeant George Felix CONRY-CANDLER 20 2nd Pilot
Flying Officer Alexander Dalgety ADAMSOM 33 Navigator

Date	Serial	Aircraft	Unit	Place	Casualties

Brief Circumstances of Accident
Casualty Details (If Applicable)

Flight Sergeant William George TOLLEY 21 Wireless Operator
Flight Sergeant Arthur G O BELLAMY 20 Air Gunner
Driver Albert E ABBOTT 30 253 (Airborne) Coy RASC

21-Sep-44	LJ843	Stirling IV	196 Sqn	Wageningen	8

Whilst starting the run up to the DZ, this aircraft was struck by enemy anti aircraft fire and crashed.

Flight Sergeant Charles Richard John GREEN 23 Pilot
Flight Sergeant Richard Glyn PHILLIPS 26 Navigator
Flight Sergeant Leonard MARSH 20 Bomb Aimer
Flight Sergeant Robert COWAN 21 Wireless Operator
Flight Sergeant David John ALLWAY 20 Flight Engineer
Flight Sergeant Donald Hay GRANT 24 Air Gunner
Driver Stanley Victor ARMAND 26 63 (Airborne) Composite Coy RASC
Driver John Robert HARRIS 27

21-Sep-44	LJ881	Stirling IV	190 Sqn	Veldstraat, Andelst	5

The aircraft was hit by flak and then attacked by several enemy fighters, setting fire to the port inner engine and causing serious damage to the tail unit. The load was jettisoned and the order to bale out given but only Driver Hughes, one of the despatchers, and the aircraft's gunner and wireless operator survived, with the Stirling breaking up into several pieces before crashing. The circumstances in which Driver Jones met his death are unclear but he is thought to have abandoned the aircraft also.

Flying Officer Brian Arthur BEBERFALD 23 RNZAF Pilot
Pilot Officer Malcolm James YARWOOD 34 RNZAF Navigator
Flight Sergeant Garnet Arthur PHILLIPS 21 RAAF Bomb Aimer

Sergeant Charles Frederick BRANSON 23 Flight Engineer
Driver George Evan JONES 253 (Airborne) Composite Coy RASC

| 21-Sep-44 | LJ916 | Stirling IV | East of Tilburg | 0 |

This aircraft was brought down after dropping its supplies and its crew then set course for base via the shortest route rather than the reciprocal course intended. At some stage it crashed and its crew were made POW.

| 21-Sep-44 | LJ928 | Stirling IV | South of Van der Molenallee | 7 |

This aircraft is believed to have been destroyed by an enemy fighter. The only survivor was Driver W Brook, one of the despatchers.

Flight Sergeant Ronald Eric George WALTRICH 23 Pilot
Flight Sergeant Robert Walter FORREST 23 Navigator
Flight Sergeant Stanley Arthur Leonard TOWNSEND 23 Bomb Aimer
Flight Sergeant Francis ORMSON 21 Wireless Operator
Sergeant Leslie Victor RATCLIFFE 28 Flight Engineer
Flight Sergeant Sidney John POOLE 24 Air Gunner
Lance Corporal Stanley LAW 28 63 (Airborne) Composite Coy RASC

| 21-Sep-44 | LJ943 | Stirling IV | Near Zetten | 7 |

The aircraft crashed at Zetten near the site where LJ982 impacted. The aircraft had fallen victim to enemy flak and only Sergeant Les Hillyard the flight engineer and Flight Sergeant Jack Thomas RCAF the rear gunner, survived.

Pilot Officer Robert Blair HERGER 23 RCAF Pilot
Flying Officer Otto Hjalmar ANTOFT 25 RCAF Navigator
Flying Officer John Kenneth MACDONNELL 21 RCAF Bomb Aimer
Warrant Officer II Leslie Innes WHITLOCK 20 RCAF Wireless Operator

Brief Circumstances of Accident
Casualty Details (If Applicable)

Flying Officer Harold Albert THORNINGTON 34 Air Gunner
Driver Ernest NOBLE 24 253 (Airborne) Composite Coy RASC
Driver Colin PARKER 31

21-Sep-44   LJ946   Stirling IV   620 Sqn   Bennekom   0

This aircraft, flown by Pilot Officer Jack Carey whose 24th birthday it was, took off after the others because of delays at its base. It was unable to catch up with the rest of the formation and so approached the DZ all alone! The load was dropped successfully despite the aircraft being hit numerous times by light flak and immediately afterward, the pilot dived the aircraft to low level and set off for home. Unfortunately, the aircraft was then hit and set on fire and the pilot climbed it and everybody baled out. The wreck of the Stirling has never been found and it is supposed to have crashed into the River Waal.

21-Sep-44   LK115   Stirling IV   295 Sqn   Wolfheze   2

The aircraft was from a mixed force of 295 and 570 Sqns, led by Squadron Leader Potter of 295 and Squadron Leader Cleaver of 570. The crew of this aircraft, captained by Pilot Officer Denis Peel, ran up to the DZ as planned but was then hit in the starboard inner engine which caught fire. The load was, however, dropped but the pilot realised he had no option but to crash land and this he did. However, the area was occupied by enemy troops and he was taken prisoner along with his crew. The 2 despatchers had jumped from the aircraft at 200 feet and were killed.

Driver Sydney CHURCHYARD 22
Driver James Francis JOHNSON 28

21-Sep-44   LK498   Stirling IV   190 Sqn   Escharen, south of Grave   0

This aircraft was hit during the sortie and when the pilot was given a course to steer afterwards, his faulty compass led him to turn back towards the DZ and the aircraft was subjected to further AA fire and attacks by fighters. Both starboard engines were set on fire and shut down by the crew. The pilot then made a text book crash landing – if such a thing is not a misnomer – and all on board escaped safely from the wreck.

| 21-Sep-44 | LK545 | Stirling IV | 299 Sqn | Near Nijmegen | 0 |

This aircraft was captained by Flight Lieutenant Reg Turner and was one of a force of only 21 aircraft which could be mustered by the Keevil squadrons; Nos: 299 and 196. Over the DZ the aircraft was badly damaged by AA fire and the pilot turned south with the aircraft on fire which forced the rear gunner to bale out. Eventually a crash landing was made to the west of Nijmegen and after a while the crew joined up with allied soldiers, with whom they spent the night. Next day, the Army provided Turner and his party with a lorry to take them to Eindhoven but their journey was far from straight forward and they had numerous adventures on the way. Eventually, Flight Lieutenant Turner and Corporal Sproston, one of his despatchers, reached safety and the former was awarded a Military Cross and the latter a Military Medal.

| 21-Sep-44 | LK208 | Stirling | 161 Sqn | RAF Tempsford | 0 |

The aircraft's undercarriage collapsed during take-off, after a swing developed. The crew was just setting out on OSRIC 900.

| 21-Sep-44 | EB345 | Whitley V | 81 OTU | RAF Sleap | 0 |

The trainee pilot approached at too low a speed and the aircraft dropped heavily onto the runway, causing damage to the undercarriage. The instructor took control and overshot for another attempt. However, on touchdown a tyre burst and the undercarriage collapsed.

| 21-Sep-44 | LL333 | Halifax V | 298 Sqn | 16 miles south-east of Resancon | 3 |

This aircraft was one of twenty eight from the Tarrant Rushton squadrons, operating on this occasion in support of SAS and SOE. The aircraft crashed whilst dropping supplies into a DZ during a moonlight

Date	Serial	Aircraft	Unit	Place	Casualties

Brief Circumstances of Accident
Casualty Details (If Applicable)

period. The pilot ignored his briefing and descended into the valley within which the DZ lay, rather than drop from the height of the surrounding hills. The official summary records that the pilot was; 'disobedient occasioned by inexperience and over enthuiasm'.

Flying Officer Alfred Fred SHEFFIELD 30 Navigator
Flying Officer Gerald BORKETT 23 Wireless Operator
Sergeant Hardy DAY 24 Flight Engineer

22-Sep-44	KH102	Liberator VI	31 SAAF	Budapest area	6

The aircraft was engaged in leaflet dropping in the area of the Hungarian capital when it was intercepted and shot down. It has to be questioned whether the use of an expensive heavy bomber and its trained crew of eight, to distribute pamphlets of propaganda material as the sole reason for flying a sortie over hostile territory makes sense. In this case six men were killed and two taken prisoner.

Lieutenant R E DEPPE SAAF Pilot
Warrant Officer I C R KLEYNHANS SAAF
Air Sergeant E HAVINGA SAAF
Sergeant Sydney WRIGHT 24 Air Gunner
Sergeant Jack BOYLE 20 Bomb Aimer
Sergeant Lawson George THOMPSON 23 Air Gunner

23-Sep-44	JP222	Halifax II	1586 Flt	At sea 1 mile north of Brindisi airfield	8

The aircraft was returning to base at the conclusion of a 7 hour resupply sortie into enemy territory over northern Italy. Despite being given and acknowledging the details of the runway in use, the pilot approached for a downwind landing but then overshot the approach and climbed away but in doing so retracted the

416

flaps prematurely. The aircraft went out of control and crashed into the sea. All those on board were killed in the crash or drowned before they could be rescued.

Flight Sergeant Rysard BEER Pilot
Sergeant Henryk MILEWSKI
Sergeant Kazimierz KUHN
Sergeant Mieczyslaw KOZLOWSKI
Pilot Officer Zygmunt MOLINSKI
Sergeant Wladyslaw MIROWSKI
Sergeant Julian MARTYNIUK
Captain Francis Patrick WOOLF Royal Artillery Army Liaison Officer

---

23-Sep-44   EF298   Stirling IV   Panoramahoeve, Ede   8

During the dropping sequence, this aircraft was hit by AA fire and the aircraft turned away from the DZ but crashed very shortly afterward.

Flying Officer William BAKER 22 RCAF Pilot
Flight Lieutenant John DICKSON 24 DFM Navigator
Flying Officer Robert Carter BOOTH 22 Bomb Aimer
Pilot Officer Francis George TOTTERDILL 24 Wireless Operator
Sergeant Richard Bert BOND 24 Flight Engineer
Flight Sergeant Dennis James BLENCOWE 20 Air Gunner
Driver Robert William HAYTON 22 253 (Airborne) Composite Coy RASC
Driver Reginald SHORE 21

23-Sep-44   KG315   Dakota   437 Sqn   South-west of Driel   8

This aircraft was seen by other crews being chased by an enemy fighter and it crashed subsequently with the loss of those on board. The squadron had just been formed by the simple expedient of taking Canadian crews from other squadrons and transferring them to the new unit.

417

Brief Circumstances of Accident
Casualty Details (If Applicable)

Flying Officer Donald Lawrence JACK 21 RCAF Pilot
Flying Officer William Richard PAGET 28 RCAF Co-Pilot
Flight Sergeant Denis Joseph O'SULLIVAN 28 RCAF Navigator
Warrant Officer I Roy Irvine PINNER 25 RCAF Wireless Operator
Corporal Thomas Henry BAXTER 35 223 Air Despatch Coy RASC
Corporal Leslie John CLARK 37
Driver Frederick Walter BEARDSLEY 29
Driver Paul WILLIAMS 18

23-Sep-44 KG370 Dakota   48 Sqn   Rosanpolder (near railway line to Nijmegan)   5

The aircraft descended from an approach height of 1500 feet and although hit by AA fire, it was not badly damaged and the approach continued. However, at 800 feet on the final run up to the DZ, the aircraft was struck by incendiary ammunition and set on fire. The pilot initially intended to turn back to the south side of the river but the fire became too intense and he decided to force land immediately. During the final stages of the approach, he was hit by ground fire and mortally wounded. Although the other seven crew members escaped from the aircraft, the wireless operator was killed by the enemy on the ground and the co-pilot received wounds from which he died in hospital. Two despatchers were taken prisoner along with the navigator but the other despatchers evaded capture initially but were killed later.

Pilot Officer Walton Ralph PRING 26 Pilot
Pilot Officer Henry Everest COLMAN 19 RCAF Co-Pilot
Pilot Officer James Le Roy SPRINGSTEELE 25 RCAF Wireless Operator
Lance Corporal Francis William Richard SIMPSON 34 253 (Airborne) Composite Coy RASC
Driver William Thomas CROSSLEY 41

23-Sep-44   LJ873   Stirling IV   620 Sqn   Oss   0

This aircraft was flown by Wing Commander D H Lee DFC, the squadron commander. During the approach to the DZ and whilst flying at 2500 feet, the aircraft was hit very severely by AA fire and the starboard wing caught fire, fuelled by the oil and petrol therein. With no other options, the pilot made a crash landing and all eight people on board escaped safely. They were fortunate to land in an area free of the enemy and were directed to allied lines by Dutch civilians.

23-Sep-44   LJ883   Stirling IV   570 Sqn   Planken Wambuis, Ede   6

The aircraft's crew had just finished dropping its load and it was down to 500 feet when it was struck by AA fire and a serious blaze started in the port wing. The aircraft continued to descend and struck the ground, causing the rear turret to break off and probably saving the gunner's life in the process because only he and a despatcher survived.

    Flying Officer William KIRKHAM 21 Pilot
    Flying Officer Morris HAND 26 Wireless Operator
    Flying Officer David Henry ATKINSON 23 Bomb Aimer
    Flying Officer Ernest Charles BROWN 20 Navigator
    Sergeant Harold ASHTON 22 Flight Engineer
    Lance Corporal Gerard REARDON 31 253 (Airborne) Composite Coy RASC

23-Sep-44   LJ949   Stirling IV   196 Sqn   Leende/Valkenswaard   0

This aircraft's crew, captained by Flying Officer W A Sparks, was making its first sortie to Arnhem along with three other new crews posted to 'B' Flight as replacements. The aircraft was badly damaged by enemy AA fire in the tail and fuselage and one engine lost a propeller but the load of twenty four containers and several panniers were successfully dropped. Having flown the damaged aircraft to a position south east of Eindhoven, the pilot crash landed it without serious injury to his crew although he and his wireless operator, Flight Sergeant J E Herring were wounded.

419

23-Sep-44   LJ991   Stirling IV   570 Sqn   Achterstaat, Heteren   5

This crew, captained by Flying Officer C Beck RCAF, had arrived on the squadron with three other crews the previous day and were sent straight into the fray! The aircraft was hit by flak over the DZ and the pilot turned away and managed to fly the aircraft across the river to its south bank. The wireless operator and one of the despatchers baled out and the pilot was thrown from the aircraft, strapped to his heavy armour plated seat, during the crash. Unfortunately, the other five occupants were killed.

Flight Sergeant Simon Pierre CORMIER 23 RCAF Navigator
Flight Sergeant Erle Mayne MILKS 20 RCAF Bomb Aimer
Flight Sergeant John MCGARRIE 20 Flight Engineer
Flight Sergeant Harold James STELL 20 Air Gunner
Driver Cyril William LIGHTWOOD 21 253 (Airborne) Composite Coy RASC

23-Sep-44   LK191   Stirling IV   570 Sqn   Randwijk   0

This aircraft was captained by Squadron Leader Richard Cleaver DSO, who a couple of weeks later would be awarded a DFC and who was one of the most successful heavy tactical transport pilots of the war and whose experiences would put a 'Boys' Own' annual to shame! The aircraft was hit by AA fire and both port engines set on fire. The situation was critical and the pilot crash landed the aircraft, guiding it between a pair of brick kilns, which promptly removed the wings. The aircraft skidded into some farm buildings, in which several Bren carriers were sheltering. The buildings were set on fire and destroyed but the carriers were swiftly removed. The flight engineer; Flight Sergeant G M Stewart, had been awarded a BEM in March 1941 for 'gallant and distinguished service in an operational theatre' and a crew photograph shows him to be wearing a second flying badge on his breast pocket.

23-Sep-44   P1435   Albemarle I   296 Sqn   RAF Long Marston   0

The crew was engaged on a glider towing sortie and during flight the starboard engine failed and was feathered successfully. The pilot attempted a single engined landing but overshot the runway and the aircraft was damaged beyond repair. Subsequent examination of the engine revealed very poor conditions in both magnetos due to some heavy pitting, over oiling and dirt, caused either at the time of manufacture or during in-service inspection.

23-Sep-44   KG435   Dakota III   117 Sqn   Imphal   0

On landing at the end of an operational sortie, the aircraft swung to port because the port brakes were binding. The pilot was unable to hold the swing and the aircraft ran into a ditch which collapsed the starboard undercarriage.

24-Sep-44   KG653   Dakota   1 FU   4 miles south west of New Leiningen   23

The aircraft was originally recorded as 'Missing' but was then found crashed in the German border area. The circumstances of its loss are not recorded but it is known that it was carrying mostly ground crew staff destined for a Canadian Dakota squadron operating in the Far East. The records also suggest that the aircraft was flown by a 437 Sqn crew to which it had been allocated prior to its flight.

Flight Lieutenant Ralph KORER 23 Pilot
Pilot Officer Lionel Alfred VEARLEY 24 Navigator
Sergeant George BECKOFF 20 RAAF Wireless Operator
Leading Aircraftman Lawrence Irwin BEACH 22 RCAF
Aircraftman 1st Class Frederick Robert Leigh GATES 21 RCAF
Aircraftman 1st Class John Dunlop MCVIE 19 RCAF
Leading Aircraftman Oliver Eugene Debs BERGEN 20 RCAF
Leading Aircraftman John Adelard Real CHEVRIER 29 RCAF
Leading Aircraftman Joseph Robert Marcel Armand COUTURIER 21 RCAF

Leading Aircraftman Michael James Foch GOOD 26 RCAF
Leading Aircraftman Fred Larsen KRISTENSEN 22 RCAF
Leading Aircraftman William John Scott LUNDY RCAF
Leading Aircraftman Donald John MACDONALD 21 RCAF
Leading Aircraftman John Cyril SUTHERLAND 37 RCAF
Leading Aircraftman Henry Studwell WATSON 19 RCAF
Corporal James CUMMING 32 RCAF
Corporal Howard John HUNTER 23 RCAF
Corporal Lorne Hamilton MOREAU 24 RCAF
Corporal Frederick William SARGENT 37 RCAF
Sergeant Walter Francis HUGHES 22 RCAF
Corporal James Ernest ALLEN 22 RCAF
Leading Aircraftman Robert Thomas BURDEN RCAF
Corporal William Howard CAMPBELL 26 RCAF

24-Sep-44   LK142   Stirling IV   196 Sqn   Near Spencourt   3
The aircraft was being used for an operational supply drop to a DZ at night and was approaching after a
transit flight of about 1½ hours. The altimeter had not been reset to the air pressure at the DZ and the pilot
initiated a descent before the DZ had been positively identified. The aircraft was flown into the ground
because it was off track and the crew was confused by some contradictory information given at the pre-
flight briefing.

Flight Sergeant Cedric Alfred WILLIAMSON 22
Sergeant Desmond Gerald Patrick KERTON 23
Sergeant James Campbell TURREFF31

24-Sep-44   P1381   Albemarle I   297 Sqn   USAAF Base Welford   0

The crew was at Welford for a glider retrieval and whilst the aircraft was taxying downhill and downwind, the brakes failed because the Bowden cable sheared at the nipple end. The pilot attempted to turn the aircraft into wind using the throttles only but this was not successful and so he raised the undercarriage to stop.

25-Sep-44   KG512   Dakota   271 Sqn   Arnhem   ?

The aircraft is recorded as being lost on a sortie to Arnhem but details could not be traced.

25-Sep-44   EE972   Stirling III   1665 HCU   Cheviot Hills   3

The aircraft was engaged on a cross country flying sortie and was carrying a crew of eight, comprising the usual six crew plus a second flight engineer and a screen pilot. After departure from RAF Tilstock it flew north eastward but encountered variable winds and some cloud and restricted visibility. Whilst flying in cloud it struck high ground at a height of 2600 feet above sea level

    Flight Sergeant Paulus Senor CORONEL 29 RAAF Navigator
    Flight Sergeant David Colville MCLACKLAND 31 Bomb Aimer
    Warrant Officer Peter Anthony ALLEN 22 Air Gunner died of injuries 29 September 1944

26-Sep-44   BD296   Whitley V   42 OTU   RAF Ashbourne   0

The undercarriage failed after a heavy landing was made in gusty wind conditions.

26-Sep-44   KG449   Dakota   575 Sqn   Paal Belgium   0

This aircraft was hit in its tail by enemy AA fire and the port elevator and rudder were damaged but the aircraft remained under control, although its port engine subsequently seized. When flying near Eindhoven, it was hit again – this time by allied AA fire – and the pilot made a crash landing in a field.

Date	Serial	Aircraft	Unit	Place	Casualties

Brief Circumstances of Accident
Casualty Details (If Applicable)

27-Sep-44   KG547   Dakota III   107 OTU   Leicester East   0

The aircraft was being flown by a pilot with 1000 hours total flying but only one hour on the Dakota. He was assisted by a co-pilot but there were no other crew aboard. Whilst making a glide approach and landing, the pilot failed to check the rate of descent soon enough and the aircraft struck the ground heavily, causing the undercarriage to collapse.

29-Sep-44   LJ932   Stirling   138 Sqn   RAF Ludford Magna   0

The crew of this aircraft, captained by Flight Lieutenant Ralph Read, had completed sorties TABLEJAM 14 and 26 over Denmark and had dropped a dozen containers on each. Setting course for UK, the crew encountered a Ju 88 over Denmark and the aircraft was attacked whilst flying at low level but the crew managed to find cloud cover. A little later and on emerging from cloud at 3500 feet, they were attacked again and the starboard outer engine was destroyed and significant other damage caused. The aircraft diverted to Ludford Magna and on approach to land, further problems were encountered and the aircraft crashed. Although two of the crew were injured, the rest survived unscathed and Read and his flight engineer, Flight Lieutenant Cyril Curtis, were both awarded the DFC. The citation for Flight Lieutenant Read's DFC, published in the London Gazette on 10 Nov 44, states:

"One night in September 1944, Flight Lieutenant Read piloted an aircraft detailed for an operation in Denmark. Soon after the target had been attacked the aircraft was intercepted by a fighter. In the ensuing engagement the bomber sustained extensive damage. The starboard engines were affected, one of them being put out of action. The starboard aileron was shot away. One of the petrol tanks was damaged. The aircraft became exceedingly difficult to control and to keep level, it was necessary for another member of the crew to assist in holding the control column. In spite of this Flight Lieutenant Read flew the aircraft to an airfield near the English coast. When coming in to land, the port engines failed. Despite this, Flight

Lieutenant Read effected a successful crash landing. In perilous circumstances this officer displayed outstanding skill, great courage and determination".

29-Sep-44   V9749   Lysander   Missing le Bourget to RAF Tempsford   4
The aircraft came down in the sea off Le Bourget and all on board were lost without trace. The circumstances of the loss are not known.

    Flying Officer John Alan LAMBERTON 20 Pilot
    Flight Lieutenant Charles Peter CLARK 35
    Squadron Leader Anthony Wilfred Alwyne COMPTON 35
    Major John Walter SAUNDERS 46 MBE Royal Corps of Signals

30-Sep-44   KG422   Dakota III   437 Sqn   B59 (see Note)   0
The pilot, who had barely 200 hours total flying time and only 50 on type, landed the aircraft on the grass and found the brakes to be ineffective in stopping the aircraft in the space available and at the landing weight involved. The aircraft ran off the grass and overshot into muddy ground, where it was damaged badly. It was commented that the pilot should have overshot the landing, when it became apparent that the brakes were proving ineffective. Furthermore, it was recommended that captains of heavy transport aircraft should have at least 500 flying hours before being appointed to command.

Note: The Accident Card refers to the airfield as B59 but this is thought not to be accurate.

30-Sep-44   KG967   Liberator VI   31 SAAF   North-east of San Severo   8
The aircraft broke up when pulling out of a dive at 700 feet. It seems probable that the aircraft had strayed into a developed cu-nim cloud which the crew had been warned to avoid and that the aircraft iced up.

    Pilot Officer George VALENTINE 23 Pilot
    Sergeant George William BRADSHAW 21 Navigator
    Sergeant Bernard REILLY 19 Air Gunner

Sergeant Elwyn STOCKFORD 21 Wireless Operator
Sergeant John Rodger Blair AIRLIE 21 Flight Engineer
Sergeant Cyril Roy KNIGHT Bomb Aimer
Sergeant Edward Frederick ROGERS 28 Bomb Aimer
Sergeant Walter Terrance WHITE 23 Air Gunner

30-Sep-44   Z6878   Whitley V   42 OTU   Perry Bridge Goole   5

The crew had been airborne for about 2½ hours on a night cross country training sortie when their aircraft crashed and burst into flames on impact. It is thought that the pilot, who was known for his slow reactions, might have failed to take action following an engine failure – for which there is post crash evidence – and allowed the aircraft to stall and then fail to recover. It is surmised that whatever the emergency, the crew were aware of the problems because they were found with their parachute packs attached to their harnesses.

Flight Sergeant George PIGOTT 28 Pilot
Sergeant Daniel HANNAN 21
Sergeant Maurice SILVER 32
Sergeant Alan Frederick WEST 20
+ one other

02-Oct-44   LL402   Halifax   644 Sqn   RAF Woodbridge   0

The crew of this aircraft, captained by Flight Lieutenant V J Blake RCAF, was undertaking an SOE operation to an area near Dordrecht. The sortie went extremely well at first and the location and approach to the DZ was accomplished without difficulty and the correct signals were observed. The load was dropped in a single pass but as the aircraft flew over the DZ it was subjected to sustained and accurate light AA fire

426

which damaged the aircraft badly, causing an engine to be lost and the hydraulics fail and also some instruments were made unserviceable and Flying Officer F R Darling RCAF the navigator, was injured. Nonetheless, the aircraft was flown clear of the area and a course was steered for Woodbridge for an emergency landing. Without flaps, brakes and undercarriage, the aircraft was crashed landed at 160 mph but all the crew survived. The pilot was subsequently awarded the DFC, with the citation reflecting his skill and determination on numerous sorties. It seems probable that this crew was just the latest in a long line of SD and transport crews who were lured into a trap sprung by the enemy, who had infiltrated the resistance movements in the Netherlands. It is worth taking Blake and his crew as an example of the sort of work the transport force did in the last years of the war. Their operational career opened at the end of April 1944, when they flew four sorties and prepared for the D-Day invasion with plenty of practice towing of gliders. Two sorties were undertaken on D-Day and followed by twelve sorties to France in support of SOE and SAS operations. Glider towing on the 1st and 3rd days of the Arnhem attack were broken by sortie to supply the SAS on 18 Sep. Later, three more transport sorties were made and the secondary role of bombing was undertaken twice and followed by several sorties to Norway or Denmark, before a glider was towed on VARSITY. A further four sorties to Norway and five to Belgium, the latter to repatriate POWs were flown and the crew finished their tour on 9 June 1945.

427

| 04-Oct-44 | FP180 | Catalina IB | 628 Sqn | Near Bentinck Island | 0 |

The aircraft was one of a pair undertaking a long range recce flight and inserting agents. Whilst landing at night in the target area, a submerged object was struck and the pilot; Flight Lieutenant J A O'Meara RAAF, opened the throttles and climbed away so that an inspection of the damage could be made. This revealed an extensive gash in the hull and made a landing dangerous, as the water ingress would likely sink the flying boat. The pilot decided to remain in the target area and cover the other aircraft, whilst its crew landed agents and ferried them to shore. Following this, both aircraft set course for base and O'Meara then positioned his landing in such a way as to allow the aircraft to be run straight onto the ramp for inspection. Unfortunately, the aircraft was beyond recovery but none of the eleven crew was injured..

Date	Serial	Aircraft	Unit	Place	Casualties

Brief Circumstances of Accident

Casualty Details (If Applicable)

05-Oct-44 KG592 Dakota 48 Sqn Missing ?

This aircraft is not recorded in the squadron Form 540 but is listed as 'missing' in the Movements Card but there is no Accident Card.

05-Oct-44 V9615 Lysander IIIA 148 Sqn Cellone 0

The aircraft, with three persons on board, was taking off for a transit flight. During the take-off the engine faltered and the take-off was abandoned but the pilot was unable to keep the aircraft on the runway because of a crosswind. It left the runway, ran into a mound of earth and turned over.

06-Oct-44 LL403 Halifax 644 Sqn Ameersfort area, Netherlands 0

The crew, captained by Flying Officer B B Baird, was engaged in Operation DODEX III to the Ameersfort area of the Netherlands. The aircraft was attacked by an enemy night fighter and it crashed in the local area. All the crew survived. This is another possible example of a trap being set for a transport aircraft dropping supplies or agents to the Dutch resistance. It is worth noting that the enemy was very clever and allowed many drops to take place unmolested, even though the DZ was compromised and all the supplies and personnel fell into their hands.

07-Oct-44 LK238 Stirling 161 Sqn Vemb Denmark 1

The aircraft; flown by Squadron Leader George Abecassis and his crew plus an extra bomb aimer, was one of 4 aircraft dropping to various TABLEJAM DZs in Denmark. Whilst flying at less than 1000 feet, the aircraft was set on fire and crashed with the death of second bomb aimer. Four of the crew evaded capture but the pilot and another man were made POW. On his release, Squadron Leader Abecassis had the consolation of being awarded a DFC for his contribution whilst with 161 Sqn.

07-Oct-44   JN956   Halifax II   1586 Flt   Brindisi   0

The aircraft was being landed at the end of a 3 hour special duties sortie but, in a strong crosswind, the pilot failed to correct a swing and the aircraft's undercarriage collapsed.

07-Oct-44   DP810   Horsa   HGCU   RAF North Luffenham   0

The glider was being used for conversion to type training.   The instructor allowed the speed to decay to an extent that the glider stalled and its undercarriage was ripped off in a heavy landing.

08-Oct-44   JN944   Halifax II   148 Sqn   Brindisi   0

The aircraft swung on take–off because the pilot handled the throttles incorrectly whilst taking off in a strong crosswind.   The aircraft ran off the runway and its undercarriage collapsed before it caught fire.   It is worth noting that several aircraft in front of this one in the take-off sequence had also swung and one would have thought this pilot might have been alive to the possibilities and been more careful.   It was commented that the pilot was more used to the characteristics of the Hercules engined Mark III, a version that handled differently to the Merlin engined version.

08-Oct-44   JP246   Halifax II   148 Sqn   Brindisi   0

Barely 3 hours after JN944 came to grief, this aircraft, returning from a 5½ hour special duties sortie crashed on landing.   The pilot made a heavy landing and the port undercarriage leg collapsed, causing the aircraft to swing and in turn fracturing the starboard undercarriage.   The pilot was found to have made an error of judgement and his CO commented that his night landings needed to be checked.

08-Oct-44   HH461   Hotspur III   5 GTS   Hereford   0

The pilot, who had carried out the exercise successfully when flying dual with his instructor, released the tow whilst out of sight of the airfield because of hazy weather. As he was also out of position, the aircraft

Date	Serial	Aircraft	Unit	Place	Casualties

Brief Circumstances of Accident
Casualty Details (If Applicable)

could not reach the airfield and it was forced landing, during the course of which it struck overhead cables and landed on its nose.

10-Oct-44 KG574 Dakota   194 Sqn   Location not known   4

The crew was engaged indropping supplies to 14th Army units in the general area of Imphal when their aircraft was shot down. Two crew and two passengers were killed but the others survived. There is some confusion and contradictions surrounding this loss, which is also reported to have happened on 12 Oct. Warrant Officer Gauthier's brother; Pilot Officer Joseph Victor Leo Gauthier had been killed in Mar 43 when a 425 Sqn Wellington, of which he was the captain, had been lost attacking Hamburg.

     Pilot Officer George Brewin WHITTAKER Wireless Operator

     Warrant Officer I Joseph Emile Armand GAUTHIER 24 RCAF Navigator

     Captain Philip Edward STAINTON 24 16 Field Reg't Royal Artillery

     Captain Donald Daman TWEDDLE 25 16 Field Reg't Royal Artillery

12-Oct-44 BT613 Hotspur III   5 GTS   Herefordshire   1

After a training sortie of 1½ hours, the glider was struck by lightning and the tow rope was burnt through and broke. The glider's fin was also struck and it failed causing the glider to spiral out of control and crash.

     Sergeant Ronald PULLMAN 20

13-Oct-44 KH158 Liberator VI   31 (SAAF) Sqn Missing   8

This aircraft was flown by one of twenty crews; sixteen from 31 SAAF Sqn and four from 34 SAAF Sqn, detailed to drop supplies on four DZs in northern Italy. This crew's particular assignment was a DZ coded 'MORRIS' in an area east-north-east of Genoa. The aircraft left base in the late afternoon of 12 Oct and flew into very bad weather with greatly reduced visibility. Those crews who returned commented on the fact that it was difficult to see the DZ fires and a number of aircraft did not drop their loads. A total of six Liberators from the force were lost and eventually the wrecks of four were found in the mountains and one near Cantalupa. However, this aircraft and its crew were lost without trace and the precise circumstances of their demise is unknown.

Major S S URY 29 SAAF Pilot
Flying Officer George Edward HUDSPITH 29 Co-Pilot
Lieutenant G A COLLARD 19 SAAF Navigator
Lieutenant N W ARMSTRONG SAAF Air Gunner
Flying Officer Thomas Roberts MILLAR 28 RAAF Bomb Aimer
2nd Lieutenant P J JORDAN SAAF Air Gunner
Warrant Officer I L B BLOCH SAAF Air Gunner
Sergeant Richard Charles FITZGERALD 19 Air Gunner

13-Oct-44	KG875	Liberator VI	31 (SAAF) Sqn	Valprato Soana	8

Lost as outlined above. The crew of this aircraft are buried in Milan War Cemetery.

Captain L VON S BEUKES SAAF
Lieutenant M C F DU P KRUGER SAAF
Lieutenant D' A SHIPMAN SAAF
Warrant Officer II D A W FRANCIS SAAF
Sergeant George Frederick Jesse ANSTEE 23 Pilot
Sergeant Charles Lea FOSTER 20
Sergeant Hubert John WOODS 20 Wireless Operator
Sergeant William Leslie PRYCE Wireless Operator

13-Oct-44	KG874	Liberator VI	31 (SAAF) Sqn	Ostana, Northern Italy	8

Lost on the same sortie as the two aircraft listed above. The crew of this aircraft are also buried at Milan War

Cemetery.

Lieutenant A H R METLERKAMP SAAF
Flying Officer John THOMSON 24 Pilot
Warrant Officer II E A JONES SAAF
Warrant Officer Robert Pender WHITELAW 22 Wireless Operator
Sergeant Leonard WHALLEY Navigator
Sergeant John Robertson SMILLIE 20 Bomb Aimer
Sergeant William Alexander ROGERS 21 Wireless Operator
Sergeant Leslie Rayburn Royston A PARKER Air Gunner

Date	Serial	Aircraft	Unit	Place	Casualties
13-Oct-44	KG999	Liberator VI	31 (SAAF) Sqn	Ala di Stura	8

This crew are also buried in Milan War Cemetery but how the aircraft came to crash is not known.

Lieutenant C P NEL SAAF
Lieutenant C B VORSTER SAAF
Pilot Officer Ronald Walter JOHNSON 21 Bomb Aimer
Sergeant Jack Edward BOSWELL Pilot
Sergeant Eric LOCKEY 20 Wireless Operator
Sergeant Henry FOY 21
Sergeant Roy BAILEY Air Gunner
Sergeant Harry AUSTIN 24 Air Gunner

Date	Serial	Aircraft	Unit	Place	Casualties
13-Oct-44	KH154	Liberator VI	31 (SAAF) Sqn	Rora, Italy	8

Lost on the same sortie as the aircraft immediately above.

Flight Sergeant Desmond Vincent WATSON 20 RAAF Pilot
Sergeant Wallace Randal YOUNG 37 Flight Engineer
Sergeant Duncan Carswell Roland SHEARER 25 Navigator
Sergeant Albery Ross BEST 21 Bomb Aimer
Sergeant Harry Heald BAWDEN 20 Wireless Operator
Sergeant Sydney Sapenne DE'LISLE 23 Air Gunner
Sergeant James HOUGHTON 19 Air Gunner
Sergeant Arthur Donald GRIFFIN 25 Air Gunner

13-Oct-44   KH239 Liberator VI   34 (SAAF) Sqn   Cantalupa   8

This aircraft was assigned to 34 (SAAF) Sqn but was being flown by a 31 (SAAF) Sqn crew.

Flight Sergeant Clarence William LAWTON 23 RAAF Pilot
Pilot Officer Thomas Dufus FOTHERINGHAM 23 Flight Engineer
Sergeant Eric Henry Albert CLIFT 20 Navigator
Sergeant David Wilfred BISHOP 20 Bomb Aimer
Sergeant Geoffrey TENNISON 20 Wireless Operator
Sergeant Dennis Raymond WELLON Air Gunner
Sergeant Stanley Edwin LOCKTON 24 Air Gunner
Sergeant John BUCKS Air Gunner

14-Oct-44   LL310   Halifax V   644 Sqn   2 miles west of RAF Tarrant Rushton   0

The aircraft was being flown on an air test by two pilots and two other crew and they had been airborne for about 10 minutes. The pilot lost both engines on the port side in succession and the aircraft was crash landed and struck trees whilst doing so. The Accident Card is rather confused about the precise sequence of events but seemingly the pilot chose a poor runway on which to land and did not feather the first engine when it cut. However, a twin engined asymmetric overshoot in a Halifax seems a remarkably risky undertaking at the best of times. The pilot was also censured for not being strapped in and this probably

Date	Serial	Aircraft	Unit	Place	Casualties

Brief Circumstances of Accident
Casualty Details (If Applicable)

contributed to the severity of his injuries.

15-Oct-44   LL293   Halifax V   298 Sqn   Hoorn, Zuider Zee, Netherlands   1

The aircraft was engaged on an SOE arms drop; RUMMY 6, to a DZ near Borger in the Emmen area of Holland. Whilst inbound to the target, it was struck by enemy AA fire and crashed into the sea. Five members of the largely Candian crew survived but one was drowned. The survivors were assisted by the Dutch people and concealed until the area was liberated the following Spring.

Warrant Officer II Harold Leonard FERGUSON 23 RCAF Bomb Aimer

17-Oct-44   KH152   Liberator VI   34 SAAF   Near Krakow, Poland   5

The aircraft was shot down whilst its crew was making a second attempt to deliver supplies to Polish resistance fighters in the Warsaw area. Whilst flying at a height of 11000 feet about 20 miles north-east of Krakow, the aircraft was attacked by a night fighter and its controls badly damaged and some fuel tanks set on fire. The order to abandon the aircraft was given and five of the crew baled out but for some reason, the three RAF SNCOs listed below did not escape from the aircraft. Lieutenant McWilliam was killed when he landed in some trees and Lieutenant Lithgow broke both legs and was badly injured. The manner of his death is uncertain, as it was alleged that he had been murdered by a German soldier after capture. Subsequent enquiries showed that the soldier had been traced but was not in the area at the time of the incident and it remains possible that Lithgow was killed by another person or that he died from his injuries. Lithgow's DFC was awarded following an attack on a German convoy off North Africa in October 1942, whilst he was flying with 15 (SAAF) Sqn. Regrettably, Lithgow's brother was killed subsequently whilst flying a Kittyhawk fighter/bomber in an attack near Casalecchio di Reno.

Lieutenant James Arthur LITHGOW DFC SAAF Pilot

Lieutenant K B MACWILLIAM SAAF Co-Pilot
Sergeant Tom MYERS Bomb Aimer
Sergeant William Francis COWAN 31 Air Gunner
Sergeant Geoffrey Frederick ELLIS Air Gunner

17-Oct-44   EW250 Liberator   34 SAAF   Near Krakow, Poland   7

The aircraft was shot down by an enemy night fighter whilst on the outbound leg of a supply dropping sortie to Polish partisans in the Radomsko area south-west of Warsaw. One member of the crew; Sergeant R T Pitcher, survived.

Lieutenant Denis O CULLINGWORTH SAAF
Lieutenant C S S FRANKLIN SAAF
Lieutenant K J MCLEOD SAAF
Lieutenant G RAY-HOWETT SAAF
Sergeant Jack Edwin SPEED
Sergeant Ronald Cecil BOWDEN Air Gunner
Sergeant Desmond Preston RICHMOND Wireless Operator

18-Oct-44   T1707 Lysander III   161 Sqn   Chailey Sussex   ?

19-Oct-44   LK207 Stirling   161 Sqn   Potton, near Biggleswade   5

The aircraft was being flown on an airtest and as this was to be conducted in the local area, the navigator and despatcher were not flying. After being airborne for 10 minutes, its tail unit was seen to fail. It dived into the edge of the village of Potton. The aircraft had been involved in a heavy landing a few days before and had been withdrawn for examination but it seems possible that the structural damage had fatally weakened the aircraft's rear fuselage. Of much greater significance was that the crew would have flown next their final sortie of the tour.

Flight Lieutenant Ross Victor LEVY 21 RNZAF Pilot

Date	Serial	Aircraft	Unit	Place	Casualties

Brief Circumstances of Accident
Casualty Details (If Applicable)

Pilot Officer James William STIGGER
Sergeant Albert James COVENEY 21 Wireless Operator
Sergeant Wilfred George ATKINSON
Sergeant Patrick KELLY 21

Date	Serial	Aircraft	Unit	Place	Casualties
19-Oct-44	JD319	Halifax	148 Sqn	Maribor, Yugoslavia	4

The aircraft was engaged in a sortie coded CUCKOLD 20 but it crashed into a 4000 feet high mountain on its return

Flight Sergeant Peter Harry EDWARDS 21 Pilot
Sergeant Kenneth Douglas DAKER Bomb Aimer
Sergeant David CLARKE 19 Flight Engineer
Flight Sergeant Charles Gibson STEELE 21 RAAF

Date	Serial	Aircraft	Unit	Place	Casualties
20-Oct-44	EW627	Liberator	511 Sqn	RAF Mauripur	4

The aircraft was undertaking a scheduled transport service from Shaibah to Karachi and was landing at the end of a 7 hour flight. The autopilot was inoperative and the co-pilot was inexperienced and so the aircraft's captain had been compelled to fly the aircraft throughout the trip. A poor approach was made and the pilot decided to overshoot for another attempt but the flight engineer set the propellers to 'Coarse' pitch instead of 'Fine' pitch and hence the aircraft had insufficient power to go around again. The pilot converted the overshoot into a forced landing and the aircraft touched down on rough ground beyond the runway, its undercarriage collapsed and it caught fire. Neither crew nor passengers were strapped in and the crew seemed to have little knowledge of the abandonment drill. The AOC was critical of both the captain and flight engineer and also commented on the crew drills and the need for modifications to this type of aircraft to prevent a repetition. Unfortunately, in early 1946 there was a similar accident involving a Liberator and again the passengers were trapped in the nose of the aircraft.

+ four non-RAF

20-Oct-44   LL148   Halifax V   1665 HCU   RAF Tilstock   0

The aircraft was being used for dual circuit training at night but the trainee pilot became confused by two sets of blue lights with which he was not familiar. He swung the aircraft off the perimeter track by mistake and the instructor pilot was unable to correct the swing before the aircraft struck a building. The confusing lights were in place to mark a short circuit for light aircraft but they were confusing to anybody not experienced with the arrangements at Tilstock. The instructor; Flight Lieutenant J A G Sizmur, was one of the early transport pilots who had been involved with the towing of gliders to North Africa in the summer of 1943. In June 1944, he had been awarded an AFC for his work with airborne forces.

21-Oct-44   V1762   Albemarle V   A&AEE   ½ mile west of Sherburn in Elmet   2

The aircraft was starting a flight test sequence when, at a height of about 500 feet in the circuit, the port engine began to vibrate violently. The pilot reduced power to about one quarter and attempted to make a short circuit to land but as he began to turn in on finals the engine failed completely and the pilot lost control. The aircraft went into a stall turn to port and dived into the ground. The cause of the engine malfunction was a displaced gudeon pin in the No: 12 cylinder which led to a fracture of the connecting rod. The Board of Enquiry was critical of the level of control and supervision which existed and the fact that the pilot had barely 3 hours solo on the aircraft type and was actually employed on glider pilot duties.

Pilot Officer James George SWAIN 37 Flight Engineer
Leading Aircraftwoman Nellie GRIFFITHS 35

23-Oct-44   BT609   Hotspur III   Shobdon, Herefordshire   0

The instructor was demonstrating a low release across wind. Unfortunately, he misjudged the wind strength and released the tow too soon. The glider undershot the landing, struck some trees and then stalled onto a hedge. It was commented that the instructor pilot had never undertaken an instructors' course!

437

Date	Serial	Aircraft	Unit	Place	Casualties
				Brief Circumstances of Accident	
				Casualty Details (If Applicable)	

24-Oct-44   FZ655   Dakota   437 Sqn   St Pol near Dunkirk   4

This aircraft was one of nine Dakotas tasked with the delivery of 57000 lbs of freight and ammunition to an airfield (B70) near Antwerp. The delivery was successful but on the return flight, this aircraft crashed. The circumstances of the loss are unclear and it appears that the co-pilot; Flight Sergeant J W Lockwood survived.

    Flight Sergeant Douglas Otto SCHNEIDER 23 RCAF Pilot
    Sergeant Sidney Alfred GUMBRELL 20 RCAF Navigator
    Warrant Officer II John Herman SOPER RCAF Wireless Operator
    Leading Aircraftwoman Margaret CAMPBELL Nursing Orderly

24-Oct-44   EF405   Stirling III   1332 CU   RAF Nutts Corner   0

The aircraft's undercarriage collapsed after a swing developed on take off and was not corrected quickly enough. The aircraft was retained as a ground instructional airframe before final disposal as scrap.

25-Oct-44   V1755   Albemarle II   22 HGCU   RAF Alton Barnes   2

The crew was engaged in a glider towing exercise and had been airborne for about 30 minutes but in conditions of poor visibility. The glider, which was being flown by an inexperienced pilot and had no radio communication with the tug crew, overshot the tug and in doing so pulled the tug's tail up, forcing it into a 70 degree angle before the rope broke. The aircraft dived into the ground and burst into flames on impact. The glider pilot should have cast of the tow when an overshoot of the tug was inevitable but he had no radio with which to warn the tug pilot.

    Flight Sergeant Thomas Christophe NEWTON 23 Pilot
    Sergeant John Albert Cotton WILSON 20 Wireless Operator

27-Oct-44   KG353   Dakota III   271 Sqn   2 miles west of B17 (Carpiquet)   0

The pilot did not realise until the aircraft was airborne that the control locks had been left in! With little control available, the aircraft crashed beyond the airfield and the crew of five were fortunate that their injuries were not severe. The pilot, co-pilot and navigator were all interviewed by the AOC because of their carelessness. An interview with one's AOC is a fairly sobering affair – sometimes called 'an interview without coffee'. It usually takes the form of a one sided discussion, during which the individual being interviewed would be ill advised to say anything more than the odd mumbled 'Yes, Sir', 'No, Sir' at appropriate points. An interesting point on the wall of the AOC's office, about 6 inches above his head or a close inspection of the pattern of the office carpet, are recommended postures for the interviewee to adopt. The interviewee is never invited to sit down or to remove their hat and will invariably be at attention throughout!

27-Oct-44   EV906   Liberatpr VI   178 Sqn   Amendola, Italy   0

The aircraft was taxying for take-off when it struck the edge of a bridge with its port wheel and dropped into a ditch, collapsing the undercarriage. The pilot was blamed for careless taxying but then the report continues by saying that the edge of the bridge gave way, no lights were available to illuminate the area and visibility was poor at the time.

29-Oct-44   JP244   Halifax   148 Sqn   Albania   7

This aircraft was amongst fourteen tasked with drops into Albania during a daylight operation. The aircraft was seen over the DZ and its crew dropped the load as planned. However, the aircraft was not seen again and its precise fate is unknown but it most probably crashed into the sea on its return flight. The crew is commemorated on the Malta Memorial.

    Flying Officer Edwin John STUBLEY 23 Pilot
    Flight Sergeant Ernest Logan BROWN 27
    Sergeant Alfred COOTE

Date	Serial	Aircraft	Unit	Place	Casualties
Brief Circumstances of Accident					
Casualty Details (If Applicable)					

Flight Sergeant Austin DONNELLY
Sergeant Richard Charles KNEE 23
Sergeant Charles MABBS 31
Flight Sergeant John THOMPSON 23

Date	Serial	Aircraft	Unit	Place	Casualties
30-Oct-44	RN894	Horsa	1 HGSU	RAF Wethersfield	0

At the conclusion of a night training sortie, the glider pilot mistook the runway in use but in rectifying his mistake, he landed downwind on the correct runway and overshot into some trees.

Date	Serial	Aircraft	Unit	Place	Casualties
01-Nov-44	BZ956	Liberator III	357 Sqn	Nam Lwi	7

During a supply dropping sortie, the aircraft struck a tree and crashed. This aircraft had been severely damaged earlier in the year and some records suggest that it had been written off at that time.

Flight Lieutenant Albert George CARLTON 25 RAAF
Flight Lieutenant Reginald Charles Joffre POWELL 27 RAAF
Flight Lieutenant Osbourn Sydney SHAVE 28 DFC RAAF
Flight Lieutenant Sydney Desmond TITTERINGTON 22 DFC RAAF
Warrant Officer I Ernest Joseph Leonard BOLINGBROKE RCAF Wireless Operator
Pilot Officer Denis Leslie FRANCIS 23
Flight Sergeant Peter George MASTERS 20 Air Gunner

Date	Serial	Aircraft	Unit	Place	Casualties
02-Nov-44	PW262	Stirling III	1332 CU	RAF Bishops Court	0

The aircraft was returning after a local weather test at night and been diverted because of bad weather at its base. The pilot landed on a short, wet runway at an airfield with which he was unfamiliar. The aircraft overshot the runway and its port wing was torn off when it ran into a ditch.

02-Nov-44 RJ256 Horsa 1 HGSU RAF Wethersfield 0

Whilst making a night landing in good visibility, the pilot failed to see another glider ahead and collided with it.

03-Nov-44 KJ986 Dakota 45 Gp Near Goose Bay 4

The aircraft crashed into a frozen river near Goose Bay whilst being ferried. Although the cause of the crash is obscure, it is thought possible that the pilot may have been banking the aircraft fairly steeply as it broke cloud, which was 10/10 ths at 500 feet, but this is conjecture.

Flying Officer Lewis Turner MORRIS Pilot
Flying Officer Archie WHITELAW RCAF Navigator
Thomas Victor WOODS Civilian Wireless Operator
Flying Officer Morley Douglas MCLAUGHLIN

03-Nov-44 LK171 Stirling IV 295 Sqn Near Oslo 1

The aircraft was engaged on a sortie to deliver supplies to the Norwegian resistance organisation in the vicinity of Oslo. Unfortunately, the crew received no confirmatory signal from the ground party at the designated DZ and in deteriorating weather the aircraft was climbed to higher altitude but encountered severe airframe icing. The pilot ordered the crew of five plus Lieutenant Michael Hicks, an Army liaison officer, to abandon the aircraft and this they did safely. Although two of these men; Flight Sergeant Mesley the flight engineer and Flying Officer Morrow the bomb aimer, were captured subsequently, the others were sheltered by the Norwegians and eventually reached safety. The pilot was unable to abandon the aircraft before it crashed and he was killed. Group Captain Surplice was station commander at RAF Rivenhall and had been awarded his DSO for his actions during the attack on Dieppe in 1942. His aircraft was painted with the letters 'WES', rather than the customary squadron codes and identifying letter. His DFC was awarded pre-War.

Group Captain Wilfred Edward SURPLICE 31 DSO DFC

441

Date	Serial	Aircraft	Unit	Place	Casualties
		Brief Circumstances of Accident			
		Casualty Details (If Applicable)			

03-Nov-44 BT508 Hotspur III 5 GTS Shobdon 1

This glider and the Hotspur listed below, collided in the circuit, probably because of an inadequate lookout. However, the Accident Card for both aircraft indicates that there was considerable pressure on the training system as the Services tried to train more glider pilots to replace the very significant losses suffered at Arnhem 6 weeks earlier.

Sergeant James Wardrobe WALKER 21

03-Nov-44 HH134 Hotspur III 5 GTS Shobdon 1

Crashed in the circumstances outlined above.

Sergeant John Frederick BOON 20

05-Nov-44 BB338 Halifax II 148 Sqn At sea near Vis, Yugoslavia 0

Whilst outbound on a supply dropping sortie to Yugoslavia and after about 1½ hours airborne, the aircraft's port outer engine constant speed unit failed but the pilot was unable to get the propeller to feather and the engine then burst into flames. Attempts to suppress the fire failed and it spread to the wing. Faced with this unpleasant situation, the pilot; Flight Sergeant Uttley, carried out a successful ditching without injury to his crew.

05-Nov-44 BD664 Whitley V HGCU RAF Brize Norton 0

Whilst parked, the aircraft was struck by a glider tow rope, which was still attached to a glider that had been cast off by its tug. The glider pilot had turned back to the airfield and was unaware that his approach would take him over the dispersal area. It was commented that the glider pilot had made a good effort to land the glider safely after being cast off.

442

05-Nov-44 KH243 Liberator   Missing on supply drop   7

This aircraft was one of twelve from the squadron, which formed part of a large force of fifty six Wellingtons and thirty five Liberators led by a single pathfinder Halifax of 614 Sqn, sent to drop supplies to partisan forces in the 'CUCKOLD' and 'TOFFEE' areas of Yugoslavia. Whilst the weather was good and over thirty Liberators dropped nearly 400 containers on 'CUCKOLD', this aircraft and the one listed below were attacked by enemy fighters and destroyed. It is believed that two of the crew survived.

    Warrant Officer Derek George STEWART 31 RAAF Pilot

    Sergeant Stanley Richard DAVIE 20 Navigator

    Sergeant William Greig BOGIE Bomb Aimer

    Sergeant Ivor MATTHEWS 26 Flight Engineer

    Sergeant Francis William LOUCH 24 Air Gunner

    Sergeant Gerald Joseph O'KANE 20 Air Gunner

06-Nov-44 KH100 Liberator   Gornigrad, Yugoslavia   8

This aircraft was lost in similar circumstances to that listed above. The whole crew died in the attack or subsequent crash.

    Flying Officer Amos Edwin Butsford DENOVAN 21 RCAF Pilot

    Flying Officer Owen Jones COX RCAF Navigator

    Flying Officer Kenneth Louis CHAPMAN 24 RCAF Bomb Aimer

    Flight Sergeant John Ward NORMAN 24 Wireless Operator

    Sergeant Evan Kenneth CORCORAN Flight Engineer

    Flight Sergeant Willaim Francis BEARY 20 Air Gunner

    Sergeant Raymond Foot Oliver JAMES 19 Air Gunner

    Flight Sergeant John Humphrey PARRY 19 Air Gunner

Date	Serial	Aircraft	Unit	Place	Casualties

Brief Circumstances of Accident
Casualty Details (If Applicable)

| 06-Nov-44 | BD436 | Whitley V | 42 OTU | Newmarket | 0 |

The aircraft's starboard engine failed at 500 feet and the pilot turned towards the nearest airfield, which was Tuddenham. The flying control at this unit refused to accept the aircraft as it did not accept emergency landings because it had FIDO installed. The aircraft was diverted to Newmarket and was landed wheels up. The pilot, Flying Officer J A Clarke – who only had 15 hours flying on the Whitley – was commended for his handling of the incident.

| 06-Nov-44 | EB188 | Halifax V | 148 Sqn | 46 degrees 19 North/14 degrees 52 East | 0 |

The aircraft with a crew of seven was engaged in supply dropping to a DZ in Yugoslavia in the position shown above. All four engines cut simultaneously and a belly landing was carried out without injury to the crew. The aircraft was destroyed by the crew, who evaded capture and returned safely in due course. There is no evidence as to the cause of the complete engine failure, although there are many possibilities such as mishandling of the fuel system, significant airlocks in the system, an unnoticed major fuel leak, water in some tanks etc.

| 07-Nov-44 | LK195 | Stirling IV | 190 Sqn | South of Enkhuizen Netherlands | 6 |

This aircraft was amongst four from the squadron sent on SOE sorties to three DZs in the Netherlands, with this crew destined for DUDLEY 3, a location east of the Zuider Zee. None of the crews was able to identify their dropping zones and three brought their loads back to a diversionary landing at RAF Earls Colne. This crew, operating together for the first time, failed to return and the aircraft was subsequently found crashed at the location shown. During his work up to full operational status, Flying Officer Hodgson had flown as second pilot to an experienced captain and their target on that occasion was the same one.

Flying Officer Edwin Davis HODGSON 32 RCAF Pilot

Flying Officer Elmer Joshua RUSENSTROM 21 RCAF Navigator
Flying Officer George Langley TOWNS 23 Bomb Aimer
Warrant Officer William KING 32 Wireless Operator
Sergeant Reginald Henry George NEVARD 20 Flight Engineer
Flying Officer Henry Edward EVANS 31 Air Gunner

08-Nov-44 FL715 Dakota   25 miles north east of Tiddem   5

The aircraft was one of fourteen aircraft sent to air drop supplies to various DZs in the Kabah (or Kabaw) Valley. This aircraft was shot down by an enemy fighter and crashed into the jungle, where it was not located for sometime. The remains of the crew of five could not be identified separately and they are buried together in a collective grave at Taukkyan War Cemetery.

Flying Officer John McArthur TAYLOR 22 RCAF Pilot
Flight Sergeant Terence Patrick BROWNE Co-Pilot
Pilot Officer Donald Alexander MACLAREN RCAF Navigator
Pilot Officer Michael Walter Warren DULEY 20 RCAF Wireless Operator
Pilot Officer Charles Knowlton DOUGLAS 21 RCAF Wireless Operator

08-Nov-44 FD949 Dakota   31 Sqn   Kabah Valley (precise location not known)   1

This aircraft, flown by Flying Officer Brian Stanbridge, was undertaking a sortie similar to FL715 and was attacked by an enemy fighter. The aircraft was severely damaged, the port engine set on fire and the wireless operator fatally wounded. Stanbridge dived the aircraft to low level and being unable to avoid the fighters and with no prospect of returning to base, he elected to force land the aircraft in one of the few paddy fields in the area. This was accomplished with little further damage and the crew escaped from the blazing aircraft and were rescued by troops from the West African Division. Subsequently, Stanbridge remained in the RAF and rose to the rank of Air Vice Marshal.

Flight Sergeant Robert Kenneth ARMSTRONG 22 RCAF Wireless Operator

445

Date	Serial	Aircraft	Unit	Place	Casualties

Brief Circumstances of Accident
Casualty Details (If Applicable)

08-Nov-44 FD924 Dakota 62 Sqn Yazagyo Burma 4

The aircraft was operating on a supply dropping sortie similar to that described above. It was also shot down by an enemy fighter but the details of the engagement are not known.

Flying Officer Bruce Sherwood CORBETT 22 RCAF Pilot
Flight Sergeant Ronald James COOK 21 Co-Pilot
Warrant Officer John Micahel DELANY 20 RCAF Wireless Operator
Warrant Officer I Michael Edmund GALLAGHER RCAF Wireless Operator

---

08-Nov-44 HH360 Hotspur III 5 GTS Hertfordshire Map Ref 785858 0

The pilot dropped the tow after being towed into cloud. In attempting to land in a field, the aircraft struck a hedge with its starboard wing and cartwheeled. It was commented that the pilot was a very large and thick limbed individual and in the restricted cockpit of a Hotspur, his thighs are so large that he could not move the control column laterally to its full deflection to operate the ailerons properly.

09-Nov-44 LJ993 Stirling 138 Sqn At sea position not known 9

On this night, the two Tempsford squadrons sent twenty four sorties to Norway, of which seventeen came from 138 Sqn and the balance from 161 Sqn. The weather conditions were absolutely appalling, with thunderstorms, icing at very low level and thick cloud. Several aircraft sustained damage from the weather and a crew was nearly lost when the captain was temporarily blinded by a lightning strike, which also disabled the aircraft's instruments. The prompt action of the aircraft's bomb aimer; Flying Officer Henry Wigley, prevented the aircraft diving into the sea and on 2 Jan 45, he was awarded a DFC. This aircraft, however, was flying sortie CRUPPER 11 with two agents, and the intention was to drop these about 60 miles north of Oslo but like the Stirling below it is thought to have been overwhelmed by the weather and was lost without trace.

Flight Lieutenant Frederick John FORD 35 pilot
Pilot Officer James Roy TANNER 23 Navigator
Flight Lieutenant Ernest HOWELL DFC Wireless Operator
Pilot Officer Donald Iain Begbie FISHER 33 Flight Engineer
Flying Officer Mostyn William OLIVER 21 Bomb Aimer
Flight Sergeant Brian Francis Frederick GRIMES 23 Air Gunner
Flight Sergeant Dennis James CORNISH 21
Peter DEINDOLL – Norwegian Agents
Arne GJESTLAND

09-Nov-44   LK198   Stirling   138 Sqn   At sea position not known   7
Lost in the circumstances outlined above. The aircraft was engaged on PUFFIN 2, a drop to a DZ about 15 miles north of Oslo but it is uncertain where or at what time the aircraft was lost

Warrant Officer Louis Alexander OULLETTE 22 RCAF Pilot
Pilot Officer Lloyd William NELSON RCAF Navigator
Flying Officer Sidney Harry SHARPE 23 Bomb Aimer
Flight Sergeant Alexander Frederick BIRDSEYE 20 Wireless Operator
Flight Sergeant Robert Augusta BEST 19 RCAF Air Gunner
Pilot Officer Peter BARNICKE 19 RCAF
Sergeant Arthur John JEFFREY Flight Engineer

09-Nov-44   EF234   Stirling IV   196 Sqn   Missing   6
The aircraft was one of eight from the squadron detailed for supply dropping to SOE targets; in this case a DZ; 'DRAUGHTS 7' at position 52 degrees 38.55 North/ 05 degrees 10.18 East. The load carried was twenty containers and three panniers.   The aircraft failed to return but there is no clear indication as to the circumstances of its loss. The aircraft wreckage was not located and the crew are commemorated on the Runnymede Memorial.

447

Date	Serial	Aircraft	Unit	Place	Casualties

Brief Circumstances of Accident
Casualty Details (If Applicable)

Flying Officer John Anthony NORTON 22 Pilot
Flying Officer Derek William EVES 21 Navigator
Flight Sergeant Harry RUSTON 27 Bomb Aimer
Sergeant John Vass THOMPSON 21 Wireless Operator
Flight Sergeant Charles Alfred MYERS 34 Flight Engineer
Sergeant Maurice Arthur GOULT 19 Air Gunner

Date	Serial	Aircraft	Unit	Place	Casualties
09-Nov-44	EM398	Master II	5 GTS	Shobdon	0

The pilot misjudged his approach and landing in a crosswind conditions and the aircraft was too fast at touchdown. Instead of overshooting for a further circuit, the pilot tried to stop but the aircraft skidded on the wet grass, went off the end of the strip and crashed into a ditch where it caught fire.

Date	Serial	Aircraft	Unit	Place	Casualties
10-Nov-44	KH153	Liberator VI	34 SAAF	Foggia	0

The aircraft crashed whilst being landed at the above airfield. Its back was broken but the crew survived. The precise cause of the accident is not recorded.

Date	Serial	Aircraft	Unit	Place	Casualties
10-Nov-44	LH384	Horsa	81 OTU	Sleap	1

Both the tug and glider were being flown by pilots under instruction. The glider pilot thought he was overshooting after casting off the tow and so commenced a 360 degree turn to bleed off the height. However, the aircraft descended too low and struck the gables of a house and crashed onto the perimeter track.

Staff Sergeant Hayden Reginald BROWNE 35 The Glider Pilot Regiment

10-Nov-44   HH294 Hotspur II   5 GTS   Shobdon, Herefordshire   ?

There are no details of this glider other than its date of write-off as the result of an accident.

10-Nov-44   LN914 Wellington X   37Sqn   2½ miles north-west of San Marco, Lamis   5

Having been airborne for about 25 minutes on the outbound leg of a supply dropping sortie, the aircraft struck a hillside at a height of about 1800 feet. The night was extremely dark and the weather absolutely appalling but why the aircraft had not been climbed above its safety height is unknown.

Warrant Officer John McDougall PIKE 21 Pilot
Warrant Officer Laurence Ratcliffe RHIND Navigator
Warrant Officer Edgar Clement THOMAS Bomb Aimer
Flight Sergeant George Arthur BETTS 23 Wireless Operator
Warrant Officer I John MACALLUM 32 RCAF Air Gunner

11-Nov-44   MF420 Wellington X   104 Sqn   At Sea   5

Having been airborne for about 50 minutes, the crew of this aircraft broadcast a message saying the aircraft was being ditched in position 42 degrees 39 North/14 degrees 27 East. No reason was given but the weather was probably a major contributing factor and several aircraft received lightning strikes and the conditions were so bad that the ASR Warwick could not take-off the following morning. Eventually, the bodies of the pilot and bomb aimer were recovered from the sea but the rest of the crew are commemorated on the Malta Memorial.

Flying Officer Jack PICKLES Pilot
Flight Lieutenant Frank TAYLOR
Pilot Officer Herbert WAITE 27 Bomb Aimer
Sergeant Reginald Milburn BADGER 21
Believed to be:
Sergeant Douglas Robert VINCENT

Date	Serial	Aircraft	Unit	Place	Casualties

Brief Circumstances of Accident
Casualty Details (If Applicable)

11-Nov-44   LP511   Wellington X   40 Sqn   20 miles north of Foggia   5

The crew of this aircraft was engaged on the same sortie as those two above. It crashed into a hillside in the position shown and was completely destroyed by fire. The loss is most probably the direct result of the prevailing weather conditions and it is assumed the aircraft was blown off course by the exceptionally strong winds.

Flight Sergeant James Potter BAKER 23 Pilot
Sergeant Basil William WESTON 20 Navigator
Sergeant Douglas William AYERS 23 Bomb Aimer
Sergeant Jack WALARON 19 Wireless Operator
Sergeant James MacPherson MACKENZIE 30 Air Gunner

11-Nov-44   MF346   Wellington X   70 Sqn   Near San Severo, Sambucelli   5

Together with the aircraft listed immediately above, this aircraft was part of a force of fifty bomber aircraft being used to drop supplies to targets in Northern Italy. Although many aircraft were able to complete their task, the force lost a Wellington ditched at sea and other three crashed in mountains just a short distance from their operating base.

Sergeant Ian Faulkland FORREST 25 Pilot
Sergeant William Geoffrey TARRANT Navigator
Sergeant Douglas Gerald MURPHY 21 Bomb Aimer
Sergeant Donald SMEDLEY 20 Wireless Operator
Sergeant John Stanley JONES 22 Air Gunner

11-Nov-44   FL554   Dakota III   216 Sqn   Burma   ?

The aircraft was lost whilst engaged on a supply dropping sortie.

11-Nov-44 KG593 Dakota III 512 Sqn Croydon 0

The aircraft was engaged on a passenger and freight carrying sortie and was approaching to land after being airborne for nearly 2 hours. The pilot had made several attempts to land in the poor weather which included thick fog. On the final approach, he was given instructions by the Flying Controller to cut his engines and land straight ahead. The pilot did as instructed and the aircraft touched down but its brakes proved ineffective on wet grass and it ran into a sandbagged dispersal point. None of the four crew or their sixteen passengers was injured but the aircraft was damaged extensively. The Accident Card comments that the station commander recommended that only pilots fully conversant with Croydon use the airfield in bad visibility. This is perhaps an alarming remark, given that Croydon was a major airport.

11-Nov-44 T1750 Lysander III 148 Sqn Florence 0

Whilst parked at the side of the runway on an airfield which was congested, this aircraft was struck by a Spitfire of 208 Sqn, which had swung off the runway.

13-Nov-44 KG591 Dakota 512 Sqn RAF Northolt 0

The aircraft was parked when it was struck by a USAAF C47, serial number 42-68806 of 1 BAD. Both aircraft were damaged and not repaired.

13-Nov-44 HH966 Hamilcar 1 HGSU North Farm, Spittisbury, Dorset 0

The aircraft was flying in gusty conditions and it got out of position with regards the tug aircraft. The instructor pilot failed to take control quickly enough and the tow rope broke whilst the combination was flying at 600 feet. The instructor carried out a forced landing in a field.

14-Nov-44 LL332 Halifax V 296 Sqn RAF Earls Colne Essex 0

The pilot, who rejoiced in the unfortunate surname of; Boghole, was converting to the Halifax and he was taxying the aircraft along the perimeter track but having difficulty maintaining directional control and over

451

Date	Serial	Aircraft	Unit	Place	Casualties

Brief Circumstances of Accident
Casualty Details (If Applicable)

corrected four swings in a row. Eventually, the aircraft left the perimeter track and struck a tractor, which was parked within the prohibited area, and the undercarriage collapsed. The station staff were criticised for sending the pilot on a solo night flying sortie after he had barely 4 hours on type but he was criticised for not stopping when he encountered trouble. The poor old tractor driver was also in trouble for parking in the wrong place! What is not clear, nor does the accident report cover it, was why the pilot was converting to the Halifax at an operational squadron rather than at 1665 HCU.

| 14-Nov-44 | MW126 | York I | MCS | le Rivier d'Allemont Near Grenoble | 10 |

This accident claimed the life of the most senior RAF officer killed in the war. Air Chief Marshal Leigh-Mallory, the brother of the well known mountaineer; George Leigh-Mallory, who had been lost on Mount Everest, was appointed to command the air forces in South East Asia and was en route to his new appointment on board a York aircraft, which would become his personal transport in Theatre. He had selected his crew but despite their general experience, they had had little time to familiarise themselves with the York before starting the journey. The aircraft took off from RAF Northolt and was escorted by fighters from 313 Sqn for the first part of the journey but these aircraft broke off and returned to base, encountering very bad conditions as they returned to North Weald. The York's route was across the English Channel and thence to Cherbourg, Poitiers and Toulouse, where the aircraft was scheduled to turn eastwards, passing Marseilles, flying north of Corsica before turning south eastwards and flying down the west coast of Italy. The aircraft was seen by the crew of a 24 Sqn Dakota but was then lost from view and that was the last sighting. When the aircraft failed to arrive in Italy, searches were organised but to no avail and a Board of Enquiry was established under the presidency of the AOC 38 Gp; AVM James Scarlett-Streatfield. With no idea as to what had happened to the aircraft, all the Board could do was to take evidence relating to the activities leading up to the disappearance and there was a wealth of evidence about the awful weather conditions encountered on that day. Although more experienced crews might have safely undertaken the

452

journey, it was judged that the pilot was not sufficiently experienced to have done so and the journey should have been delayed. The board also commented that the crew should have been trained to Transport Command standards and that the qualifications for VIP crews should be reviewed. At the time it was surmised that the aircraft could have overshot its turning point at Toulouse and crashed into the Pyrenees, been shot down over the Channel Islands after turning back, crashed or been shot down over western France or flown out into the Bay of Biscay. It was not until 4 Jun 45 that the wreckage of the aircraft and the remains of those on board were found, when a thaw set in in the French Alps. The aircraft had crashed in mountains at a height of about 6500 feet due east of Grenoble and the aircraft was some 250 miles off track! The aircraft seems to have struck the ground whilst heading in a northerly or north-westerly heading but whether this indicates the aircraft was returning or merely pointing in that direction, having spun down out of control, is not known. The reason for it being so far from its intended route has never been explained but supposes a massive error in navigation or a positive decision to 'cut the corner'. By the time the aircraft was found, AVM Scarlett-Streatfield was dead; killed in somewhat similar circumstances on 10 May 45 (see Price Of Peace, pages 35 & 36) when he accompanied a crew from 190 Sqn flying into Norway. Again, this was a senior officer on the flight deck of an aircraft operating in appalling weather conditions and flying over mountainous terrain, off course and below safety height. Leigh-Mallory and Scarlett-Streatfield have one other similarity; both had their original surnames 'double-barrelled' from Mallory and Scarlett respectively.

Squadron Leader Charles Gordon Drake LANCASTER 32 DFC & Bar Pilot
Flight Lieutenant Peter CHINN 20 Co-Pilot and ADC to Air Chief Marshal Lee-Mallory
Flight Lieutenant Keith Alan MOORING 24 Navigator
Flight Lieutenant John Austral CASEY 29 RAAF Wireless Operator
Flying Officer Alfred John ENSER 29 Flight Engineer
Sergeant Harold John CHANDLER 42 Steward
Corporal John Ellis Martin BURGESS Mechanic
Leading Aircraftman John Charles BURNETT
Air Chief Marshal Sir Trafford LEIGH-MALLORY 52 KCB DSO
Lady Dorothy LEIGH-MALLORY 52

Date	Serial	Aircraft	Unit	Place	Casualties
Brief Circumstances of Accident					
Casualty Details (If Applicable)					

14-Nov-44 V2027 Albemarle   22 HGCU   RAF Keevil   0

The aircraft, which is also shown as belonging to the ORTU, was engaged on a glider towing exercise and had been airborne for just 10 minutes when its starboard engine failed. The pilot did not feather the propeller but cast off the glider and started an approach to land, during which time the port engine failed and the pilot made a crashed landing but without injury to his crew.

14-Nov-44 EW632 Liberator   1332 HCU   RAF Nutts Corner   0

The pilot, who had been cautioned not to close the throttles until over the end of the runway, did so too early and the aircraft struck the edge of a river bank some 25 yards short of the threshold. The undercarriage was torn off and the aircraft badly damaged. The river was a recognised obstruction for aircraft landing from the south-west or overshooting from the opposite direction. A proposal to divert the river and bridge over it had been submitted and costed at £5000 but the station commander, in the comments to this accident, records that failure to do the work had cost a Fortress, a C87, a Wellington and now a Liberator!

16-Nov-44 KH153 Liberator VI   34 SAAF   Celone, Italy   0

The aircraft was landing after a 6 hour sortie to drop supplies and was being flown by an RAFVR pilot. On turning into wind for the final landing approach, the aircraft flew straight into the ground about 2000 yards short of the runway. In finding that the pilot made an error of judgement, the CO records that the HCU landing technique, mandating a turn onto finals at 1200 feet was too low and this should be a minimum of 1500 feet. In making this recommendation, there is no reference to any factors such as wind speed on approach nor when the final turn to land is made with regards the distance from the threshold.

16-Nov-44   LL311   Halifax V   298 Sqn   RAF Earls Colne   0

The ground staff were recharging the pneumatic system and the air supply had been turned off when the air bottle burst, causing significant damage to the port side of the fuselage

17-Nov-44   LA829   Whitley V   81 OTU   RAF Little Rissington   0

An engine failed whilst the aircraft was flying at 750 feet and the pilot made a wheels up forced landing.

17-Nov-44   LA873   Whitley V   21 HGCU   Coershill Farm, Ducklington Oxfordshire   3

The aircraft took off towing Horsa LG749 on a night training sortie with dark conditions prevailing. At 200 feet immediately after becoming airborne, the aircraft banked over almost vertically and with the glider still attached, dived into the ground. The crews of both aircraft were killed. The investigation was inconclusive but the accident may have been because of an artificial horizon failure or faulty instrument flying but these possibilities are conjecture since no firm evidence was found.

     Flying Officer Royston Grenville PEARCE
     Flight Sergeant Edgar Richard James WHITE 23 Wireless Operator
     Aircraftman 2nd Class Albert Edward DALE 20 Yoke Operator

17-Nov-44   LG749   Horsa I   21 HGCU   Coershill Farm, Ducklington, Oxfordshire   3

This glider was effectively dragged into the ground by its tug. The pilot would have had little time to react but at the height and darkness involved, it might have proved impossible for the glider pilot to have landed safely anyway.

     Warrant Officer John William STRANGE 22 Instructor
     Flying Officer William DAVIDSON 22 Student Pilot
     Sergeant Douglas Edwin MAWE 21 Student Pilot

Date	Serial	Aircraft	Unit	Place	Casualties

Brief Circumstances of Accident
Casualty Details (If Applicable)

18-Nov-44 LK181 Stirling IV   148 Sqn   Brindisi   0

This aircraft, previously operated by and transferred from 624 Sqn, suffered an undercarriage collapse after it left the side of the runway.

20-Nov-44 KG318 Dakota   271 Sqn   Near Dunkirk   0

The aircraft was damaged by flak and a forced landing was made with the aircraft being destroyed by fire.

20-Nov-44 LJ891 Stirling IV   299 Sqn   RAF Wethersfield   0

The aircraft was being flown on an air-sea training sortie and after about 1¾ hours airborne, its starboard inner engine began to vibrate because a cylinder had broken loose. The engine was feathered but on landing the aircraft started to swing after its starboard tyre burst. The aircraft ran into soft ground and the inevitable undercarriage collapse took place.

20-Nov-44 BT664 Hotspur III   5 GTS   Shobdon   0

Whilst landing at night, this glider struck the tractor being used to retrieve two other gliders which had landed earlier. It does seem surprising that the procedures for retrieving gliders allowed the towing of aircraft within the landing zone whilst other aircraft were still landing and in some cases having to plan a route to land between stationary aircraft, never mind 'moving targets'!!

21-Nov-44 LK276 Stirling IV   190 Sqn   Newton Field near Great Dunmow   7

This crew was being checked by an experienced pilot and was engaged in a night glider towing sortie. The glider; Horsa PF753, was cast off and landed safely and the Stirling was then flown to the rope dropping area before the pilot asked for permission to land. Having been told to hold off, the crew began to orbit the outer circle of lights but shortly afterwards, the aircraft crashed, having struck some willow trees, passed beneath overhead power lines and skidded along the ground before striking a bank and exploding. The Board of Enquiry blamed the pilot for failing to monitor his altimeter and concentrating on acquiring the lights after he had lost them. In his book: "For Your Tomorrow – Volume 2", Errol W Martyn suggests that research done many years afterwards reveals that the aircraft was shot down by an enemy night intruder, which was seen to be following the Stirling and that this fact was commonly known amongst those serving at Great Dunmow.

    Flying Officer James Ian KIDGELL 23 RAAF Pilot
    Flying Officer William Walter D'Arcy BRAIN 26 RNZAF Check-Pilot
    Flying Officer Ernest Douglas WOODS 26 Navigator
    Flight Sergeant Ronald David PAYNE 21 Bomb Aimer
    Flight Sergeant Reginald Matthew DAUNCEY 23 Wireless Operator
    Sergeant Hugh HOLT 20 Flight Engineer
    Flight Sergeant Arthur George REID 33 Air Gunner

21-Nov-44 EB410 Whitley V   81 OTU   Llechrydan Denbighshire   1

The aircraft had been airborne for just over 3 hours on a night cross country sortie and was operating over high ground, in cloudy and turbulent conditions. The crew was unsure of their position and the pilot ignored the navigator's recommended safety height of 2600 feet. The aircraft struck high ground at 1300 feet and crashed, killing one crew and injuring the others. The enquiry commented on the poor crew cooperation and the weak display of captaincy by the pilot, who was subsequently removed from training.

    Sergeant Cyril Lionel FENDER 21

21-Nov-44 P1606 Albemarle I   42 OTU   Hethel Norfolk   0

The aircraft had been airborne for nearly 2 hours on a cross country training sortie and its starboard engine was only providing power intermittently. A precautionary landing was attempted at Hethel but on the final approach the port engine failed and the aircraft crashed in the undershoot about 150 yards from the runway's end. The double engine problems were a direct result of the pilot's failure to change from the fuselage fuel tanks to the wing fuel tanks in good time and when he realised the cause of the fuel starvation, he mishandled the fuel control cocks. It is interesting to note that this accident has considerable similarities with another involving this unit, following which various edicts were issued regarding briefing and training of pilots to operate the fuel system correctly.

21-Nov-44 LL254 Halifax V   216 Sqn   Maison Blanche, Algeria   0

After about 2 hours of a ferry sortie, two engines failed because of faults in the coolant pumps. The crew jettisoned all loose equipment but the aircraft would not maintain height. The pilot was compelled to make a landing without flaps on a short runway, which had only a small overrun and the aircraft went off the end and into a ditch.

21-Nov-44 RX660 Horsa   23 HGCU   Gornall Staffordshire   0

The tug pilot had taken violent evasive action to avoid another aircraft but in doing so, the glider had got badly out of position and the tow was cast off. An attempt was made to force land the aircraft but it struck a tree and went through a hedge.

22-Nov-44 EB337 Whitley   42 OTU   Crowtrees Farm, Bradley   0

The aircraft was forced landed in a field after an engine failure during a camera gun training exercise.

22-Nov-44 KJ855 Dakota IV   436 Sqn   30 degrees 25 North/72 degrees East   0

The aircraft was operating on a night training sortie which was scheduled to be of 4½ hours duration. Unfortunately, the crew became lost for almost the entire sortie and because the pilot had decided not to carry a wireless operator, none of the radio aids was used. After just over 10 hours airborne and with the fuel almost exhausted, a forced landing was made.

22-Nov-44	T1456	Lysander IIIA	148 Sqn	20 miles north-north-east Venice	4

This aircraft was on an operational sortie (TEMPLAR) to take agents into an LZ behind enemy lines. The flight was undertaken in daylight and the aircraft was being escorted by several RAF Mustangs. Without warning and before there was any opportunity to intervene, a USAAF P51 Mustang attacked the Lysander and it was shot down with the loss of all those on board.

Flying Officer John Francis Anthony RAYNS 21
+ three non-RAF agents

23-Nov-44	EV846	Liberator	358 Sqn	Kolar	5?

The aircraft was being used for a night flying training sortie as part of the work up of the newly formed 358 Sqn. The crew was attempting an overshoot but the aircraft crashed and its crew was killed. The precise circumstances of the loss are unclear.

Flight Sergeant Forbes PORTER 23 RAAF Pilot
Sergeant Charles Victor GARSIDE 26 Navigator
Flying Officer John MCHARDY 21 Bomb Aimer
Sergeant Maurice Trevor JONES 20 Wireless Operator
Flight Sergeant William WHITE 19 RAAF

23-Nov-44	HH303	Hotspur III	5 GTS	Shobdon	0

The pilot was undertaking a night circuit detail but did not using use his landing light and so undershot the airfield.

Date	Serial	Aircraft	Unit	Place	Casualties
	Brief Circumstances of Accident				
	Casualty Details (If Applicable)				

24-Nov-44 V1847 Albemarle 23 HGCU Standon, Staffordshire 0

This aircraft was being flown as No: 2 in a stream at 500 feet and was towing Horsa glider RX614, the latter piloted by Flight Sergeant Garner. The port engine failed and the tug began to lose both height and speed so its pilot; Flying Officer Marsh, was forced to cast off the glider, which landed safely. Marsh continued to try to keep his aircraft airborne but the poor single engined performance of the Albemarle won the day and a forced landing with undercarriage retracted was made on a hill top. The tug crew escaped the crash, although the pilot sustained a slight sprained ankle.

25-Nov-44 LH237 Horsa 1577 SD Flt RAF Mauripur 0

At 50 feet immediately after being towed off, the glider's port aileron detached, followed by a mainspar failure. The glider crashed and the two Army pilots were injured.

26-Nov-44 LA914 Whitley V 42 OTU Ashbourne Derbyshire 0

The aircraft was landing after a training sortie of about 90 minutes duration. In view of the poor visibility, the pilot completed a circuit on instruments and landed faster than normal and further along the runway. In trying to stop on the wet grass, he swung the aircraft towards the perimeter track but there were cyclists on this area who distracted him and the port undercarriage collapsed as he attempted to avoid these.

26-Nov-44 T9463 Hudson 161 Sqn Belgium/Luxembourg border area 4

This crew was attempting a drop into Germany, which was completed when an agent was parachuted into a spot at Armstadt, south of Erfurt. However, during the return flight, the aircraft crashed near the Belgian/Luxembourg border having been attacked by a night fighter.

Squadron Leader Reginald Eric WILKINSON 31 DFC Pilot

Flying Officer John WEDDELL 22 Navigator
Flight Lieutenant Frederick john Joseph CHAMPION 23 DFM Wireless Operator
Flight Lieutenant George Henry ASH 30 DFC Air Gunner

26-Nov-44   FR583   Hadrian II   TSTU   3 miles south-west of Dhamial   0

The pilot was undertaking his first solo on type and he cast off the tow at 1200 feet on the crosswind leg. The glider immediately started to descend in a diving attitude and control was only recovered at 200 feet. The elevator trim was used incorrectly and the aircraft was actually nose heavy in consequence. The pilot was unfamiliar with the controls and not competent to be sent solo. Furthermore, the aircraft was carrying passengers, who should not have been allowed on such a sortie.

27-Nov-44   LK151   Stirling   138 Sqn   At sea near Assens Denmark   7

The crew of this aircraft had completed successfully the delivery of eighteen containers to a DZ at Krengerup on the Danish island of Fyn, as sortie coded TABLEJAM 69. On their return journey, the aircraft was intercepted and shot down by an enemy Ju88 and crashed into the sea near Assens on the west coast of Fyn in an area of water called the Little Belt. There were another thirteen aircraft from the squadron engaged on Danish sorties that night but all others returned safely

Flight Lieutenant Reginald Ronald WITHAM 26 DFC RAAF Pilot
Flying Officer Geoffrey Herbert Brandon SLINN 32 RAAF
Flying Officer Thomas Patrick MCHALE 24 RCAF Navigator
Sergeant Reginald Hughes BERRETT 19
Flight Sergeant Kenneth NAYLOR 21
Flight Sergeant Arthur Henry BEDGGOOD 19 Air Gunner
Pilot Officer Charles ELLEMAN

28-Nov-44   LK241   Stirling IV   299 Sqn   North Sea (location not known)   2

This aircraft was lost in the north sea but it is believed the other crew survived.

Warrant Officer John DICKIE 26 RAAF Pilot
Flight Sergeant Stanley DIXON 20

28-Nov-44   LJ470   Stirling III   1332 HCU   Missing   4

The aircraft was on a navigation exercise but never returned to base. Its radar plot faded off Stornoway and it is thought possible that the aircraft iced up and control was lost.

Flying Officer Frederick Ernest Sampson GARDINER 33
Flight Sergeant James Alexander HITCHCOCK Navigator
Sergeant James Edward Charles BUTTLE Wireless Operator
Flight Sergeant Eric William WRIGHT Flight Engineer

29-Nov-44   LL406   Halifax V   297 Sqn   ½ mile west-south-west Shepherds Grove   4

The aircraft had been airborne for about 50 minutes on a general flying practice sortie and was carrying a crew of four and one non-RAF passenger. At 1500 feet, the starboard outer engine failed because of a serious and sudden coolant leak and it then caught fire. The pilot turned the aircraft away from the live engines and it lost height in the turn when the bomb bay doors were opened instead of the flaps being lowered. The aircraft struck the ground, cartwheeled and was burnt out when the fire spread from the engine to the wing.

Sergeant Walter McKay FORBES 22 RCAF
Flying Officer Thomas Edward REILLY 24 RCAF
Sergeant William Davise COPLAND 20 died of injuries 1 December
+ 1 soldier believed to be:
Staff Sergeant Frank Joseph STARTUP 29 Glider Pilot Regiment

462

30-Nov-44 AM263 Liberator I   511 Sqn   Lagens   0

The brakes failed whilst the aircraft was landing and it collided with Dakota FZ637. This aircraft had been used quite extensively for both VIP support work and also the as part of the 'return ferry service', carrying people across the Atlantic – usually ferry crews. Although recorded as being allocated to 511 Sqn, there is some evidence that the aircraft had been transferred to 231 Sqn at the time of its accident. It was not struck off charge formally until Jan 47 but is thought to have been scrapped before then.

02-Dec-44 LP239 Wellington X   70 Sqn   Near Manfredonia, north of San Marco   5

A force of sixty five bomber aircraft, comprising fifty three Wellingtons and the remainder Liberators, were despatched to drop supplies to two DZs; FLOTSAM and ICARUS. Only four Wellingtons were able to get below the very heavy and widespread low clouds and these aircraft delivered a modest twenty four containers to the former DZ. Seven Liberators were able to get below the cloud base and these dropped supplies to the latter DZ. This work was extremely dangerous for obvious reasons of high ground and dense cloud and on this occasion a pair of Wellingtons failed to return and were eventually found crashed into high ground.

    Flying Officer Thomas Richard HAIN 21 Pilot
      Sergeant Brian COLEMAN 22
      Sergeant Jack CONSTANT
      Sergeant Edwin THOMAS
      Sergeant Arthur Robert WHIFFEN 21

02-Dec-44 MF247 Wellington X   104 Sqn   5 miles north of San Marco   5

Crashed whilst participating in the same sortie as LP239 above.

      Sergeant Albert Leonard BARNARD 21 Pilot
      Sergeant James Ferguson WALLACE 21 Bomb Aimer
      Sergeant Harry Conrad BOWLER 10 Wireless Operator
      Sergeant Cyril William James DOVER 28 Air Gunner

Date	Serial	Aircraft	Unit	Place	Casualties

Brief Circumstances of Accident
Casualty Details (If Applicable)

+ one RAF

03-Dec-44 LK143 Stirling   138 Sqn   Crashed at sea location not known   7

The crew was engaged on the double sorties; TABLEJAM 169 and 177 to DZs in Denmark. Unfortunately, the aircraft did not reach the assigned area and it crashed into the sea. The precise cause of the loss is not known.

Flying Officer George Frederick NICHOLS
Pilot Officer Charles Edward TERRELL
Flight Sergeant John George HARRIS 20
Sergeant Arthur Cecil BUTLER 25
Flight Sergeant Joseph Albert GOLDING 25
Sergeant Frederick Albert Walter FILER 20
Flight Sergeant Leslie William POULSON 20RAAF

03-Dec-44 LK273 Stirling IV   570 Sqn RAF Rivenhall   0

The aircraft was returning from a crew training sortie after about 1½ hours airborne. The base weather was very poor visibility and the pilot missed three approaches, overshooting from each before attempting a fourth. Unfortunately, the pilot lined up on the wrong runway and the aircraft overshot after touchdown. The undercarriage was retracted to stop but the starboard side collapsed first as the aircraft crossed a deep ditch and the Stirling burst into flames.

05-Dec-44 FL588 Dakota III   24 Sqn   Usson   18

The aircraft was conveying a party of glider pilots, posted from UK to the Far East and there were 3 crew and 20 soldiers aboard. The first leg of the journey involved a refuelling stop at Istres and the aircraft was en route to Toulouse and had been airborne for nearly 4 hours. Rather than fly beneath the poor weather, it appears the pilot elected to make a detour but in doing so, the aircraft struck a mountain peak in position 42 degrees 39 North/2 degrees East. It is not known whether the pilot lost control after the aircraft suffered icing problems or if there was a navigational error but there were no calls for assistance from the crew. It was acknowledged that there were few radio aids because of the enemy occupation of France. Some of the glider pilots killed in this accident were amongst the most experienced in the Regiment. Major Croot had been a Territorial Army officer and had been awarded The Bronze Lion by HM The Queen of the Netherlands whilst leading 'G' Squadron at Arnhem. In the same action, Squadron Sergeant Major Watt was awarded the US Bronze Star, whilst Captain Barclay had received his Military Cross in the fighting following the invasion of Sicily.

Flight Lieutenant Neville Oxynham CLEMENTS 30 Pilot

Flight Lieutenant Malcolm Lawrence RICHARDS Navigator

Flying Officer William Price GRIFFITHS 26 AFC Wireless Operator

Staff Sergeant Andrew Smith ANDERSON 26

Captain Frank Horace BARCLAY MC

Lieutenant Alfred John COX 21

Major Robert Shirley CROOT TD

Sergeant Geoffrey Peter DAWKINS

Sergeant Albert James GIBBS 30

Lieutenant George HORROCKS

Staff Sergeant Douglas James LAWTON 26

Lieutenant Edward Harvey William NORMAN 23

Captain Robert Victor Douglas PALMER 25

Captain Ronald Douglas TELFER 25

Sergeant Edward WAKEFIELD 23

Sergeant James WALSH 27

Warrant Officer II (SSM) William WATT 25

Date	Serial	Aircraft	Unit	Place		Casualties
Brief Circumstances of Accident						
Casualty Details (If Applicable)						

Sergeant John WOODWARD 24

05-Dec-44   RJ124   Horsa   ORTU   RAF Hampstead Norris   0

The glider was landing at the end of a night training sortie. The pilot undershot the approach and the aircraft hit two clearly marked obstructions.

05-Dec-44   BT681   Hotspur III   5 GTS   Herefordshire   0

The pilot failed to ensure the hood was properly latched and it flew back whilst the aircraft was on tow. The glider pilot then had problems with dealing with this and pulled the tug's tail up and this forced the tug pilot to jettison the tow. The glider pilot then lost control and the glider dived into the ground. It was commented that the pilot's stature made it difficult for him to latch the cockpit hood whilst sitting in the front seat.

06-Dec-44   KG639   Dakota III   109 OTU   Cumberland (location not stated)   0

The pilot was undertaking his first night solo and had been airborne for about 20 minutes when he lost sight of the airfield in poor visibility. He heard an R/T transmission which indicated there was another aircraft at the same height and in the same area and so he reduced height to 800 feet believing he was still in the circuit area. Unfortunately, whilst out of sight of the airfield (Crosby on Eden) the aircraft had drifted away towards high ground and with no safety margin it struck a hillside.

06-Dec-44   LL281   Halifax V   1665 HCU   RAF Tilstock   3

The crew was engaged on circuit training and the port inner engine failed, just as the aircraft became airborne. It swung off the line of the runway, crashed to the ground and struck a tree before catching fire and being gutted in the ensuing blaze. The engine failure was caused by not ensuring the fuel valves were fully open and the fuel supply to the port inner engine was impeded.

    Flying Officer Charles Peter ADAMS 22 Pilot
    Flying Officer Harry WEBSTER 30
    Sergeant Kenneth John HARMER 19

06-Dec-44 PW874 Horsa   11 HGSU   RAF Blakehill Farm   0

The glider had just been towed off and was barely more than 5 feet above the ground when the tow rope came off. The pilot put the aircraft back onto the ground but could not prevent an overshoot into a field beyond and via a thick hedge.

10-Dec-44 KG584 Dakota III   271 Sqn   Leith Hill Surrey   3

The aircraft had returned after a night stop on the continent and landed at Gatwick to drop off passengers. The crew then set off to return to their base, despite the very poor weather. The aircraft was being flown in and out of broken cloud, rather than at a safe height above the cloud. Despite a radio call from Gatwick to warn the pilot of the proximity of hills, no response was received and the aircraft flew into the hillside.

    Pilot Officer Edward GIBSON 24 Pilot
    Flying Officer Sydney John HOLDER 24 RAAF Navigator
    Flying Officer Robert McNeil SMITH 30 Wireless Operator

10-Dec-44 EF456 Stirling III   1665 CU   RAF Tilstock   0

The aircraft's brakes proved to be partially ineffective and the aircraft ran off the end of the runway. In an attempt to avoid running onto a main road, the pilot swung the aircraft but the usual outcome took place when the undercarriage collapsed.

Date	Serial	Aircraft	Unit	Place	Casualties

Brief Circumstances of Accident
Casualty Details (If Applicable)

11-Dec-44 RN366 Horsa 23 HGCU RAF Peplow (Childs Ercall) 0

The pilot was making a steep approach to land but he failed to check the glider's descent in time and the aircraft struck the ground heavily. It then bounced into the air, climbed sharply and stalled into a crash landing.

11-Dec-44 MF732 Wellington X 104 Sqn Foggia Main 0

The aircraft was returning from a night supply dropping sortie and its pilot was making a low approach. The aircraft touched down normally but then the pilot attempted to pull the tail down but because the speed was too high, the aircraft ballooned into the air and then stalled onto the ground. The undercarriage collapsed and the port engine caught fire. The crew escaped uninjured.

12-Dec-44 LK607 Stirling III 1332 HCU RAF Nutts Corner 0

The aircraft was engaged on a pilot training sortie and was taking off with a student pilot and instructor plus two other crew members. The aircraft swung to port and left the runway at an angle of about 10 degrees. The instructor took control and held the aircraft straight and closed the throttles. Unfortunately, on ground which had in any event been softened by rain, the aircraft ran over a filled in mill race and the starboard undercarriage sank into it and collapsed.

13-Dec-44 KG661 Dakota III 109 OTU RAF Crosby on Eden 0

The pilot, who was very keen to be punctual on the sortie, took off after a very short run for the load being carried. The aircraft became airborne in a semi-stalled state and the pilot throttled back, the aircraft crashed to the ground and caught fire.

13-Dec-44   KG710   Dakota III   44 SAAF   Missing Bari to Hassani   4

The aircraft was one of a large fleet, comprising twenty five Dakotas, fifty Wellingtons and thirty Liberators, tasked with delivering supplies to allied forces at Hassani, Athens, from airfields in Italy. The aircraft was loaded with 5032 lbs of 75 mm artillery shells and 700 gallons of petrol. The weather conditions were low cloud with rain and patches of very poor visibility but apart from this aircraft, all the others completed the sortie safely. The aircraft failed to arrive and there is no evidence as to how it was lost, although the obvious conclusion was that the aircraft had flown into the sea or been overwhelmed by the weather.

Captain A R ALDRIDGE SAAF
Lieutenant N S CAMPBELL SAAF
Lieutenant J ZURSCHMIEDE SAAF
Air Corporal C A KALIS SAAF

14-Dec-44   HH127   Hotspur III   5 GTS   Herefordshire   0

The glider was towed into cloud and the instructor released the tow but then had trouble retaining control, in part because the turn and slip indicator and the compass were situated in the front cockpit only and he was instructing from the rear seat. The aircraft crash landed.

14-Dec-44   341061   Hadrian I   22 HGCU   Upper Inglesham, Lechlade   0

The glider pilot considered that the tug was travelling too fast as it levelled out at the top of the climb and so released the tow. A forced landing was attempted but the glider overshot the field selected and crashed into a ditch. This aircraft had retained its USAAF serial number.

15-Dec-44   KH157   Liberator VI   34 SAAF   Araxos Greece   0

The aircraft had landed at this airfield and became bogged down. The Greek Peoples' Army of Liberation (ELAS) attacked the airfield and looted the aircraft and caused such damage as to render it beyond repair.

Date	Serial	Aircraft	Unit	Place	Casualties

Brief Circumstances of Accident
Casualty Details (If Applicable)

16-Dec-44   FL600   Dakota III   62 Sqn   Agartala   0

The aircraft was returning from an operational supply dropping sortie, during which the pilot had cut and feathered the starboard engine. Unfortunately, the pilot failed to select the hydraulic system to the port engine driven pump, despite the fact that the main hydraulic services are normally driven from that pump. It is possible that he made the assumption that this default selection was operative but it is good practice to confirm selections or make the necessary transfers of services if they are driven from an engine that has been shut down. On landing, neither the flaps nor brakes worked and it was impractical to attempt a go round. The aircraft overran the runway and was damaged badly. The squadron commander commented that the pilot, who had 370 hours on type, might reasonably have been able to cope with a landing without brakes and flaps but it is unclear as to how the pilot is supposed to steer the aircraft once rudder authority is lost.

16-Dec-44   340770   Hadrian I   TSTU   6 miles north-north-west of Fatehjang   0

Whilst flying at 800 feet, the combination's tow rope broke loose from the tug. The glider was damaged in the subsequent forced landing.

17-Dec-44   RJ285   Horsa   1 HGSU   RAF Rivenhall   0

The pupil pilot misjudged the landing approach and the instructor did not take control soon enough. The glider struck the ground heavily, bounced and on landing heavily a second time, broke its back.

17-Dec-44   RN881   Horsa   1 HGSU   Somerset, Map Ref 234820   0

The glider had been on tow for about 45 minutes in bumpy conditions and the glider got out of position. During evasive action by the glider pilot, the tow rope broke a few feet from the tug's connection and then wrapped itself around the glider's starboard wheel. A forced landing was made from a height of 500 feet but the glider was damaged, although without injury to either crew member.

17-Dec-44   340593   Hadrian I   ATTDU   RAF Netheravon   0

The aircraft was correctly picketed in anticipation of a severe storm but during the gale, the wind changed direction and the pickets were torn from the soft, rain soaked ground and the glider was hurled over 100 yards on its back.

18-Dec-44   P1554   Albemarle   42 OTU   North Avenue Ashbourne   1

Ashbourne airfield is located on a hill above the town and the approach to Runway 14 takes aircraft over a 'basin' before the ground rises sharply to the airfield boundary. After a 3 hour cross country sortie, the aircraft returned to land but in preparing to do so, the pilot set his altimeter incorrectly and hence believed he was higher on the approach than was the case. The aircraft struck tree tops and then crashed into the roof of a house which was situated some 46 feet below the height of the runway. The aircraft destroyed the top floor of the three storied dwelling, which was occupied by a family and several refugees. Although eight bedrooms on the top floor were affected, nobody in the house was injured. The navigator, however, had remained in the nose of the aircraft and was thrown out on impact and killed.

Pilot Officer Arthur BUNTING Navigator

18-Dec-44   BT859   Hotspur II   3 GTS   Culmhead, Somerset   2

The crew did not align the glider correctly during the approach to land and in a strong crosswind, the glider drifted further away from the landing 'funnel' and struck trees.

Flight Lieutenant Edmond Saffery CAMPBELL-COOPER
Sergeant John GIBBON 21

Date	Serial	Aircraft	Unit	Place	Casualties
Brief Circumstances of Accident					
Casualty Details (If Applicable)					

19-Dec-44 KJ884 Dakota IV 435 Sqn Gujrat, Punjab 0

The aircraft was being used as part of a squadron move and there were twenty one RAF personnel on board. The aircraft took off shortly after midnight and whilst flying at 5000 feet, its starboard engine failed and height could not be maintained. The pilot managed to fly the aircraft to an airstrip and on final approach, he cut the port engine allowing the aircraft to drift to the port side of the flare path, where it struck a large hole, crashed and caught fire. The blaze spread to the rest of the aircraft, which was gutted completely because the fire fighting equipment held at the airfield was unserviceable! All those on board escaped but about half were badly hurt.

20-Dec-44 JN958 Halifax II 148 Sqn Brindisi 0

The crew was engaged on a REBECCA training sortie and on landing in a 10 knot crosswind, the aircraft started a swing to starboard because the starboard throttles were 'lagging'. The pilot then found the aircraft was moving towards a line of Dakotas and so in trying to avoid these, a side slide developed which resulted in the undercarriage collapsing.

20-Dec-44 FR600 Hadrian II TSTU Dhamial, Punjab 0

On approach to land, the pilot allowed the aircraft to travel too quickly and it overran the strip and passed over rough ground damaging the undercarriage and lower fuselage.

21-Dec-44 KG498 Dakota III 28 SAAF 10 miles south-south-west Torretoria 22

The aircraft was evacuating wounded personnel from Athens to Italy and there were seven RAF/SAAF and sixteen others on board. The pilot descended in cloud when uncertain of the aircraft's position and the aircraft struck a hill at a height of 1200 feet about 25 miles from its destination. There was a single survivor.

Lieutenant Gerald Patrick CRONIN SAAF Pilot
Lieutenant C J JOOSTE 34 SAAF Pilot
Lieutenant P S MOORE 31 SAAF Navigator
Air Corporal H V KILBURN SAAF Wireless Operator
Leading Aircraftman Roy Farley ATKINSON
Leading Aircraftman Frank HELLAWELL
Captain John Arthur BARLOW 28 RAMC
Private Roy Douglas BROWN 24 Hampshire Regt
Sapper Herbert CUDMORE 43 RE
Private Charles Henry CULVER 21 Parachute Regt
Sapper Ivor Thomas GOODFIELD 24
Captain L HEILBRONNER 31 South African Int Corps
Lance Corporal John KIRK Parachute Regt
Signalman Alexander Dunnachie MCCORMICK 26 Royal Signals
Signalman David LAURIE 25 Royal Signals
Trooper John MASSON 28 Royal Tank Regt
Major Ian Norman PATTERSON 30 MC 'L' Sqn SAS
Sergeant Arthur Frank Gay POWELL 30 Parachute Regt
Gunner Leonard PROCTOR Royal Artillery
Sergeant Adam Edgar SCOON 31 Parachute Regt
+ two others whose details are not known

21-Dec-44 LK655 Halifax V	1665 HCU	RAF Tilstock	0

On landing in poor visibility and drizzle, the pilot mistook the 800 yard bar lights for the end of runway and so he swung the aircraft to avoid an apparent overshoot but the undercarriage collapsed.

Date	Serial	Aircraft	Unit	Place	Casualties
		Brief Circumstances of Accident			
		Casualty Details (If Applicable)			

22-Dec-44 V1823 Albemarle   22 HGCU   South Horscroft farm, Bratton Wilts   2

The aircraft was on a glider towing sortie and had been airborne for about 10 minutes. The glider got out of position and pulled the aircraft sideways. As the combination was flying at low speed, this induced a stall in the aircraft's inner wing and despite casting off the tow, the pilot was unable to recover from the stall and the aircraft crashed and caught fire. Once again the Board of Enquiry commented on the Albemarle aircraft's lack of power and also the shift in its centre of gravity when tugging gliders.

Flying Officer Vernon J BOUCHARD RCAF Pilot
Warrant Officer Arthur W BANNIER Navigator

26-Dec-44 LL484 Halifax V   148 Sqn   1 mile north of San Vito   1

The aircraft was supply dropping on a DZ at Geisha, northern Yugoslavia and the port outer engine failed due to a failure of the lubrication system. The pilot feathered the propeller but then found he was unable to maintain height and so a forced landing was made but one member of the crew was killed in the process.

Believed to be:
Flight Sergeant Frederick DAVIS 26 RAAF Navigator

27-Dec-44 FD863 Dakota III   267 Sqn   Bari   0

The aircraft was engaged on an operational sortie to Greece, carrying supplies and with an operating crew of four. The starboard engine failed and the pilot attempted a single engined approach but in doing so, he lowered the undercarriage, increasing the drag and causing the aircraft to sink and strike a tree. The pilot then raised the undercarriage and the aircraft belly landed and caught fire but there were no injuries amongst the crew.

27-Dec-44   DL467 Master II   Near Nether Stowe, Somerset   0

The pilot found the airfield fog bound suddenly and without prior forecast and so released the glider and then attempted to find an alternative landing site. Unfortunately, this was impossible and so a forced landing was made but the aircraft struck a hedge.

27-Dec-44   EM402 Master II   Bobbington Marsh, Somerset   1

The unit commander was reluctant to cancel the night flying programme and so sent a tug and glider combination to fly a weather test sortie. The weather was described as 'hopeless' but once airborne, the combination had to get down again and eventually the tug pilot was ordered to bale out. In attempting to abandon the aircraft, the pilot lost control whilst it was inverted in cloud and it crashed with him still on board.

Flying Officer Kenneth John MCDONALD 20 RCAF Pilot

27-Dec-44   HH655 Hotspur II   Temple Coombe, Somerset   0

This glider is the one involved in the accident summarised above and it was being flown by two experienced RAF pilots. They landed without injury, despite the dreadful weather but their glider was a write-off.

28-Dec-44   LL187 Halifax   301 Sqn   Czechoslovakia   8

A force of ten aircraft from this squadron, comprising four Liberators and six Halifaxes, was tasked with supply drops to Poland. Five crews: two flying Liberators and three with Halifaxs, were either successful or partially so but one of the latter aircraft was shot down by anti-aircraft fire over Czechoslovakia and all those on board were killed.

Warrant Officer Boleslaw URAM Pilot
Flight Lieutenant Franciszek KRYSZCZUK
Flight Lieutenant Tadeuzs WIANECKI
Sergeant Theodor MAJER
Warrant Officer Eugeniusz KRZECZEWSKI

Flight Sergeant Stanislaw LISIK
Flight Sergeant Wiktor MULLER
Sergeant Karol MACIERZYNSKI

29-Dec-44   LJ970   Stirling IV   620 Sqn   Sande in Vestfold 40 miles south west Oslo   7

The aircraft was shot down by Hauptmann Vogt of the Luftwaffe's Norwegian nightfighter squadron at the location shown whilst engaged in an SOE mission; TAIL 2, flying from its base at Great Dunmow in Essex to the location south south east of Oslo. The other five aircraft engaged on similar tasks returned safely. Fg Off McNamara had been awarded the Croix de Guerre by the French authorities for his work during the preceeding months.

Flying Officer John Henry MCNAMARA 23 RAAF Pilot
Sergeant Raymond POOLE 23 Co-Pilot
Flight Lieutenant Kenneth James HARRIES 24 Navigator
Flight Sergeant Wilfred HUGHES 20 Air Gunner
Warrant Officer David Wise JONES 21 RAAF Wireless Operator
Sergeant George Lyon MITCHELL 22 Flight Engineer
Flight Sergeant Sidney Walter Charles RODMAN 25 Bomb Aimer

29-Dec-44   MK367   Wellington X   70 Sqn   Italy (precise location not known)   5

The crew of this aircraft was one of thirty tasked with a mass supply drop to DZs in Yugoslavia. This particular sortie being the last of a series undertaken during the previous days. Although there was little enemy opposition, this aircraft failed to return and it was found crashed in central Italy, presumed during its return flight.

Warrant Officer Raymond Richard Lindsay HAWKE 29 RAAF Pilot

476

Sergeant John Andrew HEENAN 20 Navigator
Sergeant Donald THAYRE 22 Bomb Aimer
Sergeant Raymond Leslie CUNDY 20 Wireless Operator
Sergeant James Bernard MULHOLLAND 23 Air Gunner

30-Dec-44   V1934   Albemarle VI   Wincote Staffordshire   3

The aircraft lost an engine on take-off and the pilot attempted a forced landing straight ahead. However, the aircraft struck a barrier and burst into flames.

Flying Officer George Earl JOHNSON Pilot
Flying Officer George Gaston FLACK Air Gunner
Sergeant John William TERZZA 20 Wireless Operator

31-Dec-44   KJ958   Dakota IV   353 Sqn   Comilla Bengal   0

Almost immediately after takeoff, the aircraft's port engine caught fire and the pilot closed it down and carried out a successful wheels down landing. After the aircraft had come to a stop and all on board had left safely, the port engine fell out and the fire spread to the starboard mainplane. The cause of the initial engine failure and fire and the reason for its spread to the starboard side were not established because before an enquiry could be convened, the aircraft was partly dismantled.

31-Dec-44   LJ914   Stirling IV   620 Sqn   At sea off Denmark   6

The aircraft was engaged in an SOE sortie and had taken off from Great Dunmow but failed to return. The exact cause of the loss is unknown but it is possible the aircraft was shot down by an A-A ship off the Danish coast. Flying Officer Waring was the second of four generations of air force pilots. His father-in-law had flown in the First World War and Frederick Waring had been a soldier and police officer before joining the RAF and training as pilot. His son, who was born some months after this loss, was a helicopter pilot from 1966 and his grandson also flew helicopters before moving to something more exotic and remains in the RAF at the time of writing this account (2008).

Date	Serial	Aircraft	Unit	Place	Casualties
				Brief Circumstances of Accident Casualty Details (If Applicable)	

Flying Officer Frederick George WARING 30 Pilot
Warrant Officer Thomas Anthony LEYDEN 28 Navigator
Flight Sergeant Graham Leslie OSMOND-JONES 25 Bomb Aimer
Sergeant Kenneth CALLABY 22 Wireless Operator
Flight Sergeant Denis Carnaby FOSTER Flight Engineer
Flight Sergeant Norman Arthur WHITE 35 Air Gunner

Date	Serial	Aircraft	Unit	Place	Casualties
31-Dec-44	LK283	Stirling	138 Sqn	Shot down by enemy flak ship	7

The aircraft was flying to a DZ about 60 miles north-west of Oslo on sortie; CRUPPER10 but did not arrive. Another crew witnessed an explosion near Arendal and it is assumed that the aircraft was shot down by an enemy flak ship.

Flight Lieutenant Raymond MCGREGOR 24 RNZAF Pilot
Flying Officer George Allen COMER 22 RAAF
Warrant Officer George HARRIS 21
Flight Sergeant Derek Allen KENNINGHAM
Sergeant David James PERKINS
Sergeant Richard Edward WARD
Sergeant Geoffrey HARRISON 19

Date	Serial	Aircraft	Unit	Place	Casualties
31-Dec-44	HG909	Horsa	ORTU	Near RAF Keevil	0

The crew was engaged in a night circuits and landings but on take-off, the tug released the tow and the glider crashed outside the airfield's boundary but without injury to any of the three on board.

478

01-Jan-45   BD629   Whitley V   21 HGCU   RAF Brize Norton   0

The aircraft was being taxyed from the dispersal area to the runway for a night flying detail. Its tailwheel caught in a frozen rut, as it was moving across the grassed area, and collapsed.

01-Jan-45   K6943   Harrow II   271 Sqn   Brussels Melsbroek   0

This aircraft and the six Harrows (Sparrows) listed below were destroyed in the enemy attack on allied airfields during the early morning of 1 Jan 45. This coordinated attack (Operation BODDENPLATTE) was an attempt to neutralise the allied air forces and whilst very significant damage was inflicted, particularly on fighters and ground attack aircraft caught on the ground, very heavy casualties were suffered by the Luftwaffe forces participating. A member of the squadron ground crew was killed in the attack but there were no other fatalities from this unit.

01-Jan-45   K6973   Harrow II   271 Sqn   Brussels Melsbroek   0
Destroyed as indicated above.

01-Jan-45   K6993   Harrow II   271 Sqn   Brussels Melsbroek   0
Destroyed as indicated above.

01-Jan-45   K6994   Harrow II   271 Sqn   Brussels Melsbroek   0
Destroyed as indicated above.

01-Jan-45   K6998   Harrow II   271 Sqn   Brussels Melsbroek   0
Destroyed as indicated above.

01-Jan-45   K7024   Harrow II   271 Sqn   Brussels Melsbroek   0
Destroyed as indicated above.

Date	Serial	Aircraft	Unit	Place	Casualties
Brief Circumstances of Accident Casualty Details (If Applicable)					
01-Jan-45	K6986	Harrow II	271 Sqn	Brussels Melsbroek	0
Destroyed as indicated above.					
Leading Aircraftman Jack HYMANS 21					
01-Jan-45	KG331	Dakota	48 Sqn	Nivelles	0
01-Jan-45	KG355	Dakota	575 Sqn	Deurne	0
01-Jan-45	KG488	Dakota	271 Sqn	Brussels Evere	0
01-Jan-45	KG736	Dakota	2 TAFCS	Brussels Evere	0
01-Jan-45	KG796	Dakota	147 Sqn	Brussels Evere	0
01-Jan-45	KG800	Dakota	147 Sqn	Brussels Evere	0
01-Jan-45	KJ803	Dakota	147 Sqn	Brussels Evere	0
01-Jan-45	LJ986	Stirling IV	295 Sqn	St Denis Westram	0
Destroyed during operation BODDENPLATTE.					
01-Jan-45	LJ954	Stirling IV	196 Sqn	St Denis Westram	0
This aircraft, flown by Pilot Officer Ellis and his crew, had been forced landed on 20 Sep 44 following damage during a resupply sortie to Arnhem. Over the following 3½ months the technicians at the Repair					

& Savage Unit had worked to recover this aircraft and on 31 Dec 44 it was ready to be air tested. A pilot, who had not previously flown anything heavier than a Wellington, was persuaded to undertake the necessary airtest and he was given the Pilots' Notes with which to familiarise himself. He carried out some taxying of the aircraft and it was prepared for its test flight. However, during the German attack a low flying Me109 struck the nose of the Stirling at very high speed before crashing onto the airfield. Inevitably, the Stirling was wrecked and all the efforts to recover it were, in the end, wasted. The pilot subsequently commented that he was quite relieved not to have had to fly the Stirling!

03-Jan-45   LL355   Halifax   296 Sqn   5 miles south-west Diss Norfolk   1

The pilot, who despite having over 1600 flying hours to his credit had only 2 hours solo on the Halifax, was practicing three-engined flying when the port outer engine cut and caught fire whilst the aircraft was at 800 feet. The port wing dropped and the pilot lost control temporarily and having regained control attempted a forced landing straight ahead. Unfortuantely, the aircraft struck a tree during the forced landing and a member of the crew was killed whilst the other three on board were all injured. The engine failure was due to a connecting rod breaking and holing the crankcase. The connecting rod failed because of a failure of the engine's oil supply. It was recommended that asymmetric flying should be carried out not below 2000 feet but it is interesting to note how often a recommendation such as this is made but it was either not acted upon or ignored and was then repeated after another accident.

Flight Sergeant Frederick Charles JAMES 35

03-Jan-45   BT834   Hotspur II   5 GTS   Shobdon, Herefordshire   0

During a night training sortie, the glider landed heavily, bounced a couple of times and then landed on its nose. The RAF pilot was subsequently suspended from training following another accident.

04-Jan-45   LL380   Halifax   148 Sqn   15 miles south-west Susak   0

This aircraft was was one of eight sent to the same DZ in Yugoslavia. The crew made two passes of the DZ but on its return route to base, it was shot down by flak. The entire crew; captained by Flying Officer G

Date	Serial	Aircraft	Unit	Place	Casualties
		Brief Circumstances of Accident			
		Casualty Details (If Applicable)			

M Walker, baled out and survived.

| 04-Jan-45 | LK497 | Stirling III | 1332 CU | RAF Nutts Corner | 0 |

This aircraft suffered the usual outcome of an overshoot of the runway, when its undercarriage collapsed after it struck a ditch.

| 04-Jan-45 | FR574 | Hadrian | 21 HGCU | RAF Brize Norton | 0 |

The undercarriage was torn off in a heavy landing.

| 05-Jan-45 | DM360 | Master II | 5 GTS | Herefordshire Map Ref 980753 | 0 |

During an airtest and whilst flying at 2000 feet, this aircraft collided with an Oxford EB907. The engine caught fire and the pilot baled out. The Oxford is recorded as landing safely.

| 06-Jan-45 | Z9443 | Whitley V | 42 OTU | RAF Ashbourne | 0 |

The aircraft had been taxying from its dispersal area towards the runway for take-off on a training sortie. However, the pilot was recalled and as he was taxying back to dispersal, he initiated a gentle turn using differential engine power. The starboard undercarriage collapsed because of sheared rivets and other problems associated with fatigue damage to the undercarriage supporting structure.

| 07-Jan-45 | V1865 | Albermarle VI | ORTU | Wiggold Farm Gloucestershire | 0 |

The aircraft was being flown by an instructor, with only 68 hours on type, and a pupil pilot. The instructor was demonstrating asymmetric flying and the pupil was then handling the aircraft. As the crew attempted to unfeather the port engine at the conclusion of the phase, the constant speed unit oversped and the student stalled the aircraft at 2000 feet. The instructor took control, recovered the aircraft from the stall but was then compelled to use the starboard engine at a high power setting but was still unable to maintain height. A forced landing was made and neither crew was injured. The instructor was criticised for poor technique but it was accepted that the Pilots' Notes dealing with the feathering and unfeathering of propellers was inadequate and needed revision – this on an aircraft type which had been in service for several years and was obsolescent.

08-Jan-45 KG928 Liberator 178 Sqn Circhina, Yugoslavia 8

The aircraft failed to return from a supply dropping sortie. It was one of thirty eight aircraft, including eight from this squadron, despatched to Yugoslavia. The weather was appalling with severe icing problems and 10/10ths from 5000 feet with tops at 15000 feet. Almost all the aircraft which returned, did so without dropping but this aircraft was lost in circumstances which are not clear. Its crew did not survive and they are buried in a collective grave in Belgrade War Cemetery.

    Flying Officer James HORNOI 21 RCAF Pilot
    Sergeant Alan HELSBY 22 Navigator
    Sergeant Ronald Stewart MELTON Bomb Aimer
    Sergeant Robert Alfred REILLY 20 Wireless Operator
    Flight Sergeant Wilfred John FURNISS 32 Flight Engineer
    Flight Sergeant John Henry George MILSOM 22 Air Gunner
    Sergeant Davis Henry Brynmor NORMAN 21 Air Gunner
    Sergeant James Birnie WILSON

08-Jan-45 LP614 Wellington X 70 Sqn Near Gerova, south east of Trieste 0

This aircraft was another of the force of thirty eight Liberators and Wellingtons of 205 Gp sent to drop supplies to the same CRAYON DZ, as summarised above. On the return flight, the aircraft was forced landed because of the icing conditions but its crew survived and were eventually assisted by an allied mission to Yugoslavia.

Date	Serial	Aircraft	Unit	Place	Casualties
		Brief Circumstances of Accident			
		Casualty Details (If Applicable)			

08-Jan-45 P1651 Albemarle I 22 HGCU RAF Fairford 0

The day after making a forced landing in V1865, the pupil pilot was engaged on another sortie with a different pilot, who was also a student. A glide approach was being made to land but the aircraft landed heavily on the starboard wheel, causing the undercarriage to collapse. The aircraft bounced, landed on its port wheel, with equal force and the port undercarriage collapsed and the engine was dislodged completely from the wing. The Accident report comments that the pilot would need to be watched carefully when he became a glider tug pilot!

09-Jan-45 FZ648 Dakota 31 Sqn Kangla, Assam 0

The aircraft was taking off for a supply dropping sortie and it started to swing. The pilot failed to take immediate corrective action because he was concentrating on the aircraft ahead of his. In attempting to correct the swing, the pilot managed to lift the aircraft across a wide ditch but it did not become fully airborne and crashed into a paddy field beyond. The port engine caught fire and the blaze spread to the fuselage.

09-Jan-45 BT752 Hotspur II 5 GTS Shobdon, Herefordshire 0

The glider had just landed following a short sortie and whilst stopped and waiting to be retrieved by the tractor, it was struck by a Master II (DM381) which was taking off.

09-Jan-45 EB332 Whitley V 21 HGCU Brize Norton 0

The aircraft was taxying out for an airtest but it ran off the perimeter track and collided with a large notice board situated about 20 yards off the side.

10-Jan-45   KG599   Dakota   48 Sqn   B56   0

A USAAF B17 Fortress of the 324th Bomb Sqn of the 91st Bomb Group exploded whilst parked at the airfield and this aircraft was seriously damaged as a result.

10-Jan-45   KJ835   Dakota   108 OTU   Between Barrow on Soar and Sileby   3

The aircraft took off for a night cross country training sortie, in conditions of poor visibility and snow. Shortly after take-off and with the engines badly affected by carburettor icing, the pilot lost control and the aircraft dived into the ground and caught fire after impact. The weather was judged to have been unsuitable for night flying training and disciplinary action was instigated against the officer i/c night flying.

Warrant Officer Frederick Edward Henry DOBSON 26 Pilot

+ two RAF

11-Jan-45   HH922   Hamilcar   1 HGSU   Radnorshire Map Ref 917610   0

The aircraft was being flown on an endurance test and had been on tow for just over 2 hours. The weather was deteriorating and the glider did not have the Cable Angle Indicator (CAI) fitted and the intercom with the tug aircraft was not working. The tug towed the glider into the bad weather, rather than divert and so the glider pilot cast off the tow and forced landed.

11-Jan-45   FR577   Hadrian   21 HGCU   RAF Brize Norton   0

The glider struck a hedge on its approach to land and was damaged.

12-Jan-45   KJ435   Dakota IV   435 Sqn   3 miles from Tabingaug Airstrip   1

Seven crews were tasked to make a supply drop on a DZ near the town of Shwebo in Burma; the formation being led by Squadron Leader H J Coons DFC RCAF. The dropping would require each aircraft to make several passes, despatching part of the cargo on each circuit and this was going ahead when Coons wireless operator; Warrant Officer R O Buckmaster, spotted enemy fighters approaching. The formation was attacked

485

Date	Serial	Aircraft	Unit	Place	Casualties

Brief Circumstances of Accident
Casualty Details (If Applicable)

and Squadron Leader Coons aircraft was damaged by both enemy fire and striking a tree with its wing tip whilst taking avoiding action. Nonetheless, he attempted to draw enemy fire away from other aircraft and was subsequently awarded a Bar to his DFC. This aircraft was flown by Flight Lieutenant R F Simpson, an RAF officer serving on a predominantly RCAF unit, and it was attacked and set on fire after completing its first run. Attempts were made to jettison the cargo of ammunition but the aircraft was badly damaged and Warrant Officer Cotter wounded by a cannon shell in the stomach. The pilot made a crash landing in a clearing and the crew abandoned the aircraft before it was destroyed. Unfortunately, Cotter did not survive his injuries and died the following day: Simpson was awarded a DFC for his actions.

Warrant Officer David Grenfell COTTER 29 RCAF Wireless Operator (died of wounds 13 Jan 45)

| 12-Jan-45 | KJ899 | Dakota IV | 435 Sqn | 3 miles south of Shwebo | 5 |

This aircraft was attacked in similar circumstances to that described above. It was set on fire by a single pass from an enemy fighter and the captain ordered his crew to abandon the aircraft but only the co-pilot; Flying Officer A L Thomson survived.

Flight Lieutenant James Kenneth RAMSAY 24 RCAF Pilot
Flight Lieutenant Duncan Joseph MACKINNON 25 RCAF Bomb Aimer
Pilot Officer Edward Forseith WILLIAMS 27 RCAF
Leading Aircraftman Robert Harold PROSSER 20 RCAF
Leading Aircraftman Kenneth Allen SCOTT 19 RCAF

| 13-Jan-45 | LJ443 | Stirling III | 1332 CU | RAF Nutts Corner | 0 |

Whilst taking off for an airtest, the aircraft swung off the runway and into soft ground, causing the wheels to 'bog down' and the aircraft tipped onto its nose.

14-Jan-45   CG340?   Hadrian   361 MU   Binta, Bihar, India   0

The aircraft's serial number is not recognised and the glider is probably a US supplied machine. The pilot made his approach with the aircraft in a partially stalled condition and hence descending more rapidly than normal. It undershot and crashed through a wooden post fence and was substantially damaged.

16-Jan-45   HH147 Hostpur III   5 GTS   Shobdon, Herefordshire   0

Whilst landing from a night training sortie, the pilot was distracted when the sleeve of his flying suit snagged the flap lever. The glider flew into the ground and was damaged.

17-Jan-45   KG793 Dakota IV   435 Sqn   Tulihal, Assam   0+1

The aircraft made a normal landing at the conclusion of an operational sortie but it then collided with a native soldier who was riding a motorbike down the runway without lights. The soldier was killed and the impact caused the port undercarriage to collapse.

18-Jan-45   BT726 Hotspur II   3 GTS   Culmhead, Somerset   0

A gale was forecast and the aircraft in the open were double picketed. In gusts of over 60 mph, this glider was tossed onto its back.

18-Jan-45   LA684 Hamilcar   1 HGSU   RAF Tarrant Rushton   0

This glider and Hamilcars LA713, LA727, LA968, HH922 and HH968 were all damaged badly as a result of a severe gale.

18-Jan-45   DP599 Horsa   1 HGSU   RAF Tarrant Rushton   0

This glider, the Hamilcars listed above and Horsas RN820 and RN825 were all damaged in a severe gale.

Date	Serial	Aircraft	Unit	Place	Casualties
		Brief Circumstances of Accident			
		Casualty Details (If Applicable)			
18-Jan-45	LG731	Horsa	1 HGSU	RAF Broadwell	0
Damaged in a storm.					
18-Jan-45	LH331	Horsa	1 HGSU	RAF Great Dunmow	0
Damaged in a storm, along with Horsa RN926.					
18-Jan-45	77341	Hadrian	ORTU	RAF Fairford	0
This glider, which still carried its USAAF designation of 42- 77341, was damaged beyond repair in the gale referred to above, despite being properly picketted					
19-Jan-45	KH151	Liberator VI	301 Sqn	Off Campo Casale, Brindisi	3
The aircraft was returning from an operational sortie but on landing it overran the runway and crashed into the sea. Although four members of the crew; Pilot Officer Zygmunt Weyna, Warrant Officer Ludwik Skoczylas, Sergeant Andrzej Wandzel and Pilot Officer Jan Czarnota survived despite being injured, three others drowned.					
		Squadron Leader Witold ZURAWSKI PAF Navigator			
		Warrant Officer Edward GAGALA PAF			
		Warrant Officer Stanislaw SLOWIK PAF			
19-Jan-45	KJ931	Dakota	108 OTU	Missing	3
The aircraft took off on a night training sortie but did not return to base and its wreckage was never located. At the time the weather conditions were severe icing and the assumption is that the aircraft iced up, the relatively inexperienced pilot lost control and the aircraft crashed into the sea.					

Flight Sergeant Walter William PINFOLD Pilot
Believed to be:
  Sergeant William DEAN
  Sergeant James Lindsay CAMERON

19-Jan-45 FR655 Hadrian   343 Wg   Fatejang   0
On approach, the pilot decided there was sufficient room to land between a USAAF C47 and another glider – but there wasn't!! The aircraft struck both the other aircraft and was damaged.

20-Jan-45 KJ948 Dakota   62 Sqn   Comilla, Bengal   1
The port engine failed on take-off, just as the aircraft left the ground and it yawed violently. The pilot had no option but to throttle back and make a belly landing in a paddy field.

  Flight Sergeant Thomas James PATRICK 26 Bomb Aimer

20-Jan-45 V1848 Albemarle   22 HGCU   West Down Camp Salisbury Plain   2
The aircraft had been airborne for about 40 minutes and the crew was engaged in asymmetric flying and circuit training. Whilst flying at 500 feet, the handling pilot allowed the aircraft to stall and it entered a right hand spin, crashed and burnt out. There was no evidence of an engine failure and seems that the crew made an error of judgement in failing to maintain a safe flying speed. Neither pilot had much experience; one had 174 hours total and the other 145 hours, whilst both had barely an hour on type.

  Flying Officer Tom Urmson WILLIAMSON
  Flight Sergeant Dennis Oswald WHEATLEY 20

21-Jan-45 RX761 Horsa II   9 MU   RAF Netheravon   0
At the end of a 55 minute delivery flight, the glider was in the circuit for landing but the pilot turned too steeply and the glider stalled off the turn and crashed.

489

Date	Serial	Aircraft	Unit	Place	Casualties
Brief Circumstances of Accident					
Casualty Details (If Applicable)					

23-Jan-45   KH215   Liberator VI   358 Sqn   Missing, near Tisen   8

This aircraft and the two Liberators listed below were part of a formation of eleven aircraft from the squadron, undertaking the unit's first special duties operation since forming on 8 Nov 44. The targets for all aircraft were in French Indo China (now Vietnam) and whilst the weather at base was good, over the target areas it was appalling. Only the crews of the squadron commander; Wing Commander P G D Farr and Flying Officer Davison were successful in delivering their loads and six other aircraft returned to base with their cargoes. This crew and that of Squadron Leader Pim were lost in the same area and the wreckage of their aircraft were eventually found in positions; 23 degrees 08 North/93 degrees 46.5 East and 23 degrees 04 North/93 degrees 55 East, respectively. The theories as to the cause of loss included, fuel shortage because of loitering too long searching for the target and not being told to divert to Kunming, letting down in poor visibility over the Chin Hills in an attempt to force land in the Kalang Valley, descending to investigate a fire on the ground caused by the other aircraft's crash and striking the ground in the process.

Flight Lieutenant Kenneth Hartle BRAILSFORD 29 Pilot
Flying Officer Walter RUSSELL 22 RCAF Co-Pilot
Warrant Officer Gerard Alexander O'TOOLE 30 Navigator
Pilot Officer Leslie BLICK 35 Bomb Aimer
Warrant Officer J R SEVAIN Wireless Operator
Sergeant Joseph Charles GIBBS Wireless Operator
Warrant Officer Wwsley LEAR Air Gunne 22r
Pilot Officer Robert John WILSON 25 Air Gunner

23-Jan-45   KH277   Liberator VI   358 Sqn   Missing, near Nimzawl   8

This aircraft was lost in the position 23 degrees 04 North/93 degrees 55 East, as summarised above but the wreck was not discovered for some time. Whilst five of the crew were found in the aircraft and identified, no trace of Holt, Gittins or Robinson could be found, which opens the possibility that they had abandoned the aircraft prior to its crash.

Squadron Leader Anthony Stanley Mortimer PIM
Flight Sergeant John Hewitt HOLT 23 Co-Pilot
Flight Sergeant Erik Cairne HEARN 22 Navigator
Flying Officer William John WALLACE Bomb Aimer
Flying Officer Eric CLARKE Wireless Operator
Sergeant George GITTINS Wireless Operator
Flight Sergeant Sidney Ernest SADLER 27 RNZAF Air Gunner
Sergeant James Alfred ROBINSON 26 Air Gunner

23-Jan-45   KH278   Liberator VI   358 Sqn   Missing, location not known   8

This aircraft and its crew were lost without trace and the men listed below are commemorated on the Singapore Memorial. A USAF officer, Colonel Peter Dunn was undertaking a research project in 1986, in which he explored the origins of the Vietnam Conflict, at that time at its height. Colonel Dunn recorded that the aircraft had been deliberately shot down by USAAF fighters but what the evidence is for making that statement is not known. It was, of course, true that there were sharp differences of policy between British and US governments over how to deal with various resistance groups and the US was firmly opposed to the re-establishment of colonial rule in south east Asia post-war

Flight Lieutenant Stanley Douglas MAYHEW 28 Pilot
Warrant Officer Noel Charles EAMES Co-Pilot
Flight Sergeant William George ROBERTS 31 Navigator
Pilot Officer John HUGHES 23 Bomb Aimer
Sergeant Victor Arthur Frederick BUTT Wireless Operator
Flying Officer John Alan SCHMIDT 20 RAAF Wireless Operator
Sergeant John Richard PERRY Air Gunner
Sergeant Frank William MOORE Air Gunner

25-Jan-45   FD884   Dakota III   117 Sqn   Hathazari, Bengal   0

The pilot failed to control a swing to port during the take-off run and the aircraft hit a ditch. Both the main and tail undercarriages were ripped off by the impact.

26-Jan-45   EW142   Liberator   178 Sqn   Yugoslavia   7

This aircraft was one of fifty two tasked with dropping supplies to DZs coded TOFFEE and BALLINCLAY. Although there were no problems in the area of the DZ, aircraft routed via Senica (in what is now Bosnia) were subjected to heavy flak and it appears this aircraft fell to guns in that area.

    Flying Officer Bert JOB Pilot
    Flight Sergeant Frank TRUMAN Navigator
    Pilot Officer John BAXTER 22 Bomb Aimer
    Flying Officer Ashley Harrad NICHOLLS 22 Wireless Operator
    Sergeant Philip Vigors TIRAN Flight Engineer
    Sergeant Thomas Charles WALKER 21 Air Gunner
    Warrant Officer Alfred HUNDLEY 30 Air Gunner

26-Jan-45   JP281   Halifax II   148 Sqn   Mount Kamesnica, 40 miles south-west Knin   8

The crew was engaged on a daylight supply drop to a DZ at Virovitica in northern Yugoslavia, as part of an SOE operation ICARUS MINOR 117. The drop was completed successfully and the crew reported their ETA at base but the aircraft never arrived. It was eventually discovered at the location shown and it had flown into the mountain in heavy snow. The co-pilot, newly posted to the unit, was taking part in his first familiarisation sortie before taking his own crew on operations.

    Flight Lieutenant George Barry STRANG 25 RAAF Pilot

492

Flight Lieutenant Harry Edmund HORSFALL 26 RNZAF Co-Pilot
    Flying Officer Walter Harold WILSON 23 Navigator
    Flying Officer Raymond HOWARTH 29 Bomb Aimer
    Flying Officer Henry Oscar MASON 31 RAAF believed to be Wireless Operator
    Sergeant John Wardman HOLMES 36 Flight Engineer
    Sergeant Denis Patrick BURNS 20 Air Gunner
    Sergeant Gordon DIFFY Air Gunner

| 28-Jan-45 | KJ944 | Dakota IV | 194 Sqn | Imphal | 0 |

The port tyre burst on take-off and the aircraft's undercarriage collapsed when it swung off the runway.

| 28-Jan-45 | LL445 | Halifax V | 296 Sqn | Tuddenham Hill Near Ipswich | 0 |

The crew was engaged on an air/sea firing exercise and the aircraft had been airborne for about 20 minutes. Whilst flying at 1000 feet, the aircraft was flown into a snow storm with the engines carburettor settings in the 'cold air' position and an outside air temperature below freezing. All four engines failed because of an accumulation of snow in the air intakes and the pilot made a forced landing in a field. This sort of error is perhaps surprising from an experienced pilot who would, within a few weeks be promoted squadron leader and shortly afterwards be awarded a DFC.

| 29-Jan-45 | KG610 | Dakota | 437 Sqn | B75 | 0 |

The aircraft was landing at the conclusion of a freight carrying sortie but the pilot was making a fast approach and the aircraft bounced on touchdown. Instead of overshooting for another attempt, the pilot carried on with the landing, despite there being an aircraft ahead still on the runway. This aircraft overran and struck the other Dakota before colliding with a Mustang which had crashed earlier. Flying Control was criticised for allowing this aircraft to land when the runway was not clear and the pilot was censured for his poor handling of the situation.

Date	Serial	Aircraft	Unit	Place	Casualties
		Brief Circumstances of Accident			
		Casualty Details (If Applicable)			

29-Jan-45   RJ127   Horsa I   1 HGSU   RAF Shepherds Grove   0

This aircraft was parked on the runway and another Horsa, at the end of its landing run, ran into it. There seems to have been some disagreement as to whether this glider constituted a hazard but given the limited options available to a glider pilot, it might be judged best to keep other aircraft as far from the landing area as possible.

30-Jan-45   EW628   Liberator   1332 HCU   Standing Stones Hill, Ulster   0

The pilot, who despite having nearly 2500 flying hours, had little experience of instrument flying at night and most of his time had been spent on 'contact' flying in light aircraft. Whilst undertaking a night sortie, he found it difficult to cope with alternate conditions of bright moonlight and patches of low cloud. In consequence he did not check his altimeter and the aircraft struck high ground at 1000 feet above sea level. The aircraft was destroyed by fire but all five on board escaped with injuries. It also transpired that the pilot had been sent solo without a dual check but it is interesting that no mention is made of the actions of the co-pilot, who might reasonably have assisted his captain and warned of the proximity of the ground.

31-Jan-45   KG757   Dakota   435 Sqn   0

The aircraft was destroyed by fire whilst undergoing maintenance.

01-Feb-45   KK194   Dakota   45 Gp   Isle of Mull   3

The aircraft was approaching Prestwich at the conclusion of a 6 ¼ hour ferry flight. A descent was made into cloud without ascertaining an accurate position and the aircraft struck high ground. Although five people survived, the pilot and two others were killed.

Flying Officer F BISHOP Pilot

494

Pilot Officer Thomas Brown Milne ALEXANDER Navigator
Warrant Officer I Gilbert NICHOLS RCAF Wireless Operator

01-Feb-45	KN289 Dakota	112 Wg	Bury Quebec	0

The pilot selected the empty internal fuel tanks and the engines cut due to fuel starvation. A forced landing was made in a field

01-Feb-45	MW116 York I	511Sqn	Off Lampedusa Island	15

The aircraft crashed into the sea and was destroyed during an attempted ditching in position 35 degrees 30 North/12 degrees 35 East (off Lampedusa Island) at 1934 hours GMT. This aircraft was one of the support aircraft carrying staff and other personnel involved in the Yalta Conference. There were a series of errors in navigation, the Met forecasts obtained by the wireless operator were out of date and the crew did not obtain any reliable radio bearings to allow them to reach Malta. The aircraft circled over Lampedusa for over an hour and it seems there was some confusion about whether they thought they were at Malta and could not pinpoint their position.

Flight Sergeant Alfred Claude Jack WALKER 21 Flight Engineer
Flying Officer Arthur APPLEBY 24 Air Gunner
Warrant Officer William WRIGHT 25 Wireless Operator
Leading Aircraftman John CHICKEN 36
Lieutenant Colonel Ivor Stuart Huntly HOOPER 37 West Yorkshire Regiment
Lieutenant Colonel Wilfred George NEWEY DSO TD
Captain Albany Kennett CHARLESWORTH 52 MC Royal Armoured Corps
Captain William Henry FINCH 55 MBE General List
Group Captain Philip Stuart JACKSON-TAYLOR
Mr Armine Roderick DEW 38 MVO First Secretary Foreign Office
Mr Peter Noel LOXLEY 39 First Secretary Foreign Office
Mr John CHAPLIN 34 Second Secretary Foreign Office

Captain Robert MacDonald GUTHRIE 48 RM King's Messenger
Inspector Harry Joseph BATTLEY 36 Special Branch
Miss Patricia Maxwell SULLIVAN 23 Foreign Office

02-Feb-45   HH139   Hotspur II   5 GTS   Shobdon   0

The officer in charge of flying, ordered the gliders to be taken outside, even though there was the residue of a gale being experienced in the area. This glider was blown over and crashed into another Hotspur (BT606).

02-Feb-45   LP549   Wellington X   104 Sqn   Near Lake Lesina   5

This aircraft was one of a force of seventy three aircraft despatched to a DZ FLOTSAM. During the return flight, the aircraft crashed in Yugoslavia and its crew was killed.

Flying Officer Trevor Aston GILL 22 Pilot
Sergeant Francis Ronald FLESCH 21 Navigator
Flying Officer Robert Joseph ROWE 28 Bomb Aimer
Flight Sergeant James Melvin FREEMAN 20 Wireless Operator
Sergeant Harold LEWIS 24 Air Gunner

03-Feb-45   JP277   Halifax   148 Sqn   Yugoslavia   0

The squadron was tasked with nine daylight sorties and ten night sorties, although in fact the aircraft for two of the former went unserviceable before take-off and another returned early with engine trouble. This aircraft failed to return from a sortie to an unknown DZ in Yugoslavia. The aircraft was seen to crash onto the DZ and its crew; captained by Warrant Officer M S Bruce, was seen to escape from the wreckage and all survived. The cause of the loss is not recorded but it is not thought to have been due to enemy action.

03-Feb-45 LL351 Halifax V 297 Sqn Essex 1

The aircraft, which was fully laden for a bombing sortie , was taking off and at 100 feet on the climb severe vibration was felt. The pilot throttled back and the aircraft crashed landed and was destroyed by fire. The accident was caused by an incorrect selection of the bomb bay doors open instead of the undercarriage being retracted and this placed the aircraft in a semi stalled condition and hence the vibration.

Flight Sergeant William Edward STRACHEN 22

03-Feb-45 DL476 Master II 3 GTS ½ mile west of RAF Exeter 0

Whilst flying at a height of 150 feet and towing a Hotspur (HH460), the tug aircraft suffered an engine failure and was forced landed. The pilot; Flight Sergeant M B Morton-Smith, survived but the cause of the engine cutting is not recorded.

04-Feb-45 LL367 Halifax V 148 Sqn El Aouina, Tunisia 0

The aircraft was being delivered to the maintenance Unit and on landing its port tyre burst. The aircraft swung off the runway and into soft ground, causing the undercarriage to fail.

04-Feb-45 LJ995 Stirling IV 295 Sqn Lambas Green, 1½ miles west of Rivenhall 0

The pilot was carrying out his first night take-off with a fully laden aircraft, as part of a bombing sortie. The pilot failed to correct an initial swing and then attempted to lift the aircraft off the ground at too low an airspeed. With the undercarriage still down, the drag was significant and the aircraft struck trees, crashed and burst into flames before exploding when the fire set off the bombs. Surprisingly, the crew survived uninjured.

04-Feb-45 77262 Hadrian 1 IGS 4 miles north of Cutavecchia, Italy 0

The glider, which retained its US serial number, was cast off from its tow by the crew, when they became aware that the fabric was tearing off the glider. An emergency landing was made but subsequently it was

497

Date	Serial	Aircraft	Unit	Place	Casualties

Brief Circumstances of Accident
Casualty Details (If Applicable)

decided to scrap all the Hadrian gliders being used in this area because their general condition was so poor after a long period with minimal maintenance.

04-Feb-45   LP559   Wellington X   40 Sqn   Near Apricena, Italy   4

The aircraft was operating as one of sixty nine sent to two DZs coded FLOTSAM and CRAYON, in a late alteration to plans because of prevailing weather. Not long after take-off, this aircraft struck a spur of high ground at an altitude of 600 feet whilst turning to port but below safety height and in conditions of thick cloud from 300 feet. All crews had been briefed to maintain visual contact with the ground but if this was not possible to climb to safety height. Due to the local geography, they were warned against flying into and out of cloud.

    Flying Officer Cecil Frank WELLMAN 22 Pilot
    Flight Sergeant Alan MACLEOD 22 Navigator
    Flying Officer David Thompson BLAIN 23 Bomb Aimer
    Sergeant Daniel STOTT 22 Bomb Aimer

04-Feb-45   ME993   Wellington X   40 Sqn   Near Apricena   5

This crew was engaged on the same task as the Wellington listed above. It was returning after a sortie of 4 ¼ hours, having dropped its supplies as briefed. The aircraft was, however, off course due to the bad weather and it is thought that the pilot was descending through cloud when the aircraft struck high ground.

    Flying Officer John Noel HICKEY 25 Pilot
    Sergeant Clifford Henry JONES 20 Navigator
    Sergeant Kenneth Victor DENNIS 21 Bomb Aimer

Flight Sergeant Peter Mitchell HOLT 23 Wireless Operator
Sergeant Albert Cyril LLOYD 22 Air Gunner

04-Feb-45   MF371   Wellington X   40 Sqn   Sanni Candro   4

The aircraft crashed into high ground in circumstances similar to those described above. The rear gunner was the sole survivor.

Flight Sergeant Colin SUNDERLAND 21 Pilot
Sergeant Ralph Charles BURTON 21 Navigator
Flight Sergeant Edward MULPETER 20
Sergeant John PURDON 20 Wireless Operator

04-Feb-45   LP549   Wellington X   104 Sqn   Near Lake Lesina   5

This aircraft was another of the sixty nine sent to drop supplies to two DZs in Yugoslavia. On return the pilot attempted to spiral down through cloud, which had its base at 200 feet, although he was off course and probably unaware of his position. Whilst doing so, the aircraft struck high ground at a height of 500 feet and was destroyed.

Sergeant Norman Robert DAYNES 22 Pilot
Sergeant Laurence SMITH 21 Navigator
Flight Sergeant Boyce Herbert CHAPPELL 23 Bomb Aimer
Flight Sergeant Harold Ramsey WOODARD 20 Wireless Operator
Flight Sergeant Andrew Mark SCOTT 21 Air Gunner

05-Feb-45   Z6473   Whitley V   42 OTU   RAF Ashbourne   0

The pilot, who had little experience of flying large heavy aircraft, was attempting to land in conditions of rain, poor visibility and strong winds with violent thundery squalls. The aircraft touched down whilst drifting and its skidded sideways on the wet grass before its undercarriage collapsed. It was commented that Flying Control ought to have advised the pilot to remain airborne until the bad weather, which was

499

Date	Serial	Aircraft	Unit	Place	Casualties

Brief Circumstances of Accident
Casualty Details (If Applicable)

localised, had passed through.

05-Feb-45   KG409 Dakota III   437 Sqn   Between Alton and Winchester   0

The aircraft was on a freight carrying sortie and the pilot initiated a descent through cloud without first confirming his position accurately. In very poor visibility of less than 1000 yards and a cloud base of 300 feet, the aircraft struck the tops of trees and this caused both structural damage and put an engine out of action. The pilot climbed the aircraft to 1800 feet and the 4 occupants abandoned the aircraft by parachute.

05-Feb-45   KJ892   Dakota   117 Sqn   Hathazari   0

The aircraft swung off the runway during take-off and its undercarriage collapsed. It was not repaired.

05-Feb-45   NA120 Halifax III   298 Sqn   RAF Tarrant Rushton   0

The pilot, who had very little flying experience on the Halifax, had been briefed for a low level cross country sortie not below 500 feet AGL. At some point in the 1½ hour sortie, his aircraft struck trees and the pitot tube was broken, rendering the air speed indicator inoperative. On arrival at base, a fast approach was made to a short runway and the pilot failed to apply the brakes properly before the aircraft swung. Eventually, he selected undercarriage 'Up' after the aircraft overshot the runway and ran down a bank. The findings of the investigation conclude by stating; 'the pilot should be transferred or trained as a navigator'!

06-Feb-45   KG630 Dakota   575 Sqn   Hunters Burgh, Folkington, Sussex   23

The aircraft was one of seven from the squadron undertaking a unit move by personnel of 140 Wing from UK to the continent. As the weather was so poor and there was considerable disruption to the schedule, the move took several days. On the second day of the mission, this aircraft took off from RAF Thorney

Island at about 0935 hours and some 30 minutes later, whilst flying in cloud and below safety height, it struck a hill at about 500 feet. The starboard wing fractured and the aircraft fell into a wood at the foot of the hill and was destroyed by fire. All those on board the aircraft were killed.

Warrant Officer Peter Matthew OLEINIKOFF 34 RAAF Pilot

Flight Sergeant Edgar Alan BARSBY 20 RAAF Co-Pilot

Flying Officer Kenneth Gilbert FORSETH 22 RCAF Navigator

Flight Sergeant Ronald Arthur BROCK 21 RCAF Wireless Operator

Flying Officer Edward William CURTIS 40

Pilot Officer Colin Alexander RATTRAY 22

Corporal Colin GIBSON 21

Corporal Gerald Ernest Nelson David LEE 33

Corporal William George BLAIR 23 RNZAF

Corporal Edwin Bruce CHADD 38

Corporal David COOPER 24

Leading Aircraftman Frank BAINBRIDGE 24

Leading Aircraftman Ronald Grayham BALDRY 21

Leading Aircraftman Samuel Arthur BAMBER 30

Leading Aircraftman William Daniel DAVIES 44

Leading Aircraftman Thomas Henry FLOODY 23

Leading Aircraftman Jack NEALE 35

Leading Aircraftman Woolf NERDEN 23

Leading Aircraftman Robert SMITH 23

Leading Aircraftman Sydney MacKenzie SMITH RCAF

Leading Aircraftman George STEVENS 22

Leading Aircraftman Albert Edward Dowler WILKES 35

Leading Aircraftman George WILSON 22

Date	Serial	Aircraft	Unit	Place	Casualties

Brief Circumstances of Accident
Casualty Details (If Applicable)

06-Feb-45 KL386 Liberator 45 Gp Kindley Field Bermuda 5

The aircraft crashed into the sea shortly after take-off following a refuelling stop. It was en-route to the Middle East but its precise allocation is not known, although it was likely to have been intended for one of the heavy bomber squadrons rather than the Poles.

Hugh Murray MARTIN Pilot (Candian civilian)
Edward Craig TALBOT Co-Pilot (Canadian civilian)
Pilot Officer William Arnold COOTT RCAF Navigator
Jean-Pierre LAGADEC Wireless Operator (Canadian civilian)
Sergeant Arthur Charles Alfred GRACE 28 Flight Engineer

06-Feb-45 KN271 Dakota 45 Gp At sea 5

The aircraft disappeared without trace after departing airfield BW-1 en route to Reykjavik and there is no evidence as to the cause of its loss.

Squadron Leader Zozislaw Waclaw HIRSZ PAF Pilot
Pilot Officer Denis WASHER Co-Pilot
Flight Sergeant William Roy GREGORY Navigator
Flight Lieutenant Herbert Bond CLARKE Wireless Operator

06-Feb-45 V1752 Albemarle II 22 HGCU RAF Keevil 0

Whilst approaching to land, the aircraft was baulked by another. In his attempt to avoid a collision and overshoot, the pilot allowed a wing to touch the ground and the aircraft was damaged.

07-Feb-45 EB361 Whitley V 42 OTU RAF Ashbourne 0

The pilot was landing in strong gusty winds and the aircraft touched down on the port side of the runway, at a higher than normal speed. The aircraft swung to port and went off the side of the runway and onto rough ground before the pilot could correct he swing. The undercarriage collapsed.

07-Feb-45   KH207 Liberator VI   34 SAAF   RAF Celone, Italy   0

The aircraft had been used on a supply dropping sortie and was returning after 3¾ hours airborne. The aircraft's undercarriage was giving trouble with the nose wheel refusing to lock down and then having to be blown down by the emergency system. On landing the port undercarriage leg failed and the aircraft was damaged badly.

07-Feb-45   KJ845 Dakota   436 Sqn   24 degrees 50North/94 degrees 55 East   0

On return from an operational supply dropping sortie, the crew was unable to make contact with the various radio beacons for homing because the frequencies had been changed without prior warning! Some ground control facilities were contacted but some of these faded, whilst others passed false vectors. The pilot climbed aircraft on a safe heading but the situation was complicated because a serious oil leak had caused the port engine to cut. Eventually with fuel exhausted, the crew of five abandoned the aircraft safely and all were recovered. It has to be wondered at the arrangements which existed for ensuring that something as fundamental as changes to radio frequencies, were not properly promulgated. There are other occasions where ground control stations passed incorrect information to aircrews and again this raises serious questions as to the training given to ground control personnel.

07-Feb-45   LL384 Halifax   296 Sqn   South of Lille France   0

During an operational bombing sortie, the aircraft's port outer engine lost oil pressure but the propeller would not feather properly and continued to run at 1400 rpm, although height was being lost at the rate of 150 feet per minute. The bombs were jettisoned at low level and it was too low to bale out so the engine was unfeathered as the pilot attempted to climb to an altitude to abandon the aircraft. At this point the engine caught fire and the pilot was faced with a crash landing in the dark. The aircraft struck overhead cables and a church spire before crashing into a street. Fortunately, the entire crew survived, although they were injured.

Date	Serial	Aircraft	Unit	Place	Casualties

Brief Circumstances of Accident

Casualty Details (If Applicable)

07-Feb-45   V1970   Albemarle   22 HGCU   RAF Keevil   0

The aircraft was being landed at the conclusion of a glider training sortie but at the end of the landing run, the pilot selected undercarriage 'Up' instead of the flaps. The aircraft settled onto its belly and considerable damage was sustained.   Although neither crew member was injured, the pilot had his Flying Logbook endorsed 'Gross Carelessness', he was Reproved by his station commander and posted away to the Aircrew Refresher School.

07-Feb-45   KK712   Hadrian II   361 MU   Tajpur, Bihar, India   0

Whilst being towed at 2500 feet, the glider was cast off because the Dakota tug aircraft suffered an engine failure. A forced landing was made in a field and although the aircraft was damaged, the pilot was unhurt.

09-Feb-45   MZ980   Halifax III   298 Sqn   Donegal Bay   2

The aircraft was on a navigational training exercise and had been airborne for over 9 hours.   The crew became completely lost when unpredicted changes to wind speed and direction were encountered and it became impossible to use the radio or radar aids services.   The aircraft was badly iced up and so a climb to height was not feasible and when the crew spotted the coastline, none was able to identify its location. Eventually, the aircraft was ditched as the fuel supplies became critical but the dinghy would only inflate partially because its valves were iced up.   Two of the crew were lost; the flight engineer during the ditching and the bomb aimer dying subsequently.   This aircraft's captain was particularly unfortunate because he and his reconstituted crew were killed during Operation VARSITY 6 weeks later.

Flight Lieutenant John CARR 27 RCAF Bomb Aimer
Sergeant John Alan MCKAINE 23 Flight Engineer

504

10-Feb-45   K7000   Harrow II   271 Sqn   Brussels Evere   0

The aircraft, which was configured for its 'Sparrow' casualty evacuation role, was taxying prior to take-off when its tailwheel dropped into an unmarked hole. The pilot, who judged the impact to be commensurate with taxying across the rough ground carried on for a short distance, thus exacerbating the damage. None of the three crew or twenty others on board was injured.

10-Feb-45   KJ927   Dakota IV   357 Sqn   Near Mount Victoria, Chin Hills   4

This aircraft was one of four from the squadron operating to the same DZ during a daylight sortie. Three crews returned safely but only after being forced to climb to very high altitudes, when extremely bad weather with severe turbulence was encountered. This crew had reported their successful completion of the drop but failed to return and the wreckage of the aircraft was found eventually in the Chin Hills near Mount Victoria. The weather continued to be awful for a further 10 days before easing and allowing the crews to return to supply sorties into Indo China

    Warrant Officer James Warwick Davison REID 25 RAAF Pilot
    Warrant Officer Jack HARTLEY 22
    Flight Sergeant James Leslie LONGHURST 23
    Flight Sergeant Thomas Porteous NATHANIEL 20

10-Feb-45   LK279   Stirling   138 Sqn   Lille Balt, Denmark   7

Seven squadron aircraft were detailed for sorties to Denmark but their crews encountered very poor weather and none was successful. This crew became lost in a severe snow storm and the aircraft crashed into the Lille Balt, the stretch of water separating Jutland from the Isle of Fyn.

    Flight Sergeant Lawrence Stanley TUCKER 22 RAAF Pilot
    Sergeant William Maurice HARAGAN 20
    Flight Sergeant Geoffrey Chapman TOES 22
    Warrant Officer Ronald James BALL 22

Flying Officer Gordon Ernest MERCER
Flight Sergeant Richard York FRENCH 21
Flight Sergeant William John CARTHEW 22

11-Feb-45   KG711 Dakota III   44 SAAF   Otok, Yugoslavia   0

The aircraft, which was engaged on an operational infiltration sortie behind enemy lines, was taking off whilst heavily laden. The take-off run, which was restricted to 800 yards over very soft ground, proved inadequate and the aircraft struck a tree at the end of the strip and crashed.

11-Feb-45   LA737 Hamilcar   1 HGSU   2 miles west of RAF Tarrant Rushton   1

Shortly after take-off, the glider pilot got his aircraft out of position to the extent that the tow rope parted. An attempt was made to force land but the glider overshot the selected field, then crashed into trees whilst trying to reach another field. It was commented that the pilot had had insufficient experience before being transferred to a Hamilcar squadron. It was also noted that the flaps had not been lowered which would result in a faster approach speed. The 2nd pilot survived but the 1st pilot was killed.

Sergeant Kenneth John WILLIAMS 22

12-Feb-45   FD915 Dakota III   435 Sqn   Budalin area   5

The aircraft failed to return from a supply dropping sortie and as its wreck was never discovered, it is unclear how the aircraft was lost.

Flying Officer Thomas Gray BURTON RCAF
Pilot Officer Ward Douglas COULSON 25 RCAF
Pilot Officer Stanley Maxwell DUNCAN RCAF

Flying Officer William Andrew EDEN 20 RCAF
Pilot Officer Ralph Henry HOLTAN 29 RCAF

12-Feb-45   FL644   Dakota   194 Sqn   Imphal, Assam   0

The port tyre burst during the take-off run and the aircraft went off the left side of the runway before running into a ditch about 50 yards from the runway's edge. The burst tyre was attributed in part to the stresses imposed on it by the crosswind but also to manufacturing flaws in tyres, which were quickly exposed on hard used transport aircraft.

13-Feb-45   FD928   Dakota   62 Sqn   Near Kangla Assam   4

The aircraft was returning from a supply dropping sortie and had been diverted from its home base because of the poor weather conditions prevailing. It seems the crew did not receive the diversion message and once again the radio frequencies were changed by arrangements with the USAAF authorities but not notified to this crew in their pre-sortie briefing. On reaching the airfield the weather conditions were found to be cloud with a ceiling of 400 feet but despite knowing there were hills in close proximity to the airfield, the pilot descended into the cloud and the aircraft struck the high ground and burst into flames after impact. Subsequently, it was discovered that the signal notifying the frequency changes had not been received by the parent squadron until 5 hours after the accident. It was commented that the Wing HQ could have passed the frequency change direct to the aircraft on the existing frequency before the change was implemented.

   Flight Lieutenant Joseph Barker GOODWIN 35 Pilot
   Flying Officer Frank Hubert PICKARD 21 Co-Pilot
   Flight Sergeant Harry WOODHOUSE 23 Navigator
   Flight Sergeant Ronald James HILL 23 Wireless Operator

13-Feb-45   V1864   Albemarle VI   22 HGCU   RAF Keevil   0

The pilot was landing the aircraft at the conclusion of a 45 minute glider towing sortie but had the glare of

507

low winter sun in his eyes. He touched down to the port side of the runway and went off the side before crashing into a pair of Horsas, which had been marshalled correctly. Although there was a slight crosswind, it was judged that the pilot, who had made previous landings in similar conditions, had displayed gross carelessness and he was returned to an AFU for further training.

Date	Serial	Aircraft	Unit	Place	Casualties
13-Feb-45	LH338	Horsa I	22 HGCU	RAF Keevil	0

This glider was written off as a consequence of the accident summarised above.

Date	Serial	Aircraft	Unit	Place	Casualties
14-Feb-45	FD820	Dakota III	117 Sqn	Between Hathazart and Kan airstrip	5

The aircraft was lost in hills on its way to the Mandalay Plain where it was to have dropped supplies to 14th Army units. The aircraft would have had to cross the Chin Hills at 10000 feet, with icing conditions reported at 11000 feet and it is not thought this would have made the aircraft unstable. This particular airframe did not have de-icing boots fitted but its carburettors were supplied with hot air for de-icing. Although conjecture, it is thought possible that the aircraft struck hills due to a navigational error

Flying Officer Deckland Archibald BAYLEY RCAF Pilot
Flying Officer William Ronald THOMSON 21 RCAF Co-Pilot
Flying Officer Lloyd Elmer LONG 23 RCAF Wireless Operator
Pilot Officer Everett Elroy NEWELL 23 RCAF Navigator
Flight Lieutenant John William SLATER 29 RCAF Navigator

Date	Serial	Aircraft	Unit	Place	Casualties
14-Feb-45	JP249	Halifax	148 Sqn	Yugoslavia	?

No details of this aircraft's sortie were found.

14-Feb-45   LK236 Stirling   161 Sqn   Potton near RAF Tempsford   7+1

The crew had been engaged in a training sortie and had returned to the airfield circuit at Tempsford prior to landing in conditions of poor visibility and mist. A Mustang, serial 42-106448, of the USAAF's 383rd Fighter Squadron of the 364th Fighter Group 'bounced' the aircraft and collided with it. Both aircraft crashed and all crew members were killed.

     Flying Officer Eric TIMPERLEY 34 Pilot
     Sergeant Derrick Howard MAYERS 19
     Sergeant William George CORNISH
     Flying Officer George Colin WIGGINS 28 RAAF
     Flight Sergeant Cyril William SAUNDERS 25
     Flight Sergeant Peter Norman CARR 21
     Sergeant Peter Norman ELLIS
     Flight Officer Thomas W KILEY 20 USAAF

Note: The USAAF did not employ non commissioned personnel in the principal roles of pilot, navigator and bombardier. Those personnel who were suitable for these duties but not necessarily for the award of a commission were appointed to a sort of limbo position of Flight Officer.

14-Feb-45   V1993 Albemarle VI   21 HGCU   East of RAF Brize Norton   0

The aircraft was taking off on a glider towing and cross country exercise with a Horsa glider and as it passed about 600 feet, the port engine failed because of faulty spark plugs. The glider was cast off and made a safe forced landing with damaging the glider. However, the pilot of this aircraft was unable to maintain its height and so made a forced landing in a field.

15-Feb-45   FZ679 Dakota III   437 Sqn   Lyons, France   0

The aircraft was taking off on an operational sortie when its starboard engine cut. The pilot closed the throttles and controlled the aircraft with the rudder but swung off the runway and its starboard main tyre

Date Brief Circumstances of Accident	Serial	Aircraft Casualty Details (If Applicable)	Unit	Place	Casualties

burst when it ran over a bomb tail fin, which was lying on the ground. The aircraft's starboard wing struck a French Air Force B26 in the tail unit and then slewed sideways into another B26.

17-Feb-45	KN251	Dakota IV	238 Sqn	Castel Benito	0

On take-off the aircraft would not climb more than a few feet and tended to yaw to starboard. The pilot closed the throttles and raised the undercarriage to stop. The pilot had failed to use the full runway length and had left the starboard engine cowls open. In addition he attempted to pull off too steeply. Despite having over 2000 flying hours the pilot was inexperienced on type and had just 34 hours on the Dakota. One wonders what the 15 others on board would have said had they known in advance!

17-Feb-45	KJ890	Dakota III	117 Sqn	Burma	4

This aircraft is recorded as 'missing in the forward area' but the circumstances of its loss are not known. The crew are commemorated on the Singapore memorial and hence it is assumed the wreck of the aircraft was not located subsequently.

    Flying Officer Edward Gordon WARRINGTON 29 Pilot
    Flying Officer Denis D'Arcy BATCHELOR 29
    Flight Sergeant Frederick Richard BLIGHT
    Flying Officer Stanley Ernest HUYGENS 23

17-Feb-45	V1983	Albemarle VI	21 HGCU	Coursehill Farm, Ducklington	0

The aircraft was returning to base after just over 2 hours of a training sortie and it was on the downwind leg to land' flying at 400 feet. The port engine's Constant Speed Unit failed and the propeller went into the fully fine setting. The pilot was unable to reach the airfield and so a forced landing was attempted but the aircraft hit trees and belly landed. Subsequent examination of the wreck showed that the port propeller was in fine have proved difficult reaching the airfield in any event.

18-Feb-45   MW112   York I   511 Sqn   RAF Lyneham   0

This aircraft had a tyre burst on take-off and its undercarriage collapsed in the ensuing swing. It was categorised as a write-off and the Accident Card records it as Category 'E'. However, a reassessment of the damage led to the aircraft status being modified and it was taken to Waddington where its was rebuilt over the following 7 months and returned to service. It was eventually used by A&AEE and damaged in another accident in 1950. Four years later it was struck off charge and reduced to spares in 1954.

19-Feb-45   LJ870   Stirling IV   196 Sqn   RAF Shepherds Grove   0

Whilst making an emergency landing with engine trouble, the aircraft swung and its undercarriage collapsed.

19-Feb-45   TS436   Dakota III   107 OTU   Search Farm, 2½ miles north-west Zeals   20

The aircraft was assigned to the Glider Pick-Up Training Flt, whose role was to train crews in the 'snatch take-off' method for retrieving gliders. Those on board were mostly returning to their base in Leicester, on completion of the course of instruction at Zeals. The aircraft took off at 1523 hours in conditions of broken cloud, with some patches down to 100 feet and generally overcast, a westerly wind at 10 mph and visibility of 1 to 2 miles at ground level. The pilot made a quarter circuit of the airfield and then set course to the north-east. Three minutes later whilst flying in and out of the broken cloud and whilst in level flight, the aircraft flew into a clump of 60 foot tall beech trees on top of a knoll. The impact ripped 10 feet off the port wing and the aircraft rolled to port, hit two more trees and then impaled itself on a cluster of four mature trees, caught fire and disintegrated, scattering wreckage over a distance of 300 yards on the far side of the knoll. Destruction of the aircraft was complete but investigation revealed the engines to have been at a high power setting on impact. The Accident Report, published on 17 May 45, suggests that the pilot who was the sole survivor, had failed to climb to a safe height when flying in poor visibility, although the knoll was a well known obstruction in close proximity to the airfield. The tragic sequel to this loss is that the pilot, who had been awarded the DFC for his gallantry on operations, followed a restless career afterwards

leaving and returning to the RAF until finally joining the foreign service and being appointed an Assistant
District Officer. Whilst on an assignment in Kenya, he committed suicide.

Flight Lieutenant Reed Tilton HYDE 33 RCAF

Flying Officer James Cassells HOWDEN 29 RCAF Pilot

Flying Officer Gerard Jean GUAY 24 RCAF Wireless Operator

Flying Officer Mervyn Esmond Llewellyn SCOVELL 33 RCAF Navigator

Flight Sergeant Alan Geoffrey SHADDICK 20 RAAF Pilot

Flight Sergeant John Ogilvy ALLEN 21 RAAF Wireless Operator

Flight Sergeant Leslie Daniel SLIPPER 21 Pilot

Flight Lieutenant Thomas Arthur EVANS 23 Pilot

Flight Lieutenant Alan James ROBERTS 23 Pilot

Flying Officer Sidney Graham WILLIAMS Navigator

Flight Sergeant Donald GRANT 21 Navigator

Flight Sergeant Maxwell Vernon GILDER

Flight Sergeant James ROSS 24 Flight Engineer

Flight Sergeant Ronald Edward JELFS 23 Flight Engineer

Flight Lieutenant Douglas Elliott TURNBULL 23 Wireless Operator

Flight Lieutenant John HEYWOOD Equipment Officer

Corporal Kenneth Stanley ANDERSON

Aircraftman 2nd Class Reginald Ernest SUGGARS

Aircraftman 2nd Class Walter James COLBY 44

Flight Lieutenant Frank Joseph PLANT 27 Navigator

20-Feb-45   LV537   Albemarle VI   15 MU   RAF Wroughton   0

The aircraft was being used for conversion training with an instructor and two pupil pilots aboard. On take-off the port engine failed because of a break up of the connecting rod and a piston. The instructor straightened the aircraft but could do no more than belly land it beyond the runway. The instructor; Flight Lieutenant R V Yates-Walmsley, was awarded a 'Green Endorsement' to his Flying Logbook.

21-Feb-45   LK126   Stirling IV   196 Sqn   RAF Shepherds Grove   1

The aircraft was returning to base at about 2230 hours, at the conclusion of a bombing sortie, when it was attacked by an enemy night intruder fighter. The aircraft was set on fire but the pilot; Flight Lieutenant Campbell, was able to make a crash landing on the airfield but the air gunner was killed, although the rest of the crew escaped from the wrecked aircraft. The intruder then attacked another Stirling, flown by Flight Sergeant Payne and his crew, on four occasions but the attacks were not successful and that Stirling was diverted to Foulsham where it landed safely.

Warrant Officer John Bruce MCGOVERN 22 RCAF Air Gunner

21-Feb-45   T9405   Hudson   161 Sqn   Near Meppen   2

The aircraft was being piloted by Flight Lieutenant D T Oliver and the crew was engaged on an SIS sortie to Germany, coded CROC. About 10 miles east of the Dutch frontier, the aircraft crashed after being engaged by a night fighter at low level. There was a crew of five on board and the recently appointed squadron commander was flying with this crew. Wing Commander Watson was taken POW but died later the same day and it is assumed that he had been badly injured. Flying Officer Hartman died of very serious burns, despite an attempt to rescue him staged by Flight Lieutenant F M Jarman RAAF, the wireless operator. Jarman was awarded a DFC in Jul 45.

Wing Commander George WATSON DFM
Flying Officer John Montague HARTMAN

Date	Serial	Aircraft	Unit	Place	Casualties

Brief Circumstances of Accident
Casualty Details (If Applicable)

21-Feb-45   KG925   Liberator VI   358 Sqn   23 degrees 30 North/89 degrees 55 East   1+3

This aircraft was returning from a sortie to Indo China and had been airborne for something over 14 hours. the pilot was aware of problems with the fuel transfer system and the aircraft's reserves of fuel were fairly small anyway, at the conclusion of so long a sortie. The pilot elected to continue the flight to his base and flew over a suitable airfield on which he could have made a precautionary landing. Whilst flying at 3000 feet the starboard engines both failed because of the fuel transfer problems and it was decided to abandon the aircraft. The air gunner could not locate his parachute and so the co-pilot agreed that he would jump with the air gunner holding on to his parachute webbing. This was done but the shock of the opening parachute caused the air gunner to lose his grip and he fell to his death. The aircraft subsequently crashed into the village of Tirpol, which is near Faridpur in Bengal, and killed 3 Indian civilians when it caught fire and destroyed their huts. Sadly, an examination of the wreckage subsequently, revealed the missing parachute.

Sergeant John MCLUSKEY 22 Air Gunner

21-Feb-45   KH282   Liberator VI   358 Sqn   18 miles north-west of Bao Ha Indo-China   8

This aircraft was one of eight despatched to DZs in Northern French Indo-China and it was being flown by an experienced pilot who was acting as a screen for a new crew, recently arrived. The weather over the target area was thick cloud covering wide expanses and mountain peaks protruding through. None of the crews was able to identify their dropping points and all those which returned brought their loads back. A crew captained by Warrant Officer Adams RNZAF saw a Liberator in the same general area and noticed it make a sharp turn through 90 degrees, followed shortly by a steeply banked descending turn through a further 90 degrees, before disappearing into cloud. Adams' crew arrived over the same point and saw a break in the cloud but did not descend as they could see high ground and had already noticed the mountain peaks. From subsequent reports received from French personnel, it was concluded that the aircraft seen

514

diving into the cloud was this one and that it struck high ground in cloud.

Flying Officer John Brown SMART 23 Pilot
Flying Officer Thomas Andrew BROWN Co-Pilot
Flying Officer Herbert John Alec JOHNSON Navigator
Flying Officer Philip Percy PARKER 21 Navigator
Flying Officer James Edward Malcolm WILSON 21 Air Gunner
Sergeant William Watts SMITH Air Gunner
Sergeant Gerald Mathew PUMPHREY 24 Air Gunner

22-Feb-45   Z6665   Whitley   42 OTU   RAF Ashbourne   0

This aircraft's radio failed during the sortie and so after landing, the pilot was unable to ask for taxy clearances around the airfield. Whilst taxying across a runway, this aircraft struck another Whitley which was waiting to take-off.

22-Feb-45   LA820   Whitley   42 OTU   RAF Ashbourne   0

The crew of this aircraft, flown by Flight Lieutenant G Sawle and Warrant Officer K S Reynolds, were awaiting take-off clearance and the aircraft had its lights on, as it was 0200 hours in the morning. It was struck by Whitley Z6665 and suffered serious damage, although none of its crew was injured.

22-Feb-45   LJ894   Stirling IV   196 Sqn   De Rips Netherlands   2

The aircraft was one of a number from this squadron detailed to bomb Rees and each carried a load of twenty four 500 lbs bombs. This aircraft crashed in the Netherlands and although four of the crew survived, the pilot and the air gunner were killed.

Wing Commander Maurice William L'Isle La' V BAKER 33 Pilot & Squadron Commander
Flight Sergeant John Robert GORDON 21 Air Gunner

Date	Serial	Aircraft	Unit	Place	Casualties
		Brief Circumstances of Accident			
		Casualty Details (If Applicable)			

22-Feb-45 LJ896 Stirling IV 299 Sqn Goch Germany 2

The transport squadrons maintained their bombing capability and this crew was one of six from the squadron tasked to bomb Rees. The aircraft failed to return but it was subsequently learned that four members of the crew had survived but the pilot and one other had been killed.

Squadron Leader Arthur Nathan SPEAR 33 Pilot
Sergeant David Frederick WILSON 20 Air Gunner

23-Feb-45 LK566 Stirling IV 190 Sqn South east Norway, location not known 6

The aircraft, which was operating from Great Dunmow, was shot down by a German night fighter during a SOE sortie to resupply the Norwegian Resistance.

Warrant Officer Stanley Bernard CURRIE 28 Pilot
Flight Sergeant Kenneth Frank NEWMAN 21 Co-pilot
Flight Sergeant Donald HOLLINRAKE 23 Navigator
Flight Sergeant Lewis George BALDOCK 21 Flight Engineer
Flight Sergeant Thomas Alexander GRANT 21 Wireless Operator
Flight Sergeant Robert Edwin DAVIES 22 Air Gunner

23-Feb-45 NA656 Halifax 644 Sqn Honiley, Coventry 3

The aircraft had taken off in the early evening of the previous day to deliver supplies to a DZ at position 60 degrees 30 North/10 degrees 42 East as part of a sortie; CURB3, to Norway. The aircraft had diverted to Milltown on its return and after refuelling was returning to Tarrant Rushton. Shortly after take-off at 1507 hours the port inner engine failed and the propeller feathered. Later in the flight, the starboard inner engine also failed and the pilot diverted to Honiley. As the aircraft was turning in on final approach to land and at a height of 300 feet, the port outer engine stopped and the aircraft crashed and broke up. The subsequent investigation into the accident confirmed that the correct grades of fuel and oil had been used but as the first two engines had cut through low fuel pressure, the AIB was asked to examine why this might have happened. The results are not recorded.

Flight Sergeant Walter BROOKS 25 Navigator
Flight Sergeant James William TOMLINSON 22 Wireless Operator
Flight Sergeant Robert GENT 23 Air Gunner

24-Feb-45   KG654   Dakota   575 Sqn   RAF Broadwell   0

The pilot pulled the aircraft off the ground at too low a speed and it stalled. As it was settling back on the ground, the pilot either retracted the undercarriage or he had already done so and the aircraft crashed on its belly. None of the three crew was hurt.

24-Feb-45   LK149   Stirling   138 Sqn   At sea, location not known   7

This crew, whose captain was undertaking his first operational sortie, were lost from sortie TABLEJAM 181, when their aircraft crashed into the sea off the westcoast of Denmark

Flight Sergeant Eric William SINKINSON 24 Pilot
Flight Sergeant George COLE 20
Flight Sergeant Bertie Ronald HASLER 23
Flight Sergeant Henry Thomas BATTEN 28
Sergeant Francis William WEBSTER 22
Sergeant George Albert LETTS 25 Flight Engineer
Pilot Officer Arthur SHARMAN 33 Air Gunner

24-Feb-45   LJ459   Stirling III   1665 HCU   RAF Tilstock   0

The aircraft, with a crew of nine, was being used for circuit training and had been airborne for about 11 minutes. It landed heavily and the starboard outer engine and wing tip both fell off, followed by a swing to starboard and the collapse of the starboard undercarriage. Following the incident, the starboard wing caught fire. The Stirling had a reputation for undercarriage failures, whenever lateral loads were exerted but this incident points up the strength of the undercarriage and its structure when the forces are applied vertically. Although not stated, one must wonder whether the aircraft's mainplane had been subjected to severe strain on other occasions, if the landing did not break the undercarriage immediately but was sufficient to cause an engine and the wing tip to fracture.

26-Feb-45   LJ925   Stirling IV   196 Sqn   Holen Lake near Arendal   3

The aircraft was operating from Shepherds Grove Suffolk and was intercepted by three night fighters and badly damaged. Some of its cargo of supplies were dropped but with the starboard wing on fire, the crew decided to bale out. The navigator, bomb aimer and air gunner did this successfully but the flight engineer's parachute became entangled in the tail plane and he was killed when the aircraft crashed into a lake. The wireless operator was also killed whilst abandoning the aircraft and the pilot did not leave the aircraft and his remains were not recovered. Although two of the survivors were captured, the third was sheltered by the Norwegians.

Flying Officer Russell George TICKNER 24 RAAF Pilot
Flight Sergeant George Alfred HUMPHREY 38 Flight Engineer
Warrant Officer Joseph Dalglish STEVENSON 25 Wireless Operator

---

26-Feb-45   LL465   Halifax   301 Sqn   Risignano   0

This aircraft was one of a group of Polish Halifax and Liberator aircraft, the crews of which had been detailed for Operation STARKADDER, dropping to a DZ near Roverato. The aircraft received a 'warm reception' from enemy AA fire in the area of the DZ and the town of Treviso. Although the first two aircraft dropped a total of ten persons and a range of containers and packages, the following aircraft got no reception from the ground party and brought their loads back. Following the operation and whilst parked at the operating base, this aircraft was struck by a Wellington NC637 of 38 Sqn and the pair were destroyed by fire.

26-Feb-45   NA103 Halifax III   298 Sqn   At sea off Arendal Norway   6

The aircraft was shot down by a German night fighter as it was returning to base, having failed to find its allotted DZ because of poor weather conditions.

    Flying Officer Robert Stanley EDICK 23 RCAF Pilot
    Pilot Officer Eric Alexander INNES 21 RCAF
    Warrant Officer Chester Allen HOLMLUND 22 RCAF
    Flying Officer Alexander KOTYK 20 RCAF
    Pilot Officer Hector LOCHEAD 21 RCAF
    Flight Sergeant William George GODFREY 23

26-Feb-45   EW188 Liberator   358 Sqn   Chin Hills   8

The aircraft was one of nine squadron aircraft detailed to drop supplies into central Indo China and the crew accomplished this and a wireless message was received notifying their ETA at base. The wreckage was eventually located in the Chin Hills but there were no survivors and precious few clues as to the cause of the loss.

    Flying Officer Louise Phillippe CLOUTIER 32 RCAF Pilot
    Flight Sergeant Robert George PRYOR 21 Co-Pilot
    Flight Sergeant George Ernest FOSTER 25 Navigator
    Flying Officer Dennis Joseph BOSTON 21 Bomb Aimer
    Flight Sergeant Mervyn Rex VAGG 20 RAAF Wireless Operator
    Flight Sergeant Eric Francis WARMER 20 RAAF Wireless Operator
    Sergeant James Partric Joseph POWER 22 Air Gunner
    Sergeant George Walter MOUNT 24 Air Gunner

Date	Serial	Aircraft	Unit	Place	Casualties

Brief Circumstances of Accident
Casualty Details (If Applicable)

27-Feb-45 LK272 Stirling IV   138 Sqn   Off the Norwegian coast   7

Another crew witnessed this aircraft being shot down by enemy AA fire off the Norwegian coast. The Cornwallis crew, a very experienced bunch, was engaged on sortie CRUPPER 27, which was one of six to Norway on this date of which two failed because of deteriorating weather. Eleven sorties, flown by the same squadron to Denmark, in equally poor weather, recorded less than 50% success rate.

Flight Lieutenant Peter Brownell CORNWALLIS 24 Pilot
Pilot Officer Stanley Arthur PEPWORTH DFM
Flying Officer John Edward STANTON 28 RAAF Bomb Aimer
Flight Sergeant Brian Douglas TOVEY 25 RAAF Wireless Operator
Flight Sergeant Stuart Samuel HAGERTY 21 RCAF Air Gunner
Sergeant John Edwin CORY 23 Air Gunner
Flying Officer Leonard John GORNALL 23 DFC Flight Engineer

27-Feb-45 RX623 Horsa   22 HGCU   RAF Keevil   1

The tug and glider combination had just taken off when the tug's starboard tyre burst. The glider cast off at 250 to 300 feet and the pilot attempted a turnback, to land downwind on the airfield. However, the glider touched down about 300 yards from the perimeter, bounced, collided with a tree and then flew on for a further 200 or so yards before crashing into the airfield's bomb dump. The 1st pilot/instructor was killed and the four others on board were injured.

Flight Sergeant Keith Armstead BORE 21

28-Feb-45 KJ806 Dakota   108 OTU   Castle Donington   0

The aircraft was landing in a 90 degree crosswind and the brakes faded during the landing run. At low speed, the aircraft continued to travel down a slight incline, overshot the end of the landing area and went

520

over a 15 foot bank.

28-Feb-45   NA668 Halifax III   296 Sqn   RAF Earls Colne   0

The aircraft had been airborne for a short time during a glider towing task and had returned to land in dark conditions at night. The pilot undershot his approach and struck a tree trunk, lying on its side, but some 80 yards short of the runway. The port undercarriage was smashed and the starboard undercarriage collapsed afterwards.

01-Mar-45   KJ921   Dakota IV   357 Sqn   Hoi Ling Island   3?

The aircraft was operating over French Indo-China (Vietnam) in conjunction with a similar aircraft of the USAAF 322 Troop Carrier Sqn. This aircraft did not return from the sortie and it was discovered that it had flown into a hillside in position 21 Degrees 37 North/111 degrees 52 East. It is thought possible that the aircraft encountered poor weather. The remains of the crew were recovered eventually and they were buried in a Collective Grave in Hong Kong. There is conflicting information about the presence of a fourth person in the aircraft, thought to be an agent.

    Flying Officer Thomas Stark HUNTER 22 Pilot
    Flying Officer George Norman GILLIN 33 Navigator
    Sergeant Brian Harry MOWBRAY Wireless Operator
    Possibly plus one non-RAF

01-Mar-45   KG993 Liberator VI   34 SAAF   10 miles south of Foggia   2

The crew was carrying out a test flight and this included checking the feathering gear. At 2000 feet the feathering test was carried out by feathering the starboard outer first and this was successfully unfeathered before the process was repeated with the starboard inner. At this point, when attempting to complete the unfeathering of the starboard inner engine, the co-pilot turned off the starboard outer's magnetos. With a serious loss of power and the problems of a fully asymmetric set up, the aircraft was crash landed and two members of the crew of nine were killed.

Date	Serial	Aircraft	Unit	Place	Casualties

Brief Circumstances of Accident
Casualty Details (If Applicable)

Lieutenant M F T MAINWARING SAAF Co-Pilot
Air Mechanic H T WARE SAAF

| 02-Mar-45 | RJ314 | Horsa | 1 HGSU | Great Sampford, Essex | 0 |

The glider was being delivered to the unit as part of Exercise RIFF-RAFF. The glider was released in the wrong place and the glider pilot then found himself attempting to land in the wrong part of the airfield. At about 100 feet he was forced to change his landing path and on touchdown, collided with another Horsa.

| 03-Mar-45 | KJ848 | Dakota IV | 435 Sqn | Tulihal | 0 |

The aircraft's port tyre burst on landing at the conclusion of an operational sortie and the aircraft swung off the runway and collided with a USAAF Waco glider, serial number 341784.

| 03-Mar-45 | LJ996 | Stirling IV | 299 Sqn | Not Known | 6 |

The aircraft failed to return from a sortie FLANK 9 to Norway but its fate is not known.

Flying Officer Edward George HULL 27 Pilot
Warrant Officer Davida Kenneth JORDAN 23
Flight Sergeant Bernard William HARRIS 23
Flight Sergeant Ronald ROME 23
Warrant Officer Alexander Thomas WAINWRIGHT 21
Flight Sergeant John Michael MURRAY 31

| 03-Mar-45 | LL413 | Halifax | 297 Sqn | North Sea | 6 |

The aircraft failed to return from a search over the North Sea and is assumed to have crashed into the North

Sea. No signals or distress calls were received and no wreckage was detected.

Warrant Officer Frank RICHARDSON-JONES 25
Flight Sergeant Douglas Ward CLARKE 20
Flight Sergeant Stuart William WENTWORTH 24
Sergeant John Ford ESCOTT 19
Sergeant John Elstob KITCHEN 24
Flight Sergeant Ronald Edward SPALL 19

03-Mar-45   NA127   Halifax III   644 Sqn   Ditched in North Sea   6

The aircraft was returning to base at the conclusion of an SOE mission EARS 2 to a DZ in Norway. It ditched in the North Sea and despite an extensive search in the area of the last reported position, no trace was found. The cause of the ditching was not established and there is no information as to whether a distress call was made.

Pilot Officer Stephen Thomson WELLS 29 Pilot
Flight Lieutenant John Alfred MILLER 25 RCAF Navigator
Pilot Officer Frederick Gwilym GREY 23 RAAF Bomb Aimer
Flight Sergeant Reginald Henry BROWN 24 Wireless Operator
Flight Sergeant James Royden WEAVER 22 Flight Engineer
Warrant Officer II John CORMAN 22 RCAF Air Gunner

04-Mar-45   LA635   Hamilcar   1 HGSU   RAF Tarrant Rushton   0

The glider pilot pulled off the tow too far away from the airfield and then could not turn the aircraft over a wood. The glider crashed into parked gliders and one other aircraft was written off whilst another was only slightly damaged.

04-Mar-45   LA736   Hamilcar   1 HGSU   RAF Tarrant Rushton   0

This aircraft, together with LA708, was struck by LA635, as summarised above.

523

Date	Serial	Aircraft	Unit	Place	Casualties

Brief Circumstances of Accident
Casualty Details (If Applicable)

04-Mar-45   LA726   Hamilcar   1 HGSU   RAF Tarrant Rushton   0

At a height of 800 feet on the approach to land, the glider pilot realised he was overshooting and so he deliberately stalled the aircraft to lose height. However, in doing so he was then unable to regain effective control of the elevators to put the glider in the correct attitude for landing. The aircraft struck the ground heavily and the undercarriage was damaged.

05-Mar-45   LJ999   Stirling   138 Sqn   Tipperpold Denmark   0

The crew of this aircraft had completed successfully a sortie TABLEJAM 241 and the aircraft was being flown back to UK. An explosion is said to have taken place inside the fuselage and the aircraft, which was travelling at high speed. It struck shallow water in Ringkobing Fjord, an inland lake separated from the western seaboard of Denmark by a narrow strip of land, but remained largely intact and all the crew, captained by Flying Officer L G Sleven, survived.

05-Mar-45   LK312   Stirling   161 Sqn   At sea off Livo Island Denmark   7

On this night there were sixteen SD sorties to Denmark: a Hudson and nine Stirlings came from 161 Sqn, whilst six Stirlings were involved from 138 Sqn. This crew, captained by the squadron commander who had been in post just a few weeks following the loss of Wing Commander Watson, was engaged on TABLEJAM 209 and crashed into the sea off the Danish coast.

Wing Commander Michael Andrew BROGAN 32 DFC Pilot
Flying Officer Norman CLARKE 37 Navigator
Warrant Officer Eric Edward GRAY 21 Air Gunner
Warrant Officer Frederick MAHONY
Flight Lieutenant Harold Owen SHARMAN DFC Wireless Operator

Flying Officer Frederick John WATSON 26 DFM Flight Engineer
Flying Officer Henry Thomas WIGLEY 23 DFC Bomb Aimer

06-Mar-45 PW833 Horsa   1 HGSU   RAF Rivenhall   0
A 570 Sqn Stirling (LJ589) was landing and it swung off the runway and collided with this glider, which was correctly parked.

07-Mar-45 PW768 Horsa   Great Sampford, Essex   0
The glider was landing too fast and the pilot was faced with an obstruction caused by another glider, which had already landed. In turning to starboard, the pilot could not stop the glider before it struck a lorry.

08-Mar-45 V1995 Albemarle VI   22 HGCU   Wall Hall Farm, Hertfordshire   3
The aircraft was towing a glider on a ferrying sortie, in conditions of haze and low cloud. The combination was at about 900 feet when the glider pulled into the high position and caused the tug's tail to rise. The pilot was thought not to have cast off the tow immediately and the aircraft dived into the ground. It is also probable that the pilot was not strapped in and was thrown forward over the control column.

Flight Lieutenant Ian Marshall ROBERTSON 30 Pilot
Flight Sergeant Peter James BOURKE 19
Warrant Officer Charles WAGSTAFF 40

09-Mar-45 LK203 Stirling IV   570 Sqn   RAF Rivenhall   0
The aircraft had been engaged in a glider towing exercise for nearly 3 hours and was returning to land at the conclusion of this task. The pilot made a long and low approach to the runway and in the final stages, the aircraft struck the boundary fence with the starboard wheel, bursting the tyre. An overshoot was initiated and the pilot was instructed to land on the grass, which he did. The starboard undercarriage collapsed and the aircraft swung to the right, fracturing the starboard wing.

525

Brief Circumstances of Accident
Casualty Details (If Applicable)

09-Mar-45 NA317 Halifax VII   1665 HCU   Radmore, 1 mile east of Abbots Bromley   6+2

The aircraft was flying at low level across an airfield, in conditions of haze and low sun. It collided with a Tiger Moth serial DE473 and both aircraft crashed and were destroyed.

Warrant Officer Alexander George HEMMINGS 22 Pilot
Flying Officer John Weldon CAIRNS 24 RCAF
Sergeant George DINSDALE 33
Sergeant James FORBES 20
Pilot Officer Kenneth MILLARD 28
Sergeant Peter RICHMAN 30

The crew of Tiger Moth DE473 were:

Flight Sergeant Alan Richard EDWARDS Instructor pilot
Aircraftman 2nd Class Alan John McLaren KEAY Pupil pilot

09-Mar-45 LA646 Hamilcar   1 HGSU   1 mile from RAF Tarrant Rushton   0

The pilot realised he was undershooting his landing and raised the flaps in an attempt to gain speed but the aircraft crashed some 700 yards short of the airfield. The pilot had been flying the Horsa glider the previous day and the two gliders have significant differences in their handling characteristics and the techniques employed.

09-Mar-45 PW839 Horsa   1 HGSU   Grange Farm, Hepworth, Suffolk   0

The glider pilot allowed the glider to get too low on take-off and it was caught in the tug's slipstream. The tow rope broke and the glider crashed.

10-Mar-45 LK553 Stirling IV   295 Sqn   RAF Rivenhall   0

The pilot checked the controls for full and free movement as part of his pre take-off checks and found the controls working satisfactorily. At 110 knots on the run, the pilot attempted to pull back on the control column only to find it jammed. The throttles were closed but the aircraft overran the runway and the undercarriage collapsed in soft ground.

10-Mar-45 HH532 Hotspur II   3 GTS   Devon Map Ref 465030   0

The tow rope being used on this sortie was approaching the end of its safe working life of 44 tows. During the sortie, there were several 'snatches' and the tow rope was unable to take the strain of these and snapped. A forced landing was made in a field.

10-Mar-45 RJ255 Horsa   1 HGSU   RAF Broadwell   0

The pilot was making a flapless landing but the glider undershot the approach and struck a stone wall. It was suggested that flapless approaches should use the centre of the airfield as the point of aim for the touchdown, not a point close to the threshold.

11-Mar-45 EM408 Master II   3 GTS   Devon Map Ref 445182   2

The pilot stalled the aircraft off a steep turn at 2500 feet and it entered a spin. The pilot was able to recover from the spin but had insufficient height to pull out of the dive and the aircraft struck the ground heavily and caught fire on impact.

    Flight Sergeant Arthur Edward LEACH 20
    Sergeant James Richard EGAN 26 The Glider Pilot Regiment

12-Mar-45 DL456 Master II   3 GTS   RAF Exeter   0

The aircraft was flying at 700 feet just after take off when its engine failed because of the loss of an inlet valve seat on the No: 2 cylinder. The glider was cast off and the pilot turned his aircraft towards the airfield but

Date	Serial	Aircraft	Unit	Place	Casualties
Brief Circumstances of Accident					
Casualty Details (If Applicable)					

realising he could not reach the runway, he raised the undercarriage and converted the approach into a forced landing in a field outside the aerodrome.

| 13-Mar-45 | V2035 | Albemarle VI | 22 HGCU | RAF Fairford | 0 |

A tyre burst on take-off but the pilot was unable to stop the aircraft and so raised the undercarriage. It was later indicated that a new specification tyre was being procured for use with the Albemarle and a warning was issued regarding excessive and heavy landings. One wonders why the procurement of new tyres was not undertaken before and it seems a pretty pointless exercise for an aircraft type which was already obsolete and scheduled to be withdrawn from service.

| 14-Mar-45 | EW626 | Liberator | 246 Sqn | 4 miles west of Lagens | 19 |

The aircraft was engaged on a ferrying sortie and was taking off at night in conditions which included severe turbulence. The pilot had been briefed to turn right after take-off and was not being pressurised to take-off if he was unhappy with the prevailing conditions. After becoming airborne, the aircraft climbed ahead and then turned left and struck the high ground along this track. No reason was discovered as to why the pilot elected to ignore the briefing unless he was concerned that the aircraft was vulnerable if turned at low level in turbulence and so decided to climb straight ahead until at a safe height. However, this does not explain the left hand turn. It was decided subsequently that the runway (029) used on this occasion, was not to be used at night unless the crew was conversant with the local geography.

Flying Officer Vaclav JILEK Pilot
Leading Aircraftman William BRIDGEN 33
Warrant Officer Dalibor BROCHARD
Sergeant George Alexander CAIN

Commander Charles Alexander COLVILLE 57 RN
Squadron Leader Arthur John DAVEY 21
Leading Aircraftman Charles Stuart HUBBARD
Flight Lieutenant Leonard Fitzgerald JARVIS 34
Corporal Fredereick JECKELLS
Leading Aircraftman Edgar JONES 36
Flight Sergeant Ludvik KONDZIOLKA
Sergeant John Henry LAWRENCE 38
Leading Aircraftman David LINDSAY
Corporal William MCKENZIE 26
Flying Officer Cyril George MONTGOMERY
Flight Lieutenant Alistair Kay MURDOCH 29 Navigator
Flight Lieutenant Alois jaroslav VOLEK Navigator
Flying Officer Anthony Peter RAMSDEN
Flight Lieutenant John Edward YARNALL 37

14-Mar-45   KJ965   Dakota IV   Maunubyin, Akyab Island   0
A Beaufighter X of 27 Sqn (KW404) was making an emergency landing because of a serious oil leak in its port engine. The pilot undershot the approach and struck this aircraft's tail before striking KK126. All three aircraft burst into flames and were destroyed in the subsequent blaze.

14-Mar-45   KK126   Dakota IV   Maunubyin, Akyab Island   1
This aircraft was waiting its take-off clearance for a flight to Kangla at about 0600 hours. As summarised above, it was struck by Beaufighter KW404 and the co-pilot received severe head injuries from which he died in hospital at Comilla on 17 Mar 45.

Warrant Officer Ernest Oliver ENGLAND 25 RNZAF Co-Pilot

529

Date	Serial	Aircraft	Unit	Place	Casualties

Brief Circumstances of Accident
Casualty Details (If Applicable)

| 14-Mar-45 | KN345 | Dakota | | 45 Gp | En route El Paso – Sacramento | 5 |

The aircraft was flying between El Paso Texas and Sacramento California when it crashed near Santa Barbara. The circumstances of its loss are not known. In addition to the four crew listed, a US cadet was also killed.

Flight Sergeant Peter ANTROBUS Pilot
Warrant Officer II Floyd Eugene GEORGE 20 RCAF Co-Pilot
Flight Sergeant Frank Stanley HOLMES 23 Navigator
Flight Sergeant Edward WATKINS 21 Wireless Operator
+ one USAAF cadet whose name is not known

| 14-Mar-45 | RJ135 | Horsa | | 1 HGSU | RAF Rivenhall | 0 |

The combination were flying at 2500 feet when the glider cast off the tow because the tug developed engine trouble. The glider pilot was unable to locate the airfield because of the very poor visibility and the glider did not clear the haze until it was down to about 200 feet. A forced landing was made in a field.

| 14-Mar-45 | RX480 | Horsa II | | 1 HGSU | South of RAF Great Dunmow | 0 |

The Horsa, flown by a GPR squadron commander, was the first to cast off the tow when hazy conditions were encountered. As he was unable to locate the airfield, the pilot made a forced landing in a field. However, many of the following gliders which had also cast off their tows when encountering poor visibility, were helped by the firing of flares which indicated the location of the airfield.

| 14-Mar-45 | RX926 | Horsa II | | 1 HGSU | RAF Rivenhall | 0 |

The crew had been engaged on a towing exercise in a fully loaded Mark II glider for over 2½ hours. Having dropped the tow, the glider was being landed in poor visibility. After touchdown, the brakes seemed not to be very effective and the aircraft ran off the airfield, through a boundary fence and across the road. Although it was suggested that the pilot was inexperienced at handling a laden glider, it was also reported that the brakes of a Mark II Horsa were judged to be less effective than those of the earlier version. Sadly the two pilots of this glider were to be killed 10 days later during Operation VARSITY.

14-Mar-45 RZ139 Horsa II   1 HGSU   Mile End Green, Essex   0

Although cast off in the airfield's overhead, the pilot could not see the airfield because of the poor visibility, which was getting worse rapidly. The pilot landed his glider in a field and its nosewheel was ripped off.

14-Mar-45 LH340 Horsa   233 Sqn   RAF Blakehill Farm   0

15-Mar-45 KG525 Dakota III   28 SAAF   Maison Blanche   0

The aircraft suffered a burst starboard tyre during take-off and became airborne but stalled back onto the runway. The pilot lost control and the aircraft was damaged extensively. It appears that there was a pre-existing defect with the tyre which should have been detected had the pre-flight inspection been undertaken properly.

16-Mar-45 BT557 Hotspur II   3 GTS   ½ mile south of RAF Exeter 0

On take-off and at a height of 50 feet, the tug's engine failed. The glider pilot cast off the tow immediately and then made a forced landing in a field.

17-Mar-45 MZ632 Halifax III   1665 HCU   RAF Tilstock   0

The crew was engaged in circuit training and during one touchdown a mainwheel tyre burst. The aircraft swung off the runway and its undercarriage collapsed.

Date   Serial   Aircraft   Unit   Place   Casualties
Brief Circumstances of Accident
Casualty Details (If Applicable)

19-Mar-45   KG727   Dakota III   44 SAAF   Bari, Italy   0

The aircraft was taking off on an operational supply dropping sortie to Yugoslavia. The co-pilot misinterpreted a signal from the aircraft's captain and retracted the undercarriage too soon.

19-Mar-45   KK203   Dakota IV   238 Sqn   Kyaukpyu, Ramree Island   0

The aircraft was being used to evacuate casualties to a base area for treatment and there was a crew of three and twenty six others on board, the latter being non-RAF. On take-off, the starboard tyre burst and the aircraft swung. The pilot skilfully corrected and held the swing but he starboard tyre dug into soft sand at the side of the runway and the port undercarriage then struck a bund of earth and collapsed. There were no injuries amongst those on board but the aircraft was written off.

19-Mar-45   KN220   Dakota IV   436 Sqn   Chittagong   0

The aircraft was damaged beyond repair when it was struck by a USAAF C46.

19-Mar-45   PJ913   Stirling V   242 Sqn   Lydda Palastine   0

During the take-off, a swing to starboard developed and the flying pilot took the normal corrective action. However, without reference to the flying pilot, the aircraft captain who was in the right hand seat, closed the throttles but left the port outer at half power setting. The aircraft swung violently off the runway, struck a calvert and its undercarriage collapsed. The accident was a case of poor crew cooperation, in that the aircraft captain should not have touched the throttles without the flying pilot's request. Fortunately, none of the twelve people on board was injured.

19-Mar-45   V1862   Albemarle VI   ½ mile south of RAF Brize Norton   3

At 700 feet, whilst towing a glider, the aircraft entered an abnormally steep turn and the tow rope broke. The aircraft dived into the ground and was destroyed. The Albemarle should not have exceeded a bank angle of 30 degrees whilst towing a glider and it seems the glider got out of position and this was a major factor in the pilot losing control.

    Warrant Officer Jack SKINNER 21 DFC Pilot
    Warrant Officer George Cairns WILLINS 24 Wireless Operator
    Flight Sergeant Alastair Duncan MCGILLIVRAY 22 Pilot

20-Mar-45   T9445   Hudson   161 Sqn   Location not known   4

This crew was engaged on a sortie to Germany, coded NORVIC, and they had delivered their agent near Remagen. Whilst on the return flight, the aircraft was shot down and the crew killed.

    Flight Lieutenant Richard Nicholas FERRIS 23 RCAF Pilot
    Flying Officer James Edward TRAILL RCAF Wireless Operator
    Flight Lieutenant Allan Frayne PENHALE 24 RCAF Wireless Operator
    Warrant Officer I Robert Gerald HUTTON RCAF Navigator

20-Mar-45   AE595   Hudson   161 Sqn   Near Rheine Airfield Germany   4

The aircraft was shot down at the enemy airbase at Rheine, about 20 miles inside Germany, crashing into the airfield's bomb dump whilst engaged on SIS operation coded WALNUT. The crew had dropped an agent west of Osnabruck and were starting their return journey but probably strayed across the airfield in error.

    Flying Officer George Stoudt RAGAN 21 RCAF Pilot
    Warrant Officer I Frank Emanuel GRAY RCAF Wireless Operator
    Flight Sergeant Percy BRADLEY 21 Navigator
    Flight Sergeant Cecil Algot THOMAS 30 RNZAF Air Gunner

20-Mar-45 FK803 Hudson   161 Sqn   Maulesmuhle, Duchy of Luxembourg   6

The aircraft had left Tempsford and positioned at RAF Tangmere to collect the agents it was to deliver in a three pronged sortie coded; BENEDICT, EXPRESS and LEADER. This was the 3rd occasion that the sortie had been flown but when flying near Erfurt, the pilot; Flight Lieutenant Terence Helfer, abandoned the attempt because of the continuing bad weather and he set course for UK. When flying over Luxembourg, the aircraft was attacked, probably by a USAAF night fighter and shot down. The pilot survived with serious burns and in Jun 45 he was awarded a DFC. Once again it must be pondered at how a US pilot could have attacked an aircraft, whose profile would have been well known to American crews.

    Flying Officer Forest Harold THOMPSON 27 DFM RNZAF Air Gunner
    Flight Lieutenant Raymond Frankish ESCREET 22 DFM
    Flying Officer Henry Scurr JOHNSON 31
    Lieutenant G CORBISHER – Belgian Agent
    Lieutenant L DE WINTON
    Lieutenant J MOREL

20-Mar-45 KN228 Dakota   9 FU   6 miles north-east of Barrackpore   0

At 1000 feet after take-off, the aircraft's starboard propeller went into the fully fine position and resisted all attempts to get it to feather properly. As height was being lost, the pilot had no option but to land the aircraft and this he did on its belly. The cause of the starboard propeller problems was a loss of oil from the system because of a fractured pipe between the oil tank and the feathering motor.

20-Mar-45 KN343 Dakota   243 Sqn   In the Coral Sea   0

Whilst engaged in a ferry flight, the aircraft's starboard engine failed due to a loss of fuel pressure and a little later the port engine also failed. There was a crew of five and twenty three others on board and all survived the subsequent ditching and evacuation. There was a strong suspicion that the port engine failure was the result of water in the fuel but this could not be substantiated.

20-Mar-45   LK116   Stirling IV   620 Sqn   Near Great Dunmow   6

The crew was briefed for a night practice container drop over the DZ at Great Sampford and the Army officer who had undertaken the briefing was scheduled to fly with the crew. The first part of the sortie was completed without incident and the aircraft was returning to its base when an enemy intruder warning was received. The aircraft was shot down by one of several enemy night intruders operating in the area that night and it was attacked from below and badly damaged. The crew was ordered to abandon the aircraft but only the flight engineer survived. Captain Slater had survived an attack by a night fighter on a previous occasion, whilst Warrant Officer Bell had been the sole survivor of a 190 Sqn aircraft lost over France in Jul 44

Squadron Leader George Oliver Samuel WHITTY 23 DFC Pilot
Warrant Officer John George Joseph WILLIAMS 25
Pilot Officer George Edward AMES 22 Wireless Operator
Warrant Officer I Andrew Paul BELL 21 RCAF Air Gunner
Flight Sergeant George Robert DOUGLAS 24
Captain George Frederick SLATER 32 The Parachute Regt attached SAS

20-Mar-45   NA316   Halifax   1665 HCU   Near Wittering   3

This aircraft was on a night cross country sortie when it was intercepted and shot down by an enemy night intruder. This was the last night interception success by enemy aircraft in the east of England area. Apart for the three fatal casualties, six other men aboard the aircraft escaped uninjured.

Flying Officer Peter Edward NETTLEFIELD 21 Pilot
Sergeant Kenneth Bertie EARLL 21 Flight Engineer
Sergeant Joseph WHITBREAD 29 Air Gunner

Date	Serial	Aircraft	Unit	Place	Casualties
		Brief Circumstances of Accident			
		Casualty Details (If Applicable)			

21-Mar-45 FD900 Dakota III 45 Gp RAF Lagens 0

When lining up for take-off, the pilot failed to lock the aircraft's tailwheel and so it was castoring freely. During the initial stages of the take-off run, the aircraft swung first one way and then another before leaving the runway and colliding with a USAAF Liberator 163243.

21-Mar-45 KG534 Dakota III 216 Sqn In Flight 0

During a routine freight transport flight, an accumulator leaked quantities of acid which caused significant corrosion in the aircraft's centre section and affected the control cables, hydraulics and electrical leads. The damage was judged to be so severe as to make the aircraft uneconomic to repair and it was scrapped. Two airmen, whose task was to see the accumulator was empty of acid, were given 168 hours detention for their negligence.

22-Mar-45 PJ909 Stirling V 242 Sqn Mauripur 0

The aircraft was on a route trip between UK and Karachi and return, and was taking off at night. A swing developed and the pilot did not close the throttles and allowed the swing to continue. The aircraft's undercarriage collapsed and the starboard outer engine caught fire.

23-Mar-45 KN255 Dakota IV 238 Sqn Chandina, Begal 0

The port tyre burst on take-off, probably because the aircraft ran over a stone or sharp object. The aircraft became airborne safely but the pilot elected to land wheels up at the conclusion of the sortie rather than risk an accident with attempting to land with a flat tyre. There were no injuries amongst the three crew and eleven passengers.

23-Mar-45   LK209   Stirling IV   161 Sqn   At sea off Vlieland Island   6

The aircraft was en route to a DZ near Harlingen coded; RUMMY 31 and it was one of seven SD sorties that night of which two were for Norway and the others for the Netherlands. The aircraft was struck by enemy AA fire and crashed into sand dunes at Vieland. The pilot received injuries from which he died later but the only survivor was Flight Sergeant J T White. White jumped from the aircraft at low level but landed in some fir trees which served to cushion his landing. He made a successful escape and evaded capture until joining up with the allies.

    Flight Lieutenant Alan Henderson AITKEN Pilot
    Pilot Officer Ronald Arthur CASTON 23 Navigator
    Sergeant William HORROCKS Flight Engineer
    Flight Sergeant Alexander Robert PATON 24 Air Gunner
    Pilot Officer William Lawson SHAW 22 Bomb Aimer
    Pilot Officer Reginald Arthur SWIFT 22 Wireless Operator

23-Mar-45   HH356   Hotspur II   20(P)AFU   Not stated   0

At 400 feet whilst climbing away after take-off, the tug's engine failed. The glider cast off and the pilot attempted a turnback for a forced landing on the airfield. Unfortunately, the glider landed heavily, hitting the ground nose first.

24-Mar-45   FZ649   Dakota III   512 Sqn   Germany   3

The aircraft was towing a glider on Operation VARSITY and this was released over the LZ. As the Dakota turned away it was hit in the port side fuel tanks by enemy AA fire and a blaze started immediately, spreading along the fuselage and burning the fabric off the rudder and elevator. The wireless operator; Warrant Officer P J Hughes, baled out and was the sole survivor after the aircraft broke in two as he abandoned it.

    Flight Lieutenant Clifford Archibald CHEW AFC 27 Pilot

Flight Sergeant Harold GRAVETT 22 Co-Pilot
Warrant Officer Geoffrey Charles NEWMAN 22 Navigator

24-Mar-45   LJ997   Stirling IV   190 Sqn   RAF Great Dunmow   0

The aircraft was number 55 in the sequence of aircraft to take-off on Operation VARSITY and as a consequence it had been taxying excessively prior to starting its take-off run with a Horsa glider on tow. The port outer engine spluttered because of oiled up sparking plugs and the aircraft started to swing. The pilot was unable to resolve this without overcorrecting and the undercarriage collapsed.

24-Mar-45   MZ959   Halifax III   644 Sqn   Germany   1

The aircraft failed to return from an Operation VARSITY sortie and had been towing a Hamilcar glider with a Dodge truck and 17 pounder anti-tank gun. Five of the crew were taken POW but several were released before the end of hostilities. The pilot; Flying Officer Harold McConville, had towed gliders to Arnhem and on one occasion the Horsa he was towing had lost its tail to enemy AA fire. McConville had dived his Halifax and attempted to hold the Horsa in a stable position but the strain on the tow rope was inevitably too great and it broke.

Flying Officer Kenneth Rupert BRUCE 24 RAAF Wireless Operator

24-Mar-45   NA669   Halifax III   644 Sqn   Near Wesel, Germany   6

The aircraft was towing a Horsa glider, which was itself loaded with a jeep and 6 pounder anti-tank gun. In common with the 298/644 Sqns effort for Operation VARSITY, take-off had been from RAF Woodbridge. The Halifax/Horsa combinations numbered twelve and when included with the information below, it will be seen that the total effort was sixty tug/glider combinations. The aircraft failed to return but the circumstances of its loss are not clear.

Flight Sergeant John Philip HUGHES 21 Pilot
Flight Sergeant Tom Brook NICHOLSON 21 Navigator
Flight Sergeant Leonard William ATTEWELL 22 Bomb Aimer
Flight Sergeant William George LAWRENCE 25 Wireless Operator
Flight Sergeant Clarence MAIN 34 Flight Engineer
Sergeant Leslie Alfred DUTTON 21 Air Gunner

24-Mar-45   NA311 Halifax   298 Sqn   Near Wessel, Germany   6

This aircraft, captained by the officer whose aircraft had ditched in Donagal Bay in February, took off from Woodbridge as part of a formation of forty eight Halifax/Hamilcar combinations provided by this squadron, along with a further twelve Halifax/Horsa combinations from 644 Sqn, to participate in Operation VARSITY and to convey the heavy guns being carried into battle for 6th Airborne Division. After releasing its glider, the aircraft was seen to be hit by enemy flak and to roll onto its back and dive into the ground. The rear gunner escaped by parachute but was killed during his descent.

   Flying Officer Delmer Robert MCGILLIVRAY 29 RCAF Pilot
   Flight Sergeant James Beedham WALKER 23 Navigator
   Flying Officer Edwin Marshall HALES 21 Bomb Aimer
   Flying Officer George DIXON 24 Wireless Operator
   Flight Sergeant Augustine AHERNE 32 Flight Engineer
   Warrant Officer James Ewart BUNN 20 RCAF Air Gunner

24-Mar-45   LK137   Stirling IV   295 Sqn   Kerverlen   1

The aircraft was badly damaged by enemy AA fire and the captain ordered his crew to abandon the aircraft and he retained control whilst they did so. With port inner engine on fire, the aircraft crashed.

   Warrant Officer Horace Albert SYMMONS 27 Pilot

Date	Serial	Aircraft	Unit	Place	Casualties

Brief Circumstances of Accident
Casualty Details (If Applicable)

24-Mar-45 PJ911 Stirling 46 Sqn 37 miles south-west Perpignan 9

The aircraft was on a training sortie and was carrying the elements of several crews, who would be route flying with the squadron. Whilst a long way off course, the aircraft struck a 7800 feet high mountain whilst flying in bad visibility and below safety height.

Flying Officer Ian Rees COWAN DFC RAAF Pilot
Pilot Officer Archibald Kenzie MCMILLAN 22 RCAF Co-Pilot
Flight Lieutenant Gordon COULDRY 28 RCAF Navigator
Flight Sergeant John Martin COAD 25 Wireless Operator
Flight Sergeant Frank Reginald JONES 22 Navigator
Flight Sergeant Alexander McKenzie ROSS 21 Flight Engineer
Flight Lieutenant C COOPER DFM Wireless Operator
Flying Officer Francis William DOUGLAS RAAF
Sergeant Alan Reginald PHIPPS 20 Flight Engineer

24-Mar-45 NA814 Hamilcar 1 HGSU RAF Woodbridge 0

In common with the other glider units based normally at Tarrant Rushton, the Hamilcars and their Halifax tug aircraft were deployed to Woodbridge for Operation VARSITY. This glider was taking off when the tug suffered an engine failure immediately after lift off. The glider cast off but there was little good ground on which to make a forced landing and the Hamilcar came down in a small field, its port wing hit a tree and the aircraft disintegrated. The 2 pilots and their 7 passengers were all injured.

24-Mar-45 RN396 Horsa II 1 HGSU 1 mile west of RAF Tarrant Rushton 0

The combination had been ferrying ground crew and had been airborne for 1½ hours. On approach, the pilot made a 360 degree turn to lose height but he then found the glider undershooting and so forced

540

landed in a field. The pilot failed to set his altimeter and hence there was a significant difference between the height displayed and the actual height above the ground and had this error not happened the pilot would have realised that there was no need for a circuit to bleed off the height.

24-Mar-45 RX917 Horsa II ORTU Needham Green, Essex 0

The glider ran into the tug's slipstream on take-off and appered to be nose heavy. The glider pilot decided to cast off the tow and the aircraft crashed into a field at high speed and struck a tree before going into a ditch.

25-Mar-45 KK170 Dakota IV 194 Sqn Maunubyin 0

The aircraft was taking off on an operational supply dropping sortie and was lined up on the runway in a thick mist. The landing strip was illuminated by only 13 flares over a strip length of 2200 yards and the first two of these had been extinguished. During the roll, the aircraft swung and the pilot corrected the swing but with no visual cues, he over corrected and the aircraft swung the other way. At this stage the aircraft was running towards parked aircraft and the pilot attempted to clear these but the aircraft struck two Sentinal aircraft, went through some telegraph wires, hit the ground and ground looped.

25-Mar-45 KH397 Liberator VI 358 Sqn Bakkutia 9+8

The aircraft was taking off in the early morning on an operational supply dropping sortie. At an estimated all up weight of nearly 68000 lbs it was very heavily laden and it was thought possible that the load was badly distributed, as it was also revealed subsequently that the briefing had been haphazard, regarding the make up and stowing of loads for each DZ, as was the supervision of the actual loading. Additionally, packages recovered subsequently from the wreckage were not shown on the aircraft's load manifest and it seems probable that the aircraft was actually overweight. There was no wind to assist take-off and this would have meant the take-off run would have been longer. On take-off, the aircraft failed to climb and it crashed into some trees situated 800 yards from the runway's end before hitting a village some 200 yards further on, resulting in the deaths of 8 civilians and the injury of 10 others. The captain was experienced on type in both day and night flying but is possible that he did not adjust to flying on instruments quickly enough or that the No:1 propeller 'ran away' on take-off.

Warrant Officer Walter Roy MILLS Pilot
Flight Sergeant Leslie Charles LOVELESS 20 Co-Pilot
Pilot Officer Sidney Edward HENCHER RCAF Navigator
Flying Officer Thomas Dixon TAYLOR 26 Bomb Aimer
Flight Sergeant Gerald Desmond Townsend ROWE 21 Wireless Operator
Sergeant David Scott POTTER 21 Air Gunner
Flight Sergeant James Frederick Charles HAWKINS 24 Air Gunner
Sergeant Charles Clarence YOUNG 21 Wireless Operator/Air Gunner
Sergeant Leonard James HULSE 21

25-Mar-45   LL453   Halifax V   148 Sqn   Brindisi, Italy   0

The aircraft was being landed in the dusk, at the conclusion of a 6 hour sortie to deliver supplies into Northern Yugoslavia. The pilot misjudged his height and the aircraft landed heavily. Its starboard tyre burst and it swung off the runway, sustaining heavy damage in the process. The pilot was inexperienced on type and no further action was taken.

25-Mar-45   BT896   Hotspur II   3 GTS   Exeter   0

The pupil pilot was landing into the sun and his judgement of the approach was impaired. The glider undershot the airfield and having struck the ground in a field, it ran into the boundary fence.

25-Mar-45 HH248 Hotspur II 3 GTS Honiton Clyst, Devon 1

The glider was released from the tow at 2000 feet. It turned to starboard, went over onto its back and dived into the ground. It is thought that the starboard aileron cable had been looped over the end of the operationg lever and this caused either a jam or a sudden release.

Sergeant Ronald Mason FAULKNER 28 The Glider Pilot Regiment

25-Mar-45 DM399 Master II 3 GTS RAF Exeter 0

The pilot experienced a loss of power on take-off and so closed the throttle and raised the undercarriage to stop.

26-Mar-45 AL504 Liberator II 45 Gp CS Between Azores and Ottawa 14

This aircraft was amongst the most well known individual aircraft of the war. During its production, there was a requirement for a VIP transport version of the Liberator and this airframe was uprated to a passenger transport, although to a fairly basic standard and without pressurisation. It was then used by senior British VIPs, including the Prime Minister who flew in it to Moscow via Cairo and Tehran. The aircraft was given the name 'Commando' and was subsequently modified with an extended fuselage and a single tail fin, similar to the final versions of the Liberator. The aircraft had taken off from Northolt and is believed to have crashed off the Azores. No trace was found nor was the cause determined. However, later in the year, after another Liberator transport was lost on the Atlantic route, a comment was made about standards of workmanship at the Consolidated works and the RAF's fleet of late mark Liberators was subjected to close scrutiny.

Wing Commander William Hugh BIDDELL OBE DFC Pilot
Flight Sergeant Aubrey Norman BRODIE Co-Pilot
Flight Lieutenant Kenneth George SHEA RAAF Navigator
Flight Lieutenant David BUCHANAN RCAF Navigator
Frederick William WILLIAMS Radio Officer

Pilot Officer Douglas James SPENCE RCAF
Victor Claude James BANNISTER Steward
Air Marshal Sir Peter Roy Maxwell DRUMMOND 50 KCB DSO & Bar OBE MC
Commander Rupert Arnold BRABNER 33 DSO DSC MP Under Secretary of State for Air
Sir John Bradley ABRAHAM 61
Squadron Leader Elisha Gladdis Gladdis PLUM 47
Herbert Albert JONES 51
Eric ROBINSON 35
Edward TWENTYMAN 57

| 26-Mar-45 | K6949 | Harrow II | 271 Sqn | Gilze-Rijen Netherlands | 0 |

The aircraft had become bogged down whilst it was taxiing across soft ground. There was no towing bridle available for the aircraft so ropes were used instead during the recovery process but these contributed to the aircraft being damaged further.

| 26-Mar-45 | NA131 | Halifax | 298 Sqn | RAF Tarrant Rushton | 0 |

Crashed during circuit training.

| 26-Mar-45 | LK621 | Stirling III | 1332 CU | RAF Nutts Corner | 0 |

The pilot was undertaking his first night solo on type and with his crew, had been airborne for 1½ hours. On approach to land the aircraft was too fast and touched down too far along the runway. To avoid the overshoot, the pilot swung the aircraft violently and the undercarriage collapsed resulting in the aircraft's back being broken.

27-Mar-45   NA664   Halifax III   298 Sqn   South Farm, Smallwood, Spetisbury Dorset   6

The aircraft was returning to base at the conclusion of a night cross country sortie of nearly 5 hours duration. On the downwind leg of the landing approach, the aircraft lost speed, its port wing dropped and it dived into the ground off a stall. The most probable cause of the accident was that the pilot forgot to lower the flaps to 30 degrees before lowering the undercarriage and was not immediately concerned when the airspeed fell below 120 mph. It was commented that the Halifax bleeds off speed rapidly below 140 mph and there is a marked tendency in both Mark III and V Halifaxes for the throttles to slip back, below – 3 inches of boost. This crew had only arrived recently from 1665 HCU and were inexperienced on the type. Nonetheless, flying Halifax NA613, they had participated in Operation VARSITY and their aircraft towed a Horsa. During the return, that aircraft was struck by AA fire and suffered hydraulic problems necessitating an emergency landing at Manston.

    Flying Officer Paul Charles WILLIAMS 21 Pilot
    Flight Sergeant George Seaton REDKNAP 27 RCAF Navigator
    Flying Officer Harold Eric ACKROYD 25 Bomb Aimer
    Flight Sergeant George Cameron McKay STEWART 23 Wireless Operator
    Sergeant Jack Redman PAYNE 20 Flight Engineer
    Sergeant Henry Albert STINSON 24 Air Gunner

27-Mar-45   DL303   Master II   3 GTS   RAF Exeter   0

Whilst engaged on an airtest and flying in the circuit area at 300 feet, the aircraft's engine failed because the No: 2 cyclinder exhaust valve seating came adrift. The pilot turned in for an emergency landing but the aircraft touched down on some sharply rising ground and the undercarriage failed. The pilot; Flight Sergeant C Thomas, was commended for his efforts.

28-Mar-45   KN409   Dakota IV   45 Gp   Near Prestwick   4

The aircraft was approaching the Scottish coast at the conclusion of a 6 hour leg on the Trans-Atlantic ferry

Date	Serial	Aircraft	Unit	Place	Casualties

Brief Circumstances of Accident
Casualty Details (If Applicable)

service. The weather was 10/10 ths cloud down to 1300 feet and broken cloud to 700 feet and although clear below this height there was slight rain. The aircraft was being instructed to descend over the sea but it appears that the pilot, whose instrument flying was weak, lost control during the descent, probably after breaking out of the total cloud cover, reverting to visual flying but then entering the broken cloud and having to go back to instruments again. It was commented that the crew was not suffiently experienced for the ferrying tasks and that in future ferry pilots should have a minimum of 600 hours flying and at least 25 hours dual and solo on type. This observation is an interesting reappraisal, as the war was approaching its end, when one considers the very meagre experience of the crews who ferried aircraft across the Atlantic in the early days of the war.

Flying Officer John William NEWMAN RCAF Co-Pilot
Flight Lieutenant Hector Roy HANNAFORD 27 RAAF Pilot
Flight Sergeant Alexander Donald Cyril JAMIESON 23 Navigator
Warrant Officer II Patrick LAVIN RCAF

| 29-Mar-45 | KK121 | Dakota III | 194 Sqn | 21 degrees 43 North/92 degrees 10 East | 0 |

Having been airborne for nearly 6 hours on a supply dropping sortie, the aircraft's starboard engine failed at 3000 feet and the port engine cut a minute later. The pilot made a forced landing in a clearing but the aircraft was damaged extensively and the crew of five were injured. Although ample fuel fuel was found in the port auxiliary tank, the damage to the aircraft was so extensive that the cause of the double engine failure could not be determined. The probability, however, is that the fuel cocks were mismanaged or there was an airlock in the system.

| 29-Mar-45 | KK195 | Dakota III | 238 Sqn | Alon | 0 |

The pilot failed to lower the undercarriage and the aircraft landed on its belly. There were no injuries amongst the three crew and twenty seven passengers.

29-Mar-45   PW391   Stirling IV   ORTU   Knarr Hill Farm, Thorney Toll, Peterborough   7+1

The aircraft was 22 minutes into a cross country training flight when it collided with a Master aircraft; DM336 of No: 7 SFTS. Both aircraft crashed and were destroyed by fire. The pilot of the Master was a French NCO Corporal R de Bienkiewicz.

    Flight Lieutenant Walter John HOWES 22 Pilot
    Flight Sergeant Edward Charles ALDERSLEY 23
    Corporal John HARDY 26
    Flying Officer Kenneth Rhodes INGER 21
    Flight Sergeant Robert Henry MCALPINE 37
    Flight Sergeant Frederick William REES 33
    Sergeant Kenneth SLEEK 19

30-Mar-45   T1583   Lysander III   148 Sqn   Brindisi   0

The aircraft had been employed on crew training and the pilot had been doing circuits and bumps for about an hour. One landing was heavy and whilst taxying afterwards, the tailwheel pyramid collapsed and the stern frame structure was fractured.

31-Mar-45   LJ888   Stirling IV   196 Sqn   Near Arendal Norway   6

This aircraft was one of a batch from different squadrons operating over Norway on a bright and moonlit night. As will be seen from the following records, a Halifax and five Stirlings were lost and it must be wondered at the wisdom of operating in such weather conditions, when the aircraf would have been easily detected by the enemy. This aircraft was intercepted before reaching its dropping zone and it was shot down by a night fighter, exploding on impact and being destroyed completely. The crew are buried together in a Collective Grave at Arendal.

Date	Serial	Aircraft	Unit	Place	Casualties

Brief Circumstances of Accident
Casualty Details (If Applicable)

Flight Sergeant Derrick Vivian CATTERALL 21 Pilot
Flight Sergeant George Sidney REED 30 Navigator
Flight Sergeant Thomas Louitt BRUNTON 22 Wireless Operator
Flight Sergeant John Richard CROSS 20 Air Gunner
Flight Sergeant Reginald Sergius Paul Harding KLIMANEK 21 Bomb Aimer
Sergeant Paul Montefiore MYERS 20 Flight Engineer

Date	Serial	Aircraft	Unit	Place	Casualties
31-Mar-45	LK119	Stirling IV	161 Sqn	Hegland in Holt Norway	7

This aircraft was shot down by night fighters and exploded and burnt on crashing. The sortie was to have been the pilot's last trip of his tour and he and his crew were flying sortie; BIT 14.

Flight Lieutenant Edward Patrick Cary KIDD 32 DFC Pilot
Flying Officer Thomas Scott MACAULAY 32 Air Gunner
Flight Sergeant George Alfred HEATH 21 DFM Navigator
Sergeant Richard Arthur BURGESS 20 Flight Engineer
Flight Sergeant Harry MINSHULL 20 Air Gunner
Warrant Officer Allan Murray TAYLOR 24 RAAF Wireless Operator
Flight Sergeant Arthur Donald SHOPLAND 20 Air Gunner

Date	Serial	Aircraft	Unit	Place	Casualties
31-Mar-45	LK197	Stirling IV	196 Sqn	Location not known	6

The crew was undertaking a supply dropping sortie to Norway but their aircraft disappeared without trace and it is unclear whether it was shot down or was overwhelmed by the poor weather.

Pilot Officer Clarence CAMPBELL 25 RAAF Pilot
Flight Sergeant Kenneth William LINNEY 22 Navigator
Flight Sergeant Francis William MATTHEWS 31 Bomb Aimer

Warrant Officer George Gregory ALLMAN 22 RAAF Wireless Operator
Flight Sergeant Frederick Charles BRENNER Flight Engineer
Flight Sergeant Edward Sidney LLOYD 20 Air Gunner

31-Mar-45   LK332   Stirling IV   299 Sqn   Vegarshei   6
Lost to a German night fighter and crashed into a marsh at Vegarshei.

Flight Lieutenant Ranulf TREVOR-ROPER 29 DFC Pilot
Flight Lieutenant Herbert Wain RICKETTS 26 Navigator
Flying Officer Dennis PEAT 21 Bomb Aimer
Warrant Officer Philip Sydney BRINKWORTH 25 Wireless Operator
Sergeant James Alexander ELLIOTT 28 Air Gunner
Sergeant Kenneth Clement HAYWARD 19 Flight Engineer

31-Mar-45   PK225   Stirling IV   299 Sqn   6
The crew of this aircraft was undertaking Operation STIRRUP 8, which was a supply drop to a DZ in southern Norway but the aircraft was lost without trace.

Flight Lieutenant Arbuthnot George ANDERSON Pilot
Flight Sergeant Robert Alfred Walter DAWKINS 21 Navigator
Flight Sergeant Wilfred Ian DAVIDSON 31 RNZAF Bomb Aimer
Warrant Officer Leslie GREEN 24 Wireless Operator
Flight Sergeant David Clement Raymond SMITH 20 Air Gunner
Sergeant Leonard JEFFREY Flight Engineer

31-Mar-45   PN243   Halifax III   298 Sqn   At sea off Norway   6
The crew was briefed for an SOE sortie - OSTLER 2 - and the aircraft took off at 2026 hours en route to a DZ at 61 degrees 33 08 North/ 11degrees 48 23 East and it was lost without trace. The previous week, this crew had been involved with Operation VARSITY and had towed a Hamilcar glider successfully on that occasion.

Date	Serial	Aircraft	Unit	Place	Casualties
Brief Circumstances of Accident					
Casualty Details (If Applicable)					

Flying Officer Peter IRELAND 23 Pilot
Flight Sergeant Cyril ALEXANDER 23 Bomb Aimer
Sergeant Thomas REYNOLDS 34 Flight Engineer
Flight Sergeant Kenneth WOODHART 23 Navigator
Warrant Officer James Alexander BUZZA 24 RCAF Air Gunner
Flight Sergeant Alfred George KING 22 Wireless Operator

31-Mar-45	HH546	Hotspur II	3 GTS	Culmhead, Somerset	0

This was the RAF pilot's first solo on type and on landing, the aircraft ballooned, stalled and landed heavily causing substantial damage to itself.

01-Apr-45	KH323	Liberator	357 Sqn	RAF Jessore	15

The aircraft was being used for the infiltration of a party of Force 136 agents into Burma and was taking off at night with a crew of nine RCAF personnel, two British Army officers and four Burmese irregulars. Immediately on take-off, the aircraft climbed for a few seconds and then turned starboard through 90 degrees, lost height and crashed in flames. Although the Board of Enquiry could not come to any firm conclusions and considered pilot error and engine failure, the crash remains a mystery. However, two factors do not seem to have been explored or mentioned in the accident report. First, it was known that all the passengers and crew were located at the front of the aircraft for take-off and hence it is possible the aircraft was out of trim. Second, a crew flying the aircraft the previous day had reported its poor performance but this issue seems not to have been resolved prior to the start of this mission. It is also known, from records kept by another squadron member, that the pilot on this sortie was concerned about the state of the aircraft.

Flying Officer Leonard Stewart STOCKWELL 25 RCAF Pilot

Flying Officer James Brian MILLAR 20 RCAF Co-Pilot
Flying Officer John Nelson FRIESON 24 RCAF Navigator
Flying Officer Karl McCormick MERRIAM 20 RCAF Bomb Aimer
Pilot Officer Jack Thornber STEVENTON 20 RCAF Wireless Operator
Pilot Officer Gordon John STORKEY 22 RCAF Wireless Operator
Pilot Officer Alfred George BRETT 29 RCAF Air Gunner
Pilot Officer Robert James Smith GREEN RCAF Air Gunner
Pilot Officer Harry Ervin RICKERT 25 RCAF Air Gunner
Captain Godfrey MARCHANT 35 MC Intelligence Corps
Captain Peter Charles Henry VICKERY 24 RAC
+ four Burmese Irregulars

02-Apr-45   LK193   Stirling IV   196 Sqn   At sea off Cromer   6

The aircraft, which was at an all up weight of some 71000 lbs, was seen to dive into the sea after crossing the coast for a container dropping sortie over Europe. The cause of the accident was not determined but loss of control due to an engine failure combined with the heavy weight might have been a cause. This crew, flying Stirling LJ583, had completed successfully a Horsa tow as part of operation VARSITY.

Flying Officer Neville CARROLL 23 RAAF Pilot
Warrant Officer Stanley James Verse PHILO 22 Bomb Aimer
Warrant Officer Jack GRAIN 24 Wireless Operator
Warrant Officer Gilbert HUGHES 33 Navigator
Flight Sergeant Reginald Ernest MARSHALL 39 Air Gunner
Believed to be:
Flight Sergeant Arthur O BENNETT Flight Engineer

02-Apr-45   LK286   Stirling IV   570 Sqn   RAF Rivenhall   0

The aircraft was landing on a runway surface which was known to be rough and whose use had been

Date	Serial	Aircraft	Unit	Place	Casualties

Brief Circumstances of Accident / Casualty Details (If Applicable)

specifically authorised by Group HQ. The port tyre burst on landing and the undercarriage collapsed after the aircraft had swung off the runway.

Date	Serial	Aircraft	Unit	Place	Casualties
03-Apr-45	LJ942	Stirling IV	299 Sqn	Roskilde Fjord, Frederikssund Denmark	1

The aircraft was on a supply dropping sortie but crashed into shallow water and sank. Although most of the crew escaped and the pilot searched through the submerged wreck for the missing man, he could not be found immediately and was later discovered to have drowned. The cause of the ditching is not clear.

Flying Officer Thomas Albert MCBEATH 26 RCAF Bomb Aimer

Date	Serial	Aircraft	Unit	Place	Casualties
03-Apr-45	NA660	Halifax III	298 Sqn	Kalleberg near Farsund	6

Attacked and shot down whilst on an SOE mission from Tarrant Rushton. This crew had led the squadron's effort for Operation VARSITY and had towed a Horsa glider. Wg Cdr Law-Wright had been awarded the DSO and DFC whilst on 14 Sqn in late 1943.

Wing Commander Hubert LAW-WRIGHT 34 DSO DFC Pilot OC 298 Sqn
Flying Officer John Cranston Boyd RAE 29 Navigator
Pilot Officer Eldon Fleet CARLISLE 27 RCAF Bomb Aimer
Flight Sergeant Terence McKeown STONHAM 24 Wireless Operator
Flight Sergeant Denis Sydney Bertram DERRETT 28 Flight Engineer
Flight Sergeant Geoffrey Brasnett JOHNSON 20 Air Gunner

Date	Serial	Aircraft	Unit	Place	Casualties
03-Apr-45	PK227	Stirling IV	190 Sqn		8

The crew was flying STIRRUP 18 to Norway but the aircraft was lost without trace.

Flying Officer Sir Chandos Wren HOSKYNS Bt 21 Pilot

Flying Officer Sydney CARPENTER Navigator
Flying Officer Alan FISKEN 31 Bomb Aimer
Warrant Officer Clifford BUCKLEY 24 Wireless Operator
Sergeant Russell Ernest CHAPMAN 28 Flight Engineer
Flying Officer Peter John Rupert VINEY 21 Air Gunner
Driver Norman SMITH RASC 223 Air Despatch Coy
Driver Frederick EVANS

04-Apr-45 LK742 Halifax V   148 Sqn   Brindisi, Italy   0

Following take-off for a special duties sortie, the aircraft's undercarriage would not retract and in consequence the engines overheated. The pilot elected to return to base, since the sortie could not be continued. On landing, the aircraft touched down heavily and its port tyre burst, causing a swing from which the undercarriage collapsed.

05-Apr-45 LA742 Hamilcar   1 HGSU   RAF Tarrant Rushton   0

The crew was engaged on a dual check and after the glider had cast off the pupil selected full flap. The instructor took control and applied flap for maximum lift but the glider undershot the airfield and landed in a wood.

06-Apr-45 DP788 Horsa   1 HGSU   Stony Stratford, Northants   0

The combination was flying in a massed landing exercise and had been airborne for nearly 1½ hours. The combination passed through another combination's slipstream and the glider pilot lost control of his aircraft as it got out of position. The tow was cast off and the glider made a forced landing in a field.

07-Apr-45 KG762 Dakota III   194 Sqn   Myitke   0
The aircraft's undercarriage collapsed after it bounced on landing and went off the side of the airstrip. The 4 crew survived.

08-Apr-45 BT840 Hotspur II   3 GTS   Devon Map Ref 222088   0
The combination entered thin cloud and the glider pilot cast off the tow and made a forced landing. Although it was suggested that the glider pilot should not have pulled off when flying through thin cloud, his glider was not fitted with the Cable Angle Indicator (CAI), which would have helped him to maintain his position relative to the tug. The tug pilot was criticised for towing the glider into cloud.

09-Apr-45 AM929 Liberator   231 Sqn   St Simone, Quebec   2+1
This aircraft was one of the earliest Liberators to enter service with the RAF in 1941. It joined 120 Sqn after service with A&AEE and was involved in actions resulting in the destruction of several U-boats. Having been rejected by Coastal Command as obsolete, it was modified for transport duties and taken on charge by the unit. It was on an approach to land at Dorval that engine caught fire and fell out, after which the aircraft struck HT cables and crash landed. There was a crew of seven and eleven passengers and two of the latter were killed. During an attempt to help the casualties, a civilian was electrocuted by the downed power lines. Unfortunately, the names of the casualties have not been found.

09-Apr-45 PJ901 Stirling V   46 Sqn   Mauripur   0
The aircraft was being used for crew training and a swing to starboard developed during the take-off run. The pilot over corrected and a swing to port resulted in the aircraft running off the side of the runway and its undercarriage collapsing. As is usually the case, the most secure way to deal with a swing during the

554

early stages of a take-off, is to close the throttles and start all over again!

09-Apr-45 LK624 Stirling III 1332 CU RAF Nutts Corner 0
The pilot, who had barely 30 minutes solo on type, was faced with a burst tyre on take-off. The aircraft went off the side of the runway, into soft ground and tipped onto its nose, damaging the undercarriage in the process.

09-Apr-45 MZ506 Halifax III 296 Sqn 1 mile north of Chelveston 0
The crew was engaged in a VHF homing exercise and the pilot feathered both starboard engines whilst flying at 6000 feet. Subsequently he could not restart these engines, possibly because he did not raise the ignition switches guard. With asymmetric power it became difficult to control the aircraft and a crash landing was made but the aircraft struck a tree and burst into flames.

10-Apr-45 FL538 Dakota III 85 RSU Barrackpore 0
The aircraft overshot the runway and ended up in a pond. Neither brakes nor flaps were working but fortunately, there were no injuries to the crew.

10-Apr-45 KK110 Dakota IV 85 RSU 5 miles south of Khulna, India 0
The aircraft's radio failed in bad weather and with fuel supplies critical, the pilot made a forced landing in a river at the location shown. The crew was uninjured.

10-Apr-45 NX824 Hamilcar 1 HGSU RAF Tarrant Rushton 0
The pilot was undershooting the approach with full flaps set but did not then raise them to the half down position, where they would have provided more lift and so permitted a safe landing. The glider undershot and was wrecked in the subsequent crash.

Date	Serial	Aircraft	Unit	Place	Casualties
Brief Circumstances of Accident					
Casualty Details (If Applicable)					

10-Apr-45   HH267 Hotspur III   5 GTS   Shobdon, Herefordshire   0

The pilot, who was inexperienced, was making a night sortie and whilst landing misjudged the approach. He made an 'S' turn to bleed off some height but then allowed the glider to land heavily, causing significant damage.

10-Apr-45   DP423 Horsa   ORTU   Westwood Farm, Keevil Common   0

The pilot flew too far across wind before attempting a turn in to land. In doing so he found he was then unable to make the airfield and although undershooting he put too much flap on. The glider was put down in a field.

11-Apr-45   FD896 Dakota III   52 Sqn   3 miles north of Yelahanka   0

The aircraft took off in the early afternoon and was making a half circuit, immediately after take-off, when its starboard engine failed at 150 feet. The pilot elected to make a belly landing a few miles from the airfield and the twelve persons on board were uninjured.

11-Apr-45   FK763 Hudson   161 Sqn   Dorking Surrey   0

This aircraft was being flown on a sortie coded; FLAP to Germany and its crew was led by Flight Lieutenant Dennis Webb. The aircraft suffered an engine failure and Webb cancelled the mission and returned to UK. For reasons not shown, the aircraft was abandoned and crashed near Dorking but there were no casualties. Flight Lieutenant Webb was awarded a DFC in Sep 45 for his work with the squadron.

11-Apr-45   LK305 Stirling IV   196 Sqn   North Sea off Dutch coast   6

The aircraft is reported to have been shot down over the Frisian Islands

Warrant Officer Kenneth ATKINSON 23 Navigator
Sergeant Robert BARNES 23 Wireless Operator
Sergeant Trevor Robert JONES 19 Air Gunner
Sergeant Phillip Roy TOMLINSON 22 Flight Engineer
Flight Sergeant Frederick VERNON 26 Pilot
Flying Officer James William WHITEHEAD 22 Bomb Aimer

11-Apr-45   RR294   Hamilcar   1 mile west of RAF Tarrant Rushton   0

The pilot thought his approach was too high for a normal landing and so attempted to stall the aircraft deliberately. Unfortunately, he did not appreciate the height required to recover from a stall and he lost control at 300 feet and the aircraft crashed.

12-Apr-45   LJ638   Stirling IV   570 Sqn   Nieuwerkirk aan de Ijssel   0

This aircraft, captained by Flight Lieutenant G E Sharp, was engaged on night operations over the Netherlands, together with two other aircraft from the squadron. It failed to return but the precise circumstances of its loss are not recorded. What is known is that the sortie was coded; NICO I and the crew was to drop twenty four containers and four packages to a DZ. Depite a search conducted the following day, nothing was found immediately but the aircraft was subsequently located at Nieuwerkirk, where it had crashed but its crew survived.

12-Apr-45   PK228   Stirling IV   299 Sqn   North Sea   6

This aircraft and its crew were engaged on TABLEJAM 149, an SOE supply sortie to a Danish DZ west of Ferjitslev. There were no reports from the aircraft after its departure from Shepherds Grove and although the bodies of two crew members were washed ashore in June, there is no indication as to what happened to the aircraft.

Flight Lieutenant William Richard Fortescue CURRY 22
Flight Sergeant Sidney Ernest JONES 23

Date   *Serial*   *Aircraft*   *Unit*   *Place*   *Casualties*
Brief Circumstances of Accident
      Casualty Details (If Applicable)

Flying Officer Kenneth William Trevett RIGBY 23
Flight Sergeant Frank CAIRNS 23
Warrant Officer Sydney Norman HUNSDON 22
Flight Sergeant Robert Francis SHEEN 29

12-Apr-45   FR712   Hadrian I   361 MU   Bihta, Bihar, India   3
This glider and Hadrian KH898 were being towed by Halifax NA642 in a double tow, whilst being transferred to Bilaspur. At 200 feet immediately after take-off, the Halifax suffered an engine failure and released both gliders immediately. This glider's tow rope was not dumped by the glider pilot immediately and besides acting as a 'drag anchor', it fouled some trees and the aircraft crashed. As the gliders were turning to port at the time, it is thought possible that this pilot's visibility was obscured by the other Hadrian.

     Flying Officer John Lancelot RIDDLE 21
     Flight Sergeant Alan Frederick COOPER 21
     Believed to be:
       Sergeant Colin KING

12-Apr-45   NX838   Hamilcar   1 HGSU   1 mile west of RAF Tarrant Rushton   0
During the take-off, the tug's starboard tyre burst and so the glider pilot cast off so as not to endanger the tug. Unfortunately, the glider was poorly placed for a successful forced landing and on touchdown, the skid dug in and the glider overturned. The glider pilot; Staff Sergeant J Nunn, was commended for his prompt action and for making the best he could of a bad job.

13-Apr-45   EF272   Stirling IV   299 Sqn   RAF Shepherds Grove   0
The aircraft was taking off at night for an operational supply dropping sortie and an overcorrected swing,

which was initially to starboard, led to an undercarriage collapse and a fire in the port inner engine after the aircraft had ended up in deep ditch.

13-Apr-45   LJ931   Stirling IV   196 Sqn   RAF Shepherds Grove   0
This was another undercarriage collapse following a swing on take-off.

13-Apr-45   EJ923   Stirling III   1332 CU   RAF Nutts Corner   0
This pilot, who had already bent one Stirling during his conversion training, was landing on a runway with a strong 60 degree crosswind. A heavy landing was made with the aircraft drifting sideways and it swung into soft ground with the predictable failure of the undercarriage.

13-Apr-45   KN298   Dakota IV   238 Sqn   20 miles west of Feni, Near Chittagong   32
The aircraft was being flown by a single pilot and a wireless operator and without a navigator but with a medical attendant and another airman as crew. The flight was a routine communications sortie but the aircraft was carrying 28 sick or wounded personnel. The aircraft was flown into a developed cu-nim cloud and it suffered a structral failure and crashed with the loss of all on board.

   Flight Lieutenant E PRYKIEL PAF Pilot
   Flying Officer Robert Edward Campbell EDWARDS 36 RCAF Wireless Operator
   Leading Aircraftman Walter Robert FLETCHER 20 Air Ambulance Orderly
   Corporal Horace William LEACH 23
   + twenty eight others

13-Apr-45   NA347   Halifax A7   298 Sqn   Alphen area Netherlands   6
The aircraft had left its home base in the late evening of 12 Apr to undertake MEDICO 6; an SOE supply dropping sortie. This nearly new aircraft failed to return and crashed near the Amsterdam waterworks, amongst the coastal sand dunes. The cause of its loss was not determined.

Date	Serial	Aircraft	Unit	Place	Casualties

Brief Circumstances of Accident
Casualty Details (If Applicable)

Flying Officer John William SCOTT 23 Pilot
Flying Officer Arthur FARROW 35 Navigator
Flying Officer Samuel Alexander LYTLE 21 Bomb Aimer
Sergeant Arthur HOGG 22 Wireless Operator
Sergeant Archibald Gray GILLON 19 Flight Engineer
Sergeant Stanley THOMAS 22 Air Gunner

Date	Serial	Aircraft	Unit	Place	Casualties
13-Apr-45	RJ259	Horsa	1 HGSU	RAF Rivenhall	0

The glider pilot misjudged the landing with a heavy glider and overshot the end of the runway. The glider struck a tree stump and crashed.

Date	Serial	Aircraft	Unit	Place	Casualties
14-Apr-45	RX688	Horsa	21 HGCU	RAF Brize Norton	0

During the take-off and as the speed reached 115 mph, the glider pilot realised the tug, Albemarle V2000, was in difficulties and so cast off the tow. The pilot then flew his glider over the top of the tug but in doing so, the port undercarriage hit the tug's starboard mainplane and then crashed beyond the tug and went into a ditch.

Date	Serial	Aircraft	Unit	Place	Casualties
15-Apr-45	TS265	Stirling IV	190 Sqn	Off Norway	7

The aircraft was lost without trace on an SOE mission to Norway. Other aircraft returning from the sortie reported that severe thunderstorms and low cloud had been encountered and most diverted. However, in the general area of this aircraft's operation, an enemy night fighter had been seen and later a red glow on the surface of the sea, which might indicate that this crew fell to the night fighter. The aircraft itself was one of several Stirlings that had been rebuilt and updated from earlier marks of the aircraft, hence its unusual serial number for the period.

560

Flying Officer Arthur James LEWIS 27 Pilot
Flying Officer Ronald WELDON Navigator
Flight Sergeant Thomas William BOOKER 24 2nd Navigator
Flight Sergeant Anthony Peter Walter HILLIER Bomb Aimer
Flight Sergeant John CARTMELL 21 Wireless Operator
Sergeant Harry Victor BARROW 25 Flight Engineer
Flight Sergeant Walter Henry OGILVIE 20 Air Gunner

16-Apr-45   KN223 Dakota IV   Hathazari   0
On landing back from an operational supply dropping sortie, the port tyre burst whilst the aircraft's tailwheel was still off the ground. The aircraft tipped onto its nose but none of the crew was injured.

16-Apr-45   BT990 Hotspur II   Shobdon, Herefordshire   0
The pilot made a heavy landing and damaged the glider. This was the second accident involving this SNCO in just a few days.

16-Apr-45   HH690 Hotspur II   20(P)AFU   RAF Croughton   0
The RAF instructor pilot was giving his Army officer student his first night flying experience. On the crosswind leg, the instructor lowered full flap as he judged he was overshooting and he then raised the flaps to half setting but the glider undershot and struck an air raid shelter.

17-Apr-45   NA115 Halifax III   298 Sqn   RAF Tarrant Rushton   0
The aircraft was struck by a Hamilcar which was making a forced landing.

Date	Serial	Aircraft	Unit	Place	Casualties
Brief Circumstances of Accident					
Casualty Details (If Applicable)					

Date	Serial	Aircraft	Unit	Place	Casualties
17-Apr-45	NX874	Hamilcar	1 HGSU	RAF Tarrant Rushton	0

On take-off the tug's starboard tyre burst and the glider pilot cast off the tow. In an attempt to stay within the airfield, the pilot attempted a 180 degree turn but in doing so he turned the glider more steeply than necessary and crashed into a Halifax parked in dispersal. Had the glider pilot merely turned 90 degrees from the take-off track, the glider could have been brought to a halt safely within the airfield.

Date	Serial	Aircraft	Unit	Place	Casualties
18-Apr-45	EF274	Stirling IV	295 Sqn	RAF Rivenhall	0

Whilst taking off to ferry supplies of petrol to a European airfield, a swing developed and the undercarriage failed.

Date	Serial	Aircraft	Unit	Place	Casualties
18-Apr-45	LK202	Stirling IV	570 Sqn	Brussels	0

The aircraft was departing B58 and during the take-off run, the pilot's seat slipped back and the aircraft swung to port. In trying to correct the swing and avoid a building, the pilot swung the aircraft to starboard but its undercarriage collapsed.

Date	Serial	Aircraft	Unit	Place	Casualties
18-Apr-45	LK345	Stirling IV	196 Sqn	Hanover, Germany	0

The aircraft was landing at B120 in a strong crosswind and the pilot over corrected a swing, causing the undercarriage to fail. This airfield, recently taken from the enemy was unsuitable for a heavy aircraft such as the Stirling but the sortie was deemed operationally essential.

Date	Serial	Aircraft	Unit	Place	Casualties
18-Apr-45	LK132	Stirling IV	295 Sqn	Rheine	0

This aircraft ended in a bomb crater after it swung on landing whilst delivering a cargo of petrol in tins.

18-Apr-45   LA686   Hamilcar   1 HGSU   RAF Bentwaters   2

The aircraft was too high and the pilot realised he was overshooting the runway and so he turned the glider to line up with another runway. Again he judged he was too high and so turned in a third direction but the starboard wing dropped and the aircraft collided with the ground, catching fire on impact. There were two glider pilots and eleven RAF men aboard of whom two of the latter were killed.

   Two RAF men, names not found

18-Apr-45   HH527   Hotspur II   3 GTS   RAF Exeter   0

The crew of an experienced RAF instructor, with more than 400 hours on type, and his novice student, took off for a training exercise but whilst on tow the instructor found that the elevators would not operate as they were jamming when the control column was moved. He instructed the tug to fly over the airfield at 100 feet and then released the glider in the correct position. Unfortunately, with very little movement of the stick, the instructor had great difficulty exercising any control and the glider descended into the ground, landed heavily and broke the keel. It is thought that the elevators jammed because they had been buckled by being moved when the control locks were in and this was not apparent prior to take-off. The instructor; Flight Lieutenant H H Boddy was awarded a Green Endorsement in his Log Book in recognition of his skill in this unpleasant situation and in the New Year's Honours List 1946, he was awarded a King's Commendation for Valuable Services in the Air (KCVSA).

19-Apr-45   KN332   Dakota   28 SAAF   Vitweles Bouches, Rhone   7

The aircraft was descending through cloud in bad weather to make a landing. However, the aircraft struck a hillside at a height of 600 feet and all on board were killed.

   Lieutenant A F SMITH 30 SAAF Pilot
   Lieutenant Harry Noel GREENBERG 28 SAAF Pilot
   Lieutenant L C LORAN 26 SAAF Navigator
   Corporal Trevor GRIFFITHS 19 SAAF Wireless Operator

Date	Serial	Aircraft	Unit	Place	Casualties

Brief Circumstances of Accident
Casualty Details (If Applicable)

+ three others whose names are not known

| 19-Apr-45 | NA344 | Halifax A7 | 298 Sqn | Off Jutland coast | 6 |

The aircraft was engaged on an SOE supply dropping mission but crashed into the sea off the northern tip of Jutland. The crew was killed and it is unclear as to the cause of the loss of this aircraft which was just a few weeks old.

Warrant Officer Ronal Franklin MACKRILL 29 Pilot
Flight Sergeant Robert Henry HEALEY 21
Sergeant Albert William PANNELL 21
Flight Sergeant Douglas SMEDLEY 21
Flight Sergeant William Henry WALL 22
Flight Sergeant Frederick BRIDGE 19 Air Gunner

| 19-Apr-45 | BT892 | Hotspur II | 3 GTS | RAF Exeter | 0 |

This glider was landing behind another aircraft of the same type. The other glider weathercocked after touchdown and so the pilot of this aircraft turned to starboard to take avoiding action, which was successful. Unfortunately, as this aircraft's speed decayed, it could not be steered effectively and the pilot could not prevent a collision with a tractor.

| 20-Apr-45 | LJ930 | Stirling IV | 190 Sqn | Windlesham, Surrey | 6 |

The pilot of this aircraft was amongst the most experienced and highly decorated pilots in the RAF, never mind the transport force. The crew had landed at Odiham on return from a sortie to the continent. Knowing that the aircraft's tailwheel tyres were flat and despite being told not to do so by Flying Control, the pilot took off and the heat generated by the friction started a fire in the tail of the aircraft after it became airborne. Within minutes, the rear turret fell off and the aircraft crashed out of control, presumably because the fire had burned through the control cables.

Wing Commander Richard Henry BUNKER 25 DSO, DFC & Bar Pilot & Squadron Commander
Flying Officer George Robert Thompson TAYLOR 28
Sergeant Geoffrey ALDRED 19
Sergeant Kenneth Gerald GARDNER 22
Sergeant Frederick Charles KING 21
Flight Sergeant Ronald Lewis BAGLEY 25

20-Apr-45   PJ905   Stirling V   242 Sqn   Mauripur   0

The aircraft had taken off on a sortie from Mauripur to Palem but had returned to the departure airfield because the starboard wheel would not retract. Having landed without difficulty and whilst the aircraft was being taxyed back to dispersal, its starboard undercarriage leg collapsed.

21-Apr-45   KG326   Dakota   575 Sqn   2 miles north-east of Dessen Germany   4

The aircraft had left RAF Broadwell at about 0900 hours and was carrying a cargo of 114 containers of petrol. During the sortie the weather was very poor and the aircraft was flying in cloud with rain when it struck a hill at a height of about 1100 feet some 2½ hours after take-off. At this time the aircraft was some 18 miles south of its intended track but there is no explanation as to why the aircraft had veered off course.

Flight Lieutenant Bernard Herbert WEBB 35 RNZAF Pilot
Flight Lieutenant Duncan John STALKER Co-Pilot (shown as navigator in some records)
Flying Officer Alec Stanley Broadhurst RUSHTON 30 Navigator
Flight Sergeant Percy THOMPSON Wireless Operator

Date	Serial	Aircraft	Unit	Place	Casualties
Brief Circumstances of Accident					
Casualty Details (If Applicable)					
21-Apr-45	LJ627	Stirling IV	620 Sqn	B108 Rheine, Germany	0
Just 15 minutes before the aircraft below was damaged on landing, this aircraft had met a similar fate after it swung in a strong crosswind and ran into a bomb crater.					
21-Apr-45	LJ923	Stirling IV	196 Sqn	B108 Rheine, Germany	0
The aircraft was being landed on a very bad airfield, which was under repair because of earlier bomb damage. A strong crosswind lifted a wing and a swing developed to port, which the pilot could not control and its undercarriage collapsed.					
21-Apr-45	FR612	Hadrian	361 MU	Bihta Bihar	0
This glider and Hadrian's FR621, FR634, FR627 and FR667 were all damaged in a storm. The records show several other Hadrians as having been written off on this date because of the storm but they appear against a later storm and so it is possible that there has been some 'double counting'.					
22-Apr-45	LJ629	Stirling IV	299 Sqn	Hopsten Germany	0
This aircraft was landing at B112 in a strong crosswind, at right angles to the runway in use, over ground that was poor and unsuitable for heavy aircraft. The aircraft overran the available strip and went into a bomb crater, which promptly wiped off the undercarriage.					
23-Apr-45	LJ645	Stirling IV	570 Sqn	Skaering Denmark	4
The aircraft's crew was engaged on two drops of supplies to sites in Denmark, coded; TABLEJAM 172 and 179. There was only a reception at one of these locations and the aircraft was returning to base when it was struck by Flak. It then flew into trees and crashed. Three crew members were killed but the bomb aimer					

and wireless operator; Sergeant C Flannigan and Flight Sergeant R F Rawling, despite being injured managed to extract the pilot from the blazing wreck. Geoff Mombrun had been undertaking his operational initiation by flying as a second pilot on a sortie to Arnhem when the aircraft he was in was shot down. He and others aboard managed to avoid capture and he returned to UK.

Flying Officer Geoffrey Adrian MOMBRUN 21 Pilot died of injuries 26 April 1945
Flying Officer William George Henry HUNT 26 Navigator
Flight Sergeant John Herbert HAMILTON 24 Flight Engineer
Flight Sergeant Kenneth Ernest JOHNSON 22 Air Gunner

23-Apr-45   R9009   Lysander III   148 Sqn   10 miles south-west Udine   0

The aircraft was engaged on an operational infiltration sortie but on landing its starboard brake seized and the aircraft swung to port before the undercarriage collapsed. Subsequently, and although those on board were uninjured, the aircraft was found by enemy troops who destroyed it.

23-Apr-45   V1997   Albemarle VI   RAF Brize Norton   0

The port engine failed during take-off because the sleeve in the No: 13 cylinder was damaged when the articulated rod fractured. At this stage, the aircraft was at 350 feet on the climb with a Horsa glider on tow. The glider was immediately cast off and the pilot; Flight Sergeant W A Sealey, completed a single engined circuit and landed without further trouble – for which he received an appropriate entry in his Flying Logbook. The aircraft was not repaired, which after all only required an engine change and it languished at the base for a further 10 months before being struck off charge. This is an example of an obsolete aircraft being sidelined when there were sufficient serviceable examples to meet the requirements of the task and with the war in Europe in its final phase.

24-Apr-45   FZ685   Dakota III   233 Sqn   Rheine (B108)   0

The aircraft's port engine caught fire in the air but the pilot was able to close it down, feather the propeller and the blaze was extinguished. Whilst making an asymmetric landing, the aircraft overshot the runway and ran into a bomb crater. Although the aircraft was written off, its crew of four were uninjured.

Date	Serial	Aircraft	Unit	Place	Casualties
24-Apr-45	NA337	Halifax A7	644 Sqn	SOE operations Norway	5

Following a successful supply drop; CROP 17, the aircraft failed to return to base and it was subsequently found to have been shot down by enemy Flak, located to protect a key road and rail bridge on the Trondheim-Oslo railway at the head of Lake Mjosa. The aircraft was hit in an engine and crashed into the lake, which was partly frozen. The sole survivor was the air gunner Flight Sergeant Thomas Weightman.

Flight Lieutenant Alexander TURNBULL 27 DFC Pilot
Flight Lieutenant Walter Reginal MITCHELL 23 Navigator
Flight Sergeant Gordon Russell TUCKETT 23 Bomb Aimer
Flight Sergeant Alec NAYLOR 22 Wireless Operator
Flight Sergeant Goronwy Amman BASSETT 34 Flight Engineer

Date	Serial	Aircraft	Unit	Place	Casualties
24-Apr-45	LJ461	Stirling IV	1665 HCU	RAF Saltby	0

The pilot, who had 2500 flying hours total but only 10 on the Stirling, was practicing night landings. On take-off, he overcorrected a swing to starboard and closed the throttles to abandon the take-off. However, he allowed the swing to port to continue and the undercarriage collapsed.

Date	Serial	Aircraft	Unit	Place	Casualties
24-Apr-45	DM278	Master II	3 GTS	Devon Map Ref 460144	0

On a night take-off, the aircraft's engine failed at a height of 400 feet because the reduction gear came off. The pilot landed the aircraft straight ahead but in doing so it struck a bank and then a tree

25-Apr-45 PJ921 Stirling V 46 Sqn Mauripur 0

The pilot made an error in landing the aircraft on the taxiway, which was parallel to the runway. A wheel went off the side and into soft ground, causing the undercarriage to collapse.

26-Apr-45 LJ950 Stirling 295 Sqn Tipperne, Ringkoping Fjord Denmark 1

The aircraft was being flown on an operational SOE sortie; TABLE JAM 258. The pilot was flying at low level to avoid enemy anti-aircraft fire as he crossed the Danish coast but in a turn to starboard, the aircraft's wing tip struck the water and it crashed into the sea.

Flying Officer Geoffrey Charles SMALE 32 Bomb Aimer died of injuries 8 May 1945

26-Apr-45 LK567 Stirling IV 295 Sqn St Almstock 1

The crew, captained by Warrant Officer E A Dax, was tasked with a drop to a DZ on Danish island of Fyn but the details of the task were changed shortly before take-off and the crew went to another DZ, which proved to be unmanned. Having received no signals the crew set course for home but strayed too close to an enemy airfield and the aircraft was seriously damaged in both inboard engines. A crash landing was made on a heathland and the crew escaped from the aircraft before it was completely gutted by fire. The crew became separated and the pair helping the gravely injured bomb aimer managed to get him away from the wreck but he was left for medical assistance but died of his injuries later. Eventually, the two groups rejoined with the help of local people and they returned to England a few days after the end of hostilities.

Flight Sergeant John AYERS 22 died of injuries 30 April 1945

27-Apr-45 NA672 Halifax III 644 Sqn Lolland area Denmark 0

The aircraft was undertaking an SOE mission to Denmark; TABLEJAM 353 and carried a crew of six, captained by Warrant Officer Harry Christian. The cause of the loss is not known but the aircraft ditched in the sea just off the coast and all the crew were able to reach the shore. Two New Zealanders evaded

Date	Serial	Aircraft	Unit	Place	Casualties

Brief Circumstances of Accident
Casualty Details (If Applicable)

capture but the others were taken by the Gestapo but released at the end of the war in Europe.

27-Apr-45 RX613 Horsa   22 HGCU   Stourton Woods, Maiden Bradley   0

The combination was flying in very gusty wind and bumpy conditions on a cross country training sortie and had been airborne for 50 minutes. As he was concerned about the safety of both tug and glider, the glider pilot pulled off the tow and forced landed the glider.

28-Apr-45 KG406 Dakota III   271 Sqn   10½ miles south-east of South Foreland   5

This aircraft was transporting freight and it is believed that the pilots lost control whilst flying in cloud and the aircraft dived into the sea at the position shown. It seems probable that the intention was for the crew to return to UK with casualties as Margaret Walsh was a Nursing Orderly.

    Flight Lieutenant Rober Clifford John SOUTHEY 21 Pilot
    Flight Sergeant James Ronald FIFE-MILLER Co-Pilot
    Pilot Officer John Learned IVES 24 RCAF
    Flight Sergeant Ross Earl REYNOLDS 21 RCAF
    Leading Aircraftwoman Margaret WALSH WAAF

29-Apr-45 PJ890 Stirling V   46 Sqn   Tripoli   0

The aircraft was badly damaged during an inspection.

01-May-45 KK165 Dakota IV   194 Sqn   Mawnnubyin   0

The aircraft was engaged on a supply dropping sortie and had been airborne for about 35 minutes. Whilst flying at 8500 feet, extreme turbulence was encountered and the aircraft was lifted 5000 feet before being promptly desposited a further 3000 feet, all at very high vertical speeds which caused the pilot to lose control. The pilot managed to regain control when the turbulence abated and a safe landing was made at base. However, an examination of the aircraft revealed serious damage to the wing roots and outer wing attachment areas to an extent that the aircraft was not worth repairing.

01-May-45 KH312 Liberator VI   358 Sqn   18 degrees 38 North/93 degrees 30 East   5

This crew, who had previously set the time record for a Liberator sortie in this area of 20 hours 39 minutes, was returning to base following a successful drop, when the port outer engine failed and over Cheduba Island the starboard outer cut as well. The captain ordered his crew to ditching stations and at 0029 hours in light moonlight, the aircraft struck the water severely, smashing in the nose section and breaking up rapidly. The survivors swam ashore and after some confusion as to who had survived and who had been killed or died subsequently, it transpired that there were four survivors and five fatal casualties. Two officers of the USAAF Emergency Rescue Squadron; Lieutenants Hubbs and Puchalski, were commended for their skilful flying in rescuing some of the survivors by landing and taking off in very heavy seas.

Flight Lieutenant Richard William ROBINSON 30 Pilot
Flying Officer Rothney Alex CARTER 26 RAAF Co-Pilot died of injuries 2 May 45
Flying Officer Walter Henry BULL Navigator
Sergeant Thomas Frederick Courtney CLARKE 23 Wireless Operator
Sergeant Albert James BURLING 20 Air Gunner

03-May-45 KN202 Dakota IV   194 Sqn   Missing   6

The aircraft took off on a supply dropping sortie at 0500 hours and was never seen again.

Warrant Officer Colin Allan WALTON 29 RAAF Pilot
Flight Sergeant Edwin William WRIGHT 22 Co-Pilot
Warrant Officer Thomas Kevin Francis Xavier LEAVEY 20 RAAF Navigator
Flight Sergeant PITTENDRIGH RAAF Wireless Operator
Sergeant Roydon Maxwell KEMP Air Gunner

Brief Circumstances of Accident
Casualty Details (If Applicable)

Warrant Officer Philip Maurice GUNN 27 RAAF Wireless Operator

03-May-45 RJ245 Horsa 1 HGSU RAF Gosfield 0

After a sortie lasting 1¼ hours, the tug/glider combination arrived over the LZ but the weather was bad and there was a concentration of aircraft in the same area. The glider was cast off in a poor release position and overshot the landing, going through a hedge and being damaged in the process.

03-May-45 RX775 Horsa II 1 HGSU RAF Gosfield 0

On landing, the glider pilot took avoiding action to clear a stationary glider which was stopped in the landing area. He was then unable to turn back to his landing run. The glider ran into a ditch off the side of the runway and the nose undercarriage was forced up into the aircraft.

03-May-45 RZ403 Horsa II 1 HGSU RAF Gossfield 0

This aircraft and its crew was another victim of the poor weather and the congestion over the LZ. The tow was cast off at a bad position and the pilot was then faced with avoiding other gliders both on the way in and after landing. The aircraft overshot the landing and went through a hedge.

03-May-45 RN395 Horsa 1 HGSU ½ mile west of Pimperne, Dorset 0

The combination had been airborne for a few minutes and flew into hazy conditions. The tug pilot had one of his crew shine a red aldis lamp towards the glider as a way of assisting the glider pilot to maintain position until they reached clearer weather. Unfortunately, the glider pilot interpreted the red light as an emergency signal to cast off the tow and this he did. A forced landing followed and the glider lost its undercarriage, having run through a hedge.

05-May-45   KG491   Dakota III   Missing   6

The aircraft failed to return from a supply dropping sortie but the circumstances of its loss are not known.

Flying Officer Dennis Jack HERBERT AFC Pilot
Flight Sergeant Alexander ROBERTSON 22 Co Pilot
Warrant Officer Robert Harold DURRANT 23
Pilot Officer Sydney John ELIAS
+ two others non RAF

05-May-45   KG552   Dakota III   South of Alakwa Burma   0

This aircraft, piloted by Flight Sergeant Derrick Teify Jones, was one of nine from the squadron taking part in a supply drop in support of the attack on Rangoon, the task being to drop 48000 lbs of ammunition to a DZ at map reference QL 5038.   The supplies were to be dropped from 500 feet and on the run in all the aircraft were subjected to enemy AA fire and were hit.   This aircraft was struck in the main starboard fuel tank and petrol was lost and also a fire started, which quickly became uncontrollable.   The starboard engine caught fire and the blaze spread to the wing root before the load of supplies was jettisoned.   A crash landing was made in a paddy field and the port engine then caught fire before the entire crew abandoned the aircraft and ran for cover in the jungle.   The crew, who in addition to Flight Sergeant Jones, were; Flight Sergeant Huckins, Warrant Officer Lawrence, Warrant Officer Harrison, Flying Officer Cork and Flying Officer Jamies,   was helped by some Kerens, who warned them that the local Burmese were generally unfriendly and had recently handed a Beaufighter crew to the Japanese, who promptly murdered them. A series of adventures followed over the following several days but eventually an agent radioed for help and Jones and crew were rescued by a patrol boat.   Flight Sergeant Jones, who had flown over 130 sorties split almost evenly between supply drops and landings, was cited for the Conspicuous Gallantry Medal (CGM) Flying for his flying skill, courage and leadership of his crew.

Date	Serial	Aircraft	Unit	Place	Casualties
		Brief Circumstances of Accident			
		Casualty Details (If Applicable)			
04-May-45	LK196	Stirling IV	190 Sqn	RAF Great Dunmow	0

The pilot overcorrected a swing to starboard and closed the throttles before ground looping the aircraft in an attempt to stop it. The undercarriage failed but it was allowed that the pilot, who had only 4 hours on type, was inexperienced. It was also commented that he should not have been converted to the aircraft on a squadron, rather than a conversion unit and steps would be taken to prevent this recurring.

| 06-May-45 | V9295 | Lysander III | 357 Sqn | Meiktila | 0 |

This aircraft and the Lysander below, were both damaged badly during a severe storm at the base whilst they were parked.

| 06-May-45 | V9649 | Lysander III | 357 Sqn | Meiktila | 0 |

Damaged by a storm.

| 06-May-45 | RJ358 | Horsa | 1333 TSCU | RAF Leicester East | 0 |

On the approach to land, the pilot raised his flaps by 40 degrees and the glider stalled, landed heavily and was damaged badly. Fortunately, there were no injuries amongst the twelve people on board.

574

APPENDIX ONE

GLIDERS DESTROYED ON OPERATIONS OR ABANDONED

This Appendix lists gliders which were used on operations but were destroyed
or written off subsequently as not worth recovering. The listing does not
include Hadrian gliders being operated by British forces but allocated US
serials.

SICILY (10-Jul-43)		Horsa	DP695	Horsa	LG868
		Horsa	DP704	Horsa	LG870
		Horsa	DP706	Horsa	LG879
Horsa	LG988	Horsa	DP770	Horsa	LG880
Horsa	LT109	Horsa	DP811	Horsa	LG883
Horsa	HG878	Horsa	DP828	Horsa	LG915
Horsa	LH135	Horsa	HG858	Horsa	LG916
Horsa	DP647	Horsa	HG868	Horsa	LG917
Horsa	DG393	Horsa	HG912	Horsa	LG939
Horsa	DK199	Horsa	HG968	Horsa	LG948
Horsa	DP338	Horsa	HG971	Horsa	LG951
Horsa	DK197	Horsa	HG977	Horsa	LG985
Horsa	DP697	Horsa	HS111	Horsa	LG986
Horsa	LH202	Horsa	HS126	Horsa	LG992
Horsa	DP440	Horsa	LG675	Horsa	LG995
Horsa	LJ945	Horsa	LG679	Horsa	LH120
Horsa	LH130	Horsa	LG694	Horsa	LH132
Horsa	HG974	Horsa	LG715	Horsa	LH133
NORMANDY (06/07-Jun-44)		Horsa	LG716	Horsa	LH145
		Horsa	LG725	Horsa	LH146
		Horsa	LG736	Horsa	LH170
Horsa	DP416	Horsa	LG747	Horsa	LH173
Horsa	DP427	Horsa	LG774	Horsa	LH176
Horsa	DP438	Horsa	LG787	Horsa	LH179
Horsa	DP519	Horsa	LG790	Horsa	LH185
Horsa	DP539	Horsa	LG831	Horsa	LH189
Horsa	DP601	Horsa	LG849	Horsa	LH203
Horsa	DP628	Horsa	LG853	Horsa	LH206

Horsa	LH217	Horsa	LH402	Horsa	LH534
Horsa	LH224	Horsa	LH405	Horsa	LH553
Horsa	LH231	Horsa	LH406	Horsa	LH554
Horsa	LH234	Horsa	LH410	Horsa	LH565
Horsa	LH236	Horsa	LH429	Horsa	LH566
Horsa	LH239	Horsa	LH431	Horsa	LH568
Horsa	LH242	Horsa	LH432	Horsa	LH570
Horsa	LH243	Horsa	LH435	Horsa	LH571
Horsa	LH248	Horsa	LH437	Horsa	LH572
Horsa	LH264	Horsa	LH442	Horsa	LH575
Horsa	LH269	Horsa	LH444	Horsa	LH578
Horsa	LH271	Horsa	LH451	Horsa	LH579
Horsa	LH273	Horsa	LH453	Horsa	LH580
Horsa	LH276	Horsa	LH457	Horsa	LH582
Horsa	LH281	Horsa	LH465	Horsa	LH600
Horsa	LH295	Horsa	LH467	Horsa	LH601
Horsa	LH301	Horsa	LH469	Horsa	LH942
Horsa	LH316	Horsa	LH470	Horsa	LH943
Horsa	LH317	Horsa	LH475	Horsa	LH966
Horsa	LH321	Horsa	LH476	Horsa	LJ111
Horsa	LH324	Horsa	LH491	Horsa	LJ116
Horsa	LH328	Horsa	LH492	Horsa	LJ124
Horsa	LH329	Horsa	LH494	Horsa	LJ187
Horsa	LH339	Horsa	LH495	Horsa	LJ264
Horsa	LH344	Horsa	LH499	Horsa	LJ266
Horsa	LH349	Horsa	LH500	Horsa	LJ267
Horsa	LH353	Horsa	LH507	Horsa	LJ285
Horsa	LH373	Horsa	LH508	Horsa	LJ310
Horsa	LH375	Horsa	LH513	Horsa	LJ311
Horsa	LH378	Horsa	LH515	Horsa	LJ314
Horsa	LH379	Horsa	LH516	Horsa	LJ326
Horsa	LH380	Horsa	LH518	Horsa	PF690
Horsa	LH381	Horsa	LH519	Horsa	PF693
Horsa	LH393	Horsa	LH521	Horsa	PF694
Horsa	LH394	Horsa	LH526	Horsa	PF695
Horsa	LH397	Horsa	LH529	Horsa	PF700
Horsa	LH398	Horsa	LH532	Horsa	PF703
Horsa	LH399	Horsa	LH533	Horsa	PF705

Horsa	PF707	Horsa	PW693	Hamilcar	HH927
Horsa	PF709	Horsa	PW705	Hamilcar	HH928
Horsa	PF710	Horsa	PW706	Hamilcar	HH930
Horsa	PF715	Horsa	PW709	Hamilcar	HH932
Horsa	PF720	Horsa	PW712	Hamilcar	HH934
Horsa	PF722	Horsa	PW713	Hamilcar	HH935
Horsa	PF723	Horsa	PW714	Hamilcar	HH957
Horsa	PF724	Horsa	PW715	Hamilcar	HH959
Horsa	PF725	Horsa	PW716	Hamilcar	HH960
Horsa	PF744	Horsa	PW717	Hamilcar	HH962
Horsa	PF758	Horsa	PW720	Hamilcar	HH963
Horsa	PF760	Horsa	PW721	Hamilcar	HH964
Horsa	PF768	Horsa	PW722	Hamilcar	HH970
Horsa	PF769	Horsa	PW726	Hamilcar	LA636
Horsa	PF787	Horsa	PW732	Hamilcar	LA637
Horsa	PF790	Horsa	PW733	Hamilcar	LA638
Horsa	PF791	Horsa	PW734	Hamilcar	LA639
Horsa	PF793	Horsa	PW748	Hamilcar	LA640
Horsa	PF800	Horsa	PW758	Hamilcar	LA641
Horsa	PF803	Horsa	PW759	Hamilcar	LA644
Horsa	PF810	Horsa	PW760	Hamilcar	LA645
Horsa	PF812	Horsa	PW761	Hamilcar	LA642
Horsa	PF816	Horsa	PW770	Hamilcar	LA650
Horsa	PW637	Horsa	PW773	Hamilcar	LA651
Horsa	PW646	Horsa	PW774	Hamilcar	LA652
Horsa	PW647	Horsa	PW785	Hamilcar	LA653
Horsa	PW649	Horsa	PW786	Hamilcar	LA655
Horsa	PW652	Horsa	PW819	Hamilcar	LA669
Horsa	PW653	Horsa	PW828	Hamilcar	LA670
Horsa	PW658	Horsa	PW847	Hamilcar	LA671
Horsa	PW659	Horsa	PW871		
Horsa	PW662	Horsa	PW879		
Horsa	PW664	Horsa	PW884		
Horsa	PW665	Horsa	PW889		
Horsa	PW666	Horsa	PW897		
Horsa	PW671	Hamilcar	HH923		
Horsa	PW675	Hamilcar	HH924		
Horsa	PW676	Hamilcar	HH926		

ARNHEM
(17/18/19-Sep-44)

Horsa	HG804
Horsa	HG766
Horsa	HG930
Horsa	RN619
Horsa	HS101

Horsa	HG873	Horsa	DP555	Horsa	HG759
Horsa	RJ113	Horsa	DP558	Horsa	HG761
Horsa	DP283	Horsa	DP562	Horsa	HG766
Horsa	DP286	Horsa	DP606	Horsa	HG785
Horsa	DP290	Horsa	DP611	Horsa	HG791
Horsa	DP303	Horsa	DP613	Horsa	HG793
Horsa	DP311	Horsa	DP618	Horsa	HG795
Horsa	DP330	Horsa	DP644	Horsa	HG796
Horsa	DP335	Horsa	DP651	Horsa	HG799
Horsa	DP339	Horsa	DP658	Horsa	HG815
Horsa	DP340	Horsa	DP689	Horsa	HG819
Horsa	DP345	Horsa	DP690	Horsa	HG831
Horsa	DP368	Horsa	DP699	Horsa	HG832
Horsa	DP374	Horsa	DP720	Horsa	HG836
Horsa	DP375	Horsa	DP721	Horsa	HG847
Horsa	DP377	Horsa	DP726	Horsa	HG850
Horsa	DP385	Horsa	DP749	Horsa	HG855
Horsa	DP398	Horsa	DP754	Horsa	HG856
Horsa	DP415	Horsa	DP756	Horsa	HG871
Horsa	DP417	Horsa	DP759	Horsa	HG872
Horsa	DP422	Horsa	DP765	Horsa	HG873
Horsa	DP424	Horsa	DP774	Horsa	HG901
Horsa	DP487	Horsa	DP775	Horsa	HG910
Horsa	DP491	Horsa	DP776	Horsa	HG911
Horsa	DP492	Horsa	DP797	Horsa	HG914
Horsa	DP495	Horsa	DP802	Horsa	HG922
Horsa	DP500	Horsa	DP807	Horsa	HG924
Horsa	DP516	Horsa	DP826	Horsa	HG930
Horsa	DP520	Horsa	DP829	Horsa	HG933
Horsa	DP526	Horsa	DP833	Horsa	HG937
Horsa	DP528	Horsa	DP834	Horsa	HG939
Horsa	DP532	Horsa	DP840	Horsa	HG959
Horsa	DP533	Horsa	DP841	Horsa	HG960
Horsa	DP541	Horsa	HG736	Horsa	HG961
Horsa	DP543	Horsa	HG737	Horsa	HG962
Horsa	DP544	Horsa	HG740	Horsa	HG982
Horsa	DP548	Horsa	HG748	Horsa	HS101
Horsa	DP550	Horsa	HG749	Horsa	HS106

Gliders Lost In Action

Horsa	HS112	Horsa	LG981	Horsa	LH265
Horsa	HS116	Horsa	LG983	Horsa	LH268
Horsa	HS124	Horsa	LG987	Horsa	LH274
Horsa	HS132	Horsa	LG989	Horsa	LH278
Horsa	HS141	Horsa	LG997	Horsa	LH279
Horsa	HS148	Horsa	LH114	Horsa	LH280
Horsa	LF886	Horsa	LH127	Horsa	LH283
Horsa	LF887	Horsa	LH128	Horsa	LH285
Horsa	LF893	Horsa	LH134	Horsa	LH286
Horsa	LF897	Horsa	LH138	Horsa	LH288
Horsa	LF908	Horsa	LH140	Horsa	LH291
Horsa	LF914	Horsa	LH143	Horsa	LH292
Horsa	LF920	Horsa	LH144	Horsa	LH299
Horsa	LF921	Horsa	LH167	Horsa	LH318
Horsa	LF943	Horsa	LH168	Horsa	LH319
Horsa	LF958	Horsa	LH172	Horsa	LH334
Horsa	LF961	Horsa	LH175	Horsa	LH335
Horsa	LG663	Horsa	LH178	Horsa	LH345
Horsa	LG665	Horsa	LH180	Horsa	LH351
Horsa	LG681	Horsa	LH182	Horsa	LH355
Horsa	LG690	Horsa	LH184	Horsa	LH357
Horsa	LG697	Horsa	LH187	Horsa	LH359
Horsa	LG718	Horsa	LH188	Horsa	LH386
Horsa	LG744	Horsa	LH204	Horsa	LH387
Horsa	LG748	Horsa	LH210	Horsa	LH390
Horsa	LG767	Horsa	LH211	Horsa	LH395
Horsa	LG771	Horsa	LH216	Horsa	LH396
Horsa	LG792	Horsa	LH218	Horsa	LH400
Horsa	LG798	Horsa	LH220	Horsa	LH407
Horsa	LG837	Horsa	LH222	Horsa	LH408
Horsa	LG847	Horsa	LH227	Horsa	LH412
Horsa	LG851	Horsa	LH228	Horsa	LH414
Horsa	LG886	Horsa	LH229	Horsa	LH439
Horsa	LG892	Horsa	LH230	Horsa	LH445
Horsa	LG896	Horsa	LH240	Horsa	LH446
Horsa	LG922	Horsa	LH244	Horsa	LH448
Horsa	LG942	Horsa	LH247	Horsa	LH449
Horsa	LG977	Horsa	LH263	Horsa	LH455

Horsa	LH456	Horsa	LJ102	Horsa	PF761
Horsa	LH458	Horsa	LJ106	Horsa	PF764
Horsa	LH459	Horsa	LJ130	Horsa	PF786
Horsa	LH461	Horsa	LJ142	Horsa	PF789
Horsa	LH462	Horsa	LJ213	Horsa	PF795
Horsa	LH463	Horsa	LJ219	Horsa	PF796
Horsa	LH464	Horsa	LJ237	Horsa	PF797
Horsa	LH471	Horsa	LJ262	Horsa	PF798
Horsa	LH473	Horsa	LJ265	Horsa	PF806
Horsa	LH501	Horsa	LJ315	Horsa	PF807
Horsa	LH504	Horsa	LJ318	Horsa	PF808
Horsa	LH506	Horsa	LJ321	Horsa	PF811
Horsa	LH509	Horsa	LJ324	Horsa	PF815
Horsa	LH510	Horsa	LJ328	Horsa	PF817
Horsa	LH511	Horsa	LJ330	Horsa	PW640
Horsa	LH512	Horsa	LJ332	Horsa	PW641
Horsa	LH522	Horsa	LJ333	Horsa	PW643
Horsa	LH523	Horsa	PF691	Horsa	PW644
Horsa	LH525	Horsa	PF692	Horsa	PW645
Horsa	LH527	Horsa	PF698	Horsa	PW648
Horsa	LH528	Horsa	PF702	Horsa	PW650
Horsa	LH535	Horsa	PF704	Horsa	PW654
Horsa	LH536	Horsa	PF712	Horsa	PW655
Horsa	LH551	Horsa	PF713	Horsa	PW656
Horsa	LH552	Horsa	PF714	Horsa	PW660
Horsa	LH556	Horsa	PF717	Horsa	PW669
Horsa	LH558	Horsa	PF718	Horsa	PW672
Horsa	LH560	Horsa	PF721	Horsa	PW674
Horsa	LH561	Horsa	PF739	Horsa	PW697
Horsa	LH563	Horsa	PF742	Horsa	PW700
Horsa	LH564	Horsa	PF743	Horsa	PW703
Horsa	LH573	Horsa	PF747	Horsa	PW704
Horsa	LH577	Horsa	PF748	Horsa	PW710
Horsa	LH581	Horsa	PF749	Horsa	PW718
Horsa	LH597	Horsa	PF750	Horsa	PW727
Horsa	LH946	Horsa	PF751	Horsa	PW728
Horsa	LH956	Horsa	PF754	Horsa	PW729
Horsa	LH965	Horsa	PF755	Horsa	PW749

Horsa	PW750	Horsa	RJ160	Horsa	RJ252
Horsa	PW751	Horsa	RJ163	Horsa	RJ258
Horsa	PW752	Horsa	RJ165	Horsa	RJ261
Horsa	PW753	Horsa	RJ166	Horsa	RJ265
Horsa	PW756	Horsa	RJ167	Horsa	RJ266
Horsa	PW765	Horsa	RJ168	Horsa	RJ267
Horsa	PW766	Horsa	RJ170	Horsa	RJ268
Horsa	PW772	Horsa	RJ171	Horsa	RJ269
Horsa	PW778	Horsa	RJ173	Horsa	RJ271
Horsa	PW781	Horsa	RJ177	Horsa	RJ272
Horsa	PW782	Horsa	RJ178	Horsa	RJ273
Horsa	PW784	Horsa	RJ179	Horsa	RJ274
Horsa	PW789	Horsa	RJ180	Horsa	RJ278
Horsa	PW790	Horsa	RJ181	Horsa	RJ280
Horsa	PW816	Horsa	RJ182	Horsa	RJ281
Horsa	PW817	Horsa	RJ183	Horsa	RJ282
Horsa	PW820	Horsa	RJ184	Horsa	RJ283
Horsa	PW823	Horsa	RJ185	Horsa	RJ284
Horsa	PW825	Horsa	RJ186	Horsa	RJ286
Horsa	PW827	Horsa	RJ187	Horsa	RJ287
Horsa	PW842	Horsa	RJ188	Horsa	RJ291
Horsa	PW862	Horsa	RJ189	Horsa	RJ293
Horsa	PW866	Horsa	RJ191	Horsa	RJ294
Horsa	PW870	Horsa	RJ192	Horsa	RJ296
Horsa	PW875	Horsa	RJ194	Horsa	RJ298
Horsa	PW877	Horsa	RJ195	Horsa	RJ299
Horsa	PW885	Horsa	RJ212	Horsa	RJ301
Horsa	PW888	Horsa	RJ213	Horsa	RJ302
Horsa	PW890	Horsa	RJ214	Horsa	RJ303
Horsa	PW894	Horsa	RJ215	Horsa	RJ304
Horsa	PW895	Horsa	RJ217	Horsa	RJ305
Horsa	RJ113	Horsa	RJ223	Horsa	RJ307
Horsa	RJ115	Horsa	RJ224	Horsa	RJ308
Horsa	RJ117	Horsa	RJ225	Horsa	RJ312
Horsa	RJ126	Horsa	RJ226	Horsa	RJ316
Horsa	RJ150	Horsa	RJ227	Horsa	RJ330
Horsa	RJ153	Horsa	RJ229	Horsa	RJ332
Horsa	RJ154	Horsa	RJ230	Horsa	RJ333

Horsa	RJ334	Horsa	RN557	Horsa	RN619
Horsa	RJ335	Horsa	RN559	Horsa	RN622
Horsa	RJ336	Horsa	RN562	Horsa	RN623
Horsa	RJ337	Horsa	RN563	Horsa	RN624
Horsa	RJ338	Horsa	RN564	Horsa	RN625
Horsa	RJ339	Horsa	RN566	Horsa	RN638
Horsa	RJ340	Horsa	RN568	Horsa	RN640
Horsa	RJ341	Horsa	RN583	Horsa	RN641
Horsa	RJ342	Horsa	RN584	Horsa	RN642
Horsa	RJ344	Horsa	RN585	Horsa	RN643
Horsa	RJ345	Horsa	RN586	Horsa	RN646
Horsa	RJ346	Horsa	RN588	Horsa	RN650
Horsa	RJ347	Horsa	RN589	Horsa	RN652
Horsa	RJ348	Horsa	RN590	Horsa	RN653
Horsa	RJ350	Horsa	RN591	Horsa	RN654
Horsa	RJ353	Horsa	RN592	Horsa	RN655
Horsa	RJ354	Horsa	RN593	Horsa	RN657
Horsa	RJ355	Horsa	RN594	Horsa	RN658
Horsa	RJ356	Horsa	RN595	Horsa	RN659
Horsa	RJ359	Horsa	RN596	Horsa	RN660
Horsa	RN525	Horsa	RN597	Horsa	RN661
Horsa	RN526	Horsa	RN599	Horsa	RN664
Horsa	RN528	Horsa	RN600	Horsa	RN668
Horsa	RN531	Horsa	RN602	Horsa	RN669
Horsa	RN532	Horsa	RN603	Horsa	RN670
Horsa	RN534	Horsa	RN604	Horsa	RN671
Horsa	RN536	Horsa	RN605	Horsa	RN673
Horsa	RN539	Horsa	RN607	Horsa	RN675
Horsa	RN541	Horsa	RN608	Horsa	RN676
Horsa	RN542	Horsa	RN609	Horsa	RN678
Horsa	RN544	Horsa	RN610	Horsa	RN695
Horsa	RN547	Horsa	RN611	Horsa	RN696
Horsa	RN549	Horsa	RN612	Horsa	RN697
Horsa	RN550	Horsa	RN613	Horsa	RN700
Horsa	RN551	Horsa	RN614	Horsa	RN701
Horsa	RN552	Horsa	RN616	Horsa	RN702
Horsa	RN553	Horsa	RN617	Horsa	RN704
Horsa	RN555	Horsa	RN618	Horsa	RN705

Horsa	RN708	Hamilcar	HH971	Horsa	LH356
Horsa	RN709	Hamilcar	LA654	Horsa	LH569
Horsa	RN710	Hamilcar	LA672	Horsa	PF745
Horsa	RN714	Hamilcar	LA673	Horsa	PF762
Horsa	RN716	Hamilcar	LA674	Horsa	PF792
Horsa	RN717	Hamilcar	LA675	Horsa	PF799
Horsa	RN718	Hamilcar	LA676	Horsa	PF805
Horsa	RN719	Hamilcar	LA677	Horsa	PW673
Horsa	RN721	Hamilcar	LA679	Horsa	PW698
Horsa	RN722	Hamilcar	LA680	Horsa	PW707
Horsa	RN726	Hamilcar	LA682	Horsa	PW723
Horsa	RN728	Hamilcar	LA691	Horsa	PW757
Horsa	RN729	Hamilcar	LA705	Horsa	PW762
Horsa	RN730	Hamilcar	LA706	Horsa	PW771
Horsa	RN733	Hamilcar	LA710	Horsa	PW821
Horsa	RN734	Hamilcar	LA711	Horsa	PW826
Horsa	RN738	Hamilcar	LA712	Horsa	PW831
Horsa	RN754	Hamilcar	LA714	Horsa	PW832
Horsa	RN759	Hamilcar	LA717	Horsa	PW843
Horsa	RN761	Hamilcar	LA718	Horsa	PW880
Horsa	RN766	Hamilcar	LA720	Horsa	PW896
Horsa	RN767	Hamilcar	LA721	Horsa	RJ112
Horsa	RN769	Hamilcar	LA722	Horsa	RJ114
Horsa	RN774	Hamilcar	LA724	Horsa	RJ129
Horsa	RN783			Horsa	RJ228
Horsa	RN789	**VARSITY**		Horsa	RJ246
Horsa	RN790	**(24-Mar-45)**		Horsa	RJ247
Horsa	RN809			Horsa	RJ315
Horsa	RN811	Horsa	DP306	Horsa	RJ331
Horsa	RN822	Horsa	DP386	Horsa	RJ343
Horsa	RN828	Horsa	DP414	Horsa	RJ352
Horsa	RN835	Horsa	DP496	Horsa	RN316
Horsa	RN844	Horsa	DP497	Horsa	RN318
Horsa	RN847	Horsa	LF903	Horsa	RN319
Horsa	RN866	Horsa	LG692	Horsa	RN322
Hamilcar	HH931	Horsa	LG966	Horsa	RN324
Hamilcar	HH933	Horsa	LG993	Horsa	RN326
Hamilcar	HH958	Horsa	LH343	Horsa	RN328
		Horsa	LH352		

Horsa	RN339	Horsa	RN435	Horsa	RN494
Horsa	RN372	Horsa	RN436	Horsa	RN495
Horsa	RN373	Horsa	RN437	Horsa	RN496
Horsa	RN375	Horsa	RN438	Horsa	RN497
Horsa	RN383	Horsa	RN439	Horsa	RN498
Horsa	RN384	Horsa	RN440	Horsa	RN499
Horsa	RN386	Horsa	RN441	Horsa	RN500
Horsa	RN387	Horsa	RN442	Horsa	RN501
Horsa	RN387	Horsa	RN443	Horsa	RN502
Horsa	RN388	Horsa	RN444	Horsa	RN503
Horsa	RN390	Horsa	RN445	Horsa	RN505
Horsa	RN391	Horsa	RN446	Horsa	RN506
Horsa	RN392	Horsa	RN447	Horsa	RN508
Horsa	RN397	Horsa	RN448	Horsa	RN509
Horsa	RN398	Horsa	RN449	Horsa	RN514
Horsa	RN399	Horsa	RN450	Horsa	RN519
Horsa	RN400	Horsa	RN451	Horsa	RN651
Horsa	RN401	Horsa	RN452	Horsa	RN662
Horsa	RN402	Horsa	RN454	Horsa	RN672
Horsa	RN403	Horsa	RN456	Horsa	RN677
Horsa	RN404	Horsa	RN457	Horsa	RN679
Horsa	RN405	Horsa	RN474	Horsa	RN698
Horsa	RN418	Horsa	RN475	Horsa	RN711
Horsa	RN419	Horsa	RN476	Horsa	RN731
Horsa	RN420	Horsa	RN477	Horsa	RN736
Horsa	RN421	Horsa	RN478	Horsa	RN752
Horsa	RN422	Horsa	RN479	Horsa	RN762
Horsa	RN423	Horsa	RN481	Horsa	RN787
Horsa	RN424	Horsa	RN482	Horsa	RN794
Horsa	RN425	Horsa	RN484	Horsa	RN810
Horsa	RN426	Horsa	RN485	Horsa	RN830
Horsa	RN428	Horsa	RN486	Horsa	RN832
Horsa	RN429	Horsa	RN487	Horsa	RN834
Horsa	RN430	Horsa	RN488	Horsa	RN836
Horsa	RN431	Horsa	RN489	Horsa	RN865
Horsa	RN432	Horsa	RN490	Horsa	RN868
Horsa	RN433	Horsa	RN491	Horsa	RN871
Horsa	RN434	Horsa	RN492	Horsa	RN873

Horsa	RN879	Horsa	RX767	Horsa	RX909
Horsa	RN885	Horsa	RX768	Horsa	RX911
Horsa	RN889	Horsa	RX769	Horsa	RX912
Horsa	RN920	Horsa	RX771	Horsa	RX913
Horsa	RN921	Horsa	RX795	Horsa	RX914
Horsa	RN931	Horsa	RX808	Horsa	RX915
Horsa	RN935	Horsa	RX809	Horsa	RX916
Horsa	RN936	Horsa	RX814	Horsa	RX917
Horsa	RX534	Horsa	RX815	Horsa	RX919
Horsa	RX608	Horsa	RX818	Horsa	RX920
Horsa	RX610	Horsa	RX820	Horsa	RX921
Horsa	RX617	Horsa	RX829	Horsa	RX923
Horsa	RX647	Horsa	RX835	Horsa	RX924
Horsa	RX672	Horsa	RX850	Horsa	RX925
Horsa	RX707	Horsa	RX858	Horsa	RX927
Horsa	RX718	Horsa	RX859	Horsa	RX929
Horsa	RX719	Horsa	RX860	Horsa	RX930
Horsa	RX720	Horsa	RX861	Horsa	RX931
Horsa	RX721	Horsa	RX863	Horsa	RX932
Horsa	RX722	Horsa	RX865	Horsa	RX949
Horsa	RX723	Horsa	RX866	Horsa	RX951
Horsa	RX725	Horsa	RX868	Horsa	RX952
Horsa	RX726	Horsa	RX869	Horsa	RX954
Horsa	RX727	Horsa	RX872	Horsa	RX955
Horsa	RX728	Horsa	RX873	Horsa	RX958
Horsa	RX729	Horsa	RX875	Horsa	RX960
Horsa	RX732	Horsa	RX876	Horsa	RX963
Horsa	RX734	Horsa	RX877	Horsa	RX964
Horsa	RX735	Horsa	RX878	Horsa	RX965
Horsa	RX749	Horsa	RX879	Horsa	RX967
Horsa	RX750	Horsa	RX880	Horsa	RX969
Horsa	RX751	Horsa	RX881	Horsa	RX970
Horsa	RX754	Horsa	RX884	Horsa	RX971
Horsa	RX756	Horsa	RX885	Horsa	RX972
Horsa	RX757	Horsa	RX886	Horsa	RX973
Horsa	RX762	Horsa	RX903	Horsa	RX976
Horsa	RX765	Horsa	RX906	Horsa	RX977
Horsa	RX766	Horsa	RX908	Horsa	RX982

Horsa	RX988	Horsa	RZ230	Hamilcar	NX805
Horsa	RX991	Horsa	RZ232	Hamilcar	NX809
Horsa	RX992	Horsa	RZ241	Hamilcar	NX810
Horsa	RX993	Horsa	RZ252	Hamilcar	NX811
Horsa	RX994	Horsa	RZ254	Hamilcar	NX812
Horsa	RX996	Horsa	RZ256	Hamilcar	NX813
Horsa	RX998	Horsa	RZ288	Hamilcar	NX814
Horsa	RZ118	Horsa	RZ292	Hamilcar	NX818
Horsa	RZ119	Horsa	RZ297	Hamilcar	NX819
Horsa	RZ120	Horsa	RZ305	Hamilcar	NX820
Horsa	RZ129	Horsa	RZ307	Hamilcar	NX821
Horsa	RZ135	Horsa	RZ338	Hamilcar	NX822
Horsa	RZ136	Horsa	RZ342	Hamilcar	NX823
Horsa	RZ140	Horsa	RZ354	Hamilcar	NX825
Horsa	RZ142	Horsa	RZ356	Hamilcar	NX826
Horsa	RZ143	Horsa	RZ358	Hamilcar	NX827
Horsa	RZ145	Horsa	RZ362	Hamilcar	NX875
Horsa	RZ149	Hamilcar	LA685		
Horsa	RZ150	Hamilcar	LA689		
Horsa	RZ152	Hamilcar	LA690		
Horsa	RZ154	Hamilcar	LA707		
Horsa	RZ170	Hamilcar	LA708		
Horsa	RZ173	Hamilcar	LA715		
Horsa	RZ174	Hamilcar	LA719		
Horsa	RZ175	Hamilcar	LA723		
Horsa	RZ178	Hamilcar	LA729		
Horsa	RZ181	Hamilcar	LA730		
Horsa	RZ183	Hamilcar	LA731		
Horsa	RZ190	Hamilcar	LA733		
Horsa	RZ197	Hamilcar	LA734		
Horsa	RZ199	Hamilcar	LA735		
Horsa	RZ201	Hamilcar	LA738		
Horsa	RZ215	Hamilcar	LA740		
Horsa	RZ221	Hamilcar	LA743		
Horsa	RZ223	Hamilcar	LA745		
Horsa	RZ227	Hamilcar	LA747		
Horsa	RZ228	Hamilcar	LA748		
Horsa	RZ229	Hamilcar	LA750		

APPENDIX TWO

GLIDER PILOT CASUALTIES

The glider pilots listed below were killed whilst engaged on flying operations or in the immediate aftermath but it has not proved possible to identify the precise circumstances, nor to allocate them to a particular aircraft.

SICILY (LADBROOKE & FUSTIAN)

Sergeant Henry James AYLOTT 23
Sergeant Ernest BARKER 23
Sergeant Ralph BEDDOWS 22
Sergeant Douglas James Vincent BENNETT 22
Sergeant James Albert Arthur BENNETT 26
Staff Sergeant John Arthur BOORMAN 26
Sergeant John Matthew BROADHEAD 26
Sergeant Ronald Victor BROWN 23
Sergeant Robert Ridsdale BURTON 22
Staff Sergeant James Cyril CARR 27
Sergeant John CHURCH 23
Lieutenant Michael Bourke CONNELL
Major Astley John COOPER 31 AFC
Sergeant Duncan CRASKE 26
Captain John Neil Campbell DENHOLM 28
Sergeant Alexander GOODALL 23
Lieutenant Dereck Pease GREGG
Sergeant Robert Brown HALL 29
Staff Sergeant Peter Lawrence Gray HAMPSHIRE 22
Captain Richard M HANSON
Sergeant Jack HARMER 23
Sergeant George Albert Victor HILL 29

Sergeant Herbert Dennis John HILL 23
Sergeant William Roy HOLLAND 25
Lieutenant Gordon Charles IMPEY 23
Staff Sergeant Hedley James IRON 26
Sergeant David Goode JONES 24
Staff Sergeant Douglas Edward KENT 24
Captain Alfred Harold KITCHING 23
Sergeant Ronald Albert KNOTT 21
Staff Sergeant T G LAIDLAW
Lieutenant Owain Ernest MATHIAS 23
Sergeant Sidney Alfred MAYNARD 24
Sergeant Brendon McLennon MILLER 25
Staff Sergeant Terence MONTAGUE 21
Sergeant William John MOREL 20
Sergeant Cyril Paget MORGAN 24
Sergeant Geoffrey Edward NELSON 25
Sergeant William John PERCY 23
Warrant Officer II John Allen PRESTON 27
Sergeant Phillip Stephen PURCELL 23
Sergeant John Elliott RANDALL 22
Staff Sergeant George Arthur Leonard REEVES 29
Sergeant David William John RICHARDS
Sergeant Lawrence Nicholas RYAN 28
Sergeant Alec George SHEPHERD 30
Staff Sergeant Donald Herbert SMITH 31
Sergeant Frederick Highfield STREET 24
Sergeant Stanley Albert SURRY 24
Staff Sergeant John Russell WHEATLEY 22
Lieutenant Victor WHITTINGTON-STEINER
Staff Sergeant Eric Brian WIKNER 23
Sergeant Dennis Norman WILLIS 21
Sergeant Donald Edwin WITHAM 22

Sergeant Donald Stuart WOOD 24
Sergeant James Fortune WOOD 24
Sergeant Herbert James WOODLAND 27

NORMANDY (MALLARD & TONGA)

The casualties listed below are in addition to those named in the main body of this book.

Sergeant Richard CHADWICK
Staff Sergeant James Frederick CODDINGTON 23
Sergeant Ernest John GOODCHILD 28
Lieutenant Eric MARTIN 25
Sergeant James Harry NASH 24
Staff Sergeant Christopher Bruce ROBINSON 28
Sergeant Alec Hugh SEPHTON
Sergeant Edward STANLEY 23
Staff Sergeant Percy Pemberton TURVEY 24

SOUTHERN FRANCE (ANVIL/DRAGOON)

Sergeant William Roy JENNER 23

ARNHEM (MARKET)

The casualties suffered during the airborne phase of Operation MARKET-GARDEN are recorded in the body of this account. In addition, the Glider Pilot Regiment sustained nearly 230 fatal casualties during the ground fighting and these personnel are not recorded in this volume.

VARSITY

Pilot Officer Alfred Michael ANKERS 23
Trooper Joseph ARMSTRONG 39
Sergeant Jeffrey Frederick ASTOR 19
Flying Officer Maurice AUSTIN 21
Flight Sergeant Dennis Langdown BOND 22
Flight Sergeant Kenneth BOWLER 20

Staff Sergeant Geoffrey BRIGHT 25
Sergeant Edward Osbourne BRUCE
Captain Angus Montgomery Dingwall CARR 34
Staff Sergeant Leslie John Teddy CATT 22
Flight Lieutenant Maurice Robert CLARK 24
Sergeant Geoffrey COLLINS 25
Flying Officer Edwin COOK 21
Sergeant Herbert Walter COOMBER 22
Flying Officer Frank Horrower CUSWORTH 23
Lieutenant George John D'ARCY-CLARK 31
Sergeant Herbert Hartley DENBY 31
Staff Sergeant William Beverley DENHOLM 24
Flight Sergeant Reginald DORMER 22
Sergeant John Doughty 26
Staff Sergeant George DUNS
Flying Officer Derek Wallace EDWARDS 27
Sergeant Claude ELLERINGTON 20 RAF
Staff Sergeant John Lawrence ELLISON 25
Flight Sergeant Malcolm Frederick ESSEN 21
Sergeant George Richard EVANS 24
Flying Officer Hubert Alexander FOWLER 28
Flying Officer John William FREEMAN 20
Sergeant Harry Jack GORDON 26
Lieutenant Reginald Lionel GRAEFE
Sergeant Gordon Noel GRAHAM 24 RAF
Flight Sergeant Geoffrey John Cardross GRANT 20
Flight Lieutenant Robert Gray 27
Flight Lieutenant John Sutherland HAIG 20
Flying Officer Geoffrey Bernard HANSON
Staff Sergeant Douglas HARRISON 26
Lieutenant Laurence HARRISON 23
Sergeant William HAYMAN 20 RAF

Flight Sergeant Robert HEADS 21
Sergeant Frank HEDLEY
Sergeant David Leslie HUTCHENS 22 RAF
Flight Sergeant Percy Nicholas HYDE
Flying Officer Robert William Charles JAMIESON 21
Staff Sergeant Eric Lionel JARVIS 23
Flying Officer Kenneth Maurice JOHNSON 22
Sergeant Kenneth Albert KELSALL
Lieutenant Douglas Charles KENNARD 22
Flying Officer Edwin James KNOWLES
Flight Sergeant Thomas LAIDLAW 23
Flying Officer Joseph Patrick LEAVY 21
Flying Officer Arthur Sydney LEDBROOK
Sergeant Alexander Randolph LOGIE 26
Sergeant Andrew Bell Coliville LOVE 21 RAF
Sergeant William Samuel Edgar LOWMAN 20 RAF
Staff Sergeant Patrick Alastair MCLAREN
Flying Officer Geoffrey William MADDOCK 22
Flying Officer Stephane Peter Anthony MANSELL 20
Flying Officer Andrew MCGREGOR 29
Flight Sergeant Samuel MCINNES 21
Flying Officer Samuel MCLEAN 21
Staff Sergeant David Roger MONTGOMERY
Sergeant Walter Francis MURPHY 33
Flying Officer John Kenneth Patrick NASH 20
Staff Sergeant James NEILSON
Captain Harold Martin Rex NORTON
Sergeant Douglas NUTTALL
Flight Sergeant John Mortimer O'SULLIVAN 22
Sergeant Thomas Anthony PARKINSON 21
Flying Officer William Henry PAUL 26
Staff Sergeant William Charles PAVITT

Sergeant Roland PODMORE 25
Sergeant Philip James READ
Sergeant Gordon Knight RICHARDSON
Staff Sergeant Stanley ROBERTS
Private Andrew Clelland ROBERTSON ACC att GPR
Sergeant Christopher Verdun ROCHE
Sergeant William Lynch ROSS
Sergeant Reginald Albert ROWLEY 21
Flying Officer Robert Alfred SCRASE
Flight Sergeant Robert James SHEPHERD 22
Flight Lieutenant John Richard SHERWOOD 21
Sergeant James Alphonsus SHORE 25 RAF
Sergeant Angus Wallis SKELDON 20
Staff Sergeant John Frederick SMITH
Sergeant John Kenneth SMITH 23 RAF
Sergeant Kenneth Charles SPARKES 20
Staff Sergeant Jasper Blake SPOWART 25
Sergeant John Henry STEVENS 22
Sergeant Thomas John Alfred STEVENS 22 RAF
Captain Kenneth Fairley STRATHERN US Bronze Star
Sergeant Jack William STUBBINGS 21
Sergeant Frank SUMMERS
Sergeant Frederick Arthur TAYLOR 23 RAF
Sergeant William John TYSON 20 RAF
Sergeant Kenneth John WARREN 20
Flying Officer William John WATES 20
Flying Officer James Victor Alton WELPLEY 20
Sergeant Tom WHITELEY 20 RAF
Staff Sergeant Herbert WRIGHT

APPENDIX THREE

AIRCRAFT LOSSES

Albemarle	LV537	20-Feb-45	Albemarle	P1516	01-Oct-43
Albemarle	P1374	06-Jun-44	Albemarle	P1519	07-Aug-44
Albemarle	P1381	24-Sep-44	Albemarle	P1521	13-Jul-43
Albemarle	P1382	24-Sep-43	Albemarle	P1522	08-Jul-43
Albemarle	P1385	30-Mar-44	Albemarle	P1526	04-Sep-43
Albemarle	P1386	03-Jun-42	Albemarle	P1527	11-Jun-43
Albemarle	P1389	18-Sep-43	Albemarle	P1528	18-Sep-43
Albemarle	P1393	04-Mar-43	Albemarle	P1552	08-Jul-43
Albemarle	P1398	10-Apr-44	Albemarle	P1553	07-Oct-43
Albemarle	P1400	28-Jul-44	Albemarle	P1554	18-Dec-44
Albemarle	P1401	14-Oct-43	Albemarle	P1556	30-Apr-43
Albemarle	P1404	08-May-44	Albemarle	P1563	15-Jun-44
Albemarle	P1405	10-Oct-43	Albemarle	P1565	21-Apr-43
Albemarle	P1431	21-Oct-42	Albemarle	P1568	24-Jun-44
Albemarle	P1433	10-Aug-43	Albemarle	P1592	26-Apr-44
Albemarle	P1434	06-Dec-43	Albemarle	P1593	10-Jul-44
Albemarle	P1435	23-Sep-44	Albemarle	P1600	09-Aug-44
Albemarle	P1437	13-Jul-43	Albemarle	P1605	28-Jul-44
Albemarle	P1440	22-Jul-43	Albemarle	P1606	21-Nov-44
Albemarle	P1442	06-Jun-44	Albemarle	P1643	06-Sep-44
Albemarle	P1443	17-Jun-43	Albemarle	P1651	08-Jan-45
Albemarle	P1444	14-Jul-43	Albemarle	P1659	12-Sep-44
Albemarle	P1446	12-Jul-43	Albemarle	V1604	12-Mar-44
Albemarle	P1452	21-Nov-42	Albemarle	V1605	06-Jun-44
Albemarle	P1462	21-Dec-43	Albemarle	V1609	15-Apr-44
Albemarle	P1463	30-Mar-44	Albemarle	V1610	23-Apr-44
Albemarle	P1466	13-Jul-43	Albemarle	V1612	12-May-44
Albemarle	P1468	05-Aug-43	Albemarle	V1613	28-Apr-44
Albemarle	P1472	11-Jun-44	Albemarle	V1618	14-Jun-44
Albemarle	P1474	31-Jul-43	Albemarle	V1621	24-Jul-44
Albemarle	P1478	23-Aug-43	Albemarle	V1641	03-Mar-44
Albemarle	P1501	09-Aug-44	Albemarle	V1697	22-Dec-43
Albemarle	P1503	29-May-43	Albemarle	V1702	27-May-44

Albemarle	V1707	24-Feb-44		Bombay	L5817	01-Apr-41
Albemarle	V1709	15-May-44		Bombay	L5819	15-Jul-40
Albemarle	V1711	13-Mar-44		Bombay	L5821	17-Dec-40
Albemarle	V1739	21-Apr-44		Bombay	L5822	23-Sep-41
Albemarle	V1744	11-Jul-44		Bombay	L5823	06-May-41
Albemarle	V1745	02-Jul-44		Bombay	L5824	24-Jul-42
Albemarle	V1747	07-Mar-44		Bombay	L5826	21-Aug-41
Albemarle	V1752	06-Feb-45		Bombay	L5827	09-Aug-43
Albemarle	V1755	25-Oct-44		Bombay	L5830	14-Apr-41
Albemarle	V1762	21-Oct-44		Bombay	L5833	25-Sep-42
Albemarle	V1770	28-Apr-44		Bombay	L5834	13-Oct-41
Albemarle	V1773	06-Jun-44		Bombay	L5835	27-Jul-42
Albemarle	V1774	11-Jul-44		Bombay	L5837	06-Jul-41
Albemarle	V1781	05-Sep-44		Bombay	L5838	27-Jul-43
Albemarle	V1782	27-Aug-44		Bombay	L5841	19-Jan-43
Albemarle	V1817	29-May-44		Bombay	L5843	25-Sep-42
Albemarle	V1823	22-Dec-44		Bombay	L5844	31-Jul-43
Albemarle	V1847	24-Nov-44		Bombay	L5846	26-Nov-41
Albemarle	V1848	20-Jan-45		Bombay	L5847	17-Nov-41
Albemarle	V1862	19-Mar-45		Bombay	L5848	14-Jul-40
Albemarle	V1864	13-Feb-45		Bombay	L5849	15-Jul-40
Albemarle	V1865	07-Jan-45		Bombay	L5850	21-Jun-40
Albemarle	V1934	30-Dec-44		Bombay	L5852	17-Jun-40
Albemarle	V1970	07-Feb-45		Bombay	L5853	29-May-40
Albemarle	V1983	17-Feb-45		Bombay	L5854	31-Mar-41
Albemarle	V1993	14-Feb-45		Bombay	L5855	22-Apr-41
Albemarle	V1995	08-Mar-45		Bombay	L5857	25-Sep-42
Albemarle	V1997	23-Apr-45		Catalina	FP180	04-Oct-44
Albemarle	V2027	04-Nov-44		Catalina	FP191	16-May-44
Albemarle	V2035	13-Mar-45		Cleveland	AS468	08-Oct-40
Anson	LT191	23-Mar-44		Dakota	DG471	24-Oct-41
Anson	LT192	25-Nov-43		Dakota	DG473	14-Jun-42
Anson	LT279	27-Nov-43		Dakota	DG474	01-Jan-42
Bombay	L5811	23-Jan-42		Dakota	DG475	25-Dec-41
Bombay	L5813	11-May-40		Dakota	DG478	01-Feb-42
Bombay	L5814	07-Aug-42		Dakota	FD774	09-Jul-43
Bombay	L5815	15-Jul-40		Dakota	FD775	08-Feb-44
Bombay	L5816	19-Oct-40		Dakota	FD786	05-Sep-43

Dakota	FD790	16-Nov-43	Dakota	FD937	14-May-44
Dakota	FD793	28-Nov-43	Dakota	FD948	20-May-44
Dakota	FD802	10-Jan-44	Dakota	FD949	08-Nov-44
Dakota	FD806	19-Sep-43	Dakota	FD952	25-Apr-44
Dakota	FD811	28-Jan-44	Dakota	FD960	24-Nov-43
Dakota	FD815	11-Jul-43	Dakota	FL504	23-Jun-44
Dakota	FD820	14-Feb-45	Dakota	FL505	13-Feb-44
Dakota	FD829	01-Nov-43	Dakota	FL506	07-May-44
Dakota	FD832	18-Sep-43	Dakota	FL511	25-Mar-44
Dakota	FD835	12-Sep-44	Dakota	FL515	30-Nov-43
Dakota	FD836	22-Jul-44	Dakota	FL534	02-May-44
Dakota	FD838	15-Aug-43	Dakota	FL538	10-Apr-45
Dakota	FD846	20-Apr-44	Dakota	FL539	11-Mar-44
Dakota	FD848	10-Mar-44	Dakota	FL540	11-Apr-44
Dakota	FD850	25-Mar-44	Dakota	FL543	01-Apr-44
Dakota	FD859	13-May-44	Dakota	FL545	05-Dec-43
Dakota	FD863	27-Dec-44	Dakota	FL549	01-May-44
Dakota	FD865	19-Sep-44	Dakota	FL554	11-Nov-44
Dakota	FD866	03-Jun-44	Dakota	FL569	15-Apr-44
Dakota	FD876	09-Jul-43	Dakota	FL574	26-May-44
Dakota	FD880	10-Mar-44	Dakota	FL576	24-May-44
Dakota	FD884	25-Jan-45	Dakota	FL588	05-Dec-44
Dakota	FD888	08-Jul-43	Dakota	FL600	16-Dec-44
Dakota	FD892	18-Sep-43	Dakota	FL601	25-Apr-44
Dakota	FD893	18-Sep-43	Dakota	FL602	25-Apr-44
Dakota	FD896	11-Apr-45	Dakota	FL605	18-Aug-44
Dakota	FD899	06-Oct-43	Dakota	FL640	18-Sep-44
Dakota	FD900	21-Mar-45	Dakota	FL641	25-Mar-44
Dakota	FD903	24-Dec-43	Dakota	FL644	12-Feb-45
Dakota	FD909	23-Sep-43	Dakota	FL715	08-Nov-44
Dakota	FD910	21-Mar-44	Dakota	FZ548	11-Jun-44
Dakota	FD911	09-Apr-44	Dakota	FZ550	24-Aug-44
Dakota	FD913	12-Jan-44	Dakota	FZ552	17-Apr-44
Dakota	FD915	12-Feb-45	Dakota	FZ563	01-Jun-44
Dakota	FD921	18-Sep-43	Dakota	FZ574	19-Sep-44
Dakota	FD924	08-Nov-44	Dakota	FZ582	12-May-44
Dakota	FD928	13-Feb-45	Dakota	FZ585	05-Jul-44
Dakota	FD935	17-Jun-44	Dakota	FZ590	27-Mar-44

Dakota	FZ597	04-Aug-44	Dakota	KG374	19-Sep-44
Dakota	FZ598	23-Jun-44	Dakota	KG375	05-Mar-44
Dakota	FZ599	05-May-44	Dakota	KG376	21-Sep-44
Dakota	FZ600	19-Jun-44	Dakota	KG387	21-Sep-44
Dakota	FZ610	26-Jul-44	Dakota	KG388	19-Sep-44
Dakota	FZ620	21-Sep-44	Dakota	KG396	05-Mar-44
Dakota	FZ626	19-Sep-44	Dakota	KG399	21-Sep-44
Dakota	FZ632	17-Jan-44	Dakota	KG404	21-Sep-44
Dakota	FZ644	24-Aug-44	Dakota	KG406	28-Apr-45
Dakota	FZ644	28-Aug-44	Dakota	KG409	05-Feb-45
Dakota	FZ648	09-Jan-45	Dakota	KG413	23-Jun-44
Dakota	FZ649	24-Mar-45	Dakota	KG417	21-Sep-44
Dakota	FZ655	24-Oct-44	Dakota	KG418	20-Sep-44
Dakota	FZ656	21-Sep-44	Dakota	KG421	21-Aug-44
Dakota	FZ667	07-Jun-44	Dakota	KG422	30-Sep-44
Dakota	FZ674	05-Aug-44	Dakota	KG424	06-Jun-44
Dakota	FZ677	09-Mar-44	Dakota	KG426	06-Jun-44
Dakota	FZ679	15-Feb-45	Dakota	KG428	19-Sep-44
Dakota	FZ683	18-Apr-44	Dakota	KG429	06-Jun-44
Dakota	FZ685	24-Apr-45	Dakota	KG434	06-Jun-44
Dakota	FZ690	06-Jun-44	Dakota	KG435	23-Sep-44
Dakota	KG305	23-Sep-44	Dakota	KG444	21-Sep-44
Dakota	KG315	23-Sep-44	Dakota	KG446	06-Mar-44
Dakota	KG318	20-Nov-44	Dakota	KG449	26-Sep-44
Dakota	KG324	20-Sep-44	Dakota	KG457	02-Aug-44
Dakota	KG326	21-Apr-45	Dakota	KG461	30-Jul-44
Dakota	KG329	07-Jun-44	Dakota	KG462	25-Apr-44
Dakota	KG331	01-Jan-45	Dakota	KG471	04-Sep-44
Dakota	KG340	21-Sep-44	Dakota	KG472	16-Jul-44
Dakota	KG343	17-Jun-44	Dakota	KG480	07-Jun-44
Dakota	KG346	21-Sep-44	Dakota	KG488	01-Jan-45
Dakota	KG347	06-Jun-44	Dakota	KG489	21-Sep-44
Dakota	KG353	27-Oct-44	Dakota	KG491	04-May-45
Dakota	KG355	01-Jan-45	Dakota	KG493	23-Jun-44
Dakota	KG356	06-Jun-44	Dakota	KG494	26-May-44
Dakota	KG366	21-Mar-44	Dakota	KG498	21-Dec-44
Dakota	KG369	10-Apr-44	Dakota	KG508	15-Apr-44
Dakota	KG370	23-Sep-44	Dakota	KG508	21-Apr-44

Dakota	KG512	25-Sep-44	Dakota	KG789	19-Aug-44
Dakota	KG516	21-Sep-44	Dakota	KG793	17-Jan-45
Dakota	KG517	31-May-44	Dakota	KG796	01-Jan-45
Dakota	KG519	26-Jun-44	Dakota	KG800	01-Jan-45
Dakota	KG525	15-Mar-45	Dakota	KG801	05-Aug-44
Dakota	KG534	21-Mar-45	Dakota	KJ435	12-Jan-45
Dakota	KG547	27-Sep-44	Dakota	KJ803	01-Jan-45
Dakota	KG548	09-May-44	Dakota	KJ806	28-Feb-45
Dakota	KG552	05-May-45	Dakota	KJ835	10-Jan-45
Dakota	KG553	12-Sep-44	Dakota	KJ845	07-Feb-45
Dakota	KG566	21-Sep-44	Dakota	KJ848	03-Mar-45
Dakota	KG570	18-Sep-44	Dakota	KJ855	22-Nov-44
Dakota	KG574	12-Oct-44	Dakota	KJ884	19-Dec-44
Dakota	KG579	21-Sep-44	Dakota	KJ892	05-Feb-45
Dakota	KG584	10-Dec-44	Dakota	KJ899	12-Jan-45
Dakota	KG586	21-Sep-44	Dakota	KJ921	01-Mar-45
Dakota	KG591	13-Nov-44	Dakota	KJ927	10-Feb-45
Dakota	KG592	05-Oct-44	Dakota	KJ931	19-Jan-45
Dakota	KG593	11-Nov-44	Dakota	KJ944	28-Jan-45
Dakota	KG599	10-Jan-45	Dakota	KJ948	20-Jan-45
Dakota	KG610	29-Jan-45	Dakota	KJ958	31-Dec-44
Dakota	KG625	12-Aug-44	Dakota	KJ965	14-Mar-45
Dakota	KG630	06-Feb-45	Dakota	KJ986	03-Nov-44
Dakota	KG639	06-Dec-44	Dakota	KK110	10-Apr-45
Dakota	KG653	24-Sep-44	Dakota	KK121	29-Mar-45
Dakota	KG654	24-Feb-45	Dakota	KK126	14-Mar-45
Dakota	KG661	13-Dec-44	Dakota	KK165	01-May-45
Dakota	KG671	14-Mar-45	Dakota	KK170	25-Mar-45
Dakota	KG690	31-Jul-44	Dakota	KK194	01-Feb-45
Dakota	KG710	13-Dec-44	Dakota	KK195	29-Mar-45
Dakota	KG711	11-Feb-45	Dakota	KK203	19-Mar-45
Dakota	KG727	19-Mar-45	Dakota	KN202	03-May-45
Dakota	KG736	01-Jan-45	Dakota	KN220	19-Mar-45
Dakota	KG752	21-Aug-44	Dakota	KN223	16-Apr-45
Dakota	KG757	31-Jan-45	Dakota	KN228	20-Mar-45
Dakota	KG762	07-Apr-45	Dakota	KN251	17-Feb-45
Dakota	KG779	05-Aug-44	Dakota	KN255	23-Mar-45
Dakota	KG784	14-Aug-44	Dakota	KN271	06-Feb-45

Aircraft Losses

Dakota	KN289	01-Feb-45		DH91 Albatross		
Dakota	KN298	13-Apr-45			AX904	07-Apr-42
Dakota	KN332	19-Apr-45		DH94 Moth	W6458	23-Jul-43
Dakota	KN343	20-Mar-45		Dominie	R9553	27-Apr-43
Dakota	KN345	14-Mar-45		Envoy	X9370	08-Oct-40
Dakota	KN409	28-Mar-45		Flamingo	R2764	30-Apr-42
Dakota	LR230	06-May-42		Flamingo	T5357	04-Oct-40
Dakota	LR231	06-May-42		Ford 5AT	X5000	19-Sep-40
Dakota	LR232	04-Nov-42		Hadrian	"CG340"	14-Jan-45
Dakota	LR235	12-Jan-43		Hadrian	19704	04-Jul-44
Dakota	MA925	11-Jul-44		Hadrian	40593	17-Dec-44
Dakota	TS436	19-Feb-45		Hadrian	41061	14-Dec-44
Dakota	TS436	19-Feb-45		Hadrian	56320	19-Sep-44
DC2	AX755	13-Apr-42		Hadrian	77262	04-Feb-45
DC3	AX768	24-Jul-42		Hadrian	77341	18-Jan-45
DC3	AX769	27-Sep-42		Hadrian	FR568	02-Oct-43
DC3	MA928	25-May-43		Hadrian	FR569	20-Oct-43
DC3	MA929	27-Jan-43		Hadrian	FR574	04-Jan-45
DH 89A	P1764	16-May-40		Hadrian	FR576	31-Mar-44
DH82A	K4277	08-Oct-40		Hadrian	FR577	11-Jan-45
DH82A	K4284	08-Oct-40		Hadrian	FR596	25-Jun-44
DH86B	N6246	05-May-42		Hadrian	FR612	21-Apr-45
DH86B	X9441	17-Feb-43		Hadrian	FR621	21-Apr-45
DH89	P1765	01-May-40		Hadrian	FR627	21-Apr-45
DH89A	BD143	20-Apr-42		Hadrian	FR634	21-Apr-45
				Hadrian	FR655	19-Jan-45
DH89A	W6423	16-May-40		Hadrian	FR667	21-Apr-45
DH89A	W6424	23-Feb-40		Hadrian	FR712	14-Apr-45
DH89A	W6456	11-Apr-42		Hadrian	KK712	07-Feb-45
DH89A	W6457	31-May-40		Halifax	BB281	14-Mar-43
DH89A	X7374	21-Apr-42		Halifax	BB301	23-Nov-43
DH89A	X8505	21-May-40		Halifax	BB309	17-Sep-43
DH89A	X8506	21-May-40		Halifax	BB313	14-May-43
DH89A	X8508	20-May-40		Halifax	BB317	19-Sep-43
DH89A	X9320	12-Feb-40		Halifax	BB318	04-May-44
DH89A	X9395	29-Apr-40		Halifax	BB328	12-May-43
DH91 Albatross				Halifax	BB329	22-May-43
	AX903	11-Aug-41		Halifax	BB330	25-Feb-44

Halifax	BB334	13-Aug-43	Halifax	DG409	13-Apr-43
Halifax	BB335	26-Apr-44	Halifax	DJ989	23-Jun-43
Halifax	BB337	15-Mar-44	Halifax	DJ994	17-Aug-43
Halifax	BB338	05-Nov-44	Halifax	DK119	23-Jul-43
Halifax	BB340	13-Apr-43	Halifax	DK122	19-May-43
Halifax	BB344	11-Dec-43	Halifax	DK123	20-Feb-43
Halifax	BB363	14-Apr-43	Halifax	DK124	01-Sep-44
Halifax	BB364	19-Dec-43	Halifax	DK130	16-Jun-43
Halifax	BB378	11-Dec-43	Halifax	DK131	19-Jul-43
Halifax	BB379	24-Jun-43	Halifax	DK198	16-Mar-44
Halifax	BB386	04-Mar-44	Halifax	DK199	03-Feb-44
Halifax	BB387	01-Mar-44	Halifax	DK206	17-Dec-43
Halifax	BB389	01-Sep-44	Halifax	DK232	05-Nov-43
Halifax	BB412	11-Sep-44	Halifax	DT542	17-Dec-42
Halifax	BB422	11-Sep-44	Halifax	DT543	17-Jul-44
Halifax	BB431	28-Apr-44	Halifax	DT620	15-Mar-43
Halifax	BB435	07-Sep-43	Halifax	DT627	12-May-43
Halifax	BB437	30-Apr-44	Halifax	DT725	17-Apr-43
Halifax	BB438	05-May-44	Halifax	DT726	04-Nov-43
Halifax	BB441	06-Jun-44	Halifax	DT727	22-Jun-43
Halifax	BB444	02-Feb-44	Halifax	EB129	11-Nov-43
Halifax	BB445	10-Jan-44	Halifax	EB130	10-Sep-43
Halifax	DG244	20-Mar-43	Halifax	EB132	11-Jun-43
Halifax	DG245	15-Mar-43	Halifax	EB135	27-Jun-43
Halifax	DG252	20-Sep-43	Halifax	EB139	25-Sep-43
Halifax	DG253	18-Aug-43	Halifax	EB140	06-Dec-43
Halifax	DG271	04-Feb-43	Halifax	EB141	06-Aug-43
Halifax	DG272	23-Jan-44	Halifax	EB145	14-Jul-43
Halifax	DG283	15-Mar-43	Halifax	EB147	05-Aug-44
Halifax	DG285	16-Jan-43	Halifax	EB154	17-Aug-44
Halifax	DG286	23-May-44	Halifax	EB178	07-Sep-43
Halifax	DG350	11-May-43	Halifax	EB188	20-Sep-43
Halifax	DG354	21-Sep-43	Halifax	EB188	06-Nov-44
Halifax	DG390	16-May-43	Halifax	EB197	09-Sep-43
Halifax	DG391	21-Jul-43	Halifax	EB239	21-Oct-43
Halifax	DG393	22-Aug-43	Halifax	EV970	28-Jun-44
Halifax	DG405	23-Jun-43	Halifax	EW106	11-Oct-44
Halifax	DG406	12-Jun-43	Halifax	HR660	03-Mar-44

Halifax	HR661	02-May-43	Halifax	JP221	18-Aug-44
Halifax	HR665	25-Mar-43	Halifax	JP222	23-Sep-44
Halifax	HR666	15-Sep-43	Halifax	JP224	24-Apr-44
Halifax	HR670	09-Sep-43	Halifax	JP226	24-Aug-44
Halifax	HR674	19-Oct-43	Halifax	JP237	24-Jun-44
Halifax	JB802	18-May-43	Halifax	JP238	16-Jun-44
Halifax	JD154	15-Sep-43	Halifax	JP239	30-Jul-44
Halifax	JD155	12-Jul-43	Halifax	JP240	25-Jun-44
Halifax	JD156	17-Sep-43	Halifax	JP244	29-Sep-44
Halifax	JD171	27-Aug-44	Halifax	JP244	29-Oct-44
Halifax	JD172	31-May-44	Halifax	JP246	08-Oct-44
Halifax	JD179	18-Aug-43	Halifax	JP247	04-Jul-44
Halifax	JD180	15-Aug-43	Halifax	JP249	14-Feb-45
Halifax	JD269	14-Sep-43	Halifax	JP253	30-Jun-44
Halifax	JD312	16-Aug-43	Halifax	JP276	05-Aug-44
Halifax	JD319	18-Oct-44	Halifax	JP277	03-Feb-45
Halifax	JD362	29-Aug-44	Halifax	JP281	26-Jan-45
Halifax	JN888	14-Jul-44	Halifax	JP284	16-Jul-44
Halifax	JN889	01-Sep-44	Halifax	JP285	06-Jun-44
Halifax	JN895	29-Aug-44	Halifax	JP286	04-Jul-44
Halifax	JN896	14-Aug-44	Halifax	JP288	11-Sep-44
Halifax	JN910	15-Sep-43	Halifax	JP292	04-Jul-44
Halifax	JN911	09-Apr-44	Halifax	JP294	03-Aug-44
Halifax	JN912	18-Aug-44	Halifax	JP295	28-Aug-44
Halifax	JN921	07-Nov-43	Halifax	L9612	01-Nov-41
Halifax	JN926	15-Aug-44	Halifax	L9618	10-Dec-42
Halifax	JN944	08-Oct-44	Halifax	LK641	27-Aug-44
Halifax	JN956	07-Oct-44	Halifax	LK652	08-May-44
Halifax	JN958	20-Dec-44	Halifax	LK655	21-Dec-44
Halifax	JN959	15-Feb-44	Halifax	LK736	17-May-44
Halifax	JN960	27-Apr-44	Halifax	LK738	11-Apr-44
Halifax	JP161	11-Sep-44	Halifax	LK742	04-Apr-45
Halifax	JP162	05-Aug-44	Halifax	LK743	08-Jan-44
Halifax	JP179	04-Jul-44	Halifax	LK899	17-Dec-43
Halifax	JP180	01-Sep-44	Halifax	LL114	08-Feb-44
Halifax	JP181	05-Aug-44	Halifax	LL115	17-Dec-43
Halifax	JP206	27-Jun-44	Halifax	LL119	17-Dec-43
Halifax	JP220	15-Aug-44	Halifax	LL120	17-Dec-43

Halifax	LL129	16-Jul-44		Halifax	LL367	03-Feb-45
Halifax	LL148	20-Oct-44		Halifax	LL380	04-Jan-45
Halifax	LL182	23-Jan-44		Halifax	LL384	07-Feb-45
Halifax	LL183	10-May-44		Halifax	LL387	18-Jul-44
Halifax	LL187	28-Dec-44		Halifax	LL388	29-Aug-44
Halifax	LL192	08-May-44		Halifax	LL390	07-Jun-44
Halifax	LL228	06-Apr-44		Halifax	LL400	31-Aug-44
Halifax	LL248	05-Aug-44		Halifax	LL401	25-Aug-44
Halifax	LL251	12-Jul-44		Halifax	LL402	02-Oct-44
Halifax	LL252	01-Apr-44		Halifax	LL403	06-Oct-44
Halifax	LL254	21-Nov-44		Halifax	LL406	29-Nov-44
Halifax	LL256	20-Sep-44		Halifax	LL407	06-Jun-44
Halifax	LL273	11-Sep-44		Halifax	LL413	03-Mar-45
Halifax	LL276	01-Jun-44		Halifax	LL416	08-Jun-44
Halifax	LL279	04-Mar-44		Halifax	LL419	01-Jun-44
Halifax	LL280	08-May-44		Halifax	LL445	28-Jan-45
Halifax	LL281	06-Dec-44		Halifax	LL453	25-Mar-45
Halifax	LL284	02-Jun-44		Halifax	LL465	26-Feb-45
Halifax	LL287	31-Mar-44		Halifax	LL466	07-Jun-44
Halifax	LL289	02-Jun-44		Halifax	LL484	26-Dec-44
Halifax	LL293	15-Oct-44		Halifax	LW275	08-Feb-44
Halifax	LL300	29-May-44		Halifax	LW280	17-Dec-43
Halifax	LL306	08-Jun-44		Halifax	LW281	18-Oct-43
Halifax	LL307	03-Jun-44		Halifax	MZ506	09-Apr-45
Halifax	LL308	09-Aug-44		Halifax	MZ632	17-Mar-45
Halifax	LL310	14-Oct-44		Halifax	MZ959	24-Mar-45
Halifax	LL311	16-Nov-44		Halifax	MZ980	09-Feb-45
Halifax	LL332	14-Nov-44		Halifax	NA103	26-Feb-45
Halifax	LL333	21-Sep-44		Halifax	NA115	17-Apr-45
Halifax	LL334	06-Aug-44		Halifax	NA120	05-Feb-45
Halifax	LL343	30-Aug-44		Halifax	NA127	03-Mar-45
Halifax	LL346	27-May-44		Halifax	NA131	26-Mar-45
Halifax	LL348	06-Jun-44		Halifax	NA311	24-Mar-45
Halifax	LL351	03-Feb-45		Halifax	NA316	20-Mar-45
Halifax	LL355	03-Jan-45		Halifax	NA317	09-Mar-45
Halifax	LL356	28-Apr-44		Halifax	NA337	24-Apr-45
Halifax	LL358	09-Aug-44		Halifax	NA344	19-Apr-45
Halifax	LL364	18-Jul-44		Halifax	NA347	13-Apr-45

Halifax	NA656	23-Feb-45	Hamilcar	LA636	06-Jun-44
Halifax	NA660	03-Apr-45	Hamilcar	LA637	06-Jun-44
Halifax	NA664	27-Mar-45	Hamilcar	LA638	06-Jun-44
Halifax	NA668	28-Feb-45	Hamilcar	LA639	06-Jun-44
Halifax	NA669	24-Mar-45	Hamilcar	LA64?	06-Jun-44
Halifax	NA672	27-Apr-45	Hamilcar	LA640	06-Jun-44
Halifax	PN243	31-Mar-45	Hamilcar	LA641	06-Jun-44
Halifax	V9776	20-Apr-42	Hamilcar	LA643	26-Apr-44
Halifax	W1002	17-Dec-42	Hamilcar	LA644	06-Jun-44
Halifax	W1012	19-Feb-43	Hamilcar	LA645	06-Jun-44
Halifax	W1229	19-Jun-43	Hamilcar	LA646	09-Mar-45
Halifax	W7773	30-Oct-42	Hamilcar	LA647	01-Mar-44
Halifax	W7774	30-Oct-42	Hamilcar	LA648	23-Apr-44
Halifax	W7775	23-Dec-42	Hamilcar	LA649	25-Apr-44
Halifax	W7776	01-Oct-42	Hamilcar	LA650	06-Jun-44
Halifax	W7801	19-Nov-42	Hamilcar	LA651	06-Jun-44
Hamilcar	HH922	11-Jan-45	Hamilcar	LA652	06-Jun-44
Hamilcar	HH923	06-Jun-44	Hamilcar	LA653	06-Jun-44
Hamilcar	HH924	06-Jun-44	Hamilcar	LA655	06-Jun-44
Hamilcar	HH926	06-Jun-44	Hamilcar	LA669	06-Jun-44
Hamilcar	HH927	06-Jun-44	Hamilcar	LA670	06-Jun-44
Hamilcar	HH928	06-Jun-44	Hamilcar	LA671	06-Jun-44
Hamilcar	HH930	06-Jun-44	Hamilcar	LA683	18-Jan-45
Hamilcar	HH932	06-Jun-44	Hamilcar	LA684	18-Jan-45
Hamilcar	HH934	06-Jun-44	Hamilcar	LA685	24-Mar-45
Hamilcar	HH935	06-Jun-44	Hamilcar	LA686	18-Apr-45
Hamilcar	HH957	06-Jun-44	Hamilcar	LA689	24-Mar-45
Hamilcar	HH959	06-Jun-44	Hamilcar	LA690	24-Mar-45
Hamilcar	HH960	06-Jun-44	Hamilcar	LA691	16-Sep-44
Hamilcar	HH961	20-Jan-44	Hamilcar	LA707	24-Mar-45
Hamilcar	HH962	06-Jun-44	Hamilcar	LA708	24-Mar-45
Hamilcar	HH963	06-Jun-44	Hamilcar	LA713	18-Jan-45
Hamilcar	HH964	06-Jun-44	Hamilcar	LA715	24-Mar-45
Hamilcar	HH965	12-Apr-44	Hamilcar	LA716	09-May-44
Hamilcar	HH970	06-Jun-44	Hamilcar	LA719	24-Mar-45
Hamilcar	LA634	27-May-44	Hamilcar	LA723	24-Mar-45
Hamilcar	LA634	10-Jul-44	Hamilcar	LA727	18-Jan-45
Hamilcar	LA635	04-Mar-45	Hamilcar	LA729	24-Mar-45

Hamilcar	LA730	24-Mar-45	Harrow	K6937	13-Sep-44
Hamilcar	LA731	24-Mar-45	Harrow	K6943	01-Jan-45
Hamilcar	LA733	24-Mar-45	Harrow	K6947	23-Nov-43
Hamilcar	LA734	24-Mar-45	Harrow	K6949	26-Mar-45
Hamilcar	LA735	24-Mar-45	Harrow	K6951	14-Mar-41
Hamilcar	LA736	04-Mar-45	Harrow	K6973	01-Jan-45
Hamilcar	LA737	11-Feb-45	Harrow	K6974	06-Dec-40
Hamilcar	LA738	24-Mar-45	Harrow	K6984	07-Feb-44
Hamilcar	LA740	24-Mar-45	Harrow	K6986	01-Jan-45
Hamilcar	LA742	05-Apr-45	Harrow	K6993	01-Jan-45
Hamilcar	LA743	24-Mar-45	Harrow	K6994	01-Jan-45
Hamilcar	LA745	24-Mar-45	Harrow	K6996	20-Jun-40
Hamilcar	LA747	24-Mar-45	Harrow	K6998	01-Jan-45
Hamilcar	LA748	24-Mar-45	Harrow	K7000	10-Feb-45
Hamilcar	LA750	24-Mar-45	Harrow	K7005	14-Dec-43
Hamilcar	NA814	24-Mar-45	Harrow	K7009	08-Apr-44
Hamilcar	NX805	24-Mar-45	Harrow	K7011	19-Dec-42
Hamilcar	NX805	24-Mar-45	Harrow	K7012	15-Oct-43
Hamilcar	NX809	24-Mar-45	Harrow	K7014	11-Jun-44
Hamilcar	NX810	24-Mar-45	Harrow	K7015	20-Apr-41
Hamilcar	NX811	24-Mar-45	Harrow	K7024	01-Jan-45
Hamilcar	NX812	24-Mar-45	Harrow	K7031	17-Dec-40
Hamilcar	NX813	24-Mar-45	Hector	K8093	18-Aug-42
Hamilcar	NX814	24-Mar-45	Hector	K8097	13-Oct-42
Hamilcar	NX818	24-Mar-45	Hector	K8099	15-Nov-42
Hamilcar	NX819	24-Mar-45	Hector	K8103	16-Dec-41
Hamilcar	NX820	24-Mar-45	Hector	K8108	01-Jul-42
Hamilcar	NX821	24-Mar-45	Hector	K8112	21-Aug-41
Hamilcar	NX822	24-Mar-45	Hector	K8112	14-Sep-42
Hamilcar	NX823	24-Mar-45	Hector	K8126	11-Apr-42
Hamilcar	NX824	10-Apr-45	Hector	K8139	02-Sep-42
Hamilcar	NX825	24-Mar-45	Hector	K8140	14-Jul-42
Hamilcar	NX826	24-Mar-45	Hector	K8142	09-Dec-42
Hamilcar	NX827	24-Mar-45	Hector	K8145	16-Aug-42
Hamilcar	NX838	12-Apr-45	Hector	K8151	30-Jul-42
Hamilcar	NX874	17-Apr-45	Hector	K8154	31-Aug-42
Hamilcar	NX875	24-Mar-45	Hector	K8155	27-Aug-42
Hamilcar	RR924	11-Apr-45	Hector	K8167	22-Jan-43

Hector	K9696	23-Nov-42	Horsa	DP293	18-Aug-43
Hector	K9706	14-Sep-42	Horsa	DP303	17-Sep-44
Hector	K9721	28-Feb-42	Horsa	DP304	18-Jul-43
Hector	K9723	06-Jul-41	Horsa	DP306	24-Mar-45
Hector	K9738	13-Apr-42	Horsa	DP311	17-Sep-44
Hector	K9740	23-Jul-42	Horsa	DP312	09-Aug-44
Hector	K9742	14-Jun-42	Horsa	DP329	16-Aug-43
Hector	K9744	05-Feb-43	Horsa	DP330	17-Sep-44
Hector	K9746	02-Jun-42	Horsa	DP334	07-Apr-44
Hector	K9747	19-May-42	Horsa	DP335	17-Sep-44
Hector	K9751	18-May-41	Horsa	DP338	10-Jul-43
Hector	K9752	18-Nov-42	Horsa	DP339	17-Sep-44
Hector	K9754	17-Feb-41	Horsa	DP340	17-Sep-44
Hector	K9755	29-Jun-42	Horsa	DP345	17-Sep-44
Hector	K9760	15-Dec-41	Horsa	DP346	25-Jan-44
Hector	K9762	22-Sep-41	Horsa	DP346	28-Jan-44
Hector	K9764	01-Dec-42	Horsa	DP347	27-Apr-45
Hector	K9764	30-Nov-42	Horsa	DP348	13-Aug-44
Hector	K9765	26-Apr-42	Horsa	DP349	19-Nov-42
Hector	K9770	14-May-42	Horsa	DP349	27-Nov-42
Hector	K9775	22-May-41	Horsa	DP350	20-Feb-44
Hector	K9780	12-Sep-42	Horsa	DP368	17-Sep-44
Hector	K9781	09-Nov-42	Horsa	DP373	15-Oct-42
Hector	K9785	11-Jan-42	Horsa	DP374	17-Sep-44
Hertfordshire			Horsa	DP375	17-Sep-44
	R2510	23-Oct-40	Horsa	DP377	17-Sep-44
Hind	K6814	08-Oct-40	Horsa	DP385	17-Sep-44
Hornet Moth			Horsa	DP386	24-Mar-45
	HM498	25-Mar-42	Horsa	DP388	15-Aug-43
Horsa	?????	01-May-44	Horsa	DP396	24-Aug-43
Horsa	DG393	10-Jul-43	Horsa	DP398	17-Sep-44
Horsa	DK197	10-Jul-43	Horsa	DP414	24-Mar-45
Horsa	DK199	10-Jul-43	Horsa	DP415	17-Sep-44
Horsa	DP283	17-Sep-44	Horsa	DP416	06-Jun-44
Horsa	DP284	16-Aug-43	Horsa	DP417	17-Sep-44
Horsa	DP286	17-Sep-44	Horsa	DP418	04-Apr-44
Horsa	DP290	17-Sep-44	Horsa	DP419	07-Apr-43
Horsa	DP292	24-Jan-44	Horsa	DP422	17-Sep-44

Horsa	DP423	10-Apr-45	Horsa	DP644	17-Sep-44
Horsa	DP424	17-Sep-44	Horsa	DP647	10-Jul-43
Horsa	DP427	06-Jun-44	Horsa	DP651	17-Sep-44
Horsa	DP438	06-Jun-44	Horsa	DP658	17-Sep-44
Horsa	DP440	10-Jul-43	Horsa	DP689	17-Sep-44
Horsa	DP487	17-Sep-44	Horsa	DP690	17-Sep-44
Horsa	DP491	17-Sep-44	Horsa	DP695	06-Jun-44
Horsa	DP492	17-Sep-44	Horsa	DP697	10-Jul-43
Horsa	DP495	17-Sep-44	Horsa	DP699	17-Sep-44
Horsa	DP496	24-Mar-45	Horsa	DP704	06-Jun-44
Horsa	DP497	24-Mar-45	Horsa	DP706	06-Jun-44
Horsa	DP499	13-Feb-45	Horsa	DP714	05-Aug-42
Horsa	DP500	17-Sep-44	Horsa	DP717	11-Aug-42
Horsa	DP516	17-Sep-44	Horsa	DP720	17-Sep-44
Horsa	DP518	13-Jan-43	Horsa	DP721	17-Sep-44
Horsa	DP519	06-Jun-44	Horsa	DP726	17-Sep-44
Horsa	DP520	17-Sep-44	Horsa	DP743	24-Nov-42
Horsa	DP526	17-Sep-44	Horsa	DP743	26-Nov-42
Horsa	DP528	17-Sep-44	Horsa	DP745	17-Sep-43
Horsa	DP530	24-Apr-44	Horsa	DP749	17-Sep-44
Horsa	DP532	17-Sep-44	Horsa	DP752	02-Nov-42
Horsa	DP533	17-Sep-44	Horsa	DP754	17-Sep-44
Horsa	DP539	06-Jun-44	Horsa	DP755	31-Aug-42
Horsa	DP541	17-Sep-44	Horsa	DP756	17-Sep-44
Horsa	DP543	17-Sep-44	Horsa	DP759	17-Sep-44
Horsa	DP544	17-Sep-44	Horsa	DP763	29-Sep-42
Horsa	DP548	17-Sep-44	Horsa	DP764	05-Jun-43
Horsa	DP550	17-Sep-44	Horsa	DP765	17-Sep-44
Horsa	DP555	17-Sep-44	Horsa	DP770	06-Jun-44
Horsa	DP558	17-Sep-44	Horsa	DP772	10-Aug-43
Horsa	DP562	17-Sep-44	Horsa	DP774	17-Sep-44
Horsa	DP599	18-Jan-45	Horsa	DP775	17-Sep-44
Horsa	DP601	06-Jun-44	Horsa	DP776	17-Sep-44
Horsa	DP606	17-Sep-44	Horsa	DP777	07-Aug-43
Horsa	DP611	17-Sep-44	Horsa	DP797	17-Sep-44
Horsa	DP613	17-Sep-44	Horsa	DP798	30-Jan-43
Horsa	DP618	17-Sep-44	Horsa	DP799	06-Apr-45
Horsa	DP628	06-Jun-44	Horsa	DP802	17-Sep-44

Horsa	DP807	17-Sep-44	Horsa	HG850	17-Sep-44
Horsa	DP810	7-Oct-44	Horsa	HG855	17-Sep-44
Horsa	DP811	06-Jun-44	Horsa	HG856	17-Sep-44
Horsa	DP813	01-Dec-43	Horsa	HG857	14-Mar-43
Horsa	DP816	01-Dec-43	Horsa	HG858	06-Jun-44
Horsa	DP817	30-Oct-43	Horsa	HG868	06-Jun-44
Horsa	DP821	3-Dec-42	Horsa	HG871	17-Sep-44
Horsa	DP825	17-Apr-43	Horsa	HG872	17-Sep-44
Horsa	DP826	17-Sep-44	Horsa	HG873	17-Sep-44
Horsa	DP828	06-Jun-44	Horsa	HG873	17-Sep-44
Horsa	DP829	17-Sep-44	Horsa	HG878	10-Jul-43
Horsa	DP833	17-Sep-44	Horsa	HG901	17-Sep-44
Horsa	DP834	17-Sep-44	Horsa	HG910	17-Sep-44
Horsa	DP837	05-Jun-43	Horsa	HG911	17-Sep-44
Horsa	DP840	17-Sep-44	Horsa	HG912	06-Jun-44
Horsa	DP841	17-Sep-44	Horsa	HG914	17-Sep-44
Horsa	HG736	17-Sep-44	Horsa	HG922	17-Sep-44
Horsa	HG737	17-Sep-44	Horsa	HG924	17-Sep-44
Horsa	HG740	17-Sep-44	Horsa	HG930	17-Sep-44
Horsa	HG748	17-Sep-44	Horsa	HG930	17-Sep-44
Horsa	HG749	17-Sep-44	Horsa	HG933	17-Sep-44
Horsa	HG759	17-Sep-44	Horsa	HG937	17-Sep-44
Horsa	HG761	17-Sep-44	Horsa	HG939	17-Sep-44
Horsa	HG766	17-Sep-44	Horsa	HG959	17-Sep-44
Horsa	HG766	17-Sep-44	Horsa	HG960	17-Sep-44
Horsa	HG785	17-Sep-44	Horsa	HG961	17-Sep-44
Horsa	HG791	17-Sep-44	Horsa	HG962	17-Sep-44
Horsa	HG793	17-Sep-44	Horsa	HG968	06-Jun-44
Horsa	HG795	17-Sep-44	Horsa	HG971	06-Jun-44
Horsa	HG796	17-Sep-44	Horsa	HG974	10-Jul-43
Horsa	HG799	17-Sep-44	Horsa	HG975	03-Apr-43
Horsa	HG804	17-Sep-44	Horsa	HG977	06-Jun-44
Horsa	HG815	17-Sep-44	Horsa	HG982	17-Sep-44
Horsa	HG819	17-Sep-44	Horsa	HG985	30-Jan-43
Horsa	HG831	17-Sep-44	Horsa	HH747	31-Jan-43
Horsa	HG832	17-Sep-44	Horsa	HH753	13-May-44
Horsa	HG836	17-Sep-44	Horsa	HH909	31-Dec-44
Horsa	HG847	17-Sep-44	Horsa	HS101	17-Sep-44

Horsa	HS101	17-Sep-44	Horsa	LG697	17-Sep-44
Horsa	HS102	10-Sep-43	Horsa	LG698	01-May-44
Horsa	HS106	17-Sep-44	Horsa	LG715	06-Jun-44
Horsa	HS109	23-Sep-43	Horsa	LG716	06-Jun-44
Horsa	HS111	06-Jun-44	Horsa	LG718	17-Sep-44
Horsa	HS112	17-Sep-44	Horsa	LG722	23-Jan-44
Horsa	HS114	19-Nov-42	Horsa	LG723	29-Feb-44
Horsa	HS116	17-Sep-44	Horsa	LG725	06-Jun-44
Horsa	HS124	17-Sep-44	Horsa	LG731	18-Jan-45
Horsa	HS126	06-Jun-44	Horsa	LG733	03-Jun-43
Horsa	HS132	17-Sep-44	Horsa	LG736	06-Jun-44
Horsa	HS141	17-Sep-44	Horsa	LG744	17-Sep-44
Horsa	HS148	17-Sep-44	Horsa	LG745	03-Jan-44
Horsa	LF886	17-Sep-44	Horsa	LG746	28-Jan-44
Horsa	LF887	17-Sep-44	Horsa	LG747	06-Jun-44
Horsa	LF893	17-Sep-44	Horsa	LG748	17-Sep-44
Horsa	LF897	17-Sep-44	Horsa	LG749	17-Nov-44
Horsa	LF903	24-Mar-45	Horsa	LG767	17-Sep-44
Horsa	LF908	17-Sep-44	Horsa	LG770	24-May-44
Horsa	LF914	17-Sep-44	Horsa	LG771	17-Sep-44
Horsa	LF920	17-Sep-44	Horsa	LG774	06-Jun-44
Horsa	LF921	17-Sep-44	Horsa	LG787	06-Jun-44
Horsa	LF941	12-Feb-43	Horsa	LG790	06-Jun-44
Horsa	LF943	17-Sep-44	Horsa	LG792	17-Sep-44
Horsa	LF951	14-Apr-44	Horsa	LG798	17-Sep-44
Horsa	LF958	17-Sep-44	Horsa	LG831	06-Jun-44
Horsa	LF961	17-Sep-44	Horsa	LG833	27-Jun-43
Horsa	LG663	17-Sep-44	Horsa	LG837	17-Sep-44
Horsa	LG665	17-Sep-44	Horsa	LG847	17-Sep-44
Horsa	LG671	03-Sep-43	Horsa	LG849	06-Jun-44
Horsa	LG672	06-Jan-44	Horsa	LG850	17-Jan-45
Horsa	LG675	06-Jun-44	Horsa	LG851	17-Sep-44
Horsa	LG679	06-Jun-44	Horsa	LG853	06-Jun-44
Horsa	LG681	17-Sep-44	Horsa	LG868	06-Jun-44
Horsa	LG690	17-Sep-44	Horsa	LG870	06-Jun-44
Horsa	LG692	24-Mar-45	Horsa	LG879	06-Jun-44
Horsa	LG694	06-Jun-44	Horsa	LG880	06-Jun-44
Horsa	LG696	13-Apr-44	Horsa	LG883	06-Jun-44

Horsa	LG886	17-Sep-44	Horsa	LH134	17-Sep-44
Horsa	LG892	17-Sep-44	Horsa	LH135	10-Jul-43
Horsa	LG896	17-Sep-44	Horsa	LH136	04-Feb-44
Horsa	LG915	06-Jun-44	Horsa	LH138	17-Sep-44
Horsa	LG916	06-Jun-44	Horsa	LH140	17-Sep-44
Horsa	LG917	06-Jun-44	Horsa	LH143	17-Sep-44
Horsa	LG922	17-Sep-44	Horsa	LH144	17-Sep-44
Horsa	LG928	01-Dec-43	Horsa	LH145	06-Jun-44
Horsa	LG929	24-Aug-43	Horsa	LH146	06-Jun-44
Horsa	LG932	09-Jun-43	Horsa	LH152	06-May-44
Horsa	LG939	06-Jun-44	Horsa	LH167	17-Sep-44
Horsa	LG942	17-Sep-44	Horsa	LH168	17-Sep-44
Horsa	LG945	14-Jun-43	Horsa	LH170	06-Jun-44
Horsa	LG948	06-Jun-44	Horsa	LH171	20-Mar-44
Horsa	LG951	06-Jun-44	Horsa	LH172	17-Sep-44
Horsa	LG966	24-Mar-45	Horsa	LH173	06-Jun-44
Horsa	LG977	17-Sep-44	Horsa	LH174	03-Mar-44
Horsa	LG981	17-Sep-44	Horsa	LH175	17-Sep-44
Horsa	LG983	17-Sep-44	Horsa	LH176	06-Jun-44
Horsa	LG985	06-Jun-44	Horsa	LH178	17-Sep-44
Horsa	LG986	06-Jun-44	Horsa	LH179	06-Jun-44
Horsa	LG987	17-Sep-44	Horsa	LH180	17-Sep-44
Horsa	LG988	10-Jul-43	Horsa	LH181	03-Feb-44
Horsa	LG989	17-Sep-44	Horsa	LH182	17-Sep-44
Horsa	LG992	06-Jun-44	Horsa	LH184	17-Sep-44
Horsa	LG993	24-Mar-45	Horsa	LH185	06-Jun-44
Horsa	LG995	06-Jun-44	Horsa	LH187	17-Sep-44
Horsa	LG997	17-Sep-44	Horsa	LH188	17-Sep-44
Horsa	LG999	04-Apr-44	Horsa	LH189	06-Jun-44
Horsa	LH114	17-Sep-44	Horsa	LH202	10-Jul-43
Horsa	LH115	21-Jun-44	Horsa	LH202	25-Mar-44
Horsa	LH120	06-Jun-44	Horsa	LH203	06-Jun-44
Horsa	LH122	23-Aug-43	Horsa	LH204	17-Sep-44
Horsa	LH127	17-Sep-44	Horsa	LH206	06-Jun-44
Horsa	LH128	17-Sep-44	Horsa	LH207	06-May-44
Horsa	LH130	10-Jul-43	Horsa	LH208	07-May-44
Horsa	LH132	06-Jun-44	Horsa	LH210	17-Sep-44
Horsa	LH133	06-Jun-44	Horsa	LH211	17-Sep-44

Horsa	LH216	17-Sep-44	Horsa	LH283	17-Sep-44
Horsa	LH217	06-Jun-44	Horsa	LH285	17-Sep-44
Horsa	LH218	17-Sep-44	Horsa	LH286	17-Sep-44
Horsa	LH220	17-Sep-44	Horsa	LH288	17-Sep-44
Horsa	LH222	17-Sep-44	Horsa	LH289	04-Apr-44
Horsa	LH224	06-Jun-44	Horsa	LH290	06-Mar-44
Horsa	LH227	17-Sep-44	Horsa	LH291	17-Sep-44
Horsa	LH228	17-Sep-44	Horsa	LH292	17-Sep-44
Horsa	LH229	17-Sep-44	Horsa	LH295	06-Jun-44
Horsa	LH230	17-Sep-44	Horsa	LH297	04-Feb-44
Horsa	LH231	06-Jun-44	Horsa	LH299	17-Sep-44
Horsa	LH232	23-Aug-43	Horsa	LH301	06-Jun-44
Horsa	LH234	06-Jun-44	Horsa	LH316	06-Jun-44
Horsa	LH236	06-Jun-44	Horsa	LH317	06-Jun-44
Horsa	LH237	25-Nov-44	Horsa	LH318	17-Sep-44
Horsa	LH239	06-Jun-44	Horsa	LH319	17-Sep-44
Horsa	LH240	17-Sep-44	Horsa	LH321	06-Jun-44
Horsa	LH242	06-Jun-44	Horsa	LH323	11-Jul-44
Horsa	LH243	06-Jun-44	Horsa	LH324	06-Jun-44
Horsa	LH244	17-Sep-44	Horsa	LH328	06-Jun-44
Horsa	LH245	28-Jan-44	Horsa	LH329	06-Jun-44
Horsa	LH247	17-Sep-44	Horsa	LH331	18-Jan-45
Horsa	LH248	06-Jun-44	Horsa	LH334	17-Sep-44
Horsa	LH263	17-Sep-44	Horsa	LH335	17-Sep-44
Horsa	LH264	06-Jun-44	Horsa	LH338	13-Feb-45
Horsa	LH265	17-Sep-44	Horsa	LH339	06-Jun-44
Horsa	LH268	17-Sep-44	Horsa	LH340	14-Mar-45
Horsa	LH269	06-Jun-44	Horsa	LH342	13-Feb-44
Horsa	LH270	11-Mar-44	Horsa	LH343	24-Mar-45
Horsa	LH271	06-Jun-44	Horsa	LH344	06-Jun-44
Horsa	LH273	06-Jun-44	Horsa	LH345	17-Sep-44
Horsa	LH274	17-Sep-44	Horsa	LH349	06-Jun-44
Horsa	LH276	06-Jun-44	Horsa	LH351	17-Sep-44
Horsa	LH277	12-Apr-44	Horsa	LH352	24-Mar-45
Horsa	LH278	17-Sep-44	Horsa	LH353	06-Jun-44
Horsa	LH279	17-Sep-44	Horsa	LH354	03-Mar-44
Horsa	LH280	17-Sep-44	Horsa	LH355	17-Sep-44
Horsa	LH281	06-Jun-44	Horsa	LH356	24-Mar-45

Horsa	LH357	17-Sep-44	Horsa	LH432	06-Jun-44
Horsa	LH359	17-Sep-44	Horsa	LH434	09-Mar-44
Horsa	LH373	06-Jun-44	Horsa	LH435	06-Jun-44
Horsa	LH375	06-Jun-44	Horsa	LH437	06-Jun-44
Horsa	LH376	09-Sep-44	Horsa	LH438	28-Apr-44
Horsa	LH378	06-Jun-44	Horsa	LH439	17-Sep-44
Horsa	LH379	06-Jun-44	Horsa	LH442	06-Jun-44
Horsa	LH380	06-Jun-44	Horsa	LH444	06-Jun-44
Horsa	LH381	06-Jun-44	Horsa	LH445	17-Sep-44
Horsa	LH383	15-Mar-44	Horsa	LH446	17-Sep-44
Horsa	LH384	10-Nov-44	Horsa	LH448	17-Sep-44
Horsa	LH386	17-Sep-44	Horsa	LH449	17-Sep-44
Horsa	LH387	17-Sep-44	Horsa	LH450	24-Jun-44
Horsa	LH388	06-Jun-44	Horsa	LH450	26-Jun-44
Horsa	LH389	12-May-44	Horsa	LH451	06-Jun-44
Horsa	LH390	17-Sep-44	Horsa	LH453	06-Jun-44
Horsa	LH391	20-Feb-44	Horsa	LH455	17-Sep-44
Horsa	LH393	06-Jun-44	Horsa	LH456	17-Sep-44
Horsa	LH394	06-Jun-44	Horsa	LH457	06-Jun-44
Horsa	LH395	17-Sep-44	Horsa	LH458	17-Sep-44
Horsa	LH396	17-Sep-44	Horsa	LH459	17-Sep-44
Horsa	LH397	06-Jun-44	Horsa	LH461	17-Sep-44
Horsa	LH398	06-Jun-44	Horsa	LH462	17-Sep-44
Horsa	LH399	06-Jun-44	Horsa	LH463	17-Sep-44
Horsa	LH400	17-Sep-44	Horsa	LH464	17-Sep-44
Horsa	LH401	24-Feb-44	Horsa	LH465	06-Jun-44
Horsa	LH402	06-Jun-44	Horsa	LH467	06-Jun-44
Horsa	LH404	03-Mar-44	Horsa	LH469	06-Jun-44
Horsa	LH405	06-Jun-44	Horsa	LH470	06-Jun-44
Horsa	LH406	06-Jun-44	Horsa	LH471	17-Sep-44
Horsa	LH407	17-Sep-44	Horsa	LH473	17-Sep-44
Horsa	LH408	17-Sep-44	Horsa	LH475	06-Jun-44
Horsa	LH410	06-Jun-44	Horsa	LH476	06-Jun-44
Horsa	LH412	17-Sep-44	Horsa	LH490	09-Aug-44
Horsa	LH413	13-Feb-44	Horsa	LH491	06-Jun-44
Horsa	LH414	17-Sep-44	Horsa	LH492	06-Jun-44
Horsa	LH429	06-Jun-44	Horsa	LH494	06-Jun-44
Horsa	LH431	06-Jun-44	Horsa	LH495	06-Jun-44

Horsa	LH496	08-May-44	Horsa	LH558	07-May-44
Horsa	LH499	06-Jun-44	Horsa	LH558	17-Sep-44
Horsa	LH500	06-Jun-44	Horsa	LH560	17-Sep-44
Horsa	LH501	17-Sep-44	Horsa	LH561	17-Sep-44
Horsa	LH504	17-Sep-44	Horsa	LH562	09-Jun-44
Horsa	LH506	17-Sep-44	Horsa	LH563	17-Sep-44
Horsa	LH507	06-Jun-44	Horsa	LH564	17-Sep-44
Horsa	LH508	06-Jun-44	Horsa	LH565	06-Jun-44
Horsa	LH509	17-Sep-44	Horsa	LH566	06-Jun-44
Horsa	LH510	17-Sep-44	Horsa	LH568	06-Jun-44
Horsa	LH511	17-Sep-44	Horsa	LH569	24-Mar-45
Horsa	LH512	17-Sep-44	Horsa	LH570	06-Jun-44
Horsa	LH513	06-Jun-44	Horsa	LH571	06-Jun-44
Horsa	LH515	06-Jun-44	Horsa	LH572	06-Jun-44
Horsa	LH516	06-Jun-44	Horsa	LH573	17-Sep-44
Horsa	LH518	06-Jun-44	Horsa	LH575	06-Jun-44
Horsa	LH519	06-Jun-44	Horsa	LH577	17-Sep-44
Horsa	LH520	13-May-44	Horsa	LH578	06-Jun-44
Horsa	LH521	06-Jun-44	Horsa	LH579	06-Jun-44
Horsa	LH522	17-Sep-44	Horsa	LH580	06-Jun-44
Horsa	LH523	17-Sep-44	Horsa	LH581	17-Sep-44
Horsa	LH524	11-Mar-44	Horsa	LH582	06-Jun-44
Horsa	LH525	17-Sep-44	Horsa	LH583	06-Jun-44
Horsa	LH526	06-Jun-44	Horsa	LH597	17-Sep-44
Horsa	LH527	17-Sep-44	Horsa	LH600	06-Jun-44
Horsa	LH528	17-Sep-44	Horsa	LH601	06-Jun-44
Horsa	LH529	06-Jun-44	Horsa	LH942	06-Jun-44
Horsa	LH532	06-Jun-44	Horsa	LH943	06-Jun-44
Horsa	LH533	06-Jun-44	Horsa	LH946	17-Sep-44
Horsa	LH534	06-Jun-44	Horsa	LH956	17-Sep-44
Horsa	LH535	17-Sep-44	Horsa	LH965	17-Sep-44
Horsa	LH536	17-Sep-44	Horsa	LH966	06-Jun-44
Horsa	LH550	06-Jun-44	Horsa	LH971	16-Mar-43
Horsa	LH551	17-Sep-44	Horsa	LH971	16-Mar-44
Horsa	LH552	17-Sep-44	Horsa	LJ102	17-Sep-44
Horsa	LH553	06-Jun-44	Horsa	LJ106	17-Sep-44
Horsa	LH554	06-Jun-44	Horsa	LJ111	06-Jun-44
Horsa	LH556	17-Sep-44	Horsa	LJ116	06-Jun-44

Horsa	LJ124	06-Jun-44	Horsa	PF692	17-Sep-44
Horsa	LJ130	17-Sep-44	Horsa	PF693	06-Jun-44
Horsa	LJ142	17-Sep-44	Horsa	PF694	06-Jun-44
Horsa	LJ170	29-May-43	Horsa	PF695	06-Jun-44
Horsa	LJ175	26-Jun-43	Horsa	PF698	17-Sep-44
Horsa	LJ187	06-Jun-44	Horsa	PF700	06-Jun-44
Horsa	LJ213	17-Sep-44	Horsa	PF701	20-Feb-44
Horsa	LJ219	17-Sep-44	Horsa	PF702	17-Sep-44
Horsa	LJ235	31-Jan-44	Horsa	PF703	06-Jun-44
Horsa	LJ237	17-Sep-44	Horsa	PF704	17-Sep-44
Horsa	LJ262	17-Sep-44	Horsa	PF705	06-Jun-44
Horsa	LJ263	17-Apr-44	Horsa	PF707	06-Jun-44
Horsa	LJ264	06-Jun-44	Horsa	PF709	06-Jun-44
Horsa	LJ265	17-Sep-44	Horsa	PF710	06-Jun-44
Horsa	LJ266	06-Jun-44	Horsa	PF712	17-Sep-44
Horsa	LJ267	06-Jun-44	Horsa	PF713	17-Sep-44
Horsa	LJ275	24-Apr-44	Horsa	PF714	17-Sep-44
Horsa	LJ285	27-Oct-43	Horsa	PF714	19-Sep-44
Horsa	LJ285	06-Jun-44	Horsa	PF715	06-Jun-44
Horsa	LJ310	06-Jun-44	Horsa	PF717	17-Sep-44
Horsa	LJ311	06-Jun-44	Horsa	PF718	17-Sep-44
Horsa	LJ312	28-Mar-44	Horsa	PF720	06-Jun-44
Horsa	LJ314	06-Jun-44	Horsa	PF721	17-Sep-44
Horsa	LJ315	17-Sep-44	Horsa	PF722	06-Jun-44
Horsa	LJ318	17-Sep-44	Horsa	PF723	06-Jun-44
Horsa	LJ321	17-Sep-44	Horsa	PF724	06-Jun-44
Horsa	LJ324	17-Sep-44	Horsa	PF725	06-Jun-44
Horsa	LJ326	06-Jun-44	Horsa	PF739	17-Sep-44
Horsa	LJ328	17-Sep-44	Horsa	PF742	17-Sep-44
Horsa	LJ330	17-Sep-44	Horsa	PF743	17-Sep-44
Horsa	LJ331	07-May-44	Horsa	PF744	06-Jun-44
Horsa	LJ332	17-Sep-44	Horsa	PF745	24-Mar-45
Horsa	LJ333	17-Sep-44	Horsa	PF747	17-Sep-44
Horsa	LJ496	08-May-44	Horsa	PF748	17-Sep-44
Horsa	LJ945	10-Jul-43	Horsa	PF749	17-Sep-44
Horsa	LT109	10-Jul-43	Horsa	PF750	17-Sep-44
Horsa	PF690	06-Jun-44	Horsa	PF751	17-Sep-44
Horsa	PF691	17-Sep-44	Horsa	PF754	17-Sep-44

Horsa	PF755	17-Sep-44	Horsa	PW641	17-Sep-44
Horsa	PF758	06-Jun-44	Horsa	PW643	17-Sep-44
Horsa	PF760	06-Jun-44	Horsa	PW644	17-Sep-44
Horsa	PF761	17-Sep-44	Horsa	PW645	17-Sep-44
Horsa	PF762	24-Mar-45	Horsa	PW646	06-Jun-44
Horsa	PF764	17-Sep-44	Horsa	PW647	06-Jun-44
Horsa	PF768	06-Jun-44	Horsa	PW648	17-Sep-44
Horsa	PF769	06-Jun-44	Horsa	PW649	06-Jun-44
Horsa	PF786	17-Sep-44	Horsa	PW650	17-Sep-44
Horsa	PF787	06-Jun-44	Horsa	PW652	06-Jun-44
Horsa	PF788	07-May-44	Horsa	PW653	06-Jun-44
Horsa	PF789	17-Sep-44	Horsa	PW654	17-Sep-44
Horsa	PF790	06-Jun-44	Horsa	PW655	17-Sep-44
Horsa	PF791	06-Jun-44	Horsa	PW656	17-Sep-44
Horsa	PF792	24-Mar-45	Horsa	PW658	06-Jun-44
Horsa	PF793	06-Jun-44	Horsa	PW659	06-Jun-44
Horsa	PF794	07-May-44	Horsa	PW660	17-Sep-44
Horsa	PF795	17-Sep-44	Horsa	PW662	06-Jun-44
Horsa	PF796	17-Sep-44	Horsa	PW664	06-Jun-44
Horsa	PF797	17-Sep-44	Horsa	PW665	06-Jun-44
Horsa	PF798	17-Sep-44	Horsa	PW666	06-Jun-44
Horsa	PF799	24-Mar-45	Horsa	PW669	17-Sep-44
Horsa	PF800	06-Jun-44	Horsa	PW671	06-Jun-44
Horsa	PF803	06-Jun-44	Horsa	PW672	17-Sep-44
Horsa	PF804	31-May-44	Horsa	PW673	24-Mar-45
Horsa	PF805	24-Mar-45	Horsa	PW674	17-Sep-44
Horsa	PF806	17-Sep-44	Horsa	PW675	06-Jun-44
Horsa	PF807	17-Sep-44	Horsa	PW676	06-Jun-44
Horsa	PF808	17-Sep-44	Horsa	PW693	06-Jun-44
Horsa	PF810	06-Jun-44	Horsa	PW697	17-Sep-44
Horsa	PF811	17-Sep-44	Horsa	PW698	24-Mar-45
Horsa	PF812	06-Jun-44	Horsa	PW700	17-Sep-44
Horsa	PF815	17-Sep-44	Horsa	PW703	17-Sep-44
Horsa	PF816	06-Jun-44	Horsa	PW704	17-Sep-44
Horsa	PF817	17-Sep-44	Horsa	PW705	06-Jun-44
Horsa	PW637	06-Jun-44	Horsa	PW706	06-Jun-44
Horsa	PW638	09-Aug-44	Horsa	PW707	24-Mar-45
Horsa	PW640	17-Sep-44	Horsa	PW709	06-Jun-44

Horsa	PW710	17-Sep-44	Horsa	PW773	06-Jun-44
Horsa	PW712	06-Jun-44	Horsa	PW774	06-Jun-44
Horsa	PW713	06-Jun-44	Horsa	PW775	02-Mar-45
Horsa	PW714	06-Jun-44	Horsa	PW778	17-Sep-44
Horsa	PW715	06-Jun-44	Horsa	PW781	17-Sep-44
Horsa	PW716	06-Jun-44	Horsa	PW782	17-Sep-44
Horsa	PW717	06-Jun-44	Horsa	PW784	17-Sep-44
Horsa	PW718	17-Sep-44	Horsa	PW785	06-Jun-44
Horsa	PW720	06-Jun-44	Horsa	PW786	06-Jun-44
Horsa	PW721	06-Jun-44	Horsa	PW789	17-Sep-44
Horsa	PW722	06-Jun-44	Horsa	PW790	17-Sep-44
Horsa	PW723	24-Mar-45	Horsa	PW812	24-Apr-44
Horsa	PW726	06-Jun-44	Horsa	PW813	04-May-45
Horsa	PW727	17-Sep-44	Horsa	PW816	17-Sep-44
Horsa	PW728	17-Sep-44	Horsa	PW817	17-Sep-44
Horsa	PW729	17-Sep-44	Horsa	PW818	27-Apr-44
Horsa	PW732	06-Jun-44	Horsa	PW819	06-Jun-44
Horsa	PW733	06-Jun-44	Horsa	PW820	17-Sep-44
Horsa	PW734	06-Jun-44	Horsa	PW821	24-Mar-45
Horsa	PW748	06-Jun-44	Horsa	PW823	17-Sep-44
Horsa	PW749	17-Sep-44	Horsa	PW825	17-Sep-44
Horsa	PW750	17-Sep-44	Horsa	PW826	24-Mar-45
Horsa	PW751	17-Sep-44	Horsa	PW827	17-Sep-44
Horsa	PW752	17-Sep-44	Horsa	PW828	06-Jun-44
Horsa	PW753	17-Sep-44	Horsa	PW831	24-Mar-45
Horsa	PW756	17-Sep-44	Horsa	PW832	24-Mar-45
Horsa	PW757	24-Mar-45	Horsa	PW833	06-Mar-45
Horsa	PW758	06-Jun-44	Horsa	PW839	09-Mar-45
Horsa	PW759	06-Jun-44	Horsa	PW842	17-Sep-44
Horsa	PW760	06-Jun-44	Horsa	PW843	24-Mar-45
Horsa	PW761	06-Jun-44	Horsa	PW847	06-Jun-44
Horsa	PW762	24-Mar-45	Horsa	PW862	17-Sep-44
Horsa	PW765	17-Sep-44	Horsa	PW866	17-Sep-44
Horsa	PW766	17-Sep-44	Horsa	PW870	17-Sep-44
Horsa	PW768	07-Mar-45	Horsa	PW871	06-Jun-44
Horsa	PW770	06-Jun-44	Horsa	PW874	08-Dec-44
Horsa	PW771	24-Mar-45	Horsa	PW875	17-Sep-44
Horsa	PW772	17-Sep-44	Horsa	PW877	17-Sep-44

Horsa	PW879	06-Jun-44	Horsa	RJ178	17-Sep-44
Horsa	PW880	24-Mar-45	Horsa	RJ179	17-Sep-44
Horsa	PW884	06-Jun-44	Horsa	RJ180	17-Sep-44
Horsa	PW885	17-Sep-44	Horsa	RJ181	17-Sep-44
Horsa	PW888	17-Sep-44	Horsa	RJ182	17-Sep-44
Horsa	PW889	06-Jun-44	Horsa	RJ183	17-Sep-44
Horsa	PW890	17-Sep-44	Horsa	RJ184	17-Sep-44
Horsa	PW894	17-Sep-44	Horsa	RJ185	17-Sep-44
Horsa	PW895	17-Sep-44	Horsa	RJ186	17-Sep-44
Horsa	PW896	24-Mar-45	Horsa	RJ187	17-Sep-44
Horsa	PW897	06-Jun-44	Horsa	RJ188	17-Sep-44
Horsa	RJ112	24-Mar-45	Horsa	RJ189	17-Sep-44
Horsa	RJ113	17-Sep-44	Horsa	RJ190	04-Jul-44
Horsa	RJ113	17-Sep-44	Horsa	RJ191	17-Sep-44
Horsa	RJ114	24-Mar-45	Horsa	RJ192	17-Sep-44
Horsa	RJ115	17-Sep-44	Horsa	RJ194	17-Sep-44
Horsa	RJ117	17-Sep-44	Horsa	RJ195	17-Sep-44
Horsa	RJ124	05-Dec-44	Horsa	RJ212	17-Sep-44
Horsa	RJ126	17-Sep-44	Horsa	RJ213	17-Sep-44
Horsa	RJ127	29-Jan-45	Horsa	RJ214	17-Sep-44
Horsa	RJ129	24-Mar-45	Horsa	RJ215	17-Sep-44
Horsa	RJ135	14-Mar-45	Horsa	RJ217	17-Sep-44
Horsa	RJ143	26-Apr-45	Horsa	RJ223	17-Sep-44
Horsa	RJ150	17-Sep-44	Horsa	RJ224	17-Sep-44
Horsa	RJ153	17-Sep-44	Horsa	RJ225	17-Sep-44
Horsa	RJ154	17-Sep-44	Horsa	RJ226	17-Sep-44
Horsa	RJ156	02-Nov-44	Horsa	RJ227	17-Sep-44
Horsa	RJ160	17-Sep-44	Horsa	RJ228	24-Mar-45
Horsa	RJ162	21-Aug-44	Horsa	RJ229	17-Sep-44
Horsa	RJ163	17-Sep-44	Horsa	RJ230	17-Sep-44
Horsa	RJ165	17-Sep-44	Horsa	RJ245	03-May-45
Horsa	RJ166	17-Sep-44	Horsa	RJ246	24-Mar-45
Horsa	RJ167	17-Sep-44	Horsa	RJ247	24-Mar-45
Horsa	RJ168	17-Sep-44	Horsa	RJ252	17-Sep-44
Horsa	RJ170	17-Sep-44	Horsa	RJ255	10-Mar-45
Horsa	RJ171	17-Sep-44	Horsa	RJ258	17-Sep-44
Horsa	RJ173	17-Sep-44	Horsa	RJ259	13-Apr-45
Horsa	RJ177	17-Sep-44	Horsa	RJ261	17-Sep-44

Horsa	RJ262	26-Jul-44	Horsa	RJ332	17-Sep-44
Horsa	RJ265	17-Sep-44	Horsa	RJ333	17-Sep-44
Horsa	RJ266	17-Sep-44	Horsa	RJ334	17-Sep-44
Horsa	RJ267	17-Sep-44	Horsa	RJ335	17-Sep-44
Horsa	RJ268	17-Sep-44	Horsa	RJ336	17-Sep-44
Horsa	RJ269	17-Sep-44	Horsa	RJ337	17-Sep-44
Horsa	RJ271	17-Sep-44	Horsa	RJ338	17-Sep-44
Horsa	RJ272	17-Sep-44	Horsa	RJ339	17-Sep-44
Horsa	RJ273	17-Sep-44	Horsa	RJ340	17-Sep-44
Horsa	RJ274	17-Sep-44	Horsa	RJ341	17-Sep-44
Horsa	RJ278	17-Sep-44	Horsa	RJ342	17-Sep-44
Horsa	RJ280	17-Sep-44	Horsa	RJ343	24-Mar-45
Horsa	RJ281	17-Sep-44	Horsa	RJ344	17-Sep-44
Horsa	RJ282	17-Sep-44	Horsa	RJ345	17-Sep-44
Horsa	RJ283	17-Sep-44	Horsa	RJ346	17-Sep-44
Horsa	RJ284	17-Sep-44	Horsa	RJ347	17-Sep-44
Horsa	RJ285	17-Dec-44	Horsa	RJ348	17-Sep-44
Horsa	RJ286	17-Sep-44	Horsa	RJ350	17-Sep-44
Horsa	RJ287	17-Sep-44	Horsa	RJ351	06-May-45
Horsa	RJ291	17-Sep-44	Horsa	RJ352	24-Mar-45
Horsa	RJ293	17-Sep-44	Horsa	RJ353	17-Sep-44
Horsa	RJ294	17-Sep-44	Horsa	RJ354	17-Sep-44
Horsa	RJ296	17-Sep-44	Horsa	RJ355	17-Sep-44
Horsa	RJ298	17-Sep-44	Horsa	RJ356	17-Sep-44
Horsa	RJ299	17-Sep-44	Horsa	RJ359	17-Sep-44
Horsa	RJ301	17-Sep-44	Horsa	RN316	24-Mar-45
Horsa	RJ302	17-Sep-44	Horsa	RN318	24-Mar-45
Horsa	RJ303	17-Sep-44	Horsa	RN319	24-Mar-45
Horsa	RJ304	17-Sep-44	Horsa	RN322	24-Mar-45
Horsa	RJ305	17-Sep-44	Horsa	RN324	24-Mar-45
Horsa	RJ307	17-Sep-44	Horsa	RN326	24-Mar-45
Horsa	RJ308	17-Sep-44	Horsa	RN328	24-Mar-45
Horsa	RJ312	17-Sep-44	Horsa	RN339	24-Mar-45
Horsa	RJ314	02-Mar-45	Horsa	RN366	11-Dec-44
Horsa	RJ315	24-Mar-45	Horsa	RN372	24-Mar-45
Horsa	RJ316	17-Sep-44	Horsa	RN373	24-Mar-45
Horsa	RJ330	17-Sep-44	Horsa	RN375	24-Mar-45
Horsa	RJ331	24-Mar-45	Horsa	RN383	24-Mar-45

Horsa	RN384	24-Mar-45	Horsa	RN438	24-Mar-45
Horsa	RN386	24-Mar-45	Horsa	RN439	24-Mar-45
Horsa	RN387	24-Mar-45	Horsa	RN440	24-Mar-45
Horsa	RN387	24-Mar-45	Horsa	RN441	24-Mar-45
Horsa	RN388	24-Mar-45	Horsa	RN442	24-Mar-45
Horsa	RN390	24-Mar-45	Horsa	RN443	24-Mar-45
Horsa	RN391	24-Mar-45	Horsa	RN444	24-Mar-45
Horsa	RN392	24-Mar-45	Horsa	RN445	24-Mar-45
Horsa	RN395	03-May-45	Horsa	RN446	24-Mar-45
Horsa	RN396	24-Mar-45	Horsa	RN447	24-Mar-45
Horsa	RN397	24-Mar-45	Horsa	RN448	24-Mar-45
Horsa	RN398	24-Mar-45	Horsa	RN449	24-Mar-45
Horsa	RN399	24-Mar-45	Horsa	RN450	24-Mar-45
Horsa	RN400	24-Mar-45	Horsa	RN451	24-Mar-45
Horsa	RN401	24-Mar-45	Horsa	RN452	24-Mar-45
Horsa	RN402	24-Mar-45	Horsa	RN454	24-Mar-45
Horsa	RN403	24-Mar-45	Horsa	RN456	24-Mar-45
Horsa	RN404	24-Mar-45	Horsa	RN457	24-Mar-45
Horsa	RN405	24-Mar-45	Horsa	RN474	24-Mar-45
Horsa	RN418	24-Mar-45	Horsa	RN475	24-Mar-45
Horsa	RN419	24-Mar-45	Horsa	RN476	24-Mar-45
Horsa	RN420	24-Mar-45	Horsa	RN477	24-Mar-45
Horsa	RN421	24-Mar-45	Horsa	RN478	24-Mar-45
Horsa	RN422	24-Mar-45	Horsa	RN479	24-Mar-45
Horsa	RN423	24-Mar-45	Horsa	RN480	14-Mar-45
Horsa	RN424	24-Mar-45	Horsa	RN481	24-Mar-45
Horsa	RN425	24-Mar-45	Horsa	RN482	24-Mar-45
Horsa	RN426	24-Mar-45	Horsa	RN484	24-Mar-45
Horsa	RN428	24-Mar-45	Horsa	RN485	24-Mar-45
Horsa	RN429	24-Mar-45	Horsa	RN486	24-Mar-45
Horsa	RN430	24-Mar-45	Horsa	RN487	24-Mar-45
Horsa	RN431	24-Mar-45	Horsa	RN488	24-Mar-45
Horsa	RN432	24-Mar-45	Horsa	RN489	24-Mar-45
Horsa	RN433	24-Mar-45	Horsa	RN490	24-Mar-45
Horsa	RN434	24-Mar-45	Horsa	RN491	24-Mar-45
Horsa	RN435	24-Mar-45	Horsa	RN492	24-Mar-45
Horsa	RN436	24-Mar-45	Horsa	RN494	24-Mar-45
Horsa	RN437	24-Mar-45	Horsa	RN495	24-Mar-45

Horsa	RN496	24-Mar-45	Horsa	RN568	17-Sep-44
Horsa	RN497	24-Mar-45	Horsa	RN583	17-Sep-44
Horsa	RN498	24-Mar-45	Horsa	RN584	17-Sep-44
Horsa	RN499	24-Mar-45	Horsa	RN585	17-Sep-44
Horsa	RN500	24-Mar-45	Horsa	RN586	17-Sep-44
Horsa	RN501	24-Mar-45	Horsa	RN588	17-Sep-44
Horsa	RN502	24-Mar-45	Horsa	RN589	17-Sep-44
Horsa	RN503	24-Mar-45	Horsa	RN590	17-Sep-44
Horsa	RN505	24-Mar-45	Horsa	RN591	17-Sep-44
Horsa	RN506	24-Mar-45	Horsa	RN592	17-Sep-44
Horsa	RN508	24-Mar-45	Horsa	RN593	17-Sep-44
Horsa	RN509	24-Mar-45	Horsa	RN594	17-Sep-44
Horsa	RN514	24-Mar-45	Horsa	RN595	17-Sep-44
Horsa	RN519	24-Mar-45	Horsa	RN596	17-Sep-44
Horsa	RN525	17-Sep-44	Horsa	RN597	17-Sep-44
Horsa	RN526	17-Sep-44	Horsa	RN599	17-Sep-44
Horsa	RN528	17-Sep-44	Horsa	RN600	17-Sep-44
Horsa	RN531	17-Sep-44	Horsa	RN602	17-Sep-44
Horsa	RN532	17-Sep-44	Horsa	RN603	17-Sep-44
Horsa	RN534	17-Sep-44	Horsa	RN604	17-Sep-44
Horsa	RN536	17-Sep-44	Horsa	RN605	17-Sep-44
Horsa	RN539	17-Sep-44	Horsa	RN606	06-Sep-44
Horsa	RN541	17-Sep-44	Horsa	RN607	17-Sep-44
Horsa	RN542	17-Sep-44	Horsa	RN608	17-Sep-44
Horsa	RN544	17-Sep-44	Horsa	RN609	17-Sep-44
Horsa	RN547	17-Sep-44	Horsa	RN610	17-Sep-44
Horsa	RN549	17-Sep-44	Horsa	RN611	17-Sep-44
Horsa	RN550	17-Sep-44	Horsa	RN612	17-Sep-44
Horsa	RN551	17-Sep-44	Horsa	RN613	17-Sep-44
Horsa	RN552	17-Sep-44	Horsa	RN614	17-Sep-44
Horsa	RN553	17-Sep-44	Horsa	RN616	17-Sep-44
Horsa	RN555	17-Sep-44	Horsa	RN617	17-Sep-44
Horsa	RN557	17-Sep-44	Horsa	RN618	17-Sep-44
Horsa	RN559	17-Sep-44	Horsa	RN619	17-Sep-44
Horsa	RN562	17-Sep-44	Horsa	RN619	17-Sep-44
Horsa	RN563	17-Sep-44	Horsa	RN622	17-Sep-44
Horsa	RN564	17-Sep-44	Horsa	RN623	17-Sep-44
Horsa	RN566	17-Sep-44	Horsa	RN624	17-Sep-44

Horsa	RN625	17-Sep-44	Horsa	RN704	17-Sep-44
Horsa	RN638	17-Sep-44	Horsa	RN705	17-Sep-44
Horsa	RN640	17-Sep-44	Horsa	RN708	17-Sep-44
Horsa	RN641	17-Sep-44	Horsa	RN709	17-Sep-44
Horsa	RN642	17-Sep-44	Horsa	RN710	17-Sep-44
Horsa	RN643	17-Sep-44	Horsa	RN711	24-Mar-45
Horsa	RN646	17-Sep-44	Horsa	RN714	17-Sep-44
Horsa	RN650	17-Sep-44	Horsa	RN716	17-Sep-44
Horsa	RN651	24-Mar-45	Horsa	RN717	17-Sep-44
Horsa	RN652	17-Sep-44	Horsa	RN718	17-Sep-44
Horsa	RN653	17-Sep-44	Horsa	RN719	17-Sep-44
Horsa	RN654	17-Sep-44	Horsa	RN721	17-Sep-44
Horsa	RN655	17-Sep-44	Horsa	RN722	17-Sep-44
Horsa	RN657	17-Sep-44	Horsa	RN726	17-Sep-44
Horsa	RN658	17-Sep-44	Horsa	RN728	17-Sep-44
Horsa	RN659	17-Sep-44	Horsa	RN729	17-Sep-44
Horsa	RN660	17-Sep-44	Horsa	RN730	17-Sep-44
Horsa	RN661	17-Sep-44	Horsa	RN731	24-Mar-45
Horsa	RN662	24-Mar-45	Horsa	RN732	31-Dec-44
Horsa	RN664	17-Sep-44	Horsa	RN733	17-Sep-44
Horsa	RN668	17-Sep-44	Horsa	RN734	17-Sep-44
Horsa	RN669	17-Sep-44	Horsa	RN736	24-Mar-45
Horsa	RN670	17-Sep-44	Horsa	RN738	17-Sep-44
Horsa	RN671	17-Sep-44	Horsa	RN752	24-Mar-45
Horsa	RN672	24-Mar-45	Horsa	RN754	17-Sep-44
Horsa	RN673	17-Sep-44	Horsa	RN759	17-Sep-44
Horsa	RN675	17-Sep-44	Horsa	RN761	17-Sep-44
Horsa	RN676	17-Sep-44	Horsa	RN762	24-Mar-45
Horsa	RN677	24-Mar-45	Horsa	RN766	17-Sep-44
Horsa	RN678	17-Sep-44	Horsa	RN767	17-Sep-44
Horsa	RN679	24-Mar-45	Horsa	RN769	17-Sep-44
Horsa	RN695	17-Sep-44	Horsa	RN774	17-Sep-44
Horsa	RN696	17-Sep-44	Horsa	RN783	17-Sep-44
Horsa	RN697	17-Sep-44	Horsa	RN787	24-Mar-45
Horsa	RN698	24-Mar-45	Horsa	RN789	17-Sep-44
Horsa	RN700	17-Sep-44	Horsa	RN790	17-Sep-44
Horsa	RN701	17-Sep-44	Horsa	RN794	24-Mar-45
Horsa	RN702	17-Sep-44	Horsa	RN809	17-Sep-44

Horsa	RN810	24-Mar-45	Horsa	RX672	24-Mar-45
Horsa	RN811	17-Sep-44	Horsa	RX688	14-Apr-45
Horsa	RN820	18-Jan-45	Horsa	RX707	24-Mar-45
Horsa	RN822	17-Sep-44	Horsa	RX718	24-Mar-45
Horsa	RN825	18-Jan-45	Horsa	RX719	24-Mar-45
Horsa	RN828	17-Sep-44	Horsa	RX720	24-Mar-45
Horsa	RN830	24-Mar-45	Horsa	RX721	24-Mar-45
Horsa	RN832	24-Mar-45	Horsa	RX722	24-Mar-45
Horsa	RN834	24-Mar-45	Horsa	RX723	24-Mar-45
Horsa	RN835	17-Sep-44	Horsa	RX725	24-Mar-45
Horsa	RN836	24-Mar-45	Horsa	RX726	24-Mar-45
Horsa	RN844	17-Sep-44	Horsa	RX727	24-Mar-45
Horsa	RN847	17-Sep-44	Horsa	RX728	24-Mar-45
Horsa	RN857	19-Sep-44	Horsa	RX729	24-Mar-45
Horsa	RN865	24-Mar-45	Horsa	RX732	24-Mar-45
Horsa	RN866	17-Sep-44	Horsa	RX734	24-Mar-45
Horsa	RN868	24-Mar-45	Horsa	RX735	24-Mar-45
Horsa	RN871	24-Mar-45	Horsa	RX749	24-Mar-45
Horsa	RN873	24-Mar-45	Horsa	RX750	24-Mar-45
Horsa	RN879	24-Mar-45	Horsa	RX751	24-Mar-45
Horsa	RN881	17-Dec-44	Horsa	RX754	24-Mar-45
Horsa	RN885	24-Mar-45	Horsa	RX756	24-Mar-45
Horsa	RN889	24-Mar-45	Horsa	RX757	24-Mar-45
Horsa	RN894	30-Oct-44	Horsa	RX761	21-Jan-45
Horsa	RN920	24-Mar-45	Horsa	RX762	24-Mar-45
Horsa	RN921	24-Mar-45	Horsa	RX765	24-Mar-45
Horsa	RN931	24-Mar-45	Horsa	RX766	24-Mar-45
Horsa	RN935	24-Mar-45	Horsa	RX767	24-Mar-45
Horsa	RN936	24-Mar-45	Horsa	RX768	24-Mar-45
Horsa	RX534	24-Mar-45	Horsa	RX769	24-Mar-45
Horsa	RX602	24-Apr-45	Horsa	RX771	24-Mar-45
Horsa	RX608	24-Mar-45	Horsa	RX775	03-May-45
Horsa	RX610	24-Mar-45	Horsa	RX776	09-May-44
Horsa	RX613	27-Apr-45	Horsa	RX795	24-Mar-45
Horsa	RX617	24-Mar-45	Horsa	RX808	24-Mar-45
Horsa	RX623	27-Feb-45	Horsa	RX809	24-Mar-45
Horsa	RX647	24-Mar-45	Horsa	RX814	24-Mar-45
Horsa	RX660	21-Nov-44	Horsa	RX815	24-Mar-45

Horsa	RX818	24-Mar-45	Horsa	RX919	24-Mar-45
Horsa	RX820	24-Mar-45	Horsa	RX920	24-Mar-45
Horsa	RX829	24-Mar-45	Horsa	RX921	24-Mar-45
Horsa	RX835	24-Mar-45	Horsa	RX923	24-Mar-45
Horsa	RX850	24-Mar-45	Horsa	RX924	24-Mar-45
Horsa	RX858	24-Mar-45	Horsa	RX925	24-Mar-45
Horsa	RX859	24-Mar-45	Horsa	RX926	14-Mar-45
Horsa	RX860	24-Mar-45	Horsa	RX927	24-Mar-45
Horsa	RX861	24-Mar-45	Horsa	RX929	24-Mar-45
Horsa	RX863	24-Mar-45	Horsa	RX930	24-Mar-45
Horsa	RX865	24-Mar-45	Horsa	RX931	24-Mar-45
Horsa	RX866	24-Mar-45	Horsa	RX932	24-Mar-45
Horsa	RX868	24-Mar-45	Horsa	RX949	24-Mar-45
Horsa	RX869	24-Mar-45	Horsa	RX951	24-Mar-45
Horsa	RX872	24-Mar-45	Horsa	RX952	24-Mar-45
Horsa	RX873	24-Mar-45	Horsa	RX954	24-Mar-45
Horsa	RX875	24-Mar-45	Horsa	RX955	24-Mar-45
Horsa	RX876	24-Mar-45	Horsa	RX958	24-Mar-45
Horsa	RX877	24-Mar-45	Horsa	RX960	24-Mar-45
Horsa	RX878	24-Mar-45	Horsa	RX963	24-Mar-45
Horsa	RX879	24-Mar-45	Horsa	RX964	24-Mar-45
Horsa	RX880	24-Mar-45	Horsa	RX965	24-Mar-45
Horsa	RX881	24-Mar-45	Horsa	RX967	24-Mar-45
Horsa	RX884	24-Mar-45	Horsa	RX969	24-Mar-45
Horsa	RX885	24-Mar-45	Horsa	RX970	24-Mar-45
Horsa	RX886	24-Mar-45	Horsa	RX971	24-Mar-45
Horsa	RX903	24-Mar-45	Horsa	RX972	24-Mar-45
Horsa	RX906	24-Mar-45	Horsa	RX973	24-Mar-45
Horsa	RX908	24-Mar-45	Horsa	RX976	24-Mar-45
Horsa	RX909	24-Mar-45	Horsa	RX977	24-Mar-45
Horsa	RX911	24-Mar-45	Horsa	RX982	24-Mar-45
Horsa	RX912	24-Mar-45	Horsa	RX988	24-Mar-45
Horsa	RX913	24-Mar-45	Horsa	RX991	24-Mar-45
Horsa	RX914	24-Mar-45	Horsa	RX992	24-Mar-45
Horsa	RX915	24-Mar-45	Horsa	RX993	24-Mar-45
Horsa	RX916	24-Mar-45	Horsa	RX994	24-Mar-45
Horsa	RX917	24-Mar-45	Horsa	RX996	24-Mar-45
Horsa	RX917	24-Mar-45	Horsa	RX998	24-Mar-45

Horsa	RZ118	24-Mar-45	Horsa	RZ288	24-Mar-45
Horsa	RZ119	24-Mar-45	Horsa	RZ292	24-Mar-45
Horsa	RZ120	24-Mar-45	Horsa	RZ297	24-Mar-45
Horsa	RZ129	24-Mar-45	Horsa	RZ305	24-Mar-45
Horsa	RZ135	24-Mar-45	Horsa	RZ307	24-Mar-45
Horsa	RZ136	24-Mar-45	Horsa	RZ338	24-Mar-45
Horsa	RZ139	14-Mar-45	Horsa	RZ342	24-Mar-45
Horsa	RZ140	24-Mar-45	Horsa	RZ354	24-Mar-45
Horsa	RZ142	24-Mar-45	Horsa	RZ356	24-Mar-45
Horsa	RZ143	24-Mar-45	Horsa	RZ358	24-Mar-45
Horsa	RZ145	24-Mar-45	Horsa	RZ362	24-Mar-45
Horsa	RZ149	24-Mar-45	Horsa	RZ403	03-May-45
Horsa	RZ150	24-Mar-45	Hotspur	BT481	19-Mar-42
Horsa	RZ152	24-Mar-45	Hotspur	BT484	13-Jan-42
Horsa	RZ154	24-Mar-45	Hotspur	BT485	17-Jun-42
Horsa	RZ170	24-Mar-45	Hotspur	BT488	19-Dec-41
Horsa	RZ173	24-Mar-45	Hotspur	BT488	19-Dec-42
Horsa	RZ174	24-Mar-45	Hotspur	BT489	14-Sep-42
Horsa	RZ175	24-Mar-45	Hotspur	BT490	14-Sep-42
Horsa	RZ178	24-Mar-45	Hotspur	BT500	03-Jun-42
Horsa	RZ181	24-Mar-45	Hotspur	BT500	14-Sep-42
Horsa	RZ183	24-Mar-45	Hotspur	BT502	15-Dec-41
Horsa	RZ190	24-Mar-45	Hotspur	BT505	15-Sep-42
Horsa	RZ197	24-Mar-45	Hotspur	BT508	03-Nov-44
Horsa	RZ199	24-Mar-45	Hotspur	BT536	13-Aug-42
Horsa	RZ201	24-Mar-45	Hotspur	BT538	11-Jul-44
Horsa	RZ215	24-Mar-45	Hotspur	BT546	6-Aug-42
Horsa	RZ221	24-Mar-45	Hotspur	BT551	20-Aug-42
Horsa	RZ223	24-Mar-45	Hotspur	BT552	16-Mar-45
Horsa	RZ227	24-Mar-45	Hotspur	BT553	18-Mar-42
Horsa	RZ228	24-Mar-45	Hotspur	BT555	22-Jan-42
Horsa	RZ229	24-Mar-45	Hotspur	BT561	6-May-42
Horsa	RZ230	24-Mar-45	Hotspur	BT562	19-Mar-42
Horsa	RZ232	24-Mar-45	Hotspur	BT563	12-Mar-42
Horsa	RZ241	24-Mar-45	Hotspur	BT565	01-Jul-42
Horsa	RZ252	24-Mar-45	Hotspur	BT568	4-Jun-42
Horsa	RZ254	24-Mar-45	Hotspur	BT569	15-Jul-42
Horsa	RZ256	24-Mar-45	Hotspur	BT572	18-Apr-44

Hotspur	BT594	29-Aug-42	Hotspur	BT793	17-Aug-42
Hotspur	BT603	07-Jun-43	Hotspur	BT795	24-Apr-42
Hotspur	BT603	07-Jul-43	Hotspur	BT799	6-Aug-42
Hotspur	BT609	23-Oct-44	Hotspur	BT821	31-Oct-42
Hotspur	BT613	12-Oct-44	Hotspur	BT822	07-Dec-43
Hotspur	BT618	30-Jun-42	Hotspur	BT834	03-Jan-45
Hotspur	BT619	14-Apr-42	Hotspur	BT836	03-Mar-44
Hotspur	BT619	05-Mar-43	Hotspur	BT839	10-Jun-42
Hotspur	BT622	01-Jul-42	Hotspur	BT840	08-Apr-45
Hotspur	BT624	24-Sep-42	Hotspur	BT841	31-Mar-44
Hotspur	BT637	6-May-42	Hotspur	BT844	30-Jun-42
Hotspur	BT639	8-Mar-42	Hotspur	BT847	22-Jun-44
Hotspur	BT658	6-Nov-42	Hotspur	BT852	29-Jul-42
Hotspur	BT664	20-Nov-44	Hotspur	BT859	18-Dec-44
Hotspur	BT666	23-Aug-42	Hotspur	BT861	07-Jun-44
Hotspur	BT674	18-May-42	Hotspur	BT892	19-Apr-45
Hotspur	BT675	17-Apr-43	Hotspur	BT896	25-Mar-45
Hotspur	BT676	27-Sep-42	Hotspur	BT896	23-Apr-45
Hotspur	BT681	05-Dec-44	Hotspur	BT918	27-Oct-42
Hotspur	BT682	14-Jun-42	Hotspur	BT939	29-Jan-43
Hotspur	BT683	07-Jul-43	Hotspur	BT979	21-Apr-43
Hotspur	BT684	25-Jul-42	Hotspur	BT989	08-Apr-43
Hotspur	BT685	26-Jul-42	Hotspur	BT989	21-Apr-43
Hotspur	BT688	02-Oct-42	Hotspur	BT990	16-Apr-45
Hotspur	BT715	26-Jun-42	Hotspur	HH125	07-Jun-43
Hotspur	BT718	23-Feb-42	Hotspur	HH127	14-Dec-44
Hotspur	BT723	23-Oct-42	Hotspur	HH134	03-Nov-44
Hotspur	BT726	18-Jan-45	Hotspur	HH139	02-Feb-45
Hotspur	BT728	11-Jun-42	Hotspur	HH140	15-Sep-44
Hotspur	BT730	12-Apr-42	Hotspur	HH141	23-Jul-42
Hotspur	BT745	16-Apr-42	Hotspur	HH146	02-Oct-42
Hotspur	BT771	26-Apr-42	Hotspur	HH147	16-Jan-45
Hotspur	BT771	20-Jun-42	Hotspur	HH149	21-Oct-43
Hotspur	BT776	17-Sep-42	Hotspur	HH227	02-Oct-42
Hotspur	BT783	08-May-44	Hotspur	HH232	19-Jul-42
Hotspur	BT787	24-Apr-42	Hotspur	HH242	23-Sep-42
Hotspur	BT789	18-Jun-42	Hotspur	HH250	07-Mar-43
Hotspur	BT790	26-Aug-42	Hotspur	HH250	07-Apr-43

Hotspur	HH253	13-May-43	Hotspur	HH710	18-Jul-44
Hotspur	HH253	13-May-43	Hotspur	HH711	09-Mar-44
Hotspur	HH263	04-Sep-42	Hotspur	HH719	01-Mar-43
Hotspur	HH264	18-Jun-43	Hotspur	HH721	02-Aug-44
Hotspur	HH264	18-Jul-43	Hotspur	HH721	02-Aug-44
Hotspur	HH267	10-Apr-45	Hotspur	HH784	12-Jun-43
Hotspur	HH284	26-Nov-42	Hotspur	HH784	12-Jul-43
Hotspur	HH295	25-May-43	HP42	AS981	07-Aug-40
Hotspur	HH297	10-Nov-44	HP42	AS982	06-Dec-40
Hotspur	HH297	10-Nov-44	Hudson	AE505	21-Feb-45
Hotspur	HH303	23-Nov-44	Hudson	AE533	29-Jun-42
Hotspur	HH329	10-Aug-42	Hudson	AE578	09-Dec-42
Hotspur	HH332	04-Sep-42	Hudson	AE595	20-Mar-45
Hotspur	HH356	23-Mar-45	Hudson	AM717	28-Oct-42
Hotspur	HH360	08-Nov-44	Hudson	AM725	22-Apr-42
Hotspur	HH369	31-May-43	Hudson	AM949	15-Mar-44
Hotspur	HH376	14-Sep-42	Hudson	EW877	05-Feb-43
Hotspur	HH402	07-Sep-42	Hudson	EW900	04-Nov-42
Hotspur	HH412	13-Aug-43	Hudson	EW906	22-Feb-44
Hotspur	HH461	8-Oct-44	Hudson	EW944	05-Sep-42
Hotspur	HH519	17-Aug-42	Hudson	EW944	05-Sep-42
Hotspur	HH522	29-Dec-43	Hudson	EW945	20-Nov-42
Hotspur	HH527	18-Apr-45	Hudson	EW945	25-Nov-42
Hotspur	HH532	10-Mar-45	Hudson	EW961	14-Oct-42
Hotspur	HH539	28-Dec-43	Hudson	EW964	07-Sep-42
Hotspur	HH545	26-Feb-43	Hudson	EW964	07-Sep-42
Hotspur	HH546	31-Mar-45	Hudson	EW968	14-Oct-42
Hotspur	HH549	02-Oct-43	Hudson	FH229	13-Mar-44
Hotspur	HH556	19-Dec-43	Hudson	FH232	05-Dec-44
Hotspur	HH584	21-Aug-44	Hudson	FH254	05-Jul-44
Hotspur	HH591	15-Mar-44	Hudson	FH274	24-Dec-43
Hotspur	HH603	24-Jan-43	Hudson	FH383	02-Jul-44
Hotspur	HH604	18-Jan-44	Hudson	FH406	22-Mar-43
Hotspur	HH605	14-Feb-44	Hudson	FH417	30-May-44
Hotspur	HH649	03-Feb-43	Hudson	FH422	17-Oct-43
Hotspur	HH655	27-Dec-44	Hudson	FH431	17-Dec-42
Hotspur	HH665	19-Oct-43	Hudson	FH460	04-Aug-44
Hotspur	HH690	16-Apr-45	Hudson	FH461	04-May-44

Hudson	FH464	17-Sep-42	Hudson	T9465	21-Jul-43
Hudson	FK384	06-Apr-43	Hudson	V8983	30-Oct-42
Hudson	FK387	04-Dec-42	Hudson	V8990	13-Jul-42
Hudson	FK388	29-Nov-42	Hudson	V9104	26-Sep-41
Hudson	FK389	27-Dec-42	Hudson	V9106	18-Jul-44
Hudson	FK390	28-Apr-43	Hudson	V9115	16-Dec-41
Hudson	FK407	13-Dec-42	Hudson	V9155	31-May-44
Hudson	FK411	16-Apr-43	Hudson	V9227	21-May-42
Hudson	FK452	23-Jun-43	Hudson	V9228	11-Aug-43
Hudson	FK471	12-May-43	Hudson	V9230	02-Sep-42
Hudson	FK474	16-Dec-42	Hudson	FH168	19-May-43
Hudson	FK485	21-Feb-43	Hudson	FH275	09-Sep-43
Hudson	FK491	01-Oct-42	Hudson	FH307	29-Apr-43
Hudson	FK491	01-Oct-42	Hudson	FK803	20-Mar-45
Hudson	FK501	12-Nov-42	Lancaster	ED825	10-Dec-43
Hudson	FK507	28-Apr-43	Lancaster	ED886	10-Dec-43
Hudson	FK509	08-Oct-42	Liberator	AL504	26-Mar-45
Hudson	FK527	06-Mar-43	Liberator	AL509	04-Nov-43
Hudson	FK567	26-Mar-43	Liberator	AL513	15-Dec-42
Hudson	FK573	28-Jul-43	Liberator	AL516	31-Oct-42
Hudson	FK584	27-Aug-43	Liberator	AL523	04-Jul-43
Hudson	FK592	21-Jun-43	Liberator	AL540	18-Nov-43
Hudson	FK605	25-Dec-42	Liberator	AL545	07-May-44
Hudson	FK615	13-Mar-43	Liberator	AL574	22-Feb-42
Hudson	FK763	11-Apr-45	Liberator	AL587	23-Mar-43
Hudson	FK767	28-Mar-44	Liberator	AL595	06-Nov-42
Hudson	FK790	05-Jul-44	Liberator	AM260	14-Aug-41
Hudson	N7221	28-Mar-44	Liberator	AM261	10-Aug-41
Hudson	N7263	01-Aug-44	Liberator	AM263	30-Nov-44
Hudson	N7357	16-Aug-42	Liberator	AM911	23-May-43
Hudson	N7357	16-Aug-42	Liberator	AM913	29-Jan-43
Hudson	P5164	05-Oct-41	Liberator	AM915	01-Sep-41
Hudson	T9375	10-Oct-42	Liberator	AM929	09-Apr-45
Hudson	T9405	21-Feb-45	Liberator	BZ858	09-Oct-43
Hudson	T9429	03-Oct-42	Liberator	BZ859	06-Jan-44
Hudson	T9439	19-Apr-44	Liberator	BZ923	07-May-45
Hudson	T9445	20-Mar-45	Liberator	BZ932	08-May-44
Hudson	T9463	26-Nov-44	Liberator	BZ949	06-Jan-44

Liberator	BZ952	06-Apr-44	Liberator	EW248	17-Aug-44
Liberator	BZ956	01-Nov-44	Liberator	EW250	17-Oct-44
Liberator	BZ959	10-Jun-44	Liberator	EW261	22-Aug-44
Liberator	EV812	19-Mar-44	Liberator	EW264	15-Aug-44
Liberator	EV820	20-Apr-44	Liberator	EW275	15-Aug-44
Liberator	EV822	07-Jul-44	Liberator	EW278	11-Sep-44
Liberator	EV825	14-Apr-44	Liberator	EW280	14-Oct-44
Liberator	EV839	22-Aug-44	Liberator	EW626	14-Mar-45
Liberator	EV841	07-May-44	Liberator	EW627	20-Oct-44
Liberator	EV846	23-Nov-44	Liberator	EW628	30-Jan-45
Liberator	EV906	27-Oct-44	Liberator	EW632	14-Nov-44
Liberator	EV941	16-Aug-44	Liberator	KG826	26-Jul-44
Liberator	EV958	08-Mar-45	Liberator	KG828	15-Aug-44
Liberator	EV961	14-Aug-44	Liberator	KG836	15-Aug-44
Liberator	EV970	28-Jun-44	Liberator	KG838	13-Sep-44
Liberator	EW104	28-Jun-44	Liberator	KG839	28-Jun-44
Liberator	EW105	14-Aug-44	Liberator	KG871	15-Aug-44
Liberator	EW106	11-Oct-44	Liberator	KG873	15-Aug-44
Liberator	EW138	14-Aug-44	Liberator	KG874	13-Oct-44
Liberator	EW139	21-Jun-44	Liberator	KG875	13-Oct-44
Liberator	EW140	11-May-44	Liberator	KG887	08-Aug-44
Liberator	EW141	21-Sep-44	Liberator	KG890	15-Aug-44
Liberator	EW142	26-Jan-45	Liberator	KG925	21-Feb-45
Liberator	EW144	07-Aug-44	Liberator	KG927	28-Aug-44
Liberator	EW148	25-Apr-44	Liberator	KG928	08-Jan-45
Liberator	EW160	28-Aug-44	Liberator	KG933	17-Aug-44
Liberator	EW161	16-Aug-44	Liberator	KG934	13-Sep-44
Liberator	EW165	29-Aug-44	Liberator	KG938	21-Aug-44
Liberator	EW188	26-Feb-45	Liberator	KG939	15-Aug-44
Liberator	EW194	22-Oct-44	Liberator	KG942	05-Oct-44
Liberator	EW197	03-Jun-44	Liberator	KG967	30-Sep-44
Liberator	EW198	11-Sep-44	Liberator	KG993	01-Mar-45
Liberator	EW199	02-Jul-44	Liberator	KG999	13-Oct-44
Liberator	EW204	25-Mar-45	Liberator	KH100	06-Nov-44
Liberator	EW205	11-Sep-44	Liberator	KH101	13-Sep-44
Liberator	EW207	03-Mar-45	Liberator	KH102	22-Sep-44
Liberator	EW229	21-Aug-44	Liberator	KH151	19-Jan-45
Liberator	EW235	22-Nov-44	Liberator	KH152	17-Oct-44

Liberator	KH153	16-Nov-44	Lysander	R9009	23-Apr-45
Liberator	KH154	13-Oct-44	Lysander	R9027	21-Oct-40
Liberator	KH157	15-Dec-44	Lysander	R9106	16-May-43
Liberator	KH158	13-Oct-44	Lysander	T1456	22-Nov-44
Liberator	KH204	22-Nov-44	Lysander	T1508	29-Jan-42
Liberator	KH207	07-Feb-45	Lysander	T1583	30-Mar-45
Liberator	KH209	23-Mar-45	Lysander	T1707	18-Oct-44
Liberator	KH215	23-Jan-45	Lysander	T1750	11-Nov-44
Liberator	KH239	13-Oct-44	Lysander	T1771	28-Nov-41
Liberator	KH243	06-Nov-44	Lysander	V9295	06-May-45
Liberator	KH244	19-Mar-45	Lysander	V9316	22-Jun-43
Liberator	KH245	01-Apr-45	Lysander	V9367	17-Dec-43
Liberator	KH277	23-Jan-45	Lysander	V9373	23-Jul-43
Liberator	KH278	23-Jan-45	Lysander	V9376	03-Jul-43
Liberator	KH282	21-Feb-45	Lysander	V9405	04-Mar-44
Liberator	KH312	01-May-45	Lysander	V9490	07-Jul-44
Liberator	KH323	01-Apr-45	Lysander	V9548	16-Nov-43
Liberator	KH397	25-Mar-45	Lysander	V9595	29-May-42
Liberator	KK302	04-Apr-45	Lysander	V9597	01-Sep-42
Liberator	KK350	05-Mar-45	Lysander	V9615	05-Oct-44
Liberator	KK354	05-Mar-45	Lysander	V9649	06-May-45
Liberator	KL355	04-Apr-45	Lysander	V9664	03-May-44
Liberator	KL386	06-Feb-45	Lysander	V9672	06-Sep-43
Lockheed 10A			Lysander	V9673	10-Dec-43
	AX699	23-Dec-41	Lysander	V9674	17-Dec-43
Lockheed 10A			Lysander	V9675	14-Feb-43
	W9105	07-Nov-40	Lysander	V9723	09-Nov-43
Lockheed 12A			Lysander	V9748	05-Aug-44
	LA619	20-Feb-44	Lysander	V9749	29-Sep-44
Lockheed 14			Lysander	V9822	10-Feb-44
	AX681	22-Aug-42	Magister	L8212	08-Oct-40
Lockheed 14			Magister	L8345	08-Oct-40
	AX682	08-Apr-41	Magister	V1067	07-Feb-44
Lockheed 18			Master	DL303	27-Mar-45
	AX687	18-Sep-42	Master	DL305	25-Aug-42
Lodestar	EW984	22-Oct-42	Master	DL307	01-Jul-42
Lodestar	EW986	04-Jan-43	Master	DL368	14-Apr-44
Lysander	R1987	29-Aug-41	Master	DL373	19-Jul-43

Master	DL425	02-Sep-42	Petrel Q6	P5635	08-Oct-40
Master	DL432	07-Oct-42	Roc	L3102	08-Oct-40
Master	DL433	15-Mar-44	Roc	L3120	08-Oct-40
Master	DL456	12-Mar-45	Stinson 10C	W7878	28-Apr-42
Master	DL463	2-Apr-42	Stirling	BK771	03-Feb-44
Master	DL467	27-Dec-44	Stirling	EE944	04-Mar-44
Master	DL472	26-Mar-43	Stirling	EE944	05-Mar-44
Master	DL476	03-Feb-45	Stirling	EE948	12-Apr-45
Master	DL491	19-Jul-43	Stirling	EE972	25-Sep-44
Master	DL516	24-Sep-42	Stirling	EF117	05-May-44
Master	DL517	27-Mar-43	Stirling	EF121	28-May-44
Master	DL519	07-Sep-42	Stirling	EF215	05-Mar-44
Master	DL532	11-Sep-42	Stirling	EF234	08-Nov-44
Master	DL961	31-Jul-44	Stirling	EF244	19-May-44
Master	DM278	24-Apr-45	Stirling	EF248	19-Sep-44
Master	DM322	18-May-44	Stirling	EF256	10-Aug-44
Master	DM360	05-Jan-45	Stirling	EF260	20-Sep-44
Master	DM399	25-Mar-45	Stirling	EF263	19-Sep-44
Master	DM404	31-Aug-43	Stirling	EF267	19-Sep-44
Master	EM260	16-Sep-42	Stirling	EF268	06-Jun-44
Master	EM262	13-Sep-43	Stirling	EF269	25-Apr-44
Master	EM284	06-Nov-43	Stirling	EF272	13-Apr-45
Master	EM288	05-Aug-43	Stirling	EF274	18-Apr-45
Master	EM291	26-Feb-44	Stirling	EF295	06-Jun-44
Master	EM293	15-Aug-44	Stirling	EF296	06-Sep-44
Master	EM295	28-Dec-42	Stirling	EF297	29-Feb-44
Master	EM301	14-Nov-42	Stirling	EF298	23-Sep-44
Master	EM338	25-Oct-42	Stirling	EF305	07-Aug-44
Master	EM344	11-Nov-43	Stirling	EF311	28-Aug-44
Master	EM346	12-Aug-44	Stirling	EF319	19-Sep-44
Master	EM355	08-May-44	Stirling	EF350	12-Feb-44
Master	EM377	27-Sep-43	Stirling	EF405	24-Oct-44
Master	EM398	09-Nov-44	Stirling	EF456	10-Dec-44
Master	EM402	27-Dec-44	Stirling	EF468	20-Feb-44
Master	EM408	11-Mar-45	Stirling	EF469	06-Feb-44
Mentor	L4395	21-Mar-40	Stirling	EH897	19-Sep-44
Mentor	L4396	08-Oct-40	Stirling	EH906	05-Mar-44
Mentor	L4400	08-Oct-40	Stirling	EH923	13-Apr-45

Stirling	EJ110	05-Feb-44	Stirling	LJ851	20-Sep-44
Stirling	EJ116	06-Jun-44	Stirling	LJ864	23-Jul-44
Stirling	EJ925	13-Apr-45	Stirling	LJ867	11-Apr-44
Stirling	LJ443	13-Jan-45	Stirling	LJ868	19-Sep-44
Stirling	LJ459	24-Feb-45	Stirling	LJ870	19-Feb-45
Stirling	LJ461	24-Apr-45	Stirling	LJ873	23-Sep-44
Stirling	LJ470	28-Nov-44	Stirling	LJ878	06-Aug-44
Stirling	LJ475	13-Apr-44	Stirling	LJ880	19-May-44
Stirling	LJ503	31-Aug-44	Stirling	LJ881	21-Sep-44
Stirling	LJ564	07-Jul-44	Stirling	LJ882	23-Jul-44
Stirling	LJ594	18-Sep-44	Stirling	LJ883	23-Sep-44
Stirling	LJ618	20-Sep-44	Stirling	LJ885	06-Jun-44
Stirling	LJ627	21-Apr-45	Stirling	LJ886	08-May-44
Stirling	LJ629	22-Apr-45	Stirling	LJ888	31-Mar-45
Stirling	LJ631	25-Aug-44	Stirling	LJ891	20-Nov-44
Stirling	LJ638	12-Apr-45	Stirling	LJ894	22-Feb-45
Stirling	LJ645	23-Apr-45	Stirling	LJ896	22-Feb-45
Stirling	LJ647	19-Sep-44	Stirling	LJ897	04-Jul-44
Stirling	LJ681	20-Sep-44	Stirling	LJ913	18-Sep-44
Stirling	LJ810	21-Sep-44	Stirling	LJ914	31-Dec-44
Stirling	LJ813	21-Aug-44	Stirling	LJ916	21-Sep-44
Stirling	LJ814	26-Mar-44	Stirling	LJ920	05-Aug-44
Stirling	LJ819	06-Jun-44	Stirling	LJ923	21-Apr-45
Stirling	LJ822	11-Apr-44	Stirling	LJ925	26-Feb-45
Stirling	LJ823	21-Sep-44	Stirling	LJ928	21-Sep-44
Stirling	LJ827	26-Aug-44	Stirling	LJ930	20-Apr-45
Stirling	LJ829	20-Sep-44	Stirling	LJ931	13-Apr-45
Stirling	LJ830	21-Sep-44	Stirling	LJ932	29-Sep-44
Stirling	LJ831	20-Sep-44	Stirling	LJ939	19-Sep-44
Stirling	LJ833	21-Sep-44	Stirling	LJ940	15-Aug-44
Stirling	LJ834	16-Mar-44	Stirling	LJ942	03-Apr-45
Stirling	LJ839	28-Mar-44	Stirling	LJ943	21-Sep-44
Stirling	LJ840	20-Sep-44	Stirling	LJ944	19-Sep-44
Stirling	LJ841	06-Jun-44	Stirling	LJ946	21-Sep-44
Stirling	LJ842	04-Apr-44	Stirling	LJ947	20-Sep-44
Stirling	LJ843	21-Sep-44	Stirling	LJ949	23-Sep-44
Stirling	LJ849	06-Jun-44	Stirling	LJ950	26-Apr-45
Stirling	LJ850	18-Jun-44	Stirling	LJ954	01-Jan-45

Stirling	LJ969	02-Aug-44	Stirling	LK196	04-May-45
Stirling	LJ970	29-Dec-44	Stirling	LK197	31-Mar-45
Stirling	LJ974	07-Aug-44	Stirling	LK198	09-Nov-44
Stirling	LJ982	21-Sep-44	Stirling	LK200	09-Sep-44
Stirling	LJ984	18-Aug-44	Stirling	LK202	18-Apr-45
Stirling	LJ986	01-Jan-45	Stirling	LK203	09-Mar-45
Stirling	LJ988	20-Sep-44	Stirling	LK207	19-Oct-44
Stirling	LJ991	23-Sep-44	Stirling	LK208	21-Sep-44
Stirling	LJ993	09-Nov-44	Stirling	LK209	23-Mar-45
Stirling	LJ995	04-Feb-45	Stirling	LK236	14-Feb-45
Stirling	LJ996	03-Mar-45	Stirling	LK238	07-Oct-44
Stirling	LJ997	24-Mar-45	Stirling	LK241	28-Nov-44
Stirling	LJ999	05-Mar-45	Stirling	LK272	27-Feb-45
Stirling	LK113	29-Jul-44	Stirling	LK273	03-Dec-44
Stirling	LK115	21-Sep-44	Stirling	LK276	21-Nov-44
Stirling	LK116	20-Mar-45	Stirling	LK279	10-Feb-45
Stirling	LK119	31-Mar-45	Stirling	LK283	31-Dec-44
Stirling	LK121	18-Sep-44	Stirling	LK286	02-Apr-45
Stirling	LK126	21-Feb-45	Stirling	LK305	11-Apr-45
Stirling	LK127	20-Sep-44	Stirling	LK312	05-Mar-45
Stirling	LK131	01-Sep-44	Stirling	LK332	31-Mar-45
Stirling	LK132	18-Apr-45	Stirling	LK345	18-Apr-45
Stirling	LK133	29-Jul-44	Stirling	LK395	05-Feb-44
Stirling	LK137	24-Mar-45	Stirling	LK497	04-Jan-45
Stirling	LK142	24-Sep-44	Stirling	LK498	21-Sep-44
Stirling	LK143	03-Dec-44	Stirling	LK545	21-Sep-44
Stirling	LK149	24-Feb-45	Stirling	LK548	20-Sep-44
Stirling	LK151	27-Nov-44	Stirling	LK553	10-Mar-45
Stirling	LK170	19-Sep-44	Stirling	LK556	20-Sep-44
Stirling	LK171	03-Nov-44	Stirling	LK560	18-Sep-44
Stirling	LK177	09-Aug-44	Stirling	LK566	23-Feb-45
Stirling	LK178	18-Aug-44	Stirling	LK567	26-Apr-45
Stirling	LK181	18-Nov-44	Stirling	LK607	12-Dec-44
Stirling	LK182	07-Aug-44	Stirling	LK621	26-Mar-45
Stirling	LK187	13-Sep-44	Stirling	LK624	09-Apr-45
Stirling	LK191	23-Sep-44	Stirling	PJ890	29-Apr-45
Stirling	LK193	02-Apr-45	Stirling	PJ901	09-Apr-45
Stirling	LK195	07-Nov-44	Stirling	PJ905	20-Apr-45

Aircraft Losses

Stirling	PJ909	22-Mar-45	Wellington	W5555	03-Mar-42
Stirling	PJ911	24-Mar-45	Wellington	X9734	03-Oct-42
Stirling	PJ913	19-Mar-45	Wellington	LN914	11-Nov-44
Stirling	PJ921	25-Apr-45	Wellington	LN798	15-Nov-44
Stirling	PK225	31-Mar-45	Wellington	LN980	16-Nov-44
Stirling	PK227	03-Apr-45	Wellington	LP239	02-Dec-44
Stirling	PK228	12-Apr-45	Wellington	LP511	10-Nov-44
Stirling	PW262	02-Nov-44	Wellington	LP549	04-Feb-45
Stirling	PW391	29-Mar-45	Wellington	LP614	08-Jan-45
Stirling	R9289	10-Dec-43	Wellington	ME993	04-Feb-45
Stirling	TS265	15-Apr-45	Wellington	MF247	02-Dec-44
Tiger Moth	T5628	08-Jan-42	Wellington	MF346	10-Nov-44
Valentia	K3600	28-Jul-44	Wellington	MF371	04-Feb-45
Valentia	K3609	06-May-41	Wellington	MF420	10-Nov-44
Valentia	K3611	25-Aug-41	Wellington	MF732	11-Dec-44
Valentia	K5605	12-Nov-40	Whitley	BD228	22-Oct-42
Valentia	K8848	10-Dec-40	Whitley	BD230	24-Jul-44
Vega Gull	G-AFIE	08-Oct-40	Whitley	BD296	26-Sep-44
Vega Gull	P1749	08-Oct-40	Whitley	BD351	30-Jun-43
Vega Gull	P1750	12-Jul-40	Whitley	BD371	31-May-42
Vega Gull	P1751	16-May-40	Whitley	BD417	23-Aug-42
Vega Gull	P1752	13-Jan-40	Whitley	BD419	23-May-43
Vega Gull	P5635	08-Oct-40	Whitley	BD420	15-Feb-44
Vega Gull	P5991	15-May-40	Whitley	BD422	23-Mar-43
Ventura	AE733	11-Dec-43	Whitley	BD436	06-Nov-44
Ventura	AE733	21-Dec-43	Whitley	BD437	12-Dec-42
Ventura	AE881	07-Sep-43	Whitley	BD438	31-Aug-42
Victoria	J7710	06-Dec-40	Whitley	BD494	10-Feb-43
Victoria	K1312	25-Aug-41	Whitley	BD502	09-Nov-43
Victoria	K1313	20-Jan-42	Whitley	BD503	20-May-44
Victoria	K2795	22-Jan-41	Whitley	BD505	28-Jun-44
Victoria	K2797	09-Feb-40	Whitley	BD506	24-Nov-42
Victoria	K2798	30-Apr-40	Whitley	BD512	09-Nov-43
Victoria	K2799	19-Dec-39	Whitley	BD531	22-Sep-43
Victoria	K2807	27-Mar-42	Whitley	BD532	22-Jul-43
Victoria	K3161	01-Oct-40	Whitley	BD533	03-Apr-43
Victoria	P9129	01-Aug-44	Whitley	BD534	13-Jul-42
Warwick	BV247	17-Apr-44	Whitley	BD536	20-Aug-42

Whitley	BD538	19-Feb-43	Whitley	LA914	26-Nov-44
Whitley	BD541	08-Dec-42	Whitley	LA927	20-Feb-44
Whitley	BD543	04-Sep-42	Whitley	LA948	23-Feb-44
Whitley	BD548	07-May-43	Whitley	P5025	11-Oct-40
Whitley	BD550	16-Jul-43	Whitley	P5029	22-Oct-42
Whitley	BD554	05-Apr-43	Whitley	T4165	11-Apr-41
Whitley	BD556	08-Dec-42	Whitley	T4166	28-Mar-42
Whitley	BD629	01-Jan-45	Whitley	T4264	17-Feb-41
Whitley	BD639	03-Aug-42	Whitley	T4339	23-Aug-43
Whitley	BD664	05-Nov-44	Whitley	Z6473	05-Feb-45
Whitley	BD667	31-Aug-42	Whitley	Z6629	22-Nov-42
Whitley	BD668	29-Jan-43	Whitley	Z6653	03-Oct-42
Whitley	BL537	07-Apr-44	Whitley	Z6665	22-Feb-45
Whitley	EB287	30-Dec-43	Whitley	Z6727	25-Jul-41
Whitley	EB289	24-Dec-42	Whitley	Z6728	28-Jan-42
Whitley	EB291	17-Nov-42	Whitley	Z6747	04-Mar-43
Whitley	EB294	27-Nov-42	Whitley	Z6797	26-May-43
Whitley	EB297	20-Mar-43	Whitley	Z6878	30-Sep-44
Whitley	EB299	22-Aug-43	Whitley	Z6940	19-Sep-42
Whitley	EB300	09-Jan-43	Whitley	Z9125	10-Mar-42
Whitley	EB306	15-May-43	Whitley	Z9131	25-Sep-42
Whitley	EB308	29-Sep-42	Whitley	Z9134	19-Nov-42
Whitley	EB313	06-May-43	Whitley	Z9140	03-Jan-42
Whitley	EB332	09-Jan-45	Whitley	Z9158	01-Nov-41
Whitley	EB337	22-Nov-44	Whitley	Z9159	01-Nov-41
Whitley	EB345	21-Sep-44	Whitley	Z9160	18-Nov-42
Whitley	EB361	07-Feb-45	Whitley	Z9164	28-Apr-44
Whitley	EB399	14-Mar-44	Whitley	Z9189	27-Jul-43
Whitley	EB410	21-Nov-44	Whitley	Z9223	30-Oct-41
Whitley	LA765	31-Jan-44	Whitley	Z9224	22-Jun-42
Whitley	LA770	03-Jun-44	Whitley	Z9230	30-Jul-42
Whitley	LA774	24-Mar-44	Whitley	Z9232	25-Aug-42
Whitley	LA793	05-Mar-44	Whitley	Z9275	27-Aug-42
Whitley	LA820	22-Feb-45	Whitley	Z9275	22-Sep-42
Whitley	LA829	17-Nov-44	Whitley	Z9282	26-Jul-42
Whitley	LA856	24-Jul-43	Whitley	Z9295	03-Jan-42
Whitley	LA869	04-Jul-44	Whitley	Z9385	27-Dec-41
Whitley	LA873	17-Nov-44	Whitley	Z9419	07-Jun-43

Whitley	Z9431	04-Jun-42
Whitley	Z9443	06-Jan-45
Whitley	Z9463	13-Jul-43
Whitley	Z9490	21-Oct-43
Whitney Straight		
	BD145	10-Dec-41
Whitney Straight		
	BD168	01-Aug-44
York	IMW119	26-Jul-44
York	MW112	18-Feb-45
York	MW116	01-Feb-45
York	MW118	08-Feb-45
York	MW126	14-Nov-44

Note:

Gliders lost at Arnhem are recorded in this index with a single date of 17-Sep-44.

Aircraft Losses

ABBREVIATIONS

AFC	Air Force Cross
AFM	Air Force Medal
AK	Armia Krajowa (Polish Home Army)
Bde	Brigade
Bn	Battalion
C/N	Chalk Number
CB	Companion of the Bath
CBE	Commander of the Most Excellent Order of the British Empire
CGM	Conspicuous Gallantry Medal (Flying)
Coy	Company
DCM	Distinguished Conduct Medal
DFC	Distinguished Flying Cross
DFM	Distinguished Flying Medal
DSO	Distinguished Service Order
DZ	Drop Zone (for parachutes)
Flt	Flight
GC	George Cross
GM	George Medal
Gp	Group
GPR	Glider Pilot Regiment
LZ	Landing Zone (for gliders/aircraft)
MC	Military Cross
MM	Military Medal
ORBAT	Order of Battle
Para	Parachute (as in regiment/brigade)
RAAF	Royal Australian Air Force
PAF	Polish Air Force
RAMC	Royal Army Medical Corps
RASC	Royal Army Service Corps
RCAF	Royal Canadian Air Force
Regt	Regiment
RNZAF	Royal New Zealand Air Force
SAAF	South African Air Force
SAS	Special Air Service

SD	Special Duties
SIS	Secret Intelligence Service
SOE	Special Operations Executive
sqn cdr	Squadron Commander
Sqn	Squadron
VC	Victoria Cross
VE-Day	Victory in Europe
VJ-Day	Victory against Japan
Wg	Wing
WO I	Warrant Officer Class One
WO II	Warrant Officer Class Two

BIBLIOGRAPHY

85 Years Of South African Air Force – Winston Brent

Agents By Moonlight – Freddie Clark

Air War For Burma – Christopher Shores

Burma Liberators: RCAF In SEAC – John R W Gwynne-Timothy

Destiny Can Wait – The Polish Air Force in World War Two – various authors

First In The Indian Skies – Norman R Franks

Flights of the Forgotten – Special Duties Operations in World War II – Ken Merrick

For Your Tomorrow Volumes 1 & 2 – Earl W Martyn

Green On – The Story of RAF Re Supply – Arie-Jan van Heys

Halifax File – R N Roberts

History Of The Glider Pilot Regiment (The) – Claude Smith

Liberator In Royal Air Force and Commonwealth Service (The)

Men Who Went To Warsaw (The) – Lawrence Isemonger

Noble Pair Of Brothers (A) – Derek H Wood

One Night In June – Kevin Shannon & Stephen Wright

Peter Five – Freddie Clark

Polish Air Force At War (The) – Jerzy B Cynk

RAF Aircraft (various volumes) Compiled by James J Halley MBE Air-Britain (Historians) Ltd

Squadrons Of The South African Air Force – Steven McLean

Stirling File – Bryce B Gomersall

Stirlings In Action With The Airborne Forces – Dr Dennis Williams

They Shall Grow Not Old – Les Allison and Harry Hayward

Tugs and Gliders To Arnhem – Arie-Jan van Heys

Arnhem Sacrifice – Colin Cummings

Airlift To Warsaw – Neil Orpen

ABOUT THE COMPILER

Colin Cummings joined the Royal Air Force in 1963 and was commissioned the following year but only because of a mix up with the assessments of another officer candidate.

He blundered his way through many appointments, at home and in the Far East, usually managing to be posted elsewhere before his ineptitude was revealed. He was sent to a number of so called 'ground breaking' jobs – an air force euphemism for; 'an appointment that nobody, with half an eye on their career, would touch with a very long barge pole'. He defied all predictions and was promoted several ranks above his level of incompetence. However, in 1994 he wrote to the Air Force Board, commenting that; *'in every promotion list, there is one officer of whom all other officers remark: - "I wonder how he made it?". Should I be that officer in the next list, I should have no objection and would not be in the least embarrassed'*. This was the final straw and he was made redundant promptly.

Employed by a major business consultancy, to help win a lucrative contract - which was promptly lost, he undertook several other tasks before retiring from the fray in 1999, undoubtedly, a fraction before he would have been pushed.

In addition to working on this book and a series of tomes covering post-War RAF aircraft accidents, he has produced a missive about the Battle of Arnhem and is researching Operation VARSITY, the crossing of the Rhine in March 1945. He also has another couple of projects ongoing (a further euphemism, in this case for: 'he hasn't a clue where to start').

Having been the Wing Administrative Officer for the Staffordshire Air Training Corps for 3 years, he retired yet again (another euphemism for; 'getting out before the smelly stuff hits the fan').

He is a member of the executive committee of the RAF Historical Society and a supporter of 'Combat Stress'. In addition to his involvement at Rugby School, as an RAF Volunteer Reserve (Training) Branch officer, he is secretary of "The Old Rotors" - a group of ex-RAF helicopter operators - and is an enthusiastic owner of German Shepherd Dogs and a Burmese cat – or perhaps they own him.